Exploring Creation

with

General Science

by Dr. Jay L. Wile

Exploring Creation With General Science

© 2000 Apologia Educational Ministries, Inc.
All rights reserved.

Manufactured in the United States of America
Eighth Printing 2007

Published By
Apologia Educational Ministries, Inc.
Anderson, IN

Printed by
CJK
Cincinnati, OH

Need Help?

Apologia Educational Ministries, Inc. Curriculum Support

If you have any questions while using Apologia curriculum, feel free to contact us in any of the following ways.

By Mail:

Dr. Jay L. Wile
Apologia Educational Ministries, Inc.
1106 Meridian Plaza, Suite 220
Anderson, IN 46016

By E-MAIL: help@apologia.com

On The Web: http://www.apologia.com

By FAX:

(765) 608-3290

By Phone:

(765) 608-3280

STUDENT NOTES

Exploring Creation With General Science

Dr. Jay L. Wile

Science....what images does that word conjure up in your head? Is science dull and boring? Is it too hard for most people? Is it something that only nerds like? Well, in this course, you will begin to find out the answers to those questions. You will learn about the history of science, how to do science, the history of life, how your body works, and some of the amazing living creatures that exist in God's Creation. Like anything worth doing, this course will be hard work, but in the end, you will find it interesting and (hopefully) enjoyable. More than anything else, however, be prepared to be awed and amazed with what the Creator has made for **you!**

Pedagogy of the Text

There are 16 modules in this course. You can divide the course into 4 quarters, which works out to four modules per quarter. Each quarter should take you 9 weeks to complete, so you should shoot for finishing a module every two weeks or so. If you do that, each quarter will take you 8 weeks. Thus, you have about a week of flexibility time each quarter.

How will you know how much to do in order to spend only 2 weeks per module? Well, start by spending one half hour per day with the course. At the end of 2 weeks, if you have not completed the module, you know that you need to spend more time each day on it. If you finish a module in less than 2 weeks, then you know that you can spend less time per day on it. In the end, then, try to find the pace that will keep you on track.

There are two types of exercises that you are expected to complete: "on your own" problems and an end-of-the module study guide.

- You should answer the "on your own" problems while you read the text. The act of answering these problems will cement in your mind the concepts you are trying to learn. Detailed answers and explanations are provided for you at the end of the module, so that you may check your own work. DO NOT look at the answer to a question until AFTER you have tried to answer it!

- You should complete the study guide in its entirety after you have finished the module. The solutions to the study guides are in a separate volume which your parent/teacher has.

All definitions presented in the text are centered. The words will appear in the study guide and their definitions need to be memorized. Words that appear in bold-face type in the text are important terms that you should know.

The study guide gives you a good feel for what you need to know for the test. Any information needed to answer the study guide questions is information that you must know for the test. Sometimes, tables and other reference material will be provided on a test so that you need not memorize it. You will be able to tell if this is the case because the questions in the study guide which refer to this information will specifically tell you to use the reference material.

Experiments

The experiments in this course are designed to be done while you are reading the text. I recommend that you keep a notebook of these experiments. As you write about the experiment in the notebook, you will be forced to think through all of the concepts that were explored in the experiment. This will help you cement them into your mind. I recommend that you perform your experiments in the following way:

- When you get to the experiment during the reading, read through the experiment in its entirety. This will allow you to gain a quick understanding of what you must do.

- Once you have read the experiment, start a new page in your laboratory notebook. The first page should be used to write down all of the data taken during the experiments and perform any exercises discussed in the experiment.

- When you have finished the experiment, you should write a brief report in your notebook, right after the page where the data and exercises were written. The report should be a brief discussion of what was done and what was learned. You should write this discussion so that someone who has never read the book can read your discussion and figure out what basic procedure you followed and what you learned as a result of the experiment.

- **PLEASE OBSERVE COMMON SENSE SAFETY PRECAUTIONS. The experiments are no more dangerous than most normal, household activities. Remember, however, that the vast majority of accidents do happen in the home!**

In order to help you prepare for the experiment in the course, the next few pages list all materials needed to perform the experiments in each module. You can use this list to make sure that you have everything you need. That way, when you reach a lab in the reading, you will not be delayed for lack of supplies.

Lab Supplies Needed For Module # 1

- Vegetable oil
- Water
- Maple or corn syrup
- A grape
- A piece of cork
- An ice cube
- A small rock
- A tall glass
- Two glass canning jars or peanut butter jars, both the same size
- Food coloring, any color
- A pan and stove to boil water, and a hotpad to hold the pan
- A plastic, 2-liter bottle
- A balloon (6-9 inch round balloons work best.)
- Clear vinegar
- Baking soda
- A funnel or butter knife
- A few leaves of red (sometimes called purple) cabbage
- A saucepan
- A stove
- Measuring cups
- A pencil
- A sheet of paper (8 ½" by 11")
- Four thumbtacks or pushpins
- A piece of string 8 inches long
- A sheet of cardboard larger than or the same size as the sheet of paper
- Tape

Lab Supplies Needed For Module # 2

- A reasonably heavy book
- A sheet of cardboard about the same size as the book (The cardboard that comes on the back of a pad of paper works well. You can also cut a piece out of an old cardboard box.)
- A sheet of heavy paper (like construction paper or cardstock) about the same size as the book
- A sheet of regular paper about the size of the book
- A metal paper clip
- A small rock (It needs to weigh less than the cardboard, so it should be really small.)
- A working flashlight
- A parent or helper

Lab Supplies Needed For Module # 3

- A tall glass
- Measuring cups for measuring out one and a half cups of water
- An egg
- A teaspoon
- A spoon for stirring
- Water
- Salt
- Four sheet of reasonably thick cardboard (A cut-up cardboard box works nicely.)
- Scissors
- A sheet of facial tissue
- A chunk of soap from a bar of soap
- A stick of chewing gum
- A bathtub or large sink (A bathtub is best.)
- A reasonably large bowl
- Water
- Black pepper
- Tweezers
- A needle
- Thread
- Tape
- Someone to help you

Lab Supplies Needed For Module # 4

- A wooden pencil
- A wooden ruler
- At least 5 quarters, preferably more
- Two brooms or a broom and a mop (You basically need two implements with long handles. The experiment works best when the handles are very smooth.)
- Several feet of rope (Nylon rope works best because it is slick.)
- Two reasonably strong people to help you

Lab Supplies Needed For Module # 5

NONE

Lab Supplies Needed For Module # 6

- Alum (A powder available at any drug store - you need at least 4 ounces)
- Two small glasses (like juice glasses)
- A spoon for stirring
- Some thread
- Two weights (washers, nuts, fishing sinkers, etc.)
- A large plate
- A few rocks from outside (small rocks actually work best)
- A sheet of dark paper (blue, black, etc.)
- A magnifying glass
- Sugar (optional)
- Food coloring (optional)
- A large glass jar with a lid
- Some dirt from your yard
- Some sand
- Some gravel comprised of various sizes of rocks
- Water
- Plaster of Paris
- A medium or large margarine tub
- A few lima beans
- Water
- Paper towels
- Vinegar
- A large glass
- A limestone rock (Most gravel is limestone. You can also go to a home improvement store's garden section and specifically ask for limestone. The rock needs to be small enough to fit in the glass)
- Some steel wool
- A small bowl
- A shoebox
- A gardener's spade (or something else you can use to dig with)
- Scissors
- A spot in the yard in which you can dig
- A water hose and water
- A large rock

Lab Supplies Needed For Module # 7

- A plastic margarine tub
- Water
- A rock that will fit in the tub with a lot of room to spare
- A freezer
- Modeling clay
- Plaster of Paris
- A paper plate
- A shell or something else with a distinctive shape or design
- Vaseline® or another petroleum jelly

Lab Supplies Needed For Module # 8

- 18 index cards (The size is irrelevant, as is the presence or absence of lines.)
- A parent or someone else to write on the cards and hold the key

Lab Supplies Needed For Module #9

- Long pipe cleaners (the longer the better)
- Four different colors of beads (The beads need to have holes in them large enough for the pipe cleaners to fit through. You can get beads like that at any craft store.)
- Scissors strong enough to cut the pipe cleaners
- One slice of potato (uncooked)
- A pale green leaf (The paler the green, the better this experiment will work.)
- Rubbing alcohol (available at any drug store)
- Iodine (available at any drug store)
- One jar with a lid
- Two shallow dishes
- Tweezers
- A large jar with a lid
- A small potted plant that can fit inside the jar with room to spare
- Some water
- An area of the house that gets sunlight most every day
- A piece of masking tape or a marker
- A few earthworms
- A container that will hold the earthworms and plenty of dirt
- Dirt
- Some water
- A bright light
- Large jar (It must be large enough to fit an banana inside.)
- Nylon stocking large enough to stretch over the mouth of the jar
- Rubber band
- A banana

Lab Supplies Needed for Module #10

- One chicken bouillon cube
- Table salt
- White vinegar
- 4 small glasses
- One large glass
- One measuring cup
- One teaspoon
- Masking tape
- Marker or pen
- The four glasses from the beginning of the experiment
- White paper (no lines if possible)
- Baker's active yeast (available at any supermarket)
- Banana
- Two zippered plastic bags (like ZIPLOC® sandwich bags)
- A butter knife
- A marker or some masking tape
- A houseplant (Ivy works best, but most houseplants will work. If you have a few varieties of houseplants and ivy is not among them, you might try a few instead of just one.)
- A glass
- Scissors
- Some water
- A stalk of wilted celery with the leaves still on it
- A glass
- Some water
- A reasonably sharp knife
- Some food coloring (preferably blue)

Lab Supplies Needed for Module #11

- An uncooked chicken bone (preferably a wishbone or wing)
- A jar with a lid
- Vinegar (preferably white)
- Two houseplants. Make sure that your parents won't mind one of them looking really funny once the experiment is over.
- A few books
- A sunny window
- A plastic bandage, such as a Band-Aid®

Lab Supplies Needed for Module #12

- A small candle (It needs to be in some kind of heavy holder, but the holder should not be tall. A small tealight candle in a cup-like holder, like the one in the figure under step (F), is ideal.)
- A glass that will cover the candle
- A deep bowl (The bowl should be deep enough so that when the candle is placed at the bottom of the bowl, the sides of the bowl are well above the flame of the candle.
- One cup of vinegar
- One tablespoon of baking soda
- Matches
- A mirror (A hand-held mirror is best, but any mirror will do.)
- A paper towel
- Red (sometimes called purple) cabbage (You only need a few leaves.)
- Distilled water (You can get it at any large supermarket. You need about a quart.)
- Two drinking straws
- A saucepan
- A stove
- Three small glasses (like juice glasses)
- A ¼-cup measuring cup and a 1-cup measuring cup
- A 2-liter plastic bottle (the kind soda comes in)
- A balloon (6-inch or 8-inch round balloons work best.)
- A small spoon (like a ¼ measuring teaspoon)
- An oral thermometer (The kind you use to take a person's temperature. Do not use one of those strips that you put on your forehead. Use the kind of thermometer you stick in your mouth.)

Lab Supplies Needed for Module #13

- A saltine cracker
- A tablespoon
- Iodine (This is available at any drug store. You used it in Experiment 9.2.)
- Two small glasses
- TUMS antacid tablets (Try to get white ones, or at least a tub of TUMS that have some white ones in it.)
- Toilet bowl cleaner (It should contain hydrochloric acid as an ingredient. The best kind to get is colorless. If you cannot get colorless, get a clear kind that has a light tint of color to it. DO NOT get the kind that clings to the bowl. I used non-clinging THE WORKS® when I ran the experiment.)
- Red (sometimes called purple) cabbage
- A teaspoon
- A separate spoon for stirring
- A saucepan
- A measuring cup
- Distilled water (You can get it at any large supermarket. You need about two quarts.)
- A stove for boiling water
- Baking soda

Lab Supplies Needed for Module #14

- A watch with a second hand or (better yet) a stopwatch
- A place that you can do jumping jacks
- Flexible tubing (If you don't have some, the best place to get it is anywhere that sells aquarium products. It is typically called "aquarium tubing," and it is used to connect the aquarium air pump to the filter.)
- A plastic one gallon jug with a lid
- A sink with a plug
- A measuring cup
- A plastic, 2-liter bottle (the kind soda pop comes in)
- Strong scissors
- A plastic sandwich bag (It needs to be large enough for the bottom of the 2-liter bottle to fit into the bag.)
- Tape
- A round balloon (12-inch is ideal, but any size greater than 6-inch will do.)
- A rubber band (It should be large enough to fit around your wrist without stretching. If the rubber band is larger, it will work fine, but a smaller one will not work.)
- A reasonably fresh white carnation (Almost all big supermarkets sell them these days.)
- Two glasses
- Blue food coloring
- Red food coloring
- A knife
- Two spoons for stirring

Lab Supplies Needed for Module #15

- Three onions (any size)
- A cutting knife (In this experiment, a dull knife works better than a sharp one!)
- A freezer
- A cutting board
- A sink in which you can cut
- A tea bag
- Three small glasses (like juice glasses)
- A paper towel
- A coffee filter
- A funnel
- Scissors
- A tea kettle or pot
- A stove
- A spoon for stirring
- A pile of 2 to 3 books (The pile needs to be at least ¾ as high as one of the glasses.)

Lab Supplies Needed for Module #16

- Scissors
- A pencil
- Paper
- A ball (It needs to be small enough to be thrown with one hand, like a baseball, softball, or golf ball.)
- A coin
- Some stairs or porch steps
- A paper towel tube or rolled-up piece of thick paper
- A few people to test (8 years or older)
- A glass
- A mirror
- A room with a light switch that when closed off gets *really* dark
- A candle
- Matches
- Salt
- Sugar
- Water
- Lemon juice
- Onion juice (Tonic water is a substitute, but it is not as effective. To make onion juice, cut a few slices of onion and put them in a zippered plastic bag. Then strongly press a rolling pin back and forth across the bag several times. In this way, you will squeeze the juice right out of the onion! You do not need a lot of juice.)
- Several toothpicks
- 5 glasses
- Apple
- Onion
- Blindfold
- A knife
- Two paper towels
- Two sheets of paper
- A black marker or pen
- Two well-sharpened pencils
- Some tape

Exploring Creation With General Science

Dr. Jay L. Wile

Table of Contents

Module 1 : A Brief History of Science

Introduction 1
The First Inklings of Science 1
True Science Begins to Emerge 4
Experiment 1.1: Density in Nature 5
Experiment 1.2: Atomic Motion 7
Three Other Notable Greek Scientists 8
The Progress of Science Stalls For a While 12
Experiment 1.3: A Chemical Reaction 12
Science Begins To Pick Up Some Speed Again 16
The Renaissance: The "Golden Age" of Science 19
Experiment 1.4: Mapping the Paths of the Planets 21
The Era of Newton 23
The "Enlightenment" and the Industrial Revolution 25
The Rest of the Nineteenth Century 27
Modern Science (1900 A.D. - Present) 29
Summing it Up 31

Module 2 : Scientific Inquiry

Introduction 35
What Science is NOT 35
Experiment 2.1: How Does Weight Affect the Speed 35
Experiment 2.2: Learning More About Weight and Speed 36
The Scientific Method 40
Experiment 2.3: The Broken Flashlight 43
Failures of the Scientific Method 45
The Limitations of Science 49
Science and Christianity 50

Module 3: How to Analyze and Interpret Experiments

Introduction 59
Experiments and Variables 59
Experiment 3.1: A Floating Egg? 60
Using a Series of Experiments 63
Experiment 3.2: Which "Boat" Will Move? 63
Experiment 3.3: What Does Soap Do To Water? - Part 1 66
Experiment 3.4: What Does Soap Do To Water? - Part 2 67
Recognizing Experimental Variables When They are not Obvious 70
Interpreting the Results of Experiments 73

Module 4: Science, Applied Science, and Technology

Introduction 83
The Distinction Between Science, Applied Science, and Technology 83
Simple Machines 86
The Lever 87
Experiment 4.1: The Lever 87
The Wheel and Axle 93
The Pulley 95
Experiment 4.2: A Simulation of A Series of Pulleys 96
The Inclined Plane 99
The Wedge 100
The Screw 102

Module 5: The History of Life: Archaeology, Geology, and Paleontology

Introduction 111
How Do We Learn About The History of Life? 111
Archaeology and History 112
The Internal Test 116
The External Test 119
The Bibliographic Test 123
Archaeology in the Absence of Historical Documents 124
Relative Dating and the Principle of Superposition 129
What Do We Know About Human History? 130

Module #6: Foundations of Geology

Introduction 137
Soil, Rocks and Minerals..... 138
Experiment 6.1: The Difference Between Rocks and Minerals 140
Strata in Sedimentary Rock 142
Experiment 6.2: Separation of Sedimentation 143
Weathering of Rocks 145
Experiment 6.3: Physical Weathering 146
Experiment 6.4: Chemical Weathering 147
Erosion 149
Experiment 6.5: Erosion 149
Bringing It All Together: The Basic Structure of the Grand Canyon 154

Module #7: The Fossil Record

Introduction 161
The Making of Fossils Part 1: Casts and Molds 161
Experiment 7.1: Making a Fossil Cast 162
The Making of Fossils Part 2: Petrifaction 164
The Making of Fossils Part 3: Carbonate Residues and Impressions 165
The Making of Fossils Part 4: Avoiding Decomposition 167
Experiment 7.2: Sinking in Ice 168
Three General Features of the Fossil Record 170
A Fourth General Feature of the Fossil Record 173
Geology and Paleontology from the Uniformitarian Viewpoint 176
Geology and Paleontology from the Catastrophist Viewpoint 179
Which View is Correct? 182

Module #8: Uniformitarianism and Catastrophism

Introduction 189
Uniformitarianism and the Geological Record 189
Experiment 8.1: A Simulation of Using Index Fossils 190
Uniformitarianism and Evolution 195
Catastrophism and the Geological Record 197
Catastrophism and the Fossil Record 202
Uniformitarianism or Catastrophism: Which is Better? 206
Evolution: Another Weakness of Uniformitarianism 210

Module #9: What is Life?

Introduction 217
DNA and Life 217
The Structure of DNA 220
Experiment 9.1: Building a Model of DNA 221
Energy and Life 225
Experiment 9.2: Finding Food in Plants 225
Experiment 9.3: A Simple Biosphere 227
Sensing and Responding to Change 229
Experiment 9.4: Sensing and Responding to Change 230
Reproduction and Life 231
Experiment 9.5: Fruit Fly Reproduction 232
The Cell - Life's Smallest Unit 235

Module #10: Classifying Life

Experiment 10.1: Factors that Affect Bacterial Growth (Part 1) 243
Introduction 244
The Five-Kingdom System 245
Kingdom Monera 247
Experiment 10.1: Factors that Affect Bacterial Growth (Part 2) 249
Kingdom Protista 252
Kingdom Fungi 255
Experiment 10.2: Yeast is a Decomposer 258
Kingdom Plantae 259
Experiment 10.3: Vegetative Reproduction 259
Experiment 10.4: Turgor Pressure 261
Kingdom Animalia 262

Module #11: The Human Body: Fearfully and Wonderfully Made

Introduction 267
The Superstructure of the Human Body 267
Bones and the Human Skeleton 269
Experiment 11.1: Minerals in Bone 269
Skeletons in Other Organisms 273
Skeletal Muscles 275
Smooth Muscle and the Cardiac Muscle 281
Muscles and Movement in Other Organisms 282
Experiment 11.2: Phototropism and Gravotropism in Plants 283
Skin 284
Experiment 11.3: Skin Color 288
Skin in Other Organisms 289
Summary 289

Module #12: Energy and Life

Introduction 295
Life's Energy Cycle 295
How Do Organisms Get Energy From Food? 298
Experiment 12.1: What Combustion Needs 298
Experiment 12.2: What Combustion Makes 300
What Actually Gets Burned For Energy? 303
Energy Use in the Body 308
Experiment 12.3: Body Temperature 309
Calories and Food 311
Metabolic Rates Throughout Creation 313
How Combustion Works in Living Organisms 314

Module #13: The Human Digestive System

Introduction 321
The Process of Digestion 321
Experiment 13.1: Seeing a Part of the Digestive Process 321
The Human Digestive System 323
The Mouth, Pharynx, and Esophagus 326
The Stomach and Intestines 329
Experiment 13.2: Stomach Acid and Antacids 330
The Liver, Pancreas, and Gall Bladder 335
Experiment 13.3: The Effect of Sodium Bicarbonate on Stomach Acid 337
The Micronutrients 338

Module #14: The Human Respiratory and Circulatory Systems

Introduction 345
The Human Circulatory System 345
The Heart and Blood Flow 348
Experiment 14.1: Your Own Cardiac Cycle 352
The Components of Blood 354
Lungs and Blood Oxygenation 356
Experiment 14.2: Measuring the Capacity of Your Lungs 358
The Respiratory System 360
Experiment 14.3: A Model of Your Lungs 361
Experiment 14.4: A Model of Your Vocal Cords 362
Circulation and Respiration Throughout Creation 363
Experiment 14.5: Xylem 364

Module #15: The Human Lymphatic, Endocrine, and Urinary Systems

Introduction 369
The Lymphatic System 369
Lymph Nodes 372
Tears 375
Experiment 15.1: Working Your Lacrimal Glands Too Hard 376
The Urinary System 378
Experiment 15.2: A Model of Kidney Function 379
The Endocrine System 382

Module #16: The Human Nervous System

Introduction 387
Neurons: The Basic Unit of the Nervous System 389
The Basic Layout of the Human Nervous System 393
Our "Split" Brains 397
Experiment 16.1: Determining a Person's Dominant Side 397
The Brain and Blood 400
The Peripheral Nervous System (PNS) 402
Experiment 16.2: The Pupil of the Eye 403
The Human Sense of Taste 405
Experiment 16.3: Mapping Your Taste Buds 406
The Human Sense of Smell 408
Experiment 16.4: The Sense of Smell and the Sense of Taste 408
The Human Sense of Vision 410
Experiment 16.5: The Human Blind Spot 412
The Human Sense of Touch 415
Experiment 16.6: The Variation in Touch Sensitivity 416
The Human Sense of Hearing 417
Do We Really Use Only 10% of our Brain? 418
Summing it All Up 419

Module #1: A Brief History of Science

Introduction

This course will take you on a tour of what I consider to be the most interesting of all human endeavors: **science**. Now, of course, I am well aware that many people (perhaps even you) do not consider science to be very interesting. Nevertheless, I do believe that most people's dislike of science comes from bad curriculum and/or bad teachers, not the subject itself. Hopefully, as you go through this course, you will see why I find science so incredibly interesting, and if nothing else, you will at least develop an appreciation for this incredible field of study.

So what is science, anyway? Well, the word "science" comes from the Latin word *scientia* (sigh' en tee uh), which means "to have knowledge." It can be generally defined as follows:

Science - A branch of study dedicated to the accumulation and classification of observable facts in order to formulate general laws about the natural world

That's a nice definition, but what does it mean? It means that the *purpose* of science is to develop general laws that explain how the world around us works and why things happen the way that they do. How do we accomplish such a feat? That's where the "accumulation and classification of observable facts" comes in. The *practice* of science involves experimentation and observation. Scientists observe the world around them and collect facts. They also design experiments that alter the circumstances they are observing which, in turn, leads to the collection of more facts. These facts might eventually allow scientists to learn enough about the world around them so that they can develop a new law which helps us understand how the natural world works.

As with any other field, the only way to truly understand where we are in science today is to look at what happened in the past. The history of science can teach us many lessons about how science should and should not be practiced. It can also help us understand the direction in which science is heading today. In the end, then, no one should undertake a serious study of science without first taking a look at its history. That's where we will start in the course. This module will provide you with a brief history of human scientific inquiry. If you do not like history, please stick with this module. You will start to sink your teeth into science in the next module. Without a historical perspective, however, you will not fully appreciate what science is!

The First Inklings of Science (From Ancient Times to 600 B.C.)

Some of the earliest records from history indicate that 3,000 years before Christ, the ancient Egyptians already had reasonably sophisticated medical practices. Sometime around 2650 B.C., for example, a man named **Imhotep** (eem' oh tep) was renowned for his knowledge of medicine. People traveled from all over the Middle East to visit Imhotep, hoping that he would cure their illnesses.

Most historians agree that the heart of Egyptian medicine was trial and error. Egyptian doctors would try one remedy and, if it worked, they would continue to use it. If a remedy they tried didn't work, the patient might die, but at least the doctors learned that next time, they should try a different remedy. Despite the fact that such practices sound primitive, the results were, sometimes, surprisingly effective. For example, Egyptian doctors learned that if you covered an open wound with moldy bread, the wound would heal quickly and cleanly. As a result, most Egyptian doctors applied moldy bread to their patients' wounds. Modern science tells us that bread mold typically produces **penicillin**, a chemical that kills germs which infect wounds! Thus, even though the Egyptian doctors knew *nothing* about germs, they were able to treat wounds so that they would not get infected by germs!

Another example of the surprisingly effective art of ancient Egyptian medicine can be seen in the way they treated pain. In order to relieve a patient who was in extreme pain, Egyptian doctors would have the patient eat large numbers of seeds from a flowering plant called the **poppy**. Eating these **poppy seeds** would almost always relieve the patient's pain. Modern science tells us *why* this worked. Poppy seeds contain both **morphine** and **codeine**, which are excellent pain-relieving drugs still used today!

Now it is important to realize that although Egyptian doctors could heal people who otherwise would die, they still did not understand much about the human body. They didn't know *why* moldy bread helped wounds heal. They simply knew that it did, and therefore they used it.

Why was Egyptian medicine so advanced compared to the medical practices of other ancient nations? Well, perhaps the most important reason was the Egyptian invention of **papyrus** (puh pie' rus).

Papyrus - A primitive form of paper, made from a long-leafed plant of the same name

As early as 3,000 years before Christ, Egyptians took thin slices of the stem of the papyrus plant, laid them crosswise on top of each other, moistened them, and then pressed and dried them. The result was a form of paper that was reasonably easy to write on and store.

The invention of this ancient form of paper revolutionized the way information was transmitted from person to person and generation to generation. Before papyrus, Egyptians, Sumerians, and other races wrote on clay tablets or smooth rocks. This was a time-consuming process, and the products were not easy to store or transport. When Egyptians began writing on papyrus, all of that changed. Papyrus was easy to roll into scrolls. Thus, Egyptian writings became easy to store and transport. As a result, the knowledge of one scholar could be easily transferred to other scholars. As this accumulated knowledge was passed down from generation to generation, Egyptian medicine became the most respected form of medicine in the known world!

Papyrus photo by Harold St. John

Poppy photo from the Corel 'Fabulous Flowers' collection

FIGURE 1.1
Papyrus And Poppy Plants

Papyrus Plant
Egyptians used this plant to make a primitive form of paper.

Poppy Plant
Egyptians used the seeds from this plant as a powerful pain killer

Although the Egyptians were renowned for their medicine and for papyrus, other cultures had impressive inventions of their own. Around the time that papyrus was first being used in Egypt, the Mesopotamians were making pottery using the first known potter's wheel. Not long after, the Sumerians developed horse-drawn chariots. As early as 1,000 years before Christ, the Chinese were using compasses to aid themselves in their travels. The ancient world, then, was filled with inventions that, although they sound commonplace today, revolutionized life during those times. These inventions are history's first inklings of science.

As you progress through this course, you will see that it is divided into sections. Usually, at the end of each section, you will find one or two "on your own" questions. You should answer these questions as soon as you come to them in the reading. They are designed to make you think about what you have just read. These questions are often not very easy to answer, as you cannot simply look back on the material and find the answer. You must *think* about what you have learned and make some conclusions in order to answer the question. You will find your first "on your own" question below. Answer it on a separate sheet of paper and then check your answer against the solution provided at the back of this module.

ON YOUR OWN

1.1 Although the ancient Egyptians had reasonably advanced medical practices for their times, and although there were many inventions that revolutionized life in the ancient world, most historians of science do not think of Egyptian doctors and the ancient inventors as scientists. Why? (Hint: Look at the entire definition of science.)

True Science Begins to Emerge (600 B.C. to 500 A.D.)

As far as historians can tell, the first true scientists were the ancient Greeks. Remember, science consists of collecting facts and observations and then using those observations to explain the natural world. Although many cultures like the ancient Egyptians, Sumerians, Mesopotamians, and Chinese had collected observations and facts, they had not tried to use those facts to develop explanations of the world around them. As near as historians can tell, that didn't happen until the 6th century B.C., with three individuals known as **Thales**, **Anaximander** (an axe' uh man der), and **Anaximenes** (an axe' uh me nees). Many historians view these three individuals as humanity's first real scientists.

Thales studied the heavens and tried to develop a unifying theme that would explain the movement of the heavenly bodies (the planets and stars). He was at least partially successful, as history tells us he used his ideas to predict certain planetary events. For example, he gained a great reputation throughout the known world when he correctly predicted the "short-term disappearance of the sun." What he predicted, of course, was a solar eclipse, where the moon moves between the earth and the sun, mostly blocking the sun from view.

Anaximander was actually a pupil of Thales. He was much more interested in the study of life, however. As far as we know, he was the first scientist to try and explain the origin of the human race without reference to a creator. He believed that all life began in the sea, and at one time, humans were actually some sort of fish. This idea was later resurrected by other scientists, most notably Charles Darwin, and is today called the "theory of evolution." Later on in this course, I will discuss this theory, showing its scientific flaws.

Anaximenes was an associate of Anaximander. He believed that air was the most basic substance in nature. In fact, he believed all things were constructed of air. When air is thinned out, he thought, it grows warm and becomes fire. When air is thickened, he thought, it condenses into liquid and solid matter. We know, of course, that these ideas are wrong. Nevertheless, his attempts to explain all things in nature as being made of a single substance led to one of the most important scientific ideas introduced by the Greeks: the concept of **atoms**.

Leucippus (lew sip' us) was a Greek scientist who lived perhaps 100 - 150 years after Anaximenes. Although little is known about him, historians believe that he built on the concepts of Anaximenes and proposed that all matter is comprised of little units called "atoms." As a result, Leucippus is known as the father of atomic theory. The works of his student, **Democritus** (duh mah' crit us) are much better preserved.

Democritus used the following illustration to communicate his ideas about atoms. Think about walking towards a sandy beach. When you are a long way from the beach, the sand looks like a smooth, yellow blanket. As you get closer to the beach, you might notice that there are bumps and valleys in the sand, but the sand still looks solid. When you reach the beach and actually kneel down and examine the sand, you find that it is not solid at all. Instead, it is composed of tiny particles called "grains."

Democritus believed that all matter was similar to sand. Even though a piece of wood appears to be solid, it is, in fact, made up of little individual particles which Democritus and his teacher called atoms. Perform the following experiment to see the kind of evidence they proposed for their idea.

EXPERIMENT 1.1
Density in Nature

Supplies

- Vegetable oil
- Water
- Maple or corn syrup
- A grape
- A piece of cork
- An ice cube
- A small rock
- A tall glass

Introduction - The Greek scientists who speculated about atoms used observations such as the ones you will make in this experiment to provide evidence for the existence of atoms.

Procedure:

A. Take the glass and fill it about 1/4 of the way with the vegetable oil.
B. Add an equal amount of water to the glass.
C. Add an equal amount of maple syrup to the glass.
D. Now look at the glass from the side. What do you see? In your laboratory notebook, make a sketch of what you see.
E. Drop the rock, the grape, the ice cube, and the piece of cork into the glass. Now what do you see? Add the rock, grape, ice cube, and cork to the sketch you made in step (D).
F. Clean up the mess and put everything away.

What did you see in the experiment? If everything went well, you should have seen that the liquids formed layers in the glass. The vegetable oil formed a layer on top, the water layer was in the middle, and the syrup layer was at the bottom. In addition, the cork should have floated on top of the vegetable oil; the ice cube should have floated on top of the water layer; the grape should have floated on top of the syrup layer, and the rock should have sunk to the bottom of the glass.

How in the world is this experiment evidence for the existence of atoms? Well, according to Democritus, the water, vegetable oil, and syrup are all made of individual particles called atoms. The atoms that make up water, however, are packed together more closely than are those of the vegetable oil. Thus, when the water was poured on the vegetable oil, the atoms in the water were able to squeeze in-between the atoms in the vegetable oil, sinking to the bottom of the glass. In the same way, the atoms in the syrup are more tightly-packed than those in water or vegetable oil, so the syrup's atoms were able to fall in between the atoms of both the vegetable oil and the water and land at the bottom of the glass.

Even solid objects are made up of atoms. Thus, the cork's atoms are packed together very loosely and cannot fit in between the atoms of the vegetable oil. That's why it floats on top of the vegetable oil. The atoms in the ice cube, however, are tightly-packed enough to squeeze in between the atoms of the vegetable oil, but they cannot fit in between the atoms of the water. Thus, the ice cube falls through the vegetable oil but not the water. Similarly, the atoms in the grape are tightly-packed enough to squeeze between the atoms in the vegetable oil and the water, but not the atoms in the syrup. The atoms in the rock, however, are tightly packed enough to squeeze through all of the other atoms, and thus the rock sinks to the bottom.

At this point, I am done discussing the experiment. Now that you know what the experiment shows, you can write a summary in your laboratory notebook. Write a brief description of what you did, followed by a discussion of what you learned. You will need to do each experiment in this way. Once you have done an experiment and read the discussion that relates to it, you then need to write a summary explaining what you did and what you learned. This will help you get the most from your laboratory exercises.

Democritus was not well-received in his time, but later scientists picked up on his ideas and refined them. Today, we know that all matter is made up of atoms. Indeed, today we have a term that describes how tightly atoms are packed in a substance. We call it **density**. If a substance has a large density, its atoms are tightly-packed. If a substance has a low density, its atoms are less tightly-packed.

Although Democritus was right about all things being comprised of atoms, he was wrong about most of the details regarding what atoms are really like. He believed, for example, that atoms were indestructible. We now know that is wrong. After all, the atomic bomb and nuclear energy are both based on our ability to split atoms. In addition, he thought that the difference between one atom and another was mostly based on shape and size. We now know that atoms are mostly the same shape, and there is a distinct limit to their size. Atoms are so small that roughly 100,000,000,000,000,000,000 atoms are contained in the head of a pin! They are therefore too small for us to see. Nevertheless, we *do* know that they exist. How do we know they exist if we cannot see them? You will learn about that in a later module of this course.

There was one detail regarding atoms that Democritus was right about. He thought that atoms were in constant motion. For example, if a glass of water is sitting on a table, you might think that the water is not in motion. To some extent, you would be right. After all, the water in the glass stays in the glass, and the glass itself stays on the table. At the same time, however, the atoms that make up the water are in *constant* motion. They move around within the confines of the glass, rebounding off of the walls of the glass and colliding into each other.

You might find it hard to believe that the atoms within a glass of water are in motion when the water itself is not. However, you might find it a little easier to believe after performing the following experiment.

EXPERIMENT 1.2
Atomic Motion

Supplies:
- Two glass canning jars or peanut butter jars, both the same size
- Food coloring, any color
- A pan and stove to boil water, and a hotpad to hold the pan

Introduction - By seeing how food coloring gets distributed through two jars of water at different temperatures, you will collect evidence for the fact that atoms are in constant motion.

Procedure:
1. Boil some water. You need to boil enough water so that the boiled water will fill one of the jars about halfway.
2. Once the water is boiling, take it off of the stove (use the hotpad!) and pour it into one of the jars. Pour in enough water so that the jar is filled about halfway.
3. Take the other jar and fill it about halfway with cold water from the tap.
4. Wait one minute so that the water in each jar is still.
5. Drop a single drop of food coloring into each jar. Observe what happens over the next several minutes. Record in your laboratory notebook the difference between what happened in each jar.
6. OPTIONAL: Let the jar with the cold water sit out for a full day. Record what the jar looks like after it has set out for a full day.
7. Clean everything up.

What did you see in the experiment? If everything went well, you should have seen the drop of food coloring mix rapidly with the hot water, coloring the entire jar of water relatively quickly. In the jar of cold water, however, the food coloring should not have mixed well at all. Why the difference? The answer is the motion of atoms. When a substance is hot, its atoms move faster than when a substance is cold. When you added food coloring to the cold water, then, the atoms in the water collided with the atoms in the food coloring, moving them around. However, since the atoms in the cold water were not moving very quickly, the food coloring did not get moved around much, so it did not mix well with the water. Given enough time, the food coloring will mix well with the water, eventually becoming evenly distributed throughout the jar. When you added the food coloring to the hot water, however, the collisions between the atoms in the food coloring and the atoms in the water were much more violent, because the atoms in the water were moving so much more quickly. This moved the atoms in the food coloring around quite a bit, spreading them out evenly throughout the jar of water in a short time.

In the end, then, even though Democritus was wrong about a great many things, he was right about two important ideas. First, all things are, indeed, made up of atoms. Second, those atoms are in constant motion. Now as I said before, Democritus was not well-received in his time. Most of his fellow scientists rejected his ideas. In fact, the whole idea of the existence of atoms did not gain much popular support among scientists for almost 2,000 years! This just goes to show you that scientists do not always recognize a good idea when they see one. In fact, the history of science is filled with instances of scientists rejecting good ideas in favor of bad ones. You will see more examples of that as you work through the rest of this module.

ON YOUR OWN

1.2 Based on your results in Experiment 1.1, order the items you used in your experiment (water, vegetable oil, the grape, etc.) in terms of increasing density. In other words, list the item with the lowest density first, followed by items of higher and higher density, and end your list with the item of greatest density.

1.3 Do the atoms in an ice cube move faster or slower than the atoms in a glass of water?

Three Other Notable Greek Scientists

Ancient Greece gave us many more notable scientists. It is impossible to discuss them all in a single chapter, but there are three more that simply must be mentioned. The first is **Aristotle**, who is often called the father of the life sciences. Aristotle was born shortly before Democritus died. He wrote volumes of works on many things, including philosophy, mathematics, logic, and physics. His greatest work, however, was in the study of living things. He was the first to make a large-scale attempt at the **classification** of animals and plants.

What is classification? Well, classification is a lot like filing papers. Remember, science is a two-part process. A scientist must gather facts and then use those facts to draw conclusions about how the natural world works. As you gather more and more facts, they tend to get hard to use unless they can be ordered in some reasonable, systematic way. That's what classification is all about. By the time of Aristotle, Greek scientists had cataloged many plants and animals, but there were so many that keeping track of them was proving to be very difficult. Aristotle came up with a classification scheme that allowed him to group the known plants and animals into an easy-to-reference system. Because Aristotle was financially supported by **Alexander the Great** (you should have read about him in history books), he was able to obtain plant and animal samples from all over the known world, adding those to his classification scheme.

Although we do not use Aristotle's particular classification scheme nowadays, all fields of science are still committed to the concept of classification. Indeed, scientists who study living things today are still wrestling with producing the ideal classification system for understanding the life sciences. In a future module of this course, you will get a brief introduction to biological classification. You will then see a *lot* more of it when you reach biology in high school.

Although Aristotle was known for a great number of wonderful advances in the sciences, he was also responsible for a great deal of nonsense that hampered science for many, many years. For example, he believed that certain living organisms spontaneously formed from non-living substances. This idea was called **spontaneous generation**.

Spontaneous generation - The idea that living organisms can be spontaneously formed from non-living substances

For example, Aristotle believed that maggots (young flies) spontaneously formed from rotting meat. If you put rotting meat out, it would simply turn into maggots within a few days. He also believed that eels formed spontaneously from the muck at the bottom of a river or pond.

Of course, we now know that spontaneous generation is impossible. In all of our experience, life can only be formed by the reproduction of life. People can have children, animals can have babies, and plants can produce seeds which will grow into new plants. These are some of the ways that life is formed. Life simply cannot be formed from non-living substances. You will learn a lot more of the details regarding the story of spontaneous generation when you take biology. For right now, however, I want to make a point about how science should *not* be done, and spontaneous generation is the best example to use in order to make this point.

You see, all great scientists make mistakes. Democritus was thousands of years ahead of his time in proposing the existence of atoms, but he was wrong about most of the details regarding atoms. Aristotle made great advances in the study of living things, but he believed in spontaneous generation. Aristotle's mistake was much more damaging to the advancement of science than was Democritus' mistakes. Why? Because Aristotle was *respected*! You see, Aristotle was considered (rightly so) to be the greatest scientist of his time. Thus, his ideas (even the wrong ones) were revered for *generations*! In fact, the absurd notion of spontaneous generation lasted until *1870*, more than *2,000 years* after it was proposed by Aristotle.

Why did the idea of spontaneous generation last for so long? Because it came from Aristotle, and Aristotle was considered a great scientist. In other words, *the reputation of the author*, not scientific evidence, was the reason people believed in the idea. It took more than 2,000 years for science to show the fallacy of spontaneous generation, simply because people revered Aristotle so much. This is a great example of how science should *not* be done. Every scientist, no matter how great, will make mistakes. Thus, no scientist's work should be supported because the *person* was great. It should only be supported because the *scientific evidence* supports it! Sadly, this lesson has not been learned by many of today's scientists!

The next Greek scientist worthy of note was **Archimedes** (ark uh me' deez), who lived roughly 100 years after Aristotle. He did great work in mathematics, and he used much of what he discovered in math to advance science. He applied mathematical formulas to explain why certain things happened the way they did. Archimedes was really one of the first scientists to demonstrate how closely mathematics and science are linked.

Archimedes is probably best know for his work with fluids. He was the first to show how you could predict whether or not an object would float in a liquid. His work with liquids led to one of the more entertaining stories in the history of science. The king that Archimedes served, King Hiero, once asked Archimedes to analyze a crown that was given to the king as a gift. The crown was supposed to be made of gold, but the king was skeptical. Archimedes knew how to determine whether or not the crown was made of gold, but the process required him to know the exact amount of space that the crown occupied. This seemed impossible, as the crown was so irregularly-shaped that Archimedes could not find a way to measure it accurately.

Well, one day while taking a bath, Archimedes realized that when an item is immersed in water, it displaces the same amount of water as the space that the item occupies. Thus, all Archimedes had to do was immerse the crown in water and determine how much water it displaced. That would tell him how much space the crown occupied. Archimedes was so excited by this discovery that he grabbed the crown and ran through the streets screaming "Eureka," which means "I have found it." There was one embarrassing little problem, however. Archimedes was so excited by his discovery that he *forgot to put any clothes on*! In other words, he ran through the streets *completely naked!*

The last Greek scientist I want to discuss lived about 100 years after Christ's birth. His name was **Ptolemy** (tall' uh mee), and he studied the heavens. He was the first to try and make a complete description of the planets and stars. He assumed that the earth was at the center of the universe, and that the planets and stars orbited about the earth in a series of circles.

FIGURE 1.2
The Ptolemaic System

In the Ptolemaic system, the earth sits at the center of the universe and does not move. The planets travel around the earth in circles called epicycles. The moon is closest to the earth, followed by Mercury, Venus, the sun, Mars, Jupiter, and Saturn. Those were the only planets known in Ptolemy's day. The stars are contained in a canopy called "the heaven." Although the stars are fixed in the heaven, the heaven itself rotates, which makes the stars themselves appear to move.

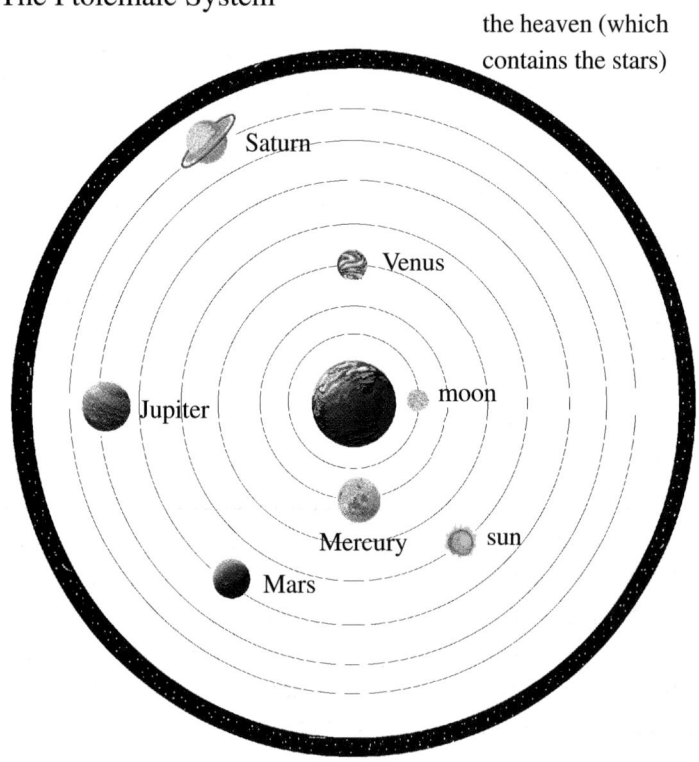

At the time, Ptolemy could explain most of the astronomical data that had been collected using his idea, so it became very popular. Sometimes, his view of the stars and planets is referred to as the **Ptolemaic system**, in an attempt to honor him. Sometimes, it is referred to as the **geocentric system**, to emphasize the fact that Ptolemy thought the earth was at the center of the universe.

The Ptolemaic system was considered the correct explanation for the arrangements of planets and stars in space until the 1700's. Thus, it was a popular theory for nearly 1600 years. Once again, however, the reason that the Ptolemaic system was so popular had less to do with the scientific evidence and more to do with other considerations. Like Aristotle, Ptolemy was (rightly) considered a great scientist. As data were collected that contradicted the Ptolemaic system, many scientists ignored it in reverence to Ptolemy.

There was actually another, probably more important reason that the Ptolemaic system became so popular. It became popular because it fit many scientists' preconceived notions of how things ought to be. In the Ptolemaic system, the earth was at the center of the universe and everything revolved around the earth. Since most people believed that the earth was the most important part of the universe, the Ptolemaic system "made sense."

Sadly, the most ardent support for the Ptolemaic system came from the church. As more and more scientific evidence came pouring in indicating severe flaws in the Ptolemaic system, the church tried to resist any movement away from it. After all, the church reasoned, since God created man, the earth must be the most important thing in the universe, so it must be at the very center, and everything else must travel around it, just as Ptolemy said. Now, of course, nowhere in the Bible is such a thing written, but that didn't stop the church from believing in it!

In the end, it took hundreds of years of scientific data (and a few people thrown out of the church) before the church was convinced to give up on the Ptolemaic system. Unfortunately, by that time, the damage had been done. The church became viewed as antagonistic to science, and some people today still hold that view. This is unfortunate because, as you will see in later sections of this module, Christianity is a friend to science. Most of the great scientists in history were Christians, and it was their Christianity that many credited for their scientific achievements. Nevertheless, because the church was unwilling to give up on the Ptolemaic system when the scientific evidence was overwhelming, many still see Christianity as an enemy of science. That's too bad.

So this little episode from history shows us another way that science should *not* be done. You should not hold fast to an idea simply because it fits with your preconceived notions. Science is built on data, not a person's beliefs. The acceptance or rejection of a scientific proposition, then, should rest solely on the data, nothing more. Today, there is a theory called **evolution**. It is popular among scientists not because there is a lot of evidence for it, but because it fits in with many scientists' preconceived notions. As you will learn in a later module, very little evidence exists for the theory of evolution, and much evidence exists against it. Nevertheless, it is still a prevalent theory because many people like the fact that it tries to explain the existence of life without ever referring to God. As a result, they believe the theory in spite of the evidence. Unfortunately, these people have not learned from the history of science. The history of science teaches us over and over again that believing in an idea because of preconceived notions hurts the cause of science; it does not help it!

ON YOUR OWN

1.4 Dr. Steven Hawking is one of the most brilliant scientists of the decade. He believes in a theory called "the big bang." This theory tries to describe how the universe was formed. If your friend tells you that you should believe in the big bang because Dr. Hawking is so smart and he believes in it, what famous example from the history of science should you tell to your friend?

1.5 What episode from the history of science tells us that we need to leave our personal biases behind when we do science?

The Progress of Science Stalls For a While (From 500 A.D. to 1000 A.D.)

From the time of the first three Greek scientists (Thales, Anaximander, and Anaximenes) until about 400-500 A.D., science progressed at a dizzying rate. Many scientists proposed many ideas trying to explain the natural world. Those ideas were debated and compared to observations. Great houses of learning were established to foster scientific inquiry. Works like those of Aristotle and Ptolemy became the guiding principles behind the progress of science.

After the first few centuries A.D., however, the progress of science stalled dramatically. By that time, the Roman Empire had a great deal of influence throughout the known world, and Rome had a distinct dislike of science. The Roman Empire did not mind the inventions, especially those that made work more productive, but it had little use for the practice of explaining the world around us. As a result, science was actively discouraged in most parts of the world.

Alchemy is one of the best examples of what passed for science during this time period. Alchemists mostly wanted to find a means by which lead (or other inexpensive substances) could be transformed into gold (or other precious substances). You see, many people had observed the fact that when you mix certain substances together, they change into other substances. Perform the following experiment to see what I mean.

EXPERIMENT 1.3
A Chemical Reaction

Supplies:

- A plastic, 2-liter bottle
- A balloon (6-9 inch round balloons work best.)

- Clear vinegar
- Baking soda
- A funnel or butter knife
- A few leaves of red (sometimes called purple) cabbage
- A saucepan
- A stove
- Measuring cups
- A few ice cubes

Introduction – During the Dark Ages, people observed that mixing several substances together could cause amazing results. This experiment shows you some of what can happen when the right substances are mixed together.

Procedure:

A. Put about 2 cups of water in the saucepan and add several leaves of red cabbage. Put it on a stove burner and heat it so that the water boils.
B. While you are waiting on the water to boil, take the balloon and put baking soda in it. You want to have about 2 tablespoons of baking soda in the balloon. The best way to do this, of course, is to use a funnel. If you do not have a funnel, try picking up the baking soda on the flat of a butter knife, pushing the knife into the balloon's opening, and then tipping the knife so that the baking soda spills into the balloon. It is tedious, but it will work.
C. Once the balloon has about 2 tablespoons of baking soda in it, pour 3/4 of a cup of clear vinegar into the 2-liter bottle.
D. Once the water in the saucepan reaches boiling, remove it from the heat. Allow the liquid in the pan to cool by adding some ice. The liquid should have a blue or pink color now.
E. Add ½ of a cup of the liquid to the 2-liter bottle.
F. Attach the balloon to the opening of the 2-liter bottle by stretching the balloon's opening over the lip of the bottle. In the end, your experiment should look like this:

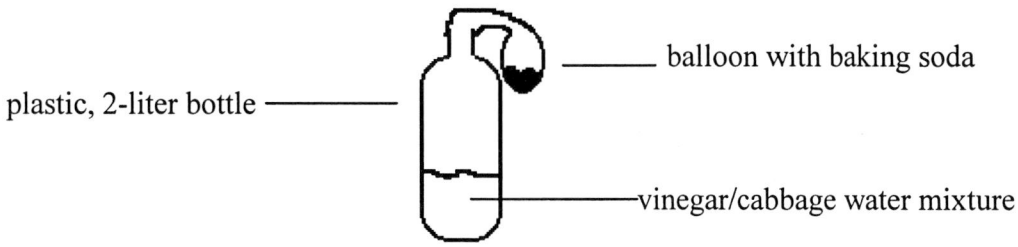

G. Once you are ready, lift the balloon so that the baking soda falls into the vinegar. Write down what you see in your laboratory notebook.
H. Clean everything up and put it all away.

What did you see in the experiment? When the baking soda hit the vinegar, the mixture began to bubble and fizz, and the balloon began to inflate. At the same time, you should have noticed a color change. The mixture should have turned from a pinkish color to a bluish color.

What happened? Well, you witnessed the effect of a **chemical reaction**. In a chemical reaction, one or more substances interact to form one or more new substances.

In your experiment, there were actually 2 chemical reactions going on. The first occurred when vinegar was mixed with baking soda. Those two substances interacted, forming two new substances: carbon dioxide and water. The carbon dioxide, which is a gas, bubbled out of the vinegar and into the balloon, filling up the balloon. The second reaction occurred as the vinegar was being used up in the first reaction. A substance in red cabbage, anthocyanin (an tho sigh' an un), interacts with vinegar to form a pink color. As the vinegar disappeared in the first reaction, the anthocyanin no longer had vinegar to interact with, so the pink color went away and was replaced by a blue color.

Alchemists in the Dark Ages saw changes like this and decided that if they were just able to find the right recipe, they could mix lead with several other substances and make gold. Of course, we now know that this is impossible, because we know that there are severe limitations on how much one substance can change in a chemical reaction. You will learn all about that when you take chemistry. The alchemists of the Dark Ages didn't know this, however, so they strove to mix substance after substance with lead, hoping one day to find that "magic" mixture which would turn lead into gold.

As alchemists began mixing and recording, many interesting things were observed. These observations were written down, and, every once in a while, one of the mixtures would form some useful substance. The recipe to make this useful substance would then be recorded, and the alchemist would proceed on to the next mixture. Like ancient Egyptian medicine, then, the alchemists (and most "scientists" of the Dark Ages) really just learned things by trial and error. They never tried to take their observations and draw conclusions about how the natural world works. Instead, they were content to just write down their observations and move on to the next experiment, searching for the next useful substance they could make.

Interestingly enough, even though the ideas of Rome held great sway in most of the known world, the Roman Empire itself began to crumble. As that happened, trade and large-scale communication became harder and harder. Since science thrives on the free exchange of ideas from one scientist to another, this put another roadblock in the way of scientific progress. Many historians refer to this period as the **Dark Ages**, because compared to the previous time period in history as well as the next time period in history, little was learned.

So here we find another lesson that we can learn from the history of science. Scientific progress depends not only on scientists, but it also depends on government and culture. Since the Romans actively discouraged science and concentrated on inventions, the progress of science slowed. Since the crumbling government caused trade and communications to become more difficult, scientific progress slowed even more. For science to proceed, then, the government and the culture must support it.

Although the progress of science slowed during this period, there are a few things worth noting. Most of the knowledge that had accumulated up to this point was carefully preserved by

Roman Catholic monks. These monks, and Christians in general, believed that God had revealed Himself to His creation in two ways: through scripture and through nature. Thus, these monks were committed to preserving *both* means of revelation. They copied and re-copied scripture so as to preserve it for coming generations. They also did the same with the accumulated scientific knowledge of the time. They created large volumes of scientific observations and speculations which came to be known as **encyclopedias**. These encyclopedias, with their vast accumulation of data and ideas, were one of the main reasons that science was able to flourish in the next period of history.

Another thing worth noting about this period is the fact that although real science stalled dramatically, there were still a lot of people making observations and inventing things. Both Arabs and Chinese during this time period were involved in making careful studies of the heavens. They made observations that were much more detailed and precise than those of the Greek scientists that came before them. Even though there were very few attempts to explain *what those data meant*, at least the data were being collected, and they would be used by later scientists to draw great conclusions about the world around us.

For example, Chinese records from 1054 A.D. include detailed observations of a phenomenon that the Chinese observers did not understand. Although they did not understand it, they recorded their observations in great detail, and modern scientists were able to use those observations to determine that the Chinese had seen a **supernova**, which is essentially the explosion of a star. The observations were so detailed that modern scientists were able to determine *where* this explosion happened, and when they looked at that part of space, they found a cloud of dust and gas which is called a **nebula**. Based on these facts, modern scientists now believe that a nebula is the remains of a star which has exploded.

Photo from the MasterClips Collection

FIGURE 1.3
The Crab Nebula

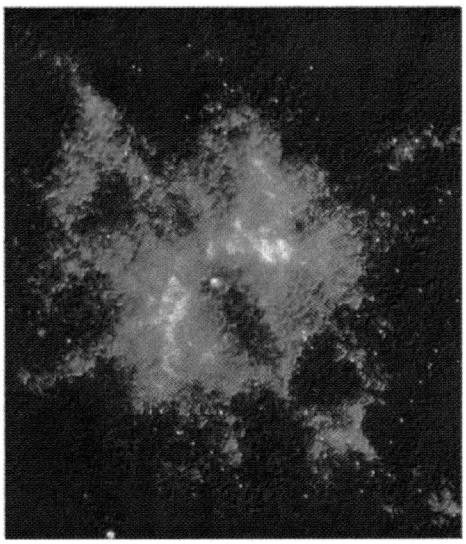

The Crab Nebula is believed to be the remains of a star that exploded. Scientists believe this because ancient Chinese records contain observations of that part of the sky consistent with a star exploding. The only thing in that portion of the sky today is the Crab Nebula.

Once again, then, we come to another lesson in the history of science. Science progresses by building on the works of previous scientists. Had the monks of this time period not cataloged and preserved the thoughts and observations of the scientists that had come before them, the scientists that came after them would not have had a foundation upon which to build. Had the Chinese not recorded such detailed observations of the night sky, modern scientists might still not know where a nebula comes from. Thus, in order for science to advance, we must study and preserve the works of the scientists that come before us. As more and more scientific knowledge is accumulated, this becomes a more and more important task.

Another thing worth noting about this time period is that the Christian church (mostly the Roman Catholic church) was instrumental in continuing the progress of medical treatment. The works of previous scientists were studied in monasteries, because Christians believed it was their duty to aid and comfort the sick. Thus, the medical advances that had been made up to this period in history were preserved and practiced throughout the Dark Ages. In addition, although no real understanding about the human body emerged, more trial-and-error medicine such as that practiced by the ancient Egyptians did lead to modest advances in the treatment of illness.

ON YOUR OWN

1.6 A great many scientists today worry that most of the younger generation does not appreciate science very much. There are those that worry about the future of science when the younger generation grows up. Although it is true that most young people today don't care for or about science, there are some who do. They will obviously become the scientists of the future. Since there will always be at least a few people who are interested in science, why are today's scientists so worried about the future of science?

Science Begins To Pick Up Some Speed Again (1000 A.D. – 1500 A.D.)

Towards the end of the Dark Ages, real science slowly began to emerge again, thanks mostly to the Roman Catholic church. Remember, science slowed considerably at the beginning of the Dark Ages due to the influence of the Roman Empire, which had little regard for real science. One of the reasons it held science in such low esteem was due to the predominate religion of the Roman Empire. The Romans believed in many gods. These gods roamed the universe, alternately torturing or helping humans, depending on the gods' whims. With such a religion, there was no reason to believe that the natural world could be explained. After all, the gods' actions were random, based on whims. Thus, the Romans reasoned, the natural world itself (which was the creation of the gods) must also be rather random. As a result, Romans believed that the natural world simply could not be explained.

By A.D. 1000, however, Christian scholars began realizing that their beliefs promoted a completely different way of looking at the world around them. They believed in a single God who created the universe according to His laws. Since they believed that God's laws never changed, they realized that the natural laws which God set into motion should also never change.

As a result, the way that the natural world worked could be explained, as long as scientists could discover the natural laws which God set into motion.

It might seem painfully obvious to you that the natural world must obey certain laws. However, that kind of thinking was relatively revolutionary at the end of the Dark Ages. Now realize that this kind of thinking wasn't really *new*. It was just different than the predominate idea of the day. After all, the Greek scientists like Aristotle and Ptolemy also believed that the natural world could be explained by laws which did not change. Nevertheless, their thinking was mostly ignored during the Dark Ages, due to the influence of Roman thought.

Perhaps the most important figure in this time period was **Robert Grosseteste** (grow' suh test ee). Grosseteste was a bishop in the Roman Catholic church in the early 1200's A.D., and he was deeply committed to the idea that the secrets of the natural world could be learned by discovering the laws that God had set in motion. He taught that the purpose of inquiry was not to come up with great inventions, but instead to learn the *reasons* behind the facts. In other words, he wanted to explain *why* things happened the way that they did. That's the essence of science.

Grosseteste taught that a scientist should make observations and then come up with a tentative explanation for *why* the observed events happened. The scientist should then come up with experiments that would test his explanation. If the results of the experiments confirmed the explanation, then the explanation might be considered reliable. If the experiments contradicted the explanation, then the explanation must be wrong.

As you will learn in the next chapter, this is essentially the method that we use today in modern science. Thus, Grosseteste is often called the father of the scientific method, because he was the first to explain and use it. Grosseteste applied his scientific method to the problem of explaining the rainbow. Although Grosseteste never developed a satisfactory explanation for the rainbow, a Roman Catholic priest who lived roughly 50 years later, **Dietrich Von Freiberg**, built on Grosseteste's work and was able to offer an explanation for why a rainbow appears in the sky. Because of that, Von Freiberg is often called "the priest who solved the mystery of the rainbow." Next year (in physical science), you will learn about how a rainbow forms.

Although Grosseteste is considered the father of the scientific method, his pupil, **Roger Bacon**, is more famous and is sometimes given that title in error. Bacon staunchly advocated the use of his teacher's scientific method. He tried over and over again to use science to break the shackles of superstition. For example, conventional wisdom in Bacon's day was that a diamond could be broken only by the application of goat's blood. He proposed experiments that, when performed, showed that goat's blood had no effect whatsoever on diamonds.

Bacon also had a strong belief that science could be used to support the reality of Christianity. A devout Roman Catholic theologian, Bacon believed that the more man learned about science, the more he would learn about God. In addition, Bacon seemed to see the potential of science when few others did. In his writings, he predicted that science would bring about marvels such as flying machines, explosives, submarines, and worldwide travel. People laughed at his ideas back then, but historians today marvel at his insight.

Roughly 70 years after Bacon (in the early 1300's), another important figure, **Thomas Bradwardine** (brad war' deen), emerged on the scene. Bradwardine was a bishop in the Roman Catholic church, and his work was important on two levels. First and foremost, Bradwardine was a theologian who questioned much of the Roman Catholic church's teachings. Most church historians consider him the first Reformer, because he emphasized salvation through faith and the grace of God. The more well-known reformers (Luther and Calvin) were heavily influenced by Bradwardine's work.

Not only was Bradwardine an important figure in church history, he was also important in the development of modern science. Bradwardine was the first scientist to examine many of Aristotle's ideas critically. He found most of them lacking. He concentrated on understanding motion. He wanted to know why things moved, what kept them moving, and what made them stop. He applied mathematics to his study of motion and actually developed equations which tried to describe the details of speed, distance traveled, and so forth. Using mathematics and experiments, he was able to show that most of what Aristotle said about motion was wrong. Although it took nearly 300 more years for science to throw away Aristotle's ideas about motion, it never would have happened without Bradwardine's work.

The last great scientist of this era was **Nicholas of Cusa**. He was also a priest in the Roman Catholic church in the mid-1400's and became an influential leader in the church towards the end of his life. He was particularly interested in the idea that God was infinite. Because he wanted to learn more about God's infinite nature, he studied the planets and the stars, thinking that they were probably the largest (and thus closest to infinite) things that he could study. His studies of the planets were revolutionary because he was the first to break from Ptolemy's geocentric view. He (correctly) believed that the earth spins while it travels around the sun. This was in direct disagreement with Ptolemy's ideas, and it laid the groundwork for the scientific revolution that would take place two hundred years later.

Before I end this section, I want to make sure that you have picked up on something. Notice that each of the great scientists of this era were devout Christians. In fact, they were all clergy (priests, bishops, etc.) of the Roman Catholic church. As you read through the rest of this module, you will notice that, with a few notable exceptions, most of the great scientists from the Dark Ages to modern times were devoted Christians. Once again, that's because the Christian worldview is a perfect fit with science. Science is based on the notion that the world works according to rational laws that do not change. Since Christians believe in a rational Creator whose laws do not change, science and Christianity work very well together.

That last statement surprises some people. Some people actually believe that science and Christianity are at odds with one another. Unfortunately, that myth has developed recently, mostly because the majority of scientists today are not Christian. However, even a quick look at science history tells us that without Christianity, science would never have gotten out of the Dark Ages. The Christian worldview was essential in turning trial-and-error based observations into true science. The more you learn about the history of science, the more you will see that this is the case!

ON YOUR OWN

1.7 Some historians call Grosseteste the first modern scientist. Why does Grosseteste deserve that honor?

The Renaissance: The "Golden Age" of Science (1500 A.D. – 1660 A.D.)

The 16th and 17th centuries (1500 A.D. to 1700 A.D.) were incredibly exciting in the history of science. The excitement began in 1543, when two very important works were published. The first (and most celebrated today) was published by **Nicolaus Copernicus**. It was a book that laid out his idea about the earth, sun, and the nearby planets. Like Nicholas of Cusa, Copernicus believed that Ptolemy's view of the universe was wrong. Rather than placing the earth at the center of everything and believing that the sun and all of the planets traveled around the earth, Copernicus placed the sun at the center of everything and assumed that all of the planets (including the earth) traveled around the sun. This view was called the **heliocentric** (he' lee oh sen trik) **system**, because "Helios" is the Greek god of the sun . Sometimes, however, it is called the **Copernican system**, in honor of Copernicus.

FIGURE 1.4
The Copernican System

In the Copernican system, the sun sits at the center of the universe and does not move. The planets travel around the sun in circles. Mercury is closest to the sun, followed by Venus, the earth, Mars, Jupiter, and Saturn. The moon is not considered a planet in the Copernican system. It travels around the earth. The stars are contained in a canopy called "the heaven." In the Copernican system, both the stars and the heaven do not move. They appear to move in the sky because the earth moves, not because they move.

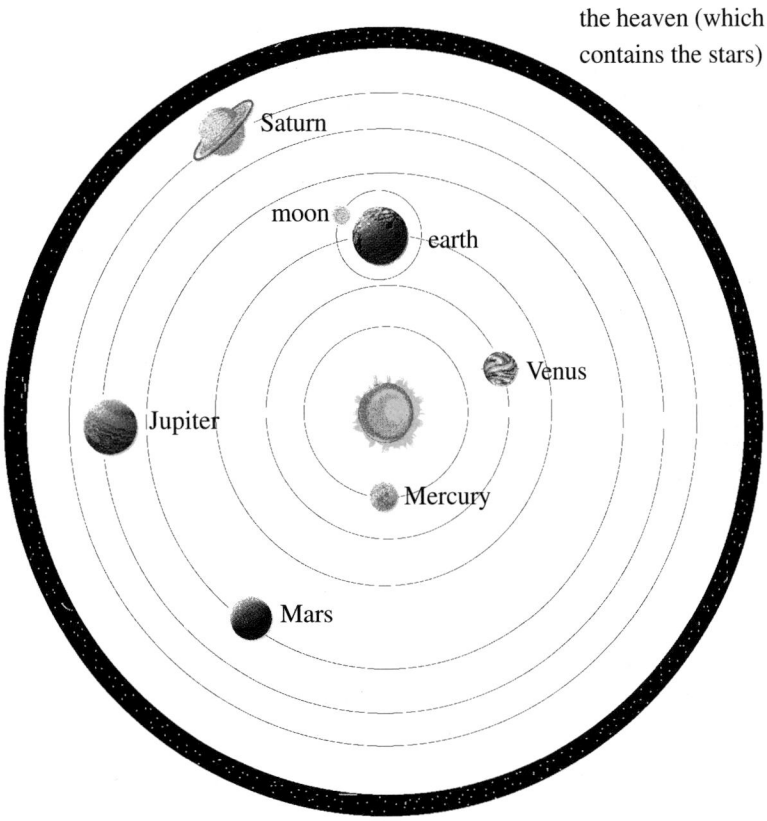

Copernicus had actually completed his studies of the planets and written his book nearly 13 years before it was published. However, Copernicus delayed its publication because the Roman Catholic church disagreed with his heliocentric system. This fact was a little ironic, as Copernicus himself was part of the clergy of the church and had actually done his work at the request of the pope, who was the head of the Roman Catholic church! Nevertheless, the Roman Catholic church publicly denounced Copernicus' work and put his book on their list of prohibited reading. As I mentioned in a previous section, the church did this not because of science, but because of preconceived notions. The church liked the idea of the earth being at the center of everything, and they therefore did not want to give up Ptolemy's geocentric view.

The other important work published in 1543 was written by a doctor named **Andreas Vesalius** (vuh sal' ee us). It was a book that tried to show all of the details of the human body. It contained incredibly detailed and amazingly accurate illustrations of the organs, muscles, and skeleton of the human body. This was the first book that illustrated all of the "insides" of the human body, and it revolutionized how medicine was taught.

Although the importance of Vesalius' book was recognized right away, it took longer for people to recognize the importance of Copernicus' work. The first reason, of course, was the fact that the Roman Catholic church banned the book. The second reason was that although Copernicus had the right idea, he had very little data to back it up. Copernicus promoted his heliocentric system not because he had made a lot of observations that supported this view, but because he knew that there was a lot of evidence *against* Ptolemy's geocentric view. Copernicus also thought a heliocentric view was easier to understand and describe, so he was attracted to it for that reason as well.

Copernicus' heliocentric view became more and more accepted as more and more evidence for it was compiled. One of the most important compilers of such evidence was **Johannes Kepler**. Kepler began making observations of the heavens in the late 1500's. He desperately wanted to be a minister, but he had terrible financial problems that forced him to accept a job as a teacher instead. While he taught, he studied the heavens, hoping that his observations would bring glory to God. In a particularly revealing letter, he wrote, "I wanted to become a theologian. For a long time, I was restless. Now, however, behold how through my effort God is being celebrated in astronomy."

Kepler made detailed observations of the planets. His observations were so detailed that he was able to deduce the basic orbits that the planets used to travel around the sun. He was even able to describe these orbits mathematically. His mathematical equations became known as "Kepler's Laws," and they became one of the most powerful arguments for the heliocentric system. Kepler's observations of the planets were so detailed and precise, that he was able to determine something very interesting about the planets. His data showed that the planets don't really travel around the sun in circles. They actually travel around the sun following an oval pattern, which mathematicians call an "ellipse." Perform the following "experiment" to learn about how the planets *really* travel around the sun.

"EXPERIMENT" 1.4
Mapping the Paths of the Planets

Supplies:

- A pencil
- A sheet of paper (8 ½" by 11")
- Four thumbtacks or pushpins
- A piece of string 8 inches long
- A sheet of cardboard larger than or the same size as the sheet of paper
- Tape

Introduction – Planets travel around the sun in ellipses, not circles. This "experiment" helps you to understand what that means.

Procedure:

A. Lay the sheet of paper on top of the cardboard.
B. Pin it to the cardboard at each corner.
C. Lay one end of the string about two inches left of center, halfway down the paper.
D. Tape it to the paper so it is held there.
E. Take another piece of tape and attach it to the string so that there are about five inches of string between this piece of tape and the one already attached to the paper.
F. Now use this piece of tape to attach the string to the paper about 2 inches to the right of center, straight across from the end of the string that is already taped down. In the end, your setup should look like this:

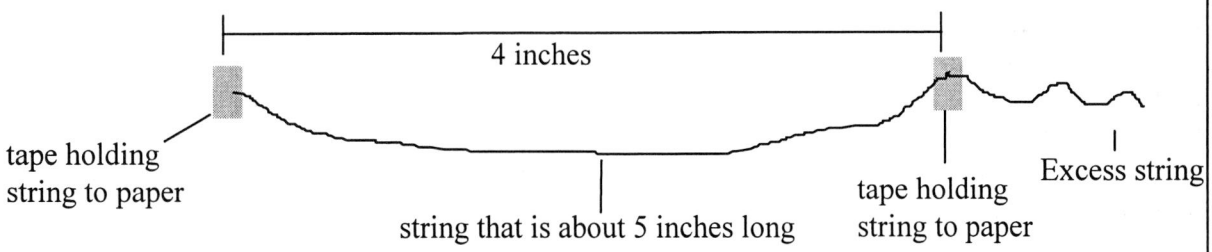

G. Now take the pencil and push the point against the string below the two pieces of tape so that the string becomes tight.
H. Keeping the string tight at all times, move the pencil from one piece of tape to the other, drawing a curve on the paper. If you keep the string tight, it will guide your pencil. The end result will be a curve that begins just under and to the left of the left piece of tape and curves around to just under and to the right of the right piece of tape.
I. Repeat the process, this time starting *above* the two pieces of tape, keeping the string straight at all times. The result will be a curve that looks like a reflection of the first curve you drew.
J. Now look at what you have drawn. It is an oval, which mathematicians call an ellipse.

K. Pull the right piece of tape off of the paper, lifting up that end of the string. Take the tape off of the string and put a new piece of tape on the very end of the string.
L. Now use that piece of tape to attach the string to the paper at the same place it was attached before. This setup should look very similar to the previous one. The pieces of tape will be in the same place, there will just be more "slack" in the string between the tape.
M. Once again, use the pencil to draw two curves: one below the pieces of tape and one above them. Keep the string straight at all times, allowing it to guide the pencil in making the curves.
N. Remove the tape and string from the paper and look at the two ellipses you drew.

Both of the drawings are ellipses. An ellipse is defined by two points called **foci** (the singular of which is **focus**). In your "experiment," the foci were the two pieces of tape. If you were to take any point on the first ellipse that you drew and measure the distance from that point to each piece of tape, the sum of those two distances would be 5 inches. That's the property of an ellipse. The sum of the distances from any point on the ellipse to each of the foci is always the same. On the second ellipse you drew, the sum of those distances would be 8 inches, because the string was longer when you drew the second ellipse.

Now don't worry if you do not completely understand ellipses. The main point I want you to understand is the difference between the two ellipses you drew. The second one is much more circular than the first, isn't it? That's because the string was longer the second time but the foci were the same. The ellipses in which the planets travel around the sun are very nearly circular. Thus, they are much more like the second ellipse than the first. Well, if the second ellipse you drew is like the orbit of a planet, where is the sun? The sun is at one of the two foci. In the end then, the planets do not travel around the sun in perfectly circular orbits. They travel in ellipses. Also, the sun is not exactly in the center of the ellipse. Instead, it is at one of the foci.

Other powerful evidence for the heliocentric view came from a scientist named **Galileo** (gal uh lay' oh) **Galilei** (gal uh lay'), who is usually referred to by only his first name. Galileo was a well-known, well-respected scientist for many reasons. He did detailed experiments about motion, confirming the work of Bradwardine and showing the flaws in Aristotle's thinking. Galileo started compiling evidence for the heliocentric system when he "invented" the telescope in 1609. I put "invented" in quotes because, in fact, he was not the first to build a telescope. Galileo was told about an invention that was displayed at an exposition in Venice. This invention was called the "optical tube." From the description he heard, he was able to determine how this invention worked and quickly built one for himself, claiming to be the first to invent it. The name of the true first inventor has been lost in history, and Galileo has been given the credit, even though he actually stole the idea.

Although Galileo came by his telescope in a less than honest way, the data that he collected with his telescope was invaluable to the advancement of the heliocentric system. He was able to show that the planets do not shine on their own. He demonstrated that the planets appear as lights in the night sky simply because they reflect the light of the sun. This fact and many others that he collected with the telescope made it clear that the heliocentric view was superior to the geocentric view. Unfortunately, the Roman Catholic church would not let go of the geocentric view and put Galileo on trial for heresy. In that trial, the church officially demanded that Galileo hold to the geocentric view in all of his writings. Because Galileo was a devout Christian, he obeyed the Roman Catholic church and stopped officially promoting the heliocentric system. Nevertheless, he kept collecting data. Well after his death, Galileo's data (along with Kepler's laws) simply proved too powerful for the church to neglect, and the heliocentric system was eventually accepted as the correct view of the heavens.

Even though the advances in understanding the heavens take center stage in the history of this period, many other scientific advances took place as well. **Blaise** (blaze) **Pascal** (pass' kal) lived in the mid-1600's. He was a brilliant philosopher, mathematician, and scientist. If you have studied Christian apologetics at all, you might remember him as the author of "Pascal's wager." This argument presents a person's worldview in terms of a bet. He then argues convincingly that Christianity is, by far, the best bet.

In addition to his philosophy, Pascal is also well remembered for his work as a mathematician and scientist. In math, he made several advances in the understanding of both geometry and algebra. In science, he spent an enormous amount of time studying the air and liquids. He demonstrated that the air we breathe exerts pressure on everything, an effect we call **atmospheric pressure** today. In his studies of fluids, he demonstrated a law which we now call "Pascal's Law." The science behind that law allowed us to develop hydraulic lifts, like the lift that a mechanic uses to raise a car so that the mechanic can get underneath it.

ON YOUR OWN

1.8 Galileo faced a very difficult decision in his life. He was convinced by science that the heliocentric system was correct. Nevertheless, his church said that it was wrong and threatened to throw him out of the church if he didn't recant his belief in the heliocentric system. Galileo, in obedience to his church, agreed to publicly recant his belief, even though he knew it was right. Did Galileo make the right choice, or should he have stayed true to his science and been thrown out of the church?

The Era of Newton (1660 A.D. – 1734 A.D.)

Although the Renaissance is often called the "golden age" of science, I personally think that science enjoyed its greatest advancement during the time of **Sir Isaac Newton**. As is the case with most of the great scientists of the past, Newton was a devout Christian. He studied science specifically as a means of learning more about God, but he never forgot that the best way to learn about God was by thorough Bible study. He wrote many commentaries on the Bible, concentrating on prophecy. He was particularly drawn to the book of Daniel. In his later years, he spent a lot more time writing about the book of Daniel than he did writing about science.

To call Sir Isaac Newton brilliant would be an understatement. In his short lifetime, Newton laid down three laws of motion that still guide the science of physics today. He formulated a universal law of gravitation, which is also still used to this day. He developed the mathematical field of calculus, which is an essential tool in many fields of science. It is little wonder that most science historians consider Sir Isaac Newton to be the single greatest scientist in the history of the world.

Newton wrote most of his revolutionary scientific work in a three-volume set call the *Principia* (prin sip' ee ah). In the first volume, Newton laid down three laws of motion. You will learn about these laws next year when you take physical science. In formulating these laws, Newton made a direct link between mathematics and science. In essence, Newton proposed that a scientific law was useless if it could not be used to develop a mathematical equation which would describe some aspect of nature. The deep link that Newton established between science and math resulted in a major breakthrough. Although many scientists in the past had used mathematics to analyze a scientific problem, Newton was the first to establish a deep link between the two. This link helped turn scientific research into a detailed, rigorous field of study.

In the second volume of the *Principia*, Newton built on the work of Pascal and added many details to the understanding of the motion of fluids. In the third volume, Newton laid down his universal law of gravitation. The term "universal" has a specific meaning here. You see, scientists in Newton's day thought that the reason an object falls when it is dropped is due to one physical process and that the reason the planets moved in the sky is due to a completely different process. Newton showed that this was not the case. In volume three of the *Principia*, Newton used detailed experiments to show that gravity was the cause of both effects. The same gravity that attracts objects to the earth (making them fall) also attracts planets to one another, keeping them in their orbits around the sun. In addition to his experimental results, Newton had (of course) developed detailed mathematical equations that describe gravity. Those mathematical equations are still considered accurate to this day. The third volume of the *Principia* essentially was the death blow to the geocentric view of the heavens.

Although Newton took center stage during this time period, there were other great scientists who brought about other great advances as well. **Robert Boyle**, the founder of modern chemistry, was a contemporary of Newton. He did many experiments with gases, formulating laws that are still used today in chemistry. In fact, when you take chemistry in high school, you will undoubtedly learn about Boyle's Laws. Boyle was also a dedicated Christian, who often wrote sermons using nature to give glory to God. His last words to the Royal Society (a group of scientists in England) were "Remember to give glory to the One who authored nature." Unfortunately, those words were eventually forgotten.

Another notable scientist from this period was **Antoni** (an' ton ee) **van Leeuwenhoek** (lew' en hook). Although not educated as a scientist, Leeuwenhoek revolutionized the study of life by building the first **microscope**. This microscope allowed him to see a world that had been completely invisible up to this point. His microscope allowed him to discover many tiny (microscopic) life forms, including bacteria. The existence of these life forms helped scientists explain many things that had been, up to this point, complete mysteries. Like Boyle,

Leeuwenhoek tried to glorify God in all of his scientific work. To him, the existence of a microscopic world was just one more testimony to the grandeur of Creation.

ON YOUR OWN

1.9 Many students think that mathematics is too difficult to learn. In order to try and teach science to such students, there are many science textbooks written today which do not use mathematics at all. What would Newton say about such textbooks?

The "Enlightenment" and the Industrial Revolution (1735 A.D. – 1819 A.D.)

This period in history marks the beginning of a change in the underlying assumptions of science. A philosopher of the time, Immanuel Kant, used the term **Enlightenment** to describe this change. Unfortunately, the change was only partially beneficial to the progress of science, so I always put the term in quotes, because the change that began in this period was only partially enlightened.

What is this change to which I refer? Well, up to this point in history, God was at the center of virtually all science that was performed. As you can see from the previous sections, most of the great scientists up to this point in history were devout Christians. Since most of the progress in science was being made by Christians, science had a very Christian flavor to it. You could hardly find a scientific book or paper written that did not mention God reverently throughout the text. Prayer was at the forefront of most scientific meetings and assemblies. Christianity was the basis of most scientific education. At this point in human history, that began to change.

What caused this change? Ironically, the great advances in science up to this point in history were indirectly the cause. You see, the advances made in science from the Dark Ages up to this point in history were the result of scientists ignoring the teachings of Ptolemy, Aristotle, and the other scientists whose works had dominated science for so long. As time went on, the scientific community began to learn that scientists should not just accept the teachings of former scientists. Instead, they realized that all scientists make mistakes, and therefore everyone's work must be examined critically. In the end, then, science stopped relying on the authority of past scientists and began relying on experiments and data.

That's the *good* part of the change that occurred during the enlightenment. Scientists stopped referring to the authority of past scientists and started examining all scientific works critically. As I have already pointed out in a previous section, that's the way science *should* be done. Unfortunately, as science began to ignore the authority of past scientists, it also began to ignore the authority of the Bible. That's the *bad* part of the change which occurred during the "enlightenment." Despite the fact that a Biblical worldview had brought about great advances in science, some scientists began to question the truth of the Bible.

Remember, up to this point in history almost all of the great scientists were devout Christians. As a result, it was difficult to find any work of science that did not mention God with great respect and reverence. During the "enlightenment," this slowly began to change. Of course, the change was not abrupt. Many scientists during this time period and beyond were devout Christians, and God was still mentioned in many scientific works. However, as time went on, fewer and fewer references to God could be found in the works of science.

Although this period can be thought of as the beginning of science's departure from a Biblical worldview, it is marked in history by the work of a devout Christian, **Carrolus** (care' uh lus) **Linnaeus** (lih nay' us). In 1735, Linnaeus published a book in which he tried to classify all living creatures that had been studied. This work is often used to mark the beginning of the enlightenment, because it revolutionized the study of living things. The basic classification scheme proposed by Linnaeus is still used today, and we still give living organisms their scientific names according to the rules set down in his book.

Linnaeus was deeply committed to performing science as a means of glorifying God. He called nature "God's private garden," and he continually glorified God in his scientific works. Here is a typical quote from his works: "One is completely stunned by the incredible resourcefulness of the Creator." In fact, it was Linnaeus' view of God that prompted him to classify living creatures. He believed that God is very organized. Thus, he believed that God's Creation should be organized as well. In his mind, the classification scheme he developed was just a means of showing the organization of Creation.

As Linnaeus was classifying living organisms, **Antoine-Laurent** (an twon' law rent') **Lavoisier** (luh vwah' see aye) was busy studying chemical reactions. He was the first to analyze chemical reactions in a systematic way. He was the first to realize that matter cannot be created or destroyed - it can only change forms. This is known as the **Law of Mass Conservation**, and you will learn a lot more about it when you take chemistry. Lavoisier was also the first to explain **combustion**, which is the process of burning.

Another important scientist in this time period was **John Dalton**. Dalton was a Quaker, who attended church at least twice each week. He did many experiments with gases, and proposed many new ideas that helped guide science in the future. Perhaps his most important work was his **atomic theory**. Building on the works of Democritus and others, Dalton proposed a detailed theory about atoms. Although a few of his ideas were wrong, most of them were right, and he is considered the founder of modern atomic theory.

As scientific knowledge grew, many inventors were able to use this knowledge to invent machines that made work faster and more productive. Up to this time period, the production of almost anything was done mostly by hand. Increased scientific knowledge, however, led to the invention of many devices that turned hours of manual labor into just a few minutes of work. This changed forever the way things were made, and so this period in history is also called the **Industrial Revolution**.

The Rest of the Nineteenth Century (1820 A.D. - 1899 A.D.)

During the rest of the nineteenth century, many great advances were made in science. Partially, this is due to the fact that people began to appreciate science more. After all, in the wake of the Industrial Revolution, people realized that the inventions which were the result of scientific knowledge made their lives better. As a result, there was much popular support for science. This popular support translated into better facilities and a better way of life for scientists, which in turn translated into great advances.

This period is probably best known for the work of **Charles R. Darwin**. In 1859, he published a book entitled *On The Origin of Species by Means of Natural Selection or the Preservation of Favoured Races in the Struggle for Life.* Typically abbreviated as *The Origin of Species*, Darwin's book caused a firestorm in the scientific community. In *The Origin of Species*, he proposed a theory that attempted to explain the diversity of life which exists on earth. This theory, now known as the theory of evolution, made no reference to God. Instead, it proposed that the same kinds of processes which we see occurring today are, in fact, responsible for all of the species on the planet. In effect, Darwin's book proposed to answer the age old question, "How did we get here?" without ever referring to a supernatural Creator.

You will learn a lot more about Darwin himself and his theory when you take biology. You will learn some of his theory in a few of the modules of this course. What I want to stress here is the impact of Darwin's work. First and foremost, Darwin's work finished the change that began in the "Enlightenment." As Darwin's ideas caught on in the scientific community, those who wanted to ignore the authority of scripture were empowered. After all, they reasoned, if science can explain how we got here without ever referring to a Creator, then why should science continue assuming that the Creator exists? As a result, it became very rare to find references to God in the scientific literature of this or the next century.

The second impact of Darwin's work was to improve the study of living things dramatically. Now it is important to realize that I (and many, many other scientists) think that Darwin's idea of evolution is fundamentally wrong. Nevertheless, even wrong ideas can help advance science! Think about what you have learned up to this point. Most of the ideas that were proposed throughout the history of science were wrong. Nevertheless, those ideas helped move science ahead, until the correct explanation could be found. Thus, even though Darwin was wrong about much of what he proposed, he still advanced biology enormously. As you learn more about evolution, you will understand better how it advanced the study of living things.

Although Darwin was wrong about much of what he wrote, he was right about one very important thing: living organisms change. Up until Darwin wrote his book, most scientists thought that living creatures stayed the same throughout history. In other words, scientists thought that every type of creature that exists today has existed throughout history. Consider dogs, for example. Scientists of this time period and before said that doberman pinchers, Saint Bernards, dachshunds, and chihuahuas always existed. Each of these breeds of dog lived throughout history, essentially unchanged. This idea was called the **immutability of the species**, and Darwin masterfully showed that this just wasn't true. He showed that all of these breeds of dog came from some original dog ancestor, through a process that he called **natural selection**. The demise of the immutability of the species was essential for a proper understanding of living organisms. Thus, although most of the rest of Darwin's ideas (as you will see later) were wrong, this one revolutionized the study of living creatures.

Even though this time period is best remembered for Darwin's work, other scientists were producing revolutionary work as well. **Louis Pasteur** was able to finally destroy the idea of spontaneous generation once and for all. He also made great advances in the study of bacteria and other living organisms. He developed a process called **pasteurization**, which he originally used to keep wine from souring. This process is now applied to milk, which is the origin of the term "pasteurized milk." Pasteur is also known for his brilliant work with vaccines. His work laid the foundation for most of today's vaccines, which have eliminated many deadly diseases.

During this time period, the study of rocks became its own field, known as **geology**. Scientists began to recognize fossils for what they really are: preserved remains of creatures that were once alive. This began to help scientists come up with a better understanding of what kinds of creatures lived in earth's past. **Sir Charles Lyell** was an important figure in this regard. He broke with the scientific view of the time that the earth was relatively young and postulated that the earth took millions of years to form. Once again, although the weight of scientific evidence goes against most of Lyell's ideas, his studies were extremely important to our understanding of modern geology. Another important aspect of Lyell's work is that it exerted a heavy influence on Darwin.

Gregor Mendel also performed his work during this time period. Mendel was an Augustinian monk. He was a devout Christian who devoted much of his life to the study of reproduction. The entire field of modern **genetics**, which studies how traits are passed on from parent to offspring, is based on his work. Although he loved his scientific pursuits, he gave them up in the latter years of his life because of a political struggle between the government and the church. He considered spiritual matters much more important than scientific matters, and he devoted all of his energy to fight what he saw as government encroachment on religious freedom.

During this period in history, science developed a much better understanding of electricity and magnetism. **Michael Faraday**'s experiments and ideas about electricity earned him the title of "the electrical giant." Many of the terms used in the study of electricity today are terms that were first used by Faraday. Faraday's Christian faith was well-known in the scientific community. Although humble, he was not ashamed of his Christianity and would argue with any scientist who tried to refute the reality of faith. In fact, his faith led him to lay the foundations of the work of another famous scientist, **James Clerk Maxwell**.

Maxwell is known as the founder of modern physics, and his importance ranks him in the same category as Sir Isaac Newton. Maxwell worked with Faraday for quite some time, and was intrigued by Faraday's work and faith. Faraday believed that nature was all interconnected at a fundamental level, because Faraday thought that all of nature derived its characteristics from God Himself. Thus, Faraday believed that electricity and magnetism were actually the result of a single process. In other words, he believed that whatever made electricity run through wires also made magnets stick to certain metals. Although Faraday could never offer evidence for this idea, he believed in it fervently. Maxwell, who was also a devout Christian, shared in Faraday's belief. He earned the title of the founder of modern physics because he was able to develop mathematical formulas which showed that Faraday was right: electricity and magnetism were both different aspects of the same process, which is now called **electromagnetism**.

Another very important scientist of this period was **James Joule**. Building on the work of Lavoisier, Joule determined that, like matter, energy cannot be created or destroyed. It can only change forms. This is now known as the **First Law of Thermodynamics**, and it is the guiding principle in the study of energy. He once penned a phrase that should be every Christian scientist's motto, "After the knowledge of, and obedience to, the will of God, the next aim must be to know something of His attributes of wisdom, power, and goodness as evidenced by His handiwork."

ON YOUR OWN

1.10 As I mentioned in the text, even scientific ideas which are wrong can still lead to advances in science. Besides the scientists mentioned in this section, name another famous scientist that proposed wrong ideas which still advanced science.

Modern Science (1900 A.D. - Present)

Near the end of the nineteenth century, there were scientists who thought that science had discovered almost all that there was to discover about nature. After all, due to the work of Newton and those that built on his work, scientists could chart the planets in their courses and knew a lot about stars and the rest of space. Those who studied living things had learned volumes about the microscopic world, and were in the process of classifying all of the organisms known to man. With the work of Mendel and others, scientists were finally understanding the complex process of reproduction. Electricity had been tamed and its relationship to magnetism was well-understood. The laws of motion as laid down by Newton seemed to explain every aspect of motion that could be studied. There were those who thought that, by the early 1900's science had essentially run its course, and that there was not much new to be learned.

All of this changed in 1900 A.D., when **Max Planck** produced a revolutionary idea. In order to explain certain experiments that could not be explained in terms of Newton's ideas, Planck proposed that energy exists in small packets, which he called **quanta** (quan' tah). Much like matter exists in tiny packets called "atoms," Planck proposed that energy exists in tiny units. This idea was revolutionary. After all, Newton and the scientists who built on his work believed that you can give *any* amount of energy to an object. If you want to throw a baseball, you can throw it at any speed you desire, as long as you are strong enough. This is not what Planck proposed. He proposed that energy comes in tiny packets. You can give one packet of energy to an object, or you can give two packets of energy to an object. You cannot, however, give an object any amount of energy in between one and two packets.

Now this idea might seem a little weird to you, but it is no more weird than the idea that matter exists in tiny packets called atoms. You can gather one atom of matter or two atoms, but you cannot gather any amount in between. It is essentially the same for energy. Planck produced a lot of evidence for his idea, and after a long while, it became accepted by the scientific community. Eventually, an entire new way of looking at energy and matter, called **quantum mechanics**, was formed as a result of Planck's idea.

One of the most famous scientists in quantum mechanics was **Albert Einstein**. Einstein used Planck's idea of energy quanta to explain a problem which had perplexed scientists for years. This problem, called the "photoelectric effect" could not be explained by Newton's laws of motion, but could be easily explained by assuming that Planck was right about energy quanta. Despite the fact that Planck produced evidence for his proposition, and despite the fact that Einstein was able to explain a supposedly "unexplainable" problem using the idea of energy quanta, scientists did not want to believe that Planck was right. After all, Newton's laws had been so successful at explaining so much of physics that scientists did not want to believe that there was something wrong with them.

As time went on, however, more and more evidence rolled in that showed Planck was right. One of the pivotal cases was made by **Niels Bohr**. Bohr developed a picture of the atom, which we call the **Bohr Model**. This picture of the atom was based in solid mathematics, and it required the assumption that energy comes in small packets. Using the Bohr Model, many of the mysteries of the atom were revealed. In the end, the weight of the evidence overwhelmed the scientific community's devotion to Newton's laws, and quantum mechanics became the new guiding principle in science.

Now it is important to note that quantum mechanics does not really contradict Newton's laws. Newton's Laws are still considered valid today. However, we now realize that Newton's laws are simply an *approximation* of quantum mechanics. When the objects you study are large, Newton's Laws are valid, because they are equivalent to the laws of quantum mechanics. However, as the size of the object decreases, there are differences between the laws of quantum mechanics and Newton's laws. In those cases, the laws of quantum mechanics are correct. Thus, Newton's laws are useful for large objects (objects we can see), but for tiny objects (like atoms, etc.), the laws of quantum mechanics must be used.

Although I first mentioned Einstein in terms of the quantum mechanical revolution, he is also an important figure in other areas of science. For example, Einstein developed a new way of looking at light, matter, and gravity. His **special theory of relativity** explained how matter is really just another form of energy. He used this theory to derive the famous equation $E=mc^2$, which says that matter can be converted to energy and vice-versa. Einstein also developed the **general theory of relativity** which explains *how* gravity works. You will learn more about both of these theories when you take physical science.

Quantum mechanics and relativity have become the guiding principles of science today. The knowledge gained from these ideas has led to numerous advances in medicine, technology, and industry. In many ways, these advances have made life easier for everyone. People live longer today, there are fewer diseases, there is more food per person today than ever before, and increased productivity has led to increased material prosperity. Also, we simply have a clearer picture of *how* Creation works. With all of these advances, however, do not fall into the trap of thinking that we have "figured it all out." Remember, scientists thought that was the case nearly 100 years ago. Look what we have learned since then! Science is constantly uncovering new ideas and new ways of looking at things. That's what makes science interesting!

Summing it Up

I hope you have gained something from this view of science history. If you don't like history, I hope that you have at least learned a few lessons from the mistakes scientists have made in the past. If you can learn from those mistakes, you will be a better scientist in the end.

Before you finish with the module, however, I need to make two points. The first is about philosophy. The history of science is rich and detailed. Entire books have been devoted to the individual eras into which I separated history. Thus, there is *no way* I could have covered everything about the history of science in just one module of this course. I am sure there will be some history experts that dispute what I have chosen to cover. Nevertheless, in my opinion, given the constraints of one module, I have presented to you a solid view of how science got to where it is today. I have certainly left a great many things out, so don't think that this is the full story. It is, however, a reasonable overview.

The second point I need to make is more practical. You are eventually going to take a test over this. You should be wondering what you need to study. Well, on the next page, you will find a study guide which helps you understand what I consider is important in this chapter. That ought to help you focus your study for the test. As you work through the study guide, you will see that I do not want you to memorize dates. Rather, I want you to remember the major names and what they were responsible for.

ANSWERS TO THE ON YOUR OWN PROBLEMS

1.1 If you look at the definition of science, it contains two parts. Science consists of collecting facts, but it also consists of using those facts to explain the world around us. The Egyptian doctors and the inventors of the ancient world collected lots of facts, but they did not use them to explain the world around them.

1.2 The more tightly-packed the atoms in a substance are, the farther it fell down the glass. Since density is a measure of how tightly the atoms are packed in a substance, the farther the substance fell in the glass, the more dense it was. Thus, the least dense item was the cork, and the most dense item was the stone. The vegetable oil was more dense than the cork, but less dense than the water. Continuing that kind of reasoning, then, the order is cork, vegetable oil, ice cube, water, grape, syrup, rock.

1.3 Experiment 1.2 demonstrated that the atoms in a substance move faster the warmer the substance is. To make ice from water, you must cool the water. Thus, ice is colder than water, which means the atoms in ice move more slowly than those in water.

1.4 Despite the fact that Dr. Hawking is brilliant, he can be wrong, just like many other brilliant scientists. The story of spontaneous generation tells how Aristotle was wrong, despite the fact that he was the greatest thinker of his time. The story of the Ptolemaic system also tells how a great thinker turned out to be wrong. Either story should illustrate that we should not make scientific decisions based on *people*. Instead, we should make them based on *data*.

1.5 The story of the Ptolemaic system tells us we must leave personal bias behind when doing science. The church held on to the Ptolemaic system too long because of bias, not data.

1.6 Today's scientists are worried about the future of science because the progress of science depends on cultural support. Science stalled in the Dark Ages due to the Roman culture. If our culture stops supporting science, science will stall again.

1.7 Grosseteste is the first modern scientist because he was the first to work with the scientific method.

1.8 There is no right or wrong answer to this question. You must decide for yourself. Personally, I would find it a tough choice. Although my church means a lot to me, I would probably get kicked out rather than give up a belief I really thought was correct. The problem is that I could be wrong, and then I would have been kicked out of the church for nothing!

1.9 Newton would not like such textbooks. Newton believed that science had to be linked to math.

1.10 There are several possible answers to these questions. Any one of the first three scientists all advanced science but were wrong. Democritus, Leucippus, Aristotle, Ptolemy, Newton, and many others all advanced the cause of science, but they were all wrong about certain things.

STUDY GUIDE FOR MODULE #1

1. Define the following terms:

a. Science
b. Papyrus
c. Spontaneous generation

2. There were 3 lessons from the history of science that I specifically mentioned in the text. What are they?

3. Who was Imhotep?

4. Although the ancient Egyptians had incredibly advanced medical practices for their time, we do not consider them scientists. Why not?

5. Who were Thales, Anaximander, and Anaximenes?

6. Leucippus and his student Democritus are remembered for what idea?

7. Who came up with the idea of spontaneous generation?

8. Who first came up with a large-scale classification scheme for living creatures?

9. What is the main difference between the Ptolemaic system and the Copernican system? Which is more correct?

10. What was the main goal of the alchemists?

11. Why don't we consider the alchemists to be scientists?

12. What was the main reason that science progressed near the end of the Dark Ages?

13. Who is considered to be the first modern scientist and why does he deserve that honor?

14. Two great works were published in 1543. Who were the authors and what were the subjects?

15. Although Galileo collected an enormous amount of data in support of the Copernican system, he was forced to publicly reject it. Why?

16. Galileo claimed to invent something that he actually didn't invent. What was it?

17. Who is the single greatest scientist of all time? What are his three biggest accomplishments?

18. A major change in scientific approach took place during the enlightenment. What was good about the change and what was bad about it?

19. What was Lavoisier's greatest contribution to science?

20. What is John Dalton remembered for?

21. What is Charles Darwin remembered for?

22. What does "immutability of species" mean, and who showed that this notion is wrong?

23. What is Gregor Mendel remembered for?

24. James Clerk Maxwell is known as the founder of modern _____.

25. What law did James Joule demonstrate to be true?

26. What is the fundamental assumption behind quantum mechanics? Who first proposed it?

27. What is Niels Bohr remembered for?

28. Einstein was one of the founders of the quantum mechanical revolution. He also is famous for two other ideas. What are they?

Module #2: Scientific Inquiry

Introduction

Now that you have a bit of historical context in which to view the human endeavor of science, it is time to figure out exactly what science is all about. You already know the definition of science, and you have already heard terms like "the scientific method," so now it's time to learn what science is, and what it is not.

What Science is NOT

The best place to start is to tell you what science is NOT. To learn a bit about what science is not, perform the following experiment.

EXPERIMENT 2.1

How Does Weight Affect the Speed at Which an Object Falls?

Supplies:

- A reasonably heavy book
- A sheet of cardboard about the same size as the book (The cardboard that comes on the back of a pad of paper works well. You can also cut a piece out of an old cardboard box.)
- A sheet of heavy paper (like construction paper or cardstock) about the same size as the book
- A sheet of regular paper about the size of the book

Introduction - This experiment will prove that heavy objects fall faster than light objects.

Procedure

A. Hold the book in one hand and the cardboard in another. Hold them both at the same height and drop them both at the same time. Note in your laboratory notebook which item hits the ground first.
B. Hold the cardboard in one hand and the heavy paper in another. Once again, hold them at the same height, and release them at the same time. Note once again in your laboratory notebook which item hits the ground first.
C. Do the same thing once again, this time with the heavy paper and the regular paper.
D. Keep the supplies. You will use them again soon.

What did you see in the experiment? If everything went well, you should have noticed that the book hit the ground sooner than the cardboard. The cardboard, however, hit the ground sooner than the heavy paper, and the heavy paper hit the ground sooner than the light paper. What does that tell you? It tells you that heavy things fall faster than light things, right? After all, the book was the heaviest item, the cardboard was the next heaviest item, the heavy paper was next, and the regular paper was the lightest item. Since they all fell the way that they did, you can conclude from this experiment that heavy things fall faster than light things, right? Well, not exactly. Perform the following experiment to see what I mean.

EXPERIMENT 2.2

Learning More About Weight and the Speed at Which an Object Falls

Supplies:

- A reasonably heavy book
- A sheet of cardboard about the same size as the book (The cardboard that comes on the back of a pad of paper works well. You can also cut a piece out of an old cardboard box.)
- A sheet of heavy paper (like construction paper or cardstock) about the same size as the book
- A sheet of regular paper about the size of the book
- A metal paper clip
- A small rock (It needs to weigh less than the cardboard, so it should be really small.)

Introduction - In this experiment, you will see that our conclusion from the previous experiment is wrong.

Procedure

A. Hold the book in one hand and the paper clip in the other. Hold them at the same height and drop them simultaneously. Note which hits the ground first.
B. Repeat step (A), this time with the cardboard and the paper clip.
C. Repeat step (A), this time with the heavy paper and the paper clip.
D. Repeat step (A), this time with the regular paper and the paper clip.
E. Repeat steps (A) - (D), substituting the small rock for the paper clip.
F. Wad up the regular paper into a tight, little ball.
G. Repeat step (A), this time using the book and the wadded up ball of paper.
H. Repeat step (A), this time using the cardboard and the wadded up ball of paper.
I. Repeat step (A), this time using the heavy paper and the wadded up ball of paper.

What did you see in this experiment? Well, most likely, the book and the paper clip hit the ground at roughly the same time. In the other trials using the paper clip, the paper clip probably hit the ground first. You should have gotten the same results with the tiny rock. Finally, in steps (G) - (I), the same paper that hit the ground last in every trial of this and the previous experiment probably hit the ground first, with the exception of step (G), when it was dropped with the book. In that step, the wadded up ball of paper might have hit the ground at the same time or just slightly later than the book.

What does all of this tell us? Well, the first thing that it tells us is our previous conclusion was wrong. After all, the paper clip was certainly lighter than the cardboard and the heavy paper, but it still fell faster than both of those objects. The rock was a *lot* lighter than the book, but it hit the ground at the same time as the book. If you chose your rock carefully enough, the rock was lighter than the cardboard, but it still hit the ground sooner than the cardboard. Finally, the same paper that took the longest time to fall in the first experiment suddenly fell faster than the cardboard and the heavy paper when it was wadded up into a ball. Thus, we obviously know that heavy things do not necessarily fall faster than light things.

The other thing you might be able to see from this experiment is that the *shape* of an object affects how it falls. After all, when the regular paper was left as a flat sheet, it fell slower than any of the other objects. When it was wadded into a tight ball, however, it fell faster than some of the objects. Also, the small rock and the paper clip had significantly different shapes than all of the other objects, and they fell at different speeds. Thus, these experiments seem to indicate that shape has something to do with how quickly an object falls.

In fact, Sir Isaac Newton was the first to use experiments to show that there is something called **air resistance**. You will learn more about this concept in physical science, but for right now, air resistance refers to the fact that air actually slows objects down as they fall. The heavier an object is, the less it is affected by air resistance. Also, the more compact an object is, the less it is affected by air resistance. Newton actually showed that if you were able to eliminate air resistance, *all objects fall at the same rate, regardless of weight, shape, or any other characteristic.* This is an important point.

In the absence of air, ALL objects, regardless of weight or shape, fall at the same rate.

Your two experiments do not demonstrate this fact, but Newton's experiments, along with his mathematics, did.

What can we learn from all of this, then? Well, after the first experiment, it seemed that we had "proven" that heavy objects fall faster than light objects. We had an experiment with several trials that seemed to demonstrate this fact. Also, the conclusion made sense. After all, if you were to tell most people that heavy objects fall faster than light objects, they would most likely agree with you. The statement makes sense and, in general, it is consistent with our everyday experience.

Nevertheless, despite the fact that we had an experiment to back up our conclusion, and despite the fact that the conclusion made sense, it was shown to be wrong. This brings up the what science is NOT:

Science is NOT a means by which something can be *proven.*

No matter what you might have thought up to this point, and no matter what you might hear or read, science has never and can never *prove* anything!

Now that last statement might shock you a bit. After all, everyone at one time or another has heard the phrase, "Science has proven that...." This is a typical phrase muttered by some people, even some scientists, but nevertheless, it is absolutely wrong. As the two previous experiments (as well as the history of science you read in the previous module) show, scientific conclusions are *continually* being changed based on new information. Ptolemy had an excellent explanation for the arrangement of the planets and stars in the sky. Other scientists had observations and experiments that backed up Ptolemy's view. It turned out, however, that Ptolemy was wrong. Even Copernicus, despite the fact that he proposed a *better* arrangement, was still wrong about a great many things. In fact, even ideas that scientists thought were true 30 years ago are now being changed or discarded due to new data.

In the end, then, all conclusions that scientists draw are *tentative*. All it takes is one experiment to destroy a conclusion that is based on thousands of years of scientific experiments. Consider another example. Suppose a student decided to go to the top of his or her house and start dropping things off of the roof. The student starts with small objects like a pen, a shoe, a ball, a pillow, etc. Eventually, the student throws bigger objects like furniture and appliances off of the roof. After the student is severely punished by his or her parents, the student makes this grand proclamation: "My experiments have proven that when an object is dropped from our roof, it will fall."

Is the student correct? Of course not. Despite the fact that the student might have dropped *every object in the house* off the roof, it still does not show that *every* object will fall off the roof when dropped. Suppose you were to drop a helium-filled balloon off of the roof. Would it fall? No, it wouldn't fall. It would float high into the air. The helium-filled balloon is what we in science call a **counter-example**.

Counter-example - An example that contradicts a scientific conclusion

The single counter-example provided by the helium-filled balloon shows that the student's conclusion was wrong. It is the same with any scientific conclusion. A single counter-example is enough to destroy a conclusion built on thousands of years of scientific work!

So what *can* science do, if it cannot prove anything? Well, when the correct method is followed, science can be used to draw conclusions that are reasonably reliable. Those conclusions will hopefully help us better understand the way Creation works, and perhaps we will be able to use those conclusions to build neat things like TV's, VCR's, and air conditioners. However, no matter how reliable we think the conclusions of science are, those conclusions are *always* tentative.

To really drive this point home, I want to give you one example from the history of science. In the late 1600's, German scientists Johann Becher and George Stahl attempted to explain the fact that some things (like paper and trees) will burn, while other things (like rocks and certain metals) will not. They proposed an idea that all substances which burn contain something called **phlogiston** (flah jis' ton). As the substance burns, it loses phlogiston and, in enough time, the burning will cease because all of the phlogiston will be used up. These scientists had detailed experiments to back up their idea, and it became the accepted scientific explanation of combustion for the next 120 years. It took the detailed experiments of Antoine-Laurent Lavoisier (whom you read about in Module #1) to provide counter-examples that showed the phlogiston explanation to be wrong. Lavoisier proposed that the process of combustion is actually a chemical reaction in which the chemicals of the substance that is burning react with oxygen in the air, and that there is no such thing as phlogiston. That's what scientists still believe today.

Photo from the MasterClips Collection

FIGURE 2.1
Combustion

For 120 years, the phlogiston idea of combustion was the generally-accepted explanation of the burning process. Counter-examples given by Lavoisier showed that the phlogiston explanation was wrong.

ON YOUR OWN

2.1 The First Law of Thermodynamics is the guiding principle of most science today. It basically states that energy cannot be created or destroyed, it can only change forms. In every experiment that has been done properly, the First Law of Thermodynamics has been obeyed. Has science succeeded in proving the First Law of Thermodynamics?

The Scientific Method

As I mentioned in the previous section, although science cannot *prove* anything, as long as you follow the correct method, science can draw conclusions that are reasonably reliable. What is that method? Well, it was first proposed by Grosseteste at the end of the Dark Ages. Today, we call it the **scientific method**. This method provides a framework in which scientists can analyze situations, explain certain phenomena, and answer certain questions. The scientific method starts with **observation**. Observation allows the scientist to collect data. Once enough data has been collected, the scientist forms a **hypothesis** that attempts to explain some facet of the data or attempts to answer a question that the scientist asks.

Hypothesis - An educated guess that attempts to explain an observation or answer a question

Once he or she forms a hypothesis, the scientist (typically with help from other scientists) then collects much more data in an effort to test the hypothesis. If data are found which are inconsistent with the hypothesis, the hypothesis might be discarded, or it might just be modified a bit until it is consistent with all data that has been collected. If a large amount of data is collected and the hypothesis is consistent with all of the data, then the hypothesis becomes a theory.

Theory - A hypothesis that has been tested with a significant amount of data

Since a theory has been tested by a large amount of data, it is much more reliable than a hypothesis. As more and more data relevant to the theory get collected, the theory can be tested over and over again. If several generations of collected data are all consistent with the theory, it eventually attains the status of a scientific law.

Scientific law - A theory that has been tested by and is consistent with generations of data

An example of the scientific method in action can be found in the life of Ignaz Semmelweis, a Hungarian doctor who lived in the early-to-mid 1800's. He was put in charge of a ward in Vienna's most famous hospital, the Allegemeine Krakenhaus. He noticed that in his ward, patients were dying at a rate which far exceeded that of the other wards, even the wards with much sicker patients. Semmelweis observed the situation for several weeks, trying to figure out what was different about his ward as compared to all others in the hospital. He finally determined that the only noticeable difference was that his ward was the first one that the doctors and medical students visited after they performed autopsies on the dead.

Based on his observations, Semmelweis hypothesized that the doctors were carrying something deadly from the corpses upon which the autopsies were being performed to the patients in his ward. Thus, Dr. Semmelweis exercised the first step in the scientific method. He made some observations and then formed a hypothesis to explain those observations.

Semmelweis then developed a way to test his hypothesis. He instituted a rule that all doctors had to wash their hands after they finished their autopsies and before they entered his ward. Believe it or not, up to that point in history, doctors never thought to wash their hands before examining or even operating on a patient! Dr. Semmelweis hoped that by washing their hands, doctors would remove whatever was being carried from the corpses to the patients in his ward.

Well, the doctors did not like the new rule, but they grudgingly obeyed it, and the death rate in Dr. Semmelweis' ward decreased *to the lowest in the hospital!* This, of course, was good evidence that his hypothesis was right. You would think that the doctors would be overjoyed. They were not. In fact, they got so tired of having to wash their hands before entering Dr. Semmelweis' ward that they worked together to get him fired. His successor, anxious to win the approval of the doctors, rescinded Semmelweis' policy, and the death rate in the ward shot back up again.

Semmelweis spent the rest of his life doing more and more experiments to confirm his hypothesis that something unseen but nevertheless deadly can be carried from a dead person to a live person. Although Semmelweis' work was not appreciated until after his death, his hypothesis was eventually confirmed by enough experiments that it became a scientific theory. At that point, doctors began washing their hands before examinations and surgery.

As time went on, more and more data was gathered in support of Semmelweis' theory. As Antoni van Leeuwenhoek's microscope became a popular tool in medical science, doctors were finally able to see the deadly bacteria and germs that can be transmitted from person to person. They were able to do experiments that showed germs infecting and harming healthy tissue. In the end, after years of experimentation by Semmelweis and others, Semmelweis' theory became a scientific law. Nowadays, doctors do all that they can to completely sterilize their hands, clothes, and instruments before performing any medical procedure.

Before we leave this story, it might be interesting to note that the Old Testament contains meticulous instructions concerning how a priest is to cleanse himself after touching a dead body. These rituals, some of which are laid out in Numbers 19, are more effective than all but the most modern methods of sterilization. In fact, Dr. S. I. McMillen, a medical doctor and author of *None of These Diseases*, states that "In 1960, the Department [of Health in New York State] issued a book describing a method of washing the hands, and the procedures closely approximate the Scriptural method given in Numbers 19." This, of course, should not surprise you. After all, God knows all about germs and bacteria; He created them. Thus, it only makes sense that He would lay down instructions as to how His people can protect themselves from germs and bacteria. If only doctors would have had the sense to follow those rules in the past centuries, countless lives would have been saved!

So you see, the scientific method (summarized in Figure 2.2 on the next page) provides a methodical, logical way to examine a situation or answer a question. If a theory survives the scientific method and becomes a law, it can be considered reasonably trustworthy. Even a scientific theory which has not been tested enough to be a law is still pretty reliable, because it is backed up by a lot of scientific data. Nevertheless, you must always remember that the conclusions of science are tentative. Just one counter-example can destroy a scientific law, and the history of science is filled with such occurrences!

FIGURE 2.2
The Scientific Method

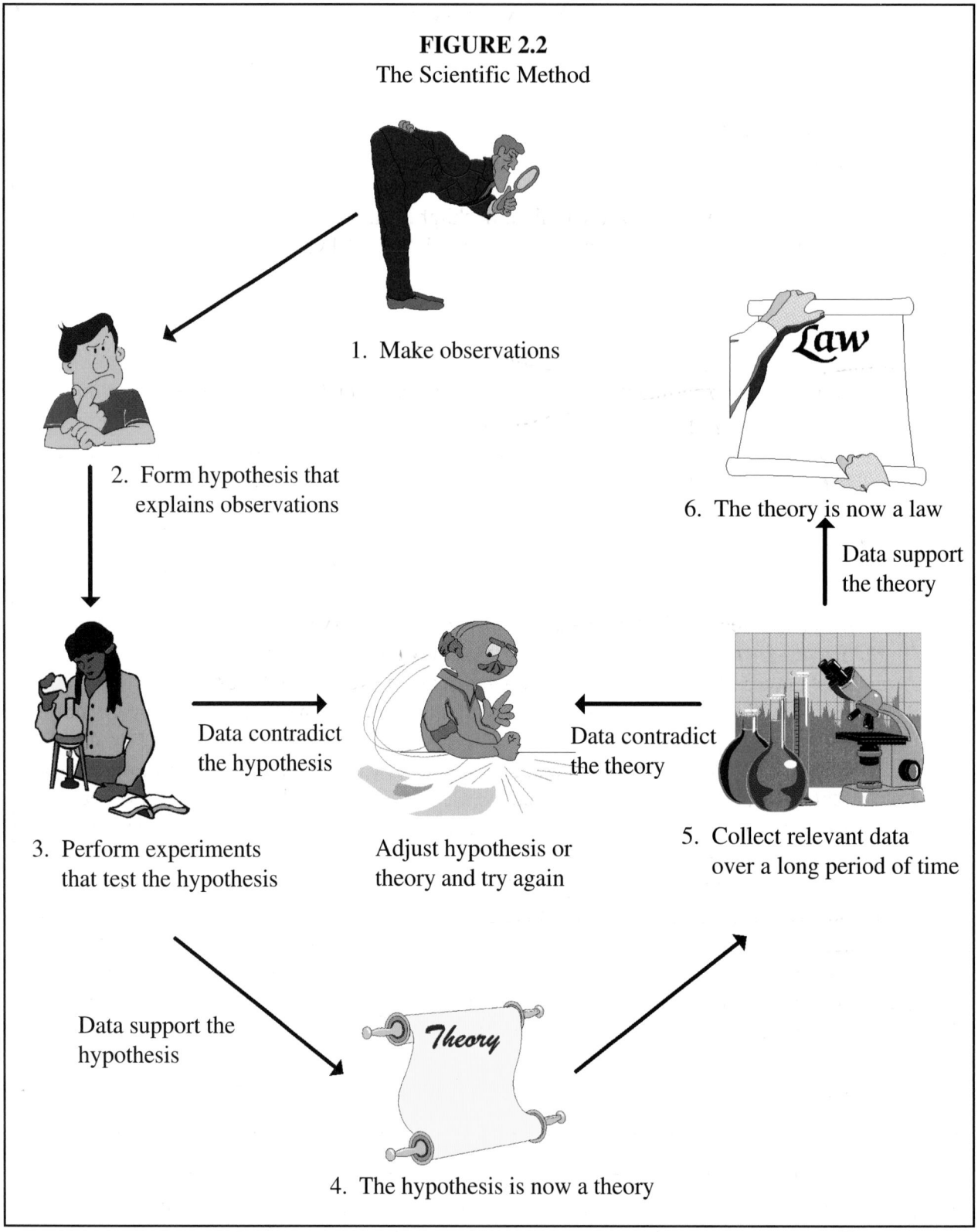

Now I want you to get some practice using the scientific method by performing the following experiment.

EXPERIMENT 2.3
The Broken Flashlight

Supplies:

- A working flashlight
- A parent or helper

Introduction - In this experiment, you will fix a flashlight that is not working. In the process, you will use the scientific method to determine what caused the flashlight to stop working.

Procedure:

A. Tell your parent or helper to look in the solutions and tests guide in order to get their instructions for this experiment. The instructions can be found in the solutions to the test for Module #2. **YOU CANNOT READ THOSE INSTRUCTIONS**. The instructions give your parent/helper an idea of how to cause the flashlight to stop working. It will be your job to find out what your parent/helper did, so if you read the instructions, you defeat the purpose of the experiment!
B. Once your parent/helper has done something to the flashlight to make it stop working, take the flashlight apart. Do this slowly, so that you can observe the parts and so that you know how it gets put back together.
C. Once you have taken the flashlight apart and made your observations, write a hypothesis in your laboratory notebook which attempts to explain *why* the flashlight is not working.
D. After you have written your hypothesis down, design an experiment to test your hypothesis. Remember, *just fixing the flashlight is not enough.* Science attempts to explain things, not just invent things. If you get the flashlight working, that is nice, but you are doing no more than the ancient Egyptians you learned about in Module #1. They had lots of great inventions and could cure lots of health problems, but they did not understand *why* things happened. In order to do science, you must *explain* the world around you, not just fix things. Thus, you must perform an experiment that specifically tests your hypothesis. Your parent/helper was given some tips, so if you are stuck, get help.
E. Once you have performed your experiment, determine whether or not the experiment confirmed the hypothesis. If so, your hypothesis is now a theory. That's about as far as you can go, because to turn your theory into a law, you would have to test it with several different flashlights, under several different conditions, for several years.
F. If your experiment *did not* confirm your hypothesis, then try to come up with another hypothesis and another experiment, and try again.
G. Check with your parent/helper to determine whether or not your theory was correct.

What did you learn from the experiment? Well, hopefully you learned why the flashlight stopped working. That's not the only thing you should have learned, however. You should have learned something about how science is done. You could have just fixed the flashlight and moved on. That would have been fast, easy, and useful. However, that's not what science is all about. When you do science, you must *explain* something, not just fix it. After all, haven't you ever taken apart something that was broken, found nothing wrong with it and then, when you put it back together, it suddenly worked again? That has happened to me more than once. Often, just taking something apart will jostle the components around enough to get them working.

That's why I stressed in the experiment that just getting the flashlight working was not enough. Think about it. You found what you *thought* was wrong with the flashlight in the course of the experiment. You then put the flashlight together and it worked. That *does not* mean that you really found the problem. It means that either you found the problem or, in the process of taking the flashlight apart and putting it back together again, you *accidentally fixed the real problem.* Had you not done an experiment to confirm your hypothesis, you would have never known which of those two possibilities actually occurred.

Now the experiment might have seemed a bit tedious. After all, if you find something that looks to be a problem, eliminate it, and then the flashlight works again, most likely you did, indeed, find the source of the problem. Science, however, must be much more precise than that. Since there were two possible explanations for why the flashlight began to work again, you had to do an experiment that would help you eliminate one of those possibilities. That's how science works. In a scientific experiment, you must be very careful to examine all possible explanations of your observations and then perform experiments to confirm just one of them.

ON YOUR OWN

The discovery of Neptune is another excellent example of the scientific method in use. Scientists had noticed that the planet Uranus did not orbit around the sun exactly as Newton's Universal Law of Gravitation predicted. French scientist Urbain Jean Joseph Leverrier assumed that this was because a previously undiscovered planet was interfering with Uranus' movement. He made some calculations using Newton's Universal Law of Gravitation and determined where this undiscovered planet had to be in order for Uranus's motion to be consistent with Netwon's law. German scientist Johann Gottfried Galle used a telescope to look in the sky at the position that Leverrier predicted, and he saw the planet on the very first night of the search! The planet was named Neptune.

2.2 What was the observation that started the use of the scientific method in this instance?

2.3 What was the hypothesis?

2.4 What was the experiment to confirm the hypothesis?

2.5 At the end of the story as written here, was the presence of Neptune in space a scientific law or a theory?

2.6 There is at least one other hypothesis that could have been made based on the observation. Experiments would have eventually shown it to be wrong, however. What is that alternate hypothesis?

Failures of the Scientific Method

Although the scientific method allows us to draw reasonably accurate conclusions about the world around us, those conclusions are not iron-clad. In fact, there have been *many* examples of how the scientific method has been used to reach conclusions which are completely wrong. In this section, I want to concentrate on two such examples. Hopefully, these examples will illustrate what I have been trying to stress both in this module and the previous one: **the conclusions of science are *always* tentative**.

In the late 1800's, Italian scientist Giovanni Schiaparelli used a powerful (for its time) telescope to observe the surface of the planet Mars. He noticed several faint lines that seemed to crisscross about the planet. When he published his observations, American scientist Percival Lowell hypothesized that the lines were actually canals which had been dug by the inhabitants of Mars. He assumed that the purpose of the canals was for water distribution. Lowell built an observatory in Arizona to make detailed observations of the planet, which he thought would confirm his hypothesis.

In the early 1900's Lowell published the results of his observations, providing what he saw as clear and convincing evidence that the lines first observed by Schiaparelli were, indeed, artificial canals. He noticed that the lines seemed to change from time to time. He saw this as evidence that the canals were, indeed, used for water distribution. After all, anyone smart enough to build canals would probably have a system by which they could open and close them based on where they wanted the water to go. Thus, the facts that the lines seemed to change from time to time was seen as strong evidence that the lines were actually canals that had been constructed by the inhabitants of Mars.

Also, Lowell noticed that there were green splotches on the planet that would also change from time to time. Sometimes their shape would change, sometimes they would disappear altogether. He assumed that the green splotches were patches of vegetation and that the changing water distribution of the canals (as well as perhaps the changing seasons on Mars) changed where the vegetation flourished and died out.

Lowell's work was received excitedly by the scientific community, and many other scientists made observations of Mars which seemed to support Lowell's idea that there were canals, vegetation, and intelligent life on Mars. Some even speculated that the inhabitants of Mars must be incredibly advanced to make a planet-wide network of canals that could be opened and closed based on need. Using that assumption, some scientists actually proposed that the two moons orbiting Mars were, in fact, not natural. Instead, these scientists believed that the moons were constructed by the inhabitants of Mars. A few even believed that they were some sort of attack vessels and that the inhabitants of Mars would actually invade earth one day!

At this point in the scientific method, Lowell's original hypothesis could be considered a theory. Based on Schiaparelli's observations, Lowell had formed the hypothesis that canals existed on Mars. He then designed experiments to test his hypothesis (building an observatory and observing Mars in detail). The results of his experiments confirmed his hypothesis. Thus, the hypothesis became a theory. Many other scientists began to produce studies that also agreed with Lowell's theory, so the theory was actually on its way to becoming a scientific law.

As time went on and more powerful telescopes were built, however, the theory of canals on Mars began to disintegrate. Scientists found that many of the "canals" Lowell and other scientists observed with their telescopes could not be observed by others. Eventually, it was determined that many of the "canals" were really optical illusions caused by the poor optics of the telescopes that Lowell and others had used, along with eye fatigue from long hours of observation through a telescope. The changing green blotches that Lowell and others saw were, in fact, simply collections of dust that were blown about by windstorms which are common on the planet. More recently, two probes have visited Mars (the Viking lander and Pathfinder). Neither of them have found any evidence of life on Mars.

Photo from the MasterClips Collection

FIGURE 2.3
Mars

Mars is named after the Roman god of war, because the red patches on its surface reminded early scientists of blood. Many scientists have thought that intelligent life once existed on Mars. Lowell believed that he saw canals on the planet's surface which had been dug by intelligent life. More recently (1996), NASA announced that a meteorite had been discovered which seemed to be from Mars. This meteorite had certain tiny structures that could be seen as evidence of microscopic life, indicating that there was, indeed, life on Mars, at least at one time. Detailed studies of the meteorite, however, indicate that the tiny structures are *not* evidence of microscopic life.

So you see that following the scientific method does not guarantee that the conclusions drawn are accurate. Lowell and those who believed as he did followed the scientific method to a tee. Nevertheless, they were wrong. Of course, the idea of canals on Mars never reached the point of a scientific law. It never rose above the level of a theory. Thus, maybe it is not surprising that it turned out to be wrong. Also, this happened a long time ago. Surely *modern* science doesn't make such mistakes, does it? Yes, it does.

In 1911, Dutch scientist Heike Onnes discovered the phenomenon of **superconductivity**. What is superconductivity? Well, when electricity travels through a wire, the wire resists the flow of the electricity. This resistance reduces the energy of the electricity in the wire, and the lost energy is converted to heat and/or light. In fact, that's how a non-fluorescent light bulb works. The filament in a light bulb resists the flow of electricity, and that resistance generates both heat and light. Onnes discovered that certain substances at *very* low temperatures (about -450 degrees Fahrenheit) did not resist the flow of electricity at all. Thus, electricity could pass through the substance without losing energy. That's superconductivity.

At that time, superconductivity was a complete mystery. Many scientists confirmed Onnes' discovery, but no one knew *how* it could be explained. Everything in science at that time in history indicated that regardless of the substance or temperature, there should *always* be resistance to electricity. As quantum mechanics (see Module #1) became more and more accepted by the scientific community, however, scientists began to see how superconductivity was possible.

In the 1950's, three scientists (Bardeen, Cooper, and Schrieffer) began work on a hypothesis that they thought would explain superconductivity. Several experiments confirmed their hypothesis and, by 1960, it was considered a scientific theory. It was actually given the name "BCS theory" in honor of the three scientists who came up with the original hypothesis. BCS theory was put to the test for the next 25 years, and it was confirmed by each and every experiment that was done. BCS theory contained detailed mathematical equations that predicted the results of every experiment done. As a result, BCS theory became accepted as a scientific law.

One of the consequences of BCS theory is that there is a certain temperature (roughly -405 degrees Fahrenheit) above which superconductivity is impossible. Regardless of the substance, there could be no superconductivity above a temperature of roughly -405 degrees Fahrenheit. Since BCS theory became accepted as a scientific law, this consequence was also considered a scientific law. Thus, scientists as a whole decided that it would be impossible to find superconductivity above that temperature.

Of course, there were a few scientists who were not so convinced about this supposed scientific law. Despite the fact that they were routinely ridiculed by the majority of the scientific community, these scientists tried to find an example of superconductivity at a temperature higher than that allowed by the scientific law. In 1986, two scientists (J. George Bednorz and Karl Alex Muller) at the IBM research laboratory in Germany found it! Since then, many more examples of superconductivity at higher temperatures than ever thought possible have been found. These superconductors are now called "high-temperature superconductors" and may someday revolutionize the way we use electricity.

So here we have an example of a very modern scientific law that was overthrown by one counter-example. As time has gone on, many more counter-examples have been discovered. Clearly the original three scientists (Bardeen, Cooper, and Schrieffer) followed the scientific method. Nevertheless, the scientific law that the vast majority of the scientific community believed in was demonstrated to be false!

Now please understand why I brought up these two examples. I certainly did not want to insult the scientists involved. Lowell made many positive contributions to the pursuit of science. For example, he was the first to postulate the existence of a ninth planet. After his death, the ninth planet (now called Pluto) was observed by the very same observatory from which he observed the planet Mars. Although BCS theory turns out to be wrong to some extent, it has still advanced our understanding of superconductivity tremendously. So please don't think I am insulting the scientists in these two stories; they have all made *great* contributions to the pursuit of science!

I also do not want to give you the impression that science is a worthless endeavor. Nothing could be further from the truth! Following the scientific method has helped us learn an enormous amount about the world around us. That knowledge has resulted in longer lifespans for people, more productivity for industries, and new inventions like automobiles and airplanes. Clearly, then, science is a *very* worthwhile endeavor.

I brought up these examples to really bring home the point that the conclusions of science are very tentative. Although Lowell had plenty of evidence for his hypothesis, the evidence was produced with poor telescopes. Thus, the evidence was worthless. Although BCS theory had a lot of experiments to back it up, it suffered from a lack of very specific data: the existence of high-temperature superconductors. Thus, no matter how firm a theory or law seems to be, new data might very well destroy it overnight!

ON YOUR OWN

2.7 Lowell's observations of Mars were used to support a theory that has been demonstrated to be false. Are those observations therefore worthless?

2.8 What caused BCS theory to become accepted as a scientific law?

The Limitations of Science

Now that you have learned a brief history of science in Module #1, and now that I have specifically discussed two examples in which the use of the scientific method led to bad conclusions, it only seems natural to discuss the limitations of science. Although science is incredibly interesting and has produced an enormous number of improvements in people's lives, it is not flawless. As I mentioned at the beginning of the module, science really cannot *prove* anything. It can provide evidence that a certain idea is true, but it *cannot* prove any idea. It is also not 100% reliable. As the history of science clearly shows, scientific laws continually get overthrown as the result of new information and ideas.

So science cannot prove anything, and it is not 100% reliable. Nevertheless, it is an interesting and useful pursuit. Science has helped us understand an enormous amount about the world around us. It has also led to the development of incredibly useful inventions. Thus, even though it has its limits, science has done a lot to make our lives better. As a result, it is important to understand what science *can* do.

There are those that have a very limited view of science. They say, for example, that science cannot be used to study anything which we do not observe happening today. In other words, we can use science to study how cancer forms in the body and how to cure it. After all, we see cancer affecting people every day. We can also design experiments in which we observe whether or not proposed cures actually work. However, these same people say that we cannot use science to examine questions such as the age of the earth, how life originated on earth, or how the earth was formed. After all, they say, no one was around to observe these events. Since the heart of science is observation, there is simply no way that science can be used to study such events.

This idea is just not true. The only limitations of science are that it cannot prove anything, it is not 100% reliable, and it must conform to the scientific method. Can we apply the scientific method to questions such as the ones I discussed above? Of course! We cannot observe the formation of the earth, but we can certainly observe the structure and composition of the earth. We can then form a hypothesis about how the earth formed. We can then do more experiments on the earth to learn more about its structure. The data collected from those experiments can be used to test the hypothesis. The hypothesis might have to be refined, but eventually, it might become a theory. More experiments on the structure of the earth can be done, and one day, the theory might even become a law.

In fact, later on in this course we will spend quite some time studying fossils and rocks. You will learn the different ways fossils and rocks form and, by studying the fossils and rocks that are here now, you can learn a lot about what happened in earth's past. Despite the fact that there was not a scientist observing the rocks and fossils forming, you will learn how the scientific method has been applied to try and determine the validity of two competing theories of earth's history.

In the end, then, science is not limited to answering only certain questions. If we apply the scientific method properly, we can use science to attempt to answer virtually *any* question. You must realize, however, that any answer you get from science is tentative. It can always be demonstrated to be wrong, with just one counter-example.

So what *can* you do with science? You can study virtually anything and attempt to answer virtually any question. As long as you adhere to the scientific method, you will be using science. You must remember, however, that no matter how well you apply the scientific method, your conclusions could be wrong. The more scientific evidence you have to support your hypothesis or theory, the *less likely* it is that your conclusions are wrong. Nevertheless, science is not 100% reliable and cannot prove anything. Thus, your conclusions are always subject to change!

Science and Christianity

Before you finish this module, I want to really emphasize that the scientific method can be applied to *any* subject. Thus, I want to spend some time applying the scientific method to the subject of Christianity. Whether you believe it or not, we can certainly apply the scientific method in studying Christianity. In fact, since the Christian world-view is largely responsible for bringing science out of the Dark Ages, it shouldn't even surprise you that we can use the scientific method to study Christianity.

Let's start with an observation. I have met many, many individuals who draw an enormous amount of strength, hope, and encouragement from the Bible. They believe that God speaks to them through the Book, and they seem quite sincere. Now, of course, there are many other people that draw strength, hope, and encouragement from other sources (other scriptures such as the Koran or the Bhagavad-Gita, crystals, humanism, etc.). Thus, just because these people claim that God speaks to them through the Bible, that doesn't mean it's true. So, we will use the scientific method to help us evaluate their claim.

Based on the observation that many people draw an enormous amount of strength, hope, and encouragement from the Bible, let's form the hypothesis that the Bible is the Word of God. Now we have to collect some data that will either confirm or deny the hypothesis. What kind of data should we collect? Well, let's look at the Bible and see if we can find any evidence that either supports or contradicts our hypothesis.

There is one really obvious place to start. Even a brief reading of the Bible will reveal that it makes a *lot* of predictions about the future. Since parts of the Bible were written a long, long time ago, some of these predictions should have already come true. This is an excellent source of data that relates to our hypothesis. After all, if the Bible is the Word of God, then God must have inspired it. Thus, any predictions that it makes about the future *must* be true. However, if the Bible was, in fact, written without the inspiration of God, then you wouldn't expect it to have a very good track record when it comes to predicting the future. So, let's look at Biblical prophecies (specific predictions about the future). Whether or not they have come true will provide us with excellent data that directly relate to our hypothesis.

The prophecies that I want to discuss were all written before the events took place. We know this as a result of certain historical facts. First, we know that the entire Old Testament was written by no later than 250 B.C., because the Greek Septuagint, a copy of the entire Old Testament, was initiated in the reign of Ptolemy Philadelphius (285-246 B.C.). This is a historical fact. Thus, we know that the Old Testament, in its entirety, existed by 250 B.C..

The first Biblical prophecy comes from the book of Ezekiel, chapter 26, verses 3-21. A subsection of that text (from the NASB, as all Biblical quotes will be) says:

> ...therefore, thus says the Lord God, "Behold, I am against you, O Tyre, and I will bring up many nations against you, as the sea brings up its waves. And they will destroy the walls of Tyre and break down her towers; and I will scrape her debris from her and make her a bare rock. She will be a place for the spreading of nets in the midst of the sea, for I have spoken...Also her daughters on the mainland will be slain by the sword...I will bring upon Tyre from the north Nebuchadnezzar king of Babylon...He will slay your daughters on the mainland by the sword; and he will make siege walls against you...Also, they will make a spoil of your riches...and throw your stones and your timbers and your debris into the water...And I will make you a bare rock; you will be a place for the spreading of nets. You will be built no more...

According to the prophecy, things do not look good for Tyre. As mentioned before, we know for certain that this prophecy had to have been written by 250 B.C.. The generally accepted date for the writing of this book, however, is 592-570 B.C. Most historians accept this as a rather strong fact because the book uses a very odd dating system that was only used for a brief time in the early sixth century B.C. Thus, the author was either writing at that time or was a very knowledgeable historian who was doing everything he could to deceive the reader.

Notice how detailed and precise this prophecy is. Ezekiel calls the city by name. He tells us that many nations will come against her and even singles out the leader of the first nation, Babylon. He is also very specific about Tyre's ultimate fate. He says that Tyre's debris will be thrown into the ocean; it will not be rebuilt; and that it will become a place where fishermen can spread their nets to dry.

The other aspect of this prophecy that must be pointed out is the fact that anyone living in Ezekiel's time would consider his predictions to be absolute lunacy. Tyre was one of the greatest cities of the ancient world. According to Dr. Wallace Fleming, Tyre was founded more than 2,000 years before this prophecy was written. During that time, it had grown into the most important trading center in that region of the world.

The city was originally built on a large island which lay one-half mile off the shore of Syria. The island had a nice port where trading ships could dock. A smaller island near the original city was eventually linked to the larger island, making the total circumference of the city approximately 2.5 miles. The outer wall of the city which faced the mainland shore was 150 feet high and was surmounted by battlements. As a result of its prominence as a major trading center, Tyre grew quickly, and an extension of the city had to be built on the mainland. The combination of Tyre's outer walls, its strategic location on an island, and the mainland city as its first line of defense made the city seem invulnerable. In the words of Dr. Fleming, "...Tyre was not only a great city but was considered impregnable." (Wallace B. Fleming, *The History of Tyre*, Columbia University Press: New York, NY, 1915, p.8)

We see, then, that Ezekiel's prophecy went against the common human wisdom of the day. Had Ezekiel been trying to "make up" a prophecy which would come true, he probably would have tried to predict the fall of a city which seemed a little weaker than the great fortress of Tyre! Instead, Ezekiel pronounced the city's doom, and specifically mentioned many facets of its destruction.

To see just how well this prophecy came true, we only need to consult the history books. According to the ancient historian Herodotus, Nebuchadnezzar, King of Babylon, laid siege to Tyre from 585-572 B.C. In the siege, Nebuchadnezzar was able to destroy and take the mainland city, but he was unable to effectively attack the island city. As a result, he simply laid a 13-year siege, stopping all supplies from entering the island city. This pressure forced Tyre to accept Babylonian rule, but the island city remained intact. These historical facts are in perfect agreement with the predictions of Ezekiel.

Since Nebuchadnezzar's siege of Tyre occurred very close to when the prophecy is assumed to be written, this particular prediction is not all that impressive. It's possible that the author wrote this "prophecy" after the fact, thereby ensuring its accuracy. Thus, if this were the only prediction made by Ezekiel, it would not be all that impressive. The prophecy continues, however, as does the history of Tyre.

The prophecy states that many nations, not just Babylon, will stand against Tyre. It states that Nebuchadnezzar will destroy the mainland city, but it says that "they" will throw Tyre's stones and timbers into the sea. In using the pronoun "they" instead of "he," the prophecy makes the distinction between Nebuchadnezzar and the others that will stand against Tyre. Thus, the pronoun "they" does not refer to Nebuchadnezzar; it refers to the other leaders which will try to destroy Tyre. As history tells us, other leaders did, indeed, march against Tyre.

In 333 B.C., Alexander the Great demanded that Tyre allow him to occupy the island city. The King of Tyre, Azemilcus, was willing to grant Alexander dominion over Tyre, but was unwilling to let him and his army occupy the city. Alexander was thus forced to attack Tyre in order to gain full control over her strategic location. According to the *Encyclopedia Britannica*, Alexander had no fleet with which to attack the island city of Tyre, so he *completely destroyed the mainland city and dumped all of its debris into the ocean.* There was so much debris that Alexander was able to construct a 200-ft wide bridge of debris from the mainland city to the island city, making it possible for his army to march straight to Tyre and conquer it.

The "bridge" that Alexander the Great constructed was predicted by Ezekiel almost 250 years before it was built! His prophecy specifically states that Tyre's debris would be thrown into the ocean by someone other than Nebuchadnezzar, and that's exactly what happened! Even the most hardened skeptic would have a hard time arguing that this part of the prophecy was not written down well before the events took place. After all, historians are convinced that the prophecy was written in the sixth century B.C. Even if a skeptic is unwilling to believe the generally-accepted date, we know for a fact that the entire Old Testament was copied less than 100 years after Alexander's battle against Tyre. It's very unlikely that a document which was so revered could be altered so significantly and that the altered version could become generally accepted in less than a century! Clearly, this part of the prophecy *had* to have been recorded well before the events took place.

Ezekiel predicted that many nations would march against Tyre, and that's exactly what happened. After Alexander the Great's conquest, the Seleucidae, the Romans, the Moslems, and finally the crusaders all took turns conquering Tyre. After all of this fighting, Tyre lay in ruins. Today, old Tyre is, indeed, scraped down to bare rock. According to historian Nina Jidejian, "The port [of Tyre] has become a haven today for fishing boats *and a place for spreading nets.*" (Nina Jidejian, *Tyre Through the Ages*, El-Mashreq Publishers: Beruit, 1969, p. 139 - emphasis mine)

Think about that for a minute. Ezekiel's prophecy was so precise that it was able to predict the only future use for the city of Tyre- a place for fishermen to spread their nets out to dry! The prophecy was written down long before Tyre was laid flat by all of its conquerors. Only after about A.D. 600 did Tyre become a haven for the spreading of nets. How can all of this be explained? How could Ezekiel have made such an impressive prediction? Was he just really lucky?

If this were the only example of a specific prophecy in the Old Testament which had come true, then luck might be a reasonable explanation. There are, however, many such prophecies in the Old Testament. For example, Josh McDowell in his book *Evidence that Demands a Verdict*, outlines 11 other Old Testament prophecies which predict the future of other major cities in the ancient world. These prophecies were all written down before the events took place, and they all came true in the smallest detail! This is very good evidence in support of our hypothesis. After all, how could anyone except the Creator of time know what will happen in the future? Since the Bible is so good at predicting future events long before they take place, that is evidence it was inspired by God.

The most impressive predictions that the Bible makes however, concern the life of Jesus Christ. These predictions, called the "messianic prophecies," provide ample evidence for the divine inspiration of the Bible, as well as the validity of the New Testament itself. The single, unifying theme of the Old Testament is God's promise that He would send a Redeemer to the world. Throughout the Old Testament, there are literally hundreds of predictions made concerning the time when the Messiah would come, the type of person the Messiah would be, the place from which He would come, and His activities on earth. Once again, we can be certain that these predictions were written down at least 250 years before Christ ever walked the earth, but they are, nevertheless, detailed prophecies which are incredibly accurate.

The most obvious example of the Old Testament's accurate predictions regarding the coming Messiah relates to His birthplace. In Micah 5:2, we read "But as for you, Bethlehem

Ephrathah...from you One will go forth for me to be ruler in Israel. His goings forth are from long ago, From the days of eternity." This verse is clearly a prediction that the Messiah will be born in Bethlehem. We know that this verse is talking about the Messiah and not a human ruler, because of the last sentence. No human ruler's "goings forth" are "from the days of eternity."

Interestingly enough, however, there is another Old Testament prophecy, found in Hosea 11:1, which says, "...and out of Egypt I called my Son." Once again, this is clearly a statement regarding the Messiah (no human was ever called God's Son in Old Testament times), but this verse seems to predict that the Messiah would be born in Egypt. This seeming contradiction, however, is easily resolved in Jesus Christ. He was, indeed, born in Bethlehem (Matthew 2:1), but He and His parents had to flee into Egypt to avoid Herod's persecution (Matthew 2:14). He ended up staying there until Herod died (Matthew 2:15). At least 250 years before Christ ever walked the earth, his birthplace and flight into Egypt had already been predicted!

The Old Testament's ability to predict events regarding the Messiah doesn't stop there, however. Another excellent example can be taken from Zechariah 11:12-13. In this passage we read:

> And I said to them, "If it is good in your sight, give me my wages; but if not, never mind!" So they weighed out thirty shekels of silver as my wages. Then the Lord said to me, "Throw it to the potter, that magnificent price at which I was valued by them." So I took the thirty shekels of silver and threw them to the potter in the house of the Lord.

This passage is a lamentation by the prophet Zechariah. He is furious that the people do not value the Lord more highly. In the end, he quotes God as saying that the people think that He (God) is worth only 30 pieces of silver. Those silver pieces are so worthless in God's sight that they should be thrown to the potter in the house of the Lord.

This passage was always a mystery to Jews, until its words were finally fulfilled in the life of Christ. Christ, who claimed to be the same as God (Matthew 27:43, John 8:58), was betrayed by Judas for the "magnificent price" of 30 shekels of silver (Matthew 26:15). Once Judas saw what was happening to Christ as a result of his betrayal, however, he returned to the temple (the house of the Lord) and threw the silver pieces on the Temple floor in a fit of remorse and rage (Matthew 27:5). The priests, knowing that the money was tainted, did not want to put it back into the treasury, so they purchased a field for the burial of strangers. The field was named "The Potter's Field" (Matthew 27:7).

In the end, then, we see that this lamentation of Zechariah was actually a prophecy of some rather intricate details related to Christ's betrayal by Judas. It is truly incredible to think that more than 250 years prior to this betrayal, the Old Testament was able to predict how much it would cost, what would eventually happen to the money, and even the name associated with the final purchase!

If these were the only Old Testament prophecies concerning the coming Messiah, it would be possible to explain them away as wildly improbable coincidences. According to Josh

McDowell, however, there are 332 distinct prophecies in the Old Testament which were fulfilled perfectly in the life of Christ! Such a large number of prophecies, all written down at least 250 years prior to the life of Christ, provides strong evidence that the Bible is, indeed, the Word of God!

So, have I just proven that the Bible is the Word of God? *OF COURSE NOT!* Science cannot be used to prove anything! Have I produced an irrefutable argument with which all scientists would agree? *OF COURSE NOT!* There are many, many scientific theories that all have strong evidence to back them up, yet they are not believed by all scientists. You see, just because a hypothesis reaches the level of a theory, that does not mean that all scientists will accept it! Indeed, many areas of study have several different theories which all compete to explain the same thing! Each theory has a group of scientists who support it and a group of scientists who do not.

What have I done, then? I have applied the scientific method to show that there is evidence for the hypothesis that the Bible is the Word of God. This means that belief in the Bible is *scientifically reasonable*. It does not prove that the Bible is the Word of God, neither does it demonstrate that all other religions are false. It simply shows that there is *evidence* for such a belief! There is a lot more evidence as well. If you are interested, you can read a book I wrote called *Reasonable Faith: The Scientific Case for Christianity*. It contains a lot more evidence to support the hypothesis. So much evidence, in fact, that the hypothesis can certainly be raised to the level of a scientific theory.

So you see that science can be used to study virtually any subject. After all, there are only three limitations to science. First, it cannot be used to prove anything. Second, it is not 100% reliable. Third, it must conform to the scientific method. As long as you keep these limitations in mind, your study of science will be thought-provoking, stimulating, and rewarding!

ON YOUR OWN

2.9 Some would say that the Bible's ability to predict the future is not all that impressive. After all, psychics predict the future all of the time. What is the difference between a psychic's predictions about the future and the Bible's predictions about the future?

2.10 In this section, I used the scientific method to provide evidence for the hypothesis that the Bible is the Word of God. Although the exercise was interesting and could easily bolster someone's faith in the Bible, science should *never* be used as a basis for determining your worldview. Why?

ANSWERS TO THE ON YOUR OWN PROBLEMS

2.1 Science has not proven the First Law of Thermodynamics, because science cannot prove anything.

2.2 The observation was that Uranus did not orbit the sun the way that Newton's Universal Law of Gravitation predicted that it should. That was something which needed to be explained.

2.3 The hypothesis was that an undiscovered planet was affecting Uranus' motion.

2.4 The experiment to confirm the hypothesis was the search for the new planet.

2.5 At the end of the story, Neptune's existence was a theory. After all, only ONE scientist had seen it. That scientist might have been seeing something else, he might have been looking in the wrong place, or he might be lying. Several other scientists had to observe Neptune over a period of time before its existence became a law.

2.6 An alternative hypothesis could have been that Netwon's Law of Universal Gravitation was wrong. After all, the observation was that Uranus did not obey Newton's law. Perhaps the problem was not another planet or planets; perhaps the problem was with Newton's law. Of course, that hypothesis would not be confirmed.

2.7 Those observations are far from worthless! They can be used for other reasons than to support the existence of canals on Mars.

2.8 BCS theory became accepted as a scientific law because many other scientists did many other experiments over the course of several years, all of which confirmed the theory.

2.9 There are 2 big differences between the predictions of the Bible and the predictions of psychics. First of all, most psychic predictions are vague, whereas the Bible's predictions are specific. Notice that the prophecies mentioned in the text name names and tell about specific events. Many psychics make vague predictions that can be applied to many events. The biggest difference, however, is that the VAST MAJORITY of a psychic's predictions never come true. A psychic will make hundreds of predictions, most of which never happen. The few that do happen, however, are trumpeted, and the rest are forgotten. ALL of the Bible's prophecies (so far) have come true!

2.10 You should never use science as the basis for your world-view because the conclusions of science are always tentative. Your worldview affects everything in your life. You should never base something that important on something as tentative as science!

STUDY GUIDE FOR MODULE #2

1. Define the following terms:

a Counter-example
b. Hypothesis
c. Theory
d. Scientific law

2. When someone tells you that "science has proven" something, what should you say?

3. Does a scientific theory have to make sense?

4. A feather and a penny are dropped from the top of a building. Which will hit the ground first?

5. A feather and a penny are dropped down a long tube which has no air in it. Which will hit the bottom of the tube first?

6. What does it take to destroy a scientific law?

Questions 7-10 refer to the following story:

In 1682, Edmund Halley studied a bright object that moved in the night sky. After searching other scientists' works, he noted that similar objects were observed in 1456, 1531, and 1607 that followed a similar path. He decided that those objects were, in fact, the same thing he was studying, and that this object passed by the earth roughly every 76 years. He then predicted that the object would be seen again in 1758. On Christmas day, the object was, indeed, seen again. It is now called Halley's comet, and it comes into view of the earth every 76 years.

7. What was the observation that Halley made to form a hypothesis?

8. What was the hypothesis?

9. What was the experiment that confirmed the hypothesis?

10. Regular appearances of Halley's comet have been found in history as far back as 2,000 years ago. Is the existence of Halley's comet a theory or a scientific law?

11. Put the following steps of the scientific method into their proper order:

a. Form a hypothesis
b. Theory is now a law
c. Make observations
d. Hypothesis is now a theory
e. Perform experiments to confirm the hypothesis
f. Perform many experiments over several years

12. If a hypothesis does not agree with the experiment which was designed to confirm it, what two choices do you have?

13. If a theory does not agree with the experiments which were designed to test it, what two choices do you have?

14. In the text, I told you about Lowell's belief that there were canals on Mars. Name the observations which led to his hypothesis and the experiments that were used to confirm the hypothesis.

15. Why was the discovery of high-temperature superconductors so startling to scientists?

16. What are the three limitations of science?

17. Can science be used to study events that will never, ever happen again?

18. Can science be used to study religious ideas?

19. What were the observations I used in the last section of the module to form a hypothesis about the Bible?

20. What was my hypothesis?

21. What were the experiments I designed to confirm the hypothesis?

22. Did I prove my hypothesis?

Module #3: How to Analyze and Interpret Experiments

Introduction

Now that you've learned about the scientific method, I want you to spend some time learning the details on how to apply it. The way you apply the scientific method affects the reliability of the conclusions that you draw from it. Think for a moment about the failures of the scientific method that you read about in the previous module. Why did the scientists come to the wrong conclusions? Well, in the case of Percival Lowell, his experiments were flawed. Indeed, he saw plenty of "canals" on Mars, but they turned out to be the result of bad telescopes and eye fatigue. Had he used better telescopes, and had he allowed more time for his eyes to rest, he might not have been fooled. In the case of BCS theory, there was data missing. High-temperature superconductors were not discovered until *after* the theory had been accepted as a scientific law. In each case, the investigators followed the scientific method, but because of flawed experiments or missing data, the conclusions they reached were wrong.

To do science well, then, you need to be very careful in designing your experiments and observations. You need to try and avoid flaws in your experiments, and you need to think of many different ways to test your hypothesis or theory so as to avoid missing data. The better you are at that, the more reliable your conclusions will be.

Experiments and Variables

In designing an experiment, it is very important that you be able to recognize all of the **experimental variables**.

Experimental variable - An aspect of an experiment which changes during the course of the experiment

In order to avoid flaws in an experiment, you must be able to recognize experimental variables and control them. For example, part of the reason Lowell saw "canals" on Mars was the fact that as time went on, his eyes became fatigued. Thus, the strain on his eyes was an experimental variable, because it changed over the course of his observations. Had he recognized that experimental variable, he could have controlled it by taking several breaks in order to rest his eyes. Since he did not recognize and control the variable, his experiments became flawed.

Now don't get the impression that experimental variables are bad. They are, in fact, very useful. Often, the only way a scientist will learn something in an experiment is by comparing the results of the experiment when different experimental variables changed. Thus, experimental variables can be very good. They are bad, however, when they are not recognized. Unrecognized experimental variables can lead to flawed experiments. Experimental variables which are recognized and controlled are often an integral part of an experiment. Perform the following experiment to see what I mean.

EXPERIMENT 3.1
A Floating Egg?

Supplies:

- A tall glass
- Measuring cups for measuring out one and a half cups of water
- An egg
- A teaspoon
- A spoon for stirring
- Water
- Salt

Introduction - Experimental variables can often be used to learn a lot from an experiment. This experiment will show you how.

Procedure

A. Fill the tall glass with one and one-half cups of water. Use the measuring cups to measure out the water.
B. Drop the egg (carefully) into the glass of water. Does it sink or float? Write that down in your laboratory notebook.
C. Use the spoon you have for stirring to pull the egg back out of the glass. Try and let it drip in the glass so that you do not lose too much water. Set the egg aside for the moment.
D. Add one teaspoon of salt to the water and stir with your stirring spoon until the salt is dissolved.
E. Once the salt is dissolved, drop the egg (carefully) into the glass of water. Note the difference (if any) between how the egg behaved before and how it behaves this time.
F. Repeat steps (C) - (E) a total of 6 times. Each time, note the difference (in your laboratory notebook) between how the egg behaves compared to the previous time. If the egg's behavior does not change even after you have repeated steps (C) - (E) 6 times, continue to repeat the steps until you see a difference.

What did you see in the experiment? If things went well, you should have seen that the egg sank in water. As you added salt to the water, however, the egg should not have sunk as quickly as it did before. Eventually, the egg should have actually floated. Now before I explain to you what this means, I want you to analyze the experiment for experimental variables. What changed over the course of the experiment?

We used the same glass throughout the whole experiment, and we used the same egg. The egg was always pulled out with the same spoon. Thus, none of those things are experimental variables. As I see it, there were two experimental variables. The first is the most important: the amount of salt in the water. In the first phase of the experiment, there was no salt in the water. Then, one teaspoon at a time, you added salt to the water. After each teaspoon of salt was added, you put the egg back into the water to see what would happen. What was the other experimental variable? It was not all that important, but it was, nevertheless, variable. The amount of water in the glass was somewhat variable. After all, each time you pulled the egg out of the water, you pulled some water out, too. You tried to let the water drip back into the glass, but there is just no way you could return *all* of the water to the glass. As a result, then, the amount of water in the glass decreased throughout the experiment. Thus, the amount of water was also an experimental variable.

How do these two variables affect what you saw in the experiment? Well, as the amount of salt in the water increased, the egg eventually started to float. Thus, we have learned something: adding salt to water helps eggs float in the water. What about the second variable? What happened as the result of the amount of water decreasing throughout the course of the experiment? Well, we can use common sense to help us out here. If you added no salt to the water but took a little bit of water out of the glass, would that change whether or not the egg floated in the water? Of course not! Thus, the second (small) experimental variable did not affect the results of the experiment.

What can we learn about all of this, then? Well, do you remember Experiment 1.1? In that experiment, you noticed that objects of low density floated on objects of higher density. Vegetable oil floated on top of water because vegetable oil was less dense than water. A cork floated on top of the vegetable oil because the cork was less dense than the vegetable oil. Well, in this experiment, an egg sank in pure water but floated once a lot of salt was added to the water. What does that tell us about saltwater? It tells us that **saltwater is more dense than pure water**.

A natural example of this fact comes from the Great Salt Lake in the state of Utah. This lake is full of saltwater rather than freshwater, and the added salt makes the water so dense that people can float in it without expending any effort, as shown in the picture below.

Photo from the MasterClips Collection

FIGURE 3.1
People Floating in the Great Salt Lake

In the experiment, then, we had two experimental variables. We thought it through to the point that we realized the second experimental variable (the amount of water in the glass) did not affect the experiment. The first experimental variable, however, did affect the results of the experiment, and we used that experimental variable to conclude something useful from the experiment.

Before we leave the discussion about this experiment, I want you to spend a little bit of time thinking about the design of the experiment itself. In this experiment, I had you use the same glass each time. If I had made you use a different glass each time, that would have introduced another experimental variable. How would that have affected the results of the experiment? It probably would not have. After all, whether or not the egg sinks in water *should* be independent of the glass in which the water is put.

We also could have used a different egg for each trial. Would that have affected the results of the experiment? It probably would have a little. After all, you learned in Module #1 that the density of an object determines whether or not it will float on water. Well, even though most eggs have similar densities, each egg's density is probably slightly different than the next. Thus, even though all eggs are dense enough to sink in pure water, the amount of salt necessary to get an egg to float in water probably varies a bit from egg to egg.

Even though using a different egg each time probably would have affected the experiment to some degree, it probably would not have affected the final conclusion. Since all eggs sink in pure water and, with enough salt, all eggs will float in salt water, the final conclusion (that salt water is more dense than pure water) would have remained the same.

Well, since using a different glass each time would not have affected the experiment at all, why didn't I have you do that? It probably would have been more convenient. Since using a different egg each time would not have affected the final conclusion of the experiment, why didn't I have you do that? Obviously, that would have made the experiment go a lot quicker. The answer to both questions is simple: *you should always reduce the number of experimental variables that are not a necessary part of the experiment.*

The amount of salt in the water is a necessary experimental variable. It is used to help us learn something from the experiment. The glass, egg, and amount of water in the glass are *unnecessary* experimental variables. We learn NOTHING from them. Thus, we need to reduce them or get rid of them. We got rid of the glass and egg as experimental variables by using the same one in each trial of the experiment. We reduced the amount of water as an experimental variable by trying to allow all of the water to drip off of the egg and into the glass before setting the egg down.

We need to reduce the number of unnecessary experimental variables because their effects on the experiment are not always predictable. Even though I explained to you how each of those experimental variables probably would not have affected the final conclusion of the experiment, there is no guarantee that I am right. There may be some subtle effect that I am not aware of or cannot think of. Thus, I need to try and get rid of them simply because they may affect the experiment in some unforeseen way.

When designing an experiment, then, we probably will have some kind of experimental variable from which we hope to learn something. We then need to analyze the experiment for all unnecessary variables. When we find them, we either need to eliminate them, or we need to think very hard about how they will affect the experiment. It is best to eliminate them, because no matter how hard we think, we might miss some subtle effect that the unnecessary variable will have on the experiment.

ON YOUR OWN

A student decides to test the effectiveness of different household floor cleaners. He marks off a section of the kitchen floor and scuffs it up with black heel marks. He then divides that section into 4 equal quarters, and he scrubs each quarter with a different brand of floor cleaner.

3.1 Identify the experimental variables.

3.2 From which experimental variable will the student learn something, and which should he try to reduce or eliminate?

3.3 Suggest ways to reduce or eliminate the experimental variables that need to be reduced or eliminated.

Using a Series of Experiments

Now that you know a bit about how to analyze an experiment, I want you to get some experience doing a series of three experiments in order to learn something. You need to start with the following experiment.

EXPERIMENT 3.2
Which "Boat" Will Move?

Supplies :

- Four sheet of reasonably thick cardboard (A cut-up cardboard box works nicely.)
- Scissors
- A sheet of facial tissue (Make sure is it not the kind that has been treated with lotion.)
- A chunk of soap from a bar of soap
- A stick of chewing gum
- A bathtub or large sink (A bathtub is best.)

Introduction - This experiment will produce an interesting effect which we will try to use other experiments to explain.

Procedure:

A. Start filling the bathtub with water. Use cold water, so as to save the heating costs. Put a plug in the drain, because you want the water to stand. You want to stop filling the tub when the water is about 3 inches deep.
B. While you are waiting for the bathtub to fill, use the scissors to cut the cardboard into four equal rectangles. The rectangles should be about 3 inches long and 2 inches wide. If you are using a sink instead of a bathtub, you probably want them to be smaller.
C. Now use the scissors to cut a point on one side of each piece of cardboard, so that each piece of cardboard looks like this:

D. Now cut a triangular notch on the side opposite the point, so that each piece of cardboard looks like this:

E. Each one of these pieces of cardboard will be a "boat" in your bathtub. Before you float your "boats," however, you need to prepare them with different "motors." Your first "motor" will be made of chewing gum. Chew the stick of gum until it is soft and pliable. Pull it out of your mouth and rip off a small chunk of it. Put the chunk of gum in the notch of one of the "boats." Use enough gum so that you can cram it into the notch and it stays there.
F. For another "boat," you will use facial tissue as your "motor." Take a small amount of facial tissue and wet it. Now roll it into a ball. The ball of wet facial tissue should be about the same size as the chunk of chewing gum you used. Cram the wet facial tissue into the notch of another "boat" so that it stays there.
G. For the next "boat," shave off a chunk of soap that is about the same size as the chunk of chewing gum you used for the first "boat." Cram it into the notch so that it stays there.
H. The last "boat" will have no "motor" in its notch.
I. By this time, the water in the tub should be rather still. If it is not, wait until it is.
J. Once the water is still, place each "boat" in the tub in this order: the one with no "motor," followed by the one with a chewing gum "motor," followed by the one with the facial tissue "motor," followed by the one with the soap "motor." Place them close to one another, pointing in the same direction. Do not put them so close that they touch one another.
K. Observe the difference between the movement of each "boat." Write your observations in your laboratory notebook.
L. Clean everything up.

What did you see in the experiment? Well, you should have seen that all of the "boats" except one didn't move much. There are stray winds in every house, and those stray winds caused some movements in *all* of the "boats." However, there should have been one "boat" that moved a lot more than the others: the "boat" with the soap "motor."

Before you try to understand why the soap "motor" actually caused the "boat" to move, I want to analyze the experimental variables and their effect on the experiment. We used the same bathtub at the same time for all "boats." Each "boat" was put in a slightly different place in the tub, but that should not have been a big effect. Each "boat" was put in at a slightly different time, but once again, that should not have been a big effect, either. Each "boat" was different. I tried to get you to reduce the effect of that variable by making each "boat" the same size. Nevertheless, the "boats" were not identical, so that is an experimental variable, too. Likewise, the "motors" were close to the same size, but not exactly the same size. That's another experimental variable. All of these were experimental variables, but they probably had little effect on the results of the experiment.

The big experimental variable, of course, was the "motor" that was used. The first "boat" that you put in the water had no "motor." In experimental terms, we call this the **control** of the experiment.

Control (of an experiment) - The variable or part of the experiment to which all others can be compared

All of the other "boats" can be compared to this one. After all, the point of the experiment was to find a workable "motor" for our "boat." To find out whether or not the "motor" we used was the cause of any motion we saw, we needed something to compare the "boats" against. As I mentioned in the experiment, random wind currents can cause all of the "boats" in the tub to move a little. Thus, in order to determine whether or not each of the "motors" *caused* any motion, we had to compare how each "boat" moved compared to the one with no "motor." Since the "boat" with the soap "motor" moved a *lot* more than the "boat" with no "motor," we could easily conclude that the soap "motor" was doing something to make the "boat" move.

In the experiment, then, the variable that we used to learn something was the type of "motor" used. We found out that soap made a workable "motor." There is obviously something special about soap, however, because both gum and facial tissue did not make the "boats" move any more than the control.

Okay, now that we have analyzed the experiment, it is time to try and learn *why* soap formed a workable "motor" for our "boat." To begin to learn this, try the following experiment.

EXPERIMENT 3.3

What Does Soap Do To Water? - Part 1

Supplies:

- A reasonably large bowl
- Water
- Black pepper
- Tweezers
- A sheet of facial tissue (Make sure is it not the kind that has been treated with lotion.)
- A chunk of soap from a bar of soap
- A stick of chewing gum

Introduction - This experiment will begin to help you to understand why soap caused the "boat" to move in Experiment 3.2.

Procedure:

A. Fill the bowl 3/4 of the way full of water. Allow it to sit so that the water becomes still.
B. Once the water is still, shake pepper onto the surface of the water. Some of the pepper will sink, but most of it will stay on the surface of the water. Shake the pepper onto the water so that the surface of the water is coated evenly with pepper.
C. Touch the surface of the water with the tip of your tweezers. What happens to the pepper? Note that in your laboratory notebook.
D. Put the tweezers down. Allow the water to settle again and, if necessary, add more pepper so that the surface of the water is still covered evenly in pepper.
E. Rip off a small amount of facial tissue, wet it, and roll it into a ball. Use about the same amount of facial tissue as you did in Experiment 3.2.
F. Grab the wet facial tissue with your tweezers and use the tweezers to dip the ball of wet facial tissue into the water. Dip the facial tissue so that about half of the ball is below the surface of the water and the other half is above the surface of the water. Note in your laboratory notebook what happens to the pepper.
G. Allow the water to settle again and, if necessary, add more pepper so that the surface of the water is till covered evenly in pepper.
H. Chew your stick of gum until it is wet and soft. Pull off a chunk of gum that is about the size of the wet facial tissue ball you used in step (E).
I. Dip the gum into the water so that about half of it is below the surface of the water and the other half is above the surface of the water. Note in your laboratory notebook what happens to the pepper.
J. Allow the water to settle again and, if necessary, add more pepper so that the surface of the water is till covered evenly in pepper.
K. Put the chip of soap in the tweezers, and wet it with some water (not the water in the bowl).
L. Dip the soap into the water so that about half of it is below the surface of the water and the other half is above the surface of the water. Note in your laboratory notebook what happens to the pepper.
M. Clean everything up.

What did you see in the experiment? Well, the empty tweezers, as well as the wet facial tissue and the chewing gum, did not affect the pepper much. However, the wet soap should have had a dramatic effect. The pepper should have moved away from the soap, as if the soap was pushing it away. This should help you understand why the soap formed a workable "motor" for the "boat." Soap does something that seems to push things on the surface of the water.

You can do one more experiment to help you see what soap does to the surface of water.

EXPERIMENT 3.4

What Does Soap Do To Water? - Part 2

Supplies:

- A bowl
- Water
- A needle
- Thread
- Tape
- Tweezers
- A sheet of facial tissue (Make sure is it not the kind that has been treated with lotion.)
- A chunk of soap from a bar of soap
- A stick of chewing gum
- Someone to help you

Introduction - This is the final experiment in a series of experiments to help you learn why soap made an effective "motor" for the "boat" in Experiment 3.2.

Procedure:

A. Cut the thread into two strips that are long enough to stretch all of the way across the bowl and still have an extra 3 or four inches to spare.
B. Fill the bowl 3/4 of the way full with water.
C. Drop the needle into the water. Note in your lab notebook whether or not the needle floats.
D. Tape one end of each strip of thread to the bowl on the side that is farthest from you. The thread strips should be taped so that they are about 3/4 of the length of the needle away from each other.
E. Stretch the two pieces of thread across the bowl so that they are tight. They should be about 3/4 of the length of the needle apart from each other. Your setup should look something like the drawing on the next page:

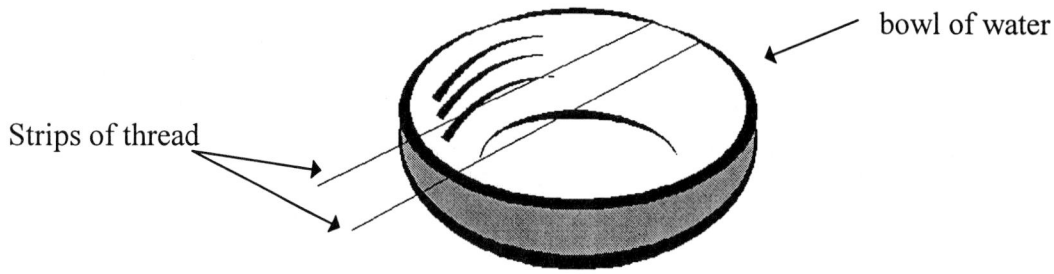

F. While you hold the threads tight, have your helper lay the needle horizontally across the threads so that the needle lies comfortably across the threads.
G. Slowly lower both strips of thread so that the needle and the strips of thread touch the water. You need to lower the threads so that the needle lies flat on the water's surface.
H. Carefully let the threads go, and the threads and needle should all float.
I. Now you need to get the threads out from under the needle and out of the water. This is tricky work. Try pulling each thread one at a time out from under the needle. You might end up sinking the needle when you do this. However, with a bit of practice, you can get both of the threads out of the way and out of the water without sinking the needle.
J. So now you should have a needle floating on the surface of the water.
K. Take the tweezers and carefully dip them in the water next to the needle. If the needle moves, follow it with the tweezers. Allow them to sit in the water for at least a full minute. Note in your laboratory notebook what happens.
L. Now take some facial tissue, wet it, and grab it with the tweezers. The ball should be about the same size as what you used in the previous experiment.
M. Dip the ball of facial tissue into the water so that half of it is submerged and the other half is not. Once again, if the needle moves, follow it. Allow the ball of facial tissue to soak in the water for at least a full minute. Note what happens in your laboratory notebook.
N. Remove the ball of facial tissue and repeat steps (L) and (M) with a chunk of chewing gum that you have softened by chewing it.
O. Remove the chewing gum and repeat steps (L) and (M) with a chunk of wet soap.
P. Clean everything up.

What happened in this experiment? The needle sank when you just dropped it into the water. However, when you laid it gently on the water with the threads, it floated. How is that possible? Well, we can learn something from what happened to the needle when you put the soap in the water. The needle moved around and eventually sank when the soap was put in the water, but it stayed afloat when you put the facial tissue, gum, and empty tweezers in the water.

What's the explanation for this? Well, first you need to realize that all of the things you saw in all three experiments occurred on the *surface* of the water. The "boats" moved on the surface of the water, the pepper moved on the surface of the water. The needle floated on the surface of the water until the soap touched the water. Thus, soap must be doing something to the *surface* of the water. What is it doing?

Well, every liquid has a property called **surface tension**. Surface tension can be thought of as a thin film that stretches across the surface of every liquid. If the film is not disturbed too much, it will tend to hold up things that would otherwise sink in water. Consider the needle, for example. It was made of metal, which is clearly a lot more dense than water. Thus, you would expect a needle to sink when it is placed in water. That's what you saw when you dropped the needle into the water. However, when you used the thread to gently lay the needle on the water, it floated. That's because of the "film" created by surface tension. The film is thin and fragile, but it is there. When you dropped the needle, you broke the "film" and the needle sank. However, when you laid the needle on the water gently, you did not break the "film," and surface tension was able to hold the needle up, causing it to float.

What happened in the experiment when you dipped the soap in the water, however? The needle sank. What does that tell you? When the empty tweezers, the facial tissue, and the gum were dipped in the water, the "film" of surface tension did not break. Thus, the act of dipping did not cause the needle to sink. It was the *soap* that caused the needle to sink. What does that tell you about soap's effect on surface tension? *Soap decreases the surface tension of water.*

How does that explain the results of Experiment 3.2? Well, think back to Experiment 3.3. When you dipped the soap into the middle pepper, the pepper pulled away from the soap. That's because surface tension had stretched the surface of the water like a thin film. When the soap touched the water, it decreased the surface tension in its general area. However, the surface of the water in the rest of the bowl still had a lot of surface tension. Thus, the "film" was broken at the center of the bowl but was still stretched hard along the edges. As a result, the "film" pulled out towards the edges of the bowl, pulling the pepper with it.

In Experiment 3.2, then, the soap in the "boat's motor" was really just reducing the surface tension at the point where the "motor" was. This caused the "film" on the water to pull back, pulling the "boat" along with it. Thus, the "boat" moved as if the soap was pushing it. Think about what we did here. We used three different experiments, all with the same important experimental variable. Comparing the results of the experiments helped us explain what soap does to the surface of water.

ON YOUR OWN

3.4 Suppose you just finished doing a lot of dishes in the sink. The dishes were dirty, so you used a lot of soap while doing them. If you put the "boat" with the soap "motor" from Experiment 3.2 in the sink after you finished the dishes, would the "boat" move like you saw it move in the experiment?

3.5 Suppose you tried to repeat Experiment 3.4 with vegetable oil instead of water. You try as hard as you can, but you simply cannot get the needle to float on the surface of the vegetable oil like you did when you used water. What does this tell you about the strength of the surface tension in vegetable oil as compared to water?

Recognizing Experimental Variables When They are not Obvious

Suppose you are sick. You go to the doctor and she tells you that you have a bacterial infection. She gives you some pills that she calls antibiotics and tells you to take two of them each day. After the very first day of taking the pills, you start feeling better. After three or four days, you feel completely healthy, but there are still pills left in the container the doctor gave you. The doctor told you to continue to take the pills until they are gone. Nevertheless, you feel fine, so you stop taking the pills. In a week, you get sick again with the same thing.

When you go to the doctor again, she examines you and immediately tells you that you did not take *all* of the pills that she gave you. She gives you some more pills and tells you to continue to take them until they are gone, no matter how you feel. This time, you follow her instructions to the letter, and you get better. Not only do you get better, but you do not come down with the same thing again.

How did the doctor know that a pill would help you get better? How did she know how many pills to give you? How did she know that you had to continue to take *all* of the pills, regardless of how you felt? The doctor knows all of these things because of the results of many *experiments* that had already been done on other people.

You see, when scientists come up with a new drug that they think will cure a particular illness, there are many, many experiments that they must do before the drug can be given to the general public. Typically, the experiments start with animals. Animals with the illness which the drug is supposed to cure are given the drug to see whether or not the drug cures the illness in the animals. If the drug has no severe side effects and is successful at curing the illness, a new series of experiments will be done with other animals. Eventually, if all of the animal-based experiments are successful, experiments are performed on people.

Now first you need to know that the people in these experiments are volunteers. Sometimes they are paid money to be in the experiment. Sometimes, they are willing to volunteer in the hopes that they will get cured of the illness. In any event, long before doctors can prescribe the drug to you and me, several experiments are performed on volunteers.

I want to discuss the typical method used in these drug studies, because it illustrates an important point about doing experiments. Suppose, for example, I came up with a new drug that was supposed to cure severe headaches. Suppose further that the drug was tested in several experiments with animals and the drug seemed both safe and effective. Eventually, it would be ready for human testing.

I would get together a group of volunteers, all of whom had trouble with severe headaches. Now, how would I go about testing the effectiveness of the drug? Well, one way I could do it is to simply give each one of them several pills and tell them that when they get a severe headache, they should take the pill. Then, they should record whether or not the headache went away and how long that took. After a few weeks, I could gather up the records of each person and then decide whether or not the drug really worked, right?

Well, I *could* do it that way, but there are a few experimental variables I would be missing. First of all, remember that I am working with a bunch of different people in this study. Each person has their own definition of a headache. Also, each person has their own idea of when a headache goes away. For some people, a headache is gone as soon as the pain is no longer distracting. For others, a headache is not gone until all of the pain is gone. Also, every person has a different level of pain which makes them uncomfortable. Some people can experience a lot of pain and barely notice it, while others can experience just a little pain and be miserable. This is called a person's **pain threshold**.

Thus, there are a *lot* of experimental variables here. How do I deal with them? Well, the first thing to do is to set up a control group. Remember, when you are trying to learn about whether an aspect of an experiment has any effect on the results, you can compare your results to a control. In Experiment 3.2, for example, the control was the "boat" with no "motor." In Experiments 3.3 and 3.4, the control was the empty set of tweezers. When you compared the results of the experiment to what happened to the control, you were able to determine when something interesting happened.

In the case of my drug study, then, I need to establish a control. So, I need to withhold the drug from a group of the volunteers. I can then compare the reports from the control group to the reports from the volunteers that took the drug. If the reports of the volunteers who took the drug differ dramatically from the reports of the control group, then the drug had an effect, right?

Well, once again, we are *still* missing an important experimental variable. There is still a big difference between the control group and the volunteers who actually took the drug. The control group *knows* that they are not taking anything that will make them better. The volunteers who are taking the drug *know* that they are taking something that I think will make them better. As a result, the control group does not *expect* anything great to happen to them, while the volunteers who take the drug do expect something great to happen to them. It turns out that this is an important experimental variable. Studies have shown that some people can be cured of an illness by simply *thinking* that they are being cured. Thus, I must control or eliminate this experimental variable as well.

How do I do that? Well, I could give my control group fake pills to take. In most drug studies, the fake pills, called **placeboes** (pluh see' bows) are usually just made out of sugar. They are made to look identical to the real drug, so that the volunteers do not know whether or not they are taking the real drug or the placeboes. As a result, they *all* think that they are being given a drug that will help them. Thus, that experimental variable is now eliminated. These kinds of studies are called **blind studies**.

<u>Blind studies</u> - Experiments in which the participants do not know whether or not they are a part of the control group

This term comes from the fact that the participants are "blind" to the details of the study.

Am I finally done? Well, not quite. You see, as long as I know who is a part of the control group and who is not, it might affect the way I examine the reports. If I know a person is a part of the control group, I don't *expect* anything great to happen to him or her. Thus, I will probably not look at his or her report very carefully. On the other hand, if I know that a person is a part of the group taking the real drug, I will probably look very closely at his or her report, noting any small decreases in headache pain.

How do I take care of this variable? That's easy. I become "blind" myself. I have someone else keep track of who is in the control group and who is taking the real drug. When I look at each report, then, I have no idea whether to expect great things or not-so-great things. Thus, I will analyze each report the same way. After I have finished my analysis, the person who knows which volunteers are in the control group can then see if my analysis of the reports differs between those in the control group and those not in the control group. These kinds of studies are called **double-blind studies** because neither the participants nor the people analyzing the results know who is in the control group and who is not.

Double-blind studies - Experiments in which neither the participants nor the people analyzing the results know who is in the control group

Notice, then, that there are at least two experimental variables that are not obvious. Both of these variables can have dramatic effects on the results of the experiment, so both have to be controlled or eliminated. Think for a moment, however, about *why* these variables exist in the experiment. They exist because the data is **subjective**. In other words, the data that is being collected depends to some extent on the opinions of people. Whether or not a headache is more or less intense is a matter of opinion from person to person. The analysis of such data is subjective as well. This leads to experimental variables which must be controlled.

Other experiments do not lead to such variables. Suppose, for example, I am testing the effectiveness of different types of fertilizers. I grow the same type of plant in several different pots which are all the same size and contain the same kind of soil. I water the plants each day with the same amount of water. To one plant, I add no fertilizer. I give each of the other plants a different brand of fertilizer, but I use the same amount of fertilizer in each case. I then measure the height of each plant each day.

I have a control in this experiment. It is the plant with no fertilizer. Do I need the study to be blind or double-blind? Of course not! The data is not subjective. The height of each plant is a measurable number. It is not subjective. Instead, it is **objective**. With objective data, there is no way opinion can affect the experimental results, so there is no need to go to the trouble of having a double-blind experiment. When designing an experiment, then, you must think carefully about whether or not the data taken is subjective. If it is, then the experiment should be done in a different way than if it is objective.

ON YOUR OWN

3.6 Many studies have been done on homeschooled students. In one popular type of experiment, the homeschooled students take the same standardized tests that publicly-schooled students take. The scores of the homeschooled students are then compared to those of publicly-schooled students. You can think of the publicly-schooled students as the control group in such a study. Should such a study be done as a blind study, a double-blind study, or neither?

3.7 Another way that homeschooled students are studied relates to their social skills. In one experiment, psychologists examined several students at play. Some of the students were homeschooled and some were publicly-schooled. The psychologists examined the students at play and determined which were well-adjusted socially and which were not. You can think of the publicly-schooled students as the control group in such a study. Should such a study be done as a blind study, a double-blind study, or neither?

Interpreting the Results of Experiments

At this point, you have a good idea of how to design an experiment. You know how to use and recognize experimental variables. You also know how to control or eliminate the experimental variables that might affect the results of your experiment in a bad way. Now it is time to look at a few experiments and get some practice interpreting their results. I want to start with an experiment that deals with ocean water.

Before you can understand the experiment, however, you need to learn a few things. In Experiment 3.1, you mixed salt with water. You mixed the salt so thoroughly with the water that it actually seemed to "disappear." It did not disappear, of course. Had you tasted the water, it would have tasted salty. Thus, the salt was still there; it was mixed so thoroughly with the water, however, that you could not see it. As you probably know, we say that the salt **dissolved** in the water.

Well, it turns out that *lots* of things can dissolve in water, including gases. When you drink soda pop, for example, the "fizz" that it has comes from carbon dioxide which is dissolved in the soda pop. Carbon dioxide is a gas, but it can dissolve in soda pop, which is a liquid. In the same way, oxygen gas can dissolve in water. In fact, that's where fish and other underwater creatures get their oxygen. Fish, for example, have **gills** which remove the dissolved oxygen from water and allow the fish to use the oxygen.

Thus, whether or not water can support fish depends, in part, on how much dissolved oxygen is in the water. If there is not enough dissolved oxygen in the water, the fish will suffocate, just like you and I would suffocate if there wasn't enough oxygen in the air that we breathe. If you have seen a fish tank with lots of fish in it, you probably saw something in the tank that was bubbling. The bubbling was caused by a pump that pumps air into the water. Most of the air bubbles out of the water, but some of the oxygen in the air dissolves in the water, keeping the amount of dissolved oxygen in the water high enough to support the fish in the tank.

A scientist studied the amount of dissolved oxygen in ocean water at different depths in the Bering Sea. After making his measurements, he graphed his results as follows:

FIGURE 1.1

The Amount of Dissolved Oxygen in the Bering Sea at Different Depths

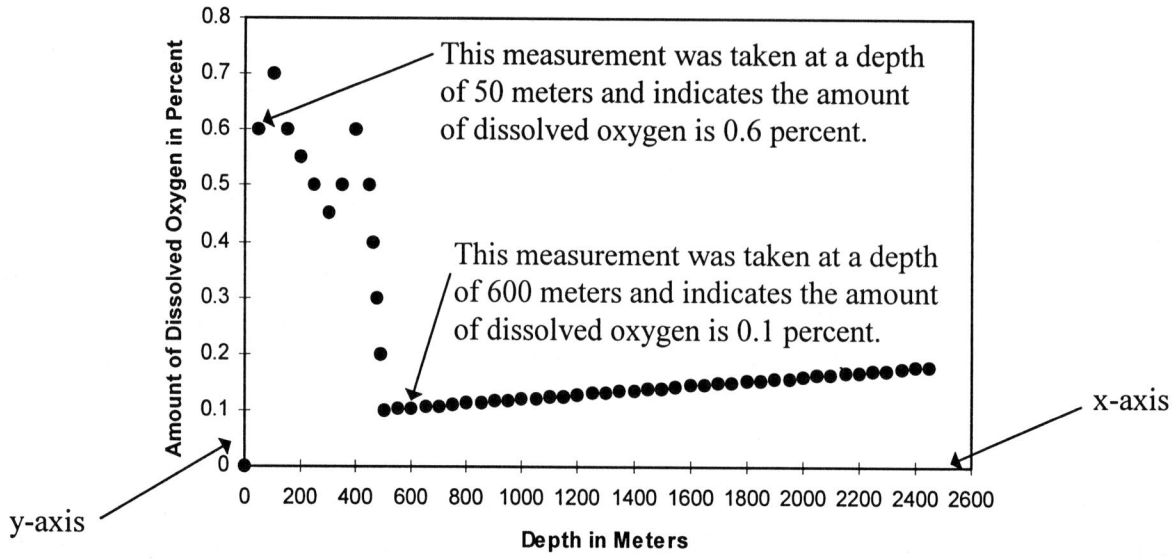

It is important for you to become familiar with reading graphs like this, as a lot of experimental data is communicated in this way. What does this particular graph show us? Well, the horizontal scale on the graph (usually called the **x-axis**) tells us the depth at which the measurement was taken. Notice that the depth is in meters. If you are not familiar with meters, don't worry. A meter is about the same distance as a yard. The important thing to see is that as you move right along the x-axis, the numbers get bigger. Thus, the farther to the right on the graph, the deeper the measurement was made. The vertical scale on the graph (usually called the **y-axis**) tells us how much oxygen was in the ocean water. Notice that this measurement was done in percent. The numbers get bigger the higher they are on the y-axis, so the higher on the graph, the more oxygen there is in the water.

Now let's look at the graph. Each dot on the graph represents a measurement. The first dot is on the bottom left-hand corner of the graph. Looking at the x-axis, it is right on the 0. This means it was taken at zero meters in depth, or right on the surface. Looking at the y-axis, it is on the zero. This means there was zero percent dissolved oxygen there. Now look at the next dot. It is not very far to the right of zero, but it is pretty high on the graph. What does that mean?

If you look at the x-axis, you will see a little vertical bar with "200" below it. This means that position on the x-axis represents a depth of 200 meters. Now the point we are looking at isn't nearly that far to the right, is it? It is somewhere between the "0" on the x-axis and the "200" on the x-axis. Thus, this measurement was made at a depth somewhere between 0 and 200 meters. Since the point is far to the left of the 200 meter mark and only a little to the right of 0, then the depth must be closer to 0 than 200. The actual depth for the measurement of that point is 50 meters. Now look at the y-axis. Based on the height of the point, we can say that it is very close to the 0.6 mark on the y-axis. So, this particular point represents a measurement made at 50 meters and indicates a 0.6 percent amount of dissolved oxygen.

Do you see how to read the graph? The horizontal position of each dot represents the depth at which the measurement was taken. The vertical position of each dot represents the amount of dissolved oxygen at that point. When the dots are between two markings on either axis, you can "guestimate" the values by noting which mark the dot is closest to.

Now that you know how to read the graph, what does it tell us? Well, once you actually get below the surface (at depths greater than 0), the amount of dissolved oxygen is pretty large. After all, the dots that are just to the right of 0 are high on the graph. Since a high vertical position indicates a lot of dissolved oxygen, depths between 0 and 400 meters seem to have a lot of dissolved oxygen. The dot just to the right of the 50 meter measurement is the highest dot on the graph. This means there is more dissolved oxygen at that depth than any other measured depth. Since that dot seems to be halfway between the 0 and 200 marks on the x-axis, that means it was made at a depth of 100 meters.

Once the measurements go below a depth of 400 meters, the amount of dissolved oxygen really starts to decrease. The dot that is halfway between 400 and 600 meters seems to have the lowest amount of dissolved oxygen. Since it is halfway between 400 and 600 meters, it probably represents the measurement made at 500 meters. Thus, we can say that of all the measurements taken, the amount of oxygen is lowest at 500 meters.

What happens for depths larger than 500 meters? Well, as the dots get farther and farther to the right of 500 meters, they start to get higher and higher. The effect is not large, but it is definitely there. This tells us that at depths greater than 500 meters, the amount of dissolved oxygen increases slowly with increasing depth.

All right. That was a lot of information, so let's review. The higher the dot is on the graph, the more dissolved oxygen is in the water. The farther to the right the dot is on the graph, the deeper the measurement was taken. The data seem to indicate that at depths less than 400 meters, the amount of dissolved oxygen in the water is relatively high. It is highest at 100 meters. At depths between 400 and 500 meters, the amount of dissolved oxygen decreases very quickly as the depth increases. Then, after 500 meters, the amount of dissolved oxygen increases slowly with increasing depth.

So what does this data tell us? Well, remember the trend of the data. The majority of the oxygen is at the smaller depths. What does that tell us about *where* the oxygen is coming from? It is, most likely, coming from at or near the surface of the water. Let's think for a moment about what's at or near the surface of the water. Air is right there at the surface of the water. What's air got in it? It has oxygen. Thus, this experiment gives us evidence that most of the oxygen in the Bering Sea comes from the air. Oxygen in the air gets dissolved in the water as it hits the surface of the water, and then it gets mixed into the water at somewhat lower depths. Since the amount of oxygen drops off quickly from 400 to 500 meters, we can say that the mixing of oxygen to depths below 400 meters is rather inefficient.

ON YOUR OWN

A student decides to try and find the ideal amount of fertilizer to add to plants. He grows ten individual plants (all of the same type), each one treated with a different amount of fertilizer. After a few weeks, he measures the height of each plant and produces the following graph:

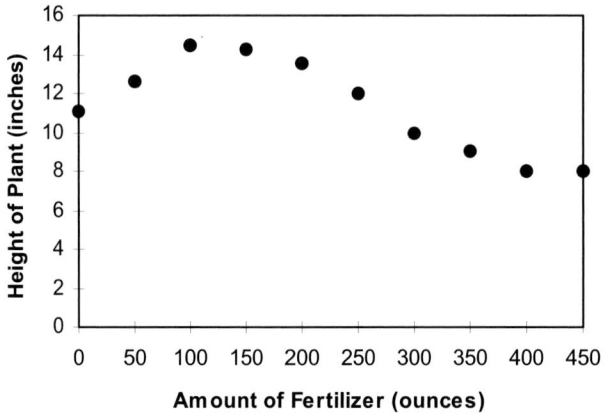

3.8 What is the ideal amount of fertilizer to use, if you want tall plants?

3.9 A student hypothesizes that no matter what amount of fertilizer you use, it's better than using no fertilizer at all. Does this experiment support or deny that hypothesis?

3.10 Suppose a farmer uses an automated fertilizing system that cannot put a precise amount of fertilizer on the plants. Instead, the farmer must indicate a range of 100 ounces. For example, the farmer can specify 25 - 125 ounces or 500-600 ounces. What range should the farmer specify?

ANSWERS TO THE ON YOUR OWN PROBLEMS

3.1 There are at least three experimental variables here. First, the brand of floor cleaner used is a variable, because he uses a different brand on each quarter. Second, the amount of black heel marks in each quarter will be different. There is just no way he can scuff up the floor equally on all quarters. Third, the amount and effectiveness of the scrubbing will vary. Most likely, he will get tired as time goes on. Thus, he will scrub less vigorously in the last quarter than on the first quarter. There may be more, but those are the ones most obvious to me. Do not worry if you didn't get them all - just use this as a learning experience.

3.2 The student will learn something from the brand of floor cleaner used. That's the whole purpose of the experiment. The cleaner quarter will indicate the better floor cleaner. He should reduce or eliminate the variable amount of black heel marks on each quarter and the variable amount and effectiveness of the scrubbing.

3.3 He can reduce the variable amount of black heel marks by examining each quarter closely and trying to even out the amount of black heel marks so they are the same on each quarter. He can reduce the variable amount and effectiveness of the scrubbing by taking breaks to ensure he is not tired. He could also count the number of strokes and make sure he scrubs with the same number of strokes on each quarter.

3.4 The "boat" will probably not move very much. Remember, the "boat" moved because of the decrease in surface tension caused by the soap. If a lot of soap is already in the water, the surface tension is already decreased substantially. Thus, the effect of the soap on the "boat" will be insignificant.

3.5 Vegetable oil has a smaller surface tension than water. If the needle could float on water because of its surface tension, then a liquid that it cannot float on must have less surface tension.

3.6 The study should probably be done as a blind study, but there is no need for a double-blind study. If you said neither, that's okay, too. The only reason I would make it blind is to reduce the competition factor. If the publicly-schooled students knew they were being treated as a control for a comparison to homeschooled students, they might try harder than they normally would in order to "beat" the homeschoolers. The homeschooled students might also have similar competitive instincts if they knew they were being compared to publicly-schooled students. Since the data are not subjective, however, there is no reason to make the person analyzing the data blind. Remember, the researcher needs to be blind only if his or her preconceived notions can affect the data. In the case of this experiment, a test score is a measurement that has no room for interpretation. Thus, there is no way the researcher's preconceived notions can affect the results. In case you are wondering, homeschooled students almost always score significantly higher than publicly-schooled students on standardized tests.

3.7 The study should be double-blind. First of all, if students knew who was homeschooled and who wasn't, that would affect how they behave. So the students have to be blind as to whether they are a part of the control or the studied group. In the same way, the psychologists analyzing the student's behavior must be blind as well. Otherwise, their preconceived ideas on homeschooling versus public schooling might affect how they analyze each student. In case you were wondering, such studies report that there are only small differences between the homeschooled students and the publicly-schooled students. The observable differences are typically that the homeschooled students don't break the rules as often as do the publicly-schooled students. Also, some of these studies have shown that homeschooled students tend to play with others regardless of race, gender, or age. Publicly-schooled students, on the other hand, tend to exclude those who are not of the same race, gender and age.

3.8 The plants grow tallest with 100 ounces of fertilizer, because the dot at 100 ounces of fertilizer is highest on the graph. Thus, that amount produces the tallest plants.

3.9 This study denies the hypothesis. With no fertilizer, the plants grow taller than with 300-450 ounces of fertilizer. You can see this because the dot for 0 fertilizer is higher than the dots for 300, 350, 400, and 450 ounces.

3.10. The range should be 100-200 ounces. Since there must be a range, you need to establish the range over which the plants grow tallest for that range. Since 100 ounces is the ideal amount, you might have thought 50 - 150 ounces would be a good range, because that would have 100 as the average amount of fertilizer. Look at the data, however. Plants grown with 50 ounces are smaller than plants grown with 150 and 200 ounces of fertilizer. Thus, the best 100 ounce range is between 100 and 200 ounces.

STUDY GUIDE FOR MODULE #3

1. Define the following terms:

a. Experimental variable
b. Control (of an experiment)
c. Blind studies
d. Double-blind studies

2. When is an experimental variable good and when should it be reduced or eliminated?

Questions 3 - 7 refer to the following story:

A consumer laboratory decides to test the effectiveness of different laundry detergents. Five white shirts are stained with grass stains and put into five different washers. In one washer, no laundry detergent is used. In the other four washers, four different types of laundry detergent are used, one type in each washer. Water from the same source is used to fill each washer. The washers are then turned on, and once they are finished, the shirts are examined by eye to see which is the cleanest.

3. What is the control for this experiment?

4. What is the experimental variable that will be used to learn something from the experiment?

5. What are the experimental variables that need to be reduced or eliminated?

6. What could be done to reduce or eliminate the unwanted experimental variables?

7. Are the data collected objective or subjective?

8. Why can a carefully-placed needle float on water, even though the needle is more dense than the water?

9. What does soap do to the surface of water?

10. A student tries to float a needle on water. He succeeds, but only after several attempts. He then tries to float the same needle on another liquid. Although the needle sinks when dropped in the liquid, it is much easier to lay the needle on the surface of this liquid and make it float than it was to get the needle to float on water. Compare the surface tension of this liquid to that of water.

11. A new, fat-free potato chip comes out on the market. A few months later, there are reports that some people get severe stomach cramps 1-4 hours after eating the chips. You must do an experiment to see if the chips cause severe stomach cramps. A group of people volunteer for the

study. Describe how you would design the experiment. Also, indicate whether the experiment should be blind, double-blind, or neither.

12. A study is done to see if a certain herb can increase a student's concentration skills. A group of students volunteer for the experiment, which consists of giving the students a pill that is made up of either sugar or the herb. The students then take a series of math tests. The test scores of the students who take the herb will be compared to those who took the sugar pills. If there is a difference between the average test scores of the groups, it could very well be the result of the herb. Should this be a blind study, a double-blind study, or neither?

13. A farmer has four different corn fields. The government pays him to experiment with 3 different kinds of herbicides (weed killers). He sprays nothing on one field, and he sprays each of the other fields with a different brand of herbicide. He then records the number of tons of corn that he produces from each field, and reports back to the government about which herbicide produced the best crop. Should this be a blind study, a double-blind study, or neither?

14. A researcher is trying to determine if there are any differences between the social skills of homeschooled students as compared to publicly-schooled students. She plans to get a group of publicly-schooled students and a group of homeschooled students together and observe how the children play with one another. She will record her observations and then try to see if the ways in which the homeschooled children interact with others are different than the ways in which publicly-schooled children interact with others. Should this be a blind study, a double-blind study, or neither?

15. A scientist comes up with a revolutionary drug that he thinks will allow people to lose weight without dieting. They simply need to take the pill and their excess weight will slowly disappear. He decides to test the pill by getting two groups of volunteers together. The first group will take a pill that is made up of sugar, and the second group will take his new drug. Each volunteer will be weighed once a week for 12 weeks. Should this be a blind study, a double-blind study, or neither? What results will indicate that the new drug is effective?

(The study guide continues on the next page.)

Questions 16 - 19 refer to the following story:

A student is playing with a spring and notices that the more weight he hangs on it, the more it stretches. He therefore decides to do an experiment. He suspends the spring from the ceiling and puts a hanger on the bottom of the spring. He then starts putting more and more weight on the hanger. He measures the length of the spring each time he adds weight, and he comes up with the following graph:

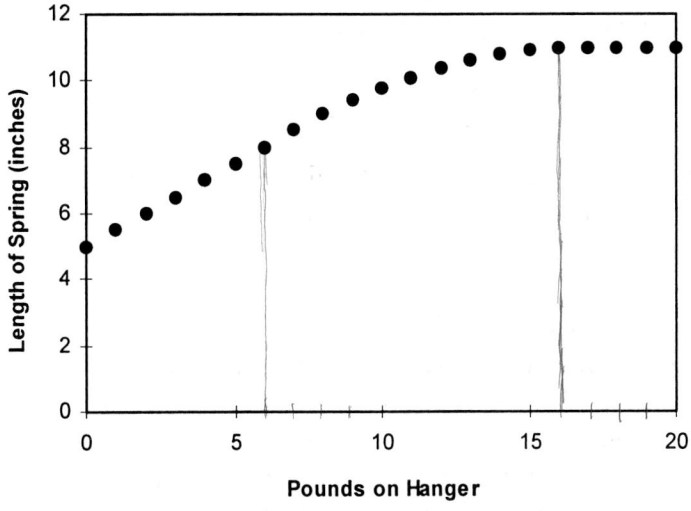

16. How long is the spring when it is not stretched out at all?

17. How many pounds are necessary to stretch the spring to 8 inches?

18. At about what weight does the spring no longer stretch in response to more weight being put on it?

19. The student does this experiment on several more springs. Although the actual numbers vary from spring to spring, the graph always has the same basic shape. What does this tell you about the ability of a spring to stretch when it is pulled?

Module #4: Science, Applied Science, and Technology

Introduction

By working through the previous three modules, you have probably gotten a good idea about what science is and how to do it. That's good, because in the next module and the three that follow it, I will introduce you to the fascinating fields of geology and paleontology. These are two of the most controversial fields in science, so you need to have a firm grounding in what science is so that you know how to deal with the controversies you will encounter. In *this* module, however, I want to spend some time on a distinction that is rarely made but absolutely critical.

The Distinction Between Science, Applied Science, and Technology

The distinction between science, applied science, and technology is rather simple. Despite the fact that it is simple, it is rarely made in textbooks today. As a result, many students grow up thinking that these three pursuits are the same. In fact, they are not. The distinction between them is the *motivation* behind each one. Science is motivated purely by curiosity. A scientist does experiments designed to explain some facet of Creation. The scientist does not care one whit about whether or not the knowledge gained is *useful*. The scientist just wants the knowledge to satisfy his or her own curiosity.

Applied science is quite different. In applied science, experiments are aimed at trying to find something useful. For example, an applied scientist will look at a job and say, "There must be an easier way to do that job." He or she will then start doing experiments aimed at the goal of building a process or machine that will make the job easier.

Do you see the difference? In science, we are just trying to answer questions. We want to know *why* something in Creation happens as it does. Thus, we make observations, form hypotheses, do experiments, and eventually come up with theories and laws that explain *why*. In applied science, we have a completely different goal. In applied science, we want to use science *to make something better*.

What about technology? Well, technology is related to, but different than both science and applied science. Technology is the invention of a new process or machine that makes life better or makes a job easier. Now although that sounds a lot like applied science, it is not. Technology is often the *result* of applied science, but it is also often the result of science. It can also be the result of accident.

Now if all of this is a bit confusing, let me clear it up with a few examples. I will start out with a simple one. You already learned that the ancient Egyptians had the best medical practices of anyone in the known world back in ancient times. One of their medical practices was to put moldy bread on an open wound. This is an example of technology that was the result of accident. The ancient Egyptian doctors tried several different treatments for open wounds. Many of those treatments made the patient more sick, so the doctors stopped using them. Eventually, someone tried putting moldy bread on an open wound. The wound healed quickly and cleanly, and eventually, the practice became a standard medical procedure.

The practice of putting moldy bread on a person's open wounds is an example of technology. The process itself makes life better because it allows people's open wounds to heal more efficiently. This should illustrate an important point. When most people think of "technology," they think of machines like computers, televisions, and automobiles. Although those are all examples of technology, they are not the only kinds of examples. Any invention or process that makes life better or a job easier is technology. Medical treatments, nutritional programs, and the like are also part of technology. The ancient Egyptians, then, had a lot of technology, but it was mostly the result of accident.

Technology can also be the result of applied science. Consider the computer, for example. The origin of computers can actually be traced back to **Blaise Pascal** in 1642. Pascal was a great scientist, mathematician, and philosopher. I mentioned him briefly in Module #1. Although he practiced science, he also practiced applied science. One of the things he wanted to do was to make the job of adding and subtracting numbers easier. After years of experiments trying to come up with a "machine" that could add and subtract, he eventually invented the **adding machine.**

As time went on, many advances were made to the adding machine, all in an attempt to make the job of keeping track of numbers easier. Eventually, adding machines were made that could multiply and divide as well. As time went on, people figured out how to make these machines "remember" previous calculations while working on more and more complex problems. All of this was done with machines that were composed of gears, rods, and shafts.

Computers eventually took another giant step forward when American scientists John Eckert and John Mauchly invented **ENIAC,** the first electronic computer. ENIAC stood for Electronic Numerical Integrator and Computer. It used electronic devices known as **vacuum tubes** (18,000 of them!) to produce several hundred multiplication steps every second. Although this computer was fast compared to all of the adding machines that had come before it, it was huge and incredibly expensive.

Applied scientists began to work on ways to reduce both the size and expense of building an electronic computer. Since vacuum tubes were both large and costly to build, they decided to attack the problem at that point. Some applied scientists worked on making vacuum tubes smaller and cheaper, while others worked on finding a replacement. In 1948, three applied scientists from Bell Telephone Laboratories (Walter Brattain, John Bardeen, and William Shockley) developed the **transistor.** It could perform the function of a vacuum tube at a much cheaper price, and it was also tiny in comparison. That discovery made it possible to build small, cheap computers, and it ushered in the computer age that we are in today.

Now look at how the computer was invented. It started out as a device that Pascal made specifically to help out people who had to keep track of a lot of numbers. Pascal did not invent the adding machine by trial and error. He used the scientific method, forming hypotheses on how to make such a device, performing experiments, etc. Thus, Pascal was doing science. However, his goal was not to learn about some aspect of Creation. Instead, it was to make life easier for certain people. Thus, Pascal was doing applied science.

In each stage of the computer's history, you can see that nearly every advance was the result of applied science. Scientists working on new computers were interested in making the adding machine faster, more efficient, and able to do more things. All with the expressed purpose of making it easier to keep track of numbers. Thus, the computer is a result of (mostly) applied science.

Although you would think that most technology we have today is the result of applied science, that's not necessarily true. Consider, for example, the use of X-rays in modern medicine. When a doctor thinks that you might have broken a bone, he or she has an X-ray done of that bone. The X-ray allows the doctor to look at the bone without cutting you open, which makes the diagnosis much faster and safer.

X-rays were discovered in 1895 by German scientist **Wilhelm Conrad Roentgen**. Roentgen was not trying to come up with a new medical procedure. Instead, he was studying electricity and trying to understand *what* it was. He was passing electricity through a tube that was partially filled with gas. He noticed that even though the tube was encased in black cardboard, whenever the electricity passed through the tube, a nearby screen would glow. He hypothesized that the tube was emitting some sort of rays whenever the electricity passed through it. Since he had no idea what those rays were, he called them "**X-rays**." He performed further tests and demonstrated that X-rays could form images on photographic film, just like light could.

Medical scientists quickly understood the value of these X-rays. After all, they could form images on photographic film even when the source was enclosed in a black box. Soon, doctors were using X-rays to form images of the insides of people's bodies. They were used to find bullets inside of shooting victims and, as the technology developed further, they were eventually used to diagnose problems with bones and internal organs.

The technology of X-rays, then, is really the result of science. A scientist who was just trying to figure out the nature of electricity ended up discovering a process that advanced medical diagnosis and treatment immensely. Not all technology, then, is the result of applied science. Some of it is the result of accident, and some is the result of science.

Sometimes, science and applied science interact to come up with technology. The history of the computer gives us an example of that. As you should remember from the history of computers that you just read, computer technology made a great leap forward when mechanical adding machines were replaced by electronic computers. The principal component of an electronic computer at that time was the vacuum tube - a glass tube from which most of the air had been removed. The tube contained electrical wires and plates and, when electricity was passed through it in a certain way, the vacuum tube could be used to run a computer. Vacuum tubes were first developed by scientists to study electricity. Later, applied scientists realized that these same tubes could be used to run computers. Thus, without scientists studying electricity, there would have been no vacuum tubes to make electronic computers! Science and applied science, then, often work together to make technology.

ON YOUR OWN

4.1 Identify each of the experiments described below as science experiments or applied science experiments.

a. Experiments designed to figure out why rainbows form in the sky science
b. Experiments designed to determine how to make a field produce more crops applied science
c. Experiments designed to make a television have a sharper picture applied science
d. Experiments designed to determine the factors that influence the speed of wind science

4.2 Which of the following would be considered technology?

a. An explanation of how clouds form
b. A microwave oven
c. A recipe to make cement
d. A description of the lifecycle of a grasshopper

Simple Machines

Since the rest of this course is going to concentrate on science, I thought I would spend the rest of this module discussing technology and applied science. The best way to discuss both of these subjects is to introduce the concept of **simple machines**.

Simple machine - A device that reduces the amount of force needed to perform a task or changes the direction of a force

To understand this definition, you obviously have to know what force is.

Force - A push or pull that changes the motion of an object

So what does all of this mean? Let's start with force.

A force is used to change the motion of an object. For example, if a car is stalled and you need to get it to a service station, you push on it to get it moving. When you do that, you are exerting a force in an attempt to change the car's motion. At first, the stalled car does not move. If you push hard enough, you will change that and cause the car to move. Thus, the push has changed the car's motion. Suppose you get the car rolling and you reach a hill. The service station is, thankfully, at the bottom of the hill. You allow the car to roll down the hill, but now it is going much too fast for you to pull into the station. What do you do at that point? You hit the brakes. The brakes push against the wheels to stop the car. Once again, the brakes apply a push to alter the motion of the car. This time, the change in motion is to stop rather than start. Nevertheless, the brakes still apply a force, and the motion of the car still changes.

Now that you know what force is, you know what a simple machine is. A simple machine reduces or changes the direction of a force that is needed to perform a task. Thus, simple machines make a task easier. There are six basic kinds of simple machines: **the lever, the wheel and axle, the pulley, the inclined plane, the wedge, and the screw**. Any non-electronic machine is really just some combination of these six simple machines.

The Lever

The lever is a simple machine that magnifies either force or motion. It consists of a rigid bar that rotates around a fixed point called the **fulcrum**. The best way to understand the lever is to do an experiment.

EXPERIMENT 4.1
The Lever

Supplies:

- A wooden pencil
- A wooden ruler
- At least 5 quarters, preferably more

Introduction - A lever allows you to use a small force to lift a heavy load. This experiment will demonstrate that fact.

Procedure:

A. Lay the pencil down on a flat tabletop or desktop.
B. Lay the ruler across the pencil so that the pencil is at the center of the ruler, as shown below:

C. Do not worry if your ruler does not stay flat. Most likely, it will tilt so that one side hits the tabletop. That's fine.
D. Place two quarters on the end that is resting on the tabletop.
E. Place a single quarter on the other end.
F. Now think about the setup. The end of the ruler that is resting on the tabletop has two quarters on it. The weight of those two quarters are pressing down on that end of the ruler.

The other side has a single quarter on it. The weight of that single quarter is pressing down on that side of the ruler.

G. Keeping the ruler still, begin moving the pencil over, towards the side with two quarters on it. Move it a little bit at a time, and stop in between each move to see what happens. Eventually, you should see the ruler tilt so that the side with the single quarter falls and hits the tabletop, while the side with two quarters is raised up in the air.

H. What did you just accomplish? You just used a lever to make the weight of one quarter lift up the weight of two quarters. The ruler is the rigid bar, and the pencil is the fulcrum. By moving the fulcrum towards the larger weight, you could actually make the small weight lift the larger weight.

I. Add another quarter to the stack of two quarters that are lifted into the air. The ruler should tilt once again, so that the side with three quarters is touching the table and the side with one quarter is in the air.

J. Begin moving the pencil towards the stack of quarters again, like you did in step (G). Continue to do this until the ruler tilts again, and the side with the single quarter rests on the table, while the side with the three quarters is in the air. You have now used a lever to make the weight of one quarter lift the weight of three quarters.

K. Continue the experiment, adding more quarters to the stack of three. Each time, move the pencil towards the stack of quarters, and you should see that the weight of a single quarter can lift many, many other quarters. I did this experiment and was able to get the weight of a single quarter to lift *20 quarters*!

L. Clean everything up.

In the experiment, you made a lever. The ruler was the rigid bar, and the pencil was the fulcrum. The single quarter represented what we call the **effort** of the lever. The effort essentially means the force being applied to the lever. The stack of quarters is called the **resistance**, which identifies the weight that's being lifted. Thus, the basic parts of a lever are the bar, the fulcrum, the effort, and the resistance.

Ill. from the MasterClips Collection

FIGURE 4.1
A First-Class Lever

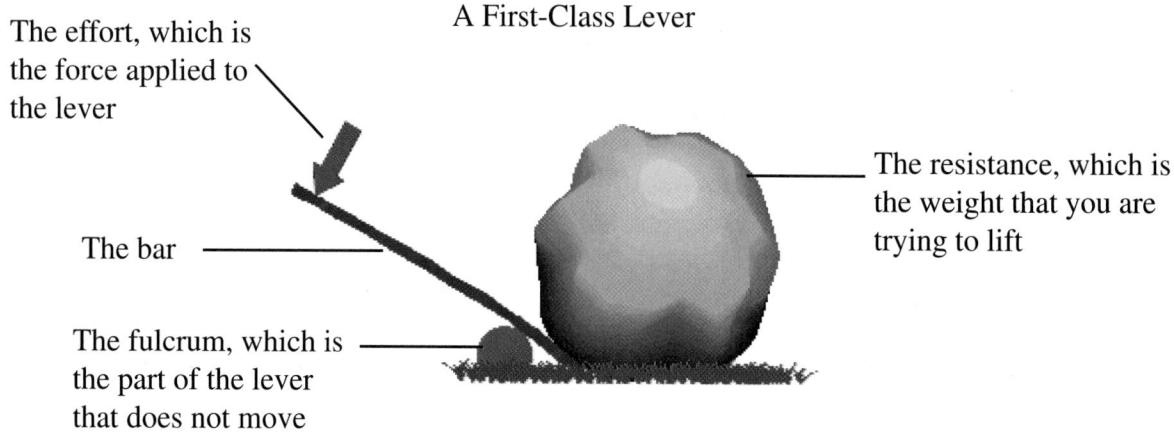

Using a lever like the one you made in the experiment, you can move objects that it would otherwise be impossible to lift. In the experiment, for example, you used an effort equal to the weight of one quarter to lift a resistance of several quarters. The lever, then, magnified the effort so that a large resistance could be lifted.

As you saw in your experiment, a lever gives the person using it an advantage. A lever like the one you used in your experiment, for example, allows a person to lift heavy objects with a relatively small force. Thus, the person receives a **mechanical advantage** by using a lever.

Mechanical advantage - The amount by which force or motion is magnified in a simple machine

In your experiment, when you used the weight of a single quarter to lift 3 other quarters, the lever was providing a mechanical advantage of 3. The effort was magnified 3 times so that one quarter could lift 3 quarters.

What determines the mechanical advantage of a lever? Mechanical advantage is determined by the distance between the effort and fulcrum as compared to the distance between the resistance and the fulcrum. Remember what happened in the experiment. In order to get the one quarter's weight to lift a stack of quarters, you had to move the pencil (the fulcrum) towards the stack of quarters (the resistance). The closer the fulcrum was to the resistance, and the farther it was from the effort, the more weight the effort could lift.

If the fulcrum is put precisely in between the effort and the resistance, there is no mechanical advantage. If you wanted to lift 100 pounds with the lever, you would have to supply 100 pounds of force. However, if you moved the fulcrum closer to the resistance, the amount of force you would have to use goes down. How much does it go down? Well, you can calculate the mechanical advantage of a lever using a rather simple mathematical formula:

Mechanical advantage = (distance from fulcrum to effort) ÷ (distance from fulcrum to resistance)

Suppose, for example, you made a lever in which the fulcrum was 6 inches from the resistance and 60 inches from the effort. In that case the mechanical advantage would be calculated by replacing "distance from fulcrum to effort" with "60" and "distance from fulcrum to resistance" with "6":

Mechanical advantage = (distance from fulcrum to effort) ÷ (distance from fulcrum to resistance)

$$\text{Mechanical advantage} = 60 \div 6 = 10$$

This means that you could lift a resistance that is *10 times as heavy as the effort*. Thus, you could lift a 100-pound rock using only 10 pounds of force!

I will come back to the concept of mechanical advantage when I do a couple of examples at the end of this section. Before I do those examples, however, I want to tell you a few more things about levers. Notice that I called the lever in Figure 4.1 a **first-class lever**. What did I mean by that? Did I mean that this is just a really great lever? No! It turns out that there are three different kinds of levers, and the one illustrated in Figure 4.1 is an example of the first kind of lever. There are also **second-class levers** and **third-class levers** as well. What separates these three classes? The position of the fulcrum relative to the resistance and effort.

In a first-class lever, the fulcrum is positioned between the effort and resistance. In a second-class lever, the fulcrum is at one end of the bar and the resistance is between the fulcrum and the effort. In a third-class lever, the fulcrum is at one end of the bar and the effort is between the fulcrum and the resistance.

FIGURE 4.2
A Second-Class Lever and a Third-Class Lever

A Second-Class Lever
In this lever, the fulcrum is at one end of the bar and the resistance is between the fulcrum and the effort.

A Third-Class Lever
In this lever, the fulcrum is at one end of the bar and the effort is between the fulcrum and the resistance.

Both a second-class lever and a third-class lever provide a mechanical advantage, and that mechanical advantage can be calculated using the same mathematical equation I showed you earlier. However, the nature of the mechanical advantage is *different* between these levers. A second-class lever, like a first-class lever, magnifies force. If the mechanical advantage is 10, you can lift a resistance of 100 pounds with only a 10 pound effort. In a third-class lever, force is not magnified. In fact, the effort is always larger than the resistance in a third-class lever. What's the mechanical advantage, then? Well, even though it takes more force to lift the resistance, the resistance moves a lot *faster* than the effort. Thus, a third-class lever magnifies speed, not force.

I want you to notice one other thing about these three classes of levers. I want you to notice what happens to the *direction* of the force that is being applied to the lever. In the first-class lever pictured in Figure 4.1, the effort pushes *down* and the resistance moves *up*. Thus, a first-class lever not only magnifies the effort, but it also changes the direction of the effort. Now look at the second-class lever pictured in Figure 4.2. Notice that the effort pushes *up*, and the resistance moves *up* as well. A second-class lever, then, magnifies force, but does not change the direction of the force. In the third-class lever pictured in Figure 4.2, the effort pushes *up* and the resistance moves *up* as well. Thus, a third-class lever magnifies speed and does not change the direction of the force.

In the last few pages, I have thrown a lot of information at you, so I want to step back and review before I continue. First, a lever consists of 4 parts: a bar, a fulcrum (the part that does not move), an effort (the force being applied), and a resistance (the load you want to move). In a first-class lever, the fulcrum is between the effort and the resistance. Because of this arrangement, the direction of the effort is reversed. If you press down, the load will move up. Also, a first-class lever magnifies the effort, providing a mechanical advantage which can be calculated. A second-class lever has the fulcrum at one end of the bar, and the resistance is between the fulcrum and the effort. This arrangement does not change the direction of the effort. If you lift up, the load moves up. It does, however, magnify the effort, providing a mechanical advantage which can be calculated. Finally, third-class levers also have the fulcrum at one end of the bar, but the effort is between the fulcrum and the resistance. This arrangement does not change the direction of the effort. It also does not magnify the effort. Instead, it magnifies the speed at which the effort moves, providing a mechanical advantage which can be calculated. Although the effort moves slowly, the resistance will move quickly.

Believe it or not, there are many, many common examples of all three classes of levers. Figure 4.3 illustrates a few of them:

Ill. from the MasterClips Collection

FIGURE 4.3

A Common Example of Each Class of Lever

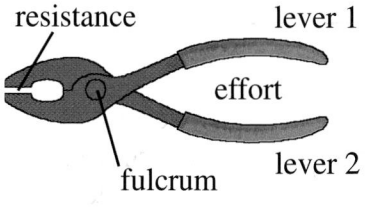

Pliers are an example of two **first-class levers**. The fulcrum is between the effort and resistance. You can grasp an object with a much firmer grasp when using pliers, because the force of your grasp is magnified.

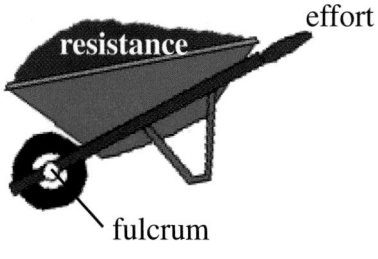

A wheelbarrow is an example of a **second-class lever**. The fulcrum is at the end, and the resistance is between the effort and the fulcrum. You can lift more weight in a wheelbarrow than you could with your arms, because the lever magnifies the force with which you lift.

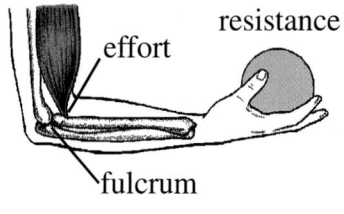

Your forearm is an example of a **third-class lever**. The fulcrum is at the end, and the effort (provided by the muscle) is between the resistance and the fulcrum. You exert more force with your muscle than the weight you lift, but the speed at which the weight moves is much faster than the speed at which your muscle moves.

Before I leave this discussion of levers, I want to revisit the equation for mechanical advantage. It is important for you to learn that the more science you do, the more you will see that math is an integral part of science. The mechanical advantage equation is your first introduction to this fact, so I want to highlight it. Study the following example to make sure you understand how to use the mechanical advantage equation.

EXAMPLE 4.1

A person constructs a first-class lever to move a 200-pound rock. The fulcrum is placed 5 inches from the rock, and the person applies force 100 inches from the fulcrum. What is the mechanical advantage of this lever?

To calculate mechanical advantage, you use the equation I gave you earlier. Since the distance between the effort (the applied force) and the fulcrum is 100 inches, we replace "distance from fulcrum to effort" with 100. Since the resistance (the load the person is trying to move) is 5 inches from the fulcrum, we replace "distance from fulcrum to resistance" with 5.

Mechanical advantage = (distance from fulcrum to effort) ÷ (distance from fulcrum to resistance)

Mechanical advantage = 100÷ 5 = 20

The mechanical advantage, then, is 20.

Now remember what we calculated here. This is far from a meaningless number. It really tells us something! It tells us that whatever force the person applies, it will be magnified 20 times to move the rock.

ON YOUR OWN

4.3 Tweezers are an example of a lever. To which class of levers do tweezers belong?

4.4 A person constructs a second-class lever in which the fulcrum is 1 foot from the resistance, while the effort is 3 feet from the fulcrum. What is the mechanical advantage of this lever?

4.5 If a lever has a mechanical advantage of 10, what does that mean?

The Wheel and Axle

The next simple machine I want to discuss is the wheel and axle. In a wheel and axle, a large circular wheel is attached to a smaller cylinder, which is like a solid tube. When the wheel turns, so does the axle. When the axle turns, so does the wheel. If both parts do not turn together, it is not a wheel and axle. It is something else.

FIGURE 4.4
A Wheel and Axle

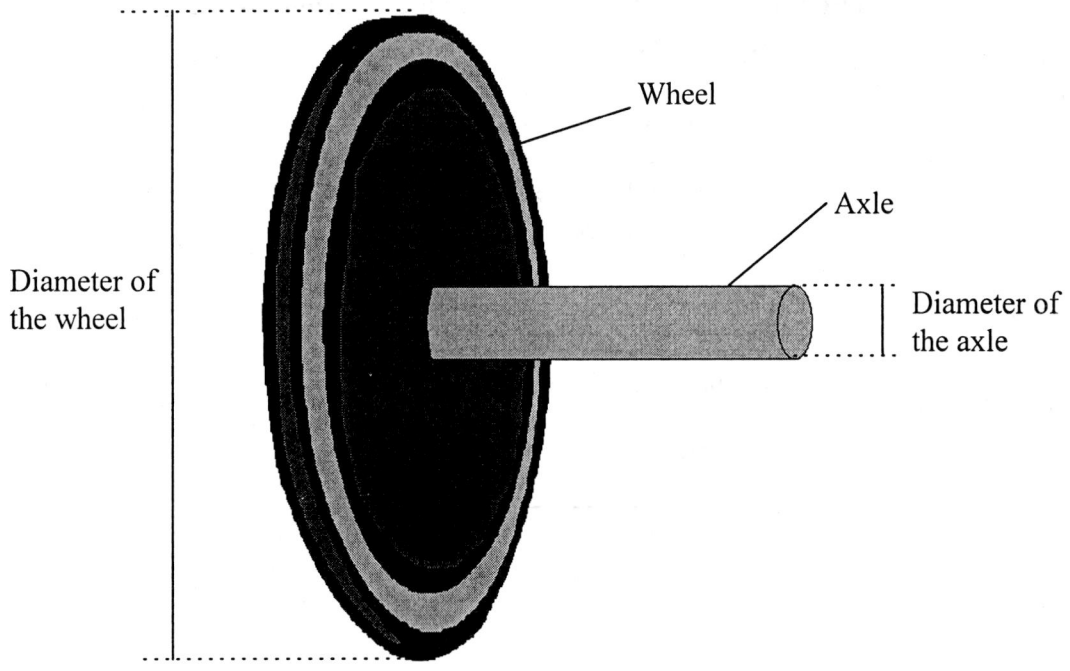

A wheel and axle has two applications, both of which can be found in an automobile. In the first application, a force is applied which turns the axle. This, in turn, causes the wheel to turn. In an automobile, the engine turns the axle of the automobile's wheels, which then causes the wheels to turn. The turning of the wheels then causes the car to move forward. In the second application, a force is used to turn the wheel, and in response, the axle turns. This application can be found in the steering wheel of a car. The driver turns the steering wheel, which causes the axle to turn.

A wheel and axle also offers a mechanical advantage. Like the mechanical advantage of a lever, it is relatively easy to calculate. First, you need to know the **diameter** of the wheel and the **diameter** of the axle. Now you might not be familiar with the term "diameter," so I want to define it.

Diameter - The length of a straight line that travels from one side of a circle to another, while passing through the center of a circle

The diameter, then, is a measure of the size of a circle. From Figure 4.4, you can easily see that the diameter of the wheel is much bigger than that of the axle.

Once you know the diameter of the wheel and the diameter of the axle, the mechanical advantage can be calculated, once again by a relatively simple equation:

Mechanical advantage = (diameter of the wheel) ÷ (diameter of the axle)

Notice that *this* equation for mechanical advantage is similar to, but different than, the equation for mechanical advantage which you learned in the previous section. This is an important point. A wheel and axle is completely different than a lever. They both offer a mechanical advantage, but because they are different, the equation for mechanical advantage is different in each case. This is very common in science. Often you can calculate the same thing for different situations, but the equations will be slightly different. You have to get used to that. Thus, if you are asked to calculate the mechanical advantage of a wheel and axle, you have to use a different equation than the one you would use for calculating the mechanical advantage of a lever.

Before I show you an example of calculating the mechanical advantage for a wheel and axle, I need to tell you what the mechanical advantage does in a wheel and axle. That depends on which way you use the wheel and axle. Suppose you turn the wheel in order to turn the axle. In that case, the mechanical advantage magnifies the force you are applying. If the mechanical advantage is 10, and you turn the wheel, the axle turns with a force 10 times as large.

Have you ever seen the inside of a big, 18-wheeler truck? If you have, you probably noticed that the steering wheel is *significantly* bigger in the truck than it is in a typical car. This is because a truck requires more force to turn than does a car. Since the mechanical advantage of a wheel and axle increases as the diameter of the wheel gets bigger, a truck's steering wheel magnifies the force with which the driver turns much more than does the steering wheel of a car.

If you use the other application of a wheel and axle (turning the axle so that the wheel turns), the force with which you turn is not magnified. In fact, you will turn the axle with a much greater force than what the wheel will turn with. However, the mechanical advantage will cause the wheel to turn with a much greater speed. In an automobile, the engine turns the axle with a certain speed. The mechanical advantage of the wheel and axle, however, magnifies that speed, so that the car can travel faster.

Have you ever compared the size of a race car's tires to that of a normal car? A race car's wheels are *much* larger than a normal car's wheels. Once again, the mechanical advantage of a wheel and axle increases when the size of the wheel increases. To get more speed, then, a race car has much bigger wheels. This increases the mechanical advantage of the wheel and axle, increasing the speed of the car.

EXAMPLE 4.2

A wheel has a diameter of 24 inches, while its axle has a diameter of 2 inches. What is the mechanical advantage of this wheel and axle?

Since this is a wheel and axle, we must use the mechanical advantage equation for a wheel and axle, not a lever:

Mechanical advantage = (diameter of the wheel) ÷ (diameter of the axle)

The diameter of the wheel and that of the axle are both given, so we can put them in the equation:

Mechanical advantage = 24 ÷ 2 = 12

The mechanical advantage, then, is 12.

What does this mechanical advantage mean? Well, it depends on the application which you use. If you are turning the wheel, the force with which you turn will be magnified by 12. Thus, the axle will turn with 12 times the force that is applied to the wheel. If you are turning the axle, the speed will be magnified by a 12. Thus, the wheel will turn with a speed 12 times faster than that of the axle.

ON YOUR OWN

4.6 When is a wheel and axle similar to a first-class or second-class lever? When is it similar to a third-class lever?

The Pulley

A **pulley** consists of a grooved wheel that rotates freely on a frame, which is usually called a **block**. A pulley is operated by laying a rope in the pulley's groove. When one end of the rope is pulled down, the wheel rotates and the other end of the rope is lifted up.

Ill. from the MasterClips Collection

FIGURE 4.5
A Pulley

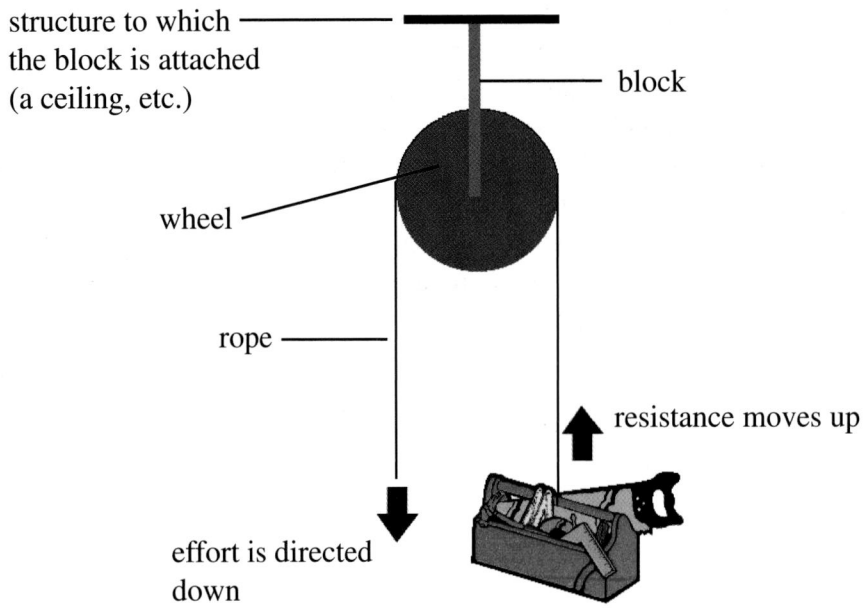

A single pulley by itself offers no mechanical advantage. However, it does change the direction of the force. This, in itself, is useful, because most people can pull down with more force than they can lift up. Thus, if you want to lift a heavy object, you can attach a rope to it, thread the rope through a pulley, and pull down on the rope. The pulley will change the direction of the force, lifting the heavy object.

Although a single pulley offers no mechanical advantage, a series of pulleys can. Perform the following experiment to see what I mean.

EXPERIMENT 4.2
A Simulation of A Series of Pulleys

Supplies:

- Two brooms or a broom and a mop (You basically need two implements with long handles. The experiment works best when the handles are very smooth.)
- Several feet of rope (Nylon rope works best because it is slick.)
- Two reasonably strong people to help you

Introduction - In this experiment, you will use broom handles to simulate pulleys, and you will see how multiple pulleys provide mechanical advantage.

Procedure:

A. Have your helpers stand about 3 feet apart, facing one another.
B. Tie one end of the rope to one of the brooms. It works best if you can tie the rope to the place where the bristles attach to the broom handle. There is usually a bulge there, and if you tie the rope just below the bulge, it will stay secure.
C. Have one helper hold the broom handle with both hands, so that the broom is parallel to the floor. Have the other helper hold on to the other broom in the same way.
D. Take the rope and loop it around the handle of the broom to which it is not tied. Make sure that the rope is between the hands of the helper holding that broom. In the end, your experiment should look something like this:

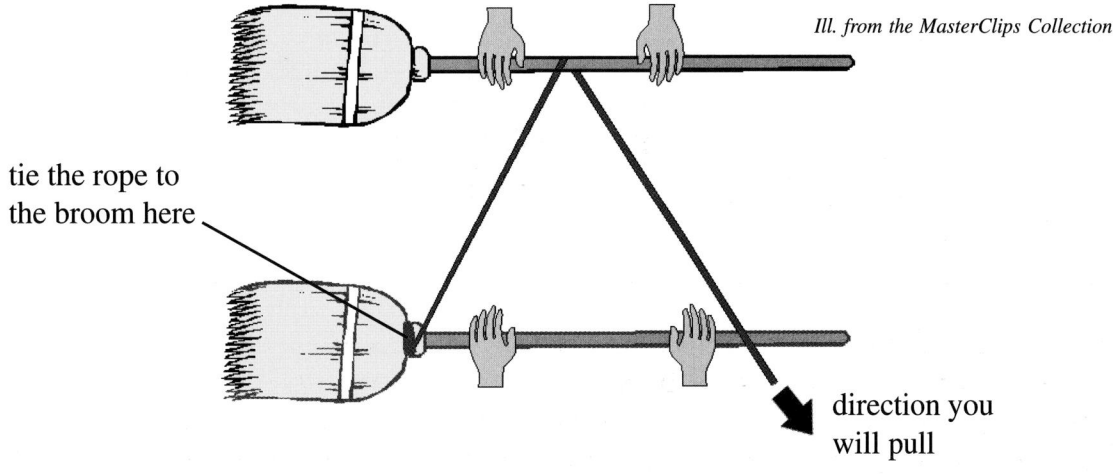

Ill. from the MasterClips Collection

E. Now tell your helpers to pull back on each broom with all of their might, and you try to pull them together with the rope. Unless you are stronger than they are, you probably will not be able to pull them together. Even if you can pull them together, get an idea of how hard it was to do so.
F. Now you need to change your experiment a bit. This time, loop the rope first around the handle of the broom to which it is not tied, then loop it around the handle of the broom to which it is tied, and then loop it again around the handle of the broom to which it is not tied. Make sure that the rope is in between the hands of your helpers when it loops around the broom handles. Now your experiment should look something like this:

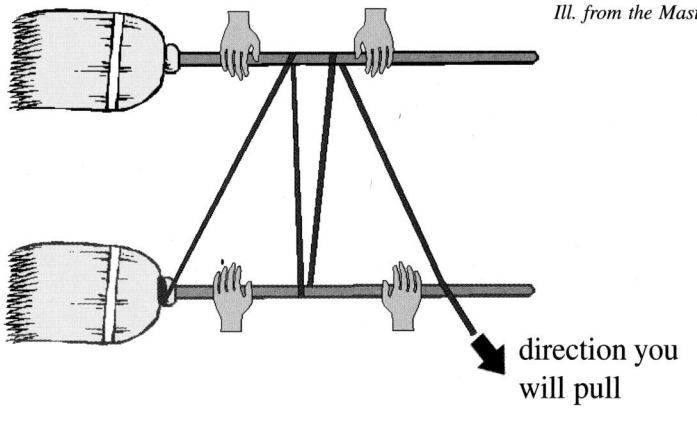

Ill. from the MasterClips Collection

G. Once again, tell your helpers to resist with all of their might, and try to pull them together with the rope. Notice any difference?
H. You can continue the experiment by looping the rope around the broom handles a few more times. You should notice a pattern to the number of times the rope is looped around the broom handles and how difficult it is to pull your helpers together.
I. Put everything away.

What did you learn in the experiment? Well, when the rope was looped around the broom handle once, it was very difficult to pull your helpers together. However, when you looped the rope around the broom handles three times, it suddenly got a *lot* easier. If you continued the experiment, you should have found that the more you looped the rope around the broom handles, the *easier* it was to pull your helpers together.

Although you were not using pulleys in the experiment, you were simulating the use of pulleys. As long as the broom handles were reasonably smooth, the ropes moved around the broom handles much as they would have moved through the wheel of a pulley. Thus, even though the ropes were not on pulleys, they behaved much like they were on pulleys. Therefore, you can think of the first trial in the experiment as a simulation of using a single pulley. When you pulled on the rope, the direction of your pull was reversed, but you gained no mechanical advantage. Thus, it was hard for you to pull your helpers together.

When you looped the rope around the broom handles a total of three times, however, things changed, didn't they? Suddenly, it got much easier to pull your helpers together, didn't it? Why was it easier to pull your helpers together? Well, when you looped the rope around the broom handles three times, you were simulating the use of three pulleys. When you use multiple pulleys, you gain a mechanical advantage. You should have noticed that mechanical advantage by the fact that it was easier to pull your helpers together. If you didn't notice a big difference, then the rope probably did not move on the broom handles very easily. In that case, your experiment didn't simulate pulleys very well, so you didn't notice the mechanical advantage.

You can, therefore, gain a mechanical advantage with pulleys by using more than one. In the second trial of your experiment, you simulated the use of three pulleys. That gave you a mechanical advantage of 3. Thus, the force with which you pulled on the rope was magnified by three. If you use multiple pulleys, the mechanical advantage is simply given by the number of pulleys that you use. When multiple pulleys are used, we often call the resulting system a **block and tackle**. A block and tackle consists of a fixed pulley and at least one moveable pulley. The more pulleys you have in a block and tackle system, the more mechanical advantage you get.

Now I want to point out something before I move on to the next section. In all three of the simple machines I have shown you so far, a mechanical advantage can be attained. In first-class levers, second-class levers, a wheel and axle (if used properly), and multiple pulleys, that mechanical advantage can be used to multiply force. The person using the simple machine, then, gets "something good" by using the machine. The person gets his or her force magnified. Is there anything "bad" they have to take in return? Is there anything negative that accompanies the positive effect of the force being magnified? Yes, there is.

As your parents have probably already told you, you almost never get something for nothing. That saying is very true when it comes to understanding Creation. The natural world will never give you something without taking something in return. Thus, when you use two pulleys, the force with which you pull the rope is magnified by a factor of two. There is a drawback, however. When you use two pulleys, you end up pulling twice as much rope in order to move your load. Thus, if you want to lift the load 5 feet, you must pull ten feet of rope. The mechanical advantage offered by several pulleys, then, makes it easier to lift a load. However, you "pay" for that by having to pull a lot more rope.

This is true of any mechanical advantage offered by any simple machine. If you use a simple machine to magnify force, you "pay" for that by having to use that force over a longer distance. When you use a lever in which the fulcrum is closer to the resistance than the effort, you have to push the lever farther than the load will raise up. If the mechanical advantage of a first-class or second-class lever is 3, for example, the force you exert is magnified by three, but you will have to push or pull the lever three times as far as the load will be lifted.

On the other hand, suppose you are using a third-class lever or you are using a wheel and axle to magnify speed. When that happens, you "pay" for the magnified speed by using a lot more force. If the mechanical advantage of a third-class lever, for example, is 3, the load will move 3 times faster than the speed at which the effort moves, but the effort will be 3 times larger than it would be if you just lifted the load without the lever. No matter what, then, you always "pay" for a mechanical advantage. If you use a simple machine to magnify force, you will have to apply that force over a much longer distance. If you use a simple machine to magnify speed, you will have to apply a much larger force.

ON YOUR OWN

4.7 A person tries to lift a load with a single pulley. He has just enough rope to get the job done. However, no matter how hard he pulls, he cannot lift the load. A smart student who just finished reading this section tells him to set up a 4-pulley system. That will make it much easier for him to lift the load. The smart student also tells him to go out and get more rope. How many times more rope will the person need?

The Inclined Plane

The inclined plane is, perhaps the simplest of the simple machines. It makes lifting a load easier, because you can slide the load up the inclined plane rather than lift it straight up. Although you may have never used a lever or a pulley, you have *certainly* used an inclined plane.

Any time you chose to walk up a ramp, roll something up a ramp, or push something up a ramp, you used an inclined plane.

The mechanical advantage of an inclined plane can be easily calculated, as long as you know the dimensions of the inclined plane.

FIGURE 4.6
An Inclined Plane

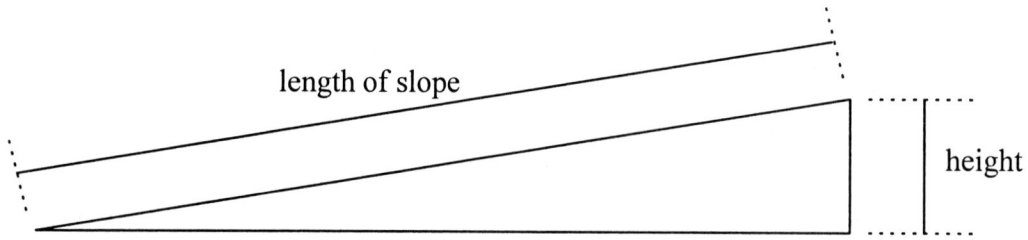

If you want to lift a load up to a certain height, an inclined plane provides the following mechanical advantage:

Mechanical advantage = (length of the slope) ÷ (height)

Like all simple machines, you "pay" for the mechanical advantage of an inclined plane. The way you pay for it is by having to push the load farther. If your goal is to raise the load up to a certain height, you can either lift it up directly, or you can push it up an inclined plane. If you lift it directly, you will move it a distance equal to the height. If you push it up an inclined plane, you will move it the length of the slope, which is always longer than the height. Thus, you push the load farther, but you need not push it as hard.

ON YOUR OWN

4.8 What is the mechanical advantage of an inclined plane whose slope is 8 feet long and whose height is 2 feet? If the slope were 10 times as long, the mechanical advantage would be huge. What would be the drawback, however?

The Wedge

The **wedge** is often confused with the inclined plane, because both simple machines look the same. They are used differently, however, so they are considered to be different machines. Figure 4.7 illustrates how these two machines are used.

FIGURE 4.7
The Difference Between an Inclined Plane and a Wedge

In an inclined plane, the force is applied parallel to the slope.

In a wedge, the force is applied to to the vertical edge.

Since these machines are used differently, it makes sense that they serve different purposes. An inclined plane is meant to ease the force required to lift a load. A wedge, on the other hand, magnifies the force that is being applied.

When you strike the vertical edge of a wedge, the pointed end of the wedge applies a magnified force to whatever it is in contact with. Have you ever watched someone split wood? If you have logs with a large diameter, you need to split those logs into smaller pieces in order to fit them into a normal fireplace. As a result, many people with fireplaces must split wood. If the wood is old enough, it is possible to split a log by simply striking it with an ax. However, most logs are not that easy to split. In order to split wood, then, most people use wedges. The pointed end of the wedge is placed in contact with the log, and a hammer is used to hit the vertical edge of the wedge. The force with which the hammer hits the vertical edge is magnified, and the wedge imbeds itself into the wood. With enough strikes of the hammer, the wedge will split the log. A more familiar example of the wedge is a knife. When you push on a knife, the edge of the knife cuts into an object with a much greater force than that with which you pushed.

A modified version of the wedge is the **double wedge**, which is shown below:

FIGURE 4.8
The Double Wedge: Two Wedges Put Together

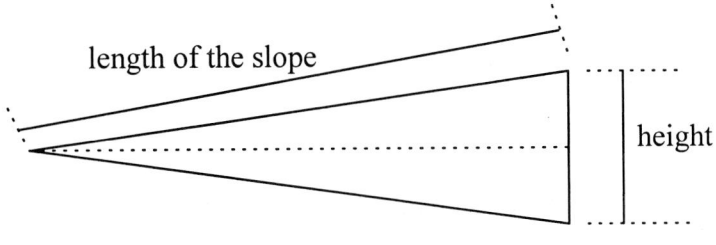

Regardless of whether it is a double wedge or a single wedge, the mechanical advantage of a wedge can be calculated with the same equation that relates to the inclined plane.

Mechanical advantage = (length of the slope) ÷ (height)

Like that of all other simple machines, the wedge's mechanical advantage must be "paid" for. In order to get the magnified force that you get from a wedge, you must apply that force over a longer distance.

ON YOUR OWN

4.9 Suppose you have two single wedges with identical slopes and heights. Do you gain more mechanical advantage by using just one of those wedges, or by using both wedges as a double wedge?

The Screw

The last simple machine I want to discuss is the screw, which is actually an inclined plane wrapped around the axle of a wheel and axle.

Ill. from the MasterClips Collection

FIGURE 4.9
A Screw

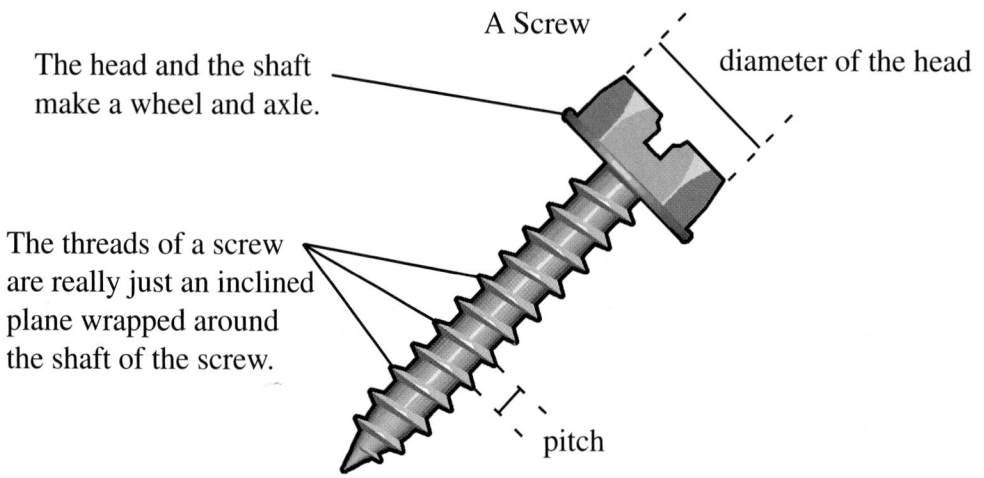

As is illustrated in the figure, the inclined planes on a screw are usually called threads. The vertical distance between the threads is called the **pitch** of the screw. A full turn of a screw will result in the screw traveling into an object by a distance equal to its pitch.

What is the mechanical advantage of a screw? Well, that's an interesting question. A screw itself has some mechanical advantage. You can calculate the mechanical advantage of a screw with the following equation:

Mechanical advantage = (circumference) ÷ (pitch)

This equation, of course, means nothing unless you know what **circumference** is.

Circumference - The distance around a circle, equal to 3.1416 times the circle's diameter

To get the circumference of a circle, then, you find its diameter and multiply by 3.1416. You might recognize that number. It is actually an approximation of a number which is called "pi." You will learn a lot more about pi when you study geometry, so I don't want to go into that now.

So what does all of this mean? Well, a "typical" screw has a pitch of 0.1 inches. The same screw might have a head whose diameter of 0.2 inches. To calculate the mechanical advantage, then, we must first determine the circumference:

Circumference = 3.1416 x (diameter)

Circumference = 3.1416 x 0.2 = 0.62832

Now that we have the circumference, we can calculate the mechanical advantage:

Mechanical advantage = (circumference) ÷ (pitch)

Mechanical advantage = 0.62832 ÷ 0.1 = 6.2832

What does this mean? It means that if you grasp the screw by the head and you turn it with your fingers, you can get the screw into the wood with 6.2832 times less force than what it would take to hammer the screw into the wood.

Now that sounds like a big mechanical advantage, but if you have ever worked with screws, you know that it is *awfully* hard to screw a screw into wood with your fingers! Instead, you typically use a screwdriver. Somehow, that's a *lot* easier. Why is it easier? Well, a screwdriver has a circumference that is much larger than the screw. Since you are using the screwdriver, then, the circumference you use in the mechanical advantage equation is the circumference of the *screwdriver*, not the screw!

A typical screwdriver might have a diameter of 1.0 inch. If you use that screwdriver to turn the same screw I discussed earlier, the mechanical advantage is totally different:

Circumference = 3.1416 x (diameter)

Circumference = 3.1416 x 1.0 = 3.1416

Mechanical advantage = (circumference) ÷ (pitch)

Mechanical advantage = 3.1416 ÷ 0.1 = 31.416

Instead of 6.2832, then, the mechanical advantage of the screw is 31.416 when you use a 1.0-inch diameter screwdriver!

Have you ever had trouble screwing a screw into wood? What did you do to get the screw into the wood? Well, if you were smart, you went to your toolbox and got a screwdriver with a larger diameter. The "fatter" the screwdriver, the more mechanical advantage you get from the screw. Thus, a larger-diameter screwdriver makes it easier to screw a screw into wood. Notice that the *length* of the screwdriver does not enter into the mechanical advantage. Only the *diameter* of the screwdriver matters when it comes to determining how easy it is to screw in a screw.

EXAMPLE 4.3

A screw has a pitch of 0.05 inches. Its head has a diameter of 0.30 inches. What is the mechanical advantage of the screw if you grasp it on the head and screw it in?

To get the mechanical advantage of a screw, we must have the circumference. To get that, we multiply the diameter by 3.1416:

Circumference = 3.1416 x (diameter)

Circumference = 3.1416 x (0.30) = 0.94248

Now that we have the circumference, we can get the mechanical advantage:

Mechanical advantage = (circumference) ÷ (pitch)

Mechanical advantage = 0.94248 ÷ 0.05 = <u>18.8496</u>

What is the mechanical advantage of the same screw if you turn it with a screwdriver whose diameter is 1.5 inches?

When you use a screwdriver, the mechanical advantage is calculated using the circumference of the *screwdriver*, not the *screw*. Thus, we need to determine the circumference of the screwdriver:

Circumference = 3.1416 x (diameter)

Circumference = 3.1416 x (1.5) = 4.7124

Now we can calculate the mechanical advantage:

Mechanical advantage = (circumference) ÷ (pitch)

Mechanical advantage = 4.7124 ÷ 0.05 = 94.248

Before I leave this section, I want to make a quick point. A screwdriver in itself is a simple machine. What kind of simple machine is a screwdriver? Well, when you turn the round handle, it turns the round shaft that turns the screw. What is it? It is a wheel and axle! Thus, the combination of a screw and screwdriver is really combination of 2 simple machines: a screw and a wheel and axle.

ON YOUR OWN

4.10 A screw has a pitch of 0.02 inches. The head has a diameter of .20 inches and the screwdriver with which the screw is being turned has a diameter of 1.0 inch. What is the mechanical advantage of the screw when it is turned with the screwdriver?

ANSWERS TO THE ON YOUR OWN PROBLEMS

4.1 Experiments (a) and (d) are science experiments, while (b) and (c) are applied science experiments. The goals of experiments (a) and (d) are simply knowledge. Now, that knowledge might be useful, but the use is not the goal. The knowledge is the goal. Thus, these are science experiments. In experiments (b) and (c), making something useful is the goal. That makes it applied science.

4.2 Options (b) and (c) are both examples of technology. Options (a) and (d) are knowledge. Option (b) is a machine, which is obviously technology. Option (c) is not a machine, but it directly makes life easier by allowing you to make sturdy structures. Thus a recipe for cement is technology, just like a microwave oven is.

4.3 Tweezers are an example of a third-class lever. The fulcrum is the part that does not move. Thus, it is the top end of the tweezers. The resistance is grasped with the other end of the tweezers. You pinch them in the middle, so the effort is in between the fulcrum and resistance. That's the definition of a third-class lever.

4.4 To solve this, we use the mechanical advantage equation:

Mechanical advantage = (distance from fulcrum to effort) ÷ (distance from fulcrum to resistance)

Mechanical advantage = 3 ÷ 1 = 3

4.5 It means different things depending on the type of lever. For first-class and second-class levers, it means that the effort will be magnified by ten. For third-class levers, it means the resistance will move at ten times the speed of the effort.

4.6 A wheel and axle is similar to a first-class or second-class lever when the wheel is turned by the effort. In that case, the effort is magnified, just as it is in first-class and second-class levers. A wheel and axle is similar to a third-class lever when the axle is turned by the effort. At that point, speed is magnified, not effort. That's what happens in a third-class lever.

4.7 The person will need 4 times the amount of rope. Since he changed to a four-pulley system, he now has a mechanical advantage of 4. He pays for that, however, by needing a lot more rope.

4.8 We can calculate the mechanical advantage using the mechanical advantage equation for an inclined plane:

Mechanical advantage = (length of slope) ÷ (height)

Mechanical advantage = 8 ÷ 2 = 4

An inclined plane with a slope tens times as long would give a lot more mechanical advantage, but you would have to push the load 10 times further. At some point, the extra pushing just isn't worth the effort you save due to the mechanical advantage.

4.9 Remember, the mechanical advantage is determined by taking the length of the slope and dividing by the height. In this case, the double wedge would have twice as large a height as the single wedge (see Figure 4.8). If you divide by a large number, the result is a small number. Thus, the larger the height on a wedge, the lower the mechanical advantage. The single, wedge, therefore would give the most mechanical advantage.

4.10 First of all, notice that the screw is NOT being turned by grasping its head. Thus, the diameter of the head is IRRELEVANT in this problem. You have to be on your guard for that. Sometimes, I will throw in useless numbers just to see how closely you are paying attention! This is one such case.

Since the screwdriver is being used, we need to know its circumference:

$$\text{Circumference} = 3.1416 \times (\text{diameter})$$

$$\text{Circumference} = 3.1416 \times 1.0 = 3.1416$$

Now we can use the mechanical advantage equation for a screw:

$$\text{Mechanical advantage} = (\text{circumference}) \div (\text{pitch})$$

$$\text{Mechanical advantage} = 3.1416 \div 0.02 = \underline{157.08}$$

STUDY GUIDE FOR MODULE #4

1. Define the following terms:

a. Simple machine
b. Force
c. Mechanical advantage
d. Diameter
e. Circumference

2. How is applied science different from science?

3. What leads to technology?

4. Identify each of the following as a science experiment or an applied science experiment:

a. An experiment to determine how to make electronic circuits smaller
b. An experiment to understand what factors affect how electricity runs in an electrical circuit
c. An experiment to figure out how to reduce electronic noise in an electronic circuit
d. An experiment to figure out the speed of electrons as they flow through an electronic circuit

5. Which of the following would be considered technology?

a. A classification scheme for all animals
b. A vaccination that will keep all animals from contracting the flu
c. A new diet for dogs that will lead to longer life
d. An understanding of what causes urinary tract infections in cats

6. List the six types of simple machines.

7. Which two simple machines look identical?

8. What is the mechanical advantage of a lever in which the fulcrum is 10 inches from the resistance and 40 inches from the effort?

9. What does the mechanical advantage in problem #8 mean?

10. A shovel is an example of a lever. To what class does a shovel belong?

11. A child's see-saw is a lever. To what class does it belong?

12. What is the mechanical advantage of a wheel and axle when the wheel has a diameter of 15 inches and the axle has a diameter of 3 inches?

13. If a person turned the wheel of the wheel and axle in problem #12, what would the mechanical advantage do?

14. If a person turned the axle in the wheel and axle in problem #12, what would the mechanical advantage do?

15. A block and tackle is composed of 6 pulleys that all work together. What is the mechanical advantage of the block and tackle system?

16. Using the block and tackle system in problem #15, how many feet of rope would have to be pulled if a person wanted to lift a load 1 foot?

17. What is the mechanical advantage of an inclined plane with a slope of 6 feet and a height of 2 feet?

18. What is the mechanical advantage of a wedge with the same dimensions as the inclined plane in problem #17?

19. A screw with a pitch of 0.1 inches is turned with a screwdriver whose diameter is 2 inches. What is the mechanical advantage?

20. If you are having a hard time turning a screw, should you get a longer screwdriver or a fatter one?

Module #5 – The History of Life: Archaeology, Geology, and Paleontology

Introduction

In the previous quarter of this course, I spent time discussing what science is and what it is not. I discussed the scientific method, how to perform and analyze experiments, and the difference between science, applied science, and technology. For the rest of the course, I want to concentrate on just one area of science: **life science**.

Life science – A term that encompasses all scientific pursuits related to living organisms

You can tell by the definition that life science is a BIG area of science. This means you've got a LOT to learn!

When I started discussing science at the beginning of this course, where did I start? I started with the history of science. After all, in order to understand something, you need to see how history has shaped its development. The same is true for a study of life science. In order to really understand what life is, we must first look at the history of life.

How Do We Learn About The History of Life?

When I discussed the history of science, it was easy to understand where I got my information. All of the things that I covered had been recorded by historians. Wait a minute, though. How do we learn about the history of life? Well, the first way is the same as before. After all, there are historical records that are several thousands of years old. Many of these records tell us about people, nations, animals, and plants that lived a long time ago. This gives us some information about the history of life. That's not the end of the story, however.

In order to really learn about the history of life, we have to go beyond historical records. After all, historical records get more and more scarce the farther you go back in history. Thus, we need something to help supplement the historical record. The first tool we can use to accomplish this task is **archaeology** (ar kee awl' uh gee).

Archaeology – The study of past human life as revealed by preserved relics

Scientists in the field of archaeology try to learn more about the people who lived in the past by studying what those people left behind.

If you think about it, even when you combine archaeology and historical records, you still don't get a good view of the history of life. After all, history usually centers on what happened to *people* in the past. Archaeology concentrates solely on studying human relics and **artifacts**.

Artifacts - Objects made by humans such as tools, weapons, containers, etc.

Thus, history and archaeology are excellent tools for learning about the history of *human* life, but how do we learn about the history of all of the animals and plants that have lived on earth in the past?

To accomplish this task, we must focus on two fields of science that do not necessarily concentrate on human life: **geology** (gee awl' uh gee) and **paleontology** (pay lee uhn tall' uh gee).

Geology – The study of earth's history as revealed in the rocks that make up the earth

Paleontology – The study of life's history as revealed in the preserved remains of once-living plants and animals

These two fields of science are incredibly interesting and can reveal much about what went on during earth's past. However, as you will come to find out, these are also two of the most ill-used and misinterpreted fields of science. Thus, we must take great pains to make sure that we understand exactly what these fascinating fields of science tell us.

Archaeology and History

I will spend the majority of this quarter discussing geology and paleontology, since those fields cover the history of all living creatures. For now, however, I will spend some time on archaeology. From a scientist's point of view, archaeology is a bit limited. It covers only a portion of the earth's history, and it concentrates on artifacts left by human beings. Nevertheless, it is still a valuable resource for learning about the history of life.

Archaeology can give us some clues about civilizations for which we have no historical records, but archaeology's main strength lies in uncovering and clarifying the history of civilizations for which we *do* have historical records. Consider, for example, some of the world history that you already know. You probably know that there was an empire called the "Roman Empire." You probably know the names of some of the emperors. You have also probably spent some time reviewing the history of great countries like Egypt and China. How do we know that the historical facts you have read about are actually true?

Think about it. I could write a history of ancient Greece tomorrow and try to get it published. It could be full of all sorts of lies and errors. How would anyone know that my history of ancient Greece is wrong? Well, you might say that it would contradict the history of ancient Greece that we already know. But how do we know *that* history is right? After all, our knowledge of history comes from books. How do we know that the authors of *those* books added only legitimate history to their works?

In historical science, any document that claims to be a work of history is put through three tests. They are called the **internal test**, the **external test**, and the **bibliographic test**. If the work passes those three tests, it is considered a legitimate work of history. If it fails even one of those tests, it is not considered an authentic historical work. It might have other values, but as a historical document, it is not reliable.

Each of the three tests I mentioned above are very important, and they each test a different facet of a supposedly historical work. The first test is straightforward and easy to describe. The **internal test** simply tests to see whether or not the document in question is internally consistent. In other words, the internal test says that a valid work of history cannot contradict itself. This, of course, makes an enormous amount of sense. After all, if a historical document makes a statement at one point and a completely contradictory statement at another point, then it probably isn't a very reliable document!

Now you might think that it is easy to determine whether or not a document passes the internal test. After all, you just have to read the document and look for any contradictory statements, right? Well, not exactly. You must remember that many documents which deal with ancient history are written in ancient languages. For example, if an archaeologist finds a scroll that claims to be a history of ancient Greece, it is probably written in Greek. Now, of course, Greek is a language which is spoken today, but most likely the *version* of Greek used in the scroll is quite different than the version of Greek that is spoken today. Languages change over time, and what people call Greek today is *significantly different* than the Greek that was spoken and written even a few hundred years ago.

I really want to drive this point home, because it is *very* important. Languages change over time, sometimes quite dramatically. Consider, for example, the following phrase:

> Whan that April with his showres soote
> The droughte of March hath perced to the roote
> And bathed every vein in swich licour
> Of which vertu engendred is the flowr

In what language is that passage written? Believe it or not, it is written in *English*! This passage is from the General Prologue of Geoffrey Chaucer's *The Canterbury Tales*. This collection of stories was written in *English* approximately 600 years ago! Does this give you an idea of how languages change over time? A mere 600 years ago, a passage from a work of English is barely recognizable as English. In fact, if you were to hear this passage read with the correct pronunciation (use Microsoft's *Encarta 99* CD-ROM, for example), you would find that it *sounds* even less like English than it looks!

The point to this discussion is quite simple. Languages change over time. The more time that has elapsed since a document was written, the harder it will be to *understand* the language. This, of course, makes it difficult to *spot* inconsistencies within a document. What seems like a contradiction might not be a contradiction once the age of the language and its usage are taken into account. Thus, when applying the internal test to a document, historical scientists always use **Aristotle's dictum**.

Aristotle's dictum - The benefit of the doubt is to be given to the document itself, not assigned by the critic to himself.

Aristotle's dictum states that when you apply the internal test to a document, you must give the document some leeway. If two passages seem to contradict each other, they are not to be counted as a contradiction if a legitimate explanation can be offered to explain away the contradiction. In the next section, you will get a concrete example of how to apply Aristotle's dictum, so for right now, you need not understand it 100%.

The second test that is applied to supposedly historical documents is the **external test**. This test asks another simple question: Does the document contradict other known historical facts? There are two ways that historical scientists apply the external test. First, they compare the document of interest to other documents which have already passed the three tests. Since those are considered reliable, anything that contradicts them is probably unreliable. Unfortunately, the older the document, the fewer the documents to which it can be compared. After all, the older the history, the less the information which we have. Luckily, however, the external test has another component. The external test also compares the statements in the document to known *archaeological* facts. For example, if a supposedly historical document references a city, archaeology might be able to confirm or deny the existence of that city. The older the document, the more important this component of the external test becomes.

The final test, the **bibliographic test**, is probably the most important of the three. To be a reliable document, the work must contain either direct eyewitness accounts or a second-hand report *based* on eyewitness accounts. The problem with such accounts, however, is that they were recorded shortly after the events took place. Given that fact, how do we know that they have not been altered over time? You see, we have *virtually no original documents from any truly ancient work of history*. This is a very important point. Nearly every document we have concerning the history of ancient Egypt, the Roman Empire, etc. are all *copies* of some original document that has been lost.

Well, if we are working with copies of the original work, how do we know that the words on the copy are truly the words from the original? This is probably the *biggest* problem with historical works. After all, back in ancient times the only way to copy was by hand. This was a time-consuming, error-riddled process. It was also usually quite expensive. In order to make a copy of a document, someone who could read and write (not always easy skills to find in ancient times) would have to carefully read a few words and then write them legibly. This would sometimes take hours for a single page! The cost of both the supplies and the person's wages could quickly become astronomical.

FIGURE 5.1
An Ancient "Copier"

Because copying was done by hand in ancient times, it took an enormous amount of time. It also took a lot of manpower. Often, to ensure accuracy, one man would copy the document, while another looked on. This helped reduce mistakes and deliberate changes.

Nevertheless, making copies in ancient times was far from perfect. Often scribes would miss errors in the copy process, and possibly just as often, the person requesting the copy would tell the scribe to make deliberate changes.

Illus. from the MasterClips collection

Anyone who had the resources and the power to command that a copy of a document be made would also be able to command the copier to change things that he or she didn't like. Suppose, for example, a king ordered his scribes to make a copy of a history of his realm. In that history, suppose that the original author made some negative statements regarding one of the king's ancestors. The king might order those statements stricken from the work or, worse yet, revised to remove their negative meaning. That would corrupt an otherwise reliable historical document.

How can we tell whether or not a historical document has been altered as a part of being copied over the years? Well, that's where the bibliographic test comes in. The bibliographic test asks two questions. First, it asks how long of a time span exists between the time that the original work was written and the time of the first available copy that we have. The shorter the time span, the more reliable the document is. After all, if only a short time elapsed between the writing of the original and the making of the copy, then there would have been little chance for alterations to occur. Alternatively, the longer the time span between original and copy, the more chance there was for alteration. Second, the bibliographic test asks how many *different* copies made by *different* people exist for the document of interest. If many copies made by many different people exist, and if they are all basically the same, then it is very unlikely that the original was modified. After all, the same modifications would have to have been made by all copiers and, given the difficulty of communication in ancient times, that is rather unlikely!

So the bibliographic test measures the time between copy and original as well as the number of copies made by different people. The shorter the timespan and the larger the number of copies made by different people, the more reliable the document is. As a point of terminology, copies of a work made by different people are often called **supporting documents**, because they can be used to support the validity of the document of interest. Thus, many historians would say it this way: the bibliographic test requires a short timespan between original and copy as well as many supporting documents for the copy of interest. If you are a bit confused about the bibliographic test at this point, don't worry too much. I will discuss it later with some concrete examples, and that will help.

In the next three sections, I want to talk about each of the three tests individually. The best way to do that is to actually apply them to a specific historical document. That will give you the best understanding of the tests and how they are used. To what document will I apply these tests? I want to use the Bible as my example. After all, the Bible is certainly a work of history. I believe it is much more than that, but it does contain many historical accounts from the ancient past. Thus, it is a good document to use as an example. There are other reasons that I want to use the Bible, however. First, I think you might be surprised at how well the Bible actually passes these tests, indicating that *science* tells us you *can* believe the accounts in the Bible. Second, I want to reinforce a statement that I made in a previous module. We can apply science to *any* question, as long as we use the right methodology. Thus, we can use historical science to evaluate the Bible, despite the fact that it is a work of religion.

ON YOUR OWN

5.1 An archaeologist discovers a document that claims to be a history of the Sumerian people. It mentions a battle that was fought at a great fortress in a certain region of the Sumerian Empire. Archaeologists look in that area and find the remains of a tiny village, but no indications of a fortress or a great battle. Which test does this document fail?

5.2 A document being evaluated as a history states that a certain city was built in 117 A.D. Later in the document, it references a battle that was fought for control of the city, and it states that the battle occurred in 105 A.D. Which test does the document fail?

The Internal Test

In order to show you how historians evaluate historical documents using the internal test, I want to apply the internal test to the Bible. Have you ever heard someone say that the Bible contradicts itself? If you haven't, you will! It is a common misconception. For example, William Henry Burr, in his book *Self-Contradictions of the Bible*, claims that the Bible contradicts itself at least 144 times. Clearly, if that is the case, then the Bible should not be considered a trustworthy source of history.

Is William Burr right? Is the Bible riddled with contradictions? Not at all. However, William Burr's examples of supposed biblical contradictions make excellent examples of how difficult it is to apply the internal test to an ancient document. Without the proper analysis, many historical documents seem to contradict themselves. However, once the linguistic and historical details of the document are investigated, these apparent contradictions disappear.

For example, one "contradiction" he lists concerns the genealogies of Christ. In the New Testament, there are two genealogies of Christ. One is presented in the book of Matthew, chapter 1, and the second is recorded in the book of Luke, chapter 3. At first glance, they seem to be completely contradictory. They don't even agree on Jesus' grandfather. Matthew 1:16 says that "...Jacob begat Joseph, the husband of Mary" whereas Luke 3:23 says that Jesus was the "...son of Joseph which was the son of Heli." One account, then, says that Jesus' grandfather was Jacob whereas another says it was Heli. The fact is, however, that these two genealogies are not contradictory, instead, they are complementary. The genealogy presented in Matthew is Joseph's family line, whereas the passage in Luke traces Mary's family line.

If you understand the culture within which the text was written, this fact becomes clear. Since women were not considered very historically important to the ancient Jews, their names did not appear in genealogies. Thus, when a historian needed to trace the family line of a woman, he would always use the name of the woman's husband in place of her own name. Most modern translations of the Bible include a footnote to this effect. We see, then, that after examining the cultural context of the passage, this apparent "contradiction" fades away. This is true of many of the supposed contradictions that occur in the Bible.

Other supposed "contradictions" occur because of the difficulty in translating the original languages of the Bible into English. A classic example of this can be found in the New Testament book of Acts. In this book, there are two accounts of Paul's conversion from Judaism to Christianity. Both say that while traveling to Damascus, Paul had a vision of Christ which temporarily blinded him. The accounts supposedly differ, however, concerning the men who traveled with him. In Acts 9:7, the Bible says that "The men who journeyed with him stood speechless, hearing a voice, but seeing no man." However, Acts 22:9 says, "And they that were with me saw indeed the light, and were afraid; but they heard not the voice of Him that spake to me."

Once again, at first glance this seems to be a contradiction. Did the men with Paul hear a voice or didn't they? The answer comes from an examination of the original language in which the New Testament was written: Greek. In each passage, the Greek word *akouo* is translated as the verb "to hear." In Greek, however, when verbs are constructed in different cases, their meanings change.

In Acts 9:7, *akouo* is constructed in the genitive case, whereas in Acts 22:9, the accusative case is used. When this word is used genitively, it implies only that sounds were heard; however, when constructed in the accusative case, the word implies that speech was both heard *and* understood. In English, we use the same construction for both cases. For example, when a person says, "I hear you, man," he may mean that your voice is reaching his ears, or he may mean that he understands what you are saying. So, once again, a detailed look at these passages yields no contradiction at all. In fact, by looking at both passages we learn something. We learn that Paul's attendants did, indeed, hear sounds coming from Paul's vision, but they could not distinguish any understandable speech from those sounds.

The vast majority of apparent contradictions in the Bible can be simply cleared away by examining linguistic, cultural, and literary context. There are some apparent contradictions that don't have such simple answers, however. An example of this comes from the book of Genesis. In the first two chapters of this book, the creation of the world is discussed. Chapter one gives an overview of the creation, while chapter two goes back and discusses the creation of the world with Adam and Eve as its focus. These two passages seem to differ on the order in which things were created. In Genesis 1:25-27 the Bible says, "And God made the beast of the earth after his kind, and the cattle after their kind...And God said, 'Let us make man'...So God created man in his own image." Thus, according to this passage, the animals of the earth were created first, and then man was created second. In Genesis 2:18, 19, however, we read:

> And the Lord God said it is not good that man should be alone; I will make a help-meet for him. And out of the ground the Lord God formed every beast of the field, and every fowl of the air, and brought them unto Adam to see what he would call them.

In this passage, it seems that the animals were created after man, not before him as was stated in the previous passage.

Is this a contradiction? No. Remember, the Old Testament was written in Hebrew. Hebrew is an especially difficult language to translate, because many of the words have several meanings and context is supposed to guide the reader as to how to interpret what is written. It has been suggested by Hebrew scholars that a proper translation of the Hebrew verb (*yatsar*) used in Genesis 2:19 is "had formed" rather than simply "formed." If this is the case, then the contradiction disappears. After all, if you replace "formed" with "had formed" in Genesis 2:19, then the passage does not imply that man was created before the animals. However, the situation is not as clear-cut as was the translation situation in Acts which was discussed above. Although this explanation is accepted by some scholars, it is rejected by others. So, unlike the previous example, there is no conclusive proof that this is not a contradiction. On the other hand, there is also no conclusive proof that this *is* a contradiction.

Do controversial passages such as these keep the Bible from passing the internal test? If they did, then no ancient work of history would pass. It turns out that all ancient works have a few difficult passages that are hard to reconcile with each other. If such a situation is not conclusively proven to be a contradiction, then historians label it a "difficulty." As I mentioned before, when applying the internal test to ancient documents, historians must follow Aristotle's dictum. Thus, a contradiction must be conclusively a contradiction in order for a document to fail the internal test. Since this is not conclusively a contradiction but most likely a problem with translation, this does not cause the Bible to fail the internal test.

If you examine the Bible in its entirety, you find no passages that clearly contradict one another. Thus, the Bible passes the internal test. In fact, the Bible has fewer "difficulties" from an internal test point of view than some of the other historical documents of its time. As a result, it passes the internal test as well as the histories of the Roman Empire, etc., which make up most of what we know concerning life at and before the time of Christ.

I do hope this brief discussion has given you some idea of how difficult it is to apply the internal test to ancient documents. What seem to be clear contradictions in the *translation* of an ancient document simply vanish when the document is examined in light of the language and culture of the time. Even apparent contradictions that do not have ironclad explanations are not enough to keep a document from passing the internal test. The contradiction itself must be indisputable.

ON YOUR OWN

5.3 Another famous "contradiction" in the Bible comes from Matthew 27:5 and Acts 1:18. They seem to give different accounts of how Judas died. Do a little research to find out why this is not a contradiction. You might want to ask a pastor, priest, or someone else that knows the Bible well; you might want to go to the library and get a book on supposed Biblical contradictions (there are many); or you might want to get on the INTERNET and find out.

The External Test

Once a document passes the internal test, the next test applied is the external test. This test determines whether or not the document contradicts any "external" sources of historical fact. If other histories of the time exist, then the document in question must be consistent with them. In fact, the document in question should, to some extent, overlap with other accepted historical works so as to lend even more credibility to the document. The more overlap that occurs, the better the document passes the external test. In addition to other accepted historical texts, the document in question must also be consistent with any archaeological discoveries for that time period. Once again, the more archaeological facts that support the document, the better the document passes the external test.

Applying the external test to the Bible is a daunting task because it is a work that covers a long time period. Many parts of the Old Testament report on events that occurred so long ago that they have no external historical works with which they can be compared. In addition, the focus of the Bible is rather narrow; thus, many contemporary historians do not comment on anything related to the Bible's accounts. Finally, a scientist must exert hefty skepticism when examining works that are contemporary with the New Testament, because many of the authors of that time period were sympathetic to the Christian church. The works of such authors cannot be considered truly objective when they speak of matters reported in the New Testament. In addition, many historical documents written over the New Testament time period were written by Jewish leaders who were vehemently anti-Christian. These accounts must also be taken with a grain of salt.

Reasons such as these lead most historians to consider archaeological discoveries as the primary data used in applying the external test to the Bible. In this section, most of the discussion related to the external test will consist of archaeological data; nevertheless, I will spend some time comparing the works of external authors to the New Testament. First and foremost, I will reject all works by authors who are sympathetic to the Christian cause. Although many of these authors (Tertullian, Iraneus, Polycarp, etc.) do provide us with accurate portraits of the events of the time, their objectivity is in question. A good scientist must always try to reduce the bias in any data with which he or she works. Thus, we must reject obviously pro-Christian authors from our external test. After disregarding these possibly biased authors, who is left?

Cornelius Tacitus, a Roman, wrote several works which are considered quite accurate histories of the first century A.D. In his major work, *Annals*, he mentions the existence of Christ and his death by Pontius Pilate, in perfect agreement with the accounts written in the Bible. He also mentions certain cities and rulers which are also discussed in the Bible. In each case, Tacitus's reports are consistent with those of the New Testament.

Another well-respected, non-Christian historian of the day was Flavius Josephus. Josephus was a Jew who wrote a history of the Jewish people in an attempt to create better feelings between the Romans and the Jews. In his major work, *Jewish Antiquities*, he not only mentions Christ's death at the order of Pontius Pilate, but he also mentions Christ's resurrection! Here is the quote from the 33rd verse of the 18th chapter of *Jewish Antiquities*:

> Now there was about this time Jesus, a wise man, if it be lawful to call him a man; for he was a doer of wonderful works, a teacher of such men as receive the truth with pleasure. He drew over to him many Jews, and also many of the Greeks. This man was the Christ. And when Pilate condemned him to the cross, upon his impeachment by the principal man among us, those who had loved him from the first did not forsake him, for he appeared to them alive on the third day, the divine prophets having spoken these and thousands of other wonderful things about him. And even now, the race of Christians, so named from him, has not died out.

Josephus also mentions rulers and cities that are discussed in the Bible, and his reports are also consistent with those of the Bible. In addition, Josephus mentions the life and execution of John the Baptist and the existence of Christ's brother James, in agreement with the New Testament.

Now it is *very* important to note that Josephus *was not* a Christian. He was a Jew that stayed devoted to Judaism. Thus, he was not trying to make Christianity "look good" in his work. Instead, he was reporting what he considered historical fact at the time. It is very interesting to note that he considered the resurrection of Christ a fact!

Two other non-Christian historians who lend support to the New Testament are Thallus and Phlegon. Both of these historians mention a darkness that covered the land on the day that Christ died, in perfect agreement with the account given in Matthew 27:45. Since neither of these two authors were Christians, they reached for "natural" explanations for this event. Thallus, for example, states that the sun was obscured by a large, black disk. We recognize that as a description of a solar eclipse. Perhaps the eclipse was God's method for darkening the earth. Who knows? What we know for sure, however, is that the darkness referenced in Matthew 27:45 has been confirmed by non-Christian historians.

With respect to archaeological discoveries, the Bible truly stands out as an accurate source of history. Whether one is studying New Testament or Old Testament-related data, archaeology provides incredibly convincing evidence for the historical validity of the Bible. For example, William F. Albright, one of the greatest archaeologists of this century, says, "There can be no doubt that archaeology has confirmed the substantial historicity of the Old Testament..." (*Archaeology and the Religions of Israel*, p.176). In addition, F. F. Bruce, author and historian, says, "...it may be legitimate to say that archaeology has confirmed the New Testament record." (*Revelation and the Bible*, p.331)

It would be an impossible task to even briefly sketch all of the archaeological discoveries that have confirmed specific passages in the Bible. As Amihai Mazar, author of *Archaeology of the Land of the Bible*, states, "The digestion of the data uncovered is overwhelming even for professional archaeologists, not to mention scholars of related subjects." (p. XV) Since the volume of such data is overwhelming, I want to concentrate on a few specific examples. These examples are ironic, because they represent cases in which archaeologists originally thought that the Bible was in error. More data, however, revealed that the archaeologists were in error, not the Bible. It is important to note that the following examples are not isolated incidents. As Edwin Yamauchi in his book, *The Stones and the Scriptures*, says, "There are a number of striking cases where specific passages have been doubted...and have [later] been confirmed." (p. 20)

A particularly startling example of such a reversal comes from the Old Testament book of Genesis, chapter 14. This chapter details a series of battles fought between two ancient alliances. During one of the battles, Abram's nephew Lot was captured. Abram led a group of men against the alliance that captured Lot, defeated the alliance, and rescued his nephew. In the early part of this century, most archaeologists believed that this account was a total fabrication. Indeed, in 1918, William F. Albright wrote an article in the *Journal of Biblical Literature* in which he stated that all of Genesis 14 was either borrowed from a legend or made up entirely.

Since 1918, however, a great number of archaeological discoveries have put the historicity of this tale beyond doubt. Discovery of the Mari Tablets in 1933 provided evidence that the kings mentioned in the account did, in fact, exist and that such long-distance battles were, indeed, fought at that time. In addition, Albright himself discovered significant archaeological evidence that the cities mentioned in the account were at war during that time. In the end, the evidence forced Albright to reverse his earlier belief. In a commentary that he wrote in 1948, Albright stated that archaeology (some of it his own) has confirmed the reliability of Genesis chapter 14.

The most important aspect of this example is that the same archaeologist who originally doubted the historical accuracy of Genesis 14 ended up being forced to change his mind in light of the evidence. Clearly, Albright did not give Genesis 14 the benefit of the doubt while studying the relevant archaeological discoveries. He believed that it was a fabrication. In the end, however, the data forced him to admit that he was in error. Remember, this is the same archaeologist that I originally quoted as saying that archaeology has confirmed the historicity of the Old Testament. This example provides a lot of credence for such a conclusion. Here is an archaeologist who did not want to believe that the Old Testament was an accurate historical work. However, after a lifetime of archaeological study, he was forced to concede the point. Clearly, he would not make such a statement if the data were not convincing.

It is important to note that the Old Testament has been shown by archaeology to be accurate not only in the "big" issues of kings, battles, cities, and dates, but also in "little" issues as well. Archaeologists are constantly being amazed at the Old Testament's accurate attention to detail. For example, in the Old Testament account of Joseph and his coat of many colors (Genesis, chapters 37-47) it is stated that Joseph's brothers sold him into slavery for the price of twenty shekels (Genesis 37:28). Many archaeologists have doubted this price, because, based on early archaeological evidence, slaves sold at slightly later times than Joseph's were significantly more expensive. Once again, however, more archaeological data vindicated the Old Testament. In 1966, the data were so convincing that author K. A. Kitchen wrote,

> ...the price of twenty shekels of silver...is the correct average price for a slave in about the eighteenth century B.C.: Earlier than this, slaves were cheaper (average, ten to fifteen shekels), and later they became steadily dearer. This is one more little detail true to its period in cultural history. (*The Ancient Orient and the New Testament*, pp. 52,53)

Finally, the New Testament is also just as archaeologically sound as the Old Testament. Consider the case of The Pavement, where the passage in John 19:13 says Christ was tried before Pilate. Prior to about 1950, there was no archaeological confirmation of such a place; thus, many archaeologists believed that it never really existed. In 1960, however, William F. Albright demonstrated that The Pavement was the court of the tower of Antonia, the headquarters of the Roman military. The reason it had not been discovered before was that it had been buried during one of the times that Jerusalem had been rebuilt, and had not been uncovered until the 1950's.

Based on the weight of the somewhat fragmentary historical evidence and the overwhelming amount of archaeological evidence, we can say without question that the Bible passes the external test. In fact, more archaeological attention has been paid to the Bible than any other source of ancient history. We can therefore say that the Bible passes the external test better than any other source of ancient history!

ON YOUR OWN

5.4 In "on your own" 5.1, I mentioned a document that seemed to fail the external test. Suppose that the passage in question is the *only* one that is not consistent with archaeology. Based on what you have read here, should we conclude that the document fails the external test? Why or why not? No. Because there may be some explanation.

The Bibliographic Test

The last test we need to apply to a document of history is the bibliographic test. Remember, a good work of history is composed of either eyewitness accounts or the accounts of those who heard from eyewitnesses. Well, if the document is old, it must have been copied several times in order to survive to the present day. The bibliographic test tries to determine whether or not the copies we have today are really true to the original.

Now remember, in order for a document to pass the bibliographic test, there must be a relatively short amount of time between copy and original, and there must be several copies made by different people. Before I examine how the Bible fares in the bibliographic test, I want you to get an idea of how other documents of ancient history fare.

The histories written by Cornelius Tacitus are considered very accurate accounts of the events which occurred in the Roman Empire during the first century A.D. His works give us a substantial amount of the facts we know concerning the Roman Empire. Currently, there are 20 copies of his major work (*Annals*) and only 1 copy of a collection of his minor works. The earliest copy of his major work was made almost 1,000 years after the original was written, and the single copy of his minor works was made roughly 900 years after the originals were penned. By comparison, consider the work of Pliny the Younger who was also a historian of the first century A.D. His *History* is currently supported by 7 different copies, the earliest of which was made 750 years after the original.

For works of ancient history, the numbers quoted above are pretty commonplace. Some works are supported by more copies, some by fewer. The works of Sophocles, for example, have 193 different copies with which they can be compared. This is one of the largest numbers you will ever see in conjunction with ancient works of history. Unfortunately, the earliest of these copies was written nearly 1,400 years after the original. Alternatively, the 750 years which elapsed between the original works of Pliny the Younger and the earliest existing copies represents one of the smallest time spans related to ancient works of history.

Compare these numbers to those of the New Testament, which is supported by *over 24,000 different copies*, the earliest of which was written a mere *25 years after the original*! The differences between the 24,000 copies are trivial, indicating that the New Testament we have today is completely faithful to the original text. Let these numbers sink in for a moment. The New Testament passes the bibliographic test *better than any other historical work of its time.*

What about the Old Testament? Does it pass the bibliographic test as well as the New Testament? Not quite, but then again, you wouldn't expect it to. After all, the works in the Old Testament are significantly more ancient. Nevertheless, the Old Testament still passes the bibliographic test better than any other historical document of its time. The best way to illustrate this is with the example of the Dead Sea scrolls.

Prior to 1947, the earliest existing copy of parts of the Hebrew Old Testament came from the *Cairo Codex* which was written in about 895 A.D. Since the last events of the Old Testament were supposed to have occurred approximately 450 B.C., this represents a significant time lag between the original writings and the first available copies. In 1947, however, the Dead Sea scrolls were discovered. These scrolls contain copies of parts of at least 500 ancient books. One of the scrolls contained a complete copy of the Old Testament book of Isaiah. The scroll was dated by archaeologists as having been written in 125 B.C. This version of Isaiah proved to be word for word identical with the standard Hebrew Bible in more than 95 percent of the text. The 5 percent of variation consisted mostly of obvious slips of the pen and variations in spelling. In over 1,000 years, then, the book of Isaiah (and presumably the rest of the Old Testament) was copied faithfully. This adds great evidence to the already convincing data which supports the bibliographic reliability of the Old Testament.

In the end, then, the Bible passes the bibliographic test better than any other work of ancient history. As William Green puts it, "...it may be safely said that no other work of antiquity has been so accurately transmitted." (*General Introduction to the Old Testament*, p. 181) Thus, we can be sure that the Bible which we read today is faithful to the original eyewitness accounts. Combine that with the fact that the Bible passes the internal test just as well as any ancient document of history and that it passes the external test *better* than any document of its time, and you come to the *scientific* conclusion that the stories and accounts in the Bible are more trustworthy than any of the other accounts we have about the Roman Empire and other facets of ancient life!

ON YOUR OWN

5.5 Suppose archaeologists found a new historical document (a copy of a much older document) in a ruin. A few years later, several copies of that same document were discovered in a nearby location, and it is determined that the same king who commissioned the first copy also commanded that the other copies be made. Would those copies help the document in passing the bibliographic test? Why or why not? Yes-If it does not contradict the original (and) No-If it contradicts the original

NO

Archaeology in the Absence of Historical Documents

Although archaeology is of immense value in determining the validity of historical documents, archaeology can also stand alone as a means of learning about people and civilizations that are not recorded in historical documents. After all, almost every civilization leaves behind artifacts. We can learn a lot about ancient people from those artifacts, as long as we are careful to understand that in just examining artifacts, we do not have a complete picture. Thus, all conclusions that we draw must be very tentative.

When an archaeologist discovers an ancient artifact, one of the first things he or she asks is, "How old is this thing?" Unfortunately, it is often difficult to provide an exact answer to this question. After all, how in the world would you know how old something is if you just dig it up from the ground? Well, sometimes, the artifact itself can give you the answer. Ancient coins, for example, might have the date they were made printed on them. Also, an artifact might be referenced in a work of history. For example, suppose a work of history mentions the date at which an Egyptian king died. If an archaeologist can find that king's tomb, then the tomb and the artifacts buried in it can be dated by the reference in the historical document.

FIGURE 5.2
Artifacts With Known Dates

This sarcophagus (a fancy name for a coffin) might hold the remains of a king who is referenced in a work of history. If so, the age of the sarcophagus is known.

This rock with Egyptian writing might have a date on it. If it does, its age is known.

Photos from the MasterClips collection

When the age of the artifact can be determined in this way, archaeologists say that the artifact has a **known age**.

Known age - The age of an artifact as determined by a date printed on it or a reference to the artifact in a work of history

Unfortunately, few artifacts have known ages. Thus, archaeologists must employ other means by which to determine how old an artifact is. One of the more reliable methods is called **dendrochronology** (den droh kron awl' uh gee).

Dendrochronology - The process of counting tree rings to determine the age of a tree

During the life of a tree, its trunk expands. If you cut down a tree and look at the inside of the trunk, you will see that it is made up of a series of rings, which are commonly called "tree rings."

FIGURE 5.3
Tree Rings

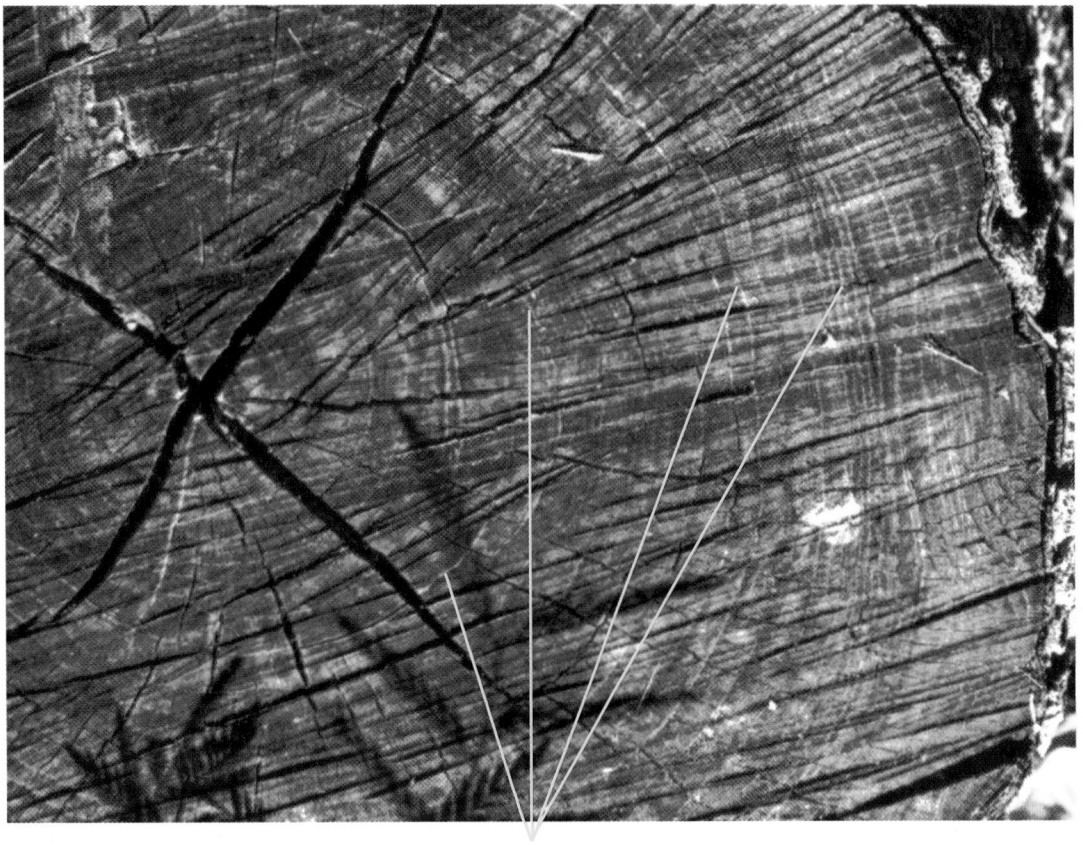

Tree Rings
Notice the variation in width and color.

Photo by Kathleen J. Wile

A tree typically grows one ring each year. Thus, if you cut a tree down and count the tree rings, you can determine how old the tree is. If there are 123 rings, the tree is, most likely, 123 years old.

Counting tree rings is a good method for determining the age of a tree, but how does that help determine the age of artifacts in archaeology? Well, the first thing that you have to realize is that the *appearance* of a tree ring depends on several environmental factors for the year in which the ring was formed. The length of the growing season, the amount of rain, the average temperature, and several other factors all play a role in determining how wide and dark the ring being grown that year will be. As you look at a tree's rings, then, you will see patterns of wide rings, thin rings, dark rings and light rings. Those patterns are a result of the weather patterns that occurred in the tree's environment over its lifetime.

Okay, fine, but how does that help an archaeologist? Well, since the weather in a given region affects the appearance of tree rings, archaeologists studying a certain region can cut down an old tree that is still alive. They can then look for distinct patterns of tree rings that correspond to several years of a given weather pattern for that region. Counting from the outside of the tree to the start of this special pattern will then tell archaeologists *how many years ago that weather pattern occurred.* Archaeologists find several such patterns and catalog them as **master tree ring patterns** for that region of the world.

So, when an archaeologist discovers a log that was once used to build a home or something like that, he or she can look at the rings in the log and try to find one of those master tree ring patterns. If the archaeologist finds one, then he or she knows how many years ago the ring patterned formed, because that has already been determined. Since the archaeologist knows when that ring pattern was formed, he or she can then count the remaining rings on the tree that was discovered and determine when that tree was cut down. That will tell the archaeologist how long ago the people who cut down the tree were alive, and that will determine the age of the artifacts left by those people.

Archaeologists have cataloged master tree rings patterns which have allowed them to date certain artifacts to as far back as 6600 B.C. Now before I go any further, I have to point out something that is very important. You must pay close attention here:

The only ages that are certain in archaeology are the KNOWN ages.

I cannot stress this point enough. Although dendrochronology is considered one of the best dating tools that exist, it is still fraught with difficulties. These difficulties lead to uncertainties in the ages calculated using this method. Thus, unless the date is written on the artifact, or unless a reference to the artifact can be found in a reliable historical document, the age determined by archaeologists is uncertain.

One of the big problems with dendrochronology is that trees *sometimes* grow more than one ring a year. This, of course, will lead an archaeologist to believe that a tree is older than it really is. The farther an archaeologist goes back in history, the worse this problem becomes. Thus, the dates that are determined by dendrochronology are usually considered *upper limits*. In other words, when dendrochronology determines that an artifact is 2,000 years old, it means that the artifact is *at most* 2,000 years old. It could be younger. This, then, is an important point:

Ages determined by dendrochronology are upper limits for the age of an artifact.

Typically, the older the artifact, the more error there will be in the process of tree-ring counting.

Even though dendrochronology allows archaeologists to get a pretty good idea of how old an artifact is, it is still a pretty limited dating method. After all, in order to use dendrochronology, an archaeologist must discover a log that has identifiable tree rings and can be linked to a master tree ring pattern for that region of the world. Thus, an archaeologist cannot use dendrochronology to date just anything! As a result, archaeologists try to use other dating methods to determine an artifact's age.

One very popular method archaeologists use is called carbon-14 dating. This dating method is actually a part of a much broader group of dating methods called **radiometric dating**.

Radiometric dating - Using a radioactive process to determine the age of an item

You will learn a lot more about radiometric dating when you take physical science next year. At that point, you will learn that radiometric dating is usually very unreliable. There is one exception to this general rule. The radiometric dating technique called carbon-14 dating is about as reliable as dendrochronology as long as the item being dated is less than 3,000 years old. You will learn the details of why this is the case next year.

When an archaeologist uses dendrochronology or radiometric dating to determine the age of an object, the archaeologist says that the object has an **absolute age**.

Absolute age – The calculated age of an artifact from a specific dating method that is used to determine when the artifact was made

Now it is important for you to understand what "absolute" means in the term "absolute age." It *does not mean* "correct" or "sure." The term "absolute age" simply means that an actual date has been assigned to the artifact. Thus, if an archaeologist uses dendrochronology to determine that an artifact was made in 40 B.C., the archaeologist will say that the artifact has an absolute age. However, any good archaeologist will be quick to point out that the age is really just an upper limit to the *true* age of the artifact, due to the problems with dendrochronology. As a result, "absolute" does not imply "true." It simply means that a dating method has been used to assign a date to the artifact. This is an important distinction to remember!

ON YOUR OWN

5.6 An archaeologist is trying to determine the age of an ancient village that has just been discovered, and she would like to use dendrochronology. What *two* things must she have in order to determine the age of the village in this way?

5.7 If an artifact has no date written on it, is there any way that you can determine its age with certainty?

Before I leave this section, I want to make a very important point. If you go to a museum or read certain history books, you will find that some archaeologists believe that they have found artifacts which are hundreds of thousands (or even millions) of years old. You need to be very skeptical about such ages. Remember, the most reliable absolute dating method is dendrochronology, and it can only provide ages of 8000 years or so. Even though such ages are pretty reliable, they still only provide an upper limit on the true age of an artifact.

About the only other absolute dating methods available to archaeologists are the many radiometric dating methods. As you will learn in physical science next year, these dating methods are incredibly unreliable. Thus, the dates obtained by using them must be viewed with healthy skepticism. The problem is, many archaeologists love to use radiometric dating because they want to believe that the earth is ancient and that man has been living on earth for hundreds of thousands or even millions of years. It turns out that radiometric dating can provide such ancient ages, and thus many archaeologists like to use radiometric dating.

In my opinion, and in the opinion of many other scientists, radiometric dates are not at all reliable, with the notable exception discussed above. Thus, any time you hear that some artifact has an absolute age of tens of thousands, hundreds of thousands, or millions of years old, you have to realize that the dating method used to calculate such an ancient age is viewed as unreliable by many in the scientific community.

Relative Dating and the Principle of Superposition

If an archaeologist is not able to find the known age or an absolute age for an artifact, he or she can still get some idea of how old the artifact is. Archaeologists often can get the **relative age** of an object by using the **Principle of Superposition**.

The Principle of Superposition – When artifacts are found in rock or earth that is layered, the deeper layers hold the older artifacts.

The Principle of Superposition is used heavily in archaeology and geology, so I want to make sure that you understand it.

When an archaeologist or geologist digs into the earth, he or she will usually find that the soil and/or the rock tend to have distinct layers, which are called **strata**. If you were to look at it from the side, it might look something like this:

FIGURE 5.4
Stratified Soil and Rock

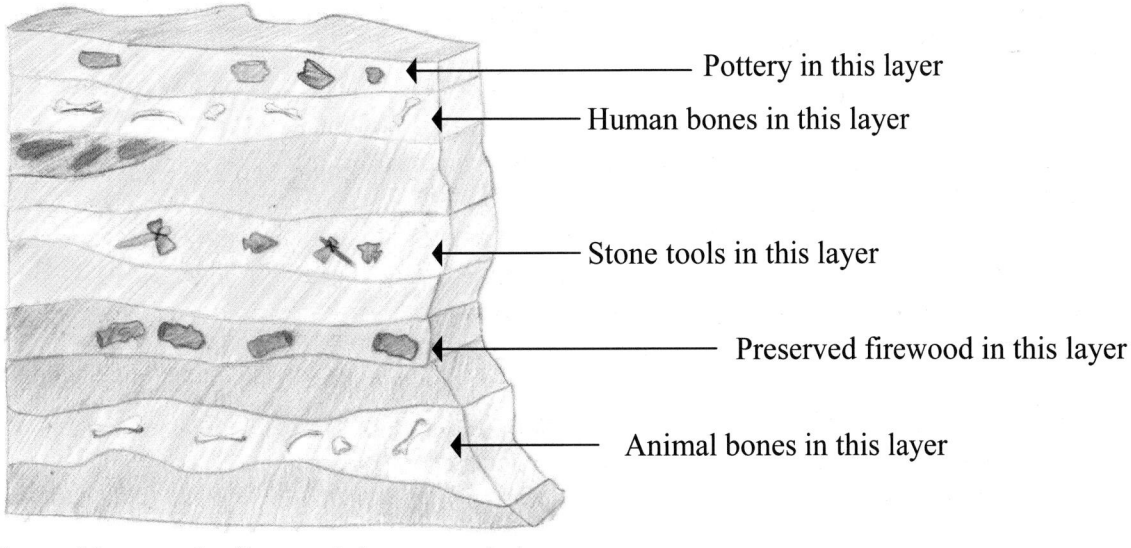

Several layers of soil or rock in an area being studied by archaeologists

Illus. by Megan Whitaker

Archaeologists assume that when these layers were formed, they were formed one at a time. As you will see later on in this course, that's not a good assumption in many cases. Nevertheless, it is an assumption that is used quite heavily in archaeology and geology.

If the layers in the soil and rock were, indeed, formed one at a time, then we can draw a rather obvious conclusion. We can say that the deeper layers are older than the shallow layers. After all, if the layers formed one at a time, then the bottom layer would have had to form first, the layer on top of it would have had to form next, and so on. Thus, the bottom layer in the figure is the oldest layer, the layer on top of it is the next oldest layer, and so on. The layer on the very top of the figure, then, is the youngest layer.

Now if this conclusion is true, then clearly any artifacts found in the bottom layer will be the oldest, and any artifacts found in the top layer will be the youngest. Thus, even though an archaeologist might not be able to determine an absolute date for any of the artifacts in the figure, he or she could say that the firewood is older than the stone tools which are older than the pottery. The archaeologist might even be able to determine more than that. Suppose, for example, that the archaeologist can use dendrochronology to determine an absolute date for the firewood. Suppose, based on dendrochronology, the firewood is determined to be 1,000 years old. The archaeologist could then say that although there is no way to give an absolute date for the animal bones, they are definitely older than 1,000 years, because they are found in a layer below the layer in which the firewood was found.

The Principle of Superposition, then, can at least give the archaeologist an idea of how old an artifact is *relative to another artifact*. This can be useful, but once again, it must be viewed with a bit of skepticism. As you will learn later on in this course, layers of rock and soil are not always laid down one by one. Sometimes, they are laid down simultaneously as the result of certain catastrophes. Thus, the underlying assumption for the Principle of Superposition is not true in all cases. Unfortunately, it is hard to tell when the Principle of Superposition is true and when it is false, so this can lead to a lot of confusion when discussing relative ages of artifacts.

ON YOUR OWN

5.8 Based on the Principle of Superposition, list the artifacts pointed out in Figure 5.4 in terms of *increasing* age. Thus, list the youngest artifact first and the oldest one last.
Pottery, Human Bones, Stone Tools, Fire Wood, + animal bones.
5.9 What is the underlying assumption of the Principle of Superposition?

What Do We Know About Human History?

I have spent a lot of time discussing archaeology and history and how they interact. However, I have not spent a lot of time discussing what archaeology and history actually tell us about human life in the past. I have done this on purpose. I think it is more important for you to learn the *science* of history and archaeology than it is to learn about their conclusions. After all, unless you know *how* history and archaeology are done, you will not know *how to interpret* the things that historians and archaeologists tell you.

Now that you know a bit about how history and archaeology are done, however, I do want to spend a few moments on what history and archaeology tell us about the past. The first thing that they tell us is that the history of human life as given by the Bible is an accurate account of what has happened in the past. Thus, one of the best things you can do to learn about human history is to read the Bible.

Now remember, the Bible passes the tests of historical science better than any other of the histories that cover the same time periods covered by the Bible. Thus, science tells us that we can believe the accounts given in the Bible better than any other accounts given in any other historical documents for the relevant time periods. This means that the overall history of human life on earth is best provided by the Bible. As a result, we have solid scientific reasons to believe in the events of the past as related to the Bible.

Now wait a minute, you might think. Doesn't the Bible give accounts of events that are rather hard to believe? What about Noah's Flood, for example? The Bible tells us that the entire world was destroyed by a flood caused by God. The only people who survived the flood were members of a family led by a man named Noah, who had built an ark by the Lord's command. Isn't that just a little hard to swallow?

Well, perhaps it might be hard to swallow for some, but there is ample reason to believe it is true. First of all, if you choose not to believe the most historically valid document of that time period, then it is awfully hard to understand how you can believe *any* history that we currently know. After all, the same historical tests that are used to evaluate all other works of history tell us that the Bible is, by far, the most reliable. If you start deciding to reject parts of Biblical history, then you have really departed from the science of history and are more or less making up the rules as you go.

Also, there is ample extrabiblical evidence (evidence from sources other than the Bible) to believe that a worldwide flood did, indeed, happen in the past. As you will learn a little later on in this course, there is quite a lot of geological evidence for a worldwide flood. History actually gives us other evidence that a worldwide flood did happen sometime in earth's past.

There are many stories of a worldwide flood from many different cultures. For example, Babylonian tablets that date back to 2000 B.C. (absolute age) contain a story called the "Gilgamesh Epic." This story tells about a ruler who seeks out a wise man. The wise man and his family are described in the story as the sole survivors of a great flood. In Greek mythology, the king of Phthia (Deucalion) and his family are said to be the sole survivors of a flood that the god Zeus sent to destroy humanity because of men's wicked ways. The natives of Polynesia, the aborigines of Central America, the aborigines of South America, the natives of South Asia, the Chinese, and the Japanese all have similar stories.

It is virtually impossible that all of these cultures learned the tale from each other! The Chinese and Japanese had no contact with the Greeks or the Jews until well after the flood stories had been written down. The aborigines of Central and South America are separated from all of the other cultures I mentioned by an ocean! How is it that all of these cultures would have such similar legends if they weren't all derived from an actual event?

Thus, the history of human life as given by the Bible is probably the best place to start if you want to find out what happened to people in the past. There is, of course, more to history than what's mentioned in the Bible, but the Bible is the best historical framework in which to view all of the other history we know.

ON YOUR OWN

5.10 Since there are many different stories about a worldwide flood that come from many different cultures, why should we believe the Bible's account? Why not believe the story of the worldwide flood as given in Greek mythology or one of the aborigine legends?

Because the Bible passes the three tests better than any other history documents,

ANSWERS TO THE ON YOUR OWN QUESTIONS

5.1 The document seems to be contradicted by archaeological research. Thus, it fails the external test.

5.2 The document contradicts itself. How could a battle be fought over a city that has not been built yet? The document fails the internal test.

5.3 These passages are not contradictory. Instead, they are complementary. One states that Judas hanged himself, and another states he fell off a cliff. In the Jerusalem area, there are many cliffs with trees that grow at the edge so that their branches hang over the edge of the cliff. These were often used for suicide, because a person could tie the rope to the branch, tie the other end to his neck, and just jump. Often times, however, the tree branch would break under the person's weight, and they would then fall to the bottom of the cliff. This is probably what happened in Judas's case. Thus, the two passages together tell us more than each individual passage. One eyewitness saw the body afterwards, and decided that Judas fell. The other might have watched the event or interviewed someone who did. He would conclude that Judas hung himself. Both are right.

5.4 The document might not really fail the external test, because later archaeological research might confirm the existence of the fortress. After all, the archaeologists could be looking in not exactly the right place, or the village that the archaeologists found could have been made on top of the ruins of the fortress, which still lie below undiscovered.

5.5 These copies would not help the document in passing the bibliographic test. The copies of a document have to be made by a different source in order to be used in the bibliographic test. Remember, one thing that the bibliographic test guards against is the process by which text is added or removed from a document at the direction of the person ordering the copies.

5.6 In order to use dendrochronology, the archaeologist must find a preserved log with identifiable rings in the remains of the ancient village. She also must find a master tree ring pattern which she can then identify in the preserved log. The preserved log gives the archaeologist something with which to use dendrochronology, and the master tree ring pattern allows her to figure out how old the log is.

5.7 There is another way to get a known age for an artifact. If the artifact is mentioned in a document of history and a date is given there, then the artifact will have a known age.

5.8 The Principle of Superposition states that the artifacts found in the lower layers will be older than those found in the upper layers. Thus, in order of increasing age, you have pottery, human bones, stone tools, preserved firewood, and animal bones.

5.9 The Principle of Superposition assumes that each layer of soil or rock is formed one at a time. We know that this is not always true.

5.10 We should believe the Biblical account because the Bible is more historically reliable than any of the other documents, as is demonstrated by the internal, external, and bibliographic tests.

STUDY GUIDE FOR MODULE #5

1. Define the following terms:

a. Life science
b. Archaeology
c. Artifact
d. Geology
e. Paleontology
f. Aristotle's dictum
g. Known age
h. Dendrochronology
i. Radiometric dating
j. Absolute age
k. The Principle of Superposition

2. If you wanted to learn about the history of life other than human life, would you use archaeology or paleontology? paleontology

3. Name the three tests used to evaluate documents that claim to be historical. internal test, external test, + the bibliographic test.

4. Give a brief description of each of the tests listed in #3.
IT - Tests to see if the document is consistant.
ET - Does the document contradict other known historical facts? or archaeological
BT - Work must contain direct eye witness accounts or second-hand reports based on eye witness accounts.

5. In what test is Aristotle's dictum used? Why must we use it?
Internal Test. Because the language might have changed over time... etc...

6. There are two reasons to believe that the copy of an ancient document might not be the same as the original. One is that the person making the copy might have made some unintentional mistakes. What is the other reason? It might have changed over time.

7. What two things help a document pass the bibliographic test?
If the copies are almost the same as the original + eye witness accounts.

8. Does the Bible contain any contradictions that make it fail the internal test?
No

9. Does the Bible have any difficult passages that might seem like contradictions?
Yes

10. Why are the two accounts given in Acts 9:7 and Acts 22:9 not contradictory? Feel free to use your Bible to look up those verses. The Greek word "akouo" changes its meaning - changing the meaning of the sentence.

11. Why are the two genealogies of Christ given in Luke 3 and Matthew 1 not contradictory? Once again, you can use your Bible. One was the Grandpa + the other was the Grandma.

12. Why can we say that the Bible passes the external test better than any other document of its time? Because it does not contradict the historical + archaeological facts.

13. Suppose a document passes the internal and bibliographic tests but some of the conclusions of archaeologists go against what the document says. If the document has some other external support (other historical documents and some archaeological evidence), why should we not automatically say that it fails the external test? Because -

14. Why can we say that the New Testament passes the bibliographic test better than any other document of its time? Because it has many more eye witness documents than any other document.

15. Does the Old Testament pass the bibliographic test?
Yes

16. The age of an ancient settlement is determined by using dendrochronology on some firewood that had been chopped down but never used by the inhabitants. Does the settlement have a known age or an absolute age? an absolute age

17. A coffin of a great king is discovered. The date of the king's death is recorded in a document of history. Does the coffin have a known age or an absolute age?
known age

18. If an archaeologist gives an absolute age for an artifact, does that mean we know for certain how old the artifact is? No.

19. Why does an archaeologist use master tree ring patterns?
To compaire and match other tree ~~and log~~ rings.

20. What is the underlying assumption of the Principle of Superposition?
The Principle of Superposition is not ~~always~~ true in all cases

21. Suppose an archaeologist uses dendrochronology to determine that a city was built in 2500 B.C. Several years later, another archaeologist is digging deeper under the site of the city and, in a lower layer of rock, he finds the remains of another city. Unfortunately, there is nothing that he can use for any dating technique. He can still conclude something about the age of the city. Assuming that the Principle of Superposition is true in this situation, what can he conclude?
That the city is older than 2500 B.C.

22. Besides being discussed in the most accurate historical document of its time, what other historical evidence exists which indicates that Noah's Flood actually did occur?
Many other cultures in the world wrote about a worldly flood.

Module #6: Foundations of Geology

Introduction

In the previous module, I spent considerable time on the science of archaeology and how it relates to history. Hopefully, you now have a better appreciation for how the "historical facts" that you have read about in your history courses have been determined. I now want to move into another science that touches on history: the science of geology. Although geology has many uses other than history, no one can truly understand the history of life or the history of this planet without understanding geology. In this module, then, I want to give you a brief introduction to this fascinating science. Once you have a firm grasp of geology, you will then be able to understand paleontology, which I will discuss in the next module.

When we start using geology to try and understand what has happened in earth's past, we immediately encounter a problem. We can make observations of the rocks, minerals, etc. that make up the earth, but we do not know for sure *how* they were formed or how they came to have the characteristics which they currently have. No one was around to observe the rocks forming, so we do not have any direct observations which will allow us to determine how the rocks we observe came to be. Nevertheless, if we want to use geology to learn about earth's history, we *must* know how the rocks we are observing today were formed.

Are we stuck, then? Of course not! As I have stressed several times in this course, science does not depend on direct observation. Science depends only on the scientific method. Thus, we can still use science to help us understand earth's history. We simply must start with a hypothesis, test the hypothesis with experiments, etc., etc. As long as we perform our geological investigations that way, we will be able to learn a lot about earth's past.

So we need to start by forming some hypotheses. This is where we run into a bit of trouble. You see, there are (at least) two different viewpoints when it comes to forming hypotheses about earth's past: **catastrophism** (kuh tas' troh fiz uhm) and **uniformitarianism** (you' nuh form' uh tair' ee uhn iz uhm).

Catastrophism - The view that most of earth's geological features are the result of large-scale catastrophes such as floods, volcanic eruptions, etc.

Uniformitarianism - The view that most of earth's geological features are the result of slow, gradual processes that have been at work for millions or even billions of years

You can think of each of these as a starting hypothesis. Most scientists take one view or the other and then start their scientific inquiries from there. This leads to two very different views of earth's past.

Well, you might be thinking, what's the problem? One of these hypotheses is right and the other is wrong. Let's use the scientific method to find out which can be confirmed by the data. *That's* the problem. Some of the geological data support one hypothesis, while other geological data support the other. Thus, there are scientific arguments which favor each of the hypotheses! Which do you choose? Well, that depends *a lot* on what data you consider to be the most important. In my scientific opinion, the most important data supports catastrophism, and the data in support of uniformitarianism is rather limited and can mostly be explained away. However, other scientists see the data in support of uniformitarianism as much more important and try to explain away the data in support of catastrophism. In the end, then, we are left with two views of geology that are quite at odds with one another.

In general, more scientists believe in uniformitarianism than catastrophism. If you remember my discussion of the history of science, however, that should not count for much in your mind. The history of science is *full* of cases in which the majority of scientists were dead wrong. We do not do science by majority vote, we do it by the data. The catastrophism view has been around for a lot longer. Once again, however, that shouldn't count for much. After all, the history of science is full of wrong ideas that stayed around for a long, long time. Thus, the only way to determine which point of view is better is to review the data for yourself and then make up your own mind.

In order to help you do this, I want to tell you about the main geological *features* of the earth. It will really take me almost two modules to complete that task. After that, however, I will dedicate more than a full module to explaining these features from both the uniformitarian view and the catastrophism view. Now remember, I think that catastrophism is the better hypothesis. Thus, my discussion will probably be slanted in that direction.

ON YOUR OWN

6.1 Many people believe that the earth is billions of years old. Many others believe that the earth is "young," which usually means less than 10,000 years old. Is it possible to believe in a "young" earth using the uniformitarianism approach to geology? Is it possible to believe in a "young earth" using the catastrophism approach to geology? Is it possible to believe in an earth that is billions of years old under the uniformitarianism hypothesis? Is it possible to believe in an earth that is billions of years old under the catastrophism hypothesis?

Soil, Rocks and Minerals

If you go out to your back yard and start digging, you will first encounter a lot of dirt, which we call **soil**. Soil is actually composed of several different things. First of all, the topmost layer of soil (called **topsoil**) is rich in **humus**.

Humus - The decayed remains of once-living creatures

Although it sounds kind of gross, humus is a very important part of the soil. It contains nutrients that plants use to stay alive. Soil that has a lot of humus is ideal for planting gardens, trees, etc. As you dig deeper in the soil, you will also find its other components: **gravel, sand, silt,** and **clay**. Not all soil has each of these components, but most does. It turns out that the relative amounts of gravel, sand, silt, and clay in soil will determine how well the soil holds water. This will also affect how well plants grow in the soil. You will learn more about that in a couple of years when you take biology.

As you dig deeper and deeper in the soil, you will eventually find rock. I don't mean a large rock buried in the soil. I mean a solid layer of rock. That's because all of the earth's soil is actually sitting on top of earth's **crust**, which is made of solid rock. Although one rock might look like any other rock to you, there are actually three different basic kinds of rocks that make up the earth: **sedimentary** (sed i men' tuh ree) **rock, igneous** (ig' nee us) **rock**, and **metamorphic** (met uh more' fik) **rock**.

Sedimentary rock is formed, as you might expect, from **sediments** (sand, silt, and other components of soil) which are laid down by water or some other agent. As these sediments begin to pile up, they can begin to fuse together due to heat, pressure, and various chemical reactions. This hardens the sediments into a solid substance, which is called sedimentary rock. Although sedimentary rock actually makes up only about 8% of earth's crust, it covers most of the earth's surface. It is usually the topmost layer of earth's crust, so it is the most common kind of rock that people encounter.

Igneous rock forms from molten rock, which is usually called **magma**. When a volcano erupts, the lava that it spews forth is magma. When that molten rock cools, it solidifies, forming igneous rock. Although the only time we see magma is when a volcano erupts, magma often flows underground as well. You will learn more about that next year in physical science. Since magma often flows underground and never reaches the surface, many igneous rocks are formed underneath the surface of the earth. You usually find igneous rock at the surface of the earth only as a result of volcanic activity. There is, however, a lot of igneous rock under the surface of the earth due to underground magma.

Metamorphic rock is rock that has undergone extreme change due to lots of heat and pressure. Both igneous rock and sedimentary rock will form metamorphic rock when exposed to these conditions. Because of the extreme heat and pressure that turns igneous or sedimentary rock into metamorphic rock, metamorphic rock is typically very hard.

Now it is important to realize that just as matter has basic building blocks which we call atoms, rocks also have basic building blocks. They are called **minerals**.

Minerals - Inorganic crystalline substances found naturally in the earth

What in the world does that definition mean? Well, first, you need to know that the term "inorganic" simply means that the substance in question did not come from a living being. Thus, it can't be the remains of some dead organism or the product of a living one. The term "crystalline" is a term from chemistry which refers to a specific kind of structure. The best way for you to understand this term is by experiment.

EXPERIMENT 6.1
The Difference Between Rocks and Minerals

Supplies :

- Alum (A powder available at any drug store - you need at least 4 ounces)
- Two small glasses (like juice glasses)
- A spoon for stirring
- Some thread
- Two weights (washers, nuts, fishing sinkers, etc.)
- A large plate
- A few rocks from outside (small rocks actually work best)
- A sheet of dark paper (blue, black, etc.)
- A magnifying glass
- Sugar (optional)
- Food coloring (optional)

Introduction - Alum is a mineral used in baking, medicine, and fireproofing. The alum that you buy has been crushed into a powder. In this experiment, you will reconstruct its natural form, which is crystalline. You will also see how different the structure of a mineral is compared to a rock.

Procedure:

A. Heat some water in a pot. You need not bring it to a boil. Just heat it to the same temperature that you might use to make hot chocolate.
B. While the water is heating, take a length of thread and attach a weight to each end. The thread needs to be 2.5 times as long as the glasses are high.
C. Pour the hot water into one of the glasses so that the glass is about half way full.
D. Now start mixing the alum into the hot water with the spoon. It should dissolve readily. Continue to add alum until you cannot get any more to dissolve. You will know that you have reached that point when the water gets cloudy and will not clear up regardless of how much you stir.
E. Let the glass stand for a few moments, and the undissolved alum will settle to the bottom of the glass, making the solution above it reasonably clear.
F. Once the solution in the glass is pretty clear, carefully pour some of the liquid into the empty glass. Do this slowly and carefully, trying not to disturb the alum that has settled to the bottom of the glass. Pour as much solution into the second glass as you can without allowing the undissolved alum to pour in. This process is called **decanting**, and it is used quite a bit in chemistry.

G. Now you should have a reasonably clear solution of alum in the second glass. Put the glass on the plate.
H. Drop one end of the thread in the glass. The weight will keep that end in the glass. Take the other end and put it on the plate. Your setup should look like this:

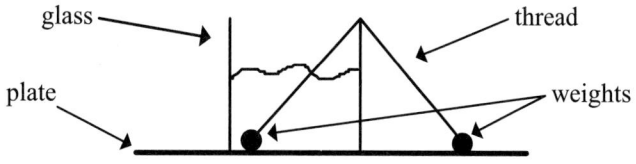

I. Draw this setup in your laboratory notebook.
J. Let the setup sit for several hours. The best thing to do is stop science today and look at it when you start science tomorrow. It will not hurt to leave it sit for several days, but you will also get great results by tomorrow.
K. After the setup has been left alone for several hours, carefully pull the thread out of the solution. Draw a picture of what the thread looks like.
L. What you see clinging to the thread are **crystals** of alum. This is an example of what a mineral looks like.
M. Lay the dark paper out on a table and shake the thread so that some of the crystals fall onto the paper.
N. Use your magnifying glass to examine the crystals.
O. Put a few rocks next to the crystals and, with your magnifying glass, compare the rocks to the crystals. You should see a difference. Write that difference down in your lab notebook.
P. **OPTIONAL**: You can use this same kind of experiment to make rock candy. If you clean out the glasses real thoroughly and use new thread, you can repeat this experiment using sugar instead of alum. The crystals that grow on the thread will be sugar crystals, which you can eat. If you want the sugar crystals to have color, add some food coloring to the solution before you put in the thread. Note that the sugar crystals are NOT minerals. Sugar is an organic substance, so it does not fit the definition of a mineral.

What did you learn from the experiment? Well, you should have seen what scientists mean by the term "crystalline." A crystalline substance has a very sharp, geometric shape. If you compared the alum crystals to the rocks, you should have noticed a strong difference. The crystals have sharp edges and smooth sides that formed an obvious geometric pattern. The rock might have had a few edges here and there, but no distinct geometric pattern.

In the end, then, minerals make up most of what we find in the earth. Sometimes, the minerals can be found in their pure form. When that happens, the minerals usually have a sharp, geometric pattern. Most of the time, however, the minerals are not found in their pure form. Instead, they are found in the form of rocks, which are usually made up of more than one kind of mineral.

ON YOUR OWN

6.2 Classify each of the following as a rock or a mineral.

a. 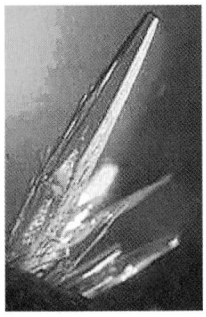

b. 

c. 

d. 

Photos from the MasterClips collection

6.3 Two rock samples look very similar. The first is much, much harder than the second. Suppose you are told that one rock is igneous and one rock is metamorphic. Which is which?

Strata in Sedimentary Rock

Now that you are familiar with the different types of rocks and minerals that make up the earth's crust, it is time to get an idea of how those rocks are arranged on the earth. The best way to do this is to study an example. Probably the best example that we can study is the **Grand Canyon**, which is located in northwestern Arizona .

FIGURE 6.1
A Portion of the Grand Canyon

Photo from the MasterClips collection

Isn't God's Creation marvelous? Not only is the Grand Canyon beautiful, it also exhibits many of the geological features that make up the earth. Thus, it is a nice tool for geology education. Take another look at the figure. Aside from the incredible beauty, what characteristic is immediately obvious in the picture? If you look at the walls of the canyon, you will see that the rocks form obvious *layers*. These layers are called **strata**, and they make up the most distinguishing aspect of sedimentary rock. The figure below shows yet another striking example of the strata that form in sedimentary rock. Notice how the layers lie straight and horizontal.

FIGURE 6.2
Strata in Sedimentary Rock

Photo from the MasterClips collection

While looking at the strata in sedimentary rock, the first thing you might ask yourself is how are those layers formed. Perform the following experiment to see one way that these strata form. This is another experiment that must sit overnight. Thus, it is best to perform the experiment as the last science you will do today.

EXPERIMENT 6.2
Separation of Sedimentation

Supplies:

- A large glass jar with a lid
- Some dirt from your yard
- Some sand
- Some gravel comprised of various sizes of rocks
- Water

Introduction - In this experiment, you will see how water can separate sediments into layers.

Procedure:

A. Fill the jar about 1/5 of the way with dirt. It is best to dig straight down into the ground so that you get dirt from many depths.
B. Add an equal amount of sand.
C. Add an equal amount of gravel.
D. Put the lid on the jar and then invert the jar to mix the contents. Invert the jar several times so that the sand, gravel, and dirt are all mixed up.
E. Draw a picture of the jar and its contents.
F. Add water to the jar so that the water level is about an inch from the top of the jar.
G. Put the lid on again and begin inverting the jar to once again mix up the contents. Invert the jar several times so that all of the gravel, dirt, and sand get shaken up in the water, and it all mixes together really well.
H. Let the jar sit for about an hour.
I. After about an hour, invert the jar again several times to once again mix everything up.
J. Repeat step (I) at least twice more before you go to bed. Be sure and let the jar sit for at least an hour between each repetition.
K. Draw a picture of the jar and its contents after it has set undisturbed overnight.
L. Dump the contents of the jar in your yard wherever your parents tell you it should be dumped and clean everything up.

What did the contents of the jar look like after it sat overnight? Well, it should look a lot different than it did before you added the water. Most likely, the gravel should now be on the bottom, and the soil and sand should have settled out in layers. The lighter substances should now be on top, and the heavier substances should be on the bottom.

So we see that water has the ability to separate sediments into layers. When you mixed up the contents of the jar, you simulated a body of water in motion. You simulated currents in rivers, tides in the ocean, etc. As water moves, it can separate sediments. When the sediments settle out of the water, they tend to settle out in layers. Although there are other processes that deposit sediments onto the ground, water processes are, by far, the most common. Thus, when water deposits sediments on the ground, the sediments tend to separate out into layers. Once water has deposited sediments onto the ground, the sediments can then form sedimentary rock as the sediments fuse due to heat, pressure, and chemical reactions.

The majority of sedimentary rock in the earth's crust, then, has been laid down by water. Because moving water tends to separate sediments, sedimentary rock usually forms strata. Now the strata formed by sedimentary rock varies greatly in thickness and appearance. For example, compare the strata shown in Figure 6.3 to those shown in the previous two figures.

FIGURE 6.3
More Strata in Sedimentary Rocks

Photo by Kathleen J. Wile

When a single layer of rock is less than 1 centimeter (0.39 inches) thick, it is called a **lamination**. Several of these layers together are called **laminae**.

ON YOUR OWN

6.4 The Grand Canyon is in the northwestern part of a state that has many of the characteristics of a desert. There is little rain in Arizona and few lakes. How in the world, then, did the sedimentary rock in the Grand Canyon get laid down by water?

Weathering of Rocks

Once you have been awed by the beauty of the Grand Canyon, and once you have learned about sedimentary rock and its strata, another thought should come to your mind. How did all of that rock in the Grand Canyon get exposed? After all, you typically find rock *underneath* the soil. Thus, you have to dig in order to get to the rock. Why, then, is the sedimentary rock in the Grand Canyon exposed?

The answer to that question begins with *weathering*. Remember, sedimentary rock forms when sediments are laid down and then, by chemical reactions, heat, and pressure, those sediments fuse to form rock. Well, if sediments can form rocks, doesn't it make sense that rocks can be turned back into sediments? We call that process **weathering**.

Weathering - The process by which rocks are broken down by the forces of nature

There are two types of weathering: **physical weathering** and **chemical weathering**. I want to give you examples of each, and the best way to do that is with some experiments.

EXPERIMENT 6.3

Physical Weathering: The Power of Plants

Supplies:

- Plaster of Paris
- A medium or large margarine tub
- A few lima beans
- Water
- Paper towels

Introduction - Plants have the power to break down rocks. This experiment will demonstrate that power to you.

Procedure:

A. Mix up the plaster of Paris like the instructions tell you to, so that you get a nice, creamy mixture.
B. Pour the plaster into the margarine tub until it is about halfway full.
C. Right away, place a few lima beans into the plaster. They should sink into it a little.
D. Allow the plaster to dry. This will take a while. You can start the next experiment while you wait for the plaster to dry.
E. Once the plaster has dried, fold a paper towel so that it will fit in the tub, covering the beans and plaster.
F. Wet the paper towel and place it in the tub so that the beans are all covered.
G. Place the tub near a window and periodically check to make sure the paper towel stays wet. If it gets dry, wet it again.
H. Every day, pull the paper towel up and check on the beans.
I. What happens to the plaster when the beans sprout?

EXPERIMENT 6.4
Chemical Weathering

Supplies:

- Vinegar
- A large glass
- A limestone rock (Most gravel is limestone. You can also go to a home improvement store's garden section and specifically ask for limestone. The rock needs to be small enough to fit in the glass)
- Some steel wool
- A small bowl

Introduction - Rocks can be broken down by chemical weathering. This experiment will show you two such processes.

Procedure:

A. Take the rock and put it in the large glass.
B. Fill the glass 3/4 of the way with vinegar.
C. Watch the rock for a few minutes. You should eventually see tiny bubbles forming around the rock and rising in the vinegar. These bubble are the result of a chemical reaction that is occurring between the vinegar and the lime in the limestone.
D. Let the glass sit overnight.
E. Place a sample of the steel wool in the bowl.
F. Pour vinegar over the steel wool. Pour in enough vinegar so that about half of the steel wool is soaking in it.
G. Let the bowl and steel wool sit.
H. A few times throughout the evening, turn the steel wool so that the other half soaks in the vinegar.
I. In the morning, examine the glass with the rock in it. Swirl the vinegar around a bit. You should see sediments in the vinegar. Those sediments have come from the rock.
J. Now examine the steel wool. What do you see floating in the vinegar?
K. Clean everything up.

Although Experiment 6.3 will take a while to finish, you will eventually see that as the beans sprout, the plaster will crack and break into pieces. This is an example of physical weathering. The plaster is an example of sedimentary rock. As plants grow on and near sedimentary rock, the roots of those plants will sink into the sedimentary rock, trying to get nutrients for the plant. The roots are strong enough to break the rock apart, turning sedimentary rock back into sediments.

There are other types of physical weathering as well. When wind picks up sand and other gritty materials and slams them into rocks, the rocks will wear away. That's another example of physical weathering. Changing temperatures also cause physical weathering. When rocks heat up, they expand. When they cool, they contract. Constant changes in temperature cause the rocks to expand and contract over and over again. This stresses rocks, causing them to crack and break. These processes and many others tend to break rocks down into sediments.

Experiment 6.4 provides you with two examples of chemical weathering. In the first example, you saw how vinegar can break down limestone into sediments. This is the result of a chemical reaction between the vinegar and the lime in the limestone. As you will learn more in biology and chemistry, vinegar is a weak acid. Lime reacts with vinegar to make carbon dioxide (a gas) and other chemicals. In your experiment, you saw the carbon dioxide in the form of bubbles that were coming out of the rock. As this chemical reaction occurred, the rock started getting broken down. The sediment you saw in your experiment was the result of that breakdown.

Another example of chemical weathering was demonstrated by the steel wool. Steel wool is made mostly of iron, which tends to rust. The vinegar in the experiment increased the speed at which the iron in the steel wool rusted, and in the end, some of the steel wool turned into an orange powder, which is commonly called "rust." There are many rocks in the earth's crust that have iron in them. As that iron rusts, it crumbles into a powder. Much of the red color that you see in Figures 6.1 and 6.2 come from this process. Well, as the iron in the rock crumbles, that makes the portions of the rock surrounding the iron crumble as well. Once again, the result is that rock breaks down.

Now wait a minute, you might be saying. There isn't a LOT of vinegar in the desert! How can Experiment 6.4 be an example of the kind of weathering that takes place in the Grand Canyon? Well, remember what I told you vinegar is. It is a weak acid. It turns out that the rain which falls from the sky is also weakly acidic. You will learn more about that when you take chemistry. Thus, the vinegar in your experiment was just a simulation of rainwater. Now rainwater is not as acidic as vinegar, but it is still acidic. The increased acidity of the vinegar just made the chemical weathering occur faster in your experiment than it occurs naturally.

In the end, then, the weak acidity of natural rainwater can cause chemical weathering, which breaks down rocks. Chemical weathering and physical weathering, then, break down rocks into sediments. Although it is probably easy to see that these processes break down sedimentary rock, they also break down igneous rock.

Can you see the difference between chemical and physical weathering? In physical weathering, the rocks get broken down, but the little pieces of rock that result still have the same basic composition as the rock had originally. After all, in Experiment 6.3, the plants broke the plaster into small bits of plaster. Thus, before the weathering you had plaster. After the weathering you also had plaster; the plaster was just in smaller pieces. In chemical weathering, the *composition* of the rock changes. In Experiment 6.4, the lime in limestone was turned into carbon dioxide bubbles and other chemicals. The sediment left over in the vinegar no longer had lime in it. Thus, any rock formed by these sediments would not be limestone any more. The same can be said about what happened to the steel wool. The steel wool turned into rust and was no longer steel.

One way to think about the difference between physical weathering and chemical weathering is to think about the sediments that remain after the weathering. If the sediments that remain are the same as the original rock but just smaller pieces, that tells you the rock underwent physical weathering. If the sediments that remain have a different composition than the original rock, that tells you the rock underwent chemical weathering.

Using that kind of thinking, you can tell that the plaster in Experiment 6.3 underwent physical weathering because the only difference between the plaster before the weathering and after the weathering was the size of the plaster pieces. Before the weathering, you had one piece of plaster. After the weathering, you had many, many small chunks of plaster. In Experiment 6.4, the rock was limestone before the weathering, but the lime in the limestone turned into gas (as evidenced by the bubbles) and other chemicals as a result of the weathering. Since the resulting sediments no longer had lime in them, they were *different in composition* than the original limestone, which had lime in it.

ON YOUR OWN

6.5 A granite rock made of quartz, feldspar, and mica undergoes weathering. Over time, it slowly changes into sand, clay, and other sediments. Did it undergo chemical weathering or physical weathering?

6.6 A rock breaks into little pieces after a larger rock falls on it. Did the rock undergo physical weathering or chemical weathering?

Erosion

Weathering is the first step in the process that causes rocks to become exposed as are those in the Grand Canyon. The next step in the process is **erosion**.

Erosion - The process by which sediments and rock fragments are carried away by wind or rain

As was the case with weathering, erosion is best demonstrated by experiment.

EXPERIMENT 6.5
Erosion

Supplies:

- A shoebox
- A gardener's spade (or something else you can use to dig with)

- Scissors
- A spot in the yard in which you can dig
- A water hose and water
- A large rock

Introduction - This experiment demonstrates erosion and two of the major factors that affect it.

Procedure:

A. On one of the short sides of the shoebox, cut out a triangle that is wide at the top of the box and narrows down to a point 1/2 of the way down the side. Your shoebox should look like this:

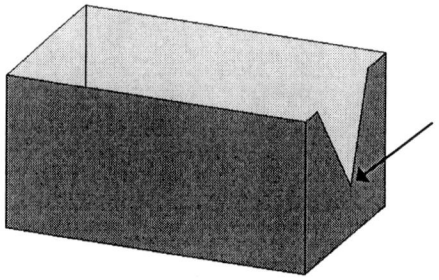

B. Ask your parents where you can dig in the yard. You will end up replacing what you dig up, but it won't look exactly the same as it did before.
C. Take the spade and peel off a layer of sod from the ground. What you want is the grass, roots, and soil that make up the top portion of the yard. You can get what you need by shoving the spade into the ground just under the grass roots and pulling up the soil, roots, and grass in one clump. You want to gather enough to cover the bottom of the box. You need not try to get all of that in one clump of sod. Get several clumps that, when laid down in the box, will cover the bottom. DO NOT actually put the sod in the box yet. Just peel it off and set it aside.
D. In the area from which you just pulled the sod, the soil underneath the grass should be exposed. Begin filling the box with that soil. Fill the box so that you have an even layer of soil in the box all of the way up to the point of the triangle that cut out earlier.
E. Now use the rock to prop up the end of the box that does not have the triangle cut out of it. This will make the soil in the box slope towards the triangle.
F. Turn on the hose so that it emits a constant, slow stream of water.
G. Hold the hose a few inches above the box near the propped-up end, so that the water strikes the soil and runs down the slope towards the triangle.
H. Hold the hose there for a few moments and observe what happens. Notice how the water forms gullies in the dirt.
I. Increase the speed of the water coming out of the hose and see how that affects the gullies being formed in the dirt.
J. After a while, stop running the hose and tilt the shoebox some more so that the excess water runs out of the box.
K. Use the spade to even out the soil so that there are no gullies and the surface is reasonably flat.

L. Now place the sod that you collected in step (C) onto the top of the soil. Arrange it so that sod covers all of the soil, leaving no bare soil exposed.
M. Pat the sod down with the spade so that it sits securely on the soil.
N. Repeat steps (E) - (I) again, and note the difference that the sod makes.
O. Return the soil to the hole that you dug and then pat the sod on top to cover the soil. That way, the part of the yard that you dug up won't look so bad.
P. Clean yourself and everything else up.

What you saw in the first part of the experiment is an example of erosion. Imagine if the soil you used in the experiment were weathered rocks rather than soil. As water ran over the weathered rocks, it would carry away the sediments formed by weathering, forming gullies in the rocks. That's (most likely) how the Grand Canyon was formed. Running water eroded the rock, digging a gully in the ground, exposing the beauty of the rocks below. Notice that in the experiment, the speed of the water strongly affected the speed at which the gully was dug out. Slow-moving water dug the gully slowly, while fast-moving water dug the gully much more quickly. That point will become important later on when I compare uniformitarianism to catastrophism.

What did you notice in the second part of the experiment? The addition of grass on top of the soil kept the water from digging a gully, right? That's because the roots of plants tend to hold soil together, and erosion cannot take the soil away. Notice that in the area of the Grand Canyon, there are not a lot of plants. Thus, erosion could work very well, cutting out the magnificent trench that tourists from around the world come to admire!

Although running water in streams, rivers, and the like is the most common agent of erosion, there are others. Rain can be an agent of erosion. As raindrops strike soil and rock, they hit hard. The hit of a raindrop can weather a tiny part of a rock, and then the flow of rainwater will carry away the sediment made from that physical weathering. Wind can also weather and erode a rock. The physical force of windborne particles can weather a rock, and the motion of the wind can pick up the sediment formed and whisk it away.

Since erosion by water is the most common form of erosion, it is worth concentrating on for a moment. One thing you might ask yourself is what happens to the sediments that are eroded by water? Well, that depends on what kind of water did the eroding in the first place. Suppose, for example, a river is rushing over some weathered rocks. The river picks up the sediments and carries them away. Where do they go? Well, a river has to end somewhere. Many rivers dump their water into a large lake or ocean. That's typically where the sediments carried by a river end up.

Consider, for example, the Nile River. The Nile is the longest river in the world, measuring 4160 miles in length from its beginning in Burundi to the Mediterranean Sea, where it dumps its water. The river carries an enormous amount of water, especially in the summer, when heavy rains in that region of the world cause the river to flood its banks every year. At the point where the Nile reaches the Mediterranean Sea, it deposits its sediments in a fan-shaped area called the river's **delta**.

Photo from the MasterClips collection

FIGURE 6.4

Satellite Photo of the Nile River's Delta at the Mediterranean Sea

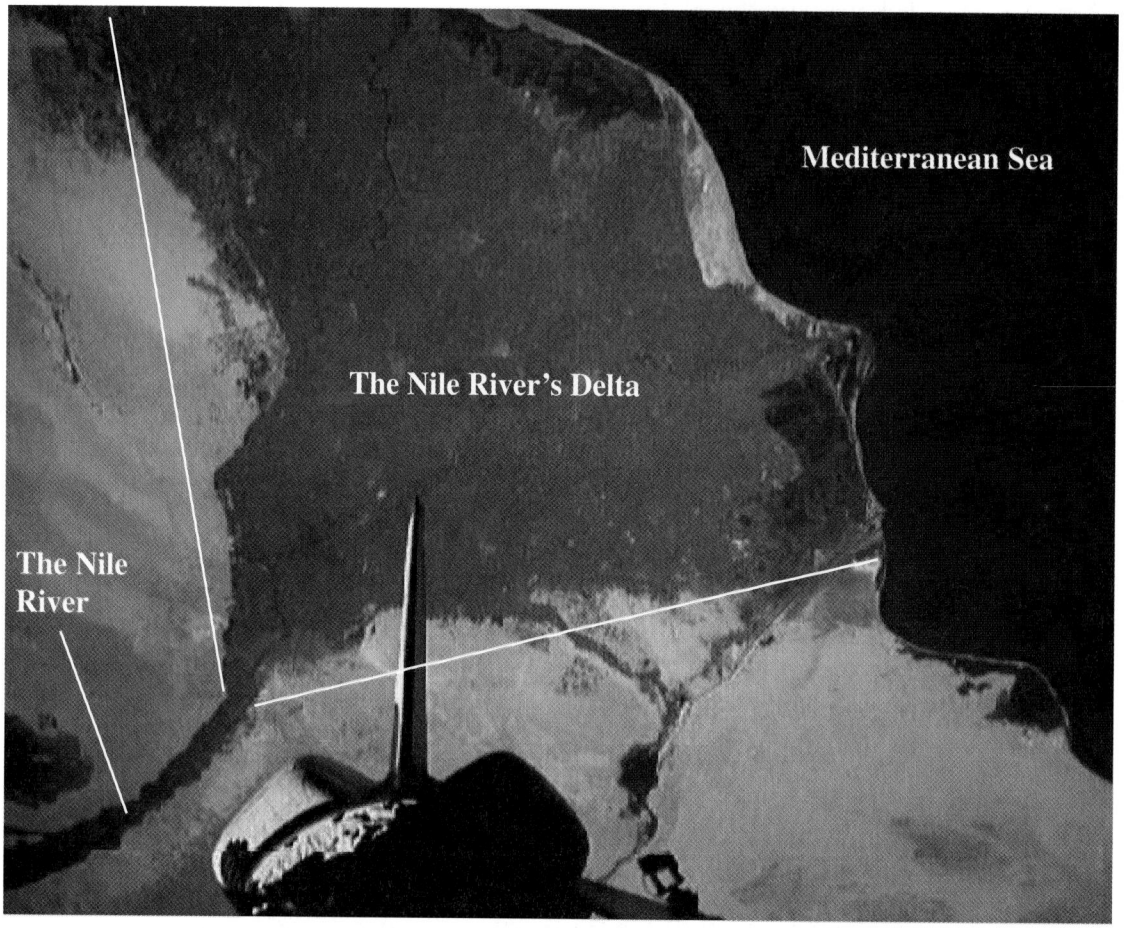

Many of the sediments carried along by rivers, then, end up getting deposited at the river's delta. Some make it past the delta and flow into the lake or sea that the river dumps into.

What about sediments in other bodies of water? When rain erodes sediments into lakes and the ocean, the sediments typically settle to the bottom of the lake or ocean. In the case of oceans, the tide might bring some sediments in and deposit them on the shore. That's where the sand comes from on the sea shore. That sand was either eroded into an ocean by rainwater or rivers or formed in the ocean itself as the result of certain chemical processes. When the tide comes in, some of that sand is deposited on the shore, forming a sandy beach.

Erosion, then, is Creation's way of "recycling" sediments. Rivers, rains, winds, etc. erode rocks that have been weathered into sediments. Those sediments then get deposited in river deltas, at the bottoms of lakes or oceans, on the shore of the oceans, etc. Those sediments, if laid down properly under the right conditions, might eventually form sedimentary rock, which might weather and get eroded again, and so on, and so on!

Although I have concentrated on the kind of erosion that occurs on the surface of the earth, there is also a great deal of erosion that occurs underground. As you will learn in physical science, a large fraction of earth's water actually flows underground. This **groundwater** can also erode rock. The result is, of course, a **cavern**. Caverns often form giant mazes under the earth which stretch for miles in all directions. In the Kentucky area of the United States, for example, there is a system of interconnected caverns that runs for a total length of 348 miles!

Caverns are often damp places. Many contain streams or lakes, and most have groundwater seeping into them from the ceiling. This water drips down to the floor of the cave. Often, as the drip forms on the ceiling, a small amount of sediment (usually calcium carbonate) is deposited on the ceiling. When the drop hits the floor, a bit of sediment might be deposited as well. Eventually, those deposits build up, sometimes forming beautiful structures in the cave.

Photo from the MasterClips collection

FIGURE 6.5

Stalactites, Stalagmites, and Columns in a Cave

When the deposits start on the ceiling and form an icicle-like structure hanging down, the structure is called a **stalactite** (stuh lak' tite). When the deposits form a structure that rises from the ground, the structure is called a **stalagmite** (stuh lag' myt). If a stalactite and stalagmite meet and form a single structure, it is called a **column**.

Caves are not the only place that stalactites, stalagmites, and columns form. Many statues made out of stone (like the Lincoln Memorial, for example) have basements underneath them.

As years of rain have eroded those statues or monuments and soaked into their basements, stalactites and stalagmites have formed there. Those stalactites and stalagmites show how powerful a force erosion can be!

ON YOUR OWN

6.7 Although erosion can form beautiful views like the Grand Canyon, it can also be a problem. Suppose, for example, a house is built near the edge of a steep hill. Heavy rains can erode the soil and rock on the hillside, taking away the support of the house and potentially causing the house to fall down the side of the hill. What could the owner of the house do to help reduce the amount of hillside erosion?

6.8 Although most caverns are underground, there are some that have been cut into mountains and thus are not really underground. Suppose you were to walk into a large cavern that was eroded in a desert mountain. Would you expect to see many stalactites or stalagmites?

Bringing It All Together: The Basic Structure of the Grand Canyon

Now that you have learned the basics of sedimentary rock, weathering, and erosion, it is time to look at the Grand Canyon in a bit more detail. Examine Figure 6.6.

FIGURE 6.6

Illus. by Megan Whitaker

A 3-Dimensional Sketch of a Portion of the Grand Canyon

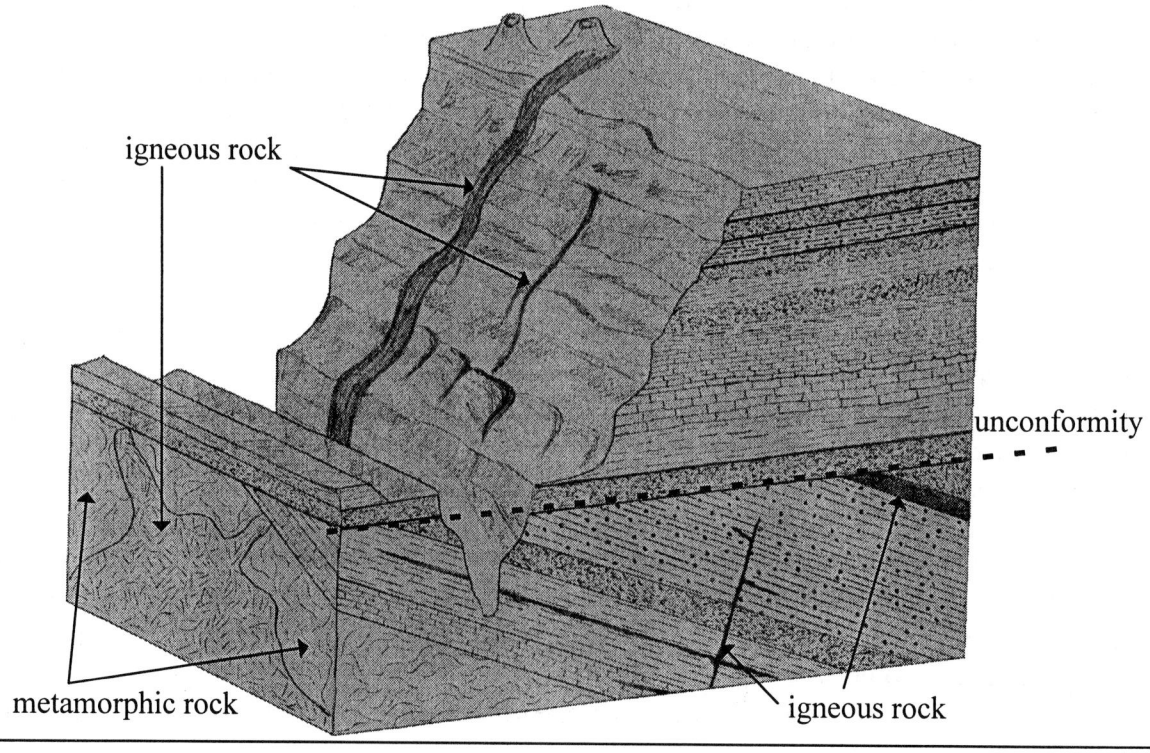

The first thing that you should notice from the figure is that the rocks which make up the Grand Canyon are stratified. The igneous and metamorphic rocks are indicated in the figure. Any strata that are not pointed out are of sedimentary rock. Thus, the majority of rock in the Grand Canyon is sedimentary. Notice the heavy, dashed line in the figure. I have labeled it with the word "unconformity." Above that dashed line, the layers of sedimentary rock lie horizontally, as you saw in Figure 6.1. Below that line, however, the rock strata seem tilted. That line is called an **unconformity**.

Unconformity - A surface of erosion that separates one layer of rock from another

There are more unconformities in the Grand Canyon than the one pointed out in the figure, but it is by far the most striking. It is striking because the rocks below are tilted relative to the rocks above. That particular kind of unconformity is called an **angular unconformity**. Because it is so striking, this unconformity is often called the **Great Unconformity** of the Grand Canyon.

There are three other types of unconformities that geologists recognize. When stratified layers rest on top of unstratified layers, the unconformity that lies between them is called a **nonconformity**. The separation between the metamorphic rock and the first layer of sedimentary rock at the bottom of the figure is an example of a nonconformity. There are also **disconformities**, where there are parallel, stratified rock layers above and below the unconformity, but there is a clear surface of erosion between them. The final type of unconformity is a bit strange. Sometimes there is a layer of rock that geologists *believe* contains an unconformity, but it cannot be identified. Such unidentifiable unconformities are called **paraconformities**. You will hear more about paraconformities in Module #8.

It is important that you understand what an unconformity is and what it is not. When you performed Experiment 6.2, you were able to see strata form out of the various sediments in the jar. Although there were clear differences between each layer, there were no unconformities between the layers. An unconformity must be a surface that has been eroded. Since the layers were deposited right on top of each other, and since there was no rushing water or blowing wind to erode the surface of one layer before the other was laid down, there were no unconformities. Thus, an unconformity is more than just a separation between layers of rock. It is a separation that has been eroded.

What formed the Great Unconformity in the Grand Canyon? Well, uniformitarians and catastrophists argue over the details, but they both agree that the rocks below the angular conformity were tilted by some major event like an earthquake, and then the rocks above the angular unconformity were laid down. I will discuss this more when I compare and contrast uniformitarianism and catastrophism.

The next thing I want you to notice in the figure is the igneous rock pointed out in the center of the figure at the bottom. These "veins" of igneous rock shoot right through several layers of sedimentary rock. This is called an **intrusion**, and it forms when magma from underneath the sedimentary rock gets injected in the cracks and fissures of the sedimentary rock. In technical terms, the "veins" of igneous rock that run in the same direction of the strata are called **sills**. The "veins" that run perpendicular to that direction are usually called **dikes**. Now I want you to see where the other major igneous rock formation is. It is on the surface of the Grand Canyon and, as you might have guessed, it is the result of volcanic activity.

Notice that the rocks in the Grand Canyon tend to fall into four basic groups. First, there are the igneous and metamorphic rocks that form the base of the canyon. Then, there is the group of sedimentary (and one layer of igneous) rock that form strata which lie below the unconformity pointed out in the figure. The third group of rocks is the sedimentary rock that is laid down in horizontal strata. Finally, there are the igneous rocks formed at the surface due to volcanic activity. The explanation of how these four groups came to be is a matter of lively debate between uniformitarians and catastrophists. When I compare and contrast those views in the next module, you will see what I mean.

The Grand Canyon is a spectacular sight in the United States, and few other sites can match its beauty and grandeur. The reason I highlighted it here is that it is a good general representation of the geological characteristics of our planet. It contains all of the three basic rock types (igneous, metamorphic, and sedimentary), it has many, many strata, and it has several unconformities, one of which is rather striking. Thus, it contains all of the major geological features that you will find on the earth.

In the next module, I will discuss the fossils that we find in rocks like those of the Grand Canyon. Those fossils tell us a lot about the history of life, but they can also tell us a lot about geology itself. Then, in the next module, I will sum all of this up with a comparison between the uniformitarian view of life's history and the catastrophism view. Hopefully, this will give you an idea of how fascinating the study of life's history is!

ON YOUR OWN

6.9 On the top, right-hand side of Figure 6.6, there in an unconformity between the very top layer of sedimentary rock and the layer right below it. What kind of unconformity is it?

6.10 Assuming that the principle of superposition is true, which group of rocks is older: the sedimentary rocks that have horizontal strata or the rocks below the angular unconformity?

ANSWERS TO THE ON YOUR OWN PROBLEMS

6.1 It is impossible to believe in a young earth with the uniformitarianism approach. The definition itself states that millions of years are assumed. It is possible to believe in a young earth with the catastrophism approach. Catastrophes can mold the geological features of the earth very quickly. It is possible to believe in a billions of years old earth with the uniformitarian approach. In fact, uniformitarians *must* believe in a very, very old earth. It is possible to believe in a billions of years old earth with the catastrophism approach. Although catastrophes cause big changes quickly, there could have been several that occurred millions or billions of years apart from one another.

6.2 Pictures (a) and (d) are of minerals while (b) and (c) are of rocks. Notice the sharp, geometric shapes in (a) and (d). That is indicative of crystals, which tend to be minerals.

6.3 Metamorphic rock is the hardest kind of rock, as it has been formed in extreme pressures. Thus, the first is metamorphic and the second is igneous.

6.4 There is not a lot of water in Arizona *now*, but at sometime or times in the past, there could have been water there. You have already learned that there is a lot of evidence for the fact that a worldwide flood occurred. There certainly would have been water in Arizona then!

6.5 This is an example of chemical weathering. The granite rock was made of three substances, and the sediments are three different substances. Thus, the composition changed, and that makes it chemical weathering.

6.6 This is an example of physical weathering. The only difference between before and after the weathering is the size of the rock. The sediments are just little versions of the original rock, so no change in composition occurred.

6.7 The home owner could plant a lot of plants on the hillside. As your experiment showed, plants tend to reduce the effects of erosion.

6.8 Remember that stalactites and stalagmites form as the result of groundwater that seeps in the ceiling of a cave and drips down. If the cave is in a mountain, there will not be any underground water running over it. Thus, you would not expect stalactites and stalagmites.

6.9 This is a disconformity. The strata are both horizontal.

6.10 The rocks below the angular unconformity are older according to the Principle of Superposition, because they are below the other rocks.

STUDY GUIDE FOR MODULE #6

1. Define the following terms:

a. Catastrophism
b. Uniformitarianism
c. Humus
d. Minerals
e. Weathering
f. Erosion
g. Unconformity

2. Which hypothesis (uniformitarianism or catastrophism) requires that the earth be billions of years old?

3. What are the three basic types of rocks?

4. How is each type of rock mentioned in #3 formed?

5. What agent is responsible for laying down most of the sedimentary rock that we see today?

6. A rock in the desert is constantly bombarded by bits of sand that are carried on the wind. The sand hits the rock so hard sometimes that tiny chips of the rock are broken off. As time goes on, the constant beating of the sand on the rock wears the rock down, and it gets much smaller. Has the rock experienced physical or chemical weathering?

7. When limestone is exposed to weakly acidic water, it breaks down, forming a gas in the process. Is this chemical or physical weathering?

8. A geologist is comparing the erosion that occurs as a result of two different rivers. The first river flows quickly while the second flows slowly. Which river do you expect to cause the most erosion?

9. Two hillsides in the same community experience a very heavy rain. The first hillside is covered with grass and flowers, while the second is mostly bare. Which hillside will experience the most erosion?

10. Where do a large part of the sediments carried by a river end up?

11. What causes an underground cavern to form?

12. What is the difference between a stalactite and a stalagmite?

13. What causes stalactites and stalagmites to form?

Questions 14 - 18 refer to the diagram below:

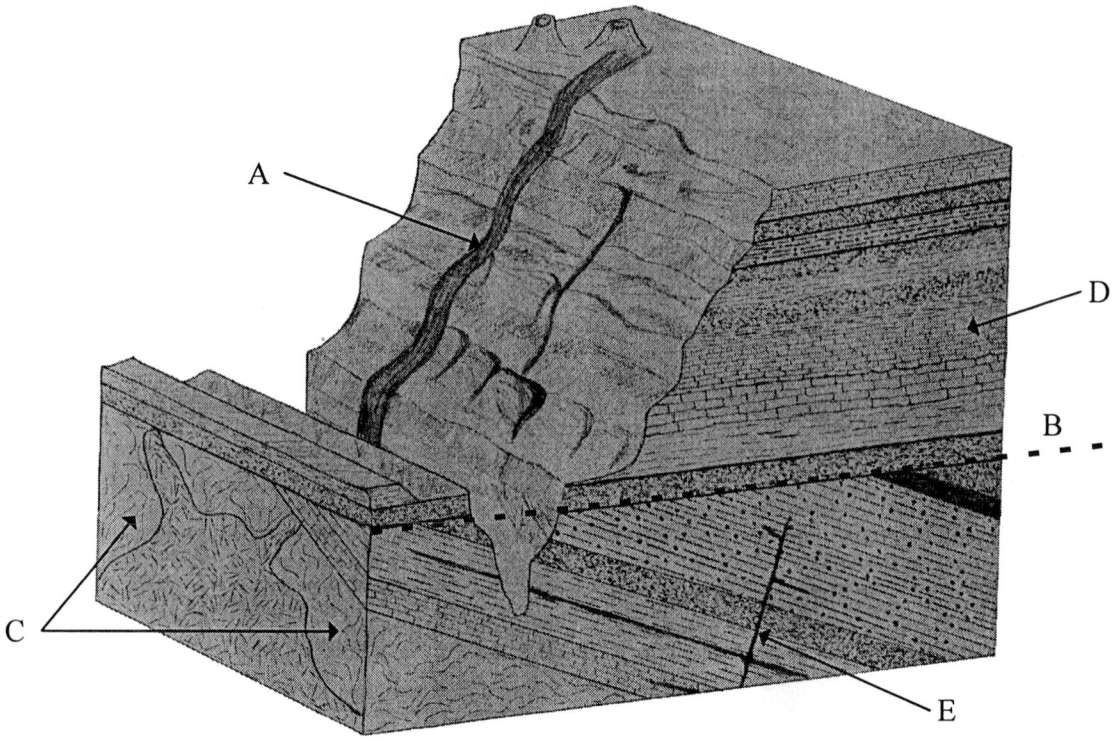

14. Which letter identifies metamorphic rock?

15. Which two letters identify igneous rock?

16. Which letter identifies sedimentary rock?

17. Which letter identifies an unconformity? What kind of unconformity is it?

18. Which letter identifies an intrusion?

Module #7 – The Fossil Record

Introduction

Now that you have learned some of the basic types and formations of the rocks in the earth's crust, it is time to look inside those rocks and see what they contain. As you have already learned, some rocks contain minerals. Minerals are interesting to study and some (like diamonds and rubies) are considered precious. From a scientific point of view, however, some rocks contain even more precious items: fossils.

As you already know, fossils are the preserved remains of once-living plants and animals. You've learned that definition already, but you might have overlooked the implication of one of the words in that definition: *preserved.* What happens when a plant or animal dies? Typically, it *decomposes*. If you have a garden, you might have even seen this process in action. Gardeners will often gather leaves in the fall and spread them over the area in which they want to plant a garden next spring. Over the course of the winter, many of the leaves will decompose, forming the nutritious humus that comprises a good fraction of the topsoil. This humus makes the soil more fertile, which can result in a more lush garden.

Remember, leaves are part of a living plant. When they fall off the plant, they die and eventually decompose to form nutritious topsoil. Although you have probably not witnessed it firsthand, the same thing happens to animals when they die. Their skin, hair or feathers, organs, and even their bones eventually decompose and form rich humus which will be later used by plants as a source of nutrition. When you take biology, you will find out that there are all sorts of living organisms (called "decomposers") which have been created by God for the specific purpose of aiding this decomposition process.

If you think about it, then, the formation of a fossil is an exception to the general rule of nature. In general, dead plants and animals are not preserved. Instead, they decompose. When you find the preserved remains of a plant or animal, then, you know that there must be something special about the way in which it was formed. The special conditions which lead to fossil formation are quite rare; thus, only a tiny fraction of plants and animals gets fossilized. The vast majority simply decompose. In the next few sections, I want to discuss the various special conditions which can lead to the formation of a fossil.

The Making of Fossils Part 1: Casts and Molds

The most common means by which a dead plant or animal can be preserved is by the formation of a **mold** and the making of a **cast**. In this process, the plant or animal itself is not actually preserved. Instead, rocks are formed in the image of the plant or animal. The best way to understand this process is to actually do it yourself.

EXPERIMENT 7.1
Making a Fossil Cast

Supplies:

- Modeling clay
- Plaster of Paris
- A paper plate
- A shell or something else with a distinctive shape or design
- Vaseline® or another petroleum jelly

Introduction - Many fossils form by a natural process that involves a mold being made and then filled with a substance which hardens into rock. In this experiment, you will use clay as the substance from which the mold is made and plaster as the rock.

Procedure:

A. Cover the outer part of the shell (the part you will fossilize) with Vaseline®.
B. Roll the clay out on the paper plate so that the clay covers an area larger than the shell.
C. Press the outer part of the shell into the clay hard, so that an imprint forms in the clay.
D. Pull the shell away, and you should see a nice impression of the shell in the clay. At this point, you have made a **mold** of the shell.
E. Mix the plaster according to the directions on the package and pour the plaster into the impression. Fill the impression so full that the plaster spills a little over the clay and onto the paper plate.
F. Allow the plaster to harden.
G. Once the plaster has hardened, pull it off of the paper plate and then remove the clay from it. What do you see? This is called a **cast** of the shell.
H. Optional: You can use this method to make a fossil of almost anything. Try making a fossil of your hand, your foot, or anything else that you would like to preserve!
I. Clean everything up.

Believe it or not, the process that you just performed in the experiment happens throughout Creation. Consider, for example, a sea shell that gets buried in sediment. As the sediment hardens and turns to rock, the rock surrounding the shell hardens around the shell. This results in a shell encased in sedimentary rock. As time goes on, water that seeps through the sedimentary rock will weather both the rock and the shell. If the shell is affected by weathering a lot more than the rock, it is possible that the shell will disintegrate before the rock. If this happens, then, you have a **mold** where the shell originally was. This mold, much like the mold you made, will have the general shape and design of the shell.

Sometimes, paleontologists will split open a rock and find an empty mold like this. Other times, the rock weathers away to reveal a portion of the mold. This can tell the paleontologist about the shell that was once there. Although it is possible to find such molds, it is relatively rare. It is much more common for something to fill the mold. For example, other sediments can seep into the sedimentary rock that contains the mold, and those sediments might fill the space left by the mold. As time goes on, those sediments will harden, forming a **cast** of the original shell. In your experiment, the plaster acted in this way. It filled the mold like sediments filling a space in a rock and, when the plaster hardened, a likeness of the shell was made.

In your experiment, then, you first formed a mold by pressing the shell into clay. If you had allowed the clay to harden, you would have had a preserved mold. That would be considered a fossil of the shell. Usually, a mold formed like the one that you made does not last very long. If an animal leaves footprints in mud, for example, you could consider those molds of the animals feet. However, as soon as the next rain comes, those footprints will, most likely, be washed away. Molds formed on the surface of mud or clay, then, rarely are fossilized, because they are likely to erode more quickly than the mud or clay that they were formed in can harden.

This, of course, is not always the case. There are fossil footprints preserved in the geological record. Thus, molds formed on the surface of mud, clay, and sediment *can* become fossilized, but such an occurrence is rather rare. Molds are much more commonly formed when the plant or animal is completely buried in the sediment. That way, the sediment can harden right around the plant or animal, and the resulting mold cannot be eroded very easily.

Once you made your mold, you then filled it with plaster, making a cast. This can happen naturally, as sediments find their way into a mold and then harden. Magma intrusions can also naturally fill a mold, making an igneous cast of the fossil. Although many casts form naturally, sometimes it is useful to make artificial casts. Crime investigators, for example, will make plaster casts of footprints made in the mud near the scene of the crime. Since the footprints in the mud will wash away quickly, making a cast of them will preserve them for use in the crime investigation. Also, paleontologists will often make casts of fossil molds that they find so that the fossils can be studied without handling the molds directly.

Although I talked about casts and molds being formed to fossilize sea shells, virtually any hard remains of a plant or animal can be fossilized in this way. Bones, for example, will often be preserved in casts. Preserved footprints have been found in both cast form and mold form. Typically, hard substances form molds and casts because a hard substance can withstand the pressure of the sediments which surround it without being crushed.

ON YOUR OWN

7.1 Is it possible for a mold to form without a cast? Is it possible for a cast to form without a mold?

The Making of Fossils Part 2: Petrifaction

Another way that the remains of once-living creatures can be preserved is through the process of **petrifaction** (pet truh fak' shun).

Petrifaction - The conversion of organic material into stone

In the definition of mineral, you learned that the term "inorganic" means "not from a living creature." Well, the term "organic" means "from a living creature." Thus, petrifaction is the process by which the remains of a once-living plant or animal are turned into stone.

Petrifaction is the result of a creature's remains being exposed to water that contains a large amount of minerals. As the mineral-rich water swirls around the creature's remains, the organic materials begin to decompose and are replaced by minerals that are deposited into the remains. If this process is allowed to complete, the remains can be entirely replaced and the result is a stony substance that is a replica of the parts of the creature that is being preserved.

Petrifaction works best on the hard remains of a creature, such as bones or wood. The figure below presents an example of the results of petrifaction.

FIGURE 7.1 *Photo from the MasterClips collection*

The Petrified Bones of a Woolly Mammoth

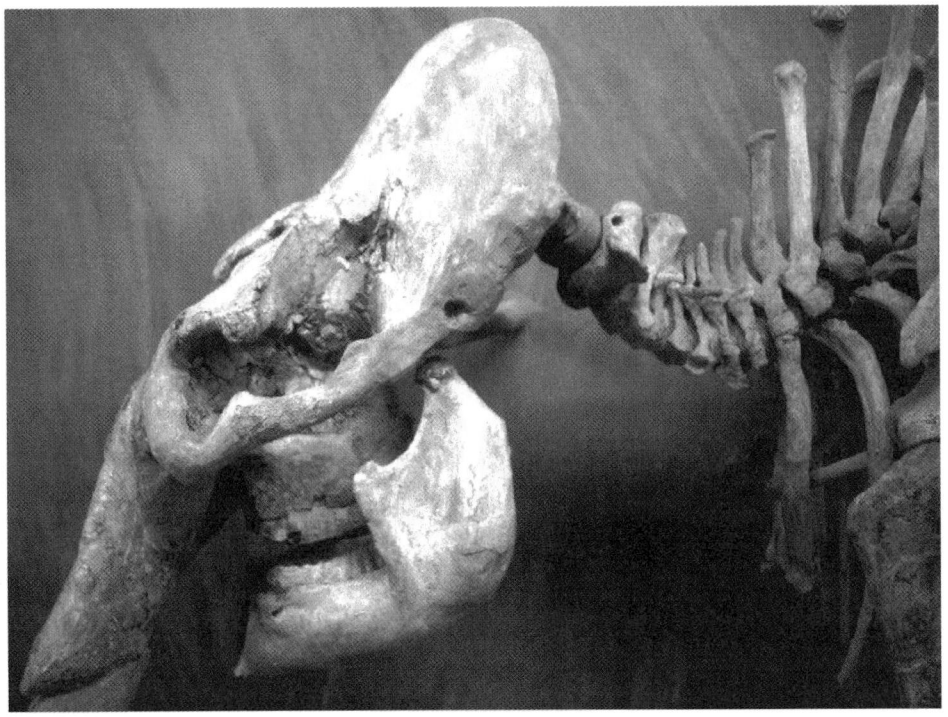

Woolly mammoths are elephant-like animals of which there are no living examples. All that we know about them comes from the study of fossils, such as these petrified bones.

Although the bones in the picture look like real bones, they are actually composed mostly of hardened minerals that replaced the bones long ago.

In certain cases, petrifaction can happen very quickly, faster than the time it takes for the creature being fossilized to decompose. Under these conditions, the minerals can combine with the organic materials in the creature's remains rather than replace them. As a result, the organic materials can be made resistant to decomposition and are therefore preserved. This is especially valuable to paleontologists, because few fossils actually have any of their organic materials preserved. Thus, petrified remains of this kind are considered quite precious!

It is instructive to compare fossils formed by casts to those formed by petrifaction. In each case, you get a hard, stony likeness of the creature's remains. However, it is important to notice the differences between the two. When a mold is formed, the shape of the creature's remains are preserved, as are any obvious bumps or grooves on the surface. When the sediments/magma that fill the mold form the cast, the result is something that has the same shape as the creatures remains as well as the same surface characteristics. The inside of the cast, however, is just solid rock. On the other hand, when petrifaction occurs, the original parts of the remains are either replaced bit-by-bit or are preserved. As a result, you get an actual replica of the creature's remains, including details that are not just on the surface of the remains. This, of course, provides more information to the paleontologist, but it is also a much rarer form of fossilization.

A very famous example of petrifaction in the United States exists in Yellowstone National Park in the state of Wyoming. In an area called "specimen ridge," there are many examples of petrified tree trunks. From a distance, they appear to be the normal kind of tree trunk that results after someone has cut down a tree. When you touch them, however, they feel like solid rock. That's because they have been petrified.

ON YOUR OWN

7.2 The Petrified Forest is part of a United States national park in Arizona. It is filled with petrified wood. Although Arizona is now much like a desert, what do we know must have been there at one time?

The Making of Fossils Part 3: Carbonate Residues and Impressions

So far, I have discussed two means of fossilization. These processes, as I have already stated, tend to preserve the hard remains of plants and animals such as wood, bones, or shells. The process that I want to discuss here can preserve much more delicate remains, examples of which are shown in the figure below.

Photos courtesy of Creation Ex Nihilo *magazine*

FIGURE 7.2
A Carbonate Residue and an Impression

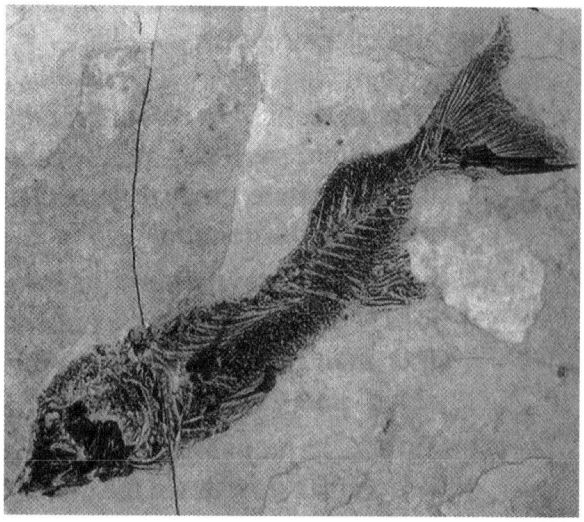

A Carbonate Residue of a Fish

An Impression of a Jellyfish

Notice what we have in both of these fossils. Instead of having a replica of the creatures' remains, we have what almost appear to be *drawings* of those remains. These apparent drawings are made in solid stone! How in the world did that happen?

These kinds of fossils form when a plant or animal is buried in sediment and then that sediment experiences a lot of pressure. When this happens, the liquids and gases in the creature's remains can be forced right out into the surrounding sediments. Since water makes up a large part of any creature (the human body is about 66% water, for example), this means the majority of the creature's remains are lost. What's left is a thin, filmy residue composed mostly of carbon. This thin, filmy residue, however, forms a detailed "picture" of the creature. When the residue is still a part of the fossil, it is called a **carbonate residue**. When the film is gone and just the impression of the film is left, the fossil is called, reasonably enough, an **impression**.

Carbonate residues and impressions can preserve the remains of creatures which cannot be preserved any other way. Consider the jellyfish fossil shown in Figure 7.2. As its name implies, a jellyfish is very soft. In fact, it has no hard, solid parts such as bones or shells. As a result, it will never form a mold, because sediments would just crush it when they buried it. In the same way, jellyfish will rarely petrify because they are so soft that they decompose much faster than their remains can be replaced by minerals. Impressions, then, are the most common means of fossilization for soft, delicate creatures.

Some carbonate residues are so incredibly well-preserved that the film can actually be lifted off of the rock and examined! This allows paleontologists to learn quite a bit about the creature that has been fossilized. Both carbonate residues and impressions have been found with such detail that even the fine veins of a leaf can be seen!

ON YOUR OWN

7.3 Would paleontologists tend to find impressions and carbonate residues in strata near the top or near the bottom of a group of stratified rocks?

The Making of Fossils Part 4: Avoiding Decomposition

Although all of the fossilization processes I have discussed so far will preserve *parts of* or the *major features of* a dead plant or animal, none of them produce ideal specimens for a paleontologist to study. Molds, casts, and petrifaction typically preserve only the "hard" parts of a plant or animal such as wood, shells, and bones. Carbonate residues and impressions can provide stunning detail as to what a plant or animal looked like, but little of the actual plant or animal is left behind. In the end, then, all of these fossils give the paleontologist information, but the information is scant at best. A living creature is full of soft tissue, organs, skin, hair, etc. that are rarely fossilized by any of these means. Without being able to analyze these parts of a plant or animal, our knowledge of that creature will always be incomplete.

Even though *most* fossils do not contain complete information about the creature that has been fossilized, there are a few strikingly spectacular specimens that come close. For example, in 1976 in a remote area of Siberia, the preserved remains of a baby mammoth were found. As mentioned in the caption to Figure 7.1, we have never found a living example of a mammoth, but we know that they existed from fossilized remains like those shown in Figure 7.1. Thus, all that we know about the mammoth comes from fossils. The more preserved a fossil mammoth is, then, the more we stand to learn about these huge creatures that once walked the face of the earth.

The fossil found in Siberia in 1976 was remarkable in that skin, hair, and many soft body parts that normally are not preserved were very well-preserved. Why? Well, the mammoth was found inside a tomb of frozen mud. The ice that surrounded the mammoth's remains protected it from the organisms that aid in decomposition, and the frigid temperature slowed down many of the chemical reactions that lead organic matter to decompose. In the end, then, the mammoth's remains were preserved because it was frozen, much like we preserve food by putting it in the freezer.

Such fossils are extremely rare but, when found, they aid paleontologists tremendously in learning about the plants and animals that lived on this earth before us. Now you might wonder how a mammoth could become surrounded by frozen mud. You can learn one explanation by performing the following experiment.

EXPERIMENT 7.2
Sinking in Ice

Supplies:

- A plastic margarine tub
- Water
- A rock that will fit in the tub with a lot of room to spare
- A freezer

Introduction - This experiment will show you how dead plants and animals can end up frozen solid.

Procedure:

A. Fill the margarine tub halfway with water.
B. Sit the tub in the freezer and wait until the water is frozen solid.
C. Once the water is frozen solid, put the rock on top of the ice in the center of the tub. Don't remove the tub from the freezer unless you have to. Just place the rock on the ice and close the door again.
D. In about two hours, go and check on the experiment. Pull the tub out of the freezer and look at the rock. What has happened?
E. Take hold of the rock and try to lift it off of the ice. What happens?

What happened in the experiment? If everything went well, you should have seen that the rock had begun to sink into the ice. If you tried to lift the rock, the entire tub would lift as well, because the rock seemed embedded in the ice.

How did the rock sink in the ice? Well, ice has a property that is very rare in Creation. When you push down on ice, it melts. No other naturally-occurring substance on earth does this. For all other substances, when you apply pressure, the substance tends to turn solid. When you apply pressure to ice, however, it turns into liquid water. Thus, when you set the rock on the ice, the weight of the rock pushed down on the ice, and the ice right under the rock turned into liquid water. The water was squeezed out from under the rock by the weight of the rock and, as soon as it came out from under the rock, it froze again.

This happened over and over again. The rock turned the ice directly underneath it to water, the water was squished out from under the rock, and the water froze again right away. This continual melting and moving of water formed a "hole" in the ice right underneath the rock, and the rock just settled into it. Thus, the rock's weight simply dug the rock into the ice.

When the baby mammoth that was discovered in Siberia died, it might have died on frozen mud. As time went on, the mammoth might have begun to sink into the ice just like the rock in your experiment. At the same time, snow might have accumulated over the mammoth, covering it. This slowed the decomposition of the mammoth, until it finally was surrounded by ice and the entombment was complete. Of course, that's just one way it might have happened. The mammoth could also have been covered with mud in a massive flood and then frozen solid afterwards. There are probably more explanations as well.

Ice tombs like the one that enclosed the baby mammoth provide excellent preservation, but they are not the only way to get beautifully-preserved fossils. Consider, for example, the fossil in the figure below.

Photo by Joachim Scheven
Courtesy of LEBENDIGE VORWELT *museum*

FIGURE 7.3
A Honeypot Ant in Amber

This remarkable specimen is encased in **amber**, which is a kind of **resin**.

Resin - A sticky, liquid substance that usually hardens when exposed to air

Many plants emit resin as a protective coating. As far as we know, the specific resin that forms amber is not emitted by any plants which are alive today. However, plants alive in earth's past obviously emitted the resin which forms amber. The ant in the figure above was, most likely, caught in the sticky liquid as it was crawling along the plant. As the plant emitted more resin, the ant was eventually covered by resin. When the resin hardened, the ant was "sealed in."

The sealed amber tomb has preserved the ant very well. You must realize, however, that although the ant appears to be intact, it is definitely not. Amber preserves the creatures entombed in it because once it hardens, amber does not allow in any of the creatures that aid decomposition. Nevertheless, the chemicals that make up this ant have been decomposing since the ant first died. Thus, many of the ant's internal structures are already completely decomposed. Nevertheless, because no creatures can aid the decomposition, it is very slow, and many parts of the ant do remain intact.

Paleontologists have actually succeeded in extracting DNA from some insects fossilized in amber. As you will learn in biology class, DNA is a huge molecule that exists in every living creature. The molecule contains all of the information that a living creature needs to grow, develop, and live. Needless to say, then, the DNA extracted from insects fossilized in amber can tell us a lot about what those insects were like in the past. Interestingly enough, the DNA that has been extracted from such fossils indicates that overall, DNA does not change very much. For example, if you compare the DNA extracted from an insect fossilized in amber to a living insect of the same species, you will see virtually no difference between the DNA from the fossil and the DNA from the living insect.

ON YOUR OWN

7.4 Some paleontologists actually classify insects fossilized in amber as fossil molds. Why is an insect in amber like a fossil mold?

Three General Features of the Fossil Record

Now that you have learned a bit about the fossilization process, it is time for you to learn some of the things that we can observe about the fossils that have been discovered. Usually, the sum total of all fossils on the earth is referred to as the **fossil record**. After all, fossils are the remains of once-living plants and animals. Thus, the fossils of these plants and animals are really a record of what was living during earth's past.

What can we observe about the fossil record? Well, one of the first things that becomes apparent when studying the fossil record is that most fossils are found in sedimentary rock. This probably should make sense to you. After all, igneous rock is formed from magma. Most creatures unlucky enough to be trapped in magma will probably be burnt to a crisp rather than fossilized. This is not always true, however. Fossil trees have been found in igneous rock, as have some fossil bones. In general, however, finding fossils in igneous rock is a bit rare. In the same way, finding fossils in metamorphic rock is rather rare, because the extreme pressure that forms metamorphic rock would tend to crush most fossils. Thus, sedimentary rock is the most likely kind of rock in which to find fossils.

Now remember that most sedimentary rock is laid down by water. Based on this fact and the fact that most fossils are found in sedimentary rock, we can easily come to the conclusion that most fossils have also been laid down by water. This is an important point. Without the action of water, most fossils would not be formed. Indeed, one of the fossilization processes (petrifaction) needs sediment-laden water in order to work! Thus, water is a very important part of the fossilization process.

The next aspect of the fossil record is usually not mentioned by any paleontologists, because it is considered a rather boring fact. Nevertheless, it is a very important feature of the fossil record. *Nearly 95% of all fossils on this planet are the fossils of clams and other hard-shelled organisms*! I suspect that you might have already read a great deal about fossils before you took this course. By the time I was your age, for example, I had read every book on dinosaurs that I could find. I had also read a lot about fossils in general. I had never, ever read about this important aspect of the fossil record, however!

Most people think about fossil dinosaurs, insects trapped in amber, and woolly mammoths when they hear about the fossil record. However, fossils like this make up a tiny, tiny minority of what's actually in the fossil record. In fact, if you really break down the fossil record, here's what you find. About 95% of all fossils that we recover are of hard-shelled creatures, like clams. They can be found in every region of the earth. Of the 5% remaining, about 95% of those are marine animals such as fish. Of the remaining 5% of those, about 95% are insects. The remaining 5% are made up of reptiles, plants, and mammals. Think about that for a moment. If you read most textbooks on fossils, you will think that there are, literally, thousands of fossils of dinosaurs and the like. There aren't. Only five percent of five percent of five percent, or about 0.0125%, of the fossils that we have discovered are of reptiles, plants, and mammals!

Now if you think about it, this should make sense. After all, the harder something is, the more likely it is to fossilize. Since clams and the like have hard shells, they are more likely to fossilize. Also, remember that water is incredibly important in the fossilization process. Thus, hard-shelled creatures that live in water *should* be the most likely kind of fossil that you find. Using the same kind of reasoning, fish should be the next most likely fossils to find, since fish have hard bones and live in water. Thus, it is not *surprising* that the vast majority of fossils are clams and fish. However, if you read most discussions of fossils, this important fact is left out!

The next thing that is easy to notice about the fossil record is that it contains the remains of some plants and animals which are still living today. For example, consider the fossilized honeypot ant shown in Figure 7.3. The same species of ant can be easily found alive today in Australia. This is true of many, many fossils. If you compare such a fossil to its living counterpart, you see that the fossil and the living counterpart are essentially the same.

Although many of the fossils that paleontologists find have living counterparts today, some do not. For example, consider the mammoth skeleton shown in Figure 7.1. Although it is easy to find elephants alive today, we cannot find a living version of a mammoth. What are the differences between mammoths and elephants? Examine Figure 7.4 below.

Illus. from the MasterClips collection

FIGURE 7.4
Drawings of a Mammoth and an Elephant

Mammoth

Elephant

Although there are many similarities between mammoths and elephants, there are important differences as well. Both have hair, but a mammoth was covered in thick, shaggy hair whereas elephants are covered mostly in bare skin with small patches of hair. The back of a mammoth was shaped rather differently than that of an elephant, and a mammoth's tusks were bigger and more curved than those of elephants.

There are no mammoths living today. Nevertheless, we know that mammoths lived at one time, because we have their fossilized remains. Thus, we say that the mammoth is now **extinct**.

Extinct - A term applied to a species of plant or animal that was once living but now is not

Although paleontologists have found several fossils of extinct plants and animals, they are the exception rather than the rule. The majority of fossils that have been discovered have living counterparts today.

Now before I go any further, I want to answer a question that you *should* be asking yourself. In Figure 7.4, I present a drawing of a mammoth. You should be wondering how in the world we know what a mammoth looks like, since no mammoths are alive today. Well, the answer is simple, but I need to make sure you really understand it. We know what mammoths used to look like because we have fossils of mammoths. Remember, however, that most of the time, fossils are terribly incomplete. A mammoth fossil such as the one shown in Figure 7.1 can tell us something about what a mammoth looked like. However, since hair, skin, and many other soft parts of an animal rarely fossilized, most fossils are not detailed enough for us to draw a reliable picture of what the animal looked like.

In the case of mammoths, however, we have a few incredibly well-preserved fossils that do have remains of hair, skin, and other soft parts. For example, the frozen baby mammoth discussed in the previous section gave paleontologists examples of mammoth hair, skin, etc.

Thus, the *only* reason we know what mammoths looked like is that we have a few incredibly well-preserved fossils. This is *very rare* in the fossil record. We do not have such fossils for most of the extinct animals we have found in the fossil record. Thus, we really do not know a lot about many of the extinct creatures for which we have fossils. The fossils are simply not well-preserved enough to provide us with examples of skin, hair, and other soft body parts. Thus, when you see drawing of dinosaurs and the like, you need to view them very skeptically. Most of the fossils from which those drawings are based contain nothing but a few bones and some teeth. Most of the details in these drawings, therefore, are the result of imagination, not data!

Before I discuss the final feature of the fossil record, I want to take a moment to discuss extinction. Scientists estimate that since 1600, 484 species of animals and 654 species of plants have become extinct. We can therefore *see* extinction occurring throughout history. Some of those extinctions are the result of human activity. Some are the result of the natural ebb and flow of Creation. Thus, we see that extinction occurred in earth's past due to the fossil record. We also can see that it occurred by examining historical records.

The reason I bring this up, however, is that extinction is a favorite source of misinformation for many people who call themselves "environmentalists." If you read the literature of such people, you will see claims that 10,000 - 40,000 species of plants and animals go extinct *every year*. Most of the time, these people blame this calamity on human activity. The problem is, such statements are outright lies. The people who call themselves "environmentalists" tend to get away with such lies, however, because their facts are rarely checked. However, if you read the literature of the scientists who are actually doing research on extinctions throughout history, you will find that in the last 400 years, just over 1,000 species of plants and animals have become extinct, and much of that is due to the natural ebb and flow of Creation (See, for example, *The Global Biodiversity Assessment*, 1995).

ON YOUR OWN

7.5 There are many creatures that have been found in the fossil record but no living specimen has ever been discovered. Thus, they are considered extinct. Can we be sure that such creatures are really extinct? Why or why not?

A Fourth General Feature of the Fossil Record

The final general feature of the fossil record that I would like to point out is that the fossils found in different strata of rock tend to be different. Remember, the majority of fossils in the fossil record are found in sedimentary rock. As you learned in the previous module, sedimentary rock tends to form layers which geologists call "strata." Well, if you find fossils in a sedimentary rock formation, you will usually find significant differences between the fossils in each layer.

For example, in the previous module, you saw a diagram of various rock strata in the Grand Canyon. If a paleontologist were to examine the fossils found in each strata, he or she would find many similarities between the fossils in each strata; but he or she would also find significant differences. First of all, nearly every layer of rock would contain fossilized clams. Remember, after all, that 95% of the fossils on this planet are of hard-shelled creatures like clams. Thus, clams are in several of the strata in the Grand Canyon. Once you get rid of all of the clam fossils, however, you notice some striking differences. Examine the figure below to see what I mean.

Illus. by Megan Whitaker

FIGURE 7.5

Certain Fossils and Where They are Found in the Grand Canyon

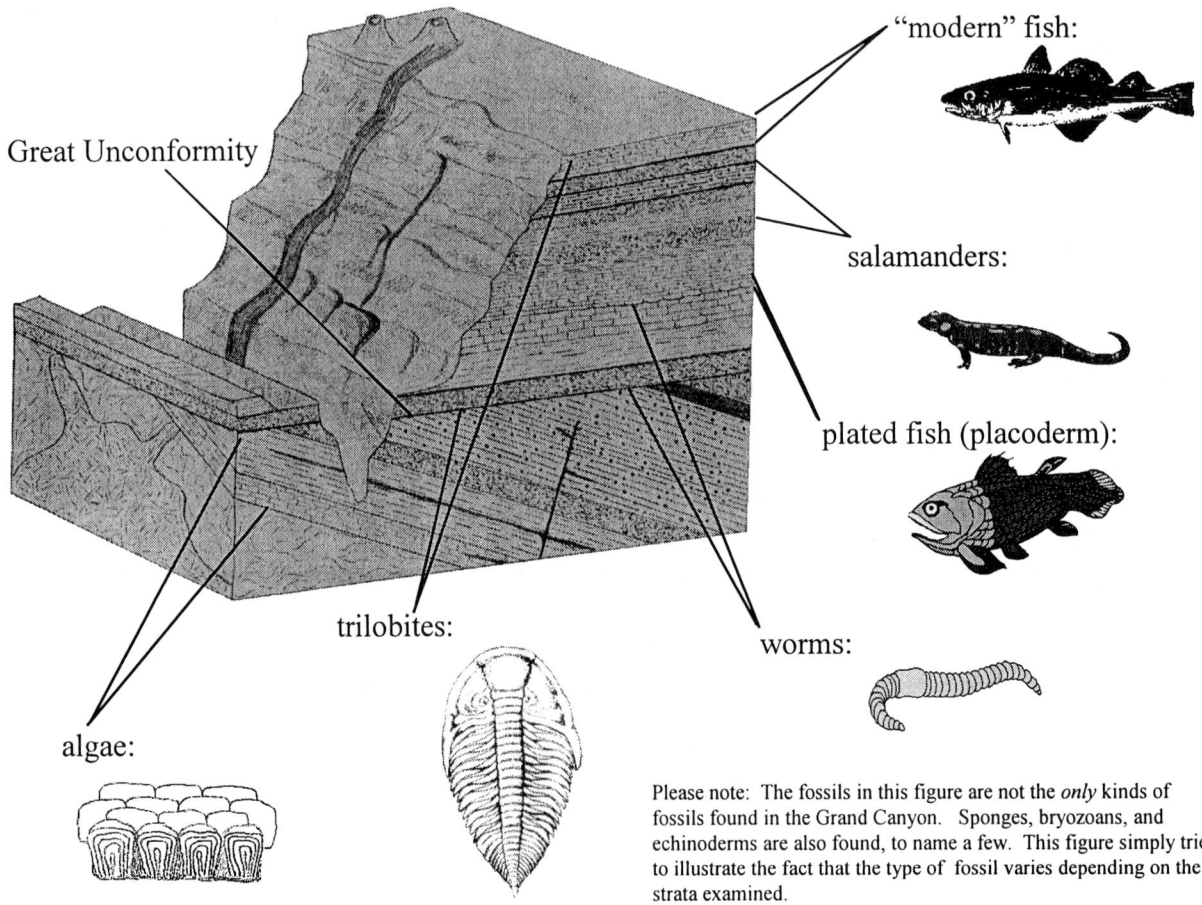

Please note: The fossils in this figure are not the *only* kinds of fossils found in the Grand Canyon. Sponges, bryozoans, and echinoderms are also found, to name a few. This figure simply tries to illustrate the fact that the type of fossil varies depending on the strata examined.

The most striking thing about the fossils in the Grand Canyon is that there are very few fossils in the strata below the Great Unconformity (pointed out in the figure). There aren't even any clams in those strata! A careful paleontologist will find a few indirect fossils of microscopic creatures such as algae (you will learn a lot about algae in biology class). Above the Great Unconformity, the strata have significantly more fossils in them.

There are fossils of **trilobites** in every layer of the Grand Canyon above the Great Unconformity. Trilobites lived in the ocean. Most lived on the ocean bottom where they plowed through the mud looking for food. They were protected by a hard outer covering known as an "exoskeleton," much like a lobster. Trilobites are assumed to be extinct, as no living trilobite has ever been discovered. The most common form of trilobite fossil is a cast fossil. In some of the layers above the Great Unconformity, actual fossils of trilobites have not been found. In those layers, however, fossils of their burrows have been found, indicating the presence of trilobites.

In the three layers just above the Great Unconformity, there are fossil casts of worms. In only one layer of the Grand Canyon (pointed out in the figure), you will find fossils of **placoderms** (plack' uh derms). Placoderms are strange-looking fish that are also assumed to be extinct. These fish had bony plates covering their heads rather than the scales that you see covering the heads of fish today. There have been no fossils of placoderms found in any other layer of the Grand Canyon. Fish that look like the ones we see today (labeled "modern" fish in the figure) are found only in the topmost layer of the Grand Canyon.

Interestingly enough, there are no fossils of mammals or birds in the Grand Canyon. However, there are fossils of **amphibians** (most likely salamanders) in the three layers which are pointed out in the figure. If you are not familiar with the term "amphibian," it refers to creatures that live both in and out of water. Frogs, salamanders, and toads are all examples of amphibians. The reason that I have to say that the fossils are "most likely salamanders" is that they are not bones, carbonate residues, or impressions of the amphibians. The fossils are simply molds of amphibian tracks. The tracks seem to be the kinds of tracks that a salamander makes; thus most paleontologists consider them to be fossils of salamanders. However, there are some who argue that the tracks might have come from a small reptile, like a lizard.

The point to this rather long discussion is very important. You *can* find fossils of trilobites in the Grand Canyon, but you cannot find them just anywhere in the Grand Canyon. You must look in the layers above the Great Unconformity. You can also find fossils of worms, but you must look in the three strata directly above the Great Unconformity. If you are looking for fish that look like the fish which live today, you can find fossils *only* in the topmost layer. It turns out that in virtually every geological formation which contains strata and fossils, the fossils found in one layer can be significantly different than the fossils found in another layer.

Why are there different types of fossils in different strata? Well, the answer to that is full of controversy. As I stated in a previous module, much of what you conclude from the sciences of geology and paleontology is dependent on whether you believe in the hypothesis of uniformitarianism or the hypothesis of catastrophism. Uniformitarians have one explanation for why the fossils found within different strata are so different. Catastrophists have another explanation. Hopefully, looking at the two explanations will help you on your way to determining which you think is the better hypothesis.

Before I move on to a discussion of the uniformitarian and catastrophism explanations for the major features of the fossil record, I want to sum them up for you so that you can remember them easily.

GENERAL FEATURES OF THE FOSSIL RECORD

1. **Fossils are usually found in sedimentary rock. Since most sedimentary rock is laid down by water, it follows that most fossils were laid down by water as well.**
2. **The vast majority of the fossil record is made up of clams and other hard-shelled creatures. Most of the remaining fossils are of either water-dwelling creatures or insects. Only a tiny, tiny fraction of the fossils we find are of plants, reptiles, birds, and mammals.**
3. **Many of the fossils we find are of plants and animals which are still alive today. Some of the fossils we find are of plants and animals which are now extinct.**
4. **The fossils found in one layer of stratified rock can be considerably different than the fossils found in another layer of the same stratified rock.**

As you read about both explanations of the fossil record, it is important to keep these features in mind.

ON YOUR OWN

7.6 A geologist shows you a rock and says that it was taken from a layer of the Grand Canyon. You can ask the geologist one question about the fossils found in the layer from which the rock was taken, and then you must tell the geologist whether the rock was found above or below the Great Unconformity. What question should you ask the geologist, and how will that help you determine from where the rock was taken?

Geology and Paleontology from the Uniformitarian Viewpoint

Any explanation of the fossil record begins with the explanation of the geological record which you learned about in the previous module. After all, since fossils are found in rocks, the formation of rocks will obviously affect the formation of fossils! Whether we are discussing uniformitarianism or catastrophism, then, we must explain both the geological record and the fossil record together.

The uniformitarian starts with a very important assumption when trying to explain the geological and fossil records. The assumption is best summed up with the phrase:

The present is the key to the past.

What the uniformitarian means by this statement is that if we want to understand what happened in the past, we merely have to see what is happening today. The uniformitarian believes that nothing "really special" happened in earth's past. Instead, the same processes we see happening today were also going on throughout earth's past. Since that is the case, then it stands to reason that the same processes we see happening today are responsible for forming the rocks and fossils that we study in geology and paleontology. What we must do, then, is see how sedimentary rock is forming today, and that will tell us how sedimentary rock formed in the past. In the same way, we need to see how fossils are forming today, and that will tell us how they formed in earth's past.

So how is sedimentary rock formed today? Well, it is hard to point to an example of sedimentary *rock* forming today, but it is really easy to point to examples of sediments *being deposited* today. For example, geologists have studied the deltas of rivers and have shown that each year, the depth of the sediment in the delta has increased. After all, rivers are constantly depositing sediment in their deltas. As time goes on, then, the sediments will get thicker and thicker. The same basic observation can be made in the shallow waters of today's tropical oceans. Geologists have analyzed mud being deposited on the bottom of the shallow parts of these oceans. As time has gone on, the thickness of the mud has increased. Based on the speed at which geologists have observed this mud accumulating, they predict that the mud gets deposited at a rate of one foot every thousand years.

Not only do we see sediments being deposited by rivers and settling out of oceans, we also see water evaporating, leaving behind accumulations of sediments. One excellent example of this is the Dead Sea which lies on the border between Israel and Jordan. Because of the weather in that region of the world, the water from the Dead Sea evaporates very quickly (at a rate of about 120 inches per year). In fact, the Dead Sea is shrinking because water is evaporating from it faster than water is being added to it by rain and rivers. The water in the Dead Sea is full of sediments (mostly salt sediments) and, as the water evaporates, those sediments accumulate. As a result, there are large accumulations of salt sediments that form a "ring" around the Dead Sea.

Observations such as these and countless others have led uniformitarian geologists to think that the sediments which make up the sedimentary rock we see today were, in fact, laid down by the same kinds of processes. For example, uniformitarian geologists think that the strata in the Grand Canyon were (with the possible exception of one layer) all laid down with the aid of water. In most cases, uniformitarians believe that these rocks are the result of oceans which slowly advanced and retreated in North America.

In the uniformitarian framework, Arizona was once (at least partially) covered by an ocean. As time went on, sediments accumulated at the bottom or near the shore of that ocean. After a long time of sediment accumulation, the ocean retreated due to several factors, and the layer of sediment remained. That layer of sediment hardened into sedimentary rock and was subject to weathering and erosion. That's how one layer of sedimentary rock formed. Eventually, the ocean advanced again and once again (at least partially) covered Arizona, and the layer of sedimentary rock that was formed before became the bottom of the ocean. Once again, sediments began to be deposited on the ocean floor or near the ocean shore; thus, sediments were deposited on top of that original layer of sedimentary rock. Eventually, the ocean retreated again, and the whole process was repeated over and over again.

A given layer of sedimentary rock in the Grand Canyon, according to uniformitarians, represents a time when that part of Arizona was covered by an ocean. The sediment that accumulated in that time period later solidified (most likely when the ocean retreated), and the result was a new layer of sedimentary rock. Thus, as you look at the many layers of sedimentary rock in the Grand Canyon, what you are really observing is the slow accumulation of sediment at the bottom of the ocean, a retreat of that ocean, a time period where there was no ocean, and then the advance of an ocean to start the process all over again. Since the oceans advanced and retreated because of differing conditions, and because they were most likely fed by different rivers at different times, the sediments they deposited on Arizona were different in composition. This explains why there are so many different kinds of rocks in the strata of the Grand Canyon.

The thing you have to remember about this view of geology is that it depends on enormous amounts of time. The sedimentation rates we observe today indicate that sediments are deposited very slowly. For example, the sedimentation in tropical seas that I mentioned earlier has been observed to occur at such a slow rate that it would take a thousand years to form a one-foot-thick layer of sediment. Thus, the sediments that were deposited over Arizona, from the uniformitarian point of view, must have taken millions of years to be deposited. Also, uniformitarians generally assume that the time it took to deposit the sediments is actually smaller than the time in between deposits. In other words, it might have taken a few million years for a layer of sediment to be deposited while the ocean covered Arizona, but once the ocean retreated, the sediments were probably exposed for as much as 100 million years before another ocean covered Arizona again.

In this framework, it is easy to see how the Great Unconformity was formed as well. After all, since uniformitarians believe that a great amount of time passes between the formation of each layer of sedimentary rock, there are many things that can happen after one layer of rock is formed and before another is laid down. Suppose, then, that after several layers of rock had been formed, an earthquake occurred, shifting the land in the Arizona area. All of those rocks which were laid down in nice, horizontal layers might have been tilted one way or the other by the earthquake. As time went on, erosion probably smoothed out any edges that were exposed as the result of the tilting. Then, when the ocean advanced across Arizona again and began depositing sediment, the sediment would be deposited horizontally, even though the strata below the ocean had been tilted.

Is it reasonable to think that Arizona was once covered by an ocean? Of course it is. We see the ocean levels rise and fall today based on different weather factors on the earth. For example, there are enormous amounts of ice in the oceans of the North and South Poles. If that ice were to melt as a result of a worldwide warming trend, the oceans would rise, and conceivably, they could rise enough to cover Arizona. Thus, even though Arizona is much like a desert now, it might not always have been that way. It could very well have been covered by the ocean at one time.

Once the rocks in the Grand Canyon had formed, something had to happen in order to cut that incredible canyon out of those rocks. Uniformitarians believe that the river we now see running through the bottom of the canyon (the Colorado River) could have done just that, given enough time. Remember, Experiment 6.5 showed you that running water can cut gorges in sediment. In the uniformitarian view, the Colorado River began slowly eroding the rocks of the Grand Canyon about six million years ago. This began cutting a gorge into the rocks. The erosion of the river was then enhanced as earthquake-like motions caused the rocks in that area to rise. These two processes plus six million years ended up forming the gorgeous canyon that we see today.

Now, given this view of how the strata in the Grand Canyon were formed, it becomes very obvious why you only find certain fossils in certain layers of rock. Since uniformitarians believe that each layer of rock was laid down one at a time, the Principle of Superposition applies to these rock layers. Thus, the lower the rock layer, the longer ago those sediments were deposited. The fact that paleontologists can only find algae and other such creatures below the Great Unconformity is an indication that only those kinds of creatures lived in the oceans of Arizona back during that time in earth's ancient history. The fact that you can find trilobites in every layer of the Grand Canyon above the Great Unconformity is simply due to the fact that trilobites lived in the waters of Arizona during all of the time that the strata above the Great Unconformity were deposited, but not before that time.

In the end, then, each layer of strata in a geological formation is, according to evolutionists, a record from a certain period in earth's history. Usually, that period is ten to a few hundred million years. If you find fossils in a layer, that tells you those creatures lived during that time period in earth's past. If you consistently do not find fossils of a creature in a layer, it might mean that the creature did not live during that time period.

ON YOUR OWN

7.7 Use the uniformitarian view to arrange the creatures in Figure 7.5 according to how long ago they lived. Start with the creature that lived during the earliest times in Arizona's past and end with the creature that lived in the most recent part of Arizona's past.

Geology and Paleontology from the Catastrophist Viewpoint

The catastrophist starts with a completely different point of view than does the uniformitarian. While the uniformitarian believes that essentially the same processes we observe today are responsible for forming most of the geological features of the earth, catastrophists believe that a good fraction of the geology we see today is the result of processes that occurred once in earth's past and will not be repeated. This is, obviously, a huge difference in viewpoint. This huge viewpoint difference usually results in a huge difference in what is concluded from the geological and fossil records.

Most catastrophists refer to the Bible's account of the creation of the world as well as the

Bible's account of Noah's flood to explain a good fraction of the geological record. For example, most catastrophists think that the layers of rock below the Great Unconformity of the Grand Canyon were formed when God first created the earth. The igneous and metamorphic rocks that lie below the Great Unconformity are assumed to have been formed as a part of the initial creation of the earth (day 1 as recorded in the Bible). Most of the sedimentary rock strata below the Great Unconformity are assumed to have been formed during the Creation Week as well, but most likely during and after the third day of the Creation Week. According to the Bible, the oceans and dry land were formed in day 3 of the Creation Week. As that happened, there would have obviously been a lot of erosion and deposition as well as earthquake-like movements. This would have formed sediment layers very quickly.

From a catastrophist point of view, there probably wasn't a lot of geologically important activity between the end of the Creation Week and Noah's flood. There were, most likely, a few volcanic eruptions and small floods that covered only certain regions of the earth. Those catastrophes (called "local" catastrophes) might well have produced some of the strata that lie below the Great Unconformity. Nevertheless, compared to the geological violence of the Creation Week and Noah's flood, these catastrophes were small and would have therefore only contributed a little to the geological features below the Great Unconformity.

The layers of rock above the Great Unconformity are assumed by catastrophists to have been formed during and after Noah's flood. Before the flood, or perhaps as a part of the early stages of the flood, the layers of rock that had already been formed could have been tilted as the result of earthquakes. The surface could then have been eroded by the enormous amounts of wind, rain, and rushing water that began to form the flood. The majority of the strata above the Great Unconformity could have then been deposited by the flood waters themselves.

Now catastrophists do not believe that Noah's flood caused a nice, calm ocean to cover the earth. Think about it for a moment. According to the Bible, God caused the "fountains of the great deep" to be broken up and opened the "windows of heaven" (Gen 7:11) in order to create the flood. This tells us that underground water shot up out of the ground to begin covering the earth, and a fierce rain fell for forty days and forty nights (Gen 7:12). Since the Bible says that even the tallest mountain of the earth was covered (Gen 7:19), there was obviously a *lot* of water released from underground and from the windows of heaven. This would have resulted in a *violent* surge of water. According to catastrophists, then, the flood covered the whole earth, but not in a gentle sea! The earth was covered in surging, rushing water that probably was composed of violently shifting currents.

These violently shifting currents would, according to catastrophists, cause huge changes in the depth, speed, and direction of movement of the flood waters. When the waters were deep and advancing, that's when one kind of sediment was deposited, forming one type of rock layer. As the waters settled down a bit and became more gentle, another kind of sediment would form, forming another type of rock layer. When the flood waters were shallow and retreating, another kind of rock layer could be formed. In the end, then, the different rock layers you see above the Great Unconformity were laid down during different stages of the flood, as the flood waters changed depth, direction, and speed.

After the flood waters retreated from the land and the rocks of the Grand Canyon were formed, catastrophists believe that another catastrophe actually cut the canyon out, exposing the rocks and forming the amazing view that we see today. Thus, catastrophists and uniformitarians believe that the Grand Canyon was cut through the rocks after they formed. The difference is that catastrophists believe the canyon was cut very quickly as a result of a catastrophe like a volcanic eruption, while uniformitarians rely on the slow erosion caused by the Colorado River. Catastrophists also believe that some of the very top layers of rock (such as the igneous rock that was formed as a result of volcanic activity) were, formed after the flood, as a result of smaller catastrophes, much like those that occurred between the Creation Week and the Flood.

Is it reasonable to believe in this kind of framework for the formation of geological structures? Of course it is. You have already seen how the scientific method shows the Bible to be an excellent source of history. Thus, it is reasonable to believe in the Creation Week as reported by such an excellent source of history. You have also already seen that there is evidence from outside the Bible that a global flood did, in fact, occur. Using these historical events to explain geology, therefore, is reasonable, as long as it is consistent with the data.

Does it make sense that so many different types of sediment could have been deposited by Noah's flood in so many layers at such thicknesses as what we see in the Grand Canyon? Of course. After all, we know that most sedimentary rock is laid down by water. We also know that the speed at which water flows affects the erosion that it causes. The violent, rushing waters of the flood could have easily eroded an enormous amount of sediment that was later deposited during different stages of the flood. Variations in depth, direction, and speed of the flood waters could easily be responsible for the different kinds of sediment that composed the Grand Canyon.

Using the catastrophism viewpoint as a reference, then, you can also see why different fossils appear in different layers. There are few fossils below the Great Unconformity because those rocks were formed in the Creation Week and afterwards. Thus, there was little to fossilize. The strata above the Great Unconformity contain many more fossils because there were plenty of creatures that could be fossilized by the time of the flood. Since the flood waters rose in different places at different times, they caught different creatures at different times. Also, since the sediment was laid down based on the depth, direction, and speed of the flood waters, the creatures being fossilized in any given layer would have, most likely, been caught in the flood waters in a given region.

In the catastrophism point of view, then, the different layers of rock do, to some extent, represent different times in earth's history. The deepest rocks are the result of the Creation Week as well as some local catastrophes which occurred between the Creation Week and the flood. Thus, they represent the earliest history of the earth. The majority of the remaining rocks were the result of Noah's flood and thus represent that portion of the earth's history. Some of the topmost rocks are the result of recent local catastrophes and thus represent the very recent part of earth's past.

However, according to catastrophists, the fact that different fossils can be found in different layers is not because each layer of rock represents a different part of earth's history.

Instead, catastrophists believe that the rocks of the Creation Week will have few fossils in them because of the very nature of the Creation Week. The rocks of the flood, however, will be teeming with fossils. The different fossils in different strata are simply an indication that the flood trapped and fossilized different creatures at different stages of the flood, depending on the depth, direction, and speed of the flood waters.

ON YOUR OWN

7.8 Suppose a paleontologist were to find fossils of trilobites in a layer of Grand Canyon rock below the Great Unconformity. Using the catastrophist framework, was the rock most likely formed during the Creation Week or during a local catastrophe between the Creation Week and the Flood?

Which View is Correct?

You have just been given a very sketchy introduction to both the uniformitarian view and the catastrophist view. They are very different, so either one or both of them is wrong. Assuming that one is correct, which one is it? Well, the fact is that no one knows for sure. Remember, the nature of science is that it cannot prove anything. Thus, we cannot say for sure that one is right and one is wrong. Even though we cannot say *for sure* which is right and which is wrong, we can examine the data and see which viewpoint is consistent with the data and which is not. That's what I want to do in the next module. I want to look at each view and see how it stands up to some relevant data.

Before I leave this module, however, I want to make one very important point about catastrophism and uniformitarianism. You might think that the hypothesis of catastrophism is not as testable as the hypothesis of uniformitarianism. After all, uniformitarians believe that we can explain most of the geological and fossil records in terms of processes that we see today. Thus, we can test some of the ideas of the uniformitarian view by observing how sedimentation and fossilization occur today. Catastrophism, on the other hand, refers to events that took place once in history and will not be repeated. Thus, we cannot test the catastrophist view because we have nothing to observe today.

This idea is a common misconception. First of all, although we will never be able to observe Noah's flood, we can observe smaller catastrophes which occur around the world. If we see how those catastrophes have affected the geological record, we can predict what a much greater catastrophe might have done. Indeed, some great advances in catastrophic geology have occurred as the result of detailed studies of Mount St. Helens' eruption in 1980 and hurricanes such as hurricane Donna in 1960. You will learn more about that in the next module.

Well, you might say, although we can have *some idea* of what a global flood would do to the geological record, we still must include some speculation. A local flood might allow you to observe changes in the local geology, but you still must speculate on how those changes would be amplified by a global flood. We will never know that for sure, so there is an enormous amount of speculation involved. In uniformitarianism, there is no speculation needed. After all, we *see* those events occurring right now. Thus, uniformitarianism uses a much more direct approach.

Once again, that is a common misconception. Although it is true that uniformitarians can directly view those processes that they think formed all of the geology that we see today, they also have to speculate. You see, using all of the history at our disposal, we can only see how those processes have worked for, at most, a few thousand years. Uniformitarians, however, require hundreds of millions of years in order for the processes we see today to form the geological and fossil records. Thus, uniformitarians must also speculate. They must speculate on how these processes are affected by the timespan of hundreds of millions of years.

In the end, then, uniformitarians and catastrophists both must speculate. They must speculate on different things, but they both do it. Neither framework is any more direct than the other. Each relies on many assumptions and even more speculation.

ON YOUR OWN

7.9 As you can see from the previous section, catastrophism (at least the kind that I discuss in this course) relies heavily on the Bible. Some would say, therefore, that catastrophism requires quite a bit of faith, since a catastrophist must believe in the events that are described in the Bible. It is important to point out that uniformitarians must exercise a lot of faith as well. List an article of faith in which a uniformitarian must believe. Indicate (based on your own bias) which view (catastrophism or uniformitarianism) requires the most faith.

7.10 Consider the explanations given by uniformitarians and catastrophists regarding why the fossils found in different strata are so different. Which one appeals more to you? Why?

ANSWERS TO THE ON YOUR OWN PROBLEMS

7.1 A mold can form without a cast, but a cast cannot form without a mold. Remember, the mold is made first, when the creature's remains disintegrate and the surrounding rocks retain the shape of the remains. After the mold is formed, a cast can be formed when new sediment fills the mold. Thus, a mold can form and, if no sediment fills the mold, a cast will never form. A cast must have a mold, however, so no cast will form unless a mold forms first.

7.2 At one time there must have been a lot of water there. Petrifaction will not occur without a good supply of mineral-laden water. Thus, there must have been a lot of water in Arizona at one time.

7.3 Carbonate residues and impressions are more likely to be found in strata near the bottom of a series of stratified rock. Remember, to make a carbonate residue or an impression, there needs to be a lot of pressure. There will be more pressure on the rocks at the bottom of the stratified rock, because all of the upper layers are sitting on top of them, weighing them down.

7.4 An insect in amber is like a mold because the amber surrounds the insect and then the insect begins to decay. As a result, there is an insect-shaped hole in the amber, with some organic material still inside. The insect-shaped hole can be thought of as a mold.

7.5 We can never really be sure that they are extinct. All we know is that no one has *found* a living example of the creatures in question. Since we have not searched every nook and cranny of the earth, we might have missed them. You will learn in the next module of a few creatures which were thought to be extinct but later living examples were found.

7.6 You need to ask the geologist whether or not fossil trilobites were found in that layer of rock. If the answer is yes, you know it comes from above the Great Unconformity. If the answer is no, you know it comes from below the Great Unconformity.

7.7 In the uniformitarian view, the Principle of Superposition applies. So, the deeper the layer, the older it is. Thus, the fossils found at the bottom are the oldest and the fossils found at the top are the youngest. This means that the order of fossils from oldest to youngest is: algae, trilobites and worms, plated fish, salamanders, and modern fish. You really can't make the distinction between trilobites and worms, because they are both found in the layer right above the Great Unconformity and neither is found any lower. Thus, you have to say that they lived at the same time.

7.8 The reason catastrophists believe that there are few fossils below the Great Unconformity is because most of the layers were formed during the Creation Week, when there were few things to fossilize. However, if a local catastrophe were to have occurred between Creation and the flood, then there would have been the chance that creatures such as trilobites would be fossilized. Thus, the layer of rock was probably formed in a local catastrophe that happened between the Creation Week and the flood.

7.9 There are at least two articles of faith that I can think of. You need only list one. One thing that a uniformitarian must have faith in is that the Bible is NOT literally true. After all, if the Bible is literally true, then there was a worldwide flood, and that would radically alter the geology of the earth in a single, non-repeatable event. That cannot fit into the uniformitarian view that the present is the key to the past. I consider this a hard article of faith to believe. Since the Bible has been shown to be so historically accurate, it is very hard to believe that the flood was just made up. Others have a different view, however. Another article of faith for uniformitarians is that the earth is old enough to allow for the hundreds of millions of years that they need for their view. There is no solid evidence that the earth is that old (you will learn more about that in physical science), so that must be taken on faith. Once again, I find it very hard to believe in an earth that is so old. Others, however, have a different view. Thus, I would think that the uniformitarian view requires the most faith, but others may differ with me on that point.

7.10 There is no right or wrong answer here. I want you to think about it deeply enough to write an answer, though. That will help you prepare for the next module.

STUDY GUIDE FOR MODULE #7

1. Define the following terms:

a. Petrifaction
b. Resin
c. Extinct

2. When a plant or animal dies, what is the most likely thing that will happen to its remains?

3. Which forms first, a fossil mold or a fossil cast?

4. Describe the process of a cast forming, indicating when the mold has formed and when the cast has formed.

5. What is required in order for petrifaction to occur?

6. Why does petrifaction usually produce fossils with more information than fossil casts?

7. What is the difference between a carbonate residue and an impression?

8. How are carbonate residues and impressions similar?

9. What is so nice about fossils which have been encased in amber or ice?

10. What are the 4 general features of the fossil record?

11. What kinds of creatures make up 95% of the fossil record?

12. Approximately how many species of plants and animals have gone extinct in the last 400 years: a hundred, a thousand, ten thousand, or a hundred thousand?

13. What is a trilobite? Are trilobites extinct?

14. What is a placoderm? Are placoderms extinct?

15. What is the uniformitarian explanation for how most sedimentary rocks formed?

16. What is the catastrophist explanation for how most sedimentary rocks formed?

17. What is the uniformitarian explanation for why different fossils are found in different strata?

18. What is the catastrophist explanation for why different fossils are found in different strata?

19. What major speculation must uniformitarians make when studying geology?

20. What major speculation must catastrophists make when studying geology?

Module #8: Uniformitarianism and Catastrophism

Introduction

Now that you have learned the basics of uniformitarianism and catastrophism, I want to spend some time contrasting those two views of earth's history. The contrast will be very interesting, because you will see how these two hypotheses lead to dramatically different views on what happened in earth's past. Hopefully, I will be as even handed as possible, but please remember that *all* scientists are biased. It is impossible to be otherwise. Thus, I am biased as well. In my scientific opinion, the data leans heavily in favor of catastrophism. Thus, I am sure that my discussion will as well! Please remember that as you read.

Uniformitarianism and the Geological Record

Remember what uniformitarians believe about the strata that we see in the geological record. They believe that each one of those strata represents a certain period of time in earth's past. The deeper layers represent time periods far back in earth's past, whereas the layers near the top represent more recent periods in earth's past. From a uniformitarian point of view, then, it would be very useful to know *which* layers represent *which* time period.

How do uniformitarians do this? Well, the first thing you have to realize is that uniformitarians do not believe that sedimentary rock formed in *all* regions of the earth during *all* time periods. After all, in order for sedimentary rock to be formed, sediments must be deposited. In order for sediments to be deposited, there must be some agent to do the depositing. Typically, that agent is water, but it also could be wind. Thus, for sedimentary rock to form in a certain region, there must be water or the right kind of wind around to deposit sediments to begin with. Well, those conditions are not going to be in *all* regions of the world during *all* time periods.

Thus, when you look at the rock layers in a given part of the world, uniformitarians do not expect to find a layer of rock for each time period in earth's past. Instead, they expect to find some layers in some regions of the world and other layers in other regions of the world. How do they determine which layers belong to which time period? They use **index fossils**.

Index fossils - Fossils considered to represent a certain period in earth's past

Remember, there are many fossils of plants and animals which are now extinct. Since uniformitarians believe that each layer of rock represents a given time period, then the fossils in that layer are of plants and animals that lived during that time period. Well, if you find certain fossils in one layer of rock and not in other layers of rock, then *that* fossil can be related to *that* layer of rock and therefore *that* time in earth's past.

In the end, then, uniformitarian geologists have certain index fossils that they think indicate certain times in earth's past. If a paleontologist finds an index fossil in a certain layer of rock, that tells the geologists *what time period* the layer of rock represents. Now this is a difficult concept, so if you are having trouble understanding it, don't worry. I want you to perform a simple "experiment" to help you see what I mean.

"EXPERIMENT" 8.1

A Simulation of Using Index Fossils to Order Rock Layers

Supplies:

- 18 index cards (The size is irrelevant, as is the presence or absence of lines.)
- A parent or someone else to write on the cards and hold the key

Procedure:

A. Your parent needs to set up this experiment. He or she needs to draw a symbol on each index card. Six symbols should be used: a star, a circle, a square, a triangle, a straight line, and an "X." Each card should have only one symbol on it. Thus, your parent needs to draw a star on three index cards, a circle on three other index cards, etc. In the end, your parent will have three index cards with a star on each, three index cards with a circle on each, three index cards with a square on each, and so on.

B. Now your parent needs to put these cards in three piles. Your parent should do this while you are somewhere else, so you do not see the way your parent makes the piles. Each pile needs to have one card with each symbol on it. Thus, each pile will have a card with a star, a card with a circle, a card with a square, and so on. The *order* in which these symbols appear in each pile must be the same. Thus, your parent can put the card with the star on the bottom of the pile, the card with the circle next, the card with the square next, the card with the triangle next, the card with the line next, and the card with the "X" on top. If the first pile has those cards in that order, then *each of the other piles must have those cards in the same order*. Once that is done, your parent needs to write down the order in which the symbols appear in each pile and hide that list from you.

C. Now your parent needs to remove 2 cards from each pile. He or she should remove the card with the star and the card with the "X" from one pile, the card with the square and the card with the line from the next pile, and the card with the circle and the card with the triangle from the last pile. Your parent *should not* change the order of the cards that remain: he or she should just remove the 2 cards from each pile.

D. There should now be 3 piles, each with 4 cards.

E. Now it's your turn. You need to look at the three piles of cards and use them to determine the order in which your parent originally laid down all 6 cards. Remember, each pile is missing two cards, so you are missing two symbols in each pile. Nevertheless, the cards that remain are still in the same order in which they were laid down. There are just 2 cards missing from each pile. Using all three piles, however, you should be able to reconstruct the order in which the six original cards were laid down.

F. Write down your reconstruction and check with your parent to see if you are right.

Did you get the reconstruction right? It really doesn't matter. What's important is that you thought through the process. This gives you an idea of how uniformitarians interpret the fossil record. When they look at the strata in any region of the earth, they see several layers and assume that each layer represents a certain period of time in earth's history. They know, however, that there is not a layer from *each* period of earth's history. Thus, much like each pile of cards in your experiment was missing a couple of cards, each geological structure in each region of the earth is missing some layers of rock. However, just like you were able to reconstruct the order in which the cards were laid down by your parent, uniformitarian geologists think that they can reconstruct the order in which the rocks were laid down by comparing different geological formations from different regions of the earth.

How do they do that? Well, they do it the same way you reconstructed the order of the cards in your experiment. Remember, each card had a symbol on it. According to uniformitarian geologists, each layer of rock contains index fossils which indicate what time in earth's past the rock was formed. Thus, just like you used the symbols on the cards to determine the order in which the cards were originally laid down, uniformitarian geologists use the index fossils in each layer to determine the order in which the rock layers were laid down.

Because this is such an important point, and because you still might be a bit confused, I want to explain this again with a figure.

Illus. by Megan Whitaker

FIGURE 8.1

The Geological Record in Different Regions of the Earth

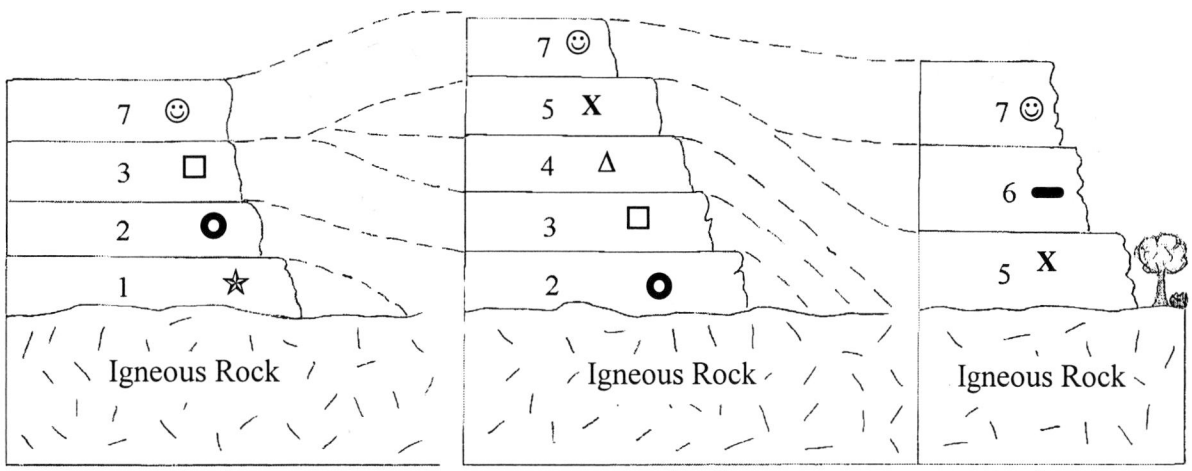

In this figure, regions "A," "B," and "C" represent different regions on the earth. In each region, a geologist finds sedimentary rock strata sitting on top of igneous rock. The sedimentary rock layers all have fossils in them. The index fossils that they contain are represented by the symbols in each layer. Thus, the star in the bottom layer of region "A" represents the type of index fossils found in that layer. If two layers have the same symbols, that means they have the same index fossils.

Suppose you were a uniformitarian geologist. How would you interpret the geological records in these three regions of the earth? Well, first you would look for layers that had the same index fossils. The layer that is second to the bottom in region "A" and the layer at the bottom of region "B," for example, both have circles in them. This means that they have the same index fossils. Thus, a uniformitarian geologist would assume that these two layers represent the *same time period* in earth's past. Why are there no layers with circles in region "C?" Well, the uniformitarian would assume that during this time period in earth's past, the conditions were not right for the formation of sedimentary rock in that region of the world. Thus, there are no layers of rock representing that time period.

Since these two layers in regions "A" and "B" have the same index fossils (represented by circles in the figure), then they are assumed to represent the same time period in earth's past. Thus, they should be labeled the same. I labeled them with a "2." Why? Well, in region "A," there is a layer *below* the layer with the circle. What does the Principle of Superposition indicate? It indicates that the older rocks are lower than the younger rocks. Thus, the layer *under* the layer with circles must be *older*. I therefore labeled *that* layer as "1" and the layer with the circles as "2." According to a uniformitarian, then, the layer labeled "1" is the oldest layer of rock, while the layer labeled "2" is a bit younger. Why is there no layer "1" in regions "B" and "C?" Once again, the uniformitarian would say that at that time period in earth's past, there was no water or wind, or perhaps there were no large amounts of sediments in those regions of the earth. Thus, sedimentary rock was not formed in regions "B" and "C," but it was formed in region "A."

Using this same kind of reasoning, the uniformitarian geologist can determine the order in which each layer in regions "A" through "C" was laid down. Think about how you determined the order in which the cards were laid down in your experiment. You matched the symbols on the cards to determine which cards were equivalent. In the same way, a uniformitarian matches rock layers based on the index fossils found in each layer. After matching the symbols, you used the fact that the cards were laid down one at a time. Thus, if one card was *under* another card, you knew that it was laid down *before* the other card. In the same way, a uniformitarian geologist assumes that the Principle of Superposition is true. Thus, the geologist assumes that if one layer is *under* another, it is the *older* layer.

In the end, then, the uniformitarian geologist can use the same reasoning you used in your experiment to determine the order in which all of the layers in Figure 8.1 were laid down. By matching the index fossils from layer to layer, the geologist assumes that he or she can identify which layer in each region of the earth represents the same time period as a layer in another region of the earth. In the figure, for example, the top layer of each region has the same index fossils (represented by smiley faces). Thus, they all represent the same time period in earth's past. Also, the geologist uses the Principle of Superposition to determine which layer was laid down first, which was laid down second, etc. Once again, think about the top layer in the figure. Since it is on the top in each region of the earth, it must represent the most recent time period in earth's past.

Using this kind of reasoning, the uniformitarian can order each layer in terms of when it was laid down in earth's past. That's what the numbers in the figure represent. The layers with the low numbers were laid down first, followed by the layers with the larger numbers. If a certain number does not appear in a region, that means the conditions simply were not right for forming sedimentary rock in that region of the earth at that time in earth's past. The dashed lines, then, connect the layers in one region of the earth with the corresponding layers in another region, if those layers exist.

If the uniformitarian assumptions are correct, you can use this kind of reasoning to order all of the sedimentary rock layers of the earth in terms of when they were laid down. When you do that, you notice a pattern. It seems that the kind of creatures that lived at different times in earth's past were quite different. The figure below illustrates what I mean.

Illus. by Megan Whitaker

FIGURE 8.2

The Geological Record Reconstructed According to Uniformitarian Assumptions

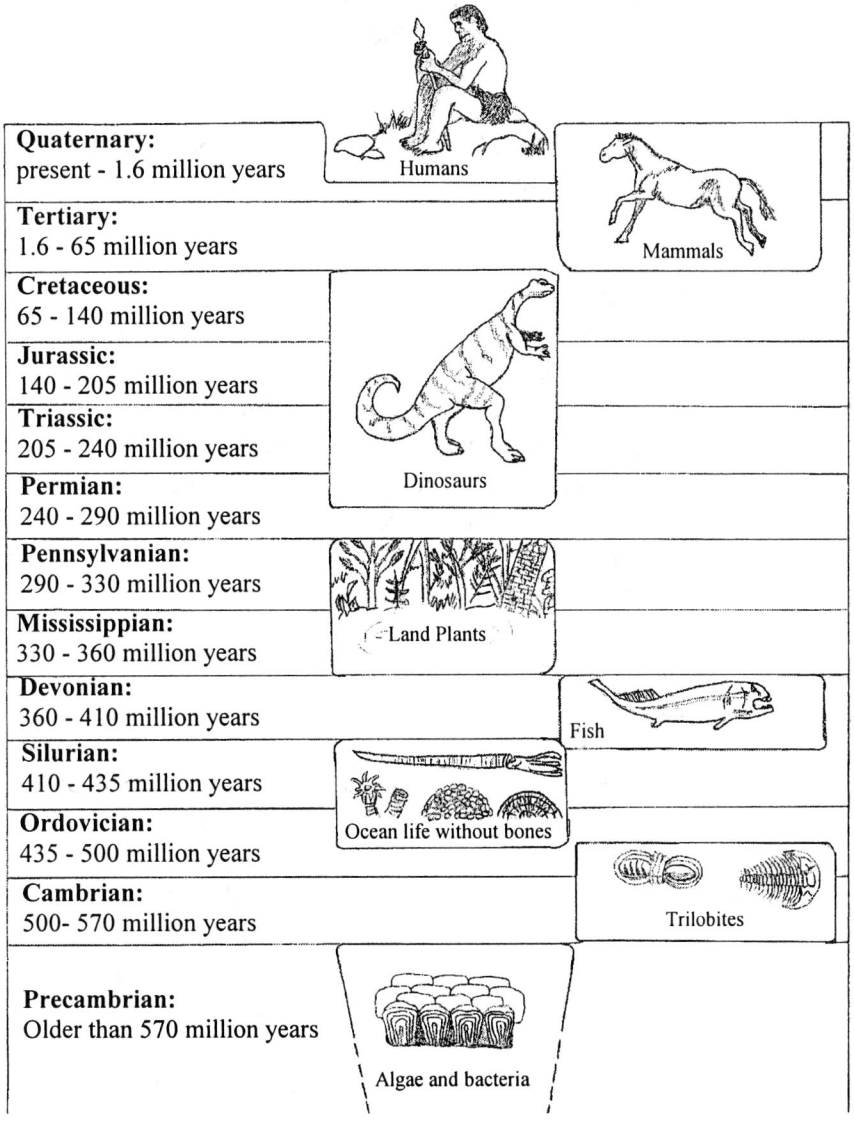

A figure like this is typically referred to by uniformitarian geologists as a **geological column**.

Geological column - A theoretical picture in which layers of rock from around the world are meshed together into a single, unbroken record of earth's past

Although this is rarely pointed out in most geology textbooks (even the ones written at the college level), it is *very* important that you understand there is no such thing as a *real* geological column. You cannot go anywhere on earth and find all of the layers of the geological column. This is a theoretical picture. It assumes that each layer of rock represents a period in earth's past, and it further assumes that the index fossils found in a given layer of rock are, in fact, accurate indicators of *which* time period the rock was formed. If either of these assumptions is wrong, then the geological column is pure fiction.

In the figure, each horizontal rectangle represents a layer of rock. Many of these layers have layers *within* them, so a more detailed geological column would have several more rectangles. However, the rectangles in this figure represent what most uniformitarian geologists consider the "major" layers of the geological column. According to uniformitarian assumptions, each layer represents a time period in earth's past. These time periods are usually referred to as **eras**, and they are each given names, as listed in the figure.

Notice that each layer in the figure also has a range of years associated with it. These years represent how long ago uniformitarian geologists assume that these layers were laid down. The Precambrian layer of rock, for example, is assumed to have been laid down more than 570 million years ago, while the Cambrian layer right above was laid down during a time period that started 570 million years ago and ended 500 million years ago. How do uniformitarian geologists get these ages? Well, that's a complicated process to explain. It relies heavily on radiometric dating, which you will learn more about in physical science. For right now, you just need to know that the dates are determined by a process more complicated than the process used to determine the order of the layers, and it relies heavily on radiometric dating, which is not very accurate under most circumstances.

Now notice in the figure what kinds of plant and animal fossils are found in the different layers of rock. In Precambrian rock, for example, typically fossils of only algae, bacteria, and other "simple" forms of life exist. In Cambrian rock and the lower layers of Ordovician rock, however, fossil trilobites are found. In the upper parts of Ordovician rock and in Silurian rock, ocean-dwelling creatures with no backbones (a creature without a backbone is called an "invertebrate") are found. As you get into rocks that are younger (according to the geological column), you eventually find fossils of fish. Younger rocks reveal fossils of plants, then dinosaurs, and then mammals. Finally, the youngest rocks (Quaternary rocks) contain fossils of human beings. It is important to note that although trilobites are shown only in Cambrian and Ordovician layers in the figure, they are actually found in rock layers all the way up to the Permian era. However, in Cambrian and lower Ordovician layers, they are the most common fossil you find. Thus, the pictures of fossils in the figure represent the most common fossils found in those layers.

ON YOUR OWN

8.1 What are the two major assumptions that uniformitarian geologists use in constructing the geological column?

8.2 If either assumption listed in 8.1 is wrong, what can you conclude about the geological column?

8.3 In the previous module, you learned that the layers which lie below the Great Unconformity in the Grand Canyon contain few fossils. The fossils which are found there are typically of algae and bacteria. What time period would a uniformitarian say that those layers represent?

Uniformitarianism and Evolution

Now if you look once again at Figure 8.2, notice that according to the geological column, there seems to be a "progression" in the plants and animals that lived during earth's past. In the oldest rocks (Precambrian), we see only "simple" life forms such as algae and bacteria. In the younger rocks layers (like the Cambrian rocks, for example) there are more complicated life forms such as trilobites. In even younger rocks (Ordovician), there are more complicated ocean-dwelling creatures. Even younger rocks (Devonian) show the rise of fish, which are some of the most complicated ocean-dwelling animals. Eventually, fossils of plants, dinosaurs, and even mammals begin to appear as the rocks get younger and younger. Finally, in the youngest rock layers, we see fossils of human beings.

According to uniformitarians, this provides excellent evidence for the **Theory of Evolution**.

The Theory of Evolution - A theory which states that all of life on this earth has a single, common ancestor that existed a long time ago

Now what does this definition mean? Well, the Theory of Evolution states that long, long ago, there was only one simple life form on this planet. As that life form began to reproduce, certain differences appeared between the parent and some of the children. In human beings, for example, we know that two brown-haired parents can have a baby with blonde hair. Thus, even though a child will have many things in common with his or her parents, there will be differences between the parents and the child as well.

The Theory of Evolution states that as millions of years passed and the children of this simple life form continued to reproduce, and their children reproduced, and so on, these small differences between parent and child began to "pile up." As this went on, there were eventually so many differences that the children being produced looked nothing like the original life form that began this process. In this way, a "simple" life form gave rise to a more complicated life form.

For example, consider the case of a fish. Suppose a fish was born which had slightly longer fins than its parents and its brothers and sisters. This might make the fish able to swim faster than all of its brothers and sisters. Thus, this fish could get food faster than its brothers and sisters. It also would be better able to swim away from other fish who were trying to eat it. As a result, this long fin would give the fish an advantage. That advantage would ensure that the fish lived to reproduce. When the fish did reproduce, most likely, a few of its children would have long fins as well.

Now suppose that one of those children reproduced and one of its children had a bit more control over the end of its fin compared to all of the other fish. Suppose it could open and close the end of the fin, almost like it was a hand. This would be an advantage for the fish, because it could dig in the sand at the bottom of the ocean for food. When that fish reproduced and its children reproduced and so on and so on, the fin might continually change so as to start looking more and more like a leg or arm rather than a fin. Eventually, then, after millions and millions of years of reproduction with plenty of differences cropping up between parent and child, a fish with legs and arms might be produced. If, as time went on, this fish and its children kept reproducing, a fish with legs and arms and the ability to breathe air might eventually be born. At that point, the creature would no longer be a fish. Instead, the creature would be some other life form, perhaps a frog.

In the end, then, The Theory of Evolution states that starting with a single life form and progressing through hundreds of millions or perhaps billions of years of reproduction, the differences that occur between parent and offspring can "pile up" so as to make completely new life forms. If you look at the geological column in Figure 8.2, that's what the fossil record seems to indicate. After all, the oldest rocks contain only simple life forms, while the younger and younger rocks contain more and more complicated life forms.

According to the uniformitarian geologist, then, the simple life forms that you see in Precambrian rock began reproducing. As the differences between parents and children continued to pile up, the life forms began to change. Those changes piled up to such a degree that eventually, trilobites were formed. A uniformitarian, then, would say that over millions of years, bacteria and algae **evolved** into trilobites.

Continuing this line of reasoning, the creatures that lived in Cambrian times eventually evolved into the ocean-dwelling creatures with no backbones which we see in the Ordovician and Silurian rocks. Those creatures eventually evolved into the fish that we see in Devonian rock. The plants that lived in Devonian times eventually evolved into the land plants of the Mississippian and Pennsylvanian eras. Eventually, the fish in the oceans evolved into amphibians (like frogs) and then into the dinosaurs that you see in the Permian, Jurassic, Triassic, and Cretaceous eras. The creatures in those eras eventually evolved into the mammals of the Tertiary period, which eventually evolved into humans. All of the life forms that we see today, then, are really just the descendants of a single simple life form that existed hundreds of millions or billions of years ago.

The geological column, then, seems to be a record of how this evolution occurred. You start with very simple life forms in the oldest rocks and you simply follow the fossils through to see how those life forms evolved into what we see today. Of course, you have to remember that the geological column itself is simply a theoretical construct. It doesn't actually exist anywhere. It is based on certain assumptions and a particular way of looking at the geological record. If the assumptions upon which it is based are not true, then The Theory of Evolution is not true, either.

There is one other thing that I must stress. I told you this in the last module but I need to remind you of it now. Remember, the fossil record looks very little like what is drawn in Figure 8.2. In fact, what you are looking at in Figure 8.2 constitutes less than 5% of the fossil record. The other 95% is composed of clams and other similar, hardshelled creatures. Thus, what you are looking at here is a tiny, tiny subset of the entire fossil record.

In summary, then, following uniformitarian assumptions provides you with two major conclusions. First of all, uniformitarians believe that you can construct a theoretical geological column that provides you with a chronological record of life on this earth. According to this record, life started out simple and gradually got more and more complex. Second, uniformitarians believe that the great number of plants and animals we see today were formed from a single simple life form that existed hundreds of millions if not billions of years ago. That process is called evolution. You will learn *a lot* more about evolution in biology class.

ON YOUR OWN

8.4 Many students who first hear about The Theory of Evolution ask, "If evolution happened in the past, why don't we see one life form evolving into another today?" How would a uniformitarian answer this question?

8.5 Since the geological column is only a theoretical construction, the Theory of Evolution would be better served by more direct evidence. If the Theory of Evolution is true, what kind of direct evidence for it would you expect to find in the fossil record?

Catastrophism and the Geological Record

Now that you have seen the way a uniformitarian interprets the geological record, it is time to see how a catastrophist interprets the geological record. Now remember, the catastrophist believes that most of the geological record that we see today was formed as the result of one or more catastrophes. The worldwide flood as described in the Bible (and confirmed by legends in many other cultures) is the biggest of these catastrophes and thus is responsible for a good fraction of the geological record. In addition to that catastrophe, however, other local catastrophes such as a hurricane or the eruption of a volcano have produced some of the geological structures that we see today.

The first thing you might ask a catastrophist is whether or not there is any evidence that geological structures can form in this way. Uniformitarians, after all, have some evidence for their view. We see sediments accumulating today that fit right in with the uniformitarian view. Thus, uniformitarians have some present evidence for their ideas about the past. Do catastrophists have any such evidence? Yes they do, and the evidence is rather dramatic.

On May 18, 1980, an earthquake started in southwest Washington state. That earthquake caused a landslide which ripped the top off of one of the most beautiful mountains in the region: **Mount Saint Helens**. Geologists knew that Mt. St. Helens was a volcano, but it had been inactive since 1857. However, in early 1980 a column of magma began pushing up the inside of the mountain, causing the northern face of the mountain to bulge outwards. When the top of the mountain was ripped away in the earthquake, that released the magma, and the volcano erupted. The eruption lasted from May 18 to October 18. It killed 57 people, severely damaged life in an area of about 70 square miles, and covered an even larger area with ash and debris. The total energy released in the explosion is estimated to be equivalent to the explosion of *430 million tons of TNT*, which is about the same as the energy released in the explosion of *33,000 atomic bombs*. During the main part of the eruption, the volcano was releasing energy at the rate of *one atomic bomb per second*. This energy release leveled entire forests and caused massive mudflows.

What were the geological results of this amazing sequence of events? Well, geologists are *still studying the data* to completely understand it. However, there are a few rather amazing things that we have learned. First and foremost, Mt. St. Helens has taught us that stratified rock can be laid down in a matter of hours: not days, not years, not millions of years, not billions of years. Consider, for example, the following photo:

Photo by Dr. Steven A. Austin *Copyright Institute for Creation Research*

FIGURE 8.3

Stratified Rock That Formed in Less Than 5 Hours (The woman in the photo provides scale)

During the eruption, there were periods when huge volumes of steam were released. This ground-hugging steam, mixed with volcanic ash, formed a virtual "river" of mud that moved across the ground at speeds greater than 100 miles per hour. As sediments were deposited by this "river," they hardened and formed rock. You can clearly see from the photograph that this process formed stratified rock. If you look closely at the rock, you can see that the strata are of varying thickness. Some strata are reasonably thick, and others are very thin.

Photo by Dr. Steven A. Austin **FIGURE 8.4** *Copyright Institute for Creation Research*

A Close-up of the Rocks in Figure 8.3

Much like the photos shown in the previous module, then, these rocks are stratified. Regular strata of different thickness, as well as laminae, are both present.

So we see that the same kind of stratified rocks that uniformitarians assume take millions of years to form can, in the case of a catastrophe, form in a matter of hours. Stratified rocks are not the only kinds of geological formations that were formed rapidly as a result of the Mt. St. Helens eruption. Remember how uniformitarians assume that the Grand Canyon was formed? Once the rocks of the Grand Canyon were formed, uniformitarians believe that the Colorado River began eroding those rocks. They estimate that this took approximately 6 million years.

While it is certainly conceivable that a river could slowly erode a canyon like the Grand Canyon over a period of millions of years, Experiment 6.5 demonstrated that the speed at which erosion takes place depends on the speed at which the eroding agent travels. In that experiment, you saw that a slowly-flowing stream eroded a landscape slowly, while a quickly-flowing stream eroded the landscape very quickly. In the eruption of Mt. St. Helens, there were many, many agents of erosion (water, steam, mud, etc.) that traveled very quickly over the landscape. If you look at the results of these eroding agents, you will be amazed.

In the figure below, there are two canyons. The canyon on the right is known as

"Engineers' Canyon." The canyon on the left was formed in less than a day as a result of a mudflow that took place during the Mt. St. Helens eruption.

Photo by Dr. Steven A. Austin *Copyright Institute for Creation Research*

FIGURE 8.5
A Canyon Formed in a Day

Interestingly enough, the canyon that formed in a day has much in common with the Grand Canyon. The general shape of the canyon is the same, and the size of the canyon is roughly one fortieth that of the Grand Canyon. This has led some geologists to call this newly-formed canyon the "Little Grand Canyon."

We see, then, that canyons can be formed rapidly as the result of catastrophic events. In fact, Mt. St. Helens has taught us something else about canyon formation. It has taught us that appearances can be *very* deceiving. You see, the reason that uniformitarians believe the Colorado River eroded the Grand Canyon is that the Colorado River is at the *bottom* of the Grand Canyon. Thus, it seems only logical to conclude that the river formed the canyon. Although this seems like a logical assumption, we now know that it is not necessarily a *correct* assumption. Consider, for example, the photo in Figure 8.6.

Photo by Dr. Steven A. Austin **FIGURE 8.6** *Copyright Institute for Creation Research*

Another View of Catastrophic Erosion

If a uniformitarian geologist were to study this canyon without the benefit of knowing what happened, he or she would assume that the river pointed out in the figure eroded the canyon over a period of millions of years. After all, that's what makes sense. The river is at the bottom of the canyon, and the rock on both walls of the canyon is exposed. Thus, the river carved the canyon through a slow process of erosion, right? Wrong! You see, people *observed* this canyon form as a result of the Mt. St. Helens eruption, and it was formed *first* as a result of the eruption's mudflows. *Later on* the river was formed in the canyon. In this case, then, the river did not form the canyon. *Instead, the canyon formed the river*!

What does all of this tell us? Does it tell us that the uniformitarian assumptions about the formation of stratified rock and canyons are wrong? Of course not! It just tells us that they are not the *only possible explanation*. This is a very important point and cannot be overemphasized. Uniformitarian geologists are fond of explaining *exactly* what happened in earth's past to form this layer of rock or that canyon. If you go to the Grand Canyon and take a tour, for example, the tour guide will tell you without a doubt that the Colorado River carved the Grand Canyon out through the slow process of erosion over a period of six million years. However, the only canyons whose formation people have *actually observed* did not form that way. Why, then, are uniformitarian geologists so confident that the Grand Canyon formed that way? They are confident only because they fervently believe in the uniformitarian hypothesis. Direct observation, however, tells us that the catastrophism hypothesis can also explain such formations!

Now think about all that you've learned for just a moment. When I mentioned that the total energy released as a result of the Mt. St. Helens eruption was roughly equivalent to the explosion of 33,000 atomic bombs, you probably decided that the Mt. St. Helens eruption was an enormous catastrophe. Well, in terms of loss of life and damage to the surrounding area, that is probably true. On a *geological scale*, however, the Mt. St. Helens eruption was rather ordinary. Several much more severe catastrophes have happened during the course of recorded history. Thus, the geological features that formed as a result of the Mt. St. Helens eruption are, most likely, *rather limited* compared to the geological features that would be formed by a *serious* catastrophe!

So, let's take the word of the most historically accurate document of ancient history and assume that there was a worldwide flood. In addition, let's make the logical conclusion that every major culture has a worldwide flood story because there was, indeed, a worldwide flood. Think of the enormous geological implications of such a catastrophe! Compared to a worldwide flood, the Mt. St. Helens catastrophe would be hardly noticeable! If the Mt. St. Helens catastrophe can build layers of stratified rock that are several feet high, it stands to reason that a worldwide flood could form layers of stratified rock that are hundreds of feet high. If the Mt. St. Helens catastrophe can carve out canyons that are one-fortieth the scale of the Grand Canyon, then some large, post-flood catastrophe could certainly carve out the Grand Canyon itself!

ON YOUR OWN

8.6 Does the data from the Mt. St. Helens eruption prove that the Grand Canyon was formed quickly as a result of a catastrophe?

8.7 The Mt. St. Helens catastrophe was a volcanic eruption, not a flood. Nevertheless, catastrophists assume that many of the structures formed by the volcanic eruption could also be formed by a flood. Why is this a reasonable assumption?

Catastrophism and the Fossil Record

Now remember what you learned in the previous module. Many catastrophists believe that the rocks you see in the geological record belong to four distinct groups. First, there are the rocks that are associated with God's creation of the world. Many of the igneous and metamorphic rocks are the "foundations" of the earth that God initially formed. The sedimentary rocks that sit directly on top of those rocks are, in general, the result of the creative acts involving water. Most of those happened between days 3 and 6 of the creation event as described in the Bible. Second, a few of those sedimentary rocks and igneous rocks might have resulted from certain local catastrophes (like volcanic eruptions) that occurred after the creation week but before the worldwide flood. Third, the majority of sedimentary rock that we see is a direct result of the flood itself. Fourth, there are some sedimentary and igneous rock formations that are the result of local catastrophes that have occurred since the flood. Mt. St. Helens is an example of such a catastrophe.

In this view, then, the fossils found in these rocks can be split into three basic groups. The fossils in the pre-flood rocks are the remains of the creatures that lived before the flood. The fossils in the rocks that were laid down by the flood are the remains of the creatures that lived at the time of the flood. Fossils in the post-flood rocks are the remains of creatures that lived after the flood. In some ways, then, the catastrophist believes that the geological record does provide you with a glimpse into different periods of earth's past. However, unlike the uniformitarian view, those periods represent three broad eras rather than several periods of time.

Now remember, catastrophists think that most of the sedimentary rocks (and therefore most of the fossil-bearing rocks) that we see today were laid down during the flood itself. Thus, when the catastrophist looks at the fossil record, he or she assumes that most of the fossils are the result of the kinds of processes that happened during the flood. As I mentioned in the previous module, catastrophists explain the fact that different fossils appear in different layers of the geological record not because each layer represents a separate period in earth's history, but because each layer was formed during different stages of the flood. The creatures caught in these layers would be different, depending on the details of the flood and the region of the earth. Using this assumption, there are certain aspects of the fossil record that become quite easy to understand.

First of all, there is the existence of the fossils themselves. It is important to note that paleontologists have uncovered huge numbers of fossils in the geological record. Sometimes, those fossils are concentrated into enormous deposits often called **fossil graveyards**. In a series of rocks in Africa called the Karoo Beds, for example, the fossils are so plentiful that paleontologists estimate that there are more than 800 billion fossils of creatures that had backbones (which biologists call "vertebrates"). Many of these creatures were fish.

Now think about that for a moment in terms of the fossilization processes you learned about in the previous module. In order for something to be fossilized, it must be buried in sediment, amber, mineral-rich water, or ice very quickly. In the case of the Karoo Beds, the creatures had to be covered in sediment in order to be preserved, because they are found in sedimentary rock. In the catastrophism viewpoint, this is not at all surprising. After all, the flood probably forced these creatures to move in an effort to escape the nasty conditions caused by the rapidly-moving flood waters. This probably concentrated them into a small region. Eventually, the huge amounts of moving sediment and mud caused by the raging floodwaters overtook the creatures, burying them quickly. As the flood waters continued to deposit more and more sediment on top of the creatures, the creatures were preserved and fossilized.

In terms of what we know about fossilization, this makes an enormous amount of sense. We know for a fact that fossil deposits like the ones seen in the Karoo Beds are simply not formed today. In the Gulf of Mexico, for example, there is a phenomenon called a **red tide**. You will learn more about red tides in biology class. For right now, you just need to know that red tides kill massive numbers of fish when they occur. In the Gulf of Mexico, it is not unusual for a single red tide to kill a million fish. What happens to those fish once they die? Do they fossilize? NO! They simply decay away. Thus, there must have been something *special* that fossilized billions of fish in the Karoo Beds. In the catastrophist view, that something special was a worldwide flood. The flood would tend to concentrate creatures which tried to escape its wrath, and then the huge amounts of sediments carried by the flood could bury and preserve these creatures rapidly.

Fossil graveyards are incredibly common in the fossil record. It would be impossible for me to mention even a small fraction of the fossil graveyards uncovered by paleontologists. However, I must mention another one because it provides still more evidence that many fossils were formed by a worldwide flood. Consider, for example, the fossil graveyard that is found in the Cumberland Bone Cave in Maryland. In this cave, there are thousands of fossils that range through dozens of different types of creatures. In this *one cave*, paleontologists have found fossils of wolverines and grizzly bears, both of which are found in very cold climates. In addition, they have found fossils of peccaries (a form of pig) and antelopes, which are found in warm, wet climates. They have found fossils of ground hogs, rabbits, and coyotes, which are found in temperate, dry prairies. Finally, they have found fossils of water-loving creatures such as beavers and muskrats.

Now think about that for a moment. In this single cave, paleontologists have found fossils of land creatures from very cold climates, land creatures from warm and wet climates, land creatures from temperate and dry climates, and water creatures. These fossils are not found in different strata. They are found all mixed up together in the Cumberland Bone Cave. Other caves *in the very same part of Maryland* exhibit no fossils at all! How can we explain all of this? In the catastrophism view, it is quite simple. Remember, Noah's Flood was supposed to have covered the entire world. Thus, the flood would have killed creatures from *all* climates. The waters could have easily mixed these fossils together and, as a result of currents from the flood waters either advancing on the land or retreating, those mixed-up fossils would end up being deposited in just one area. While the explanation for these fossil graveyards is simple in the catastrophism framework, it is hard to explain them in terms of uniformitarianism.

The massive fossil deposits in fossil graveyards, then, are evidence for the catastrophist view of the geological record. In addition, the mere existence of the number of fossils we see today is best understood in the catastrophist framework. As you learned in the previous module, fossilization is the exception, not the rule. Under normal conditions, a dead plant or animal will decay. In order to be preserved, the animal must be buried rapidly. The catastrophist view provides the easiest way to understand how this could happen to the extent that we see in the fossil record. Also, sometimes the fossils themselves indicate that they were buried very rapidly.

Dr. Joachim Vetter, for example, has collected several fossils of fish that are in the process of swallowing other fish! (*Creation Ex Nihilo* magazine, Vol 12 (Sept-Nov 1990), pp. 10-14) Typically, these fossils are carbonate residues or impressions. Unfortunately, I could not secure the rights to publish photos of the fossils, but they are extraordinary. These fossils clearly preserve a moment in time: the moment when one fish is eating another fish. In each case, the fossil contains a small fish partly encased by the mouth of a larger fish.

Think about what this means in terms of how that fossil was formed. The large fish that were preserved in this way did not die in the middle of a meal and then lie around for millions of years while they were encased in sediment. That simply could not happen! The fossils indicate that the fish were *buried in an instant*, without warning. Most likely, the large fish were in the midst of eating when the flood waters brought in a huge amount of sediment, burying the fish in mid-swallow. This killed both the fish and their potential meals. Since they were buried by sediment, the process of forming a carbonate residue or impression began.

Finally, it is important to note that just as Mt. St. Helens has demonstrated that geological formations can occur quickly, certain fossils have demonstrated that the fossilization process occurs very quickly. Consider the three photos in the figures below:

FIGURE 8.7
A Fossilized Water Wheel

Photo by Bev Lunt
Courtesy of Creation Ex Nihilo *magazine*

This water wheel was built roughly 60 years ago. Today, it is almost completely petrified, due to the mineral-rich water that has been flowing over it. If such a large water wheel can be petrified in just 60 years, there is no reason to require millions of years for the petrifaction of a fossil.

FIGURE 8.8
Fossilized Pliers and Hat

Photos Courtesy of Creation Ex Nihilo *magazine*

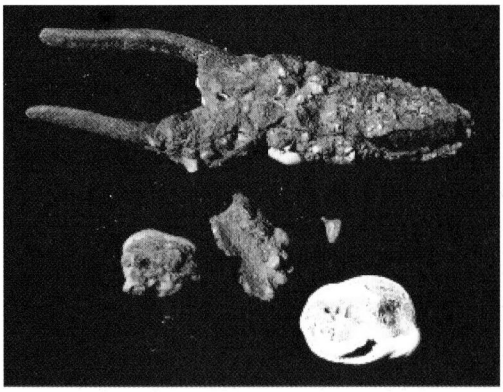

These pliers were found by Kevin Skerman completely encased in rock. The bottom of the rock was broken (the pieces are still in the figure) to reveal the handles.

This petrified hat was found in a mine in Tasmania. The original material has been completely replaced by minerals, making this a rock-hard, heavy hat. It will never rot away!

The unusual fossils in the photos demonstrate that fossilization can occur quickly, given the right conditions. Clearly, none of these fossils are very old. Pliers haven't been around for millions of years. Neither have hats or water wheels. Nevertheless, these recently-made things have been fossilized, all because they were exposed to the proper conditions. Catastrophists think that this is the *normal* mode of fossilization. Without the proper conditions, fossils will not form at all. If the proper conditions exist, catastrophists think that fossils will form rapidly!

ON YOUR OWN

8.8 Why are fossil graveyards a problem for uniformitarians?

Uniformitarianism or Catastrophism: Which is Better?

Now that I have given you the basics of both uniformitarianism and catastrophism, I now want to examine them in the light of certain data which I consider important. Now remember, as I have warned you several times, I think that catastrophism is a superior view with which to analyze the data. Thus, my examination of these two viewpoints will be biased towards catastrophism. That is unavoidable. If you pick up a uniformitarian's book on geology, catastrophism might not even be mentioned. If it is mentioned, it will probably be shown in a poor light. In the end, every book is biased because every author is biased. If you truly want to be educated in the subjects of geology and paleontology, you should probably read authors from both viewpoints and try to come to your own conclusions.

So given the fact that I am biased, how do these two theories stack up in light of the data? To begin with, catastrophism seems to do a much better job at explaining the number of fossils found in the fossil record, including fossil graveyards. As I have said before, most dead plants and animals decay. They do not fossilize. Thus, fossilization is a rare event. Usually, something special must occur in order for a dead plant or animal to fossilize. Catastrophes such as volcanic eruptions and floods, especially the worldwide flood, would provide lots of these special events. This explains well the huge number of fossils that exist. Uniformitarianism has a much harder time explaining such things. When it comes to fossil graveyards such as the Cumberland Bone Cave, this becomes very important. How did so many fossils from so many climates come to rest in a cave, especially when the other caves in the surrounding area have no fossils at all? Catastrophism offers a ready explanation – uniformitarianism does not.

Next, let's take a look at the uniformitarians' geological column. Remember, this is a construct, based on uniformitarian assumptions. The construct is assembled using index fossils. According to uniformitarians, there are certain fossils which are representative of certain times in earth's history. For example, trilobites are used as index fossils. Trilobites are assumed to have existed from Cambrian times (570 million years ago) through Permian times (240 million years ago). Thus, when a paleontologist finds a trilobite in a layer of rock, he or she assumes that the rock represents an age from Cambrian to Permian times. If the number of trilobites is particularly large, then it is usually considered Cambrian rock.

Now think about that for a moment. In order for this to really be true, trilobites must be extinct now. After all, if they represent the eras mentioned above, they *could not have lived before or after those eras*. The problem is that we *don't really know* whether or not trilobites are extinct. We assume they are because we have not *found* any living examples. That doesn't mean they don't exist, however. It only means that we have not found them!

You see, there are many examples of fossils which paleontologists thought were of extinct creatures but later learned that such creatures still exist. An example of that is the **tuatara** (too uh tar' uh). The tuatara is a reptile which belongs to a class called the "beakheads." Paleontologists long thought that all beakheads died out in the Cretaceous period. However, biologists found living tuataras in New Zealand. Not long ago, tuataras thrived in that region of the world. Nowadays, because of some effects brought about by Europeans, they are slowly dying out. However, there are still tuataras alive today.

Two questions come to mind when faced with such a fact. First, if tuatara fossils are used to identify Cretaceous rock, how accurate can such an identification be? We know that tuataras are alive today. How, then, can they be used to identify rock that is supposedly 570 to 240 million years old. Second, *why can't paleontologists find fossil tuataras in other strata*? After all, 240 million years is a long time. Shouldn't one or two tuatara fossils be found in strata from more "recent" times, since they have been living all along? In my opinion, this brings the whole idea of the geological column into doubt. If those strata *really do* represent different eras in earth's past, then you *should* find some fossil tuataras in rocks that are more recent than Cretaceous rock. Nevertheless, paleontologists cannot. Why? Uniformitarians do not have a satisfactory answer to that question.

Now if this was the only example of such a situation, you might be able to explain it away. However, it is not. A more well-known example is the coelacanth (see' luh kanth). This was a kind of fish whose fossils are very prevalent in the geological column from Devonian (410 million years ago) times to Cretaceous times (65 million years ago). No fossils of coelacanths can be found in rock "younger" than Cretaceous rock or "older" than Devonian rock. Therefore, uniformitarian geologists just assumed that there have been no living coelacanths on earth for the last 65 million years. However, in the winter of 1939, *The London Illustrated News* reported on the discovery of a living coelacanth. We now know they are relatively common in a region off the coast of South Africa and in another region between Africa and Madagascar. Once again, you have to ask the question why the geological column seems to indicate that no coelacanths have existed for 65 million years when, in fact, living coelacanths exist today! Is it really possible that coelacanths avoided being fossilized for 65 million years when they were fossilized with such regularity prior to that? There are many, many examples of both plants and animals which were assumed to be extinct but have now been found alive today. This remains a difficult problem if you choose to believe the uniformitarian viewpoint.

Not only are these kinds of fossils difficult to understand in terms of uniformitarian assumptions, there is another disturbing use of index fossils which is often necessary in order to interpret the geological record in terms of uniformitarian assumptions. In Module #6, I introduced the term "unconformity." As you should recall, an unconformity is a surface of erosion that separates one layer of rock from another. I mentioned that there were four types. The first three were easy to understand, but then I mentioned the last type of unconformity: a **paraconformity**.

Paraconformities are rather common in geology. In the Grand Canyon, for example, there are layers of rock that contain Cambrian index fossils in the lower parts of the layer and Mississippian index fossils in the upper parts of the same layer. According to uniformitarian assumptions, Cambrian times were supposed to have ended 500 million years ago and Mississippian times were not supposed to have begun until 360 million years ago. Thus, these time periods should be separated by a clear unconformity. After all, in other parts of the Grand Canyon, there is a clear unconformity between Devonian and Cambrian rock. Thus, the uniformitarian MUST assume that there was a break in the deposition of sediments after the Cambrian time period. Nevertheless, in many parts of the Grand Canyon, you find a single layer of rock with both Cambrian index fossils and Mississippian index fossils.

The way the uniformitarian gets around this problem is to suggest that there is a paraconformity in the rock. A paraconformity is an unconformity which has been "disguised" so that it does not look like an unconformity at all. Thus, even though the layer in question has no evidence of erosion, and even though the rock seems to be the same throughout the entire layer, the uniformitarian geologist assumes that there *must* be an unconformity there because there must be something separating these index fossils. As a result, the uniformitarian geologist simply assumes that a paraconformity exists there. Paraconformities are, perhaps, one of the biggest problems for uniformitarians. One reason they are such a problem is that there are so many of them. The other reason is that there is simply no evidence for them. Regardless of the lack of evidence, however, uniformitarians must believe in them, or the whole geological column is useless.

Please note that index fossils and paraconformities are of no worry to the catastrophist. The catastrophist thinks that the different fossils that are found in different strata represent different conditions and stages of the worldwide flood. Thus, it is not surprising to find fossils of tuatara and coelacanths in some geological strata but not others. After all, whether or not a creature gets fossilized depends on where it is and what the conditions of the flood are in that region. If a catastrophist finds coelacanths in deep strata but not shallow ones, that just means that coelacanths were fossilized early in the flood and not later in the flood. Nevertheless, there is no reason to assume that they do not exist any more. In the same way, there is no reason for a catastrophist to assume the presence of an unconformity that does not seem to exist. If "Cambrian" index fossils and "Mississippian" index fossils are found in the same layer, it tells the catastrophist that in that region of the world, those creatures lived near one another during the time of the flood and that they were caught by sediment deposits at roughly the same stage of the flood.

The whole concept of unconformities does bring me to a problem with the catastrophist viewpoint. Catastrophists have yet to offer a clear description of how unconformities can exist between certain layers of rock that were formed in the flood. After all, an unconformity requires erosion. There was not a lot of time during the flood for erosion to take place. Thus, the way in which some unconformities formed can be a problem in the catastrophist viewpoint.

There are, of course, other difficulties with catastrophism. For example, there are many limestone formations in Europe and North America that have what geologists call "*in situ* growth structures." These structures have the appearance of being formed slowly over time by creatures that were living in the sediments as the sediments were being deposited. If we assume that these sediments were laid down by the flood, it is hard to understand how these fossil structures could have formed. The problem is even more significant due to the fact that these fossils are found in what seem to be their *natural* growth positions. Thus, it really *does* look like they were formed during a "business as usual" period in earth's past. Noah's Flood would certainly not be "business as usual," so this presents catastrophists with a problem.

Speaking of limestone brings me to another problem with catastrophism. There is an enormous amount of limestone stretching over vast regions of the earth. In the minds of many geologists, there is simply too much limestone to have been laid down at one time. Catastrophists have never provided a detailed model to account for the large amounts of limestone formed all over the world.

So, *both* uniformitarianism and catastrophism have difficulties. Regardless of which view you take, you will run into what seem to be unsolvable problems. Which, then, is the better framework in which to view geology? Well, that depends on how many problems you see with each assumption and how important those problems are to you. In my opinion, for example, the problems with catastrophism are small compared to the problems associated with uniformitarianism. Thus, I think that the more scientifically accurate viewpoint is the catastrophist viewpoint. Nevertheless, knowledgeable scientists can view the same data and come to the opposite conclusion. Thus, this is a decision that you must make on your own, depending on how you view the data.

ON YOUR OWN

8.9 If the whole idea of index fossils is ignored, what evidence exists for paraconformities?

Evolution: Another Weakness of Uniformitarianism

One of the most important aspects of the uniformitarian viewpoint is the concept of evolution. If you believe that the geological column is real, then you probably believe that life on this planet started out as a simple life form and then slowly evolved into all of the creatures we see today. After all, that's what the geological column indicates happened. Of course, if you think that the construct of the geological column is not correct because of problems like the ones I pointed out in the previous section, then you have no real reason to believe in the process of evolution.

Evolution, then, becomes something that we can use to support or deny the reality of the geological column. If there is independent evidence for evolution, then that would be evidence in favor of the reality of the geological column. If there is not any independent evidence for evolution, then that is further evidence against the reality of the geological column. So, which is it? Is there independent evidence for the process of evolution or not? Well, the short answer to this question is "**no**." You will learn more about evolution when you take biology. For right now, however, let's look at what should be the main line of data that relates to evolution.

Now remember what evolution says. It says that life started out simple and through hundreds of millions (or perhaps billions) of years, the simple life forms became more complex. This happened as differences between parent and child began "piling up" in generation after generation. In this way, fish evolved into frogs, frogs evolved into reptiles, reptiles evolved into birds and mammals, and mammals evolved into humans. If this really happened, then at some time in earth's past, a creature had to exist which was part fish, part frog. This kind of creature is called an **intermediate link**, because it represents a "link" between one type of creature and another. If evolution really happened, then, there should be evidence of such creatures in the fossil record. The fact is, however, paleontologists can find only a few examples of such creatures, and those are highly questionable.

The scientist who first proposed a strong argument for evolution (Charles Darwin) noticed this lack of intermediate links in the fossil record. To him, it was the most difficult problem that he had with his hypothesis. In fact, in his book, he stated:

> Geological research, though it has added numerous species to existing and extinct genera, and has made the intervals between some few groups less wide than they otherwise would have been, yet has done scarcely anything in breaking the distinction between species, by connecting them together by numerous, fine, intermediate varieties; and this not having been affected, is probably the gravest and most obvious of all the many objections which can be raised against my views. (*The Origin of Species*, 6th ed, 1962, Collier Books, NY, p.462.)

Notice what he says here. Evolution says that one species eventually led to another. Thus, there should be "fine, intermediate varieties" of fossils in between species. The fact that there weren't was a problem that he called "grave."

Although Darwin could not find any good examples of intermediate links in the fossil record, he had a hope. He wrote his book in the mid 1800's. As a result, he figured that geology was still in its infant stage as a science and that geologists just hadn't found the intermediate link fossils yet. He was convinced that as time went on, geologists would find these intermediate links. Thus, he said that the intermediate links were currently just "missing" from the fossil record, but they would be found in time. Critics of evolution quickly coined the phrase "missing link" to emphasize that the fossil record was devoid of any evidence for evolution.

Well, what of these missing links? Has geology uncovered them? The answer to that is an unequivocal **NO**. Read, for example, the words of Dr. David Raup, the curator of the Chicago Field Museum of Natural History and an expert on the fossil record.

> Well, we are now about 120 years after Darwin, and knowledge of the fossil record has been greatly expanded…ironically, we have *even fewer examples* of evolutionary transition than we had in Darwin's time. By this I mean that some of the classic cases of Darwinian change in the fossil record, such as the evolution of the horse in North America, have had to be discarded or modified as the result of more detailed information. (*Field Museum Bulletin* January, 1979)

So Dr. Raup says (and most experts on the fossil record agree) that the missing links are still missing! Darwin saw this fact as strong evidence against evolution, and Dr. Raup says that the situation is worse now than ever! The fossil record, then, is strong evidence against evolution.

At this point, you might be thinking, "Wait a minute, haven't I seen museum exhibits, television programs, and books with detailed, evolutionary sequences? Where have they come from if the fossil record is so devoid of evolutionary intermediate links?" Well, they come either from misinterpretations of the fossil records or from the imaginations of those who really want to believe in evolution. In biology, you will learn about some of these misinterpretations. In this module, I want to concentrate on the imagination part. Perhaps the most famous fossil presented as evidence for evolution is *Archaeopteryx* (ark ee' op ter icks), which evolutionists want to believe is an intermediate link between reptiles and birds. The figure below shows you a photograph of an impression fossil of *Archaeopteryx* and a drawing of what paleontologists think that *Archaeopteryx* might have looked like.

Photo Courtesy of Creation Ex Nihilo *magazine* *Illus. by Megan Whitaker*

FIGURE 8.9

A Fossil and an Artistic Interpretation of *Archaeopteryx*

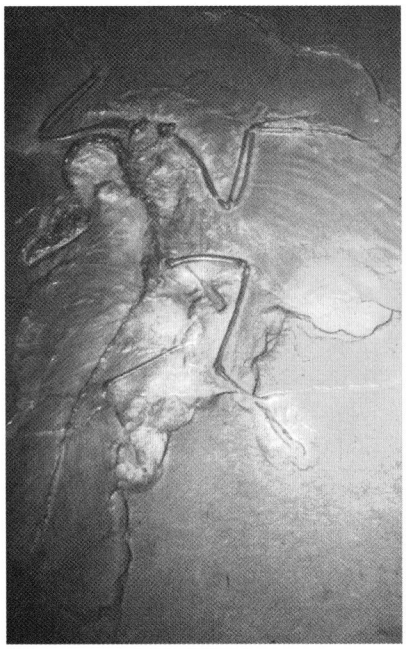

Picture of an *Archaeopteryx* fossil impression

Sketch of what *Archaeopteryx* might have looked like

Those who believe in evolution think that *Archaeopteryx* is an intermediate link between reptiles and birds. They think this because *Archaeopteryx* has some unique features which you don't see in any living birds today. The fossil impression clearly shows teeth in the mouth. No living bird has teeth, but reptiles have teeth. In addition, there are claws on the wings. No living bird has claws on its wings. Reptiles, however, have claws for their front feet. The tail is also longer and has more bones than that of the living birds we see today. Reptiles usually have long, bony tails. Thus, since this fossil is clearly a bird (the impression shows feathers), but it has some characteristics which we normally associate with reptiles, many think that this fossil qualifies as an intermediate link between reptiles and birds.

The problem is, that intermediate link status is mostly in the imagination of those who want to believe in evolution. Look at the sketch of what *Archaeopteryx* might have looked like. If you saw something like that today, what would you call it? You would call it *a bird*. That's what *Archaeopteryx* seems to be. It seems to be a bird with certain special features that no living bird today has.

Along with *Archaeopteryx*, there are a few other supposed intermediate links that paleontologists can find. In each case, however, the fossil looks so much like one of the two creatures it is trying to link, that it is hard to believe it is evidence for evolution. For example, paleontologists believe that a creature called *Australopithecus* (aw stray' low pih thih cus) is an intermediate link between apes and humans. Since apes are similar to humans in many ways, evolutionists believe that apes evolved into humans. The problem is that *Australopithecus* is almost entirely ape. If you saw one, you would consider it to be an ape. Nevertheless, because of a few minor differences between the apes we see today and the fossils of *Australopithecus*, it is assumed to be an intermediate link. However, since it looks like an ape, it probably is nothing more than an ape with a few special characteristics.

In the end, then, there are almost no intermediate links in the fossil record, and the few that paleontologists believe are intermediate links are highly questionable. If evolution really occurred, however, there should be *many* intermediate links. The fact that only a few questionable ones can be found is strong evidence against evolution. The fact that the fossil record casts doubt on evolution is another reason to believe that the geological column is really just a myth.

ON YOUR OWN

8.10 If a scientist believes that God created each type of creature individually, would he or she expect to find intermediate links in the fossil record? How does that expectation compare to the data we have?

ANSWERS TO THE ON YOUR OWN PROBLEMS

8.1 First, they assume that the Principle of Superposition works for all sedimentary rock. Second, they assume that the index fossils found in a layer of rock will indicate which time period that layer represents.

8.2 If either of those assumptions is wrong, the geological column is not real.

8.3 Uniformitarians would say that those are Precambrian rocks. Looking at Figure 8.2, you can see that the simple fossils like algae are found in Precambrian rocks.

8.4 The uniformitarian would say that you do not see evolution happening today because evolution occurs too slowly to see it happening. Remember, evolution takes place over hundreds of millions of years. True science has only been around for a few thousand years. That's such a small time compared to the millions of years required for evolution that you would not be able to see evolution happening.

8.5 You would expect to see fossils of creatures that look like a cross between creatures that we see today. For example, if fish evolved into frogs, then there should be fossils that are part fish and part frog. I will talk about such expectations in the final section of this module.

8.6 No, it does not prove anything. Remember, science does not prove anything. What the data from Mt. St. Helens does is provide evidence for a catastrophic formation of the Grand Canyon. This evidence is not conclusive, but to many scientists it is very convincing.

8.7 There are many similarities between the Mt. St. Helens eruption and a flood. Remember, most of the pictures I showed you are formations that resulted from mudflows. Well, there would have been wildly energetic mudflows in the flood.

8.8 Fossil graveyards are a problem for uniformitarians because they assume that creatures are fossilized one at a time by accident. To make a fossil graveyard, then, that accident would have to happen over and over again in a certain region. Also, when fossil graveyards contain creatures from many climates, there is no way to understand how this could have happened.

8.9 There is no evidence for paraconformities other than index fossils. If there are no such things as index fossils, then there is no reason to believe in paraconformities.

8.10 If God created each creature, a paleontologist would expect no intermediate links. This is what we see in the fossil record.

STUDY GUIDE FOR MODULE #8

1. Define the following terms:

a. Index fossils
b. Geological column
c. The Theory of Evolution

2. How are index fossils used by geologists?

3. Explain, in your own words, how the geological column is constructed.

4. Is it possible to go somewhere in the world and see all major layers of the geological column in one geological formation?

Using Figure 8.2 as a guide, answer questions 5-7:

5. According to the uniformitarian view, which creatures lived on earth first: trilobites or fish?

6. If a paleontologist finds only fossil algae in a layer of rock, roughly how old does the geologist think the rocks are?

7. A geological formation with only two layers of rock is studied. One has fossils of mammals only and the other has fossils of fish only. According to uniformitarian assumptions, which layer should be on the bottom and which should be on the top?

8. Why is the geological column considered to be evidence for evolution?

9. Why is the geological column not really evidence for evolution?

10. What does the data from Mt. St. Helens tell us about the time it takes to form stratified rocks?

11. If you see a canyon with a river flowing at the bottom of it, should you assume that the river eroded the canyon?

12. On a geological scale, was the Mt. St. Helens eruption a major catastrophe? What does that tell you about the kinds of geological formations which can be formed in a major catastrophe?

13. What did the Mt. St. Helens eruption have that a major flood would also have?

14. What is so important about the Cumberland Bone Cave when it comes to the question of uniformitarianism versus catastrophism?

15. Do fossils require millions of years to form?

16. What is a paraconformity?

17. List at least four problems with uniformitarianism as discussed in the text.

18. What are the three problems with catastrophism that were discussed?

19. Why does the fossil record offer no evidence for evolution?

20. Why does the fossil record offer evidence for the idea that God created each plant and animal individually?

Module #9: What is Life?

Introduction

Now that you've gotten a good view of the history of life, I want to examine the whole concept of life in a little more detail. After all, if we are going to study life science, we need to know what life is! Now to some extent, you already have an idea of what life is. If I were to ask you whether or not a rock is alive, you would easily answer, "No!" On the other hand, if I were to ask you whether or not a blade of grass is alive, you would quickly answer, "Yes!" Most likely, you can distinguish between life and non-life by just giving examples of what is alive and what is not.

Even though this is the case, scientists must be a little more detailed in defining what it means to be alive. Thus, scientists have developed several criteria for life. If something meets all of these criteria, then we can scientifically say that it is alive. If it fails to meet even one of the criteria, it is not alive. These criteria are:

1. **All life forms contain deoxyribonucleic (dee ahk' see rye boh new klay' ik) acid, which is called DNA.**

2. **All life forms have a method by which they take energy from the surroundings and convert it into energy that helps them live.**

3. **All life forms can sense changes in their surroundings and respond to those changes.**

4. **All life forms reproduce.**

When put together, these criteria define life, as far as science is concerned. Anything that meets these criteria is called a **living organism**. Now if you're not sure exactly what each of these criteria mean, don't worry. I will discuss each of them in detail.

DNA and Life

Our first criterion states that all life contains **DNA**. Now you've probably heard about DNA before (I mentioned it briefly in Module #7). Most likely, however, it is still a big mystery to you at this point. Why is DNA so special when it comes to life? Well, DNA provides the *information* necessary to take a bunch of lifeless chemicals and turn them into a living system. You see, if we were to analyze an organism and determine every chemical that made up the organism, and if we were then to go into a laboratory and make all of those chemicals and throw them into a big pot, we would not have made something that is alive. We would not have even made something that resembles the organism we studied. Why?

In order to make life, we must take the chemicals that make it up, and we must *organize* them in a way that will promote the other life functions mentioned in our list of criteria for life. In other words, just the chemicals themselves cannot extract and convert energy (criterion #2), sense and respond to change (criterion #3), and reproduce (criterion #4). In order to perform those functions, the chemicals must be organized so that they work together in just the right way. Think about it this way: suppose you went to a store and bought a bicycle. The box said "some assembly required." When you got it home, you unpacked the box and piled all of the parts on the floor. At that point, did you have a bicycle? No, of course not. In order to make the bicycle, you had to assemble the pieces in just the right way, according to the instructions. When you got done, all of the parts were in just the right place and worked together with just the right parts. This made your bike.

In the same way, DNA is the set of instructions that takes the chemicals which make up life and arranges them in just the right way so as to produce a living system. Without this instruction set, the chemicals that make up a living organism would be nothing more than a pile of goo. However, directed by the information in DNA, these chemicals can work together in just the right way to make a living organism. Now of course, the exact way in which DNA does this is a little complicated. When you take biology, you will learn a great deal about how DNA does its job. In this course, I want you to concentrate on what DNA looks like instead of the details of how it does its job. If you really learn about the structure of DNA now, it will be easier for you to understand how DNA works when you take biology.

Okay, then, what does DNA look like? Well, first of all, you need to know that DNA is a **molecule**. In physical science next year, you will learn a lot more about atoms and molecules. For right now, just remember that atoms are the basic building blocks of matter.

Atom - The smallest stable unit of matter in Creation

Everything you see (this book, the chair upon which you sit, your body itself) is made up of little units of matter called atoms. Currently, scientists have found about 109 different kinds of atoms in Creation. This number increases as time goes on because, every once in a while, scientists discover a new kind of atom. In a few years, then, the number of basic kinds of atoms in Creation will probably be a little larger. That's why I say "about" 109 different kinds of atoms in Creation.

If this were the end of the story, Creation would be pretty boring. After all, if everything that you see is made up of atoms, and if there are only about 109 different kinds of atoms in Creation, then there are only 109 different substances in Creation, right? Of course not! Although God used atoms as the basic building blocks of Creation, He designed those atoms to link together to form larger building blocks called **molecules**.

Molecule - Two or more atoms linked together to make a substance with unique properties

These larger building blocks make up most of the substances with which you are familiar. Table salt, water, wood, etc., are all made up of molecules which are, in turn, made up of atoms.

DNA is a molecule. This means that it is made from several atoms that link together. Well, it turns out that DNA is actually a *really big* molecule. The majority of molecules in

Creation are made up of somewhere between 2 and 100 atoms linked together. DNA, however, is made of *millions* of atoms linked together! Now if you think about it, that should make sense. After all, DNA contains all of the information necessary to make life. Thus, DNA must contain a *lot* of information. It has been estimated that if one could translate into English all of the information in a single human DNA molecule, it would fill up *1,000 books, each of which would be 600 pages long*! That amount of information requires a large molecule!

Now let me point out that although DNA is large *compared to other molecules*, it is remarkably small when you consider that it stores all of that information. A DNA molecule, in fact, represents the most *efficient means of storing data* in all of Creation. Many people today marvel at how much information can be stored in a tiny, laptop computer. However, the best computer disk made today cannot even *come close* to storing information as efficiently as does DNA. In fact, computer scientists have been trying for years to make computers that store information the way DNA does, and they *can't even do it*.

Now think about that for a moment. Human science can't produce anything that stores information as efficiently as DNA does. In fact, it cannot even produce anything that stores information *in the same way* as does DNA. Suppose one of your friends showed you a computer disk and then loaded it into a computer. Suppose further that you used the computer to look at the information on the disk and found that the disk contained detailed drawings and instructions for assembling a bicycle. If your friend told you that the disk and all of its contents were formed as the result of lightning striking a pile of garbage that contained plastic and metal, would you believe him? Of course not. Why?

Well, first, the disk itself is a complicated piece of technology which can be used to store a lot of useful information. Things like that do not result from accidents. They are made as a result of careful design and manufacturing. Also, the instructions for assembling the bike (which are stored on the disk) could not form by accident, either. There is just too much information there. The instructions were clearly *created* by someone who knows how to make bicycles. Thus, it would be obvious to you that neither the disk nor the information on that disk could be the result of some accidental event like lightning striking a pile of plastic and scrap metal. Nevertheless, if you are a scientist and do not believe in God, you are *forced* to believe that a data storage device *significantly more advanced* than humankind's best computer disk, and information *significantly more extensive* than the instructions for assembling a bicycle both came about as the result of an accident! Scientists who believe in God need not believe such absurd things! Just as computer disks and bicycle assembly instructions are designed and made by very intelligent engineers, DNA and the information necessary for life are designed and made by the most intelligent engineer of all, God!

ON YOUR OWN

9.1 In general, which is smaller: an atom or a molecule?

9.2 Think about a cookbook. A cookbook is, in some ways, very much like DNA. How?

The Structure of DNA

In the previous section, you learned that DNA stores an enormous amount of information. How does it store information? The answer to that question lies in the structure of DNA. The figure below represents a simplified view of a portion of a DNA molecule.

FIGURE 9.1
A Simplified View of a Portion of DNA

Illus. by Megan Whitaker

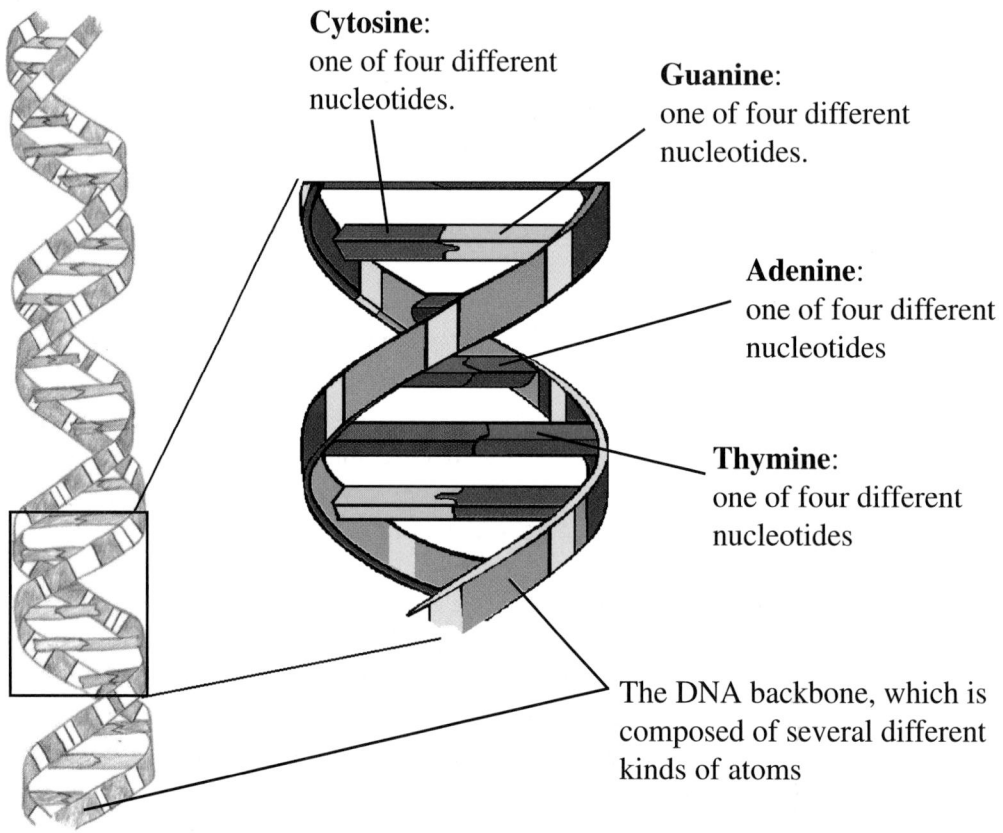

A DNA molecule is shaped like a **double helix**. If you don't know what that means, don't worry. You will be making a model of DNA in a little while, and you will see what that means then. The double helix is formed by two long strands of atoms linked together in just the right way. These strands are called the **backbone** of the DNA. Each strand has little units attached to it. These units are called **nucleotides** (new' klee oh tides). There are four different nucleotides in a DNA molecule. Their names are adenine (ad' uh neen), thymine (thy' meen), guanine (gwa' neen), and cytosine (sigh' tuh zeen).

In the figure, the DNA backbone is represented by the blue and white ribbons. Adenine is represented by the purple bars; thymine is represented by the red bars; cytosine is represented by the green bars; and guanine is represented by the pink bars. Notice that the four nucleotides link together. This is what holds the double helix together. Notice that in the figure, there are no cases of pink bars linking with red bars or purple bars. In each case, green bars link with pink bars and red bars link with purple bars. This represents the fact that the four nucleotides of DNA cannot link together in just any way. Only adenine and thymine can link together, and only cytosine and guanine can link together. You will learn more about this in a moment.

Now how in the world does this molecule store information? Well, have you ever heard of something called **Morse code**? Morse code was developed by Samuel F.B. Morse in 1836. He invented it as a way of communicating by telegraph. In a telegraph, electrical signals are sent over a wire whenever a button on the telegraph is pressed. The electrical signal generates a sound on the receiving end. That sound is a single "beep." When the beep is short, it is called a "dot," and when the beep is long, it is called a "dash." Morse developed a code that represents all 26 letters in the alphabet as well as the numerals 0 through 9 in terms of just dots and dashes. For example, the letter "S" is represented by 3 dots, and the letter "O" is represented by 3 dashes. If you were in trouble and had a telegraph, you could send three short beeps followed by 3 long beeps followed by three short beeps. The person receiving your transmission would say that he received 3 dots, 3 dashes, and 3 dots. He would translate that as "SOS," which is the internationally-recognized abbreviation for "I need help."

Although Morse code is often used to send short messages like "SOS," it can also be used to send very detailed messages as well. After all, using just dots and dashes, you could spell out *any* word in the English language. Thus, if you wanted to, you could send this entire book (just the words, not the pictures) to someone via Morse code. It would be *very* tedious, but it *could* be done. Well, just as all of the information in this book could be represented by a series of dots and dashes in Morse code, all of the information necessary for life is stored in a coded series of the four nucleotides (adenine, thymine, cytosine, and guanine) in DNA.

Just as someone must *translate* from Morse code back to English so that you can understand a message sent in Morse code, the series of nucleotides in DNA must also be translated into something that a living organism can understand. It turns out that there is a host of chemical processes that occur in order to translate the information stored in a series of nucleotides into something that a living organism can use. The details of these processes are far beyond the scope of this course, but when you take biology, you will learn about some of them. For right now, I want you to really understand the structure of DNA. The best way for you to do that is to build your own model.

EXPERIMENT 9.1

Building a Model of DNA

Supplies:

- Long pipe cleaners (the longer the better)
- Four different colors of beads (The beads need to have holes in them large enough for the pipe cleaners to fit through. You can get beads like that at any craft store.)
- Scissors strong enough to cut the pipe cleaners

Introduction - Although a drawing of DNA is nice, a model is even better. In this experiment, you will build a model of DNA to help you understand its structure.

Procedure:

A. Sort the beads out by color. Assign each color to represent a nucleotide. In the pictures of the DNA that that you see below, for example, red represents thymine, and green represents adenine. Blue represents guanine, and yellow represents cytosine.
B. Take a pipe cleaner and make several small loops in it. The best way to do this is to wrap the pipe cleaner once around a pencil. Shape the pipe cleaner so that it is straight and so that all of the loops are on just one side. Your pipe cleaner should look something like this;

C. Do the same thing with another pipe cleaner, and then lay them side by side so that the loops face each other:

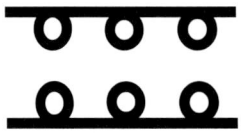

D. Now you need to connect the loops with small pieces of pipe cleaner. Cut a pipe cleaner into small segments. You need to make one segment for each pair of loops that face each other. Each segment should be long enough so that two beads can be threaded into the pipe cleaner and there will still be extra pipe cleaner on each end. There should be enough extra pipe cleaner so that each side can be wrapped into a loop.
E. You then want to actually put two beads (each a different color) on each pipe cleaner segment. On a given segment, you should put either one bead that represents adenine and one bead that represents thymine or one bead that represents guanine and one bead that represents cytosine.
F. Once the beads are threaded into a pipe cleaner segment, use the excess pipe cleaner on each side of the segment to attach the segment to the loops. The segment will therefore join the first pipe cleaner with loops to the second pipe cleaner with loops. In effect, then, you will make a "ladder" that looks something like this:

Photo by Kathleen J. Wile

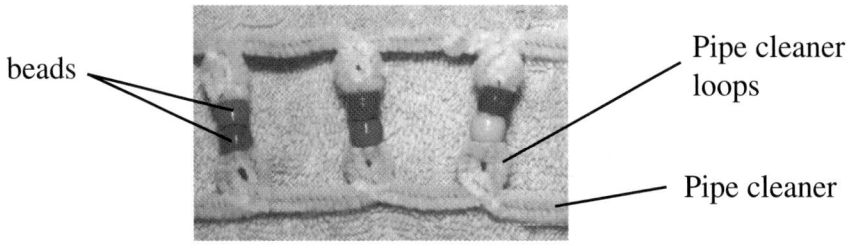

Remember, in this example, red represents thymine and green represents adenine. Thus, on a given segment I can have a red bead and a green bead, but not a red and yellow nor a red and blue bead. The two beads can be in any order, but only red and green (representing thymine and adenine) or blue and yellow (representing guanine and cytosine) can be together.

G. You have now built the basic structure of DNA. The pipe cleaners with loops in them represent the backbone of the DNA, and the beads represent the nucleotides. There are only two things left to do. First, you need to make your model longer. Do this by making another "ladder" like the one you just made. Then, twist the pipe cleaners on the end of the first "ladder" with the pipe cleaners on the end of the second "ladder" so that you now have a single "ladder" which is twice as long:

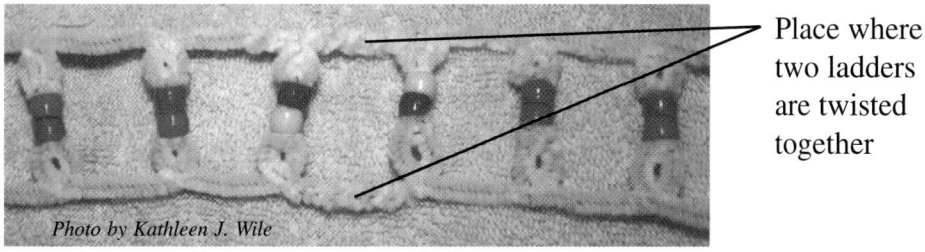

H. Do this as much as you want, so that your "ladder" grows longer and longer.

I. The final step is to twist the "ladder" into a double-helix like DNA. Do this by holding each end and twisting them in opposite directions. In the end, your DNA model should look something like this:

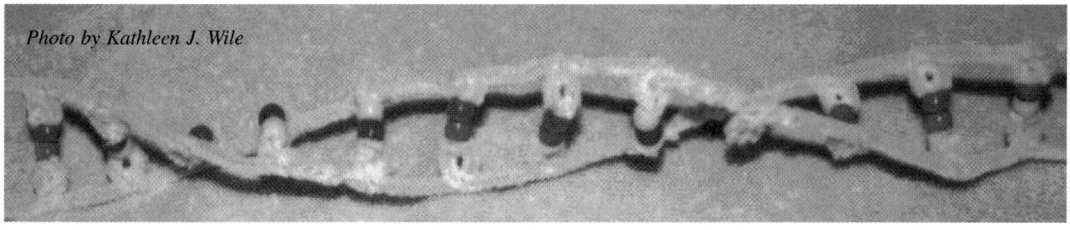

J. Your DNA model will not stay twisted unless you hold it in its twisted form for quite some time. You can do this by twisting the DNA model so that it looks right and then anchoring the ends to a table or other surface with tape. That will hold the model in its shape. After a few hours, you can release the tape and the model should stay twisted.

Now I want you to look at your DNA model. First of all, as I have said before, the pipe cleaners with the loops in them represent the backbone of the DNA. The twists in the model show you what a "double helix" structure looks like. The beads represent the nucleotides. As you have constructed the model, only the nucleotides representing adenine and thymine or the nucleotides representing guanine and cytosine touch each other. This represents the fact that in DNA, adenine only links to thymine and cytosine only links to guanine. In living organisms, the sequence of nucleotides in the DNA (represented by the sequence of colored beads in your model) is a code that can be translated into all of the information necessary for life. When you take biology, you will learn basically how this is done.

I need to make one more point about your model. In real DNA, each side of the "ladder" is really it's own molecule. The reason that the two sides of the "ladder" stay together is because adenine likes to link up to thymine and guanine likes to link up to cytosine. Thus, two backbones are connected by the nucleotides that link up. In your model, then, the place where the beads touch each other is really a link that holds one side of the ladder to the other side. If you were to cut the pipe cleaner in between the two beads, your model would begin to unravel into two halves. In real DNA, this happens as a part of the process that decodes the sequence of nucleotides into information. You will learn more about this process when you take high school biology.

What I want you to understand right now is that in order to figure out the sequence of nucleotides in DNA, you only need to know about the sequence of nucleotides on one half of the DNA. Suppose, for example, some mean person cut your DNA model right in between each bead. As I told you before, this would cause your model to unravel into two halves. Suppose further that this mean person took one half of your DNA model and left the other half. When you see the half that he left sitting on the table, you see the following:

Using just what you see there, you can figure out what the sequence of nucleotides on the other half of the DNA model was.

Remember, thymine (represented by red) links only to adenine (represented by green). Thus, the first bead there is red. This means that the first bead on the half that the mean person stole must have been green, because thymine (red) links only to adenine (green). Similarly, since yellow represents cytosine and blue represents guanine, the second bead on the side of the DNA that was stolen must have been blue, because cytosine (yellow) links only to guanine (blue). Using this kind of reasoning, you could completely reconstruct the other half of the DNA, even though it was stolen:

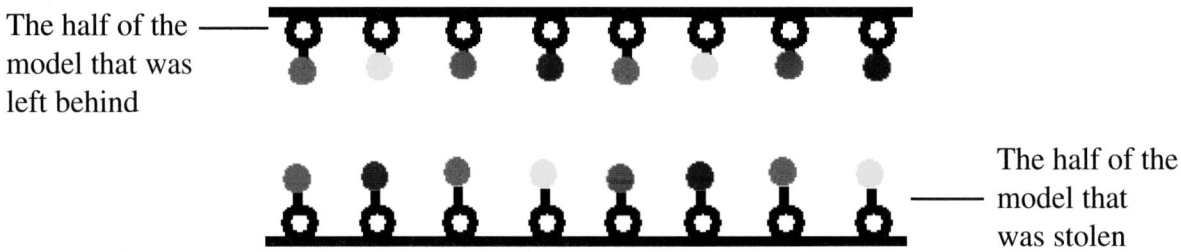

The point of this discussion, then, is that since we know thymine links only to adenine and cytosine links only to guanine, if you know the sequence of nucleotides on one half of a portion of DNA, you can determine what the sequence of nucleotides on the other half of DNA is.

ON YOUR OWN

9.3 A scientist analyzes one half of a portion of DNA. She determines the following sequence:

adenine, thymine, cytosine, adenine, guanine, cytosine, thymine

thymine, adenine, guanine, thymine, cytosine, guanine, adenine

What is the sequence of nucleotides on the other half of this portion of DNA?

9.4 Suppose that any nucleotide could link up with any other nucleotide. If this were the case, would there be any way of reconstructing the nucleotide sequence from one half of a portion of DNA, like you did in the previous problem?

Energy and Life

I have spent so much time talking to you about DNA that you probably have forgotten what I was originally discussing. In the first section of the module, I gave you four criteria for life. DNA was involved in the first criterion. I now want to proceed to the second:

2. All life forms have a method by which they take energy from the surroundings and convert it into energy that helps them live.

What does this mean? Well, it basically says that all living organisms have to "eat" in some way. You see, everything around you (plants, paper, rocks, wood,..everything) has energy in it. When you eat food, you are actually taking energy from the food and transferring it to your body. Thus, you are taking in energy from the surroundings (food) and you are converting it to energy that helps you live.

Why didn't I just word this criterion for life as "all living organisms must eat to survive?" Well, that's because the word "eat" is too restrictive. You see, some living organisms (plants, for example) actually produce their own food, so that they do not need to eat in the strict sense of the word. Perform the following experiment to see what I mean.

EXPERIMENT 9.2

Finding Food in Plants

Supplies:

- One slice of potato (uncooked)
- A pale green leaf (The paler the green, the better this experiment will work.)
- Rubbing alcohol (available at any drug store)
- Iodine (available at any drug store)
- One jar with a lid
- Two shallow dishes
- Tweezers

Procedure:

A. Place the leaf in the jar and fill the jar with about one cup of rubbing alcohol.
B. Put the lid on the jar and let it sit overnight. This should end your science work for today.
C. The next day, open the jar and dump out the alcohol. Keep the leaf.
D. In one shallow dish, place a potato slice. Pour just a little iodine on the white part of the potato slice.
E. Place the leaf in the second shallow dish. Pour enough iodine into the dish so that the leaf is covered.
F. Wait for a few moments and then grab the potato slice with the tweezers. Wash the potato with water. Try to avoid getting iodine on your hands, because it will stain them. Notice the color change that has occurred on the white part of the potato. Be sure and wash out the sink you are using with LOTS of water. Any iodine left in the sink will rust flatware and other metal objects placed in the sink, so you need to get rid of ALL iodine.
G. Wait about 2 hours and then pull the leaf out of the iodine with the tweezers. Once again, wash the leaf with water and look at it. Do you see a color change?
H. Clean everything up. Be sure and clean the sink with plenty of water!

In the experiment, you took a potato and added iodine to it. The result was that the white part of the potato turned blue. Why? Well, the potato contains **starch**. That's why we eat it. Starch is a chemical that we use as a food source. The starch contains energy, and our bodies break the starch down and convert the energy contained in it into energy that our bodies use to keep us alive. Iodine is often used to test for the presence of starch because when iodine is mixed with starch, the mixture turns a deep blue color. That's the blue color you saw on the potato.

Well, when you put the leaf in the alcohol, the alcohol broke down the protective coating that leaves are covered in. It also partially pulled out a chemical (chlorophyll) that gives the leaf its green color. This left a pale leaf with no protective coating. When you added iodine to the leaf, you should have seen part or all of leaf turn blue. That's because starch is also in the leaf. Leaves actually produce food in the form of a chemical called **glucose** (glew' kose). If the plant that the leaf is on needs energy, it takes the energy from the glucose and converts it into energy it uses to survive. If the plant has plenty of energy, it converts any unused glucose into starch, which can be broken back down into glucose when the plant needs energy.

Plants (potatoes, house plants, trees, or any other kind of plant), therefore, produce their own food. Thus, they don't "eat" in the same way you and I eat. Nevertheless, they do convert energy from their surroundings into energy which sustains them. Therefore, they do meet that criterion for life. How do plants produce their own food? Well, they take water from the ground and a gas called carbon dioxide from the air. Aided by the energy of sunlight, they chemically combine carbon dioxide and water to make glucose, the chemical I mentioned above. This process is called **photosynthesis** (foh' toh sin' thuh sis).

Photosynthesis - The process by which a plant uses the energy of sunlight and certain chemicals to produce its own food

You will learn a lot more about that process in biology. One of the by-products of photosynthesis is oxygen. Thus, plants help renew our oxygen supply so that we can continue to breathe.

Since plants make their own food, they do not need to get food from their surroundings. This long-term experiment demonstrates this fact.

EXPERIMENT 9.3
A Simple Biosphere

Supplies:

- A large jar with a lid
- A small potted plant that can fit inside the jar with room to spare
- Some water
- An area of the house that gets sunlight most every day
- A piece of masking tape or a marker

Introduction - Since plants produce their own food, they need not get it from an outside source. Under the right conditions, then, plants are self-sustaining.

Procedure:

A. Water the plant so that the soil in the pot is moist.
B. Put the potted plant into the jar and close the lid so that the plant is enclosed in the jar.
C. Mark the height of the plant on one side of the jar. You can do this with a piece of masking tape or a marker.
D. Place the jar next to a window or in some other area that is well-lit. It can even be left outside as long as the outside temperature stays pleasant.
E. Check on the plant every few days. Note whether or not it grows. Let it sit for at least 30 days. You can even let it sit for longer if the continued experiment is interesting to you. In fact, you can use this kind of experiment for a science fair project.

In the experiment, you will see that the plant will stay alive and even grow, despite the fact that it is enclosed in the jar. If a mouse, insect, or any other animal were to be unlucky enough to be enclosed in the jar, it would quickly die due to lack of food and water. Nevertheless, the plant will live and grow. Why? Well, you provided it with some water, and there was some carbon dioxide in the air that was in the jar. Since you placed the plant in sunlight, the plant will use the energy of sunlight, the water in the soil, and the carbon dioxide in the air surrounding it to make glucose and oxygen.

When the plant needs energy, it will convert the glucose into energy. It takes oxygen to do that, but oxygen will be produced when the glucose is made, so there will be plenty of oxygen available. When the glucose is converted to energy, water and carbon dioxide will also be produced. You probably will see some of that water as droplets that form on the side of the jar. That water and carbon dioxide will then be used later to produce more glucose. Do you see what will happen, then? The plant will use carbon dioxide and water to make glucose, but those two chemicals will be made when the glucose is used. In the same way, it will use up oxygen to convert the glucose to energy, but that oxygen will be made again when the glucose is made. Thus, the plant will be almost self-sustaining.

It will not be completely self-sustaining, however. It will need the energy from the sunlight. Thus, the plant takes energy from its surroundings (in the form of sunlight) and converts it into glucose, which it can use to make energy to sustain itself. Whenever you have a living system that is isolated from its surroundings and its contents continue to live and grow, that system is called a **biosphere** (by' oh sfear). In your experiment, then, you have created a very simple biosphere.

You probably should be asking yourself a question at this point. What about fertilizer? You know that farmers and gardeners often use some form of fertilizer in order to help their plants grow. Why won't your plant need fertilizer? Well, contrary to popular belief, fertilizer does not *feed* a plant. A plant uses only water, carbon dioxide, and light to make its food (glucose). Any excess food is stored as starch. Thus, fertilizer is not something that a plant eats. Fertilizer has several chemicals in it that help some of the plant's other functions (fighting disease, repairing injuries, etc.). Thus, fertilizer is kind of like a vitamin pill for plants. Just like you and I don't *need* vitamin pills to stay alive, a plant does not *need* fertilizer to stay alive. However, just as vitamin pills can help make us more healthy, fertilizer can make a plant more healthy.

Whether a living organism makes its own food or gathers its food, it then converts the food into energy. The process by which food is broken down and converted to energy is called **metabolism** (muh tab' uh liz um).

Metabolism - The process by which a living organism takes energy from its surroundings and uses it to sustain itself, develop, and grow

The process of metabolism is incredibly interesting. You will learn a lot more about it when you take biology.

As you continue to check on your biosphere, you will probably notice water droplets on the side of the jar from time to time. As I mentioned before, that is because water and carbon dioxide are produced when the plant converts glucose into energy. In fact, water and carbon dioxide are produced by the metabolism of nearly every living organism. You can see that human metabolism produces water. Just hold a glass surface near your mouth and exhale onto the glass. You will see the glass cloud up. That's because you exhale water as a product of your metabolism. The water then forms tiny droplets on the glass, clouding it. I also noted that in converting its food to energy, the plant needed oxygen. That is true for the vast majority of living organisms (not all, but most) on the earth. Most of them need oxygen in order to convert their food into energy. That's why most living things need oxygen to survive.

ON YOUR OWN

9.5 Some fertilizers are advertised as "high-quality plant food." What is wrong with such an advertisement?

9.6 Several science-oriented stores will sell you an "aquatic biosphere," which is a closed glass container that holds water, underwater plants, underwater snails, and perhaps some shrimp. The biosphere is completely closed off, but the occupants will live for quite a long time, as long as you provide the biosphere with one thing. What one thing must you provide?

Sensing and Responding to Change

Moving on down the list of our criteria for life, we come to the third criterion:

3. All life forms can sense changes in their surroundings and respond to those changes.

It is important to realize that in order to meet this criterion, an organism's ability to sense changes is just as important as its ability to respond. After all, even a rock can respond to changes in its environment. If a boulder, for example, is perched on the very edge of a cliff, a slight change in the wind patterns around the boulder might be enough for it to fall off of the cliff. In this case, the boulder is responding to the changes in its surroundings. The reason a boulder doesn't meet this criterion for life is that the boulder cannot sense the change.

Living organisms are all equipped with some method of receiving information about their surroundings. Typically, they accomplish this feat with **receptors**.

Receptors - Special structures or chemicals that allow living organisms to sense the conditions of their surroundings

Your skin, for example, is full of receptors. Some allow you to distinguish between hard and soft substances when you touch them. Other receptors react to hot and cold temperatures. Thus, if you have your hand under a stream of water coming from a water faucet, your receptors react to the temperature of the water. The receptors send information to your brain and you can then react to the temperature. If the water is too hot or too cold, you can remove your hand from the stream to avoid the discomfort.

Of course, *all* living organisms can sense and respond to change, so they *all* have receptors. Perform the following experiment to see that even earthworms can sense and respond to change.

EXPERIMENT 9.4
Sensing and Responding to Change

Supplies:

- A few earthworms
- A container that will hold the earthworms and plenty of dirt
- Dirt
- Some water
- A bright light

Introduction - All living organisms sense and respond to change in their environment. This experiment shows how earthworms respond to light and water.

Procedure:

A. One way you can get earthworms is to go to a live bait shop and buy them. If you do so, you will also get the container and dirt as a part of the package.
B. Fill your container at least halfway with dirt.
C. Put the earthworms on top of the dirt.
D. Put the container under the light.
E. Let the whole system sit for 30 minutes or more and see what happens to the earthworms.
F. Turn off the light and make the room reasonably dim.
G. Pour water on the dirt so as to make the dirt really wet.
H. Once again, wait for 30 minutes or so and see what happens to the earthworms.
I. Clean everything up. Let the earthworms go, or use them as an excuse to go fishing!

What did you see in the experiment? If all went well, you should have seen that in the first phase of the experiment, the worms dug themselves into the dirt. Why did they do that? Well, worms do not have eyes like you and me, but they can sense light, because they have light-sensitive receptors on their skin. When they sense light, they crawl away from it. Why? Earthworms actually breathe through their skin (you will learn more about that in biology). In order for that to work, their skin must stay moist. When earthworms sense light, they think that it is the sun. Since the sun tends to dry out things that are moist, the earthworms know that they must flee the sun, or their skin will dry, suffocating them. Thus, when earthworms *sense* light, they *respond* by moving away from it.

In the second part of the experiment, the earthworms should have crawled out of the dirt to the top of the soil. Once again, this is because they sensed a change in the environment and responded to it. In this case, the change was that the dirt started to get wet. In response, the earthworms came up to the surface. There are at least two reasons for this. First, if the dirt gets too wet, the earthworms can have trouble breathing through their skin. Also, when the dirt is wet, there is less danger of the earthworm's skin drying out. Thus, being on the surface is safer for the earthworm when the dirt is wet. Earthworms often come up out of ground at night (once again, because there is less chance of their skin drying out then), and that is why some people call earthworms "nightcrawlers."

Have you ever heard of leprosy? It is mentioned several times in the Bible. This terrible disease causes people's skin receptors to cease functioning properly. This causes them to lose the sense of touch, pain, etc. that comes from their skin. Thus, if a person has leprosy on his or her arm, he or she cannot feel pain when the arm is cut. Well, you might think that is a good thing, but it is not! Pain tells us that something is wrong. Thus, we can investigate the problem and fix it. If your arm gets cut, you know it, and you can clean and bandage the wound before it gets worse. Since people with leprosy cannot *feel* the pain, they can be cut and not even know it. If left untreated, the wound will become infected. In some cases, the infection can become so severe that the arm is lost or the person dies! People with leprosy must examine themselves several times each day to detect injuries that you or I would immediately know exist!

A living organism's ability to sense and respond to changes in its surrounding environment is a critical part of survival. If earthworms could not sense and respond to light, they would die. If we did not experience pain, the consequences could be terrible. You see, God's Creation is always changing. Weather changes, seasons change, landscape changes, and the community of organisms in a given region changes. As a result, living organisms must be able to sense these changes and adapt, or they will not be able to survive.

ON YOUR OWN

9.7 Although it might be hard to believe, plants sense and respond to change in their surroundings. After all, they are living organisms. Name at least one example that shows how plants sense and respond to change.

Reproduction and Life

We now come to the final criterion that determines whether or not something is alive:

4. All life forms reproduce.

We instinctively know this, of course. After all, dogs have puppies, cats have kittens, and people have children. There is, of course, a very simple reason *why* living organisms must reproduce. If they do not, they will eventually die out completely. Thus, reproduction is a means by which living organisms ensure that their kind will continue. Of course, sometimes this is not enough. As we learned from geology and paleontology, some organisms do go extinct. Nevertheless, this is rare when compared to the huge number of living organisms in Creation. Overall, reproduction is God's way of ensuring that a type of living organism will not die out.

In order to get a little bit of experience observing the process of reproduction, perform the following experiment:

EXPERIMENT 9.5
Fruit Fly Reproduction

Supplies:

- Large jar (It must be large enough to fit an banana inside.)
- Nylon stocking large enough to stretch over the mouth of the jar
- Rubber band
- A banana

Introduction - In this experiment, you will see the process of reproduction in fruit flies. **Please note:** If you are on a "normal" homeschooling schedule, you might have to delay this experiment, as it will not work well in the winter unless you live in a warm state like Florida.

Procedure:

A. Peel the banana.
B. Open the jar and stick the banana in the jar.
C. Leave the jar open and look at it daily. Eventually, you should see some small flies hovering around the banana. As you might expect, they are **fruit flies**.
D. Trap some of the flies in the jar by stretching the nylon stocking over the mouth of the jar and holding it in place with the rubber band. The stocking must cover the entire mouth of the jar. It has tiny holes that will allow air into the jar so that the flies can breathe, but the holes are too small for the flies to squeeze through. Thus, they will stay in the jar and continue to live. In case you are wondering, this is not cruel. The flies have a huge food source and are not bothered by anything trying to eat them. They are as content as flies can be.
E. Observe the jar daily over the next two weeks. Note what you see. Make drawings of what the flies look like initially, and then make drawings when the situation changes.
F. You need to observe things for at least 2 weeks. After that, you can release the flies outside or continue to observe, whichever you prefer. This is another experiment that can be used as a science fair project.

What did you see in the experiment? Well, if things went well, you should have seen that after a few days, little white crawling things appeared on the banana. Those are **maggots**. When flies reproduce, they make maggots. Thus, the maggots are "baby" flies. As the maggots mature, they become the flies that you originally saw in the jar. Over the period of 2 weeks, you should have seen maggots form and mature into adult flies. The process of maggots turning into flies is called **metamorphosis** (met uh more' fuh sis). When you take biology, you will learn more about this fascinating process.

Since reproduction is something common to all living organisms, and since there are so many different kinds of living organisms in Creation, you can imagine that reproduction takes many different forms. Consider, for example, the difference between reproduction in dogs and reproduction in humans.

FIGURE 9.2
Reproduction in Dogs and Humans

Photos from the MasterClips collection

When dogs reproduce, *several* puppies are born to a single mother dog each time. There are so many puppies, that they are typically called a **litter**. The schnauzer puppies in the picture above all came from the same litter. Thus, they have the same mother and father and were all born over a period of a few hours.

When people reproduce, usually only one baby is born at a time. Every once in a while there will be two (we call the babies **twins**), and even more rarely more than 2 will be born. One baby at a time, however, is the norm.

Why do dogs produce so many puppies at one time when people usually produce only one baby at a time? Well, the answer is simple. God has designed each living organism's reproduction in order to meet that individual organism's survival needs. In the wild, dogs die frequently, because they live reasonably dangerous lives. As a result, if dogs had few puppies, more dogs would die each year than the number of puppies born that year. As a result, every year there would be fewer and fewer dogs until there were no more dogs. Thus, since a dog's life is dangerous, dogs must have several puppies in order to keep the population of dogs steady. Human beings, however, have significantly less dangerous lives. As a result, the population of people will stay steady even when most people have only two babies or so their entire lives.

The number of offspring that a living organism has, therefore, depends on how many offspring are necessary to keep the population level up. Rabbits, for example, have a *lot* of babies. The typical rabbit can begin producing babies about six months after birth. They produce 3-8 babies in each litter. A mother rabbit can have as many as *6 litters each year*! Since the average rabbit lives about 10 years, you can see how many baby rabbits can be produced! Why do rabbits need to reproduce so much? They lead incredibly dangerous lives. There are *many* other animals that hunt and eat rabbits. As a result, *a lot* of rabbits die each year. Thus, they must produce lots of baby rabbits to keep the rabbit population steady.

Have you heard anything about earth's "population problem?" There are many people out there that think that there are just too many people on the earth. They consider this a real problem, arguing that eventually, the earth will not be able to support the number people that it holds. As a result, they say, there will be widespread famine and disease because there will be simply too many people on the earth.

Is this a real problem? Not at all! Anyone who does any research into this supposed problem will find out that there is no need to worry about the human population growing too quickly for the earth to support it. Why? Well, first and foremost, you need to know that the earth's population is growing. There is a simple reason for that. More babies are born each year than the number of people who die each year. It turns out that the average mother must have 2.2 babies in order to keep the population of humans steady.

Why does the average mother have to have 2.2 babies in order to keep the human population steady? Well, it takes two people (a mother and a father) to have a baby. Thus, each mother and father needs to have 2 babies, one to "replace" each of them when they die. However, there are *some* children that die due to disease or accident. These children will not "replace" the adults that they are supposed to replace, because they did not live long enough to have their own children. If there aren't a few "extra" babies born each year, the parents of those children will not get "replaced" when they die, and the human population will slowly decrease. Thus, the average mother must have just a little more than 2 babies in order to "replace" the mother, the father, and those whose children die early.

It turns out that in *many* countries like the U.S., the United Kingdom, Canada, and Italy, mothers are having *fewer* than 2.2 children in their lifetimes. As a result, mothers in these countries are not having enough babies in order to keep the human population steady. In addition, the *number* of countries in which mothers are having fewer than 2.2 babies is actually *increasing*! Thus, there are many countries in which the mothers are not having enough babies to replace the people who are dying, and the number of countries in that situation is growing!

Despite these facts, the human population is still growing because of countries like India in which mothers are having significantly more than 2.2 babies in their lifetime. However, the average number of babies being born to mothers in countries such as India is also *decreasing*. Thus, even though the human population is still increasing, it is not increasing all that quickly. In addition, the speed at which the human population is growing *decreases every year*. As a result, it is only a matter of time before the human population stops growing.

"Wait a minute," you might think. Even if the speed at which the population is growing is slowing down, the population will still increase for a while. Are we in danger of the population becoming too large *before* it stops growing? The answer to that question is a very firm, "No." How can I say that? Well, all I need to do is point out a few facts to you. First, the biggest indicator of whether or not there are too many people on earth is the amount of food per person. After all, if there really are too many people for the earth to support, the first thing that you would see is massive starvation. There would simply not be enough food for every person on the planet.

Well, is the food supply running out? Are we seeing that the amount of food per person is decreasing as time goes on? Absolutely not! In fact, the opposite is true. Every year since it has been studied, the amount of food per person on the earth actually *has increased.* Over the past 250 years, for example, the population of the earth has increased by a factor of 6. This means there are 6 times as many people living today than there were in the mid-1700's. Now that sounds like a lot, but consider this: *The amount of food produced over that same time period has risen by a factor of 1700!* Thus, there is more food per person on earth now than there *has ever been in history*.

If this is the case, why are there people who are starving today? That is the result of evil - not food shortage. People starve because they are in countries whose leaders hoard the wealth and food. In countries where the leaders do not horde the food and wealth, people starve because they refuse to work, or because they do not take advantage of the charitable organizations that will feed them. If all of the food on earth were divided equally among the people of the earth, we could all eat to our hearts content and still have extra.

There are other indicators you can look at to determine whether or not there are too many people on earth. The price of raw materials used in manufacturing is also a great indicator. After all, if there were too many people on earth, people would have to fight over the materials we use for building things. If that were the case, the price of these materials would go up and up. In fact, the price of *almost all* raw materials has *decreased every generation* since these things have been measured.

In the end, then, the human population on earth is *not* a problem. The rate at which it is growing decreases every year. We therefore know that the population of people will eventually level off and then, most likely, decrease slowly. Meanwhile, the amount of food per person on earth is increasing, and the cost of raw materials is decreasing. Thus, there are no population problems to worry about. God has designed the earth as our home, and He would not skimp on the design. His gift to us will provide for our needs as long as He sees fit!

ON YOUR OWN

9.8 The bombardier beetle is a very interesting insect that you will learn about in biology class. It is an ugly beetle with a powerful chemical weapon that wards off any creatures wanting to eat it. As a result, bombardier beetles live a very safe life. Would you expect bombardier beetles to produce a lot of baby beetles or only a few?

The Cell - Life's Smallest Unit

Now that you know the basic criteria that determine whether or not something is alive, it is important for you to see *how* living organisms meet these criteria. For example, all living organisms have DNA. Where is the DNA? All living organisms convert energy from their surroundings into energy that sustains them. Where and how does that happen? All living organisms sense and respond to change in their surroundings. How? All living organisms reproduce. What are the details?

Well, the answers to many of those questions are too detailed for this course. You will learn some of the answers when you take biology. However, I can *begin* to answer some of those questions by introducing you to life's most basic unit: the **cell**.

Cell - The smallest unit of life in Creation

What is a cell? Well, it is a tiny blob of a jelly-like substance called **cytoplasm** (sigh' tuh plaz um) with other structures inside. Usually (not always) the cytoplasm is surrounded by an enclosure called a **membrane**. The structures inside a cell are called **organelles**.

FIGURE 9.3
A Simplistic Representation of a Cell

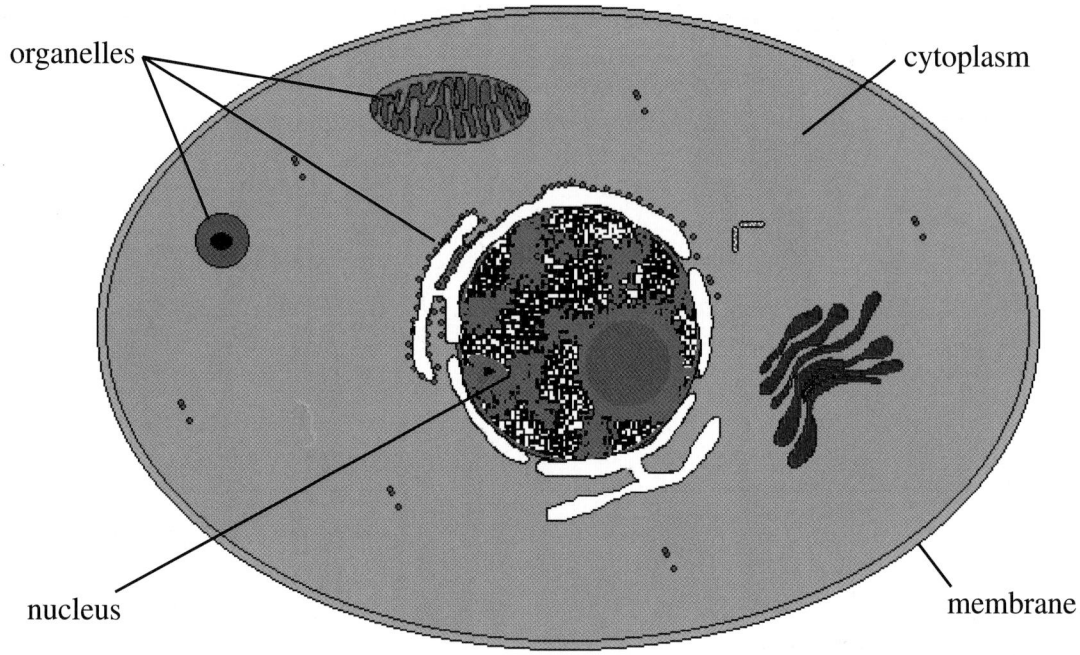

Believe it or not, your entire body is made up of cells. In fact, just as everything you see is made up of atoms, all life is made up of cells. There are, roughly, one hundred trillion cells that make up your body! These cells work together to make you the person that you are. You see, every cell in your body has particular tasks that it must accomplish. You have cells in your eye that detect light and, based on what they detect, they send electrical signals to your brain. You have cells in your skin that protect your body from foreign substances. You have cells in your blood that transport oxygen to all of the cells in your body. These cells work together along with millions of other different cells to make you the person that you are!

Interestingly enough, the cells that are in you are very similar to the cells that we find in cats, dogs, and other animals. Even the cells in an elephant are very similar to the cells that you have in your body. Of course, it takes many more cells to make an elephant than to make you, and it takes fewer cells to make a dog or a cat. Also, the tasks that these cells perform and the ways in which they work together are different. That's a large part of why a dog is different than a cat and an elephant is different than you. Nevertheless, the cells themselves are very similar.

You will study cells in *great detail* when you take biology, but I do want you to know a few things about them right now. First of all, they are very small. That is obviously the case, since there are about a hundred trillion of them in your body! The cells in your body range in size, but the average cell is about *one ten thousandth* of an inch across. That's pretty small! The largest cell in the body is about four hundredths of an inch across. Thus, you cannot see cells with your naked eyes. You must use a microscope.

The second thing you need to know about cells is that it does not necessarily take lots of cells to make a living organism. Although humans, cats, insects, and many, many other living organisms are composed of trillions of cells, there are literally *millions* of living organisms that are composed of *only one* cell. Indeed, there is an entire microscopic world of which you are mostly unaware. You will learn a lot more about that world when you take biology. The organisms that make up this microscopic world are often made up of just one cell! Thus, a single cell *can* perform all of the functions of life. Thus, a *single cell* is considered alive!

The third thing that I want to point out is that cells themselves can reproduce. They must be able to, or they would not be considered alive. What you might not have considered, however, is that there are certainly cells in your body that are reproducing *right now* as you read this text. After all, in order to grow, you need more cells. Where do those cells come from? They come from the reproduction of other cells. Also, you have cells in your body that die all of the time. When you scratch your skin, for example, you destroy hundreds of skin cells. Those cells must be replaced. Thus, cells are constantly reproducing in your body in order to replace cells that have died and in order to make new cells so that you can grow.

The fourth thing that I want you to know is the identity of one of the organelles in the cell. It is called the **nucleus** (new' clee us), and it is pointed out in Figure 9.3. Usually near the center of the cell, the nucleus is probably the most important organelle in the cell. It is where you will find the DNA of the organism.

The last thing that you need to know about cells is that there are three basic kinds of cells in Creation. The one sketched in Figure 9.3 is called an **animal cell**. It is the basic cell that you find in animals. Plants have a slightly different kind of basic cell, and it is called, as you might imagine, a **plant cell**. Finally, there is a third kind of cell that is typically found in the tiniest single-celled living organisms. These organisms are called **bacteria**, and a cell from such an organism does not have a nucleus. There is still DNA in the cell, it is just not housed in the nucleus, because there is no nucleus. This is one reason that the nucleus is considered an important organelle in the cell. The presence or absence of a nucleus in a cell can help identify what kind of cell it is. You will learn more about cells without a nucleus in the next module.

In order for something to be living, it must meet all of the criteria listed at the beginning of this module. If that is the case, then it will *definitely* be comprised of cells. Thus, you could add a fifth criterion for life: All life forms are comprised of at least one cell. This, however, is usually not done, since anything that meets the other criteria *must* be comprised of cells. Since the cell is the smallest unit that can satisfy all four criteria for life, the cell is considered the most basic unit of life itself.

ON YOUR OWN

9.9 A mule is a cross between a horse and a donkey. Most mules are sterile, which means they cannot produce offspring. Does this mean they are unable to meet the fourth criterion for life and are therefore not considered alive? Why or why not?

9.10 Suppose a scientist is looking at the following cells under a microscope:

a. a cell from a bacterium (the singular form of bacteria)
b. a cell from an onion
c. a cell from a mouse
d a cell from a blade of grass
e. a cell from a horse

Which cells would look very similar to each other under the microscope?

ANSWERS TO THE ON YOUR OWN PROBLEMS

9.1 Remember, atoms link together to make molecules. Therefore, molecules must be bigger than atoms, because there are two or more atoms in a molecule. Thus, atoms are smaller.

9.2 A cookbook has many recipes in it. These recipes have information that tells you how to take many individual things that you would probably not eat and put them together in such a way as to make them something you would eat. Like a cookbook, DNA has information that takes many individual chemicals which are not alive and puts them together in such a way as to make life.

9.3 Remember, DNA is held together by nucleotides on one half of the molecule linking up with nucleotides on the other half. Only adenine and thymine can link together, and only cytosine and guanine will link together. Thus, the other side must be:

thymine, adenine, guanine, thymine, cytosine, guanine, adenine

9.4 There would be no way to do it. The way we determined the first nucleotide on the other half of the DNA molecule in the previous problem was by recognizing that only thymine can link to adenine. If any nucleotide could link to adenine, there would be no way to know which nucleotide would be there.

9.5 Fertilizers are NOT plant food. Plants make their own food. Fertilizers are plant vitamins.

9.6 You must provide light. The plant will make food for itself, and the other creatures will eat either the plant or tiny organisms that you cannot see which eat the plant. The plant will also make enough oxygen for all the organisms, but it needs light to do that.

9.7 There are many ways that plants sense and respond to change. Here are a few:

Plants can sense where the greatest amount of light is and they will grow towards that light.

Plants can sense when they touch a structure and, if the structure is right, they will wind themselves around the structure for support.

Plants can sense which way is up and they will always grow that way.

Plants can sense when it is night and respond. For example, many plants close their flowers at night and open them in the morning.

There are other examples, but these are the most common. You will experiment with some of these later on in the course.

9.8 Since the bombardier beetle leads a pretty safe life, there will not be a lot that die before having babies. Thus, they do not need a lot of extra "replacements." Therefore, you would think that bombardier beetles have few offspring.

9.9 Although the mule itself cannot produce baby mules, each of its cells can reproduce. Otherwise, it would not grow or be able to heal if it is hurt. Thus, the mule still meets the fourth criterion of life, but it does so because of its cells' ability to reproduce.

9.10 Cells (b) and (d) would look very similar, because they would be plant cells. Similarly, cells (c) and (e) would look very similar, because they are animal cells.

STUDY GUIDE FOR MODULE #9

1. Define the following terms:

a. Atom
b. Molecule
c. Photosynthesis
d. Metabolism
e. Receptors
f. Cell

2. What are the four criteria for life?

3. What does DNA provide to a living organism?

4. Compared to other molecules, is DNA big or small?

5. Does DNA store its information more efficiently or less efficiently than a computer?

6. DNA is made up of two basic parts: the backbone and the nucleotides.

   a. Which part stores the information?

   b. Which part forms the double helix structure?

7. Which nucleotide will link to adenine? Which will link to cytosine?

8. One half of a portion of DNA has the following sequence:

cytosine, guanine, adenine, guanine, thymine, thymine

What is the sequence of nucleotides on the other half of this portion?

9. One half of a portion of DNA has the following sequence:

thymine, guanine, cytosine, adenine, thymine, guanine

What is the sequence of nucleotides on the other half of this portion?

10. What is the name of the chemical that plants make for food?

11. What is the name of the chemical that plants store their food as?

12. What is a biosphere?

13. Metabolism requires food and something else. What is that something else?

14. Metabolism produces energy and usually two other things. What are they?

15. An organism's receptors no longer work. Which of the 4 criteria of life will the organism not be able to perform?

16. Consider the difference between a shark and an anchovy. Both are fish. The first is a fierce hunter that rarely is eaten by any other animal. The second is a major source of food for many other fish in the sea. Which would you expect to have more babies: two shark parents or two anchovy parents?

17. Every once in a while, a female cat will be born sterile. This means that the cat cannot have kittens. Does this mean that the cat is not alive, since it cannot reproduce?

18. Is the population of people on this earth becoming a problem?

19. In the following picture:

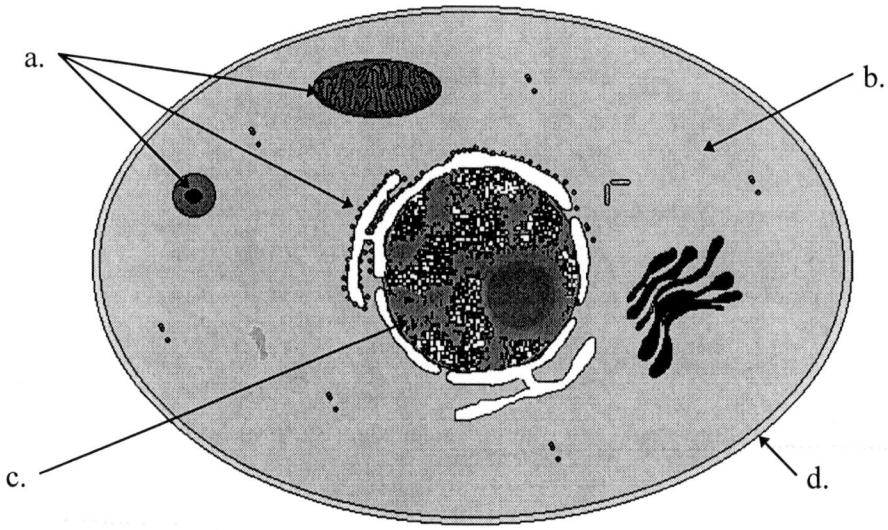

Indicate what the arrows are pointing out.

20. In the picture above, where is the DNA stored?

21. How many basic kinds of cells are there?

22. If a scientist uses a microscope to examine a cell from a mouse, a cell from a leaf, and a cell from a cat, how many different basic kinds of cells will she see?

Module #10: Classifying Life

Initial Experiment Setup

In the third section of this module (Kingdom Monera), you will be studying bacteria. Although it is impossible to see bacteria without the aid of a nice microscope, I want you to perform an experiment that will help you learn a bit about bacteria. This experiment must sit for 2 days, however, so I want you to start it now so that it is ready when you reach that section of the module.

EXPERIMENT 10.1 - Part 1

Factors that Affect Bacterial Growth

Supplies:

- One chicken bouillon cube
- Table salt
- White vinegar
- 4 small glasses
- One large glass
- One measuring cup
- One teaspoon
- Masking tape
- Marker or pen

Introduction - This experiment allows you to see how bacteria grow despite the fact that you cannot see bacteria without a microscope.

Procedure:

A. Dissolve the bouillon cube in one and one-third ($1\frac{1}{3}$) cup of hot water from the faucet. Do this in the large glass. The entire cube may not dissolve. That's fine.
B. Equally divide the solution between the four glasses.
C. To one glass, add a teaspoon of salt and stir until the salt is dissolved. Label this glass with masking tape that has the word "salt" on it.
D. To another glass, add a teaspoon of vinegar and stir. Label this glass with masking tape that has the word "vinegar" on it.
E. Label the third glass with masking tape that has the word "control" on it.
F. Label the last glass with masking tape that has the word "cold" on it.
G. Put that glass in the refrigerator.
H. Do not cover any of the glasses.
I. Allow the glasses to sit for 2 days. While the glasses are sitting, continue with the module.

Introduction

In the previous module, you learned in detail the different criteria that must be met in order to consider something to be alive. If something satisfies the four criteria you learned in the last module, it is alive. If it fails to meet even one of the criteria, it is not alive. Thus, based on those four criteria, we can *distinguish* between life and non-life. In other words, we have formed a **classification system**. In this classification system, we identify all things around us as either alive or not alive. A rock is not alive, but a houseplant is alive. Thus, there are two categories in this classification system.

If you think about it, you use classification systems all of the time. You classify other students as publicly-schooled, privately-schooled, or homeschooled. You also classify them as people you like, people you can tolerate, or people you don't really like. In both of these classification systems, other students belong to one of three categories. In the end, then, you are already familiar with the use of classification systems.

Why do you use classification systems? Well, a classification system takes an enormous amount of data and orders it in an easy-to-access, meaningful way. Consider, for example, the idea of classifying students based on how they are educated. Although there are many differences from one homeschooled student to the next, homeschooled students share much in common. In the same way, all publicly-schooled students share common experiences, despite the fact that every individual student is unique. Finally, privately-schooled students also have many things in common, despite their individual characteristics. By placing students into one of those three categories, you are "ordering" them in an easy-to-access system of reference.

So what? What does that do for you? Well, suppose you wanted to study different kinds of educational methods. If you gave a bunch of students a few standardized tests, you could then take all of the publicly-schooled students and average their test scores, take all of the privately-schooled students and figure out a separate average test score for them, and finally, you could compute the average test score of the homeschooled students. If you then compared those three averages, you might learn something about the effectiveness of each type of learning. In fact, many such studies have been done. In general, homeschooled students have the highest average test scores, privately-schooled students have lower average test scores, and publicly-schooled students have the lowest average test scores.

See what this classification system has allowed us to learn? By grouping students together in a few distinct classifications, we have been able to learn something about the effectiveness of the various types of schooling. Without the classification system, having a bunch of students take standardized tests doesn't tell you anything except the amount of knowledge that each individual has. By putting the students in categories and comparing the test score between categories, however, you have learned something more.

Classification, then, is a way of grouping things in terms of similarities that they share. This takes a large amount of data and organizes it in a way that helps us learn something about those things that we are classifying. Well, since the goal of science is to learn, it makes sense that scientists like to classify things, too. In fact, you have already learned some classification systems in this course. In an earlier module, you learned that there are three kinds of rock: sedimentary, igneous, and metamorphic. That's a classification system for rocks which contains three distinct categories.

In this module, you will learn a five-category classification system for living organisms. This classification system is used throughout the life sciences, in an attempt to take the enormous amount of information that pertains to life and order it in some meaningful, easy-to-use way.

The Five-Kingdom System

The study of life is often referred to as the science of **biology**. In biology, the **five-kingdom system** is the standard classification system used in classifying living organisms. In this system, the main categories are called "kingdoms." As you might expect, there are five of them. The names of these kingdoms are **Monera** (muh nihr' uh)**, Protista** (pruh tist' uh)**, Fungi** (fun' jye)**, Plantae,** and **Animalia**. The proper names of all the classification groups are Latin, and when we use those names, we capitalize them to emphasize that these are proper classification names.

Now first of all, you should not be afraid of these names. I expect that they are mostly new to you, but that's okay. You will be studying these five kingdoms throughout this entire module, so you have plenty of time to learn the names. Instead, you should focus on the things that you recognize about them already. For example, look at the last two. Those are just Latin names for "plants" and "animals." Thus, you really know two of these five kingdoms already. They are the kingdoms that contain plants and animals. You might even be familiar with the third kingdom as well. Have you every heard a mushroom referred to as a fungus? Well, "fungi" is just the plural form of "fungus." Thus, kingdom Fungi contains mushrooms. It contains other organisms as well, but I will get to that a little later on.

What about those other two kingdoms? Well, remember in the last module I said that there is a tiny, microscopic world of which you are mostly unaware? Those two kingdoms (Monera and Protista) contain most of the organisms in that microscopic world. The five-kingdom system, then, isn't so bad. The first two kingdoms are Monera and Protista, which contain mostly microscopic organisms. The third kingdom is Fungi, and it contains organisms like mushrooms. The fourth kingdom (Plantae) contains plants, and the fifth kingdom (Animalia) contains all of the animals. I will be discussing each kingdom individually, so do not be worried if you are still a bit confused.

Now, how do we know what organisms go into what kingdom? Well, we group organisms together based on similar characteristics. Since we are trying to put *all* living organisms in Creation into one of five categories, these similarities have to be pretty basic. For example, the first and most basic distinction that we make between organisms is based on the number and type of cells that the organism has.

Remember from the previous module that there are three kinds of cells: plant cells, animal cells, and cells without a nucleus. I now want to expand on that fact. Cells that have a nucleus (plant cells and animal cells) are called **eukaryotic** (yoo kehr ee aht' ik) cells. Cells without a nucleus are called **prokaryotic** (pro kehr ee aht' ik) cells. Now remember, the nucleus is an organelle. Well, if a cell has no nucleus, it will not have any other organelles. Thus, we can define these two types of cells as follows:

Prokaryotic cell - A cell that has no organelles

Eukaryotic cell - A cell with organelles

Study the following figure to see the difference between prokaryotic and eukaryotic cells.

FIGURE 10.1
The Difference Between Prokaryotic and Eukaryotic Cells

Sketch of a Prokaryotic Cell

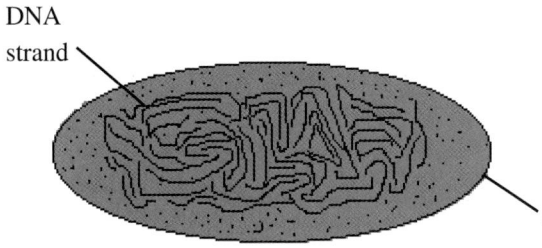

A prokaryotic cell contains no organelles. The main feature of a prokaryotic cell is the DNA strands visible throughout the cell.

Sketch of a Eukaryotic Cell

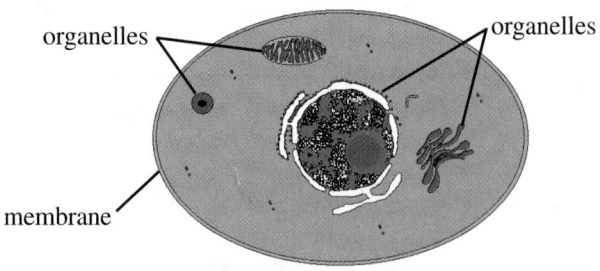

A eukaryotic cell has organelles. These organelles have their own tasks to perform in order to maintain the life of the cell. The DNA of a eukaryotic cell is stored in the nucleus of the cell.

Now that you know the distinction between these two basic cell types, I can finally discuss how to split organisms up into the five different kingdoms. Kingdom Monera contains all organisms that are composed of prokaryotic cells. Bacteria are the most well-known members of kingdom Monera. They are made of a single, prokaryotic cell. I will discuss bacteria in more detail in the next section of this module.

The next kingdom is called Protista. It contains those organisms that are composed of only one eukaryotic cell. It also contains organisms which are referred to as **algae** (al' jee). Algae are composed of eukaryotic cells and look like water plants, but they are not really plants. Plants have specialized components like roots, leaves, stems, etc. Algae do not. Seaweed is an example of algae. Notice, then, that although many of the organisms in this kingdom are microscopic, others are not. The single-celled organisms contained in this kingdom are microscopic. Even some of the algae contained in this kingdom is microscopic. However, there are certain forms of algae (like seaweed) that are not microscopic and can therefore be seen with the naked eye.

Moving out of the microscopic world (for the most part) and into the macroscopic world (the world we can see with the naked eye), we come to the kingdom Fungi. This kingdom is comprised mostly of organisms that feed on dead organisms. As I have noted before, mushrooms are placed in kingdom Fungi. Most fungi are visible to the naked eye and therefore are composed of trillions of cells. However, there are examples of single-celled organisms that we place in kingdom Fungi. Yeast is the most common example of a single-celled member of kingdom Fungi. Whether they are made of one cell or many, all fungi have eukaryotic cells.

The next kingdom, Plantae, is composed of organisms that produce their own food. Almost all members of kingdom Plantae are made of many eukaryotic cells. Trees, grass, bushes, etc., are all members of kingdom Plantae.

The last kingdom, Animalia, also contains organisms made of many eukaryotic cells. Members of kingdom Animalia are separated from kingdom Plantae by the fact that they eat other (usually living) organisms (fungi, plants, or other animals) rather than making their own food. Of course, members of kingdom Animalia are called "animals." Grasshoppers, birds, cats, fish, and snakes are all members of kingdom Animalia.

ON YOUR OWN

10.1 An organism is made up of one prokaryotic cell. To what kingdom does it belong?

10.2 An organism is made up of many eukaryotic cells. It makes its own food and has specialized structures like roots, stems, and leaves. To what kingdom does it belong?

10.3 An organism is made of many eukaryotic cells. It eats only dead organisms. To what kingdom does it belong?

Kingdom Monera

With kingdom Monera, we begin to discuss the incredible microscopic world that exists all around us. This world, unknown to human beings until 1675 when Anton van Leeuwenhoek crafted a crude magnifying lens, is home to an incredibly large number of microorganisms. Amazingly enough, the combined weight of all microscopic organisms far exceeds the combined weight of all other living organisms on earth! Bringing this fact a little closer to home, the number of organisms in kingdom Monera that live in your gut and on your skin is larger than the number of cells in your entire body! Thus, even though microorganisms are small, they are an important part of life on earth.

Organisms in kingdom Monera are interesting on many different levels. First of all, these organisms are not well-understood by biologists. There are several facets of their structure and function that we simply do not understand. Secondly, these organisms can survive in habitats that are deadly to other organisms. For example, they live on dust particles floating 6 kilometers (20,000 ft) above the surface of the earth. They thrive and multiply in temperatures that are too extreme for any other organism. In fact, microbiologists have found certain organisms from kingdom Monera living on the core of a nuclear reactor, *which can attain a temperature of up to 2000 °F*! Finally, members of kingdom Monera represent the smallest organisms in Creation. The average member of this kingdom is less than *one ten-thousandth of an inch* across! Clearly, then, these interesting organisms are worth studying.

Without a very nice microscope, you will never be able to see bacteria. To give you an idea of what bacteria look like and how small they are, look at the following photograph, which was taken with a very specialized microscope called an "electron microscope." The organism pictured is a bacterium (that's the singular form of bacteria) which is called *Pseudomonas* (sue' doh mohn' us). The picture made by the electron microscope is 36,000 times the actual size of the bacterium shown!

FIGURE 10.2
The Bacterium *Pseudomonas* Magnified 36,000 Times

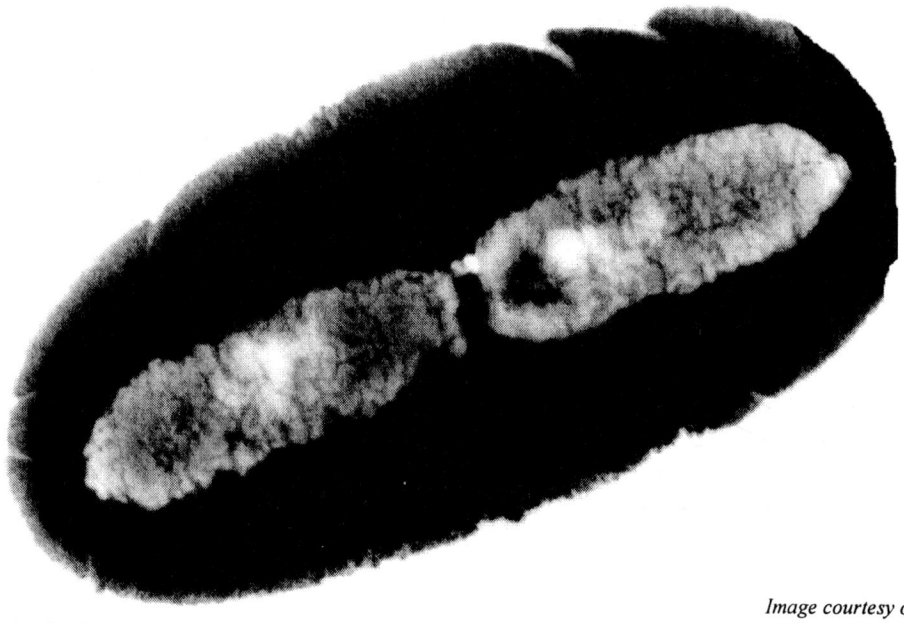

Image courtesy of Beth Verhostra

Even though it is impossible to see bacteria without the aid of a nice microscope, the experiment you started at the beginning of this module should allow you to see them indirectly. The instructions below tell you how to finish that experiment.

EXPERIMENT 10.1 - Part 2

Supplies:

- The four glasses from the beginning of the experiment
- White paper (no lines if possible)
- A brightly-colored marker or crayon

Introduction - This is a continuation of the first experiment. You will now be able to see bacteria in an indirect way.

Procedure:

A. Take the white paper and, at the very bottom, write "HELLO" with the brightly-colored marker or crayon. The letters should not be taller than the level of liquid in each of the glasses.
B. Put the paper behind the glass labeled "control" so that the word "HELLO" is behind the liquid in the glass.
C. Try to look through the liquid and see if you can read the word from the other side of the glass. Note whether you can clearly see it, mostly see it, barely see it, or not see it at all.
D. Repeat steps (B) and (C) with the other glasses. Each time, note how easy it is to see the word "HELLO" through the liquid in the glass.
E. Dump the liquids down the drain, thoroughly rinsing the sink with HOT water.
F. Wash your hands *thoroughly* with soap and warm water.

What did you see? If things went well, you probably were not able or were just barely able to see the word "HELLO" through the control. However, you were probably able to see the word somewhat through the liquid that had salt in it as well as the liquid that had been in the refrigerator. In addition, you should have been able to see the word very clearly through the liquid that had the vinegar in it.

How does all of this relate to bacteria? During the two days that the liquid sat out, bacteria were able to enter the glasses. Most likely, they were deposited in the glass by dust particles that settled in the liquid. There were also probably some in the glass BEFORE you added anything else to it. The chicken bouillon acted as a food source for these bacteria, allowing them to grow and reproduce. As the two days went by, more and more bacteria began populating the liquid. Their presence caused the liquid to become cloudy. Thus, the cloudier the liquid, the more bacteria there were in the liquid.

Since the control was the cloudiest, we can conclude that bacteria grow and reproduce very well in water with bouillon at room temperature. Since the liquid with salt was not as cloudy, we can conclude that salt tends to hurt the growth and reproduction of bacteria. In the same way, since the refrigerated liquid was less cloudy than the control, we can conclude that low temperatures tend to hurt the growth and reproduction of bacteria. Finally, since the liquid with vinegar was pretty clear, we can conclude that vinegar really hurts the growth and reproduction of bacteria.

I want to get back to that point in a minute. First, however, I want to explain why I told you to rinse the sink out thoroughly with HOT water and to wash your hands thoroughly with soap and warm water. You see, it was very important that you get rid of all the bacteria that grew in your experiment. That's because many bacteria are **pathogenic**.

Pathogen - An organism that causes disease

Pathogenic bacteria, then, are bacteria that cause disease. In fact, many of the ailments that plague humanity, plants, and animals are caused by pathogenic bacteria.

The bacterium *Clostridium* (claw strid' ee um) *botulinum* (bot' yool in um), is one of the principal causes of food poisoning. If food has not been properly cooked to rid it of bacteria, this is one of the most likely contaminates. Eating food with this bacteria will cause botulism. Mild cases of botulism involve severe nausea, diarrhea, and high fever. However, severe cases of botulism can cause you to stop breathing entirely, which will lead (of course) to death.

Bacteria known as *Salmonella* (sa muh nihl' uh) are common contaminates of eggs and poultry. People are infected by these bacteria when the poultry or eggs that they have eaten have not been cooked thoroughly. Since these bacteria are present in nearly every bird, about the only way to make sure you get rid of them is by really cooking the meat or eggs thoroughly. The heat will then kill the bacteria. Once again, while mild cases of *Salmonella* poisoning cause just nausea and diarrhea, severe cases can cause death.

This list could go on and on and on. Since many bacteria are pathogenic, it is important to try and limit our exposure to them. That's why I told you to rinse the sink thoroughly, so that all of the bacteria would go down the drain. If any bacteria were left in the sink and you used a dish that had been in the sink and not washed well, you could be exposing yourself to the bacteria that you grew in the experiment. It was also important to wash your hands so that any bacteria which got on your hands during the second part of the experiment (or during cleanup) also went down the drain.

Since it is important for us to limit the amount of exposure we have to bacteria, it is instructive to look at the results of the experiment again. The experiment demonstrated that bacteria grow and reproduce reasonably well in liquid that has a food source at room temperature. You can reduce the growth and reproduction somewhat by adding salt or refrigerating the liquid. You can reduce the growth and reproduction more by adding vinegar.

Now think about those results in terms of what we do with our food. When you buy meat, eggs, milk, and things like that at the store, what do you immediately do when you get home? You put the food in the refrigerator. Why? Well, most people would say that it keeps the food from spoiling, at least for a while. That's true, but why? The answer is that a *lot* of what we call "food spoilage" is caused by bacteria. Milk goes sour and curdles because of bacteria. Meat gets rancid because of bacteria. Thus, putting food in the refrigerator reduces the growth and reproduction of bacteria, which keeps the food from spoiling for a while.

Do you know how people stored meat before we had refrigeration? Typically, they *salted* it. As your experiment demonstrated, salt seems to reduce bacteria growth and reproduction just about as well as refrigeration. As a result, salt was a precious substance before refrigeration was widely available. Of course, the problem with using salt is that it does change the taste of the food you are trying to store. For meat, salt usually adds flavor, so that's not a problem. However, you would definitely *not* want to salt milk! Thus, although salt did help increase the time that some foods could be stored, it is not as widely applicable as refrigeration!

What about using vinegar? After all, your experiment demonstrated that the addition of vinegar reduced bacteria growth and reproduction even more than salt or refrigeration. Well, some people still use vinegar to preserve food for long periods of time. We call it "pickling." When you pickle food, the process involves adding vinegar, which nearly stops bacteria growth and reproduction. Pickling, then, is an excellent way to store food. Like salting, however, is it not reasonable for many foods, because it affects the taste significantly.

There are other ways to reduce the growth and reproduction of bacteria. For example, bacteria *must* have moisture to survive. Thus, **dehydrated food** (food in which almost all of the water has been removed) can be stored for a long, long time without fear of significant contamination by bacteria. In addition, you can severely reduce the amount of bacteria growth and reproduction by killing most of the bacteria in the food initially and then sealing it away from the outside. Remember, the liquids in your experiment were exposed to the air, and bacteria were introduced into them from the dust particles floating in the air. If you had sealed the liquids, they would have not had as many bacteria in them. In addition, had you boiled the liquid to kill most of the bacteria and *then* sealed it, the bacteria growth and reproduction would be almost non-existent. That's the idea behind canned foods. Canned foods are cooked or treated in some other way to kill the bacteria already in the food. Then, when they are put it the can, they are sealed away from the air. Thus, no bacteria can get in, and therefore canned foods can be stored for a long time.

Before I finish this section, I want to make sure you understand that *not all bacteria are pathogenic*. I have spent so much time talking about pathogenic bacteria and how to limit your exposure to them that you might get the idea that all bacteria are bad for you. That's just not true.

There are bacteria which live inside you that help you immensely. For example, one of the by-products of a gut-dwelling bacterium's metabolism is vitamin K, a substance your body needs. Gut-dwelling bacteria also secrete a chemical that helps your body digest fat. In addition, some bacteria in your gut actually keep pathogenic bacteria from growing and reproducing there. These bacteria, then, actually keep you healthy!

We also use certain bacteria to help us make food. Bacteria called *Lactobacillus* (lak' toh buh sil us') help us make cheese. When a starter bacterium is added to milk, it turns the milk into a chemical called lactic acid, and it begins to separate the milk solids (called "curds") from the liquids in the milk (called "whey"). If most of the whey is drained away, the moist curds left over are cottage cheese. Adding butter to the curds will make creamed cheese. Finally, if other bacteria are allowed to grow and breed on the curds, cheese forms. Cheddar cheese, for example, is the result of a certain bacteria type growing for a long period of time at moderate temperatures. If the bacteria type, temperature, or time of growth is changed, a different type of cheese will be produced. Cheese isn't the only thing that we use bacteria to help us make, however. Bacteria are also used in the making of sauerkraut, vinegar, yogurt, and buttermilk.

ON YOUR OWN

10.4 A biologist looks at three milk samples under a microscope. The milk samples were all taken from the same bottle of milk, but they were put in three different glasses. The first glass was covered and placed in the refrigerator for 5 hours. The second was left sitting on a counter uncovered for 5 hours. The third was left sitting out on the same counter for 5 hours, but it was covered during that time period. In which sample would the biologist find the most bacteria? In which sample would the biologist find the least bacteria?

Kingdom Protista

The next kingdom that I want to discuss has some things in common with kingdom Monera. For example, like kingdom Monera, most of the organisms in kingdom Protista can be seen only with the aid of a microscope. There are two major differences, however. First, members of kingdom Protista are made of eukaryotic cells, while the members of kingdom Monera are composed of prokaryotic cells. Second, the members of kingdom Protista are much bigger. Typically, single-celled organisms in kingdom Protista are about 10 - 100 times larger than the single-celled members of kingdom Monera.

This kingdom is usually split into two groups: **protozoa** (proh' tuh zoh' uh) and **algae**. Protozoa are mostly single-celled and tend to behave like little animals. They can move around, and most of them eat other organisms. Algae, on the other hand, are more like plants. They do not have a plant's specialized structures like roots, stems, and leaves. However, they do make their own food, just like plants.

As I mentioned in the previous module, plants (and algae) make their own food through the process of photosynthesis. One of the substances that is used up in the process of photosynthesis is carbon dioxide, and one of the by-products is oxygen. Thus, the process of photosynthesis uses up carbon dioxide and produces oxygen. It turns out that this is very useful for animals, because when animals breathe, they use up oxygen and produce carbon dioxide. Thus, the process of photosynthesis gets rid of the excess carbon dioxide produced by animals and puts more oxygen back into the air so that the animals can breathe it again.

A lot of students already know that. They know that photosynthesis is absolutely essential to keep the earth's supply of oxygen plentiful. What most students *do not know*, however, is that *algae* are the most important source of photosynthesis on earth. Plants (trees, grass, etc.) produce about 25% of the earth's oxygen supply through photosynthesis, while algae produce nearly 75% of the earth's oxygen supply through photosynthesis. Thus, in terms of earth's oxygen supply, the members of kingdom Protista are extremely important!

To give you an idea of what kinds of organisms belong to this kingdom, I want to show you the following two figures.

FIGURE 10.3
Protozoa From Kingdom Protista

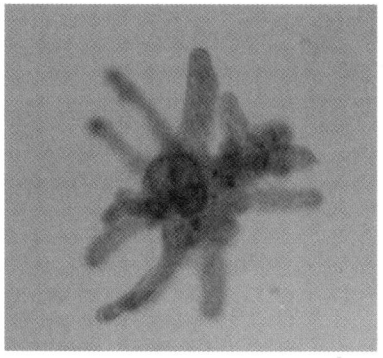

Amoeba (ah mee' buh) - magnified 400 times

These organisms do not have any defined shape. Instead, they exist as a "blob" that is constantly changing its shape. The "arms" that you see there are called pseudopods (soo' doe pods). In order to move, amoebas stretch a pseudopod out and force all of their cytoplasm into the pseudopod. By repeating this process several times, amoebas can slowly move from one place to another.

Photo by Kathleen J. Wile

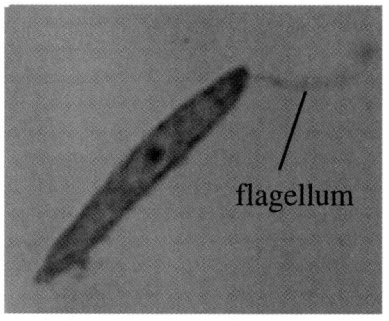

Euglena (yoo glee' na) - magnified 1000 times

These organisms are typically smaller than amoeba. They move themselves with a tail called a flagellum (flah gel uhm'). Although these organisms do eat other organisms, they also can produce food with photosynthesis.

Photo by Kathleen J. Wile

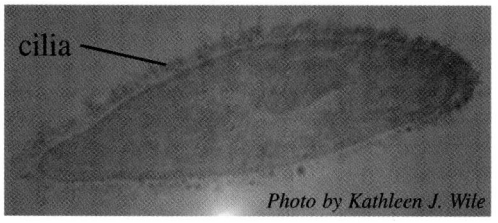

Paramecium (pehr uh mee' see um) - magnified 350 times

These organisms are typically the largest of the protozoa. They move by beating the "hairs," called cilia (sil' ee uh), back and forth like little oars in the water.

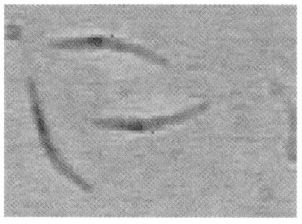

Plasmodium (plas moe' dee um) - magnified 700 times

These organisms cause the disease known as malaria. They are usually transmitted through mosquito bites.

Photo courtesy of Pathologists Associated

FIGURE 10.4
Algae From Kingdom Protista

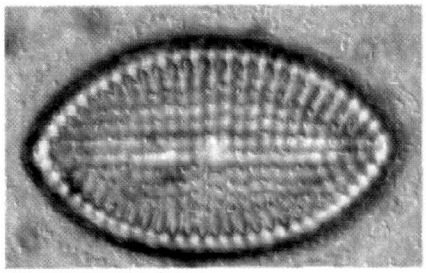

Diatom - magnified 400 times

This organism is just one of many different kinds of diatoms. Diatoms are the most important group of organisms on the planet when it comes to photosynthesis.

Photo by Kathleen J. Wile

Kelp - (no magnification)

Although this looks like a water plant, it is not. It has no specialized structures like roots, stems, or leaves. It is one of the many forms of what is commonly called "seaweed." Unlike the microscopic members of kingdom Protista, kelp can grow to be very large. Kelp as long as 100 feet have been seen!

Photo by Cyber Sea Photography

Red algae - (no magnification)

This is another form of seaweed. It is interesting because of its red color. Most organisms that perform photosynthesis are green. Red algae is one of the exceptions to that general rule.

Photo © Mike Guiry, NUI, Galway

Like bacteria, members of kingdom Protista need moisture to live. Wherever there is water, there will probably be protozoa, algae, or both. They live in freshwater ponds, streams, and lakes as well as saltwater oceans and lakes. They even live in soil and inside the bodies of animals and human beings. Some members of this kingdom are pathogenic. As pointed out in the Figure 10.3, plasmodium are single-celled protozoa that cause malaria. One particular kind of amoeba (*Entamoeba histolytica)* causes severe dysentery. It is often spread through contaminated water. Countries that do not carefully sterilize their water supply often have lots of this amoeba in their water. This is where the phrase, "don't drink the water" comes from. If you drink water that is contaminated with this amoeba, you will experience diarrhea, nausea, exhaustion, and dizziness, which are all symptoms of dysentery. In some cases, it can even spread to the liver and brain, causing death!

ON YOUR OWN

10.5 A scientist shows you an organism that was pulled from a lake. It is large and green and cannot move on its own. It makes its own food by photosynthesis. How can you tell whether this organism is a plant (and therefore belongs to kingdom Plantae) or an algae (and therefore belongs to kingdom Protista)?

Kingdom Fungi

Have you ever gone mushroom hunting? I mean, other than in a store. Where did you search for the mushrooms? Most likely, you looked for them in decaying mats of leaves, piles of dead tree limbs, or other places where the remains of dead plants and animals are found. Why? Well, mushrooms are a part of kingdom Fungi, and most of the organisms in this kingdom feed on dead organisms. By feeding on dead organisms, they decompose dead matter. As a result, these organisms are called **decomposers**.

Decomposers - Organisms that break down the dead remains of other organisms

Guess what results from decomposers breaking down the dead remains of organisms? Nutrients for plants and other organisms! Fertilizer, for example, can be made simply by taking dead matter from other organisms and adding some decomposers. In a few months, you will have rich fertilizer which will act as a source of vitamins for plants.

The role of the decomposers in Creation is very important. In a single autumn, the average elm tree will drop as much as *400 pounds* of leaves on the ground. If it were not for the members of kingdom Fungi, those leaves would continue to pile up, until the tree choked on its own dead leaves in just a few seasons! Because of the decomposers, however, the leaves will be broken down into fertilizer that can then be re-used by the tree.

The very presence of decomposers in Creation is another example of the Creator's ingenuity. Think about it for a moment. The planet that He gave us has its own recycling system built right into it! Think about the design and planning that had to go into such a system. Suppose a team of brilliant scientists spent their careers trying to devise a system in which many different organisms could survive for a long period of time. Do you think that they could come up with a plan this elegant and this well-designed? Of course not!

Indeed, a team of scientists tried to design and build a self-contained system for supporting life. It was called "Biosphere 2" and was supposed to be a microcosm of life on earth. It contained a variety of animals and plants and was designed to be completely self-supporting. The scientists thought they had it all worked out. They spent 7 years and 200 million dollars designing and building this air-tight, enclosed facility which spanned 3.15 acres in Arizona. Despite the best that technology and science had to offer, however, Biosphere 2 could not support life for even two years! After about 1 year and 4 months, oxygen levels could not be maintained. They had to start pumping oxygen in from the outside. Many of the animal species that had been put in Biosphere 2 became extinct, at least within the confines of the biosphere. In the end, Biosphere 2 was a failure.

Why was Biosphere 2 a failure? Well, there were many reasons, but one of them was that the designers had not anticipated the number and variety of decomposers that they needed. As a result, the dead matter in Biosphere 2 was not decomposed quickly enough. This meant that there were not enough nutrients available to be used by the plants and members of kingdom Protista that were supposed to supply oxygen through photosynthesis. Without those nutrients, these organisms could not live in a healthy manner, so they in turn could not produce oxygen efficiently.

If a team of brilliant scientists could not come up with a workable system for sustaining life (even after spending 7 years and 200 million dollars), how in the world could this perfectly-balanced system we call earth have come about by chance? Nevertheless, any scientist who does not believe in God is forced to believe that very thing! In all of our experience, well-designed systems do NOT occur by chance. They only result from careful design and construction. This planet is the most well-designed system that anyone has ever studied. Thus, it is only logical to assume that it is the result of careful design and construction as well!

Since decomposers are an important part of Creation, you should learn a little bit about them. Let's start with the decomposer that you know best: the mushroom. A mushroom, since it is a part of kingdom Fungi, is more appropriately called a "**fungus**" The figure below is a sketch of the individual parts of the fungus that you and I call a mushroom.

Ill. from the MasterClips Collection

FIGURE 10.5
The General Structure of a Mushroom

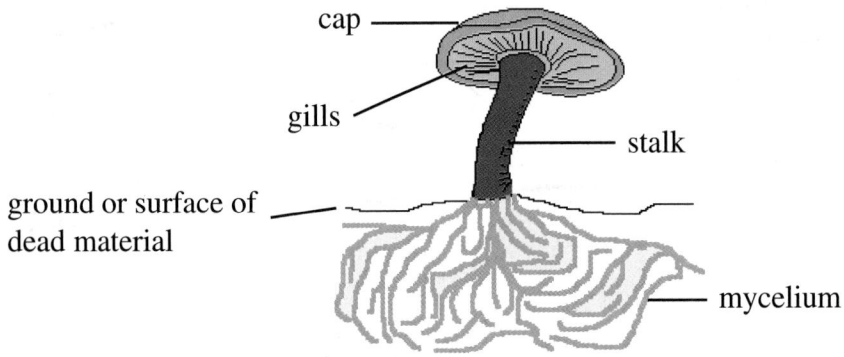

You should notice from the sketch that the part you call the mushroom is really only a portion of the fungus. Underneath the ground (or underneath the surface of the dead material), there is a vast network of interwoven filaments. This network is called the **mycelium** (my sell' ee uhm), and believe it or not, the mycelium is *the actual fungus*.

The part that you call the mushroom (the stalk, gills, and cap) is the only part of the fungus that is visible above the surface. Thus, it is the only part that you see. However, that part is really just a means by which the fungus reproduces. Thus, the stalk, gills, and cap are only present for a short amount of time: the time during which the fungus reproduces. The fungus is always around, however. It just lives beneath the surface where you can't see it unless you really look for it. Next time you see a mushroom, carefully dig around it, looking just beneath the surface. It might help if you have a magnifying glass. Look for thin filaments that weave in and out of each other. *That's* the real fungus!

Now don't be fooled by this drawing. The mycelium is *not* a root system for the mushroom. Although it might look a lot like roots in the drawing, there are *many* differences between a root system and the mycelium of a mushroom. A root system, for example, has one purpose: to pull nutrients and water from the soil so that they can be transported to the rest of the plant. The mycelium of the mushroom, on the other hand, is the *main part* of the fungus. The stalk, cap, and gills of a mushroom exist only at a certain stage of the mushroom's life. The mycelium, however, exists throughout the entire life of the mushroom. Thus, whereas the root system is really just an extension of the tree; a mushroom's stalk, cap, and gills are really just an extension of the main body - the mycelium. One more point: the gills on a mushroom are NOTHING like the gills on a fish. The gills on a fish help the fish breathe. The gills on a mushroom are necessary for reproduction - not breathing, so don't get them confused. You will learn more about *both* kinds of gills when you take biology.

Although mushrooms are probably the most familiar members of kingdom Fungi, there are other kinds of organisms in this kingdom. Figure 10.6 gives you three examples.

Shelf Fungi Photo from the MasterClips Collection *Mold and Yeast Photos by Kathleen J. Wile*

FIGURE 10.6

Three Other Kinds of Organisms From Kingdom Fungi

Shelf Fungi

These fungi are typically found growing out of dead (or dying) trees. The mycelium is underneath the tree bark.

Mold

There are many different kinds of molds. They grow on rotting fruit, stale bread, and many other decaying food items. This mold is growing on a tomato.

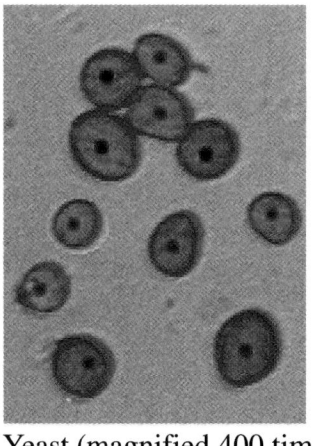

Yeast (magnified 400 times)

The yeast used in baking bread is actually a single-celled fungus. The dark circle in each cell is the nucleus of the cell.

You have probably seen **shelf fungi** growing on dead or dying trees when you have taken walks in the woods. Much like mushrooms, the "shelves" that you see are only extensions of the *real* fungus, which grows beneath the bark of the tree. Just as you've seen shelf fungi before, I am sure that you have seen **mold** before. Mold is a general term used for many different fungi that grow on fruit, bread, and other foods.

You might be surprised to see yeast pictured in Figure 10.6. Yes, yeast are indeed fungi. They are one of the examples of fungi that are composed of a single cell. Just so you understand that yeast are, indeed, fungi, and also so you can see what decomposers do, perform the following experiment.

EXPERIMENT 10.2
Yeast is a Decomposer

Supplies:

- Baker's active yeast (available at any supermarket)
- Banana
- Two zippered plastic bags (like ZIPLOC® sandwich bags)
- A butter knife
- A teaspoon
- A marker or some masking tape

Introduction - This experiment will demonstrate the function of decomposers using yeast, one of the members of kingdom Fungi.

Procedure:

A. Peel the banana and cut two slices from it with the butter knife. The slices should be roughly the same thickness and size.
B. Use the teaspoon to scoop out some yeast. Sprinkle the yeast on one of the two slices. Do not put any yeast on the other slice.
C. Place each slice of banana in a different zippered plastic bag. Label the one that contains the banana slice which has yeast on it. You can label it with the marker or some tape. Just be sure it is labeled in a way that you know means "this bag contains the banana slice upon which I sprinkled yeast."
D. Seal the bags with the zippers.
E. Place them on a counter or a shelf.
F. Check the bags daily for about a week. Note the differences you see in the two bags.
G. After a week (you can observe them for longer if you like), throw the bags away.

Although it will take up to a week for you to see results, you should notice a big difference between the contents of the two bags. Wait until then to answer the second "on your own" question (question 10.7) below.

ON YOUR OWN

10.6 A student wants to study a mushroom to learn more about the organism. He finds a mushroom growing in his back yard and pulls it out of the ground, getting the entire stalk, cap and gills. What is the student missing? What must he do to get what he is missing?

10.7 After a few days of checking the bags in Experiment 10.2, what difference did you see between them? How can you explain the difference?

Kingdom Plantae

Now I want to move on to a kingdom with which you are more familiar. Kingdom Plantae contains the plants of Creation. In the beginning of this module, I said that kingdom Plantae contains the organisms which make their own food. You learned, however, that kingdom Protista also contains a few organisms which make their own food (algae). Do you remember what distinguishes algae from plants? To help you remember, perform the following experiment.

EXPERIMENT 10.3
Vegetative Reproduction

Supplies:

- A houseplant (Ivy works best, but most houseplants will work. If you have a few varieties of houseplants and ivy is not among them, you might try a few instead of just one.)
- A glass
- Scissors
- Some water

Introduction - In this experiment, you will be reminded what distinguishes plants from algae. You will also see one way in which plants reproduce.

Procedure:

A. Fill the glass ¾ of the way full of water.
B. Use the scissors to cut a stem from the plant. The stem should have at least a couple of leaves on it, and the stem should be reasonably long.
C. Place the stem in the glass so that a large part of the stem is in the water but the leaves are hanging on or above the top of the glass.
D. Sit the glass somewhere that it is comfortably warm and well-lit. The best place would be somewhere near where the plant is kept.
E. Check the glass daily, keeping it ¾ of the way full of water. Note any new developments.

What will you see in the experiment? Eventually, you should see roots forming in the water. If you see this happening, you can actually plant the stem in some soil. As long as the newly-formed roots are underneath the soil and you take care to keep the soil moist, the stem should eventually grow into another full-fledged plant. This process is called **vegetative reproduction**.

Vegetative reproduction - The process by which the stem of a plant can form new roots and develop into a mature plant

This is not the only way plants reproduce, of course. Plants typically reproduce by forming seeds. However, this is another form of reproduction that plants have at their disposal. Gardeners often use this to grow several plants from one. They usually refer to it as "growing a new plant from a cutting of an old plant." You will learn a lot more about how plants reproduce when you take biology.

Although Experiment 10.3 demonstrates the process of vegetative reproduction rather well, it is not the real point of the experiment. The real point is to visually show you the difference between algae and plants. As I mentioned in a previous section of this module, plants have very specific parts. The **roots** absorb water and nutrients from the soil, and the **stems** help transport them to the **leaves**. The leaves are the main place that photosynthesis takes place in most plants. Thus, there are three specific kinds of structures in plants (roots, stems, and leaves), and they each perform their own tasks. Algae is not like that. Although one portion of an algae might look different than another portion, there are not specific structures that have their own tasks to perform.

I want to make one other point about the members of this kingdom before moving on. As I mentioned in Module #9, plants have cells that are a bit different than animal cells. A simplified sketch of a plant cell is shown in the figure below:

FIGURE 10.7
A Simplified Sketch of a Plant Cell

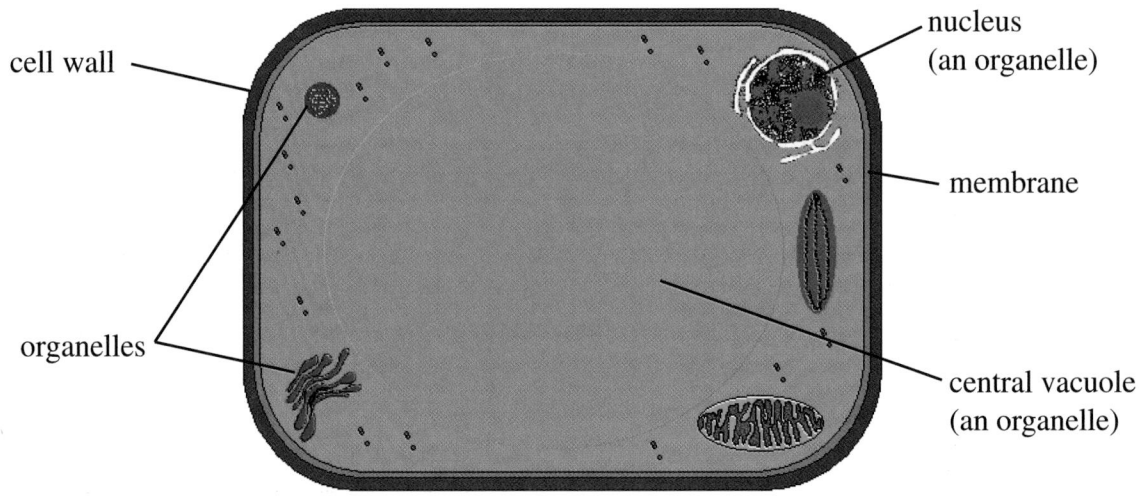

Notice some of the differences between an animal cell (such as the one on the right-hand side of Figure 10.1) and a plant cell. First of all, most plant cells are a bit more square than animal cells. This isn't always true, but it is true for the majority of plant cells. Second, notice that while a plant cell has a membrane around it (like an animal cell), it also has a **cell wall** surrounding the outside of the membrane. Animal cells do not have cell walls. Also, notice that the nucleus (the organelle which contains the cell's DNA) is not near the center of the cell. In most animal cells, the nucleus is near the center. Instead, at the center of most plant cells is a container called the **central vacuole** (vac' you ol).

The central vacuole can be thought of as a kind of water balloon. It fills with water, increasing in size. This pushes the organelles and cytoplasm in the cell against the cell wall. The cell wall is strong, however, so the cell wall goes rigid, pushing against the force created by the expanding central vacuole. When a plant cell is functioning normally, the pressure caused by the expanding central vacuole pushes against the cell wall, and the cell wall pushes back against the pressure. This results in a rigid cell. What happens when the cells are rigid? Perform the following experiment to find out.

EXPERIMENT 10.4
Turgor Pressure

Supplies:

- A stalk of wilted celery with the leaves still on it
- A glass
- Some water
- A reasonably sharp knife
- Some food coloring (preferably blue)

Introduction - The pressure inside a plant cell due to the increasing size of the central vacuole is called **turgor pressure**. This experiment will show you what turgor pressure does for a plant.

Procedure:

A. Fill the glass ¾ of the way with water.
B. Add a few drops of food coloring to the water and stir so that the water is now blue.
C. Take the wilted celery stalk and cut a small slice off of the bottom, which is the side opposite of the leaves.
D. Put the stalk of celery into the water so that the bottom of the celery (the place that you cut the piece off of) rests at the bottom of the glass.
E. Allow the celery to stand in the water overnight. This should end your science work for today.
F. Check the celery the next morning. What differences do you notice?
G. Clean everything up.

What happened overnight? Well, you should have noticed two differences between the celery yesterday and the celery today. First, you should have noticed that the leaves and some of the top of the celery stalk turned blue. Second, you should have noticed that the celery is no longer wilted. Why? Well, when you cut a small slice off of the bottom of the celery, you made a "fresh cut," allowing the celery to absorb some water. That water traveled all of the way to the top of the celery, being absorbed by cells wherever it was needed. The blue color shows that the water from the cup was, indeed, transported to the very top of the celery.

Why was the celery no longer wilted? Well, as the cells that needed water absorbed it, their central vacuoles began to expand. This increased the turgor pressure in the cells, causing the cells to go rigid. That rigidity allowed the celery to stand straight up. Thus, the turgor pressure in a plant's cells helps the plant to stand upright. Without turgor pressure, plants would always look wilted and would never stand up straight.

ON YOUR OWN

10.8 I told you that *most* of a plant's photosynthesis takes place in its leaves. Does the rest of the photosynthesis take place in its stems or its roots?

10.9 What would happen to a plant cell if it did not have a cell wall?

Kingdom Animalia

If an organism is not a single-celled prokaryotic cell, not a single-celled eukaryotic cell, not a form of algae, not a fungus, and not a plant, then it is an animal and it belongs in kingdom Animalia. This tells us that *most* of the organisms with which we are familiar are animals. Earthworms, for example, are animals. Insects are animals. Fish are animals. Cats and dogs are animals. Birds are animals. In fact, from a biological point of view, even humans are a part of kingdom Animalia.

Now don't get all upset here. I am not saying that humans are animals. Clearly, humans are more than animals. Humans are made in the very image of God. Animals are not. Thus, there is a huge difference between humans and animals. However, from a *biological point of view*, humans belong in the same kingdom. We are made up of the same basic kind of cells that the animals are, and we do not have any characteristics that place us in the other kingdoms. Thus, we *are* members of kingdom Animalia.

As you can see, then, there is a lot of diversity in this kingdom. Everything from earthworms to butterflies to turtles to blackbirds to cats to humans belong in it. Because there are so many different kinds of organisms in this kingdom, I don't want to spend a lot of time on it right now. Also, this kingdom is, by far, the one with which you have the most experience. Thus, you already have a working knowledge of many of the organisms in this kingdom.

In the next module, I will start talking about the incredible human body and some of the amazing processes that go on to keep you and me alive. As I discuss how humans perform all of the functions of life, I will also show you how other organisms accomplish those same essential tasks. In that process, you will learn a lot more about other members of kingdom Animalia, along with organisms in other kingdoms as well.

ON YOUR OWN

10.10 Suppose you were able to look at a single cell under a microscope. The cell might be just one cell from an organism that has many cells, or it may be the only cell in the organism. There are 2 kingdoms which you could automatically assign the organism to based *only* on the cell that you see. What two kingdoms are they?

ANSWERS TO THE ON YOUR OWN PROBLEMS

10.1 All organisms made of prokaryotic cells belong to kingdom Monera.

10.2 It most likely belongs to kingdom Plantae. It could belong to kingdom Protista. As you will learn later, there are some organisms (algae) in kingdom Protista that are made up of many eukaryotic cells and make their own food. However, these organisms do not have specialized structures like roots, stems, and leaves.

10.3 If the organism eats only dead organisms, it is most likely a member of kingdom Fungi. It is not a part of kingdom Monera, as it is made of eukaryotic cells. It is not in Protista, as it is made of more than one cell. It is not in Plantae because it does not make its own food. It could be in Animalia, but most organisms that feed only on dead organisms are in kingdom Fungi.

10.4 The biologist will see the most bacteria in the sample from the glass that was left sitting uncovered on the counter. The biologist will see the least bacteria in the sample from the glass that was placed in the refrigerator. As you learned from Experiment 10.1, refrigeration slows the growth and reproduction of bacteria. What about the glass that sat covered on the counter? Well, that will have a lot of bacteria in it, but not as much as the uncovered one. Remember, I told you in your experiment that bacteria were introduced into the liquid through dust particles in the air. By covering the glass, you reduce the number of bacteria introduced in that way.

10.5 You can tell the difference by looking for specialized structures like roots, stems, and leaves. If it has such structures, it is a member of kingdom Plantae, not kingdom Protista.

10.6 The student is missing the mycelium, which is the most important part of the fungus. The student must dig into the ground and get the filaments that make up the mycelium.

10.7 The banana slice with the yeast on it should be mushy and squished, while the other banana slice should just look brown, but should have retained its original shape. This is because the yeast decomposed the banana, turning it into mushy goo. Since the banana without yeast did not have a decomposer on it, it did not decompose very rapidly. The bag with the yeast in it will probably be partially inflated, too, since gas is also a product of decomposition.

10.8 The rest of the photosynthesis takes place in the stems. It could not take place in the roots, because the roots are underground, and there is no light underground.

10.9 Without a cell wall, a plant cell would explode. There would be nothing to fight against the turgor pressure caused by the central vacuole.

10.10 Members of kingdoms Monera and Plantae can be classified based only on their cells. After all, if the cell is prokaryotic (lacking organelles), the organism comes from kingdom Monera. If it is a plant cell (having a central vacuole and a cell wall), the organism comes from kingdom Plantae. Members of the other kingdoms are made of animal cells. Thus, identifying it as an animal cell only narrows the classification down to three kingdoms.

STUDY GUIDE FOR MODULE #10

1. Define the following terms:

a. Prokaryotic cell
b. Eukaryotic cell
c. Pathogen
d. Decomposers
e. Vegetative reproduction

2. Name the five kingdoms.

3. An organism is made up of several eukaryotic cells and eats only dead organisms. To which kingdom does it belong?

4. An organism is made up of several eukaryotic cells and makes its own food. It has specialized structures that perform individual tasks. To which kingdom does it belong?

5. An organism is made up of one prokaryotic cell and eats only dead organisms. To which kingdom does it belong?

6. An organism is made up of several eukaryotic cells and makes its own food. It has no specialized structures. To which kingdom does it belong?

7. An organism is made up of one eukaryotic cell and eats other, living organisms. To which kingdom does it belong?

8. An organism is made up of several eukaryotic cells and eats only living plants. To which kingdom does it belong?

9. Why can dehydrated food be stored for a long time without worry of it being contaminated by bacteria?

10. Why did people salt meat before refrigeration was available?

11. When you store food for a long time, why does covering it reduce the amount of bacterial contamination?

12. A member of kingdom Protista can move on its own. Is it protozoa or algae?

13. Are there any pathogenic organisms in kingdom Protista?

14. Why are decomposers essential to Creation?

15. Are all members of kingdom Fungi made of many cells? If not, give an example of a single-celled member of kingdom Fungi.

16. Icebergs are dangerous to ships because the visible part of an iceberg is actually very small. Most of an iceberg is underwater where it cannot be seen. How is a mushroom like an iceberg?

17. What is the main part of a mushroom: the cap, the stalk, the gills, or the mycelium?

18. A cell has a cell wall and a central vacuole. Is it a prokaryotic cell, a plant cell, or an animal cell?

19. What is turgor pressure and what does it do for a plant?

20. To which kingdom do human beings belong?

Module #11: The Human Body: Fearfully and Wonderfully Made

Introduction

Now that you know a little bit about the amazing diversity of life in Creation, I want to try and communicate to you how incredibly well God has designed it all. The best way to do this is to show you God's ultimate feat of design: the human body. As I discuss some of the most basic aspects of the human body, you will get a deep appreciation for how carefully and how thoughtfully God has designed his Creation. As the scripture says, we are indeed "fearfully and wonderfully made." (Psalm 139:14)

In order to give you a slightly broader view of Creation, from time to time I will compare the structures of the human body to the structures of other organisms. Hopefully, this will allow you to learn the details of many other organisms in Creation. I also hope that it will teach you one of the most important facts of biology: **there is no such thing as a simple life form**. As human beings, we tend to think about organisms like insects and microorganisms as "simple" organisms. Although you can argue that such life forms are, indeed, simpler than human beings, it is very apparent that they are not simple at all. Even the most basic organism in Creation is exceedingly more complex and well-designed than the most impressive piece of technology produced by the human race!

The Superstructure of the Human Body

Where do I start? The human body is so amazing and so detailed that one of the hardest aspects of teaching about it is deciding where to begin. I have decided to start with what holds your body up and keeps it together: the human body's **superstructure**.

The body's superstructure is composed of three basic units: **the skeleton, the muscles,** and **the skin**. There are 206 separate bones in an adult's skeleton. Children actually have more bones than adults, because while children mature, some of the separate bones in the body fuse together to become one. These bones work together to support the body. They also work with the muscles to allow you to move. In addition, some bones are specifically designed to protect vital organs. Finally, a substance inside your bones, the **bone marrow,** actually produces the cells that are in your blood.

In order to help you move, your body has about 640 different kinds of **skeletal muscles.** In addition to those muscles, there are also **smooth muscles,** which control the movements necessary for your body's organs to function. Finally, there is a special muscle called the **cardiac** (kar' dee ack) **muscle.** This muscle is found only in the heart, and it controls how the blood is pumped throughout your body.

The last element of your body's framework is the skin. It has two functions. First, it protects the body by not allowing certain things to get inside you. Second, it interprets the outside world and sends those interpretations to the body. This can also be thought of as a means of protecting the body. For example, if you put your hand in hot water, your skin tells your brain that the water is hot, and then the brain instructs your skeletal muscles to pull your hand out. This protects your body from the heat of the water.

Although you probably think that you are pretty familiar with your skin, you probably are not aware that your hair, fingernails, and toenails are all really a part of your skin. You see, skin cells harden according to a process called **keratinization** (kuh' rat uh nuh zay shun). This process is what forms your hair, nails, and the outer layer of your skin.

Consider how these three elements of your superstructure (skeleton, muscles, and skin) work together. Go find a ball. Pick it up in your hand, and then throw it (preferably outside!). Now think about what had to go on in order to allow you to perform this relatively simple act. Your skin sent information to your brain telling it about the size, shape, and texture of the ball. Your brain then sent instructions to your skeletal muscles to move in such as way as to grasp the ball. Your muscles then moved the bones in your hand according to those instructions, allowing you to grasp the ball.

Okay, all of those processes were necessary just for you to grasp the ball! In order to throw it, your brain sent lots of different instructions to the muscles along your arm. The muscles moved according to those instructions, causing the bones in your arm to move. As your arm moved, the skin kept sending information to your brain, and at some point, your brain decided it was time to let go of the ball. Thus, while still sending instructions to the muscles in your arm, the brain sent instructions to your hand muscles to move in a certain way. When the muscles followed those instructions, the bones in your hand moved so as to release the ball, and the ball then flew through the air, hopefully where you intended it to go.

Now think about all of that for a moment. The actions that I just described are all very precise. They require incredible coordination between your brain, muscles, skeleton, and skin. As you think about that, remember that your body is performing *millions of other processes at the same time.* After all, while you were throwing the ball, you continued to breathe, your blood continued to flow, and you continued to see, smell, and hear. All of these things continued on as normal while your body performed this well-coordinated set of actions!

Do you think that we could build a robot that could accomplish all of this? Absolutely not! We could build a robot that has an arm which can grasp and throw a ball. However, in order to perform all of the coordinated actions it takes to throw a ball, it would require a large amount of computing power. There is no way we could give the robot enough computing power and functionality to also go on performing other tasks that require a large amount of coordination.

In other words, despite the amazing technology that can be designed and created by us today, we cannot make a machine that can do even a fraction of what you can do with your own body! Nevertheless, if you do not believe in God, you have to assume that this incredible machine that we call the human body – a machine that far surpasses anything our best applied scientists can build – had to have been the result of *random chance.* After all, without God, you have to believe that the human body is the product of evolution, and evolution occurs by random chance. If our greatest applied scientists cannot build anything that comes anywhere close to performing the functions of the human body, how likely is it that the human body evolved by chance? In my opinion, the answer is "no chance whatsoever".

ON YOUR OWN

11.1 One treatment for certain types of cancer is a bone marrow transplant. In this procedure, a portion of the patient's bone marrow is replaced with different bone marrow. Besides the bone marrow itself, what else would change in the patient's body as a result of this procedure?

Bones and the Human Skeleton

As you know, your skeleton is comprised of bones. However, you are probably not aware of how incredible your bones really are. First of all, bones are as strong as steel but at the same time as light as aluminum. To this day, applied scientists cannot come up with any material that is both as strong and light as bone. If they could come even close, the building industry would be revolutionized! Second, your bones never really stop growing. Thus, they can change and adapt to fit your body's changing needs. Finally, they can repair themselves when they break!

How are these amazing feats of design put together? The following experiment helps illustrate the answer to that question.

EXPERIMENT 11.1
Minerals in Bone

Supplies:

- An uncooked chicken bone (preferably a wishbone or wing)
- A jar with a lid
- Vinegar (preferably white)

Introduction – Bones are both strong and light. They are also somewhat flexible. In this experiment, you will learn what makes them strong and how flexible they would be without it.

Procedure:

A. Clean the bone of all meat and tendons. Make it as bare as possible.

B. Allow the bone to dry overnight.
C. The next day, test the bone by trying to gently bend it. Do not use so much force that you break it! Notice that the bone bends a bit, but it is still mostly rigid.
D. Next, fill the jar with enough vinegar so that the bone will be fully immersed.
E. Drop the bone in the jar and close it.
F. Every day, pull the bone out of the vinegar and test it as you did in step (C).
G. Note the difference that you observe.
H. Put the bone back into the vinegar and close the jar again.
I. Continue this process for 7 days or more.

What will you see over the course of seven days? Well, at first, the ends of the bone will get soft. As time goes on, the entire bone will get rubbery so that it can be bent and flexed very easily. It is a nice effect, so you should definitely keep the experiment going until the bone reaches that state.

Why will the bone get rubbery? To answer this, I need to tell you what bones are made of. Bones consist of cells that are surrounded by a substance called the **bone matrix.** This matrix is composed principally of two things: **collagen** (kahl' uh gin) and **minerals.** Collagen is a flexible, rubbery substance that belongs to a class of chemicals know as **proteins.** The minerals in bones are rigid, hard chemicals which usually contain calcium. I'm sure you've heard that milk builds strong bones. That's because milk contains calcium, and the minerals in your bones are made with calcium. Thus, drinking milk helps supply your body with the calcium it needs to make the minerals in your bones.

Collagen and minerals work together to make your bones both strong and flexible. The collagen gives bones their flexibility while the minerals give bones their hardness. In your experiment, the vinegar dissolved the minerals which made up the chicken bone. As time went on, then, there were fewer and fewer minerals in the chicken bone, so the bone got more and more flexible. Eventually, the vinegar dissolved nearly all of the minerals in the bone, and you were left with a bone made mostly of collagen. Without the minerals, your bones would be as rubbery as that chicken bone. Without the collagen, your bones would be strong but not flexible. Thus, if you fell, your bones would break instead of bend. Because of the unique blend of collagen and minerals in bones, however, your skeleton is both flexible and strong.

Figure 11.1 illustrates the makeup of a typical bone in the human body. Now don't get worried. I am not going to require you to memorize this drawing. I just want you to see the general structure of a typical bone.

FIGURE 11.1
A Typical Bone

3D Illustration by Michael Dailey

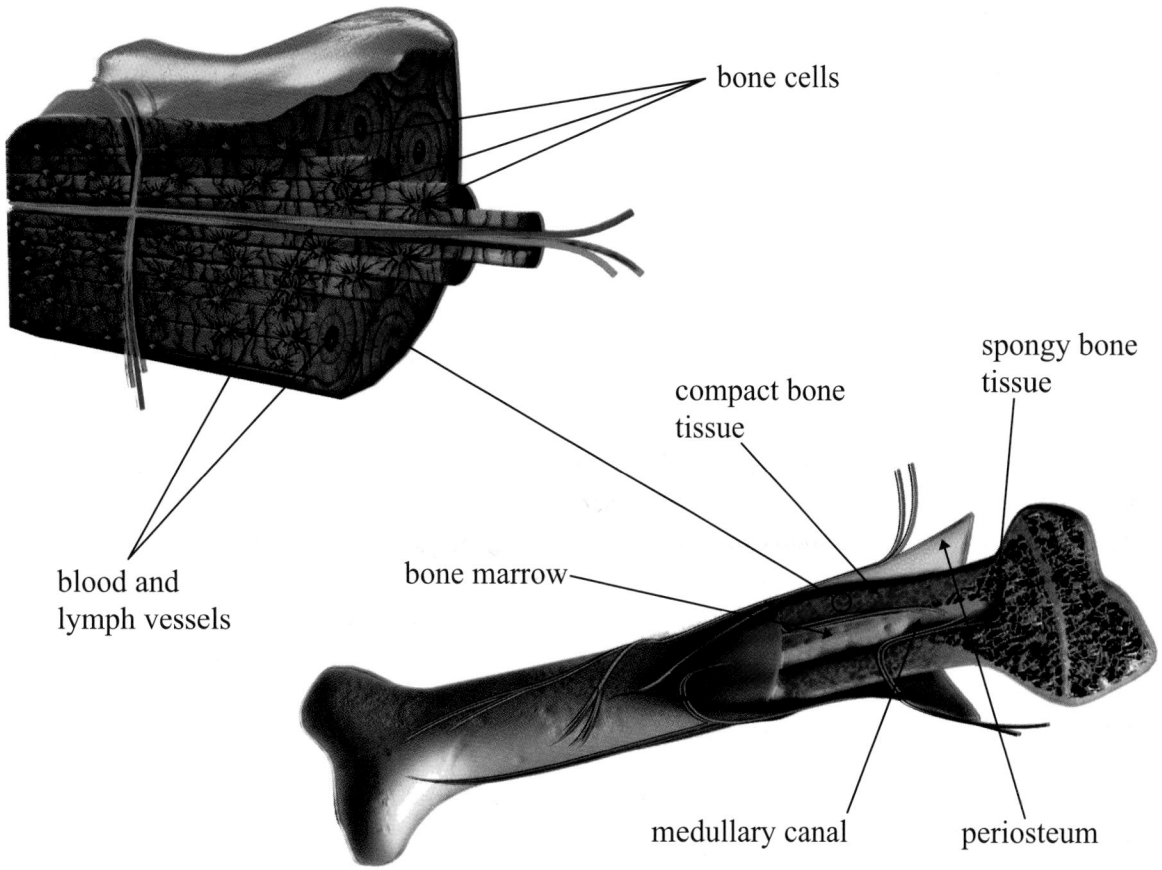

The center of the bone is called the "medullary (med' you lar ree) canal." This canal contains bone marrow and blood vessels. If the bone marrow is young, it is red and produces the blood cells that are in your blood. If it is old, the bone marrow is yellow and can no longer make blood cells. The medullary canal is surrounded by two types of bone: **spongy bone** and **compact bone.** Both of these kinds of bone are made of the same substances. The main difference between compact bone tissue and spongy bone tissue is how their mineral-hardened fibers are packed together. In compact bone tissue, they are packed together tightly, forming a hard, tough structure that can withstand strong shocks. In spongy bone tissue, on the other hand, the fibers are packed loosely, with a lot of space in between. This gives the tissue a spongy look. Although the bone looks spongy, it is quite hard, providing support to the bone without adding much weight. It also contains red bone marrow, which produces red blood cells.

The compact bone tissue is made up of tiny "rods" that are packed together. A more detailed view of these rods is shown in the upper left-hand portion of the figure. Notice that there are blood vessels running through the center of each rod as well as out to the edges of the rods. These are necessary because there are living **bone cells** which need oxygen and nutrients. The bone cells are those spidery-looking things in the figure. Thus, even though you might not think of them that way, your bones are actually alive. In fact, specialized cells can continue to make more spongy and compact bone tissue, allowing your bones to grow along with your body. Also, there are other cells that can break down bone tissue in case your body needs the minerals which the bones contain. Thus, your bones change throughout your life, growing and changing shape based on the needs of your body. Do not worry about what a "lymph vessel" is. You will learn about that in an upcoming module.

The compact and spongy bone tissue are both surrounded by a thin layer called the "periosteum" (pehr' ee ah' stee uhm). This layer contains blood vessels which supply nutrients to the bones, and it also contains nerves which can send pain signals to your brain when the bone is damaged.

As I mentioned in the previous section, your bones grow as you grow. In fact, some bones actually fuse together as you mature. As a result, babies are born with 350 bones, but mature adults have only 206 bones. These bones come in all shapes and sizes. The smallest bone in an adult's body is found in the middle ear and is only one-tenth of an inch long. The largest bone is the femur, and is represents nearly 25% of a person's height. The skull, which you might think is only one bone, is actually composed of 29 separate bones. Figure 11.2 gives you an overview of the bones in an adult's body.

FIGURE 11.2
The Bones in the Adult Human Body

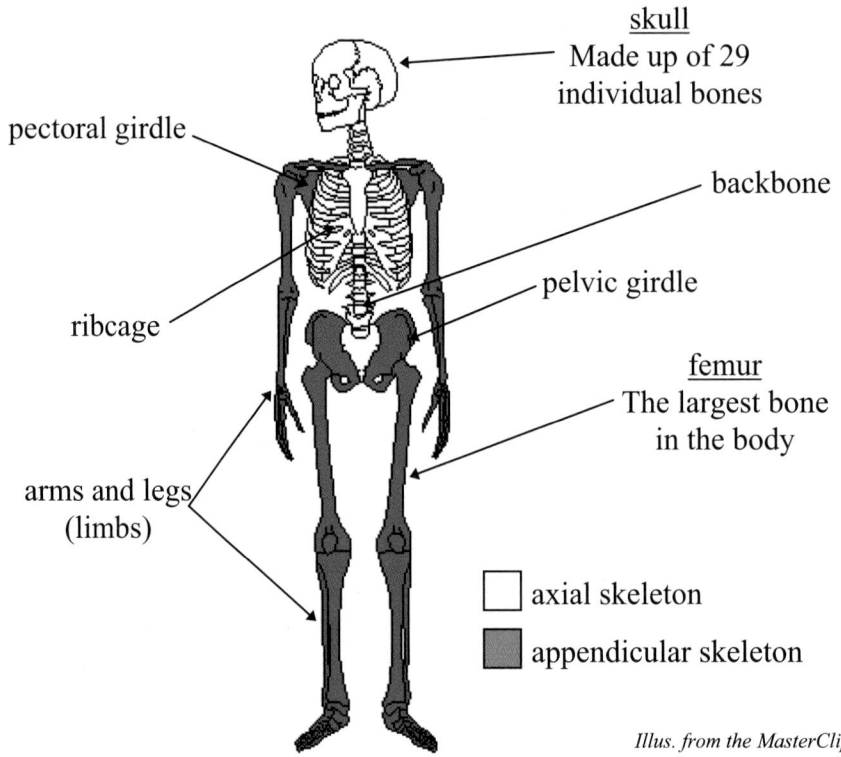

Illus. from the MasterClips collection

The sum total of all bones in the body is called the **endoskeleton.** You have probably heard it called just the "skeleton", but in the next section of this module, you will see why it needs to be called the "endoskeleton". From a biologist's point of view, the most important part of the endoskeleton is the backbone. The presence or absence of a backbone in a creature is one means of classification in biology. All creatures with backbones are called **vertebrates** (ver' tuh brayts). Humans, therefore are vertebrates, since they have backbones. Cats, dogs, elephants, fish and most of the other animals with which you are familiar are vertebrates.

Like most vertebrates, humans have endoskeletons which can be split into two major sections: an **axial skeleton** and an **appendicular** (ah pen dihk' you luhr) **skeleton.**

Axial skeleton – The portion of the skeleton that supports and protects the head, neck, and trunk

Appendicular skeleton – The portion of the skeleton that attaches to the axial skeleton and has the limbs attached to it

As you can see from the figure, the backbone, ribs, neck, and skull make up the axial skeleton. On the other hand, the pectoral girdle and the arms that attach to it as well as the pelvic girdle along with the legs that attach to it make up the appendicular skeleton (shaded gray in the figure).

ON YOUR OWN

11.2 When people get older, their bones break more easily. For example, if you trip and fall, it will most likely hurt, but your bones will almost certainly not break. However, a very old person can easily break a bone simply by tripping and falling. What substance must be lacking in an older person's bones?

11.3 Suppose you are holding two bones in your hand. They are roughly the same size and shape; however, the first bone is significantly heavier than the second. Which bone has more compact bone tissue?

Skeletons in Other Organisms

Now that you know a little bit about the human skeleton, you should learn about the other kinds of support structures that God has used in Creation. As I mentioned in the previous section, all creatures which we call vertebrates have a backbone. In fact, the skeleton of most vertebrates is similar to that of humans. Most vertebrates have both an axial and an appendicular skeleton, for example. Most vertebrates have ribs, a skull, and limbs as well. Thus, animals such as cats, dogs, fish and the like all have endoskeletons which are similar in many ways to the human skeleton.

Now even though most of the animals with which you are familiar are vertebrates, there are a host of organisms throughout Creation which are not. In fact, the vertebrates belong to only one kingdom: Animalia. The organisms in the other four kingdoms have no backbone or endoskeleton at all. In addition, not even all animals have backbones. Organisms from kingdom Animalia with no backbone are called **invertebrates** (in ver' tuh brayts). Believe it or not, there are more invertebrates in kingdom Animalia than there are vertebrates! Figure 11.3 shows some examples of invertebrates.

FIGURE 11.3
Examples of Invertebrates

Photos from the MasterClips collection

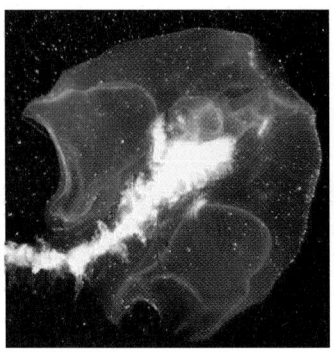

Jellyfish

Snail

Grasshopper

An invertebrate does not have an endoskeleton for one of many reasons. In the case of a jellyfish, for example, there is no need for one. A jellyfish floats in the water. The water helps to support the creature, so the jellyfish and invertebrates like it do not need a support structure of their own. Snails, clams, and other shelled animals find protection and support in their shells. Finally, insects (grasshoppers, for example) have an external support structure call an **exoskeleton.**

Exoskeleton – A body covering, typically made of a tough, flexible substance called chitin, that provides support and protection

Actually, grasshoppers represent just one of the many kinds of animals with exoskeletons, which biologists call **arthropods** (ar thrah' pods). There are more arthropods in Creation than *all other animals combined*! Crayfish, lobsters, spiders, scorpions, and insects are all examples of arthropods.

As the definition above states, an exoskeleton is generally made of **chitin.** This chemical has the useful property of being both tough and flexible (much like the chemical mixture that makes up bone). In addition to chitin, there is usually a mineral substance in the exoskeleton of an arthropod that makes it hard (much like the calcium minerals in bone). The hard, tough, exoskeleton can be thought of as a suit of armor that an arthropod wears. It is flexible enough to move with the creature, but it is tough enough to provide a good measure of protection and support. Some biologists say that the best way to get an idea of what an arthropod's exoskeleton is like is to examine your own fingernails. The structural qualities of an arthropod's exoskeleton is much like those of your fingernails.

Now remember, invertebrates are not the only organisms in Creation without a backbone. Invertebrates are *the members of kingdom Animalia* which do not have a backbone. The organisms in the other four kingdoms do not have backbones, either. Why not? Well, think about it. The members of kingdoms Monera and Protista are mostly composed of one cell. The cell membrane gives them the support that they need. The members of kingdom Protista which are comprised of many cells (algae) all float in the water. Like the jellyfish, then, the water supports algae. As you learned in Experiment 10.4, the members of kingdom Plantae have turgor pressure in their cells that help support them.

What about the members of kingdom Fungi? Well, like arthropods, they are covered in chitin. Biologists do not consider this an exoskeleton because, unlike endoskeletons and exoskeletons, the chitin covering of fungi cannot move around. Nevertheless, it does support the fungi. Without its chitin covering, for example, the mushroom part of a fungus could never stand up. It would simply flop over on its own weight, much like a wilted plant.

ON YOUR OWN

11.4 Classify the following as vertebrates, invertebrates, or neither:

a. worms b. alligators c. grass d. yeast e. starfish

Skeletal Muscles

As I mentioned briefly in the second section of this module, there are three main types of muscles in your body: skeletal muscles, smooth muscles, and the cardiac muscle. In this section, I want to concentrate on the skeletal muscles. Figure 11.4 gives you an overview of the skeletal muscles in the human body. Now don't get all worried here. I am not going to make you memorize these muscles. I just want to give you an idea of how complex this all is.

Illus. from the Future Graph biology collection

FIGURE 11.4
The Major Skeletal Muscles in the Human Body

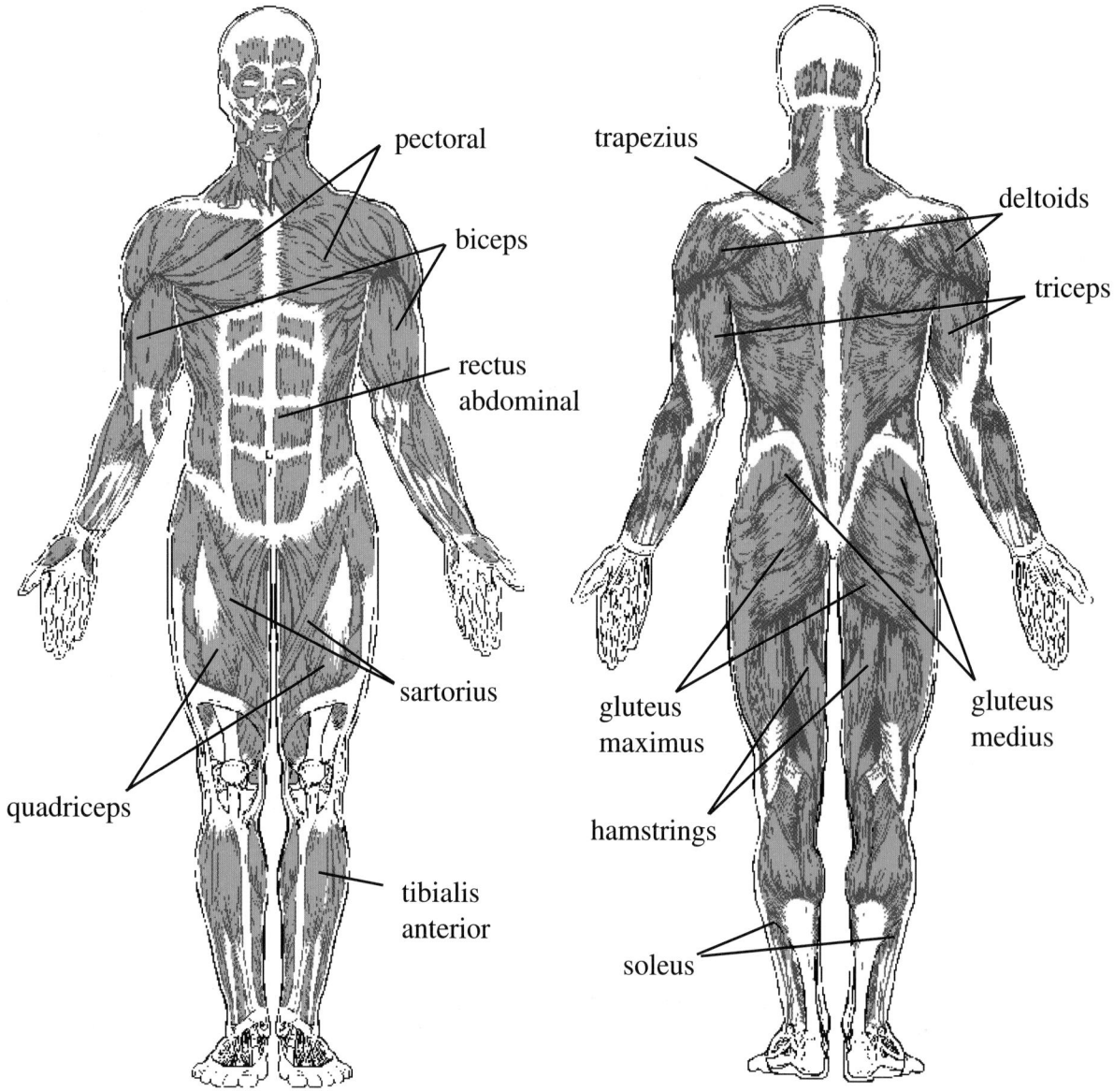

Now the first thing to realize about skeletal muscles is that they do not attach directly to the skeleton. Instead, the muscles typically taper as they get near to the skeleton, and they end in a **tendon**, which attaches to the skeleton. The second thing to realize about skeletal muscles is that they would do little good if it were not for the **joints** in the skeleton.

Muscles allow us to move because the skeleton is jointed. Think about it. Suppose your arm was supported by one long bone that went from your shoulder to your hand. If that were the case, you could not bend your arm without breaking the bone! Thus, your arm is *jointed* about midway between your shoulder and your hand. This joint, called the "elbow joint," separates the upper arm bone (the humerus) from the two forearm bones (the radius and ulna). Because that joint is there, you can bend your arm at the elbow. There are four major kinds of joints in the human body, and they are illustrated in Figure 11.5.

Illus. by Megan Whitaker

FIGURE 11.5
Major Types of Joints in the Human Body

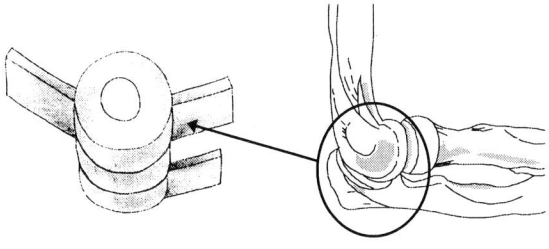

Hinge Joint

Elbows and knees are hinge joints. They offer a limited range of motion but are very stable.

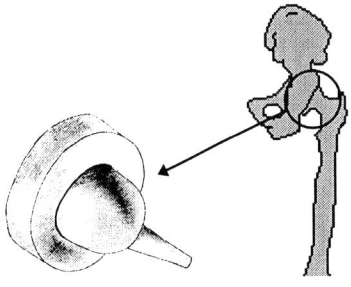

Ball-And-Socket Joint

Hips and shoulders have ball-and-socket joints. They offer a wide range of motion but are less stable than hinge joints.

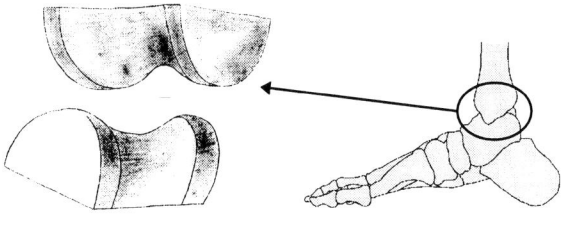

Saddle Joint

The ankle has a saddle joint. The range of motion is less than a ball-and-socket but more than a hinge.

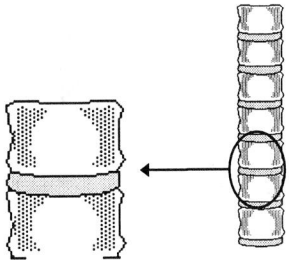

Washer Joint

Washer joints appear only in the backbone. They allow you to bend and twist your back.

As mentioned in the figure, **hinge joints** can be found at the elbow and the knee. They act like the hinges on a door, allowing up and down (or left and right) motion, but that is all. For a joint, that is fairly limited motion. However, because the motion is limited, the stability of the joint is enhanced. This is especially important for the knee, because it holds an enormous amount of weight.

Ball-and-socket joints have a ball-shaped head that fits into a bowl-shaped socket. This design allows for a large range of motion. The ball can roll around in the socket, providing left and right motion *along with* up and down motion. The hip joints and shoulder joints are good examples of ball-and-socket joints. Although ball-and-socket joints all have the same basic design, there are differences between one ball-and-socket joint and another. For example, the socket part of the shoulder joint is rather shallow. That allows for a large range of motion. However, the ball can be pushed or knocked out of the socket, causing a dislocated shoulder. In the hip joint, the socket is deeper. This results in slightly less freedom of motion for the hip, but the ball is more secure in the socket, so there is less chance of dislocating the hip joint as compared to the shoulder joint.

To understand the difference in the amount of motion provided by ball-and-socket joints as compared to hinge joints, try moving your forearm without moving *anything* else. Keep your wrist, hand, and shoulder rigid and still, and just move your forearm at your elbow. Notice the rather limited range of motion that you have. Now, keep your entire arm, wrist, and hand still, and move your entire arm at the shoulder. Notice how much more you can do by moving your arm at the shoulder. You can move your arm in circles, up and down, back and forth, etc. That's the difference in motion between a hinge joint (elbow) and a ball-and-socket joint (shoulder).

The **saddle joint** is sort of in-between a hinge joint and a ball-and-socket joint. Saddle joints are composed of two saddle-shaped bones that fit together. The saddles can slide along each other allowing left to right motion as well as up and down motion, but the bones are not as free to move as they are in a ball-and-socket joint. Your ankle joint is a good example of a saddle joint. Notice that your ankle joint does allow more motion than your elbow, but not nearly as much as your shoulder.

The last major kind of joint is the **washer joint**, and it exists only in your backbone. Your backbone is made up of individual bones called **vertebrae** (ver' tuh bray). Each vertebra is connected to the other with a washer joint. Each joint allows a small range of motion. Together, however, they allow you to bend and arch your backbone.

Now joints by themselves are not as useful as you might think. They allow the skeleton to bend at certain places, but they cannot *cause* the motion. Also, remember that bone is hard. If joints were made of bone and nothing else, there would be a *big* problem. The bones in the joint would rub against each other. This would cause LOTS of pain and severe bone damage. To get around this problem, the bones in a joint do not actually touch. Instead, the bones in a joint are covered with a tough, flexible substance called **cartilage** (car' tih lej). The cartilage in joints is similar in feel to hard plastic. It is firm but resilient. As a result, the cartilage-covered bones of a joint can rub up against each other without damage. In addition, the resilient nature of the cartilage allows it to act as a shock-absorber so that jarring movements (such as jumping) do not destroy the joints.

Now that's amazing enough, but I am not done yet! If two bones are jointed together, the cartilage will allow them to rub against each other without damage, but the joint would not necessarily stay together, would it? Consider a ball-and-socket joint, for example. What keeps the ball in the socket? The answer is that the two bones which are jointed together are held together by strips of tissue called **ligaments** (lig' uh mints). Ligaments are much like strips of strong elastic that go from one bone to the other. This holds the bones in the joint, but because of the nature of ligaments, the bones can be pulled apart from one another for brief times due to large stress, and then they will "snap" right back into place, provided that the stress does not last too long or is not too severe.

Okay, that's all there is to a joint, right? WRONG! Although cartilage and ligaments allow joints to move and keep the bones together, our bodies are designed to be incredibly efficient as well. If a joint had just cartilage in between the two bones, the joint would be able to move, but not without a lot of effort. Thus, in order to make the motion in joints smooth as well as not too difficult, the joints are also *lubricated*! Most joints are surrounded by a "bag" called the **articular** (ar tik' you lur) **capsule**. The tissue that makes up this bag produces a fluid, which is called **synovial** (sih no' vee al) **fluid**. The synovial fluid in the articular capsule is slippery, like egg white. This slippery quality allows the fluid to lubricate the joints so that their motion is smooth and easy.

Now that you know about joints and how they work, I can finally describe to you how skeletal muscles move your bones around those joints. They accomplish this by relaxing or contracting in concert with other muscles. This is a very complicated process which is best illustrated by example. I want to use the figure below to show you how your arm muscles work to move your forearm at the elbow.

Illus. by Megan Whitaker

FIGURE 11.6
Moving the Forearm at the Elbow

Extension of the forearm:

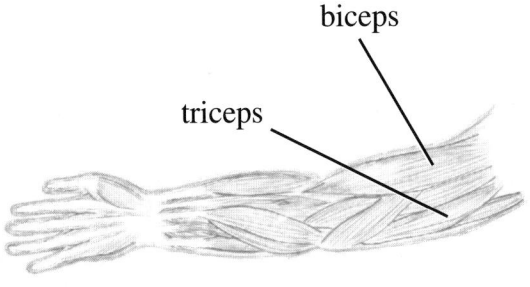

When the forearm is *extended*, the triceps muscle is contracted, pulling the forearm down. The biceps muscle is relaxed, which allows the forearm to go down without resistance.

Flex of the forearm:

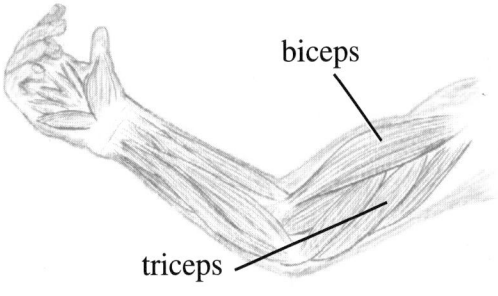

When the forearm is *flexed* at the elbow, the biceps muscle is contracted, pulling the forearm up. The forearm can move up without resistance, because the triceps muscle is relaxed.

When you want to flex your forearm, the biceps muscle contracts and, at the same time, the triceps muscle relaxes. Since your biceps muscle is attached to the top of the forearm, its contraction pulls your forearm up. Since the triceps muscle relaxes, there is nothing fighting that motion. The hinge joint thus allows your forearm to flex. To extend your forearm, the precisely opposite actions happen. The triceps contracts and the biceps relaxes. The contraction of the triceps extends the forearm, since it is attached to the outside of the forearm at the elbow. Since the biceps relaxes, there is nothing fighting that motion.

This is typical of how skeletal muscles work. They work in pairs of partners which are opposite of one another. When the first partner contracts, the second relaxes and motion in one direction is caused. Motion in the other direction is caused when the two partners switch jobs and the first relaxes while the second contracts. In reality, this is an oversimplification. Muscles tend to work in large groups of 10, 20, even thirty or more, depending on the joints involved.

Now I want you to sit back and think about all of this for a moment. The human skeleton is full of joints. There are four basic designs for these joints, depending on the motion that the joint needs. In addition, there are variations within those designs (shallow or deep sockets in the ball-and-socket joint, for example) in order to meet the individual requirements for the joints. The bones within the joints are cushioned with cartilage to reduce wear and pain. The bones are held together with ligaments which secure the bones to the joints but allow for some flexibility when the joint is stressed. The joint is then encased in a bag that makes its own fluid which lubricates the joint. Finally, the joint is moved by muscles that work *in concert* with other muscles. Sometimes the muscles work in pairs, but many movements we make require the concerted motion of more than *thirty* individual muscles.

Has applied science ever come up with anything so marvelous? Of course not! Think about an automobile, for example. An automobile has several moving parts that rub up against each other, much like the bones in a joint rub up against each other. Those parts are not cushioned like bones are, however. If they were, the automobile would not break down and need replacement parts nearly as often. Also, automobiles use oil, like joints use synovial fluid, to lubricate the moving parts. However, automobiles don't make their own oil! Instead, you have to buy it and put it in the engine. Joints make their own! Even a marvel of technology like an automobile is *primitive* compared to the human muscular and skeletal systems.

Have you ever seen a robotic arm? Several industries use robotic arms to perform repetitive tasks over and over again. Have you ever watched how jerky their movements are? That's because the hydraulics which control their motion are not nearly as smooth or efficient as muscles. Also, the energy required to move a robotic arm is *thousands of times larger* than the energy required to move your arm, because the joints that engineers can make for robots are not *nearly* as smooth-moving as your joints.

In the end, then, the human muscular and skeletal systems produce motion much more efficiently, much more elegantly, and at a much lower energy cost than the best machines that applied science can produce. Despite this fact, there are scientists who believe that the human body is the result of evolution, which requires *random chance*! Think about that for a moment. Suppose I showed you a car and told you that it was formed as the result of a tornado that ran through a junkyard. Suppose I told you that all of the metal in the junkyard was thrown together in just the right way by chance, and a car was produced. Would you believe it? Of course not! The car is just too well-designed to be the product of random chance. How, then, can anyone who has really studied the human body (which is much more elegantly-designed than a car) ever believe it is the result of evolution?

ON YOUR OWN

11.5 Athletes and other people who stress their joints can destroy the cartilage and ligaments of the joints. If the cartilage of a joint is destroyed, what bad thing can happen to the bones of the joint? If the ligaments are destroyed, what bad thing can happen?

11.6 Suppose a person's triceps muscle stops working properly. The triceps can never contract. It can only relax. Will the person be able to flex his or her forearm at the elbow? Will the person be able to extend the forearm?

Smooth Muscle and the Cardiac Muscle

Smooth muscles are quite different in both structure and function than skeletal muscles. As their name implies, smooth muscles are smoother than skeletal muscles. Under a microscope, skeletal muscle tissue has a rough, striped appearance. Smooth muscle tissue, on the other hand, looks smooth and unstriped. Smooth muscles are not connected to the bone. Instead, smooth muscle tissue forms layers that are arranged so as to make your organs work.

Consider, for example, what happens when you eat. Food that you eat goes down into your stomach. You will learn the details of this in an upcoming module, so I don't want to dwell on how that happens right now. I just want to talk about what happens when the food lands in your stomach. In order to do its job, the stomach must churn the food around, mixing it with the liquid in the stomach. How is that accomplished? It is accomplished through the action of smooth muscles which line the stomach. They contract and relax, squeezing and kneading the food to spur on the digestion process.

Unlike your skeletal muscles, your smooth muscles are controlled by your brain without any conscious thought. Thus, the movements that they cause are called **involuntary movements**, because you do not do them by choice. They happen as a normal part of life with no thought on your part. Since smooth muscles cause involuntary movement, they are often called **involuntary muscles**. Because the stomach is controlled by smooth muscles, you never have to think about "working" your stomach. It happens involuntarily. That's how all of your organs work. If you always had to think about contracting and relaxing the muscles that control your organs, you would die right away. That doesn't happen, because your brain does it all for you, without you having to think about it at all!

The cardiac muscle is another muscle that works involuntarily. Under a microscope, a cardiac muscle cell is striped like a skeletal muscle cell, though it is much smaller. However, since it is controlled involuntarily, it is something of a cross between a skeletal muscle and a smooth muscle. The heart muscle is controlled by both the brain and a small patch of cells, called the **sinoatrial** (sine' oh aye' tree uhl) **node**, which resides on the heart. The sinoatrial node sets the pace at which the cardiac muscle contracts and relaxes. It does this by generating an electrical signal that turns on and off at about 100 times each minute. When the electrical signal is turned on, the cardiac muscle contracts. When it turns off, the cardiac muscle relaxes. That's how your heart beats. Because the sinoatrial node sets the "pace" at which your heart beats, it is often called the **pacemaker**.

"Wait a minute," you should be thinking. My heart doesn't usually beat 100 times a minute! That's right. Remember, I said that the brain also has some control over the cardiac muscle. Based on the information that your brain is getting from the receptors all over your body, the brain can slow down or speed up the rate at which the sinoatrial node produces electrical signals. Under normal circumstances, the brain usually slows a person's heartbeat to between 60 and 80 beats per minute. When you exercise heavily, or when you are nervous, the brain can speed the rate up so that the heart beats faster.

You probably know of someone who has an artificial pacemaker. More than 80,000 artificial pacemakers are surgically implanted into Americans every year. Thus, the odds are that you know of or at least have heard of someone who has one. These people have a condition that causes their sinoatrial node to malfunction. As a result, the implanted pacemaker generates the electrical signals which cause the cardiac muscle to contract and relax. A pacemaker, then, is an artificial sinoatrial node. Like most of the marvels of technology, however, it pales in comparison to the biological wonder that it imitates. A pacemaker can vary the rate at which it produces signals, but only somewhat. It cannot react to meet the body's needs like the sinoatrial node can. Thus, those who have pacemakers must watch their activity level, because their heart cannot adjust to the demands of the body the way it would if the sinoatrial node were working properly.

ON YOUR OWN

11.7 There are muscles in your blood vessels that expand and contract in order to regulate the way that blood flows throughout your body. Are these muscles smooth or skeletal? What about the muscles that cause the head to turn one way or the other? Are they smooth or skeletal muscles?

Muscles and Movement in Other Organisms

Most animals have muscles which allow them to move. Although many details differ between the muscles of a frog and the muscles of a human, the basic structure and function of muscles are reasonably consistent throughout most of kingdom Animalia. One thing that I would like to point out, however, is that the *placement* of the muscles can be quite different in some animals as compared to others. Consider the arthropods, for example. Remember, these animals have exoskeletons. Thus, while our muscles (and all vertebrate muscles) lie *on top of* our skeleton, the muscles of arthropods are attached *underneath* their skeleton. In other words, while our muscles pull on the skeleton from on top of the bone, arthropod muscles pull on their skeleton from underneath the chitin.

What about the other kingdoms? Well, the members of kingdom Monera can, indeed, move from one place to another. They do not utilize muscles, however. Most members of kingdom Monera have little tails called **flagella** (fluh gel' uh). They spin these tails like little outboard motors, allowing them to move through the water (or liquid) they inhabit. Some members of kingdom Protista (the algae) do not really move much on their own. Others (the protozoa) rely on specific structures which allow them to move. Some have flagella, while others have tiny hairs called **cilia** (sil' ee uh). These hairs beat back and forth, acting like oars which row the organism through the water.

The members of kingdom Fungi do not move around a lot. They certainly have no muscles. The members of kingdom Plantae do not have muscles, but they manage to move in a few ways. Perform the following experiment to see what I mean.

EXPERIMENT 11.2

Phototropism and Gravotropism in Plants

Supplies:

- Two houseplants. Make sure that your parents won't mind one of them looking really funny once the experiment is over.
- A few books
- A sunny window

Introduction – Plants can move in response to certain situations. In this experiment, you will see two specific situations which cause plants to move.

Procedure

A. Take the first plant and set it in front of the window, a few feet away from it. Allow it to set for three days.
B. Take the books and make a pile on the floor. Then, tilt the second plant so that the pot it is in lies against the books. Steady it so that the plant stays tilted, leaning against the books.
C. After three days, turn the first plant (the one that is not tilted) 180 degrees, so that the side of the plant which did not face the window now faces the window.
D. Note what you see in both plants after a few days.

For the first plant, you will see that it moves so that all of its leaves face the window. The tendency of plants to grow so that they face the light is called **phototropism** (fo' toh trope' iz uhm). Although most houseplants take a few days in order to move so that they face the light, some plants can do so much more quickly. Sunflowers actually turn throughout the day so that they follow the sun as it travels across the sky!

What will happen to the second plant is an illustration of **gravotropism** (grav' uh trope iz uhm), which is the tendency for a plant to sense which way is "up" and to grow that way. Both gravotropism and phototropism are caused by special growth hormones which accelerate plant growth. These hormones are affected by gravity and light. As a result, different parts of plants grow at different rates depending on the position of the plant. This has the net effect of "moving" the plant so that it faces the light and always grows upward. You will learn more about these two effects when you take biology.

Skin

The body is covered by a thin layer which we call the **skin**. Although you might think of skin as fragile, it is *anything* but that. Skin is the primary line of defense for our body. It protects our inner tissues, provides us with a sense of touch, grows hair and nails, and even excludes microorganisms from our bodies. Figure 11.7 is a cutaway representation of a block of human skin. It is truly amazing to think that something as thin as our skin has this much detail!

Illus. from the MasterClips collection

FIGURE 11.7
A Simple Diagram of Human Skin

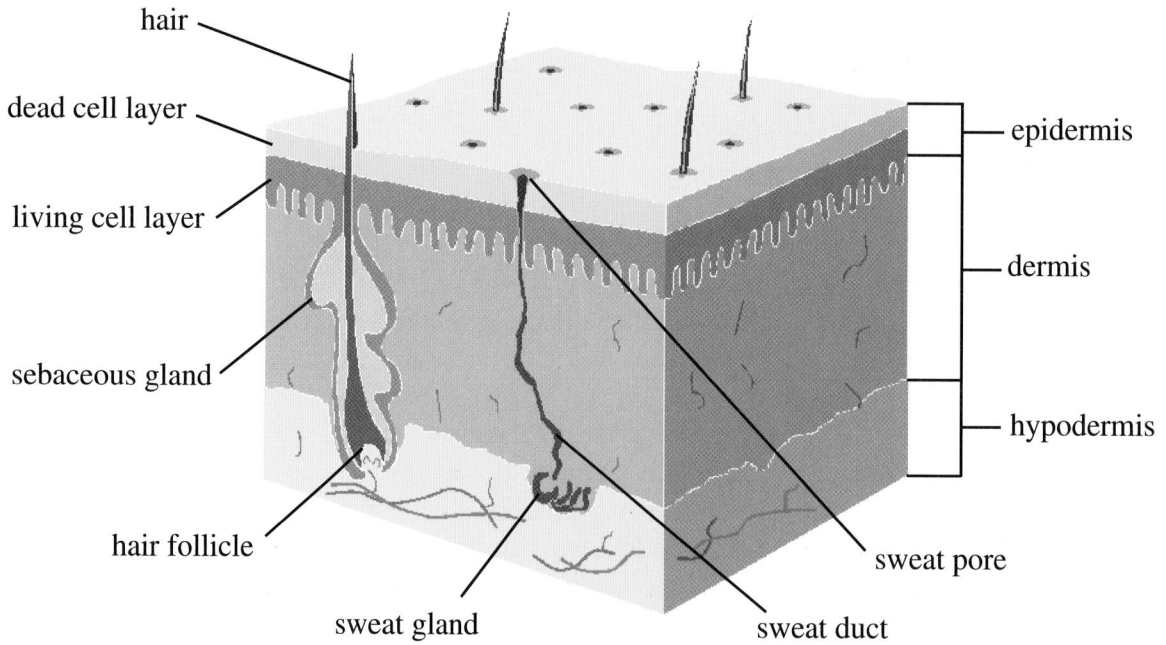

Your skin is composed of two basic layers. The outer layer is called the **epidermis** (ep uh dur' miss). It protects our inner tissues. The other layer, the **dermis**, is composed of fibrous connective tissue. Below the dermis lies the **hypodermis** (hi poh dur' miss). Composed mostly of fat, it is not technically considered part of the skin. It's job is to provide insulation for your body.

Notice that the epidermis is composed of two layers: a layer of dead cells and a layer of living cells. As living things tend to do, the living cells of the epidermis are continually reproducing. After a new living cell is formed, it is pushed towards the top of the epidermis and, as it moves upward, its cytoplasm is transformed. Now remember, the cytoplasm of a cell (as described in Module #9) is a jelly-like substance that makes up most of the cell. The cell's organelles are located in the cytoplasm, and the cell's membrane holds the cytoplasm in place. Well, as a living skin cell moves upward in the epidermis, the cytoplasm is transformed into a waterproofing protein called **keratin** (kare' uh tin). This process, called **keratinization** (kuh' rat uh nuh zay shun), kills the cell, but makes the cell quite sturdy and hard to destroy.

The dead cells in the epidermis are what really do most of the skin's protective work. Because these cells are firm and sturdy, it is difficult for pathogenic organisms (mostly bacteria and fungi) to penetrate the epidermis. Because they are dead, however, they are constantly falling from the skin's surface. Thus, the layer of living epidermis cells must continually reproduce so that new cells can be keratinized and sent to replace the cells that fall off. A good fraction of the dust that you find in your home is actually composed of the dead epidermis cells that have fallen from your family's (and your pets') skin.

Notice that your skin also has **hair**. Almost all of your skin produces hair. Even though you might not be able to see it without the aid of a magnifying glass, there is hair on almost every part of your body, except for certain areas such as the palms of your hands and soles of your feet. Like the outer layer of the epidermis, hair is made from keratinized cells, but the keratin is harder in these cells than in the skin's cells. Thus, hair is dead as well. The cells that are keratinized to make hair do not come from the lower layer of the epidermis. Instead, they come from a structure known as a **hair follicle** (fall' uh kul) which lies deep within the dermis. The hair follicle is comprised of cells that rapidly reproduce. The cells formed in this reproduction are keratinized and formed into a cylinder, which then grows through the skin.

Hair grows at different rates based on the activity of your hair follicles. The hair follicles on your head, for example, are very active for months at a time. As a result, the hair on your head can grow very long. The hair follicles on your arms and legs, however, are active for only short periods of time and have long periods of "rest." Thus, they produce hair that is much shorter than the hair on your head.

Why does your skin grow hair? Well, hair has two main functions: insulation and sensation. First of all, your hair helps keep you warm. Hair helps trap warm air next to your skin. Have you ever gotten goose-pimples? Typically, they are caused by cold air or by nervousness. Goose-pimples are formed by hair. You see, each hair is connected to a small, smooth muscle in the dermis. When you get cold (or when you are very nervous), this muscle contracts, pulling the hair straight up. This increases the amount of warm air trapped next to the body. It also stresses the epidermis where the hair sticks out, causing a little bump to form. That bump is what we call a goose-pimple.

Hair's second purpose is sensation. The hair is surrounded by nerves in the dermis. When your hair is moved, those nerves send signals to your brain, telling it that the hair is being moved. Your brain then tells you that something is touching your skin. Since hairs move so easily, this is a very sensitive system. Even a gentle breeze will move your hair, sending signals to your brain so that you know a gentle breeze is blowing. The skin has other receptors (which I will discuss in a later module) which provide your sense of touch. However, your hair is a very sensitive receptor when it comes to something touching you.

The **sebaceous** (suh bay' shus) **gland** is connected to the hair follicle in the dermis. This gland produces oil which coats the hair and also gets ejected onto the skin at the opening where the hair emerges. This oil softens the hair and the skin. If you have ever experienced dry, chapped skin, you know how painful it can be. This oil keeps that from becoming an everyday occurrence. The oil also helps protect the body from harmful organisms, as it makes it harder for certain bacteria to attach themselves to the skin. These glands are absolutely necessary for healthy skin, but they are also a nuisance for young people. During most students' teen years, the sebaceous glands are extremely active, producing a *lot* of oil. Sometimes, because so much oil is produced, the opening on the surface of the skin gets plugged up. This causes irritation, which swells into blackheads and pimples.

The last set of structures illustrated in the figure govern the process of sweating. Sweat is produced in your sweat glands, travels up through the dermis in the sweat duct, and then pours out onto your skin through your sweat pores. Sweating serves at least two purposes. When we sweat, we cool ourselves down. You will learn more about *how* sweating cools you down next year when you take physical science. For right now, just realize that sweating cools your skin. Secondly, sweat provides food for bacteria and fungi which *live on your skin!* Now wait a minute. Doesn't the skin do everything it can in order to keep bacteria and fungi out of your body? Well, not exactly. The skin does everything it can to keep *pathogenic* bacteria and fungi out of your body. However, not *all* bacteria and fungi are pathogenic. In fact, many are beneficial to us.

You see, there are certain bacteria and fungi which produce acid (primarily a substance called lactic acid) as a by-product of the processes which keep them alive. This lactic acid is an incredibly effective defense against many types of pathogenic bacteria and fungi. Thus, your body encourages these acid-producing bacteria and fungi to live on your skin by producing food for them in the form of sweat. These beneficial bacteria and fungi then cover your skin in acid, protecting it from harmful bacteria and fungi. A healthy person has as many as 65,000 bacteria living on almost *every square inch of his or her body!*

If you don't know much about chemistry, you might wonder how in the world having acid covering your skin could possibly be good for you. Well, when you take chemistry in a few years, you will learn that only a few acids are dangerous. Many are quite gentle. In fact, if you drink fruit juice, soda pop, or milk, you are drinking acid. Thus, acids are not necessarily dangerous chemicals. Many are quite good for your body, including the lactic acid produced by bacteria and fungi which feed on your sweat.

Now I want you to think about this for a moment. Your skin's primary function is to protect your body from harm. One of the most obvious threats the body faces is infection by pathogenic bacteria and fungi. Although your skin alone provides a lot of defense against such infections, it is just not enough. Thus, your skin actually produces *food* for bacteria and fungi that can *help* it do its job! Isn't that amazing? Without your skin producing food, the bacteria and fungi that live on it would die. Without those bacteria and fungi, your body would be much more susceptible to infection. In other words, this is a case in which *several organisms help each other* so as to benefit all of the organisms concerned. The bacteria and fungi on your skin benefit from the food your sweat provides, and you benefit by staying healthier.

Although this process is rather surprising, it is very common throughout Creation. In fact, it is so common that biologists have a term for it. The term is **symbiosis** (sim by oh' sis).

Symbiosis – Two or more different organisms living together so that each benefits from the other

Symbiosis is an incredible testament to God's forethought in designing his Creation. You see, survival is all about solving problems. The better an organism can solve the problems related to staying alive, the longer and more productive the organism's life will be. Thus, in order to help these organisms solve problems, God has made it so that many organisms can work together. Just as a volleyball team is much more effective than a single player, the "teams" that are formed via symbiosis make all of the organisms involved more effective at living.

Can you imagine how such "teams" could form by chance? After all, teams are formed when a leader (coach, team captain, etc.) begins choosing players and assigning them to play certain positions. The team leader has some idea of the capabilities of each player, and he or she assigns each player to a position which the player has the ability to play. The same thing must be true of symbiosis. Organisms don't just randomly go around looking for other organisms to help! Think about it. There are a host of bacteria and fungi that your skin fights off. How would your body know to make a special type of food (sweat) that only attracts *certain types* of bacteria and fungi? Well, the "team captain" (God), designed your body to attract the correct players (the beneficial bacteria and fungi) and then "assigned" those players to the position of making an acid that is good for your skin and fights off pathogens.

The idea that such a team could be put together by random chance is absurd. Nevertheless, if you do not believe in God, you are forced to believe that the process of symbiosis has happened over and over again in nature as the result of random chance! Those who do not believe in God truly have amazing faith! They have enormous faith in the ability of random chance to mimic the awesome design we see in Creation.

Now that I have shown you the basics of your skin, I want to address one subject that you are probably wondering about: skin color. Why is it that people have such a wide range of skin color? Skin has a chemical in it called **melanin** (mel' uh nin). This chemical is called a

pigment, because it tends to give color to whatever it is in. This particular pigment tends to darken skin. If someone has a lot of melanin, he or she has dark skin. If someone has only a little melanin, he or she will be very light-skinned. There is a certain condition call **albinism** (al' bine iz uhm), in which a person has no melanin at all. These people have skin that is extremely light.

What affects how much melanin a person has in his or her skin? There are many factors, and the following experiment demonstrates one of them.

EXPERIMENT 11.3
Skin Color

Supply:

- A plastic bandage, such as a Band-Aid®

Introduction - In this experiment, you will see how light affects the production of melanin.

Procedure:

A. Put the bandage around one of your fingers so that is covers your skin.
B. Leave the bandage on for two days.
C. At the end of two days, pull the bandage off and compare the skin that was under the bandage to the rest of your finger.

After you are done with the experiment, answer "on your own" question 11.10, which asks whether light tends to increase or decrease the amount of melanin in your skin.

Hair gets its color essentially the same way that skin does. Dark hair has a lot of melanin in it, while light hair has very little. Red hair contains a mixture of melanin and red pigment made by the bodies of certain people. If the person produces a lot of red pigment and only a little melanin, his or her hair is "strawberry blonde." The more melanin produced, the deeper the red color becomes. Without any melanin (in the case of albinism, for example), hair is white.

ON YOUR OWN

11.8 A medical researcher comes up with a way of shutting down the activity of the sebaceous gland. Although teenagers everywhere rejoice, the Food and Drug Administration (FDA) decides not to allow the process to be performed in the United States. Why would teenagers everywhere rejoice at such a discovery? Assuming that the procedure itself is safe, why wouldn't the FDA allow it to be performed in the United States?

11.9 If your body is always cold, your sweat glands will not produce sweat, because your skin does not need to be cooled down. With what you have learned in this module, explain one reason *why* you can get sick if you are cold for too long.

11.10 Based on the results of Experiment 11.3, does sunlight tend to increase or decrease the amount of melanin in your skin?

Skin in Other Organisms

Most organisms in Creation have some kind of outer covering which protects them. Thus, almost all organisms have some kind of "skin." However, the "skin" of many organisms is not nearly as complex as human skin. Most members of kingdoms Monera and Protista, for example, have just a membrane surrounding their single cell. Some bacteria (kingdom Monera) have a sheath of sticky goo (called a "capsule") that covers their membrane. This capsule protects them to a greater degree than does the membrane by itself.

Most plants (kingdom Plantae) have an epidermis. Unlike human skin, however, the epidermis of plants is often just one layer of cells. Even though that's pretty simplistic when compared to human skin, it does offer a lot of protection for the plant. In kingdom Fungi, the organisms are typically covered with chitin. This covering is strong. It serves to hold parts of the fungus up (as I mentioned previously), but it also offers excellent protection for the fungus.

Most of the organisms in kingdom Animalia also have a skin of some sort. The makeup of the skin is often used to help classify organisms in this kingdom. For example, if an organism's skin produces hair, it is considered a **mammal**. Mammals are a group of organisms which all have similar characteristics, one of which is skin that makes hair. In addition, most mammals give birth to live young (as opposed to laying eggs), nourish their young with milk that they produce, and possess a heart with four chambers. As you can tell from the description, humans are mammals, as are cats, dogs, elephants, rabbits, etc. You will learn more about mammals when you take biology.

If an organism's skin produces feathers, it is a **bird**, not a mammal. On the other hand, if the organism's skin produces scales, the organism is probably either a **fish** or a **reptile**, depending on other characteristics that the organism has. If the organism's skin is an exoskeleton, the organism is an **arthropod**. Some organisms, like **amphibians** (frogs, toads, and salamanders), even *breathe* with their skin. Obviously, then, the structure and function of an organism's skin varies quite a bit in Creation!

Summary

Before you finish with this module, I want you to take a moment and think about what you have learned. The human body is truly amazing in its design! Think of all of the structures I have taught you about in this module, and then consider this: I have *barely even scratched the surface* of the human superstructure. I have deliberately left out many of the more difficult aspects of the human skeletal system, the human muscular system, and human skin, simply because you do not have the chemistry to understand them! Now I want you to think about one other fact: The human body is so amazingly complex that there are still many aspects which are a *complete mystery* to science! Despite our best efforts, we have yet to understand the majority of the processes which make the human body work! This should give you profound respect for the God who actually designed and created it, and it should also convince you that there is simply no way such an elegantly-designed system could ever be formed by random chance!

ANSWERS TO THE ON YOUR OWN PROBLEMS

11.1 The patient's blood would change as well. Since bone marrow produces blood cells, a bone marrow transplant will actually change the patient's blood. That is, in fact, the reason bone marrow transplants are done.

11.2 As a person gets older, the relative amount of collagen in his bones decreases. Remember, the minerals in bone make them hard but brittle. The collagen makes them flexible. Bones with the right amount of each are hard but do not break easily. With too little minerals, the bones are too soft (like the chicken bone in your experiment). With too little collagen, the bones are too hard and brittle.

11.3 Compact bone tissue is much heavier than spongy bone tissue. Thus, the first bone has more compact bone tissue, because it is heavier.

11.4 You don't have to know a lot about these creatures to determine whether or not they are vertebrates. You just have to remember a couple of things. First, if the organism is in ANY kingdom other than Animalia, it is neither a vertebrate nor an invertebrate. If it is an animal, then it is a vertebrate if it has a backbone. For your purposes, you can assume that if it has a skeleton at all, it has a backbone and is therefore a vertebrate.

a. Worms are animals, and they are too squishy to have a skeleton. Thus, they are invertebrates.
b. Alligators are animals, and they have skeletons. Thus, they are vertebrates.
c. Grass is a plant. Thus, it is neither an invertebrate nor a vertebrate.
d. Yeast is a fungus. Thus, it is neither an invertebrate nor a vertebrate.
e. This is a hard one. Starfish are covered with a hard, outer covering, If you look inside, there are no bones. Thus, they are invertebrates. Don't worry if you got that one wrong!

11.5 Cartilage cushions the ends of the bones so that they don't scrape together in the joints. A loss of cartilage will cause great pain and bone damage as the bones of the joint scrape together. Ligaments hold the bones in the joints. Thus, a loss of ligaments will make it easy to dislocate the joint.

11.6 The triceps contracts to extend the forearm and relaxes so that the biceps can flex the forearm. Thus, the person will be able to flex the forearm at the elbow but not extend it.

11.7 The muscles that regulate blood flow are smooth. You know that because you don't have to think about regulating your blood flow. Your body does it for you. Thus, they are involuntary muscles and are therefore smooth. The muscles that turn the head are skeletal muscles. You know this because you have to think to move your head. Thus, the muscles are voluntary. Also, the head is a part of the skeleton. To move the skeleton, you have to use skeletal muscles.

11.8 Teenagers everywhere would rejoice because without the oil from the sebaceous gland, there would be no pimples or blackheads. Remember, a pimple or blackhead is formed by a plugged up sebaceous gland. The FDA would not approve the procedure because you need that oil for healthy skin. It keeps the skin from painfully cracking, and it also makes it harder for harmful bacteria to attach to your skin.

11.9 If you do not sweat, the bacteria and fungi which feed on your sweat will die. Without the bacteria and fungi that cover your skin in lactic acid, you will be more susceptible to pathogenic bacteria and fungi which make you sick.

11.10 In your experiment, the skin covered with the bandage should have been lighter than the rest of your skin. Since the rest of your skin was exposed to light, that means light makes skin darker. That's why you can suntan. Since increasing the amount of melanin in skin makes it dark, light must increase the amount of melanin in your skin.

STUDY GUIDE FOR MODULE #11

1. Define the following terms:

a. Axial skeleton
b. Appendicular skeleton
c. Exoskeleton
d. Symbiosis

2. What three things make up the human superstructure?

3. What are the two main differences between smooth muscles and skeletal muscles?

4. Where is the cardiac muscle found? Is it an involuntary muscle or a voluntary one?

5. What is produced in the bone marrow?

6. What is keratinization? What is it used for?

7. What two principal substances make up bone? What qualities do they each provide to the bone?

8. What is the difference between compact bone tissue and spongy bone tissue?

9. Are bones alive?

10. What is the difference between an invertebrate and a vertebrate? Is it possible to be neither?

11. Are your arms part of the appendicular skeleton or the axial skeleton? What about your neck?

12. What is the difference between an endoskeleton and an exoskeleton? What do we call organisms with exoskeletons?

13. Order the following joints in terms of increasing range of motion. Then order them in terms of increasing stability:

Ball-and-socket, hinge, saddle

14. What purpose do ligaments serve in the joints? What about cartilage?

15. How do skeletal muscles attach to the skeleton?

16. Describe how the biceps and triceps work together to move the forearm.

17. Is the stomach composed of smooth muscle or skeletal muscle?

18. A sunflower will actually turn throughout the day so that it follows the sun across the sky. What is the term we use to describe this?

19. What are the two main functions of hair?

20. What are the two main functions of sweat?

21. Why do your skin cells constantly fall off your body?

22. What do the sebaceous glands produce, and what are the substance's two main purposes?

23. For the following animals, classify each as mammal, bird, reptile, or amphibian.

    a. The animal has hair.
    b. The animal breathes through its skin.
    c. The animal has scales.
    d. The animal has feathers.

Module #12: Energy and Life

Introduction

Now that you know a little bit about the skeleton, muscles, and skin, I want to discuss something that they all use: energy. The muscles use energy to contract and relax; the bones use energy to grow and make blood cells; and the skin uses energy to produce hair, skin cells, and nails. In fact, energy is used in all parts of our bodies. Indeed, energy is such an important component of life that it is central to our second criterion for life:

All life forms have a method by which they take energy from the surroundings and convert it into energy that helps them live.

In this module and the next, I want to give you an introduction to how that happens in our bodies and in many other organisms.

Life's Energy Cycle

Before I start discussing the way in which our bodies satisfy the second criterion for life, I want to spend some time on a few fundamental concepts. First, I want to answer a very simple question: Where does all of this energy come from? After all, the second criterion for life says that living organisms take energy from the surroundings and convert it into energy which helps them live. Well, if living organisms take energy from the surroundings, then the energy must already be there. Where did it come from?

Almost all of the energy used by living organisms comes from one place: the sun. There are a few very exotic bacteria that get their energy from certain chemical reactions which occur at the bottom of the ocean. However, the vast majority of the energy used by living organisms in Creation comes from the sun.

Now that might sound a little strange to you. After all, you know that you get your energy from the food that you eat and the liquids you drink. If you were to stop eating and drinking and simply lay out in the sun all day, you would die. You wouldn't be able to satisfy your energy needs that way! How, then, can I say that the energy in your body originated in the sun?

Well, think about it. When light from the sun hits the earth, plants (and other organisms like algae) convert that energy into food for themselves. We call such organisms **producers**, because they produce food for themselves.

Producers - Organisms that produce their own food

It is easy to see how the energy that a producer uses comes from the sun. Through the process of photosynthesis, producers take energy from the sun, carbon dioxide, and water and they make a sugar called glucose. That glucose is then used by the plant as food. The plant, then, converts the energy of the sun into glucose, and then it uses the glucose as food for energy.

That's not the end of the story, however. God has designed the producers to make a lot more food than they need. They store this excess food, usually in some chemical form other than glucose. Plants, for example, usually store their excess food as starch. When animals eat those plants, they are using that starch to produce their energy. Thus, even though these animals cannot get energy *directly* from the sun, they get it indirectly, by eating the food that plants manufactured from the sun. We call such creatures **consumers**, because they consume other organisms to get their food.

Consumers - Organisms that eat living producers and/or other living consumers for food

Human beings are consumers. We eat plants, and we eat meat, which comes from animals. Those animals either ate plants or ate creatures which ate plants. In the end, then, the energy of life comes from the sun, because the producers produce the food from the sun's energy, and the consumers eat the producers or other consumers which have eaten the producers.

Photos from the MasterClips collection

FIGURE 12.1
Producers and Consumers

Lettuce is a producer. It produces its own food from sunlight.

Cows are consumers, because they eat producers such as grass.

Humans are also consumers, because we eat plants and animals.

There is actually a third group of organisms which I have not mentioned yet. They are the **decomposers** that you learned about in Module #10. Although you *could* classify such organisms as consumers (after all, they do not produce their own food), they are classified separately because they play a distinct role in Creation. Decomposers actually "recycle" dead organisms. You see, when a decomposer eats a dead organism, the organism is broken down into chemicals that act as fertilizer for producers. Now remember, fertilizer is *not* plant food. However, fertilizer does act as "vitamins" that make plants more healthy. Thus, producers use the products of the decomposers.

Not all organisms that eat dead organisms are decomposers. Vultures, for example, eat dead organisms. However, the process of a vulture eating a dead animal does not produce fertilizer for plants. Thus, a vulture is not a decomposer. As you will recall from Experiment 10.2, yeast is a decomposer. That's because when yeast eats dead organisms, the organisms are broken down into substances used by producers.

An organism can be classified by whether or not it is a producer, consumer, or decomposer. However, if an organism is a consumer, it can be further classified. Remember, cows are consumers because they eat producers. Lions are also consumers, even though they do not eat producers. They are consumers because they eat *other* consumers. Also, humans are consumers, and we eat *both* producers and consumers.

If a consumer eats only producers, it is called a **herbivore** (hur bih' vor).

Herbivore - A consumer that eats producers exclusively

If a consumer eats only other consumers, it is called a **carnivore** (kar nih' vor).

Carnivore - A consumer that eats only other consumers

Finally, if a consumer eats both producers and other consumers, it is an **omnivore** (ahm nih' vor).

Omnivore - A consumer that eats both producers and other consumers

From these definitions, then, you can see that cows are herbivores, lions are carnivores, and humans are omnivores.

ON YOUR OWN

12.1 Classify each of the following as a consumer, producer or decomposer.

a. grass b. horse c. tree d. yeast e. sparrow f. shark

12.2 A creature's diet includes leaves, fruits, and certain bugs. Is this creature a carnivore, herbivore, or omnivore? If one of the three items from that list were removed, the creature would be classified differently. What one thing would have to be removed, and what would the new classification be?

How Do Organisms Get Energy From Food?

Okay, you now know that producers make their own food from the sun's energy, and consumers eat that food by eating plants or eating animals that have eaten plants. Also, you know that decomposers eat dead organisms and "recycle" those dead organisms back into Creation. However, I still haven't told you *how* organisms actually get energy from food. Well, that's not an easy question to answer. In fact, I will spend the rest of this module *and the next* just giving you an introduction to how this is done. The process is quite fascinating and well worth the time it will take to discuss!

In short, organisms get energy from food by *burning* their food. Now don't get the wrong idea here. There aren't little fires going on in your body. Nevertheless, the chemical process by which organisms get energy from food is a **combustion** reaction. Combustion reactions are what occur when wood, paper, and other flammable materials are burned. Thus, much like we can get energy to heat our home by burning wood in a fireplace or gas in a furnace, organisms get the energy they need for life by burning their food.

Of course, the burning process that goes on in organisms is different than the burning process that goes on in a fireplace or a furnace. Nevertheless, there are quite a few similarities. I want you to perform the following experiments to see some of those similarities.

EXPERIMENT 12.1
What Combustion Needs

Supplies:

- A small candle (It needs to be in some kind of heavy holder, but the holder should not be tall. A small tealight candle in a cup-like holder, like the one in the figure under step (F), is ideal.)
- A glass that will cover the candle
- A deep bowl (The bowl should be deep enough so that when the candle is placed at the bottom of the bowl, the sides of the bowl are well above the flame of the candle.
- One cup of vinegar
- One tablespoon of baking soda
- Matches

Introduction - In this experiment, you will see that oxygen is essential for combustion.

Procedure:

A. Please note that you are going to be working with open flames in this experiment. **BE CAREFUL!!**
B. Put the candle on a table or countertop and light it.
C. Put the glass upside down over the candle, so that it covers the candle completely.
D. Watch the candle for about a minute or so. Note what happens.

E. Next, add one cup of vinegar to the bowl.
F. Place the candle in the bowl. The candle holder needs to be heavy enough so that the candle rests on the bottom of the bowl. It should not float in the vinegar. Then light the candle. In the end, your setup should look like this:

Notice how the vinegar surrounds the candle but the candle is taller than the height of the vinegar. Also notice that the sides of the bowl are significantly taller than the candle.
G. Get a tablespoon of baking soda and SLOWLY sprinkle it into the vinegar. Make sure that the baking soda lands in the vinegar, not in the candle. You will immediately see bubbles in the vinegar. Add the baking soda slowly so that the bubbles do not rise high enough to spill over into the candle. Distribute the baking soda all of the way around the candle so that the bubbles surround it.
H. Watch the candle. What happens?
I. Wait until the bubbling stops, and then use a match to try and re-light the candle. Don't move the candle. Try to re-light it right where it is. What happens?
J. Clean everything up.

What did you see in the experiment? If everything went well in steps (A) - (D), you should have watched the flame on the candle slowly dim until it went out altogether. Why did that happen? The flame of a candle comes from the combustion of the wax that makes up the candle. Combustion requires oxygen. When you put the glass over the candle, the oxygen in the air surrounding the candle could not be replenished. Thus, when all of the oxygen was used up, combustion could no longer occur, and the flame went out.

The second part of the experiment demonstrates the same fact, but in a much more interesting way. You see, when baking soda and vinegar mix, a chemical reaction occurs. This chemical reaction produces carbon dioxide gas. That's what the bubbling was all about. The bubbles you saw were the result of carbon dioxide gas forming in the chemical reaction between baking soda and vinegar.

Well, as the baking soda and vinegar produced carbon dioxide gas, the gas began to fill up the surrounding area. In other words, the carbon dioxide gas began filling up the bowl. This pushed the air that was in the bowl out, in order to make room for the carbon dioxide. As you will learn in physical science, air is a mixture of gases. One of the gases in that mixture is oxygen. Since the air was pushed out by the carbon dioxide, the oxygen was pushed out along with it. Once most of the oxygen was pushed out of the bowl, the flame went out, because combustion requires oxygen.

Now, what happened when you tried to re-light the candle? Well, you struck a match and it began to burn. However, as you moved the match towards the candle, it suddenly extinguished. Why did that happen? The carbon dioxide will stay in the bowl for a while, until the breezes that blow in your home eventually mix air back into the bowl. Now, as long as the match was exposed to air, it would burn. As you lowered the match into the bowl, however, the match eventually was surrounded only by carbon dioxide. At that point, there was no longer any oxygen near the match, so combustion could not occur. Once again, at that point, the flame went out.

Hopefully, then, the experiment demonstrated to you that combustion requires oxygen. This is an important point.

Combustion requires oxygen.

Now let me ask you a question: Why do we need to breathe? Nearly everyone can answer that question. We need to breathe in order to get oxygen. Okay, then let me ask you another question: Why do we need oxygen? The answer to that question should be a little more obvious now. We need oxygen in order to burn our food for energy. Without oxygen, combustion cannot occur. Combustion is what our bodies use to convert the food that we eat into energy that our bodies can use. In order for that conversion to occur, we must have oxygen. Without oxygen we die. After all, we can be completely full of food, but if we have no oxygen with which to burn the food, we can never get energy from it. Without energy, all of the systems that keep us alive simply stop. That's why we need oxygen.

Okay, so you now know that combustion requires two things. First, it requires something to burn. In the case of a candle, the wax is what burns. In our bodies, food is what burns. The second thing that combustion needs is oxygen. Well, we know that combustion produces energy. After all, the flame of a candle gives off both heat and light. Those are both forms of energy. In our bodies, combustion produces the energy that we need to live. Does combustion produce anything else besides energy? Yes, it does. Perform the following experiment to find out the other products of combustion.

EXPERIMENT 12.2

The Products of Combustion

Supplies:

- A mirror (A hand-held mirror is best, but any mirror will do.)
- A paper towel
- Red (sometimes called purple) cabbage (You only need a few leaves.)
- Distilled water (You can get it at any large supermarket. You need about a quart.)
- Two drinking straws

- A saucepan
- A stove
- Three small glasses (like juice glasses)
- A ¼-cup measuring cup and a 1-cup measuring cup
- A 2-liter plastic bottle (the kind soda comes in)
- A balloon (6-inch or 8-inch round balloons work best.)
- A small spoon (like a ¼ measuring teaspoon)
- Vinegar
- Baking soda

Introduction - Combustion produces energy and two substances. This experiment will help you learn what those substances are.

Procedure:

A. Rinse the saucepan out twice with distilled water.
B. Place a few leaves of red cabbage in the pan.
C. Rinse out the measuring cups twice with distilled water.
D. Use the 1-cup measuring cup to add 2 cups of distilled water to the saucepan.
E. Put the saucepan on the stove and heat it until the water boils.
F. While you are waiting on the boiling, perform the first experiment, which is described below.

Steps (G) - (J) detail the first experiment:

G. Use the paper towel to clean and dry the mirror.
H. Hold the mirror close to but not touching your mouth.
I. Breathe on the mirror three or four times.
J. Examine the mirror. Note what happened.

Steps (K) - (Z) detail the second experiment:

K. Once the water begins to boil, turn off the stove and remove the pan from the heat. Allow the pan and water to sit and cool.
L. While the pan and water are cooling, fill the 2-liter bottle about 1/8-full of vinegar.
M. Get a balloon ready.
N. Use the small spoon to add baking soda to the vinegar in the bottle. Add two or three spoon's worth. As soon as you've added the baking soda, quickly cover the opening of the bottle with the mouth of the balloon. Make the seal between the balloon and bottle as airtight as possible, so that the balloon begins to fill up with the carbon dioxide that is being produced. You do not need to fill the balloon very full at all. As long as the balloon is at least partially inflated, you have all the carbon dioxide that you need.
O. Let the balloon and bottle sit for a while. As long as the seal between the balloon and bottle is airtight, you will not lose the carbon dioxide inside the balloon.
P. Next, rinse the three small glasses out twice with distilled water.
Q. Use the ¼-cup measuring cup to scoop out ¼ cup of the solution in the saucepan. Try to

avoid getting cabbage leaves in the cup, but it will not hurt the experiment if you do. **BE CAREFUL. THE SOLUTION WILL BE HOT!!!**

R. Pour that solution into one of the small glasses.
S. Repeat steps (Q) and (R) twice more so that all three glasses have ¼ cup of cabbage water in them.
T. Take out a straw, and remove the balloon from the 2-liter bottle. Pinch the neck of the balloon so that you do not lose much carbon dioxide.
U. Place one end of the straw in the cabbage water solution in one of the three glasses. Next, use the balloon to blow carbon dioxide through the other end of the straw and into the cabbage water. Do this slowly, so that the solution does not splatter you! Don't worry about getting ALL of the carbon dioxide into the straw. You will lose A LOT in the process. The main thing is to make sure that at least SOME of the carbon dioxide goes through the straw and into the cabbage water. You will know this is happening because you will see bubbles coming out the end of the straw.
V. After you are done, note the color change as compared to the cabbage water in either one of the remaining solutions.
W. Get another straw and place one end in the cabbage water that is in one of the two remaining glasses.
X. Blow through the other end with your mouth so that your breath goes down the straw and bubbles up through the cabbage water. Do this several times.
Y. Compare the color of the cabbage water to the color you saw in step (V) as well as the color of the cabbage water in the remaining glass.
Z. Clean everything up.

So what did you see in the experiments? Well, let's start with the first one. When you breathed on the mirror, it fogged up, didn't it? What made that fog? Water vapor made it. When you breathe out, one of the things that you are exhaling is water vapor. Where did that water vapor come from? Some of it came from the combustion reactions that are burning up your food. That's one of the products of combustion: water vapor. When you go outside on a cold day, you can "see your breath." In a way, that's true. On a cold day, the water vapor that you exhale immediately becomes liquid water as soon as it leaves the warm confines of your mouth. The "fog" that you see coming out of your mouth is composed of little droplets of exhaled water. There are other gases you are exhaling which you do not see. However, you do see one gas that is being exhaled: water. Some of that water comes from the combustion reactions which burn your food.

Okay, so you now know two of the things produced by combustion: energy and water. There is one more thing, and it is illustrated by the second experiment. What happened in that experiment? Well, you should have seen that the cabbage water in all glasses initially had a blue/purple color. When you used the balloon to bubble carbon dioxide through the cabbage water in the first glass, it turned a pink/red color. The same thing should have happened when you blew your own breath through the cabbage water in the second glass. The cabbage water should have turned pink/red. Especially when you compared the color of the cabbage water in the first two glasses to the cabbage water in the third glass, the color change should have been rather striking.

What does this mean? Red cabbage contains a chemical that changes color based on other chemicals to which it is exposed. You will learn more about this in chemistry, but the chemical in red cabbage is called an "indicator," because it indicates the presence of other chemicals known as acids and bases. Well, when carbon dioxide is bubbled through water, a chemical reaction occurs which makes an acid (carbonic acid). In the presence of acid, the chemical in red cabbage turns pink/red. So, when you bubbled carbon dioxide through the cabbage water, the carbon dioxide reacted with the water to make an acid. That acid caused the chemical from the red cabbage to turn pink/red.

Well, what happened when you blew your own breath through the cabbage water? It turned the same pink/red color. What does that tell you? It tells you that your breath also contains carbon dioxide. Where does the carbon dioxide come from? You guessed it. It comes from the combustion reactions which burn your food! Thus, I can now tell you:

Combustion produces energy, carbon dioxide, and water.

So, to sum all of this up, we burn our food in order to give our bodies energy. We inhale oxygen because combustion requires oxygen. Without that oxygen, we could not burn our food and therefore we could not get the energy we need to live. We exhale carbon dioxide and water because carbon dioxide and water are both produced by combustion.

ON YOUR OWN

12.3 There are many different kinds of fire extinguishers. However, one type of fire extinguisher is simply a canister filled with carbon dioxide. When you push the lever, the carbon dioxide rushes out the nozzle. How does this extinguish a fire?

12.4 There are several studies which indicate that plants grow better when their caretakers talk to them. Assuming that plants can't really hear us when we talk, what have you learned in this section that might explain the results of these studies?

12.5 Describe an experiment which would provide evidence for the explanation that you provided in question 12.4.

What Actually Gets Burned For Energy?

Now that you know a few details about the combustion process itself, I want to discuss *exactly* what our bodies burn for energy. After all, we eat *a lot* of things for food (meat, vegetables, fruits, breads, dairy products, sweets, etc.). Do our bodies just take it all in and burn it? No! In fact, our bodies are rather picky about what they burn. There are only three things that our bodies can burn: **carbohydrates** (car boh hi' drayts), **fats**, and **proteins**. Our bodies even have a preference. They would rather burn carbohydrates. If they can't burn carbohydrates, they will resort to burning fats. If they can't get either of those, they will burn proteins. In the end, then, our bodies are very picky about what they burn.

Collectively, carbohydrates, fats, and proteins are called the **macronutrients** (mack' roh new' tree uhnts), because we must eat a lot of them every day. I want to discuss each of the macronutrients individually, and since the body prefers to burn carbohydrates, I want to discuss them first. There are many different forms of carbohydrates. Simple carbohydrates are called **monosaccharides** (mon' oh sack' uh rides). Sometimes, they are also called **simple sugars**. Glucose, the chemical that plants produce for food, is an example of a monosaccharide. The monosaccharide called "fructose" (frewck' tohs) is the sugar which gives fruits their sweet taste. There are other carbohydrates, however. Two monosaccharides can link together to become a **disaccharide**. Perhaps the best know disaccharide is table sugar, which is formed when glucose links up with fructose. The scientific name for table sugar is "sucrose" (sue' crohs). Finally, if many monosaccharides link together, they form a **polysaccharide**. The polysaccharide with which you are most familiar is starch, which is the main component of a potato. Figure 12.2 illustrates the different kinds of carbohydrates.

FIGURE 12.2
Carbohydrates

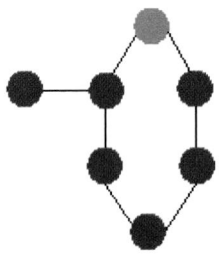

Monosaccharide

These are the simplest carbohydrates. Glucose is pictured as an example. When you take biology, you will learn why we picture glucose like this.

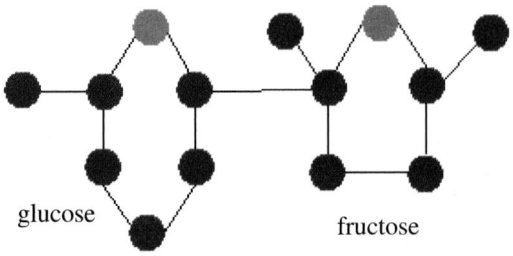

Disaccharide

When two monosaccharides link up, they form a disaccharide. The one pictured here is sucrose. It contains one glucose and one fructose linked together.

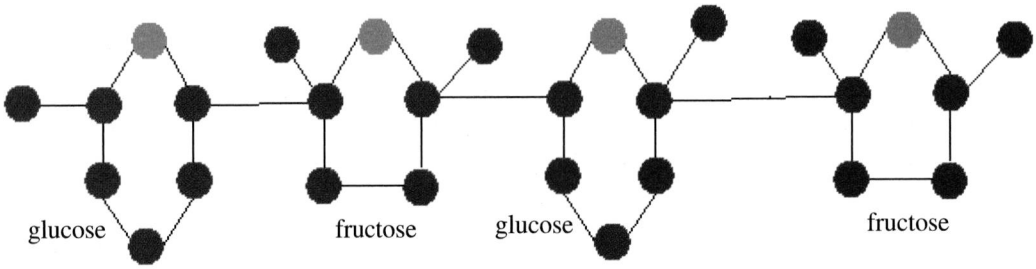

Polysaccharide

When several monosaccharides link up, they form a polysaccharide. There is not enough room to picture a real polysaccharide, as they typically have many, many monosaccharides linked together. Starch is an example of a polysaccharide.

As I mentioned before, if there are any carbohydrates (monosaccharides, disaccharides, or polysaccharides) available, your body will burn those first. In fact, the cells in your brain will *only* burn carbohydrates for energy. They cannot burn fats or proteins. As a result, when your body starts to run low on carbohydrates, it will burn fat and proteins in other parts of the body and save the carbohydrates for use by the brain! Interestingly enough, however, when it comes to carbohydrates, the cells in your body can only burn monosaccharides. Thus, in order for the body to use disaccharides and polysaccharides, it must first break them down into monosaccharides.

The next macronutrient I want to discuss is fat. There are many, many different types of fats in the food that we eat, but they can all be put into one of two classifications: **saturated fats** or **unsaturated fats**. Generally speaking, saturated fats are solid at room temperature, while unsaturated fats tend to be liquid at room temperature. Fried foods are cooked in hot fat. If the fat is solid at room temperature (such as butter or shortening), it is most likely made of saturated fats. If it is liquid at room temperature (such as vegetable oil), it is most likely made of unsaturated fats.

Although many weight-conscious Americans think of fat as a bad thing, it is absolutely essential for a healthy body. As you learned in the previous module, your skin has a fat layer that is used to insulate the body. Without that insulation, we could not keep our bodies at the proper internal temperature. Many organs also have a layer of fat for cushion and insulation. Also, the fat that our bodies store serves as a great storehouse of energy in case we are unable to eat for an extended amount of time. Finally, there are certain vitamins (A, D, E, and K) that can *only* be stored in the body's fat reserves. Thus, fat is a necessary part of life.

Your body can actually produce most of the fats that it needs from excess carbohydrates and proteins. In other words, if you eat more carbohydrates than your body needs, it will convert those carbohydrates into fats as a way of storing them for future use. There are a few fats that your body needs but cannot produce itself. Those fats, called "essential fats," are typically found in vegetable oils. They must be eaten, since your body cannot produce them. A balanced diet contains plenty of those fats. Even though fat is a necessary part of life, too much fat can be bad for you. A host of health problems can be traced back to too much fat in the body. Thus, like most things in life, you need to be moderate in your fat intake. Except for certain people with specific conditions, everyone needs to eat fat. In fact, many "low fat" foods neglect the essential fats that you must eat, and some nutritionists call essential fats the most neglected nutrient in the United States. Eating too much fat (or eating so many carbohydrates that your body makes too much fat), however, can be bad for you as well.

Proteins are the third macronutrient. Your body burns these molecules only if you have too many of them, because they are essential to many other chemical processes which occur in your body. Like polysaccharides, proteins are formed when smaller substances, called **amino** (uh me' no) **acids**, link together in long chains. Nearly every chemical reaction that occurs in the body is affected by proteins. Even the reactions that burn food for energy are controlled by proteins. Thus, next to DNA, proteins are probably the most important chemicals for life.

In fact, the information stored in DNA is used to tell the cells in your body how to make proteins. How does it do that? Well, you will learn the details when you take biology. For right now, however, just realize that each cell in your body is full of amino acids. The cell reads the information contained in DNA and, based on that information, starts linking its stored amino acids together into long chains to make proteins.

To make the proteins necessary for life, then, the cells in your body need two things: DNA and amino acids. The DNA is in the nucleus of the cell, but where do the amino acids come from? Well, your cells can actually manufacture 12 of the 20 amino acids that they need. However, there are 8 amino acids, called **essential amino acids**, which your cells cannot manufacture. In order to get these amino acids, you must eat proteins which contain them. The best source of these essential amino acids is meat, milk, fish, or eggs. That's because animal proteins contains all 8 essential amino acids.

Have you ever talked to a true vegetarian (someone who not only refrains from eating meat, but does not eat *any* animal products)? True vegetarians will tell you that they must work hard to get protein in their diet. Actually, that's not quite true. All living organisms contain proteins, because proteins govern virtually all of the chemical reactions of life! Thus, there are plenty of proteins in plants. The problem is that plant proteins rarely contain all 8 essential amino acids which our bodies cannot produce. Thus, what vegetarians really have trouble getting is *the right kind of proteins* in their diet. They can eat all of the protein they want, but unless the proteins they eat contain the 8 essential amino acids, it does little good. In order to get all 8 essential amino acids, true vegetarians must eat a wide range of plants and seeds.

The main reason we must eat proteins, then, is not as a source of energy. Instead, the proteins we eat are a source of the amino acids that our bodies cannot produce themselves. Without a steady supply of amino acids, our bodies would not be able to manufacture the proteins that they need to manufacture, and the consequences can be terrible. Children who do not get the 8 essential amino acids, for example, typically suffer severe brain damage, resulting in mental retardation.

When we eat proteins, then, our bodies do not keep them intact. Our bodies break the proteins down into their individual amino acids. Those amino acids are then sent to the cells throughout our bodies, so that the cells can use them to manufacture the proteins that they need. Under normal circumstances, that's how our bodies use the amino acids in the proteins we eat. If we eat too many proteins, our bodies end up having more amino acids than they need. If that happens, the excess proteins are converted into carbohydrates and fats. If our bodies suddenly run low on both carbohydrates and fats, however, they can burn the amino acids directly for energy.

Athletes can very often have situations in which they burn amino acids for energy. Typically, an athlete stresses his or her body by demanding a large amount of energy in a short time period. Under those circumstances, the athlete's muscles may need energy faster than the body can supply monosaccharides and fats to those muscles. As a result, the muscles will begin to burn the amino acids which are there in the muscle cells. So athletes often eat high protein diets, because they burn more proteins than the average person.

In the end, then, the food that we eat provides us with three macronutrients, which in turn provide energy for our daily lives. These macronutrients are used in different ways, depending on the situation. Figure 12.3 illustrates this.

FIGURE 12.3
Food and the Macronutrients

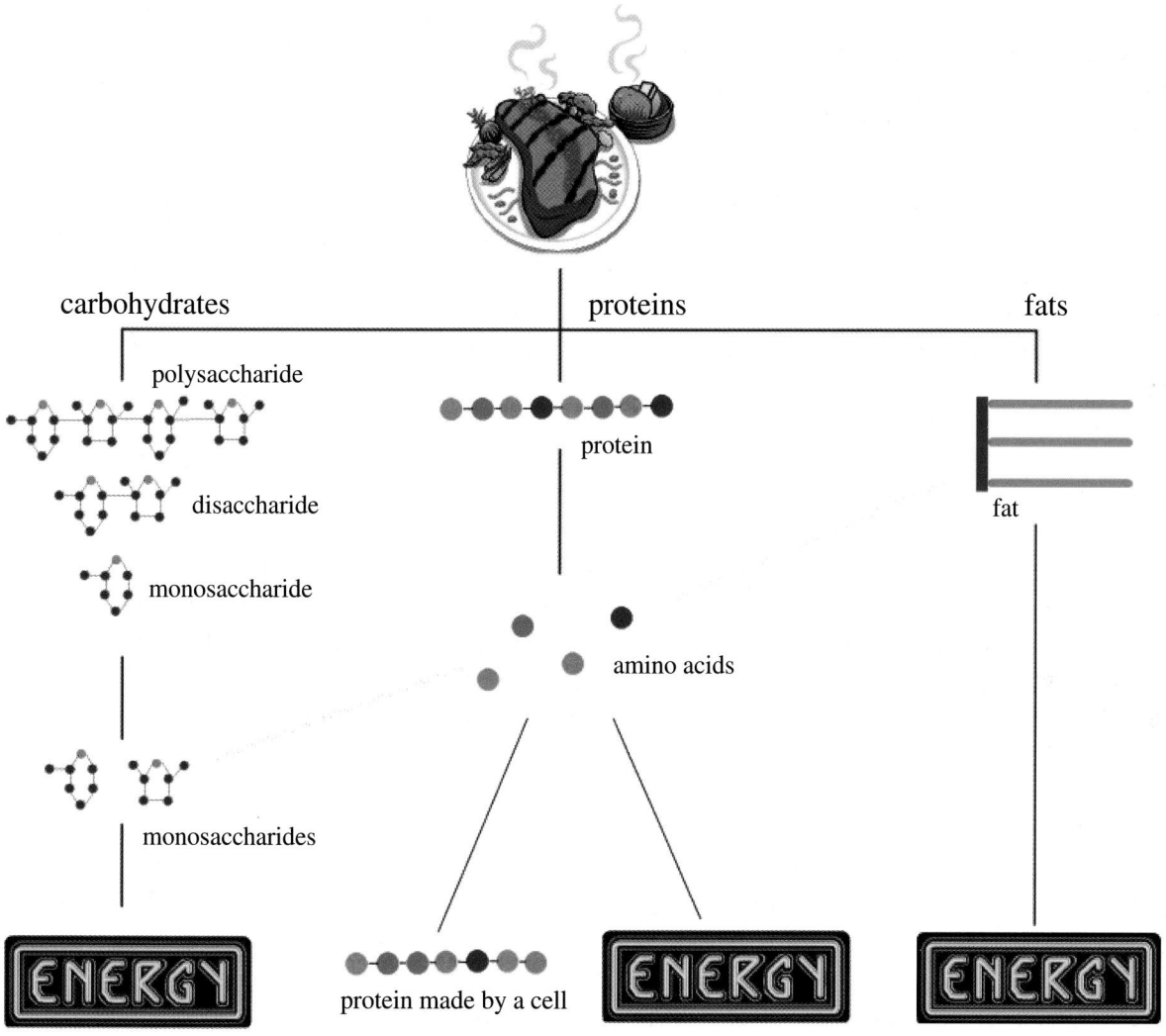

The carbohydrates in our food get broken down into monosaccharides and then burned for energy. Excess carbohydrates can be converted to fats in order to store the energy for later use.

The proteins in our food get broken down into amino acids. If the body has too many amino acids, they will be converted into fats or carbohydrates. If the body needs amino acids, they will be used by the cells to make the specific proteins that the cells need to make. Under conditions of low carbohydrates and fats, they can be burned for energy.

The fats in our food can be used for insulation, cushioning, vitamin storage, or energy storage. Some fats are essential for other body functions as well. They can also be burned for energy. Fats will only be burned when the body runs low on carbohydrates.

Before I finish with this section, I want to make two points. First, please realize that food contains other things that our bodies need besides just the macronutrients. In fact, food contains a huge number of chemicals which we call **micronutrients**. These micronutrients are important for healthy bodies as well. However, micronutrients are not used for energy, and energy is what I am stressing in this module. Thus, I am ignoring the micronutrients, even though they are important. In case you are wondering, we call carbohydrates, fats, and proteins "macronutrients" because you need a lot of them every day. The prefix "macro" means "large," so "macronutrients" refers to the substances that we need in large quantities. The micronutrients are important, but we need them in much smaller quantities. That's why we call them micronutrients.

Second, I want to remind you of something I have said before. The chemical process by which we convert the macronutrients into energy is combustion, but it is unlike any combustion you have ever seen. Thus, do not think that there are little fires going on in your body! True, we do burn the macronutrients for food, but the burning process is carefully controlled and regulated by a whole host of chemical machinery. Although the end result is identical to combustion, the process is completely different than anything you have ever seen. I will discuss that process to some degree at the end of this module. You will learn even more about it when you take biology. For now, just realize that it is a very unique form of combustion and is unlike any burning process with which you are familiar!

ON YOUR OWN

12.6 A man puts himself on a no-fat diet. As a result, his macronutrient intake is almost all carbohydrates and protein. An analysis of his body's fat content was done before he started the diet and several weeks afterwards. To his shock, the level of fat in his system actually *increased* after being on the diet. Where did the excess fat come from?

12.7 A woman goes on a high-protein diet. As a result, she begins eating a lot more protein than she used to eat. If her cells were short of amino acids before she went on the diet, what will happen to the extra protein she is now eating?

Energy Use in the Body

The macronutrients in food provide us with the energy that we need to survive, but for what purposes do our bodies use this energy? Well, remember in the last module I told you about involuntary muscles. They control the workings of our organs. Even though we don't need to think about their actions, they are continually contracting and relaxing in order to keep our bodies working. Thus, our bodies need energy to keep the involuntary muscles going.

There is another thing that we never think about but nevertheless requires an enormous amount of energy. Perform the following experiment to see what it is.

EXPERIMENT 12.3
Body Temperature

Supply:

- An oral thermometer (The kind you use to take a person's temperature. Do not use one of those strips that you put on your forehead. Use the kind of thermometer you stick in your mouth.)

Introduction - You know that your body stays warm. In this experiment, you will see that your internal body temperature does not change significantly, regardless of the conditions.

Procedure:

A. Take your temperature while you are sitting down. Follow the normal instructions for your thermometer. It usually involves keeping the thermometer under your tongue for 3 minutes.
B. Once you have taken your temperature, put the thermometer back in your mouth, and go somewhere cold. It could be outside; it could be right next to an air conditioner; you could even open the refrigerator door and stand as close as you can to the refrigerator. **Now be reasonable about this.** The idea is to get uncomfortably cool, but NOT dangerously cold! If the temperature outside is sub-zero, don't go outside. Instead, go to a room in your house than it uncomfortably cold. If you have a garage attached to your house, that will be cool if it is really cold outside. Like I said, be uncomfortably cool, not dangerously cold!
C. Allow the thermometer to stay in your mouth for another three minutes while you are uncomfortably cold. Then, go to a warm place and look at the temperature reading again. Compare it to your previous temperature reading.
D. Put the thermometer down and put on a sweater. Then, do 5 minutes of vigorous exercise. You could do jumping jacks, run in place, or something like that. The point is to get uncomfortably warm as a result of the exercise.
E. Take your temperature right after you are finished with the exercise. **Be careful**! You are probably not used to taking your temperature when you are out of breath.
F. Compare your temperature now to the other two measurements.
G. Wash the thermometer and put it away.

What did you see in the experiment? Well, as long as you took your temperature correctly each time, you should have seen very little difference between the three temperature measurements. The measurement you made in step (C) might be a bit lower than the first one you made, and the measurement in step (E) might be a bit higher than the first one you made. In general, however, even though you felt uncomfortably cold in step (C), your *internal temperature* did not change much. Once again, even though you felt uncomfortably warm in step (E), your *internal temperature* did not change much.

Why is that? Well, human beings are **endothermic** (en doh thur' mik). This means that we use energy for the purpose of keeping our internal temperature the same. In other words, we are "warm-blooded." Not all organisms are like that. In fact, the *vast majority* of organisms are

ectothermic (ek toh thur' mik), which means that they do not have a constant internal temperature. In other words, they are "cold-blooded." If it is cold outside, ectothermic creatures get cold on the inside. If it is warm outside, ectothermic creatures are warm on the inside. Now don't get me wrong. The internal temperature of an ectothermic creature is not necessarily *the same* as the outside temperature. However, the outside temperature strongly affects the internal temperature of an ectothermic creature, but it does not strongly affect the internal temperature of an endothermic creature.

Ectothermic organisms require less food than endothermic organisms, because the energy required to maintain a constant internal temperature is very large. Since ectothermic organisms do not maintain a constant internal temperature, they expend less energy in order to stay alive and thus require less food. Endothermic creatures, however, generally are faster at responding to the outside world than are ectothermic creatures. That's because high temperatures increase the rate at which most chemical reactions occur. Thus, a higher internal temperature means faster chemical reactions inside the body. Since an organism is ultimately controlled by chemical reactions, the faster the reactions go, the faster the organism can react.

A good way to see the effect of outside temperature on the movement of ectothermic creatures is to go to a zoo and watch how the reptiles move on a cool day. Typically, they move very slowly if at all. On cool days, most reptiles try to find a sunny rock upon which to lay, because a sunny rock is the warmest place to be. On warm days, however, the reptiles move around a lot more. That's because reptiles are ectothermic. On warm days, their internal temperature is higher, so the chemical reactions in their bodies run faster. This allows them to move more quickly.

Our bodies, then, use energy to control all of the involuntary muscles which keep our organs and internal processes functioning properly. They also use energy to keep our internal temperatures at a constant 98 to 99 degrees Fahrenheit. Of course, that's not all that our bodies use energy for. We also use energy to move our voluntary muscles. When we sit quietly, the majority of the energy that our bodies use is concentrated on the involuntary muscles and in keeping our internal temperature constant. However, when we get up and move around, we are contracting and relaxing our voluntary muscles. That takes energy as well. In the next section, I will explain how we measure the energy that our bodies use.

ON YOUR OWN

12.8 An animal tends to move around very quickly in the snow. Is this animal most likely ectothermic or endothermic?

Calories and Food

I am sure that you've heard about calories. If you have ever tried to lose weight, or if you have ever talked to someone who is trying to lose weight, you have probably heard about "counting calories." In this section, I want to tell you what a calorie is and what it measures. A **calorie** is actually a unit used to measure energy. You will learn a lot about that unit when you take chemistry, so I don't want to go into the definition of calorie and all of that right now. I just want you to realize that a calorie represents a certain amount of energy.

Well, since food provides us with macronutrients, and since macronutrients provide us with energy, one way to measure the macronutrient content in food is to measure the number of calories worth of energy the food gives us. The more macronutrients in the food, the more calories it provides. The fewer the macronutrients, the fewer the calories. Now it turns out that there is a bit of confusion in the scientific world over the definition of a calorie. Chemists have a very specific definition, and nutritionists have another. The result of this confusion is that a food calorie is actually worth 1,000 chemistry calories. Thus, please realize that in this discussion, I will always talk in terms of food calories. When you take chemistry later, you will see the difference in the definitions and the confusion that it causes.

Since the calorie is a unit of energy, it can be used to measure both the amount of macronutrients in food as well as the amount of energy our bodies need in order to live. I want to talk about both of those things in this section. First, let's talk about the energy that our bodies use. The total energy that our bodies use each day is called our **metabolic** (met uh bah' lik) **rate**. A person's metabolic rate has two factors. The first factor is the amount of energy that a person's body needs every day just to survive. It is called the **basal** (bay' sul) **metabolic rate**, which is often abbreviated as **BMR**.

Basal metabolic rate - The minimum amount of energy required by the body every day

Now please realize that the BMR is not a measure of the total energy used by the body in a day. Notice the definition. The BMR is a measure of the *minimum* energy required by the body every day. A person's BMR varies based on many things including height, weight, general athleticism, age, and gender. Two very similar people can have significantly different BMRs.

The second factor in determining our metabolic rate is the amount of activity we engage in every day. For example, suppose you sleep in on Saturday. Once you get up, you sit quietly and read for a while, and then you spend the rest of the day in quiet conversation with your family. On a day like that, you don't burn up much more energy than that which is determined by your BMR. Suppose that on Sunday, however, you get up early and go to church. After church, you get together with your friends and play some games, rough-house a little, and generally cause a ruckus. All of that activity requires a lot of energy above and beyond what is demanded by your BMR. On Sunday, then, you would use a lot more energy than you did on Saturday. Thus, your total metabolic rate is the sum of your BMR and your activity level on a given day.

Scientists have done a lot of work studying human metabolic rates. Although metabolic rates vary from person to person, there are some general trends that tend to be pretty accurate on average. Table 12.1 lists the average energy requirements for people of different ages and genders.

TABLE 12.1
Average Daily Energy Needs (in calories) Based on Gender and Age

Gender	7-10 yrs	11-14 yrs	15-18 yrs	19-24 yrs	25-50 yrs	51 yrs +
Male	2000 cal	2500 cal	3000 cal	2900 cal	2900 cal	2300 cal
Female	2000 cal	2100 cal	2200 cal	2200 cal	2200 cal	1900 cal

Notice that, in general, girls and women need less energy than boys and men. That's because, in general, a woman's BMR is lower than a man's BMR. Also notice that as children grow, they need more energy. Once they reach maturity (after age 18), however, their energy needs level off and even go down a bit.

Now remember, calories can be used to measure your macronutrient intake as well. For a healthy life, the number of calories worth of macronutrients you eat every day should roughly equal the number of calories you use every day. Thus, the average 13 year-old male should eat roughly 2500 calories worth of macronutrients, because that's what Table 12.1 says the average 13 year-old male uses each day. If you eat significantly fewer calories than you use, you will lose weight. If you eat significantly more calories than you use, you will gain weight.

As you might imagine, however, a healthy life requires more than just eating the proper number of calories every day. Because the three macronutrients are used differently in the body, you need a certain distribution of macronutrients in your food. Many nutritionists in the United States think that about 70% of the calories you eat each day should come from carbohydrates. Roughly 21% should come from fat, and the balance (9%) should come from protein. According to these nutritionists, this mixture of macronutrients is ideal for the human body. However, there is no real consensus among nutritionists. That's because there are still too many things we do not understand about the human body! Now please remember that I am not addressing the micronutrients at all. There are many micronutrients that you need in order to stay healthy as well. Thus, all of the information I am giving you in this module relates only to the macronutrients, not the micronutrients.

ON YOUR OWN

12.9 Consider two roommates in college. They eat essentially the same amount of the same cafeteria food each day. They also participate in essentially the same activities each day. However, one roommate loses weight during the college year while the other gains weight. How is that possible?

Metabolic Rates Throughout Creation

The metabolic rates of organisms vary greatly throughout Creation. In general, ectothermic organisms have lower metabolic rates than endothermic organisms, because ectothermic organisms need not expend energy in order to keep their internal temperature constant. As I mentioned previously, however, that lower metabolic rate comes at a cost. Ectothermic creatures are, in general, slower to react to the outside world than are endothermic creatures.

However, metabolic rates vary dramatically even among similar creatures. For example, consider the organisms in kingdom Protista. In Module #10, I told you about different protozoa in this kingdom. All protozoa are composed of a single cell. Thus, you would think that they are all pretty similar. Nevertheless, their energy needs vary dramatically from creature to creature. For example, the paramecium pictured in Figure 10.3 has significantly higher energy needs than does the euglena pictured right above it.

Perhaps the best example of how metabolic rates vary among similar creatures is to consider the metabolic rates of different mammals. Remember, I already told you that mammals are animals which share similar characteristics. They all have skin which produces hair, they are all endothermic, and they all nurse their young with milk that they produce. Thus, mammals are similar in many ways. Look, however, at the metabolic rates of a few mammals.

FIGURE 12.4

Metabolic Rates in Mammals (Normalized to Body Weight)

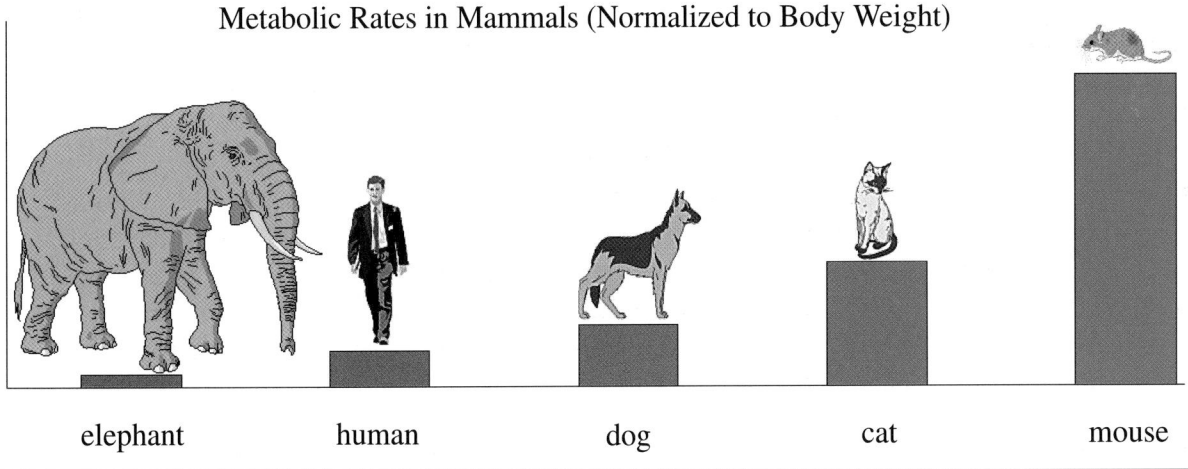

Do you see a trend in the figure? The smaller the mammal, the larger the metabolic rate. That's a general trend among mammals throughout Creation. Why? Well, it turns out that small creatures have a larger percentage of their total body exposed to the outside air. Thus, a mouse has a large portion of its body in contact with the air as compared to an elephant. As a result, a mouse loses more heat than an elephant. Well, since both animals must keep their internal temperatures the same, the mouse must expend more energy for that purpose than the elephant. As a result, the metabolic rate of a mouse is much higher than that of an elephant.

How Combustion Works in Living Organisms

Throughout this module, I have been telling you that we burn our food for energy. I have also been telling you that the combustion which occurs in your body is significantly different than the combustion that occurs in a candle, fireplace, or furnace. In this last section of the module, I want to give you a simplistic view of how combustion occurs in most living organisms.

First, you have to realize that your food is burned in your cells. Remember, the cell is the basic unit of life. Thus, all of your energy needs originate in your cells. Your muscle cells need energy in order to contract and relax your muscles, your living skin cells need energy to react to outside stimuli, etc. Thus, the combustion that takes place in living organisms takes place inside the organism's cell or cells.

In order to simplify things somewhat, I am going to concentrate only on how monosaccharides are burned for energy. Amino acids and fats can be burned for energy, but those processes are even more complicated. As you will see in a moment, the combustion of monosaccharides is hard enough to understand, so I don't want to get any more complex than that. I will also choose the specific monosaccharide called glucose.

The combustion of a monosaccharide takes place in three steps. This is already significantly different than the combustion of wax in a candle or wood in a fireplace. Those kinds of combustion happen very quickly. If the combustion of monosaccharides were to happen that quickly, the cell would instantly burn up! Thus, in order to make the release of energy more gentle, cells break up the combustion process into three steps.

The first step is called **glycolysis** (gli kol' uh sis). In this step, glucose is broken into two parts. This results in a small release of energy and a little bit of hydrogen. The two parts of the glucose and the hydrogen are then sent to a particular organelle in the cell called the **mitochondrion** (my' toh kon' dree uhn). The next two steps happen there.

In the mitochondrion, the second step, called the **Krebs cycle**, occurs. In this step, the two pieces of glucose are broken down into their two main elements: carbon and hydrogen. Oxygen combines with the carbon to make carbon dioxide. That results in a small release of energy as well. The hydrogen from glycolysis and the hydrogen released in the Krebs cycle then go through the third step, called the **electron transport system**.

In the electron transport system, oxygen combines with the hydrogen to make water. This results in a large release of energy. Since the majority of energy release occurs in this step, and since this step takes place in the mitochondrion of the cell, the mitochondrion is often referred to as the "powerhouse" of the cell.

Now don't worry if some of this is too hard to grasp. This is difficult stuff. However, it is important enough to look at again, so I want you to study the following figure.

FIGURE 12.5
A Simplified View of Combustion in Living Organisms

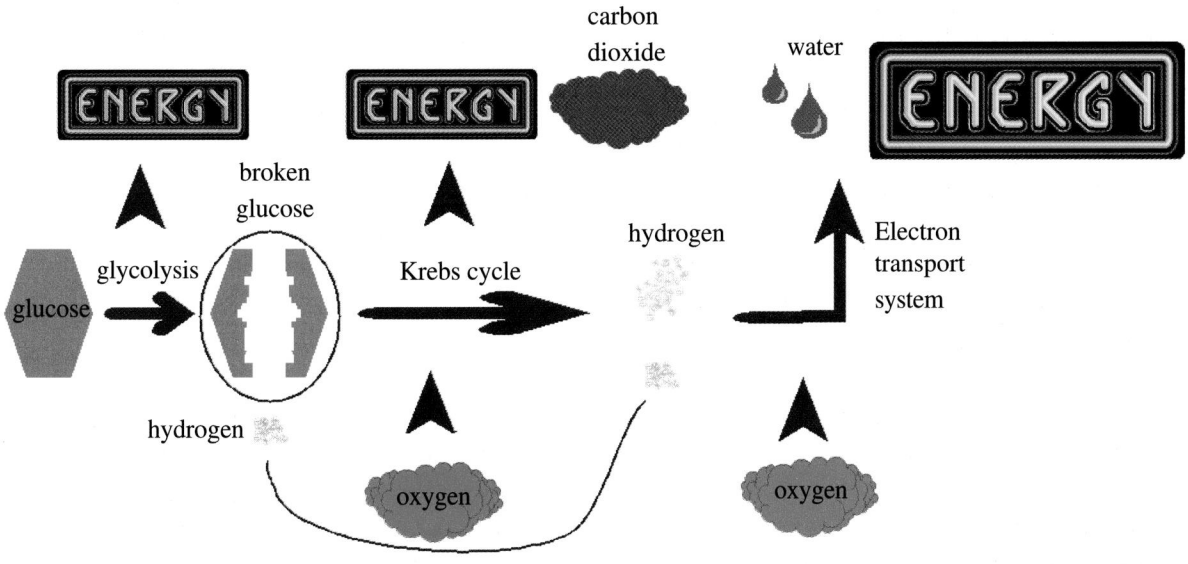

Step1: Glycolysis

Glucose is broken into two parts. This produces two smaller substances, hydrogen, and some energy.

Step2: The Krebs Cycle

Oxygen combines with the carbon in the broken glucose. This produces energy, carbon dioxide, and more hydrogen.

Step3: Electron Transport System

The hydrogen that was produced in steps 1 and 2 combines with oxygen. This produces water and a large amount of energy.

Although this figure is complicated, try to break it down. In the first step, a glucose molecule is broken into two parts. This results in two pieces of a glucose molecule, some hydrogen, and some energy. The hydrogen produced in this step makes its way to step 3. The two pieces of the broken glucose molecule proceed to step 2. In step 2, oxygen is added to the two broken pieces of the glucose. This makes carbon dioxide, more hydrogen, and some energy. Finally, in step 3, oxygen is added to the hydrogen made in both of the previous steps. This produces water and significantly more energy than the other two steps combined.

Notice how I have arranged the figure. The items in the bottom part of the figure are ADDED to the process. Notice what's being added: oxygen. It is added in steps 2 and 3. On the other hand, the items in the top part of the figure are PRODUCED by this process. Notice what's produced: carbon dioxide, water, and energy. Think about it. This process takes oxygen and a fuel (glucose) and makes carbon dioxide, water, and energy. What process is that? It's **combustion**!

So, this very complex process is simply a *gentle* way of burning monosaccharides. Through this process, an organism can produce energy the same way a fire produces energy, but in a much more controlled and gentle way. Now don't worry if this is all a little above your head. I wanted to expose you to it for two reasons. First, when you take biology, you will need to learn this process in more depth. If you are exposed to it now, it will be *easier* to learn the next time. Second, I wanted to give you an idea of how *complicated* this all is.

Think about it for a moment. The process by which living organisms get energy from food is amazingly complicated. Even the "simple" organisms in kingdom Protista burn food this way! Make no mistake about it. I have not even scratched the surface of this incredible process. The details of each step of the process are amazingly hard to understand. They are so hard to understand, in fact, that many scientists *never* learn the process in depth. There are so many chemical processes governing each step that it takes a detailed knowledge of both chemistry and physics to truly understand it.

Are you beginning to see why I told you that there is no such thing as a simple life form? One of the most basic processes which occurs in all living organisms is exceedingly complex. It has to be. Otherwise, living organisms could not get the energy that they need in a way that keeps them from burning up! Nevertheless, if you deny the existence of a divine Creator, you are *forced* to believe that this exceedingly complex system, a system which very few scientists truly understand, has all come about *by chance*! How can anyone possibly believe such a thing? The design inherent in this system alone cries out in witness of a Supreme Designer!

Like I said before, don't be concerned if this is all a little over your head. The main things I want you to pull from this section are as follows:

1. **The process of combustion in living organisms is amazingly complex. It has to be, in order to provide energy in a gentle enough fashion.**

2. **The combustion process occurs within the cell.**

3. **Two of the three steps in the combustion process occur in an organelle called the mitochondrion.**

4. **Since the majority of the combustion process takes place within the mitochondrion, biologists refer to the mitochondrion as the powerhouse of the cell.**

ON YOUR OWN

12.10 If there were no oxygen available to an organism, could the organism produce any energy?

ANSWERS TO THE ON YOUR OWN PROBLEMS

12.1 a. Grass is a producer, because it is a plant and therefore makes its own food.

b. A horse is a consumer, because it eats other organisms (grass, for example).

c. A tree is a plant and is therefore a producer.

d. Yeast is part of kingdom Fungi, so it is a decomposer.

e. A sparrow eats other organisms, so it is a consumer.

f. A shark eats other organisms, so it is a consumer.

12.2 The creature is an omnivore. However, if you removed bugs from the list, the creature would be an herbivore.

12.3 Much like what you observed in experiment 12.1, the carbon dioxide rushes out and pushes all oxygen away from the fire. Without oxygen, the fire can no longer burn.

12.4 We know that plants use carbon dioxide, water, and energy from the sun to make their own food (glucose). Well, when we talk to plants, our exhaled breath tends to hit the plants. The carbon dioxide from our exhaled breath increases the amount of food that the plant can make, and that makes the plant more healthy.

12.5 There is an easy way to test the hypothesis in question 12.4. Make three groups of plants. The first you take care of without talking to them at all. To the second, you play a tape of someone talking, but you do not actually talk to them. To the third, you do not talk to them, but you breathe on them for the same amount of time that you play the tape to the second group. If the theory is right, the first and second group will look nearly the same, but the third group will be healthier.

12.6 Remember, excess carbohydrates and proteins can be converted to fat. The fat came from excess carbohydrates and/or proteins.

12.7 The extra proteins she is now eating will be broken down into their amino acids, and the amino acids will be sent to the cells so that the cells can make their own proteins.

12.8 Most likely, the animal is endothermic. If the animal were ectothermic, cold temperatures would slow it down, because the animal's internal temperature would be low.

12.9 Their BMRs are different. Although they basically do the same activities, their BMRs are determined by many other factors (age, gender, overall athleticism, etc.). Thus, the energy they need *above their BMRs* is essentially the same. However, since their BMRs are different, the TOTAL amount of energy they need daily is different.

12.10 Yes, the organism could still produce *some* energy. Look at the figure. Oxygen is not added until step 2 (the Krebs cycle). Thus, step 1 does not need oxygen. Since there is some energy produced in step 1, then the organism could produce that energy, regardless of whether or not oxygen is present. The problem, however, is that for the vast majority of organisms, the energy produced in step 1 is not enough. Thus, the organism would still die.

STUDY GUIDE FOR MODULE #12

1. Define the following terms:

a. Producers
b. Consumers
c. Herbivore
d. Carnivore
e. Omnivore
f. Basal metabolic rate

2. From where does the energy in living organisms ultimately originate?

3. Label each of the following as a consumer, producer, or decomposer:

a. mushroom b. evergreen bush c. worm d. algae

4. What is the name of the chemical process that converts food into energy?

5. What does combustion require?

6. What does combustion produce?

7. What are the three macronutrients?

8. What is the main thing that macronutrients provide?

9. Do we need to eat more macronutrients or micronutrients?

10. Which is larger: a monosaccharide, a disaccharide, or a polysaccharide?

11. Is glucose a monosaccharide, a disaccharide, or a polysaccharide?

12. What are the two basic kinds of fat? How can you distinguish them?

13. What are proteins made of?

14. In what order does the body prefer to burn the macronutrients?

15. When proteins are eaten, they are broken down into their amino acids. If your cells are short on amino acids, what happens to the amino acids that come from the proteins you eat? What happens if your cells have plenty of amino acids?

16. Why is it important to eat either animal protein or a wide variety of plant protein?

17. Which type of animal has a higher BMR: an endothermic animal or an ectothermic animal?

18. Which type of animal is less active on a cold day: an endothermic animal or an ectothermic animal?

19. What do calories measure?

20. Consider two men. While they sleep, they burn about the same number of calories. However, the first man needs significantly more calories than the second in order to keep his weight constant. Which man is less active during the day?

21. If Jean needs to eat more calories than Wanda in order to keep her weight constant, can you immediately conclude that Jean is more active than Wanda?

22. Which has a higher BMR: a horse or a pig?

23. Where does the combustion of food take place?

24. Why is the mitochondrion called the "powerhouse" of the cell?

Module #13: The Human Digestive System

Introduction

In the previous module, I spent a lot of time discussing the energy that we get from food. I discussed the process of combustion, the three macronutrients, and how combustion occurs in living organisms. However, I really didn't tell you *how* the food that you eat gets broken down into the three macronutrients that you end up burning for energy. That's what I want to cover in this module. Along the way, you will also learn a little bit more about the micronutrients. In the previous module, I sort of glossed over them. In this module, I want you to learn a little more about them as well.

The Process of Digestion

When you eat your food, your body must break it down in order to get the macronutrients contained within. That process is called **digestion**.

Digestion - The process by which an organism breaks down its food into small units which can be absorbed

The process of digestion starts, of course, with **ingestion**. When you eat food (or drink liquids) you are ingesting the food or liquid. The process of digestion then starts right away. To get an idea of what the process of digestion entails, perform the following experiment.

EXPERIMENT 13.1
Seeing a Part of the Digestive Process

Supplies:

- A saltine cracker
- A tablespoon
- Iodine (This is available at any drug store. You used it in Experiment 9.2.)
- Two small glasses

Introduction - The process of digestion involves two different kinds of action. In this experiment, you will see both of them.

Procedure:

A. Take a saltine cracker and break it in half. Crumble half of the cracker and allow the crumbs to fall into one of the two glasses.
B. Add two tablespoons of water to the cracker crumbs and swirl the glass to mix the cracker crumbs with the water.

C. Take the other half of the cracker and chew it up really well. **DO NOT SWALLOW**. Just chew the cracker well.
D. Now spit the stuff in your mouth out into the other glass. Okay, it's gross, but science is gross sometimes. Deal with it!
E. Add two tablespoons of water to the chewed-up mess and swirl the glass.
F. Note any differences you see in the two glasses.
G. Add equal amounts of iodine to both glasses. It doesn't need to be a lot - just a drop or two.
H. Swirl each glass.
I. Note any difference you see in the two glasses.
J. Clean everything up.

What did you see in the experiment? Well, the first thing that you noticed was that the cracker you chewed should have been reduced to much smaller pieces than the cracker that you crumbled. In fact, that's the first part of digestion: breaking up food into small pieces. We call that **physical digestion**, because it does not change the chemical nature of the food. It simply breaks food into tiny pieces.

The second thing that you should have noticed is how differently the two "cracker solutions" acted in response to iodine. The unchewed half of the cracker should have produced a dark blue color. Depending on how well you chewed the other half of the cracker, it should have produced a much lighter blue. If you chewed the cracker really well, you might have seen no blue color at all in that glass.

What do the results of this experiment show us? When iodine mixes with starch, it produces a deep blue color. The deep blue color you saw when you put the iodine in the glass with the unchewed cracker, then, tells you that saltine crackers have starch in them. Remember what starch is. It is a polysaccharide. When you put the iodine with the chewed cracker, the much lighter blue or absence of blue tells you that there was less starch in the chewed up cracker.

Where did the starch go? Well, the **saliva** (some people call it "spit") that your mouth produces contains chemicals which break starch down. Remember, our bodies must break polysaccharides (like starch) down into monosaccharides before they can be used. The saliva in your mouth starts this process by breaking starch down into disaccharides. This is the second component of digestion: **chemical digestion**. It is not enough to just break the food down into tiny pieces. Your body must also change the chemical nature of the food in order to extract what it can use.

Digestion, then, has two different components. Some parts of the process of digestion are aimed simply at breaking down the food you eat into smaller pieces. Other parts of the digestive process are designed to take those pieces of food and chemically alter them so that the body can extract those chemicals which it can use. The unusable parts of the food then get ejected.

ON YOUR OWN

13.1 In which part of the digestive process are your teeth a major participant: physical digestion or chemical digestion?

The Human Digestive System

As you might imagine, the human digestive system is large and complex. It is illustrated in the figure below.

Illus. from the Future Graph collection

FIGURE 13.1
The Human Digestive System

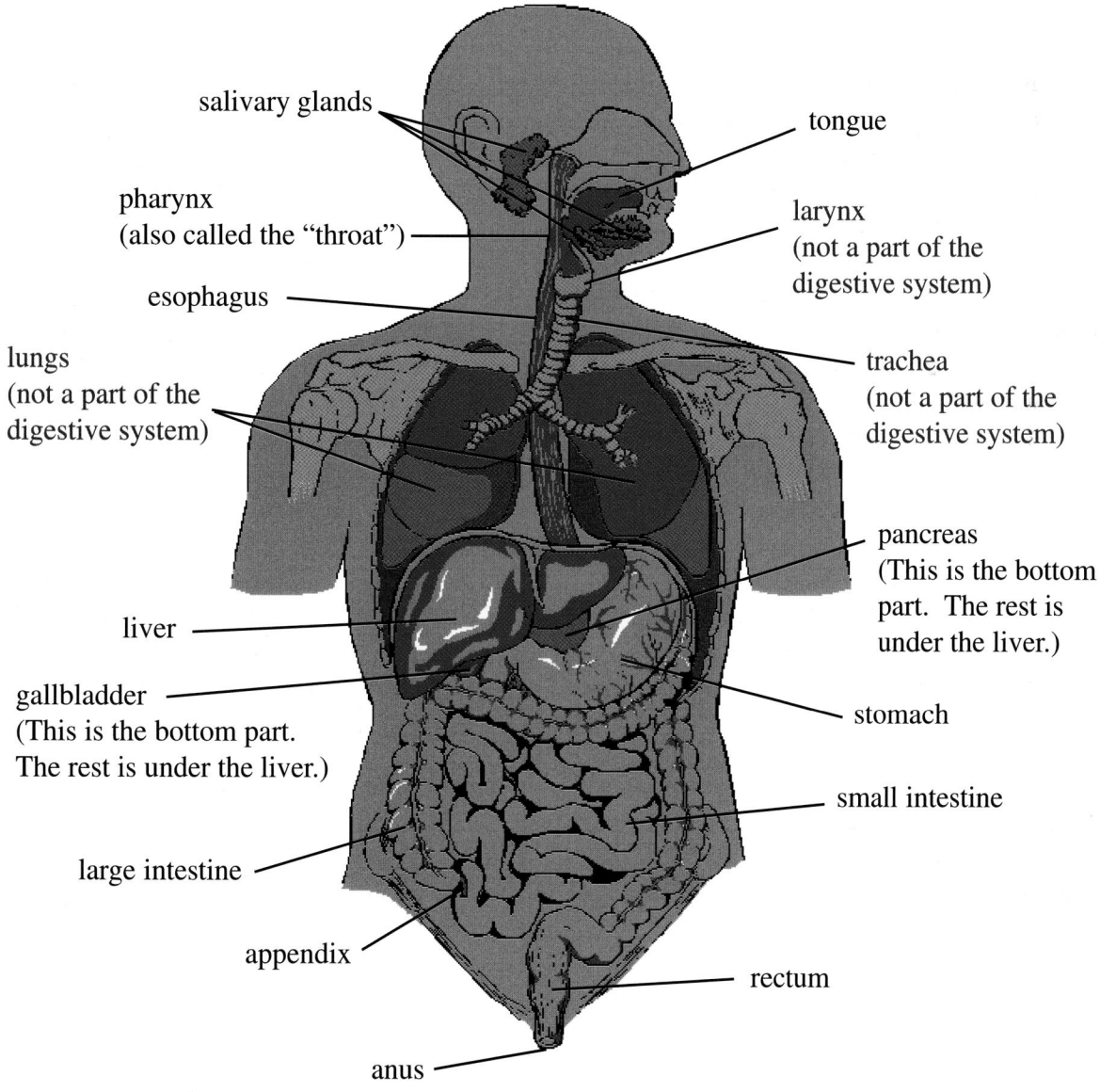

I want to discuss many of the parts of the digestive system in greater detail, but for now, I want to give you an overview of what each structure pointed out in the figure does in terms of digestion. Note that the lungs, larynx (lare' inks) and trachea (tray' key uh) are in the figure for reference but are not a part of the digestive system.

Food enters our bodies through the **mouth**. It is cut, crushed, and ground into little pieces by the **teeth**. It is also moistened by saliva. The **tongue** moves food around in the mouth. It also provides most of the taste sensation that we get when we eat. The food is then passed from the mouth to the **pharynx** (fare' inks), where it is then passed into the **esophagus** (ee sof' uh gus). Notice in the figure that the pharynx actually has a fork in it. One path leads to the esophagus and the other leads to the larynx. When I talk about the mouth, pharynx, and esophagus individually, I will talk about the incredible process that occurs to make sure that food goes down the fork which leads to the esophagus, while air goes down the fork that leads to the larynx.

Once in the esophagus, the food is sent to the **stomach**. In the stomach, the food is churned and mixed with juices which are made by the stomach lining. The stomach temporarily stores the food that has been thoroughly mixed and sends it into the **small intestine** (in test' in). In the small intestine, the food is broken down chemically, and most of the micronutrients and macronutrients are absorbed by the bloodstream through the lining of the small intestine. The nutrient-filled blood then passes through the **liver**, which picks up many of those nutrients. That's not the only thing the liver does, however. It is one of the largest organs in the human body. It also cleans the blood of poisons and wastes, and it produces a substance called **bile**, which is necessary for the digestion of fats. In addition, it makes certain proteins that the body needs from the amino acids absorbed in digestion, and it stores many of the micronutrients and macronutrients that it picks up from the blood.

The bile from the liver is concentrated (to make it stronger) and stored in the **gall bladder**. The gall bladder then injects this concentrated bile into the small intestine, where it aids in the digestion of fats coming from the stomach. The **pancreas** (pan' kree us) produces other digestive juices, which are also injected into the small intestine to aid in the digestion of the macronutrients.

Once the food is digested, it is sent to the **large intestine**. By the time food reaches the large intestine, most of the micronutrients and macronutrients have been removed. At this point, then, the food must be ejected from the body. Water is absorbed from the waste, and the waste is turned into **feces** (fee' sees), which are then sent to the **rectum** and expelled from the body through the **anus**.

That's the basic outline of what happens in order for your body to digest the food you eat. How long does all of this take? Well, it depends on the individual as well as the kind and amount of food that is ingested. However, on average, it takes less than 1 minute for food to get chewed in the mouth and transferred to the esophagus. It is in the esophagus for only a couple of seconds, and ends up in the stomach. Typically, a meal remains in the stomach for 2 to 4 hours before being sent to the small intestine. The small intestine usually takes 1 to 4 hours to digest the food, and then the food gets sent to the large intestine. The amount of time the waste products stay in the large intestine varies *greatly* depending on the person involved or the food that was eaten. The shortest time the waste products from food spend in the large intestine is about 10 hours, but some waste products take *several days* to make it through the large intestine. In the end, then, the food that you eat can spend as little as 13 hours in your body or as long as several days. Remember, however, that all of the micronutrients and macronutrients have been absorbed by the time the food leaves the small intestine. Thus, your body gets the nutrients from the food you eat within 3 to 8 hours.

Notice that within this entire discussion, I have not mentioned the **appendix**. This little worm-shaped tube branches off of the large intestine at its opening. Scientists are not sure what the purpose of the appendix is. The cells within the appendix are the same kinds of cells we find in the infection-fighting systems of the human body, so there are some biologists who think that the appendix is an infection-fighting organ which specifically fights off infections of the large and/or small intestine. Only apes and humans have an appendix, so it is obviously a very specialized organ.

For reasons that we do not understand, the appendix can become infected and filled with pus. This results in pain and cramps near the right hip bone. This pain is usually accompanied by fever, nausea, and vomiting. If the appendix is not removed at that point, it will eventually burst, and the infection can be spread throughout the stomach area. If untreated, this can actually lead to death. As a result, infected appendixes are usually removed with a surgical procedure called an "appendectomy."

There are many scientists who believe that the appendix actually serves no purpose whatsoever in the human body. They call the appendix a **vestigial** (ves tid' gee uhl) **organ**, which means it is a useless remnant of the process of evolution. In other words, these scientists think that at one time, the appendix did serve some useful purpose. According to these scientists, apes probably needed their appendix at one time. However, as they changed through the process of evolution, some other organ (or process) took over the appendix's job. However, the appendix continued to form in apes, but there was no longer anything for it to do. Since these same scientists think that humans evolved from apes, they think that humans inherited the ape's useless appendix.

There is a very good reason to believe that these scientists are dead wrong in their assessment of the appendix: *history*. At one time, evolutionists listed 180 organs in the human body as vestigial organs. These supposed vestigial organs included such things as the thyroid gland, the thymus, the pineal gland, and the tonsils. All 180 organs were thought to be vestigial because science had supposedly demonstrated that they served no useful purpose. We now know that all of those organs (except perhaps the appendix) are useful, important, and sometimes *vital* organs. You see, the human body is so complex and well-designed that there are still aspects of it which are a *complete mystery* to modern science. Thus, just because we do not know the function of the appendix does not mean that is has no function. Just as science has learned important functions for 179 of the supposed vestigial organs in the human body, it will eventually learn the function of the appendix!

ON YOUR OWN

13.2 Name the parts of the digestive system through which food never really passes.

13.3 Blood vessels run all around the organs of the body, supplying nutrients and oxygen to the cells of the organs as well as picking up the cells' waste products. One organ of the digestive system, however, has blood vessels that *pick up nutrients* in order to distribute them throughout the body. Which organ has these blood vessels?

The Mouth, Pharynx, and Esophagus

Now that you have seen the digestive system as a whole, I want to break it down into several parts so that you can learn more of the details of how it works. I'll start, therefore, with a more detailed view of the mouth, pharynx, and esophagus.

Illus. from the Future Graph collection

FIGURE 13.2
The Mouth, Pharynx, and Esophagus

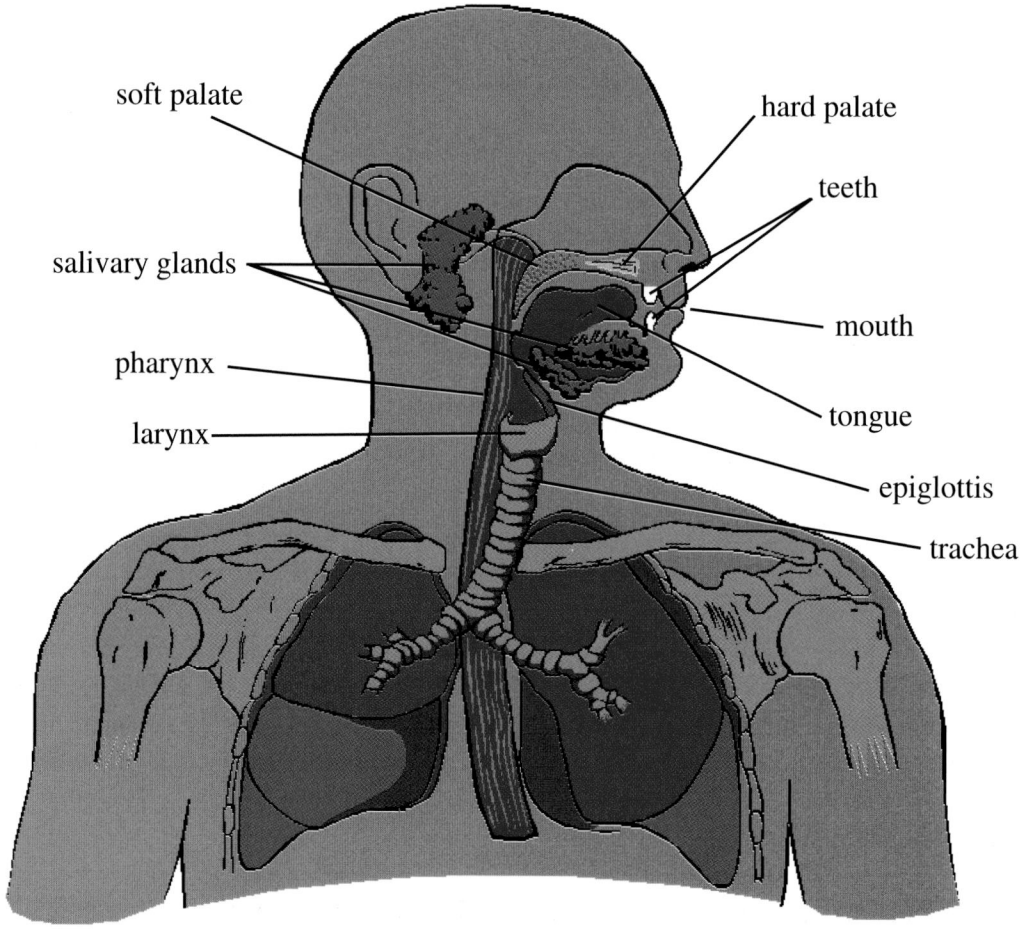

As you learned in Experiment 13.1, the digestion of food starts in the mouth. The teeth cut, grind, and crush the food into small bits. It is important to realize that your mouth has specific kinds of teeth, each designed for a different purpose. Figure 13.3 illustrates this fact.

Illus. from the Future Graph collection

FIGURE 13.3
The Basic Kinds of Teeth in the Adult Human Mouth
(This is a drawing of the lower jaw.)

The teeth on this side of the mouth (and in the upper jaw as well) are arranged in the same way as pointed out on the other side of the figure.

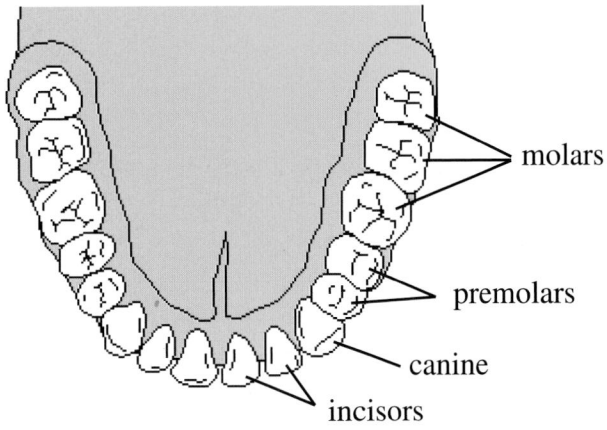

The teeth are made of hard, bone-like material and are surrounded by soft, shock-absorbent gums. The **incisor** (in size' or) teeth are sharp and are used to cut food. The **canine** (kay' nine) teeth are used to tear food, while the **premolars** and **molars** are used to crush and grind food.

Once the food is cut, torn, and ground into small bits, those bits are mixed with saliva that comes from the salivary glands. Saliva contains a digestive juice that begins to chemically digest the food. As you learned in the experiment, one thing that saliva helps to do is break down starch. It also lubricates the mouth, making chewing and swallowing easier, and it aids in physical digestion by moistening the food.

How do your salivary glands put saliva into your mouth? Well, there are several ducts that run from the salivary glands to your mouth cavity, both underneath and above your tongue. The saliva that has been produced in the salivary glands travels through those ducts and into your mouth. It is important to realize that the salivary glands do not put saliva into your mouth all of the time. Instead, they do it mostly when you are eating. How do the salivary glands know that you are eating? Well, the senses of taste and smell (you will learn about these senses later in the course) and the feeling of hunger send signals to the salivary glands, telling them to "turn on." That causes the salivary glands to release saliva into your mouth. You can actually see how this works the next time you are really hungry. Before you start eating, smell your food by inhaling deeply through your nose. What happens? Your mouth begins to fill with saliva, even though you haven't put food in your mouth!

A Russian physiologist (a scientist who studies how the systems of the body work) by the name of Ivan Pavlov demonstrated that a body can be **conditioned** to produce saliva using senses other than taste and smell. In 1889, he did experiments in which he rang a bell every time that he fed a dog. Eventually, the dog's salivary glands would produce saliva whenever the bell was rung, regardless of whether or not there was food for the dog to eat. Pavlov called this a **conditioned response**, because the dog had become conditioned to expect food whenever the bell was rung. As a result, its body responded by salivating.

Once the teeth have cut, crushed, and ground the food, and once the food has been mixed with your saliva, the tongue moves the food around so that it forms a soft lump called a **bolus** (bowl' us). The tongue then rises to move the bolus to the back of the mouth, and the **soft palate** rises, sealing off the nose. If you laugh while you are drinking, you may break that seal, and the liquid will squirt out your nose! Assuming that doesn't happen, the bolus then moves out of the mouth and into the pharynx.

The muscles in the pharynx contract, squeezing the food so that it moves into the esophagus. Now although that *sounds* pretty simple, it is actually a rather complex procedure involving the coordination of several muscles at once. You see, the pharynx is a passageway for two things: air and food. When you inhale, air passes through the pharynx to the larynx and then into the lungs. However, when you eat, the bolus moves through the pharynx and then into the esophagus. How does your body know that air goes down one "pipe" and food goes down the other?

Well, the act of swallowing causes the muscles at the base of the larynx to contract, causing the larynx to rise up. If you put your hand on your larynx as you swallow, you can feel it rise. This motion causes a small flap of cartilage called the **epiglottis** to cover the larynx. When the food passes into the pharynx, then, there is only one opening: the esophagus. Thus, the bolus goes into the esophagus, because the larynx is covered by the epiglottis. When you inhale, the muscles at the base of the larynx relax. This causes the epiglottis to uncover the larynx, and air can pass down through the larynx, into the trachea, and on into the lungs.

Although this is an incredibly well-coordinated system, every once in a while something goes wrong, and the trachea can be uncovered when food gets into the pharynx. When this happens, part or all of the bolus can fall into the larynx instead of the esophagus. However, God has designed a backup mechanism for this system. The linings of the larynx and trachea are *very* sensitive. If anything other than air passes down the larynx, a signal is sent to the brain and muscles cause you to cough. This pushes any food that is in the larynx back into the pharynx. If you have ever eaten and then started coughing uncontrollably, someone probably asked you if the food "went down the wrong pipe." In fact, that's most likely what happened! Food probably got into your larynx, and your body's cough mechanism kicked in, making you expel the food.

Once the bolus is in the esophagus, the muscles of the esophagus contract above the bolus and relax below it. As you might expect, this is a well-coordinated system in which several groups of muscles contract and relax in perfect time relative to one another, making a "wave" of muscle activity which pushes the bolus down the esophagus and into the stomach.

ON YOUR OWN

13.4 Although many animals have teeth, they don't necessarily have all of the teeth that humans have. For example, there are certain animals which do not have canine teeth. Would you expect carnivores, herbivores, or omnivores to lack canine teeth?

13.5 Why do you cough when you inhale smoke?

The Stomach and Intestines

Once the bolus of food gets to the end of the esophagus, it is deposited in the stomach. The rest of the digestive process takes place either there or in the intestines.

Illus. from the Future Graph collection

FIGURE 13.4
The Stomach and Intestines

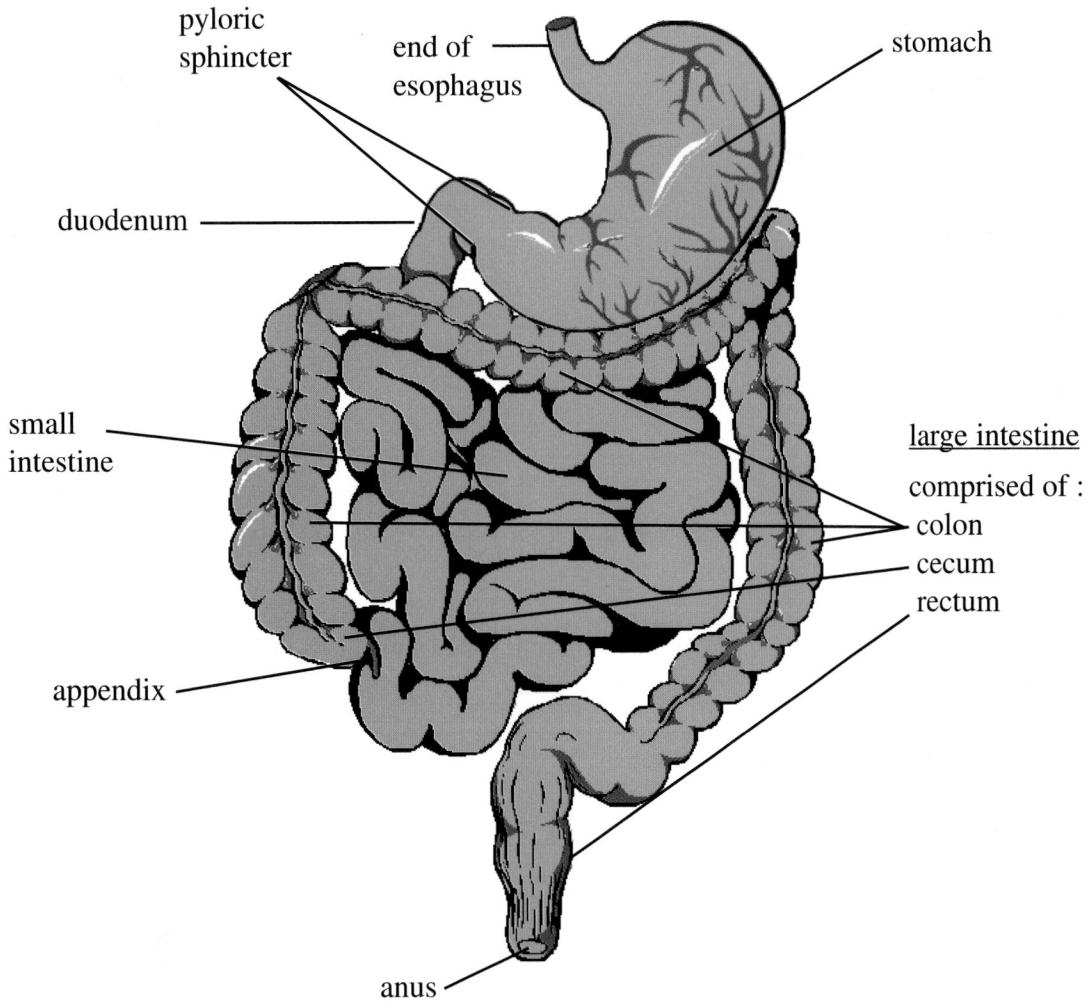

When the bolus lands in the stomach, it is mixed with a liquid called **gastric juice**. Gastric juice is actually a mixture of many different liquids. The most important of those liquids is **hydrochloric** (hi' droh klor' ick) **acid**. This chemical is a powerful acid whose main function is to activate digestive chemicals that are in the gastric juice. It also kills any pathogenic microscopic organisms that might have been eaten along with the food. In addition, hydrochloric acid helps dissolve the food so that it is easier to digest. The hydrochloric acid found in the stomach is often called "stomach acid."

If you have ever eaten too much food, you might have felt your stomach acid in the form of heartburn. Heartburn is a burning sensation that you feel in the middle or upper part of your chest. It is called heartburn because you feel a burning sensation in the general vicinity of your heart. Although it is called heartburn, it has nothing to do with the heart. Instead, it is the result of excess stomach acid leaking up and out of the stomach into the esophagus, irritating the lining of the esophagus. When you feel heartburn, you are told to take an antacid. Why? Perform the following experiment to find out.

EXPERIMENT 13.2

Stomach Acid and Antacids

Supplies:

- TUMS antacid tablets (Try to get white ones, or at least a tub of TUMS that have some white ones in it.)
- Toilet bowl cleaner (It should contain hydrochloric acid, also called hydrogen chloride, as an ingredient. The best kind to get is colorless. If you cannot get colorless, get a clear kind that has a light tint of color to it. DO NOT get the kind that clings to the bowl. I used non-clinging THE WORKS® when I ran the experiment.)
- Red (sometimes called purple) cabbage
- A small glass (like a juice glass)
- A teaspoon
- A separate spoon for stirring
- A saucepan
- A measuring cup
- Distilled water (You can get it at any large supermarket. You need about a quart.)
- A stove for boiling water

Introduction - In this experiment, you will get a good idea of the properties of stomach acid as well as the function of antacids.

Procedure:

A. You need to make the same indicator solution that you made in Experiment 12.2. Start by rinsing the saucepan, measuring cup, stirring spoon, and small glass with distilled water.
B. Place several leaves of red cabbage into the saucepan and add 2 cups of distilled water.
C. Heat the saucepan until the water boils and then allow it to boil for a few minutes.

D. Turn off the heat and allow the pan and its contents to cool for a while.
E. Add one teaspoon of toilet bowl cleaner to the small glass. **BE CAREFUL WHILE HANDLING THE TOILET BOWL CLEANER**. If you get it on your hands, immediately rinse them with LOTS of water. The toilet bowl cleaner will burn skin.
F. Once the saucepan and its contents have cooled somewhat, fill the measuring cup with the cabbage water. **BE CAREFUL - IT COULD STILL BE VERY HOT**. If you get a few cabbage leaves in the measuring cup, use the stirring spoon to remove them.
G. Pour the cup of cabbage water into the small glass. Use the spoon to stir the contents, so that the teaspoon of toilet bowl cleaner mixes with the cabbage water. The color of the contents should be pink or red. If not, the color of your toilet bowl cleaner is too strong and you need to try a different kind of toilet bowl cleaner.
H. Add an antacid tablet to the small glass. Try to use a white one.
I. Note what happens when the tablet hits the cabbage water/toilet bowl cleaner mixture.
J. After you have watched the tablet for a few moments, start stirring it. You want the tablet to completely disappear. This will take a little while. You can speed the process up by using the spoon to cut up and crush the tablet.
K. Note the color change that begins to occur.
L. Once the tablet is gone, note the color. If you do not see purple or blue, add another tablet and continue to stir. Your goal is to get the solution to be purple or blue.
M. Once you get to the purple or blue color, add another teaspoon of toilet bowl cleaner. What happens?
N. Clean everything up.

What did you see in the experiment? Well, if everything went well, the antacid tablet or tablets should have turned the toilet bowl cleaner/cabbage water solution from red/pink to blue/purple. The addition of more toilet bowl cleaner should have turned the color back to red/pink. Why did this happen?

If you remember from Experiment 12.2, red cabbage contains a chemical which we call an "indicator," because it indicates the presence of two other types of chemicals: **acids** and **bases**. You will learn a lot more about acids and bases when you take chemistry. For right now, you can think of these two chemicals as opposites of one another. Acids have certain chemical properties that cause them to react in certain ways, and bases have different chemical properties that cause them to react in different ways. The key point to know right now is that acids and bases tend to cancel one another out. If you take an acid and add just the right amount of base to it, the base will cancel out the chemical properties of the acid, and the acid will cancel out the chemical properties of the base. This is called **neutralization**, because acids neutralize the properties of bases, and bases neutralize the properties of acids.

In your experiment, you started with toilet bowl cleaner. The active ingredient of toilet bowl cleaner is usually an acid. In many toilet bowl cleaners, that acid is hydrochloric acid, which is the same acid that your stomach produces. In the experiment, then, the toilet bowl cleaner represented stomach acid. When the chemical in red cabbage is exposed to acids, it turns a red/pink color. When it is exposed to bases, it turns a blue/purple color.

In the experiment, then, you added the cabbage water to the toilet bowl cleaner. Since the toilet bowl cleaner had acid in it, the cabbage water turned red/pink in response to the acid. When you added the TUMS® tablet, however, things should have gotten interesting. The tablet should have started bubbling and fizzing, getting smaller and smaller. This is because the TUMS® tablet (or any traditional antacid tablet) contains a base. In the case of TUMS®, the base is calcium carbonate. Another popular base in antacid tablets is magnesium hydroxide. The base in the tablet was chemically reacting with the acid in the toilet bowl cleaner. This chemical reaction allowed the base to start neutralizing the acid.

As the neutralization took place, you should have noticed the color of the solution begin to change. It got less red and more blue. Eventually, it turned either blue or purple. This indicated that the base had neutralized all of the acid. That's what antacid tablets do in your stomach. They add a base to your stomach which neutralizes some of the acid in your stomach. That gets rid of extra acid, which hopefully then removes the cause of heartburn. In your stomach, there is a *lot* more acid than in the experiment, so even several antacid tablets will not neutralize *all* of the acid in your stomach. However, they will neutralize some of it, so that there is not as much acid that could leak out into the esophagus.

In your experiment, you did one more thing. After you saw the color change to blue/purple, you then added more toilet bowl cleaner. This should have turned the solution red again. Why? Well, think about it. The reason that the solution had turned blue was because all of the acid had been neutralized by the base. When you added more toilet bowl cleaner, however, you added more acid. That extra acid neutralized all of the base in the solution and left it with extra acid. Thus, the solution had acid in it again, and the chemical from the cabbage water turned red/pink again. This will happen over and over again if you keep adding base and then acid.

Okay, then. One thing that the stomach produces is hydrochloric acid. In addition, it produces a few chemicals that begin chemically digesting the bolus of food. Smooth muscles in the stomach relax and contract, churning the bolus with the gastric juice until it is turned into a liquid mush called **chyme** (kime).

Chyme passes to the small intestine in spurts that are controlled by a ring of muscles called the **pyloric** (pie lor' ik) **sphincter** (sfink' ter). There, the chyme is mixed with several more digestive chemicals which come from the **gall bladder** and **pancreas**. One other interesting thing takes place at this point. The chemicals that continue the digestion process in the small intestine cannot work properly in the presence of acid. The chyme, however, is full of hydrochloric acid from the stomach. Thus, as the food passes through the small intestine, it is mixed with a base that comes from the pancreas. This base neutralizes the stomach acid, allowing the digestive chemicals in the small intestine to do their job.

Most of the rest of the digestion takes place in the first part of the small intestine. After that, the digested food continues through the intestine and, along the way, the blood absorbs the digested food so that it can be transported to different places in the body. This absorption process is slow and time-consuming. That's why the small intestine is so long - nearly 20 feet long! Since it is long, it takes the digested food quite a while to pass through it. That way, there is plenty of time for the absorption of nutrients.

In fact, the small intestine is a great testimony to the design ingenuity of our Creator. As I mentioned, the absorption of digested food is a slow and painstaking process. Thus, the digested food must spend a long time in the small intestine to get absorbed. However, that time would have to be *significantly* greater if it weren't for the clever design of the small intestine. Unlike many organs, the inside wall of the small intestine is not smooth. Instead, it is covered with millions of projections called **intestinal villi** (vil eye'), illustrated in the figure below:

Illus. by Megan Whitaker

FIGURE 13.5
Intestinal Villi

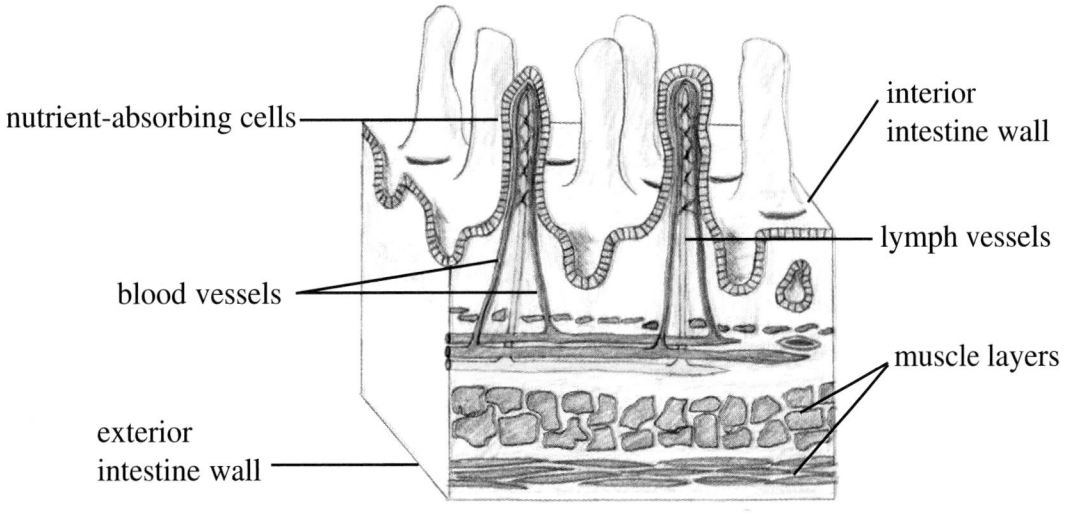

These villi increase the amount of intestine that comes into contact with the food, speeding up the absorption process. If the inside wall of the small intestine were smooth rather than covered with villi, the small intestine would need to be *2 ¼ miles long* in order to allow enough time for the absorption of food!

Altogether, the intestinal villi make the wall of the small intestine look like it is covered with velvet. Each one looks like a tiny finger which waves around the interior of the small intestine. This mixes the chyme and allows the villi to come into contact with it. Each one of these villi is covered with a layer of cells that specialize in absorbing nutrients. As nutrients are absorbed by these cells, they pass to the blood vessels or lymph vessels that eventually send the nutrients throughout the body. Don't worry about what "lymph vessels" are. You will learn about them in a later module.

The small intestine, because of its amazing design, can absorb almost all of the useful nutrients from food by the time the food has traveled the entire length of the small intestine. Thus, when the chyme passes from the small intestine into the large intestine, it is mostly composed of indigestible material that the body considers waste. The large intestine's job, then, is to treat this waste so that it can be expelled from the body.

The large intestine is actually composed of three parts: the **cecum** (see' cum), the **colon** (kole' un), and the **rectum**. It is called the "large" intestine because its diameter is larger than the diameter of the small intestine. It is actually about ¼ the length of the small intestine, or roughly 5 feet.

The cecum is at the beginning of the large intestine. Smooth muscles in the cecum push chyme into the colon. The main function of the colon is to absorb water that is in the chyme. This consolidates the waste in the large intestine and provides water for your body. Other things happen in the colon, however.

For example, there are many bacteria which live in your large intestine. These bacteria feed on the chyme which travels through the large intestine. Since they digest some of the chyme for their own life processes, the chyme is further reduced, consolidating the waste even further. Not only that, but some of the by-products of the bacteria feeding on the chyme are useful to our bodies. One particular vitamin, vitamin K, is produced by bacteria which live in both the large intestine and the small intestine. You will learn a little more about vitamin K in the final section of this module. Other chemicals called biotin and folic acid are also the by-products of bacteria feeding off of the chyme in the large intestine.

These chemicals (vitamin K, biotin, and folic acid) are absorbed in the large intestine and distributed throughout the body. Without the bacteria living in your large intestine, your body would not have enough of these chemicals and your health would suffer. The bacteria living in your large intestine (and small intestine) are yet another example of the Creator's forethought in His design. Just like the bacteria on your skin, the bacteria in your intestines help to keep you healthy. In exchange, your body provides food for them. As you learned in Module #11, this is called "symbiosis." The total number of bacteria in your intestines is *over 100 trillion (100,000,000,000,000)!* Together, they weigh about 3 pounds!

Although your body *benefits* from having bacteria in your large and small intestines, those same bacteria would be pathogenic in other parts of your body. In healthy individuals, then, the bacteria are confined to your intestines. However, if the walls of the intestines are torn or begin to leak, those bacteria that were being helpful can invade other parts of your body and cause serious damage!

The last part of the large intestine is the rectum. Any waste products that make it to this point are called **feces** (fee' sees) and must be expelled from the body. The feces are pushed into the rectum via the contraction and relaxation of muscles in the colon. Once feces have entered the rectum, they pass out of the body through the anus. About one third of a person's feces are composed of bacteria that were originally in the large intestine. Most of the bacteria are dead by the time that they leave the body.

Although I have not gone over every part of the digestive system yet, the parts that I have covered (mouth, teeth, esophagus, stomach, small intestine, and large intestine) are collectively called the **digestive tract**. Any internal structure through which food actually passes is part of the digestive tract. Although other organs such as the liver and pancreas are a part of the digestive system, they are not a part of the digestive tract, because food does not pass through them.

ON YOUR OWN

13.6 Where in the digestive tract does most of the absorption of nutrients occur?

13.7 Although there are bacteria in the small intestine and the large intestine, there are essentially none in your stomach. Why?

The Liver, Pancreas, and Gall Bladder

Although not a part of the digestive tract, the liver, pancreas, and gall bladder are nevertheless essential to the human digestive system. They are illustrated in the following figure. On the left-hand side of the figure, you see them along with the stomach and liver. However, in that arrangement, the gall bladder and pancreas are almost completely hidden. Thus, the right side of the figure shows you the view with the stomach, liver, and large intestine removed.

Illus. from the Future Graph collection

FIGURE 13.6

The Liver, Pancreas, and Gall Bladder (Two Views)

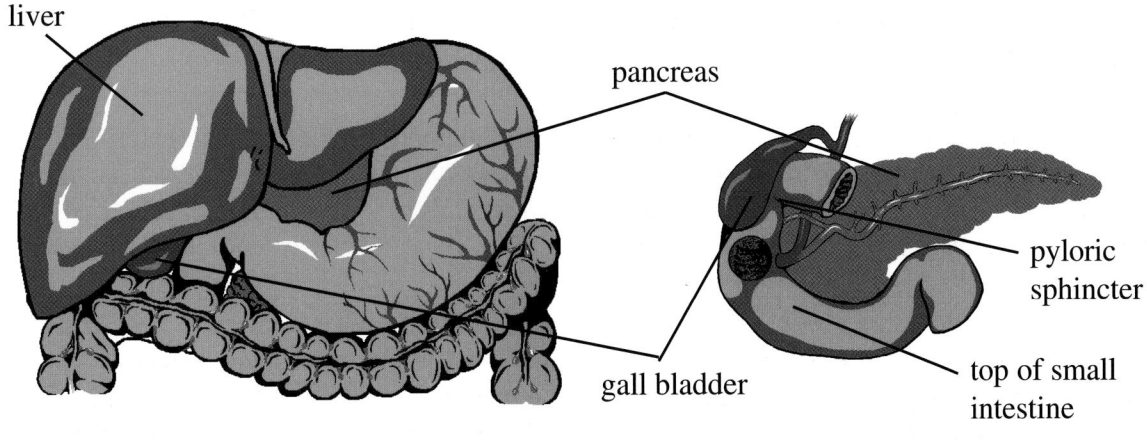

View as it looks from the front

View from the front with the liver, stomach, and large intestine removed

The liver is, by far, the most complicated organ in the digestive system. It has an enormous number of jobs, yet it is able to perform them all with incredible efficiency. Its most direct role in terms of digestion comes from the fact that it makes bile. Bile is a mixture of chemicals that prepares fats for digestion. The bile made by the liver is sent to the gall bladder. The gall bladder's job is twofold. First, it removes about 90% of the water from the bile. Chemists say this makes the bile "concentrated," which increases its strength. Then, while chyme enters the small intestine, the gall bladder contracts, shooting bile into the chyme. The bile then prepares the fats in the chyme so that other chemicals can digest them.

The liver performs many more functions than just making bile! For example, the blood vessels that carry nutrients from the small intestine to the rest of the body pass through the liver. If the body is not in need of a large amount of energy, the liver takes the monosaccharides coming from the intestines and converts them into the polysaccharide known as **glycogen**. It then stores the glycogen until the body needs energy. When energy is needed, the liver breaks down the glycogen and sends it to where it is needed. The liver can also store fats and amino acids. When energy is needed and no glycogen is readily available, the liver can chemically transform the fats and amino acids into glucose.

Not only does the liver store and transform macronutrients, it can also produce other chemicals that the body needs. The principal components of cell membranes, for example, are produced in the liver. Thus, the liver is much like a chemical plant/chemical warehouse. It takes raw materials coming from the small intestine and then, based on conditions in the blood, it decides what to do with those chemicals.

When the liver receives monosaccharides other than glucose, it changes them into glucose. If the blood supply already has plenty of glucose in it, the liver will convert it to glycogen and store the glycogen. If the blood supply runs low on glucose, the liver will convert the stored glycogen into glucose to bring the blood supply to the proper level of glucose. If the liver receives amino acids, it might use those amino acids to make proteins. It also might convert the amino acids to glucose in order to be used for energy. If the liver receives fats, it might store those fats or convert them to glucose, depending on what the blood supply needs.

The liver is also something of a detoxification center. There are certain chemicals that we get from our food which can be dangerous. In addition, there are chemicals that we inhale from the air (like pollutants) which are poisonous. Either way, there are dangerous chemicals that make their way into the bloodstream. The liver takes those chemicals and either recycles them for use in making bile, or it transforms them into urea, which the body can then get rid of in urine.

If that's not enough, there is at least one more task that the liver performs. It warms up the blood. Remember, humans are endothermic. That means our internal temperature is held relatively constant. One of the reasons our body temperature stays constant is the function of the liver. Blood that passes through the liver is warmed so that its temperature stays the same.

All of this should give you a good idea of why the liver is so large. It has many, many functions that are absolutely essential to the body. A typical liver is 9 inches wide, 7 inches tall, and 5 inches thick. A healthy adult liver weighs about 3 pounds. An enormous amount of blood (about 1 ½ quarts *each minute*) passes through the liver.

The pancreas is the only organ in the digestive system which I have not yet covered. A typical adult pancreas is roughly 5 inches long. It is widest at the small intestine and tapers down significantly along its length. The pancreas has two main functions. It makes several digestive juices which are squirted into the small intestine as chyme passes through the pyloric sphincter. In addition, it also produces a base know as sodium bicarbonate. You know this chemical better as "baking soda." Perform the following experiment to see what the sodium bicarbonate does.

EXPERIMENT 13.3

The Effect of Sodium Bicarbonate on Stomach Acid

Supplies:

- Baking soda
- Toilet bowl cleaner (the kind you used in the previous experiment)
- Red (sometimes called purple) cabbage
- A small glass (like a juice glass)
- A teaspoon
- A separate spoon for stirring
- A saucepan
- A measuring cup
- Distilled water (You can get it at any large supermarket. You need about a quart.)
- A stove for boiling water

Introduction - This experiment will show you what happens when the sodium bicarbonate from your pancreas is mixed with the stomach acid in the chyme that comes from the stomach.

Procedure:

A. You need to make the same indicator solution that you made in Experiment 13.2. Start by rinsing the saucepan, measuring cup, stirring spoon, and small glass with distilled water.
B. Place several leaves of red cabbage into the saucepan and add 2 cups of distilled water.
C. Heat the saucepan until the water boils and then allow it to boil for a few minutes.
D. Turn off the heat and allow the pan and its contents to cool for a while.
E. Add one teaspoon of toilet bowl cleaner to the small glass. **BE CAREFUL WHILE HANDLING THE TOILET BOWL CLEANER**. If you get it on your hands, immediately rinse them with LOTS of water. The toilet bowl cleaner will burn skin.
F. Once the saucepan and its contents have cooled somewhat, fill the measuring cup with the cabbage water. **BE CAREFUL - IT COULD STILL BE VERY HOT**. If you get a few cabbage leaves in the measuring cup, use the stirring spoon to remove them.
G. Pour the cup of cabbage water in the small glass. Use the spoon to stir the contents, so that the teaspoon of toilet bowl cleaner mixes with the cabbage water. The color of the contents should be pink or red. If not, the color of your toilet bowl cleaner is too strong and you need to try a different kind of toilet bowl cleaner.

H. Take the other spoon and scoop some baking soda out of the box. **SLOWLY** add the sodium bicarbonate to the mixture in the glass. Note what happens.
I. Continue to slowly add baking soda to the mixture in the glass until the color of the mixture changes from red/pink to blue/purple.
J. Clean everything up.

What happened in the experiment? Well, when you added baking soda to the mixture, you should have seen a LOT of bubbles. In fact, if you did not add the baking soda slowly enough, the bubbles probably spilled out of the glass. When sodium bicarbonate (baking soda) reacts with acids, it neutralizes the acid. The color of the mixture in the glass changed because, just as was the case in Experiment 13.2, the cabbage water acted as an indicator. Before the acid was neutralized, the indicator was red/pink. After the acid was neutralized, the indicator turned purple/blue. One of the products of the neutralization process is carbon dioxide. That's where the bubbles came from.

Essentially the same thing happens in your small intestine when sodium bicarbonate from your pancreas mixes with chyme coming from the stomach. The chyme has hydrochloric acid in it, just as the toilet bowl cleaner does. When the sodium bicarbonate from the pancreas mixes with the chyme, a reaction occurs which neutralizes the acid and produces carbon dioxide gas.

ON YOUR OWN

13.8 Some people, because of certain problems, must have their gall bladder removed. If this happens to a person, he or she is sometimes put on a special diet. What macronutrient must be reduced in the diet?

13.9 Suppose your pancreas could no longer make sodium bicarbonate. You would no longer be able to digest most of your food. Why?

The Micronutrients

In the previous module, I spent considerable time discussing the macronutrients but barely touched on the micronutrients. I want to finish this module by making up for that a bit. Although we do not need micronutrients in the quantities that we need macronutrients, they are incredibly important to the human body.

Most of the micronutrients that our bodies need are absorbed in the small intestine. They are called **vitamins** and **minerals**. You already know what a mineral is. You learned that in Module 6. You don't yet know what a vitamin is, however.

Vitamin - a chemical substance essential for the normal working of the human body

Vitamins are effective in extremely small amounts and act mainly as regulators of the chemical processes which occur in the body. Vitamins are classified as either fat-soluble or water-soluble. A fat-soluble vitamin cannot be dissolved in water. It can only be dissolved in fat. A water-soluble vitamin cannot be dissolved in fat but can be dissolved in water.

The fat-soluble vitamins are vitamin A, vitamin D, vitamin E, and vitamin K. The water-soluble vitamins are vitamin C, the vitamin B group (B_1, B_2, B_3,B_5, B_6, B_{12}), biotin, folic acid, and pantothenic acid. The body cannot make most of these vitamins, so they must be eaten with our food. There are at least 2 exceptions. Although your body can also absorb it from food, vitamin D is actually manufactured in the body through the skin's exposure to sunlight. In addition, vitamin K is produced by bacteria in the large intestine.

So what do these vitamins do? Well, each kind of vitamin has its own unique support role in the human body. Vitamin A, for example, is a component of the process that allows your eyes to detect light. Without sufficient vitamin A, you would not see properly. It also maintains the cells that protect your body, such as skin cells. Vitamin D allows calcium that you eat and drink to be absorbed for your bones. Vitamin E is an "antioxidant," which means it helps protect certain important chemicals in your body from being destroyed through the chemical process called "oxidation." The B vitamins help your body's metabolism in different ways, as do biotin and folic acid. Vitamin C helps build collagen in bones and teeth, and there is a lot of evidence that it supports the processes which help us fight disease.

The last vitamin I want to discuss is vitamin K. When you cut yourself, you bleed. What keeps all of your blood from leaking out of your body through the cut? Well, the answer is that your blood **clots** so that it cannot leak out of the cut anymore. Vitamin K is an important part of that blood clotting process. If you didn't have enough vitamin K in your blood, you could easily bleed to death from even a small cut. Now it turns out that there are *several* chemicals involved in the blood clotting process, so don't get the idea that it is all the result of vitamin K. Nevertheless, vitamin K is a necessary part of the blood clotting process!

Now as I mentioned before, you have already learned a definition for minerals. Are the minerals your body needs the same as the inorganic crystalline substances found naturally in the earth? Well, your body doesn't need *all* of the inorganic crystalline substances found naturally in the earth, but it does need some. Does that mean you should go eat rocks? Of course not! Remember, these are micronutrients. You need them only in small quantities, and you only need certain minerals.

The minerals you need the most are those which contain calcium, chlorine, magnesium, phosphorus, potassium, sodium, sulfur, chromium, copper, fluoride, iodine, iron, selenium, and zinc. Without enough minerals containing these elements, you would have problems. For example, too little calcium in your diet will lead to bone problems. Remember, calcium minerals are used to harden bone. Without enough, bones will not form properly. A constant lack of calcium intake can, later in life, lead to a malady called "osteoporosis."

Iron is an important part of the system that transports oxygen throughout your body. With too little iron, your body will not be able to distribute oxygen efficiently. As a result, you will not be able to burn the macronutrients as quickly as you need to. This leads to shortness of breath, dizziness, feeling worn-out all of the time, and a host of digestive problems. This malady is called "anemia."

Now although vitamins and minerals are an important part of the digestive process, you have to remember that your body is an incredibly efficient, finely-tuned "machine." Even though vitamins and minerals are good for you, they are called micronutrients for a reason. You only need a small amount! In fact, too many vitamins and minerals can be just as hazardous as too few.

For example, your liver stores the fat-soluble vitamins (A, D, E, and K). If you take too many of these vitamins, your body doesn't use them and they end up building up in the liver. They can build up to such high quantities that they actually become *toxic*! The liver can become damaged, and there can be other terrible consequences. Too much vitamin A will lead to liver damage, hair loss, blurred vision, and headaches. Too much vitamin D can lead to liver damage and calcium deposits. These deposits can interfere with the smooth muscles and the cardiac muscle. Now remember, vitamin D is produced by our own bodies when our skin is exposed to the sun. However, that cannot cause us to have too much vitamin D, because our bodies will not make it if they don't need it. However, if you eat too much vitamin D, then there are consequences.

The fat-soluble vitamins are the most important ones to watch, because they tend to build up in your body easily. The water-soluble vitamins can be dissolved in the urine if there are too many of them, and thus your body can get rid of them. However, even water-soluble vitamins can be dangerous in large doses. Too much vitamin B_6, for example, can cause numbness in the mouth and hands and can interfere with the muscles that control walking.

So should you be terrified about eating too many vitamins? No, of course not. It is very hard to overdose on vitamins from the *food that you eat*. You would have to eat an incredibly unbalanced diet to overdose on a particular vitamin. However, you *can* overdose on vitamins if you take *too many* vitamin pills, herbs, or other dietary supplements. The U.S. government has issued recommended daily allowances (RDAs) for each of the vitamins. As long as you stay within those guidelines, you will be safe. Thus, you can take a multivitamin, as long as you do not take too many. In general, you should not take more than three or four times the RDA of any vitamin. For example, the bad effects mentioned for vitamin A can begin to occur if you regularly take 5 times the RDA of vitamin A.

ON YOUR OWN

13.10 Certain nutritional companies sell pills with amino acids in them. Sometimes, they are called vitamin pills. Why is that name wrong?

ANSWERS TO THE ON YOUR OWN PROBLEMS

13.1 Your teeth crush, tear, and grind food into little pieces. This does not change the chemical nature of the food; it just makes the food smaller. Thus, the teeth are involved in physical digestion.

13.2 Food never passes through the gall bladder, the liver, the salivary glands, the appendix and the pancreas. Nevertheless, with the possible exception of the appendix, these are important parts of the digestive system. You will see that in a later section of the module.

13.3 The small intestine has these blood vessels. Remember, most of the micronutrients and macronutrients are absorbed by the bloodstream through the lining of the small intestine. Thus, there must be blood vessels there ready to transport what was absorbed.

13.4 Remember, the incisor teeth are sharp and are used to cut food. The canine teeth are used to tear food, while the premolars and molars are used to crush and grind food. If you think about it, an herbivore can get away without canine teeth. They need to be able to cut food (so that they don't need to eat the whole plant at once) and they need to grind food to make it small, but meat is generally what needs tearing. Since herbivores eat no meat, they don't need canines. The other way to think about it is to think where the name "canine" comes from. "Canine" means dog. Dogs eat meat. Thus, an animal without canines can't eat meat.

13.5 You cough when you inhale smoke because, since you are inhaling, your epiglottis stays open. Thus, the smoke gets into your larynx, and the little particles in the smoke irritate the sensitive lining of the larynx, making you cough. This is much like what happens when food "goes down the wrong pipe." Your larynx has something other than just air going down it, and the lining is irritated.

13.6 Most of the absorption of nutrients occurs in the small intestine.

13.7 The acid in your stomach kills bacteria. Thus, the bacteria can't live in your stomach because of the stomach acid.

13.8 The gall bladder concentrates bile and injects it into the small intestine. Bile helps you digest fat. Without the gall bladder, you might have to reduce the fat in your diet. Interestingly enough, without a gall bladder, bile is sent directly from the liver to the small intestine. If you increase your fat intake slowly enough, the constant release of bile from the liver to the small intestine becomes manageable for the body. In time, then, even someone without a gall bladder can eat a normal amount of fat.

13.9 You learned earlier that the digestive chemicals in the small intestine will not work in the presence of acid. Without the sodium bicarbonate to neutralize the acid, the acid stays in the chyme, destroying the effectiveness of the digestive chemicals.

13.10 Amino acids are not micronutrients. Remember, amino acids are the building blocks of PROTEINS. Thus, they are macronutrients, not vitamins.

STUDY GUIDE FOR MODULE #13

1. Define the following terms:

   a. Digestion b. Vitamin

2. Using the following figure, label organs (a) through (p) with the following names:

liver, stomach, trachea, tongue, salivary glands, pharynx, small intestine, esophagus, large intestine, gall bladder, rectum, pancreas, anus, lungs, larynx, appendix

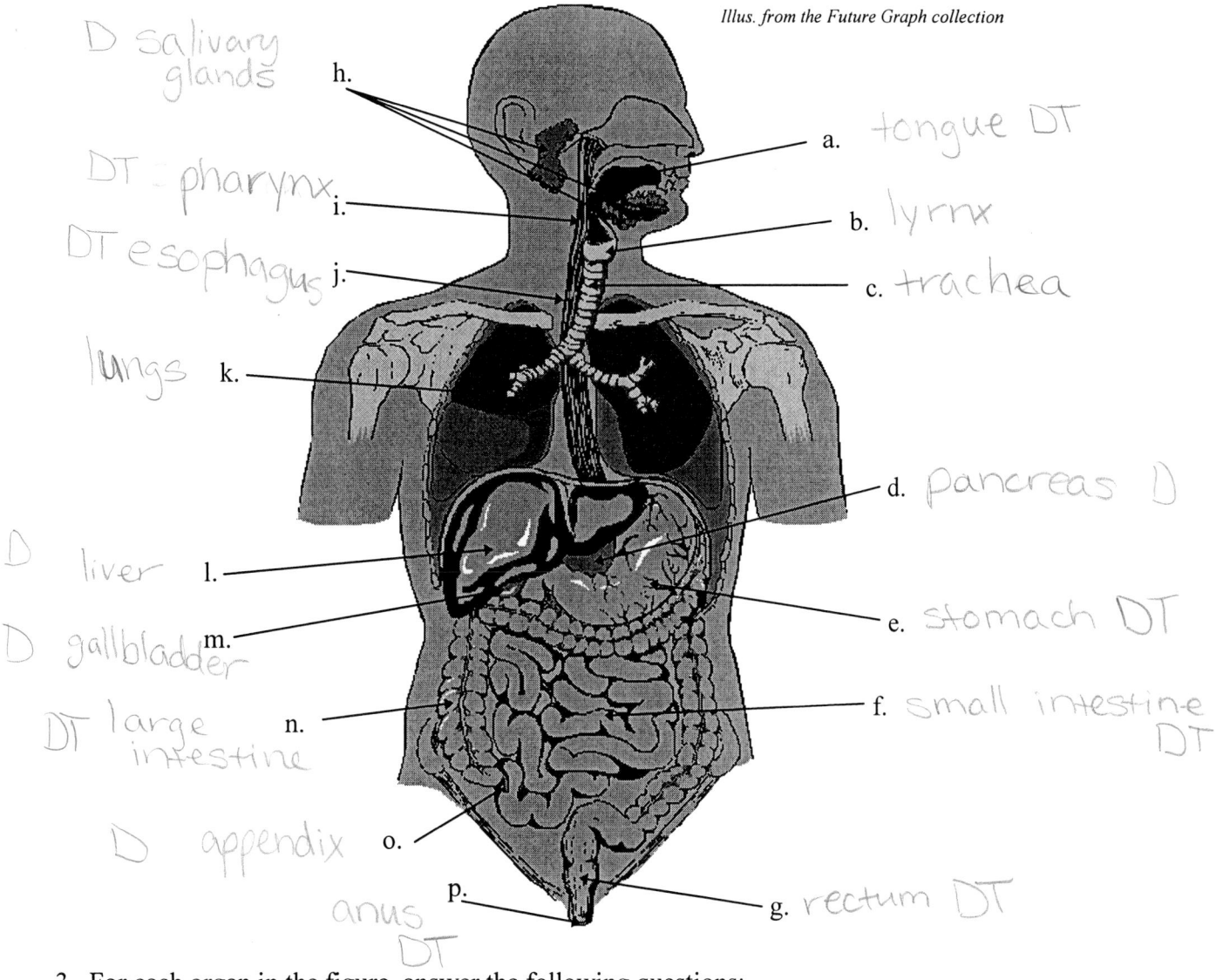

3. For each organ in the figure, answer the following questions:

   Is it a part of the digestive system?
   If it is a part of the digestive system, is it a part of the digestive tract?
   If it is a part of the digestive system, what is (are) its function or functions?

4. What keeps food from going down into your larynx?

5. What would happen to the digestive process if the pancreas stopped making the base that it uses to neutralize stomach acid?

6. What are the fat-soluble vitamins?

7. Which vitamins (fat-soluble or water-soluble) are the most likely to build up to toxic levels in the body if you take too many?

8. What kind of role do most vitamins play in the body?

9. Which two vitamins can the body absorb without eating food that contains those vitamins?

Module #14: The Human Respiratory and Circulatory Systems

Introduction

In the previous two modules, I covered nutrition and the human digestive system. As you know, the entire purpose of the digestive system is to convert the food we eat and the liquids we drink into micronutrients and macronutrients. The micronutrients play a support role in chemical processes throughout the body, while the macronutrients are burned as a source of energy. As a result of studying those two modules, you should have developed a deep appreciation for the design and complexity of the human body.

Of course, the entire digestive system would be useless if the body had no way of transporting the nutrients to the cells that needed them. In addition, a body can have as many macronutrients as it wants, but without a good supply of oxygen, those macronutrients can never be burned for energy. Also, if there were no way to get rid of the carbon dioxide produced when the macronutrients are burned, the body would rapidly poison itself!

That's where the human circulatory and respiratory systems come in. The human circulatory system, comprised primarily of the **heart** and the **blood vessels**, transports oxygen and nutrients to all of the tissues in the human body. Also, it picks up waste from the body's cells and transports them to organs which can get rid of them. The respiratory system, composed primarily of the **lungs**, allows the body to take in oxygen from the surrounding air and expel carbon dioxide. Since these two systems are intertwined, it only makes sense to talk about them together. That's what I will do in this module.

The Human Circulatory System

The human circulatory system transports nutrients and other vital chemicals around the body. It also picks up waste to be expelled from the body. The circulatory system carries all of these things in the **blood**. I will discuss the makeup of blood later. First, however, I want to concentrate on what carries the blood. The blood flows around the body in "tubes" which are generally called "blood vessels." Scientists, however, have a more precise vocabulary. Blood vessels are actually separated into three categories: **veins, arteries**, and **capillaries**.

Veins - Blood vessels that carry blood back to the heart

Arteries - Blood vessels that carry blood away from the heart

Capillaries - Tiny, thin-walled blood vessels that allow the exchange of gases and nutrients between the blood and cells

I first want to discuss veins and arteries, and then later I will tell you about capillaries.

Veins and arteries are relatively large blood vessels in which the blood flows at a reasonably brisk pace. The figure below gives you a general idea of how these vessels are arranged in the human body.

FIGURE 14.1
The Major Veins and Arteries in the Human Body

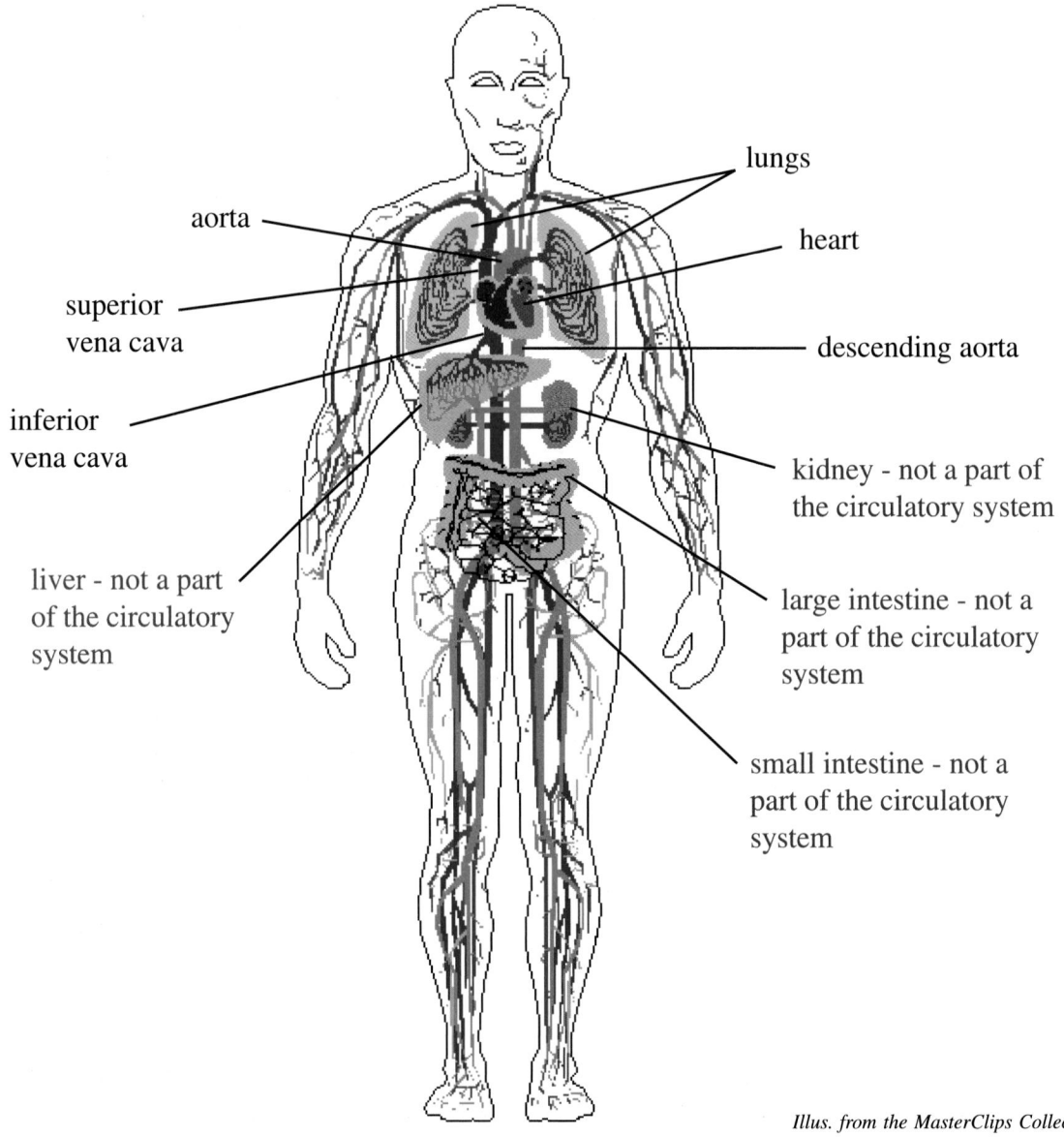

Illus. from the MasterClips Collection

Now the first thing I want you to notice is the color scheme. Some of the blood vessels are blue and others are red. This is a standard color scheme in biology. Why do we use this color scheme? Well, one of the most important things that the blood carries is oxygen. Thus, it is important for scientists to distinguish between blood that is rich in oxygen (called **oxygenated blood**) and blood that doesn't have much oxygen (called **deoxygenated blood**). They do so with this color scheme. In this figure, the red blood vessels carry oxygenated blood, while the blue blood vessels carry deoxygenated blood.

How did biologists come up with this color scheme? Well, look at your wrist. If you look closely, you should see what appear to be blue blood vessels in your skin. Those are blood vessels which contain deoxygenated blood. Although they *appear* blue when you look at them through the skin, they really are not blue. Deoxygenated blood is dark red while oxygenated blood is bright red. However, when we look at blood vessels through the skin, the color gets distorted. Thus, blood vessels carrying deoxygenated blood appear to be blue, when in fact they are dark red. Even though this is a distortion of color caused by viewing the blood vessels through the skin, the blue color is still used as a means of representing deoxygenated blood.

The red blood vessels in the drawing, then, carry oxygenated blood. The blue blood vessels carry deoxygenated blood. What about the pink blood vessels which run between the small intestine and the liver? Those are blood vessels which are rich in nutrients. Remember, most of the nutrients we get from food are absorbed by the blood vessels in the small intestine and then transported to the liver. Thus, the pink color denotes blood which is rich in nutrients.

Okay, so now you know that there are blood vessels which carry oxygenated blood and other blood vessels which carry deoxygenated blood. In general, the *majority* of the veins in your body carry deoxygenated blood while the *majority* of the arteries in your body carry oxygenated blood. Please note that this is ***not always*** the case, however. The definitions of veins and arteries have *nothing* to do with whether the blood inside them is oxygenated or deoxygenated. Instead, the definitions are based on which *way* the blood flows. If a vessel carries blood *towards* the heart, the blood vessel is a vein. If it carries blood away from the heart, it is an artery. However, once you understand how blood flows in the body, you will understand why most veins carry deoxygenated blood and most arteries carry oxygenated blood.

In the next section of this module, I will tell you about how the blood flows through the body. Before I do that, however, I need to talk about the third kind of blood vessel: the capillary. Compared to arteries and veins, capillaries are incredibly small. Their walls are also very thin. In fact, capillary walls are only one-cell thick. In between these cells, there are spaces through which clear fluid can escape the capillary and bathe the cells of the surrounding tissue. This way, oxygen and other nutrients are passed from the blood to the cells that need them. Also, as the fluid bathes the cells, the cells deposit waste products into the fluid. When the fluid is then reabsorbed by the capillaries, it has little oxygen and few nutrients, and it is full of waste products.

If you look at the entire system for a moment, then, blood is carried away from the heart in large blood vessels called arteries. Those arteries eventually branch into smaller arteries (called "arterioles") which branch into tiny capillaries. As the blood flows through the capillaries, clear fluid "leaks" out of the capillaries into the surrounding tissue. This fluid deposits oxygen and nutrients into the surrounding cells. It also picks up waste products from the cells. That fluid is then reabsorbed by the capillaries, which eventually dump the deoxygenated blood full of waste into small veins (called "venules"). Those small veins carry the blood to larger veins which then carry the blood back to the heart. If you were to take every artery, vein, and capillary in an adult human body and lay them end-to-end, the resulting "string" of blood vessels would be about *90,000 miles long*!

Sit back and think about that for a minute. In the average adult, there are 90,000 miles worth of arteries, veins, and capillaries. It takes about 1 minute for a single drop of blood to start at the heart, travel to where it is needed in the body, and return to the heart again. In that amount of time, it supplies cells with the oxygen and nutrients they need, picks up waste products from the cells, and gets rid of those waste products so the whole process can start all over again! Isn't that amazing?

Compare this to something like the water system in a large city. The buildings in the city (houses, places of business, etc.) receive water from a central facility. That water is delivered to them through a network of large and small pipes. These pipes start from the central facility and branch out to all of the buildings. After the water is used, pipes from the toilets, tubs, and sinks of the buildings dump their waste water into pipes which eventually lead to a network of tunnels. In addition, rain water and other kinds of runoff from the streets dump either directly into the tunnels or into pipes which eventually lead to tunnels. All of this waste water is then dumped into a sewage treatment facility and then into a nearby river or lake.

Now, if you were to lay all of the pipes and tunnels in a city's water system end-to-end, would they make a 90,000 mile-long string? Probably not. Would they be nearly as complex as the blood system in the body? Not even close! After all, this water system carries only one thing: water. Blood carries a whole host of things (oxygen, nutrients, etc.). Also, the water system does not need to deliver water to all parts of each building. It delivers water only to kitchens, bathrooms and certain other specialized rooms. The circulatory system in the body, on the other hand, supplies blood to *every part* of the body! Now if you were to look at a drawing that showed the network of pipes and tunnels which make up a city's water system, you would *never* conclude that this network just appeared as the result of some random process! Nevertheless, there are people who want to convince you that this significantly more complex system (the circulatory system) did result from a random process called evolution! Clearly anyone who looks at the details of the circulatory system and believes that it is the result of evolution must have an *enormous* amount of faith!

ON YOUR OWN

14.1 Blood is flowing through a vein in the leg. Is it flowing up or down the leg?

14.2 Fill in the blank below with arteries, veins, or capillaries:

Wherever you find living tissue cells in the body, you will find _____ very near.

The Heart and Blood Flow

The heart is a truly amazing organ! Remember from Module #11 that it has its own special muscle, called the **cardiac muscle**. This muscle is controlled involuntarily (like a smooth muscle) but has many of the visual characteristics of a skeletal muscle. Thus, I told you in

Module #11 that it was sort of a cross between a smooth muscle and a skeletal muscle. What does this muscle do? Well, it pumps blood, of course!

Before I get into how the heart pumps blood, I want to spend a little bit of time on the structure of the heart. A simple sketch of a human heart is shown in the figure below.

FIGURE 14.2
The Human Heart

Illus. from the MasterClips Collection

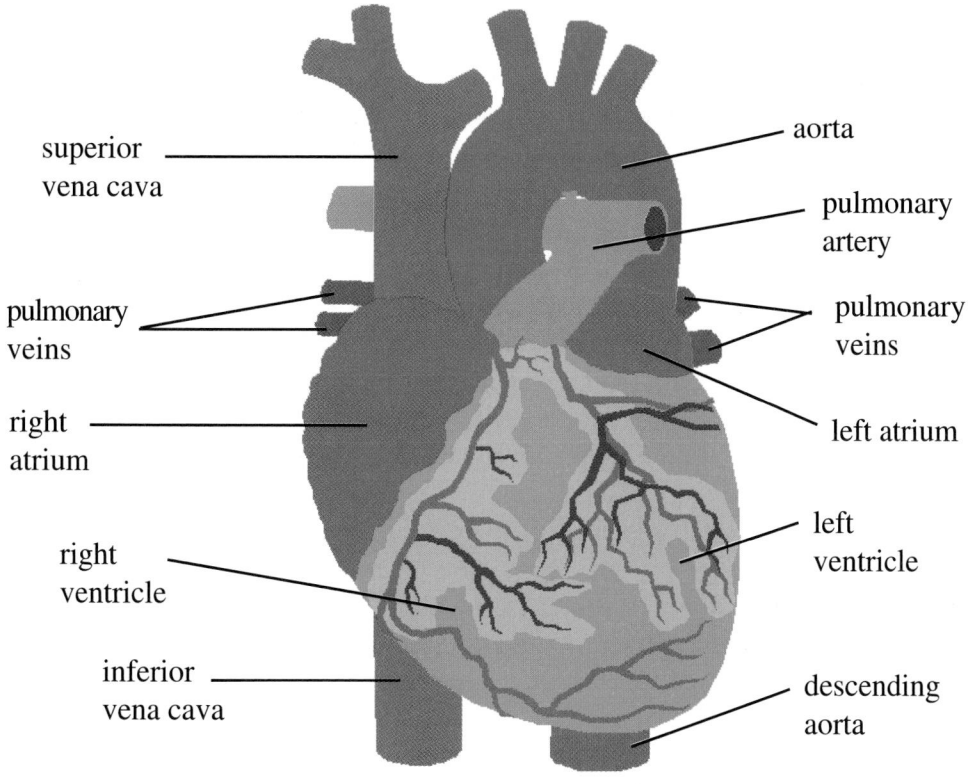

In order to match up parts in this sketch compared to Figure 14.1, notice that the **superior and inferior vena** (vee' nuh) **cava** (cave' uh), the **aorta** (aye or' tuh), and the **descending aorta** are in both figures.

The human heart is called a **four-chambered heart**. It turns out that this is something which all mammals have in common. Birds also have a four-chambered heart. As its name implies, this kind of heart is divided into four chambers: the **left atrium** (aye' tree uhm), the **right atrium**, the **left ventricle** (ven' trih kuhl), and the **right ventricle**. This kind of heart is different than the hearts of most other animals in Creation. Some animals (such as sponges - yes, sponges are animals) have no heart at all. Some animals (such as lobsters) have a heart that is made up of one chamber. Other animals (like most fish) have a heart made of two chambers. Other animals (like frogs) have three-chambered hearts. Finally, animals like lizards have hearts which look like a cross between a three-chambered and a four-chambered heart.

Why do different animals have different kinds of hearts? Well, different animals require different things from their circulatory system. Remember, for example, that mammals are endothermic. This means that their internal temperature stays rather constant. As you learned in Module #12, this requires a lot of energy. Since bodies cannot get energy without oxygen, that means it also requires a lot of oxygen. Thus, mammals and other endothermic animals (like birds) must have a very efficient circulatory system. It turns out that a four-chambered heart is extremely efficient, since it keeps deoxygenated blood entirely separate from oxygenated blood. Hearts with less than four chambers mix deoxygenated blood with oxygenated blood, which is a less efficient way of getting oxygen to the cells. Thus, mammals and birds need four-chambered hearts because they need very efficient circulatory systems. A frog doesn't need quite as efficient a circulatory system, so a three-chambered heart will do. A fish needs even less from its circulatory system, so a two-chambered heart works fine.

Notice in the figure that there are several blood vessels running across the surface of the heart. Remember, the heart is full of living cells (mostly cardiac muscle cells), so it must also have its own supply of blood. Thus, blood flows through the chambers of the heart so that the heart can pump it throughout the body, but it also flows through arteries, veins, and capillaries that supply the tissues of the heart with the oxygen and nutrients that it needs.

Okay, then, how does all of this work? Well, I want to start by showing you one more figure.

Red = Oxygenated
Blue = Deoxygenated

FIGURE 14.3
Blood Flow in the Heart

Illus. from the MasterClips Collection

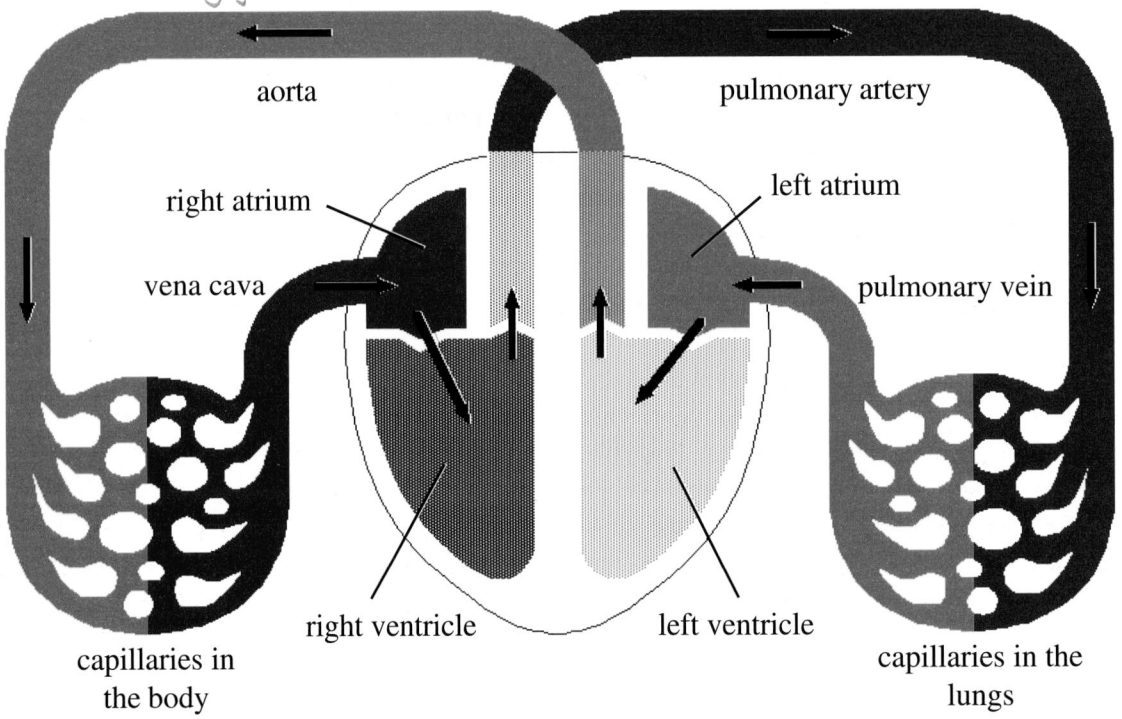

Veins = Deoxygenated Blood
Arteries = Oxygenated Blood

Figure 14.3 is a simplified diagram of blood flow in the human body. It focuses in on the heart, which is the most important part of the circulatory system. Notice first that the same color scheme I used in Figure 14.1 is employed here. Oxygenated blood is represented in red and deoxygenated blood is represented in blue. Also, notice the four chambers of the heart as pointed out in the figure. Notice that the terms "right" and "left" refer to the right and left sides of the *person to whom the heart belongs*, not the person looking at the heart.

Now that you know the general layout of the figure, I want to use it to explain how blood flows throughout your body. Blood flow begins in the right atrium. The main veins of the body (the **superior and inferior vena cava**) bring deoxygenated blood in from the various tissues of the body. That blood fills the right atrium. When the right atrium receives a signal from the sinoatrial node (you learned about that in Module #11), it contracts. This pushes blood out of the right atrium and into the right ventricle. The atrium then relaxes to fill with blood again, and the ventricle contracts, pushing the deoxygenated blood out of the right ventricle and into the **pulmonary** (pull' muhn air' ee) **artery**.

The pulmonary artery sends the deoxygenated blood to the capillaries of the lungs. That's what the "web" of blood vessels on the right side of the figure represents. As the blood flows through the lung capillaries, it releases carbon dioxide and picks up a new supply of oxygen. Thus, after passing through the lung capillaries, the blood turns from deoxygenated blood into oxygenated blood. This newly-oxygenated blood is then carried back to the heart through the **pulmonary veins**.

The pulmonary veins dump blood into the left atrium, which then contracts and sends the blood into the left ventricle. The left atrium then relaxes and the left ventricle contracts, pushing the oxygenated blood out into the **aorta**. The blood travels out the aorta to the rest of the body. If it goes to the upper parts of the body, it travels up through the arteries that branch from the aorta. If it goes to the lower parts of the body, it travels down the **descending aorta** to the various arteries which branch off it.

Eventually, the blood makes it to capillaries in the various tissues of the body. That's what the web of blood vessels on the left side of the figure represents. In the capillaries, the blood gives oxygen and other nutrients to the cells and picks up waste from the cells. At that point, the blood is once again deoxygenated, and it travels back to the heart in the body's veins. Those veins all lead to the superior vena cava (if the blood is in the upper portion of the body) or the inferior vena cava (if the blood is in the lower portion of the body). These vessels take the blood back to the right atrium, where the whole process starts all over again.

Now as if that wasn't difficult enough, you need to realize something about this whole process. Although I started the story of blood flow with the right atrium and then followed the blood through the right ventricle and *then* into the left atrium, that's only what happens if you follow the same drop of blood through the circulatory system. In reality, the right and left atrium fill *at the same time* (with different blood, of course) and then contract *at the same time*, dumping blood into each ventricle *at the same time*. The ventricles then contract *at the same time*, pushing blood either into the pulmonary artery or the aorta, depending on which ventricle you look at.

Each atrium, then, is either filled or empty at the same time, as is each ventricle. The left side of the heart controls blood flow throughout the body, while the right side of the heart controls blood flow into and out of the lungs.

The entire cycle of a heartbeat - the contraction of the two atria (plural of "atrium"), the relaxation of the atria and the contraction of the ventricles, and the relaxation of the ventricles - is then followed by a slight pause. This entire procedure, including the pause, is called the **cardiac cycle**. When the average person is at rest, his or her cardiac cycle usually takes about three quarters of a second. I want you to spend some time learning a little bit about your own cardiac cycle by performing the following experiment.

EXPERIMENT 14.1
Your Own Cardiac Cycle

Supplies:

- A watch with a second hand or (better yet) a stopwatch
- A place that you can do jumping jacks

Introduction - Each person has his or her own cardiac cycle time depending on metabolic rate and other factors. In this experiment, you will determine your own cardiac cycle under different conditions.

Procedure:

A. You have probably been sitting down quietly (or at least reasonably quietly) reading this incredibly interesting course. Although you have, most likely, been excited about all of the wonderful things you have been learning, chances are good that you are close to your "resting" cardiac cycle. Thus, I want you to measure that now.
B. To measure your cardiac cycle, place the index finger of your right hand at the inside of your left wrist on the thumb side. Lightly push around the area until you feel a constant beat. That's your **pulse**. Count the number of times your pulse beats in 30 seconds.
C. When your heart pumps blood into your aorta, the increased pressure in your arteries causes them to expand. That expansion travels through the arteries. When you feel your pulse, you are touching an artery, and the beat that you feel is caused by the artery expanding and contracting in response to the heart pumping blood into the aorta. In the end, then, each beat you feel corresponds to a *heartbeat*. If you double the number of beats you felt in 30 seconds, that will tell you how many times your heart beats per minute. However, I want you to do something else. Divide 30 by the number of beats you counted. This will give you your *cardiac cycle*, which essentially tells you how long your heart takes to make one beat. The average person your age has a cardiac cycle of about 0.75, which corresponds to 80 beats per minute.
D. Now, of course, the cardiac cycle you just measured corresponds to your *resting* cardiac cycle. If your body starts expending lots of energy, the blood must flow more quickly so that

the cells in your body can get enough oxygen to make the energy they need. This changes your cardiac cycle. To measure this, do one full minute of vigorous jumping jacks right now.

E. As soon as you are done with the jumping jacks, put your finger back on your wrist and count the beats you feel in your pulse for 30 seconds.
F. Wait for one full minute, sitting quietly, and count your pulse beats again for a period of 30 seconds.
G. Repeat step (F) at least 4 more times.
H. Once you are done, go back and divide 30 by each of the number of pulse beats that you counted. This gives you your cardiac cycle during the time that you rested after completing the jumping jacks.

What did you see in the experiment? Well, unless your heart rate is abnormal, your resting cardiac cycle was probably less than 0.9 and greater than 0.6. Most likely, it was around 0.75. However, after you did your jumping jacks, your cardiac cycle should have been smaller than your resting cardiac cycle. Why? The cells in your body (specifically your muscle cells) needed extra energy. Thus, they had to start burning macronutrients. To do that, they needed more oxygen and perhaps more macronutrients. Thus, the blood needed to get to them more quickly than normal. Thus, your heart started pumping *faster*. Since your heart started pumping faster, it had to take less time to make each beat, so the cardiac cycle *decreased*. As you rested, however, your cells needed less and less energy, so your cardiac cycle should have started to slowly increase again.

Before I leave this section, I want to point out something that you might have missed. Look again at the right side of Figure 14.3. Notice that the pulmonary artery has *deoxygenated* blood in it and that the pulmonary vein has *oxygenated* blood in it. Now based on the functions of these two blood vessels, that makes sense. The pulmonary artery takes blood to the lungs to be oxygenated, and the pulmonary vein returns the oxygenated blood to the heart so that it can be pumped out to the entire body. However, remember that I said *most* veins carry deoxygenated blood while *most* arteries carry oxygenated blood. These two blood vessels represent notable exceptions to that general rule of thumb.

Now that you understand blood flow in the body, you should understand both the general rule of thumb and why these two blood vessels are exceptions. Remember, arteries carry blood away from the heart. When blood is going to parts of the body *other than the lungs*, it comes out of the heart oxygenated. This oxygenated blood moves away from the heart until it moves into capillaries and deposits its oxygen and nutrients into the cells. At that point, it is picked up by the veins so that it can be taken back to the heart, because veins carry blood towards the heart. Thus, most arteries carry oxygenated blood because while blood travels away from the heart, it usually has not dropped off its supply of oxygen and nutrients. Once it does that, it is picked up by veins to be carried back to the heart. Since veins are defined as those blood vessels which carry blood back to the heart, most veins carry deoxygenated blood.

A notable exception to this is the system that carries blood to the lungs. While blood is traveling away from the heart and towards the lungs, it is deoxygenated. Thus, the arteries from the heart to the lungs carry deoxygenated blood. They are arteries because they carry blood away from the heart. They carry deoxygenated blood, however, unlike most arteries. Once the blood is oxygenated in the lungs, it is carried back to the heart. At that point, then, it is traveling in veins, because only veins carry blood back to the heart. However, since the blood is oxygenated at that point, the veins that carry blood from the lungs to the heart carry oxygenated blood, unlike the majority of the veins in the body.

ON YOUR OWN

14.3 When the left atrium is mostly empty, is the right atrium mostly full or mostly empty? What about the right ventricle?

14.4 The heart of a certain fully-grown animal has deoxygenated blood and oxygenated blood mixed together inside the heart. Is the animal endothermic or ectothermic?

The Components of Blood

Now that you have learned a bit about blood vessels and blood flow, you might want to learn a bit about blood itself! Blood is an incredibly complex mixture of chemicals and cells. More than half of any given sample of blood is made up of a pale yellowish liquid called **blood plasma**. Suspended within the plasma are three main types of cells: **red blood cells, white blood cells,** and **blood platelets**.

Blood plasma contains many chemicals, including micronutrients and macronutrients. The levels of many of these chemicals are carefully controlled by the **kidneys**, because the body is *very* sensitive to the composition of blood plasma. Even tiny changes in the concentration of many salts in the blood plasma could have fatal consequences! Thus, the kidneys have complex chemical sensing and regulating mechanisms, keeping the salt concentration in blood plasma at very precise levels.

Red blood cells are the cells which transport oxygen from the lungs to the tissues. They give the blood its overall red color, because they contain a protein called **hemoglobin** (heem' uh glow bin), which is red. This protein is inside red blood cells and receives oxygen from the lungs. It then carries the oxygen until the blood reaches cells in need of oxygen. At that point, it releases the oxygen to the cells. Without red blood cells, the blood running through your circulatory system would never be able to perform its most important function: the transport of oxygen from the lungs to the tissues of the body.

Red blood cells are short-lived, typically lasting 80 to 120 days within the circulatory system. There are so many red blood cells in our blood that roughly *2,000,000 red blood cells die every second* in a typical adult. If red blood cells are dying all of the time, why don't we run out of them? Well, our bodies continue to make more in order to replace those that are dying. Where are they produced in the body? You should remember that. You learned in Module #11 that blood cells are manufactured by the **bone marrow**.

White blood cells make up only 1% of blood, but they perform a vital function. They are responsible for protecting the body from agents of disease which are in the bloodstream. You can think of white blood cells as little guards which continually "patrol" the bloodstream. When they recognize an organism that should not be in the bloodstream, they often attack the organism by engulfing it and killing it. These little guards have other "weapons" at their disposal, however. Sometimes, rather than directly attacking an invading organism, certain white blood cells will produce chemicals called **antibodies**, which act like poisons to invading organisms.

Have you have ever been given an "antibiotic" when you were sick? An antibiotic is simply a collection of antibodies. From where did the antibodies in that antibiotic come? Well, the *vast majority* of antibiotics come from bacteria and fungi! Only a tiny fraction of antibiotics are actually made by medical scientists. The vast majority of them are produced by fungi and bacteria, and scientists simply collect them for use in antibiotics. This brings up an important point. Despite the fact that medical science is amazingly advanced today, it cannot artificially produce most of the antibodies that are used to make antibiotics. Instead, it must *harvest* those antibodies from other organisms that make them *naturally*!

Think about that for a moment. Bacteria and fungi are *better* at producing chemicals than our best scientists today! If bacteria and fungi are better at making disease-fighting chemicals than are our *best* scientists, how in the world can you believe that these organisms were produced by a random process such as evolution? If you walked into a laboratory filled with scientists making disease-fighting chemicals, would you think that the laboratory was the result of a tornado running through a junkyard? Of course not! A laboratory can only be made with forethought and design. Well, "simple" organisms like bacteria and fungi are better at producing chemicals than the best laboratory science can design! How, then, can anyone ever believe these organisms developed by chance?

The smallest cells in your blood are **blood platelets**. These cells have one purpose: to aid in the process called **coagulation** (co' ag you lay' shun). Coagulation is an incredibly complex chemical mechanism which clots blood when a blood vessel is broken. This vital process keeps us from bleeding to death when we are cut.

In simple terms, the blood coagulation process has three steps. In the first step, the smooth muscles in the blood vessel contract to make the hole as small as possible. In the second step, the blood platelets immediately begin to clump together and stick to the edges of the injury. This makes a soft clot over the hole. Finally, a host of chemicals work together to transform the proteins in the blood plasma into a protein called "fibrin," which forms a tight web that seals off the injury in the blood vessel.

The blood clotting mechanism begun by blood platelets is universally recognized as one of the most stunning, complex chemical processes which exists in the world. It is a finely-tuned, amazing system that has several checks and counter-checks to make sure that the blood clots *only* when a blood vessel is damaged and *only* in the area of the injury. Think about it. Blood cannot just clot anywhere at any time! Blood clotting causes blood to stop flowing! When a blood vessel is cut, that's a good thing. At any other time or place in the circulatory system, that would be a very *bad* thing. The blood clotting process only occurs when necessary, however, due to an incredibly complex chemical mechanism.

Dr. Michael Behe, one of the most respected scientists in the world, says that the blood clotting mechanism alone is very strong evidence that something is wrong with the whole idea of evolution (which he calls "Darwinian theory"). In his book, *Darwin's Black Box*, he makes this important statement:

> Blood coagulation is a paradigm of the staggering complexity that underlies even apparently simple bodily processes. Faced with such complexity beneath even simple phenomena, Darwinian theory falls silent. (Michael J. Behe, *Darwin's Black Box*, Touchstone, 1996, p. 97)

According to Behe, this statement can be made about thousands of processes which we see in nature. Just as I have tried to show you over and over again, there is simply no way to explain the marvels of technology which we see in the natural world without assuming that they were designed and created by God!

ON YOUR OWN

14.5 Sickle cell anemia is a genetic condition which causes the body to produce an altered form of the protein hemoglobin. This affects the shape of one of the types of blood cells, causing them to have a difficult time passing through the blood vessels. This leads to "logjams" in the blood, which can have severe consequences. Which type of blood cell is affected by sickle-cell anemia?

14.6 There is a rare problem during the birth of some babies in which the baby's blood platelets are destroyed by an inconsistency between the baby's blood and the mother's blood. When this happens, the baby can die from even the slightest injury. Why?

Lungs and Blood Oxygenation

From the previous discussion, it should be clear to you that the lungs play a vital role in your body. As a result, you need to learn a few things about your lungs and how they work. A simplified sketch of human lungs is provided in the figure on the next page.

Lung Illus. from the MasterClips Collection **FIGURE 14.4** *Alveoli Illus. by Megan Whitaker*

Human Lungs

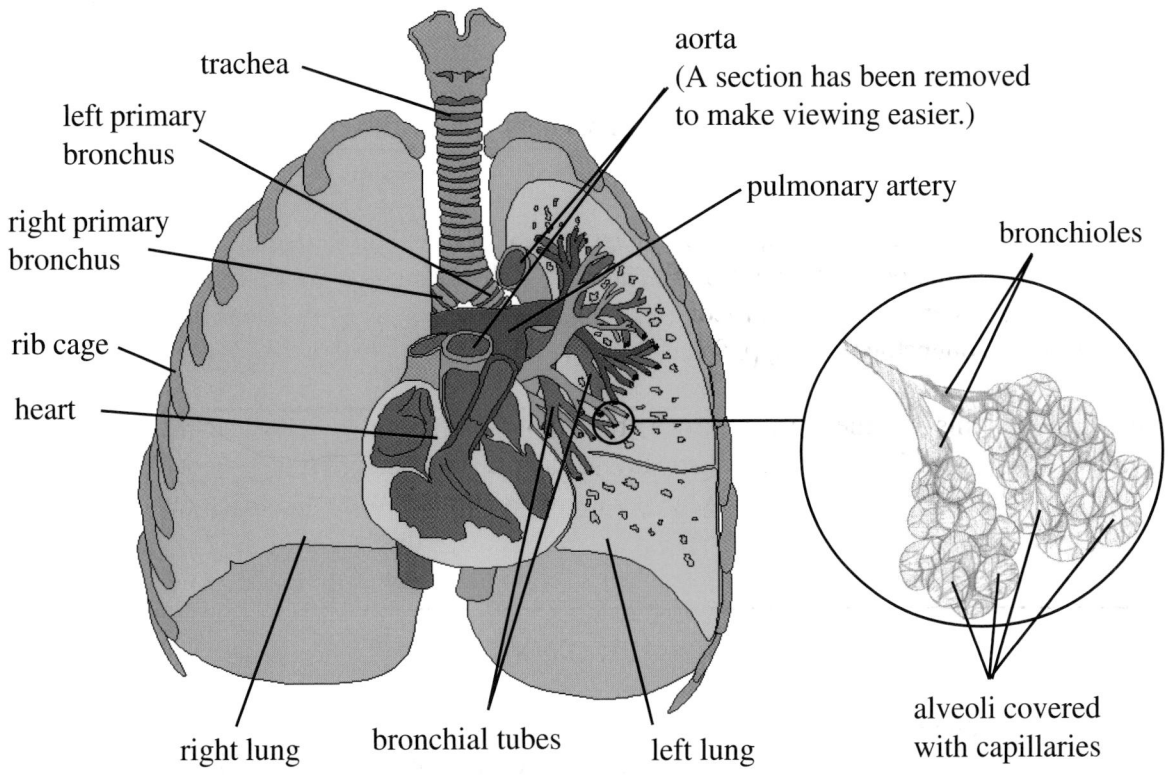

As are all organs in the body, the lungs are incredibly complex, efficient, and well-designed. Remember, their main job is to oxygenate the blood and to allow the blood to release carbon dioxide. If you think about it, then, the lungs need to have tubes that transport air and tubes that transport blood. Well, we already know about the tubes that transport blood. Arteries carry blood to the lungs; they branch into smaller and smaller arteries until they branch into capillaries. The capillaries then allow the blood to pick up oxygen from the lungs and release carbon dioxide into the lungs to be expelled. Veins then carry oxygenated blood back to the heart.

What about the air tubes? In general, the tubes in the lungs that carry air are called **bronchial** (bron' kee uhl) **tubes**. As you should remember from Module #13, air travels from the mouth or nose into the **trachea**. The air passes through the trachea, eventually reaching a branch. That branch is the end of the trachea and the beginning of the lungs' bronchial tube system. A little more than half of the air travels through the right branch into the **right lung**, and a little less than half travels through the left branch into the **left lung** of the lung. The right branch is called the **right primary bronchus** (bron' kus), and the left branch is called the **left primary bronchus**. These two primary tubes branch into smaller and smaller bronchial tubes. The branches become so small that there are about 30,000 of them in each lung. At the end of these tiny bronchial tubes, called **bronchioles** (bron' kee ohls), there are little sacs called **alveoli** (al vee' oh lie). There are about 300 *million* alveoli in a typical adult's lungs!

Most of the "action" in the lungs takes place in the alveoli. The alveoli are covered with capillaries. The deoxygenated blood that has come into the lung through the arteries flows through these capillaries, getting rid of carbon dioxide and accepting oxygen from the air that has been brought into the alveoli by the bronchioles. The carbon dioxide travels back out of the alveoli, through the bronchioles, into the bronchial tube system, and out the trachea each time you exhale.

One of the most important diseases associated with cigarette smoking is **emphysema** (em' fuh zee' muh). In this disease, the alveoli become overlarge and merge with other alveoli. This causes the lungs to have a few large alveoli rather than many small alveoli at the end of each bronchiole. This results in significantly less efficient oxygen exchange with the blood. As a result, the blood cannot carry as much oxygen as the cells of the body need. This results in shortness of breath, wheezing, and extreme difficulty in breathing. Severe emphysema is deadly.

Interestingly enough, the left lung and right lung are different from one another. Each lung is composed of "lobes" that house the arteries, veins, and bronchial tubes. The right lung is made up of three lobes while the left lung is made up of only two. Why the difference? Well, look at Figure 14.4 again. Notice that the heart is not exactly in the center of the two lungs. It takes up more space on the left side of the trachea as compared to the right side. The left lung is smaller to allow the heart to take up that extra room.

Since the two lungs together make up one of the largest organs in your body, you might want to know how big your lungs really are. Well, it's hard to measure the exact dimensions of your lungs, but it is relatively easy for you to measure the *air capacity* of your lungs. Perform the following experiment to determine how much air your lungs can hold.

EXPERIMENT 14.2

The Capacity of Your Lungs

Supplies:

- Flexible tubing (If you don't have some, the best place to get it is anywhere that sells aquarium products. It is typically called "aquarium tubing," and it is used to connect the aquarium air pump to the filter.)
- A plastic one gallon jug with a lid
- A sink with a plug
- A measuring cup

Introduction - Your lungs hold air so that your blood can be oxygenated. This experiment helps you determine about how much air your lungs hold.

Procedure:

A. Fill the sink about halfway full of water and plug it so that the water stays in the sink.

B. Fill the jug completely with water. Try to get all of the air bubbles out.
C. Close the jug's lid and invert it so that the opening of the jug is completely under water.
D. Keeping the jug completely inverted and the opening of the jug under water at all times, take the lid off of the jug. Essentially no water should escape from the jug.
E. Keeping the jug completely inverted and the opening of the jug under water at all times, insert one end of the tubing so that it goes into the jug through the opening. Don't put the end of the tube too high in the jug. The opening of the tube should be just inside the jug.
F. Take the deepest breath you can and then blow into the tubing. Blow in one, continuous breath without pausing to breathe in again. Blow until there is no air left to blow.
G. As you blow, the air will travel into the jug, displacing water. The more you blow, the less water will be in the jug. If you are reasonably athletic or large, you might blow all of the water out of the jug. Most students will not, however.
H. Put the lid back on the jug while the jug is inverted and the opening is under water.
I. Remove the jug from the water, turn it rightside up and take off the lid.
J. Pour what water is left into the measuring cup. Try to fill the measuring cup to exactly one cup. If there is still water in the jug, empty the measuring cup and fill it again. Do that until the jug is empty, counting the number of cups of water in the jug. The last time you fill the cup from the jug, it will probably not fill the cup exactly full. Try to estimate the amount of water to the nearest quarter. In other words, if the cup is not very full, estimate that there is ¼ cup of water there. If it's nearly half full, then estimate ½ cup. If it is more than ½ but noticeably less than 1 cup, estimate it to be ¾ cup.
K. There are 16 cups in a gallon. Subtract the number of cups of water that were in the jug from 16, and that will tell you roughly how many cups of air your lungs can hold.
L. Clean everything up.

So what was your lungs' capacity? Most students have a capacity between 12 and 16 cups. However, as I stated in the experiment, athletic people and larger individuals can have capacities greater than a gallon. Interestingly enough, when we are resting, we use only about 1/15 of our lungs' capacity. When we exercise, however, we start breathing more deeply, using more and more of our lungs' capacity.

ON YOUR OWN

14.7 Which would be more efficient in terms of getting oxygen into the blood: a lung with lots of little alveoli or a lung with fewer, larger alveoli?

14.8 Bronchitis (bron kye' tis) is a breathing disorder which plagues many people. Based on the name, what part of the lungs is affected by bronchitis?

The Respiratory System

Although I mentioned the lungs when I discussed the circulatory system, they are usually considered a part of a separate system called the **respiratory** (res' per uh tor' ee) **system**. This system, as illustrated in Figure 14.5, contains all of those structures which help us breathe.

Illus. from the MasterClips Collection

FIGURE 14.5
The Human Respiratory System

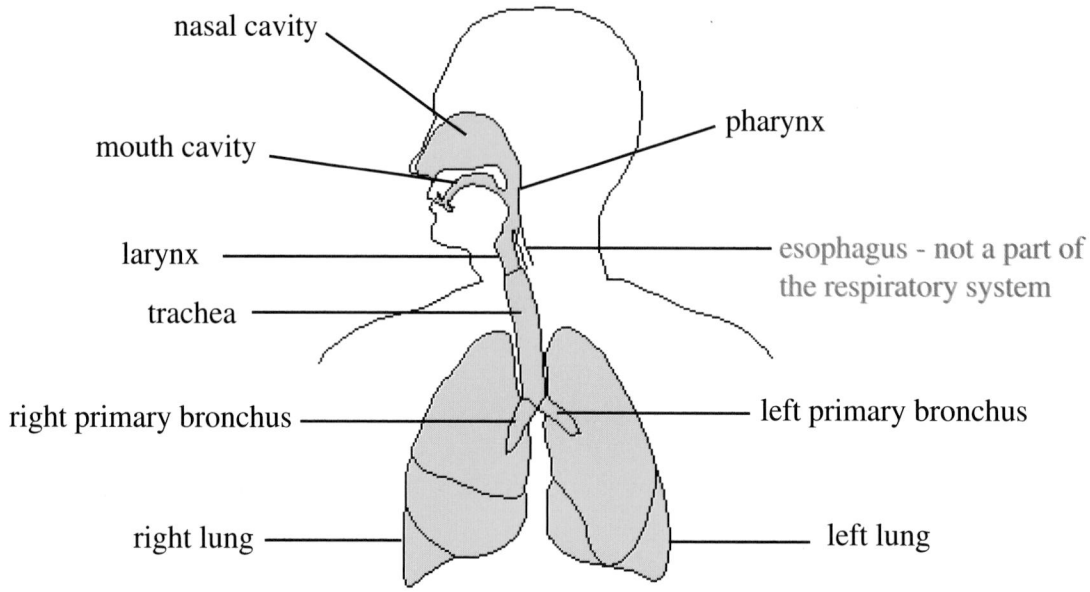

The respiratory system controls how we breathe. Air travels either through the **nasal cavity** or the **mouth cavity** into the **pharynx** (which you learned about in the previous module). Most of the time, we breathe through our nose, so most of the air we breathe passes through the nasal cavity. This is actually very important. You see, the nasal cavity is lined with a sticky substance called **mucus**. This mucus is designed to trap particles which are in the air. That way, the particles do not make it into your lungs. When you have a cold, the cold virus stimulates your body to produce too much mucus. When that happens, the mucus leaks out your nose, and people say that "your nose is running."

When particles are trapped by the mucus, they are pushed along by tiny hairs called "cilia" (sill' ee uh). These hairs push the particles towards the front of the nose, where they will be blown out or sneezed out. If you have a "stuffy nose," that means a lot of mucus and trapped stuff has been pushed to the front of your nose, waiting for you to blow your nose and get rid of it. Sometimes, the body takes over and sneezes, essentially blowing your nose for you.

When the air passes through the nasal cavity or the mouth cavity, it then travels through the pharynx. As you learned in the previous module, an automated "gatekeeper" called the epiglottis makes sure that the **larynx** is open when you breath, so that air can be passed into it. Air then travels through the larynx into the **trachea** and then into one of the lungs via either the left primary bronchus or the right primary bronchus. When you swallow food, however, the epiglottis closes the larynx so that food travels only into the esophagus.

Now one thing I have not described is how your respiratory system actually pushes air in and out of the nasal cavity, pharynx, larynx, trachea, and lungs. That is controlled by a skeletal muscle called the **diaphragm** (die' uh fram). When the diaphragm contracts, it gives your lungs extra room, pulling them out. This sucks air into your respiratory system, and you inhale. When the diaphragm relaxes, it forces your lungs to get smaller. This forces air out of your respiratory system, and you exhale. To give you a visual indication of how this works, perform the following experiment.

EXPERIMENT 14.3

A Model of Your Lungs

Supplies:

- A plastic, 2-liter bottle (the kind soda pop comes in)
- Strong scissors
- A plastic sandwich bag (It needs to be large enough for the bottom of the 2-liter bottle to fit into the bag.)
- Tape
- A round balloon (12-inch is ideal, but any size greater than 6-inch will do.)

Introduction - In this experiment, you will be able to see how your diaphragm controls breathing.

Procedure:

A. Use the scissors to cut the 2-liter bottle across the middle so that the bottom falls away.
B. If the sandwich bag is zippered, cut the zipper off of the top. Then open the bag and put the top half of the bottle (bottom first) into the bag. You should make it so that bag fully surrounds the bottom of the bottle but has plenty of slack in it.
C. Use tape to secure the bag to the bottle. You should put tape all the way around, making a good seal between the bottle and the plastic bag.
D. Push the bag's slack into the bottle.
E. Blow up the balloon relatively large and then let all of the air out. Squeeze the balloon to make sure all of the air is gone. The purpose of this step is to stretch the balloon, that's all.
F. Now put the balloon in the top opening of the bottle upside down. Stretch the opening of the balloon over the opening of the bottle, so that the balloon hangs upside down in the bottle. Your final setup should look like this:

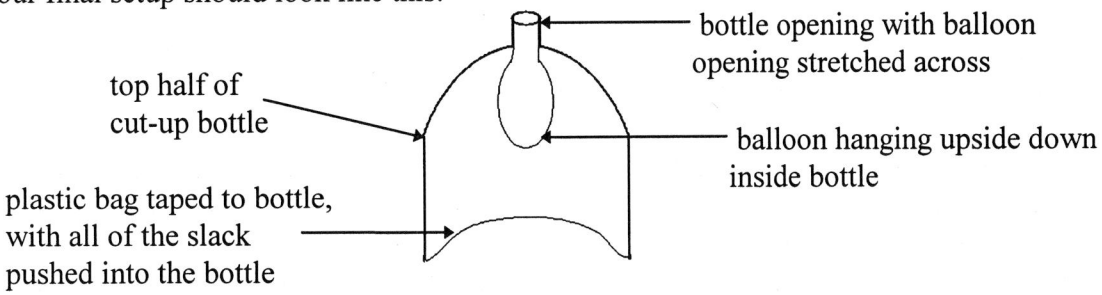

G. This is actually a reasonable model of a lung. To watch your lung "breathe," pull the slack in the plastic bag down and watch the balloon. Then, push the slack up and watch the balloon.
H. When you pull the slack in the plastic bag down, that provides more room in the system. This allows the balloon to expand, and you should see it inflate a bit with air. When you push the slack back into bottle, you get rid of the extra room. This squeezes the balloon, pushing the air out of it.
I. Clean everything up.

In your model of a lung, the plastic bag represents your diaphragm. When you push the slack of the plastic bag into the bottle, you are simulating the relaxation of the diaphragm. This squeezes your lungs (represented by the balloon), forcing air out of them. Just as the balloon deflates, so do your lungs. This causes you to exhale. When you pulled the slack in the bag down, that simulated the diaphragm contracting. This provided more room for the balloon (your lungs), allowing it to fill with air. This, then, simulated inhaling. As your diaphragm contracts and expands, then, your lungs fill and empty, causing you to breathe. Your lungs never fully empty when you exhale. That might have happened in your model, but in your body, there is always air in the lungs, because there is always blood in need of oxygen flowing through them.

There is one other aspect of the respiratory system that I want to discuss. When you exhale, air passes through the larynx, out of your body. The larynx is often called your **voice box**, because it contains your **vocal cords**. Your vocal cords are two thin fibers of tissue which stretch across the sides of the larynx. As you exhale, air is pushed out the trachea and into the larynx, passing over these fibers. When the vocal cords are relaxed, air passes through the larynx silently. When the vocal cords are tightened, however, the air makes them vibrate, producing sound. That sound is the basis of speech, singing, humming, etc. To get an idea of how your vocal cords work, perform the following quick experiment.

EXPERIMENT 14.4
A Model of Your Vocal Cords

Supply:

- A rubber band (It should be large enough to fit around your wrist without stretching. If the rubber band is larger, it will work fine, but a smaller one will not work.)

Introduction - The passage of air over a stretched rubber band simulates how your vocal cords make noise.

Procedure:

A. Hold the rubber band so that it loops around all of your fingers (not your thumb) on each hand.
B. Pull your hands apart a little, stretching the rubber band slightly.
C. Hold the top strand of the rubber band in front of and very near your mouth and blow on it

hard. You might have to move your hands up and down to position the strand properly, but you should be able to get the rubber band strand to hum, because the air coming from your mouth will vibrate the rubber band, and that causes a humming noise.

D. Now you should stretch the rubber band tighter. **BE CAREFUL - DO NOT STRETCH IT HARD ENOUGH TO BREAK IT!!!!!** Repeat step (C), and try to note the difference in the hum that is produced.

E. Play a little with the strength at which you blow. See if you can find a relationship between the volume of the humming noise and the strength at which you blow.

In this experiment, the rubber band represented a vocal cord. When it was stretched tight and air passed over it, it began to vibrate, making a humming noise. Essentially the same thing happens in your larynx, producing the sound which is the basis of speech, singing, humming, etc. When you stretched the rubber band harder, the hum should have changed slightly. It probably sounded a bit higher in pitch than the previous hum. That's what controls the pitch of your voice. When your vocal cords get stretched tightly, they vibrate faster, producing a higher-pitched noise. This makes your voice sound higher. In the last step, you should have noticed that the harder you blew, the louder the hum. That's essentially how you control the volume of your voice. The more air you use, the louder the sound you produce. In the end, then, the amount of air passing through your larynx essentially controls the volume of your voice, while the tightness of your vocal cords controls the pitch of your voice.

ON YOUR OWN

14.9 When a person cannot breathe due to an obstruction in the nasal and mouth cavities or the pharynx, a surgical procedure called a "tracheotomy" is performed. In this procedure, an opening is cut through the neck and into the trachea. At that point, the person breathes through the hole in the trachea. People who have tracheotomies cannot speak unless they block that hole. Why?

Circulation and Respiration Throughout Creation

Although I have concentrated on circulation and respiration in humans, obviously *all* organisms have to have some means of getting the necessary chemicals to the right place in the body. For some organisms, the job is not as hard as others because they are smaller. Members of kingdoms Monera and Protista, for example, are typically only one cell. These organisms still must have systems that transport nutrients and oxygen from outside of the cell to different parts within the cell and transport waste products back out. The chemical nature of these systems are *incredibly* complex. In fact, in the same book I mentioned previously, Dr. Behe uses the cell transport mechanism as another system that is so complex it defies evolution. Nevertheless, even though it is *incredibly* complex, it is still not as complex as the circulatory and respiratory systems in larger creatures.

What is amazing about God's creation is the diversity among its organisms. For example, even within kingdom Animalia, there are many different means by which organisms get and transport the chemicals they need throughout their bodies. You already know that hearts vary from one-chambered to four-chambered, depending on the needs of the animal. Some animals, such as sponges, don't even *have* a heart or a circulatory system. They have mobile cells that travel freely throughout their bodies, digesting food, transporting the nutrients to where they are needed, and exchanging oxygen for cell waste products.

Other examples of the diversity of the creatures in Creation include the many ways that organisms get oxygen for the combustion of macronutrients. Animals like fish have to extract the oxygen which is dissolved in the water. They use **gills** instead of lungs to accomplish this feat. Other animals, such as worms, actually breathe through their skin! Then there are the insects. They have neither lungs nor gills. They have an intricate network of tubes which runs throughout the body. These tubes are connected to holes in the insects' sides. Air simply passes into the network from the holes in the insects' sides and gets distributed throughout the body through the network of tubes!

Even plants have a "circulatory" system. They must get water from the roots to the rest of the plant. In addition, photosynthesis occurs in a plant's leaves. Since *all* parts of the plant need food, and since the food for a plant is made in photosynthesis, there must be a way for plants to transport food from the leaves to the rest of the plant. To see a plant's "circulatory" system at work, perform the following experiment.

EXPERIMENT 14.5
Xylem

Supplies:

- A reasonably fresh white carnation (Almost all big supermarkets sell them these days.)
- Two glasses
- Blue food coloring
- Red food coloring
- A knife
- Two spoons for stirring

Introduction - This experiment will show you the "circulatory" system of a plant at work.

Procedure:

A. Take the carnation and cut about ½ an inch from the bottom of the stem. Then, split the stem in half lengthwise using the knife. **BE CAREFUL!!! CUT THE STEM, NOT YOURSELF!!!!** You should split the stem only about halfway up the flower.
B. Fill each glass ¾ of the way with water
C. Add a few drops of red food coloring to one glass and a few drops of blue to the other.
D. Stir them with different spoons.

E. The color of the solutions in the glass should be deep - not pale. If the colors are pale, add more food coloring and stir until you get deep colors.
F. Place the flower in the glasses so that one half of the stem soaks in the red water and the other half soaks in the blue water. The flower should be stable and stand on its own. If not, you can tape each half of the stem to its glass.
G. Leave the flower like this overnight.
H. Note what you see the next day. You might have to wait as long as two days to see a result.
I. Clean everything up.

When the experiment is complete, you will see the results of part of the carnation's "circulatory" system. Most plants have tubes running throughout the entire plant. One set of tubes, called **xylem** (zy' lum), transports water up from the roots to the rest of the parts of the plant. That's what caused the results of your experiment. Some of the water in the glasses was transported from the bottom of the carnation stem all the way up to the flower's bloom through the xylem. Plants have another system of tubes called **phloem** (floh' ehm). These tubes are responsible for carrying food from the leaves down to the rest of the plant.

In the end, then, all organisms have transport mechanisms that allow nutrients and essential gases (like oxygen) to be distributed throughout the organism. This is essential to satisfying the second criterion of life. The way that this happens in *all* organisms is exceedingly complex, and it defies the very foundation of the theory of evolution, which essentially states that all of life has been constructed based on chance. Whether we are talking about the "simple" transport mechanisms that exist in a single-celled creature, the "moderately complex" xylem and phloem in a plant, or the incredibly complex human circulatory system, the mechanisms required to satisfy just the second criterion of life show us that life is clearly beyond the reach of chance!

ON YOUR OWN

14.10 There are certain plants (called "bryophytes") that do not have xylem and phloem. Compared to plants that do have them, would you expect bryophytes to be larger or smaller?

ANSWERS TO THE ON YOUR OWN PROBLEMS

14.1 It is flowing up the leg. Remember, veins carry blood back to the heart. Thus, the blood is traveling towards the heart, which means up the leg. If it were flowing down the leg, it would be moving away from the heart.

14.2 Wherever you find living tissue cells in the body, you will find capillaries very near. Cells need oxygen and nutrients. They cannot get them from the blood unless the blood is traveling in capillaries. Thus, wherever there are living cells, there must be capillaries.

14.3 Remember, both sides of the heart work simultaneously. Thus, when the left atrium fills, the right atrium will fill as well. Then, they both empty the blood into the ventricles, also at the same time. Thus, when the left atrium is mostly empty, the right atrium will also be mostly empty and both ventricles (including the right ventricle) will be mostly full.

14.4 As stated in the section, endothermic animals MUST have the most efficient heart, which is a four-chambered heart. This kind of heart separates oxygenated blood and deoxygenated blood. Since this animal has a heart which mixes both types of blood, it is not a four-chambered heart, and the animal is NOT endothermic. Thus, the animal is ectothermic.

14.5 Only red blood cells contain hemoglobin, so sickle-cell anemia must affect them.

14.6 Without enough blood platelets, the child's blood cannot clot. Even the slightest injury can cause the child to bleed to death. This happens very rarely, but if not caught, the child can bleed to death even as the result of a few bruises.

14.7 Remember what happens in emphysema. The alveoli grow large and merge, making larger alveoli. This results in poor oxygen transfer to the blood. Thus, many small alveoli are better than a few large ones.

14.8 The bronchial tubes are affected by bronchitis. You could have said the bronchioles or the primary bronchus as well. Bronchitis is the inflammation of tissue on the inside of the bronchial tubes. This causes swelling of the tissue, which makes less room for air to travel. Typically, neither primary bronchus is affected by bronchitis. It is usually the smaller bronchial tubes which are affected.

14.9 The trachea is below the vocal cords. If air passes in and out of the hole, the air never passes over the vocal cords. Without air to vibrate the vocal cords, no sound will be produced.

14.10 Bryophytes are very small compared to other plants. Without xylem and phloem, there is no way to transport nutrients. Thus, the plant has to be small and thin so that all cells are very near the oxygen in the air and the water that drips on the plant.

STUDY GUIDE FOR MODULE #14

1. Define the following terms:

a. Veins
b. Arteries
c. Capillaries

2. What purpose do the lungs serve?

3. What purpose does the heart serve?

4. How many chambers are there in a human heart? Name them.

5. What is special about a four-chambered heart as compared to a three-chambered heart or a two-chambered heart?

6. In what kind of blood vessels does the blood transfer oxygen to the cells and pick up wastes?

7. When deoxygenated blood is returning to the heart, into what chamber does it enter the heart?

8. After entering the heart, the deoxygenated blood is then transferred to a second chamber. What chamber is that?

9. When deoxygenated blood leaves the heart, where does it go?

10. When oxygenated blood comes into the heart, what chamber does it fill?

11. Once the oxygenated blood is back in the heart, it is then transferred to another chamber. What chamber is that?

12. When oxygenated blood leaves the heart, through what artery does it travel first?

13. Most veins carry what kind of blood (oxygenated or deoxygenated)? Are there any exceptions to this general rule of thumb?

14. Name the three types of blood cells and their main job in the blood.

15. What makes up more than half of your blood?

16. What is hemoglobin and where is it found?

17. Where are blood cells produced?

18. What are alveoli? What happens in the alveoli?

19. What kind of blood vessels surround the alveoli?

20. Where are bronchial tubes found and what travels in them?

21. When you inhale, air travels through the following parts of the respiratory system:

pharynx, nasal cavity, trachea, larynx, alveoli, bronchial tubes

List these parts in the order in which inhaled air passes through them.

22. Which of the parts listed in the problem above contains the vocal cords?

23. What controls the volume of the sound produced by the vocal cords? What controls the pitch of the sound produced?

24. A sample of fluid is taken from a tube within a plant. If it is mostly water, which was it taken from: a xylem or phloem tube?

Module #15: The Human Lymphatic, Endocrine, and Urinary Systems

Introduction

In this module, I want to discuss three systems in the human body which help maintain a balanced condition of health. The **lymphatic** (lim fa' tik) **system** removes excess fluid from body tissue and returns it to the bloodstream. At the same time, it cleans the fluid of microorganisms and other contaminants which can cause health problems. The **endocrine** (en' doh krin) **system** produces the **hormones** which help regulate several of the chemical processes that occur in the body. The **urinary system** controls and regulates the water in our bodies and maintains the proper balance of chemicals in that water.

Although I have lumped these three systems into one module, do not think that they are less important than the other systems of the body. Without even one of these systems working properly, you would die within a matter of days. Indeed, a full study of human anatomy and physiology would require many pages devoted to each of these systems. However, in this course, I want to just give you a brief overview of human anatomy without a lot of chemical details. Understanding these three systems requires a great deal of chemistry knowledge. Thus, since I cannot go into chemistry in this course, I cannot spend a lot of time on any of these systems.

There is one other reason I want to touch on these systems only briefly. The next module is the final one of the course. In that module, I want to discuss the most amazing aspect of the human body: its nervous system. Since that is such an incredibly complex and interesting system, I want to spend a lot of time on it. Thus, you will find that this module is a little short. That will allow me to make the final module of the course a bit longer, so as to really concentrate on the human nervous system.

The Lymphatic System

Did you know that there are vessels in your body other than those which carry blood? Indeed, there is a vast network of **lymph** (limf) **vessels** which travel throughout your body. What do these vessels carry? They carry a watery fluid that is found in between the body's cells. This clear fluid, called **interstitial** (in ter stitch' yul) **fluid**, leaks out of the capillaries and passes in and out of cells, facilitating the exchange of gases between the cells and the blood. This fluid must be collected and cleaned before it can return to the blood. That's what the body's lymphatic system does.

You can think of the lymphatic system as the "drainage system" of the human body. Just as a drainage ditch is very important to a farm, the lymphatic system is very important to the human body. Without it, tissues would become waterlogged and full of toxic chemicals and pathogenic organisms. In addition to these tasks, the lymphatic system also acts as an "early warning" system, telling the body about potential disease-causing situations. After all, since the lymphatic system carries the fluid that has just been in and out of the body's cells, it is well-equipped to detect potential threats to the body.

A schematic illustration of the body's lymphatic system is given below. Don't worry, you will not be required to memorize its various parts. I just want to show it to you in order to give you an idea of its complexity.

FIGURE 15.1
The Human Lymphatic System

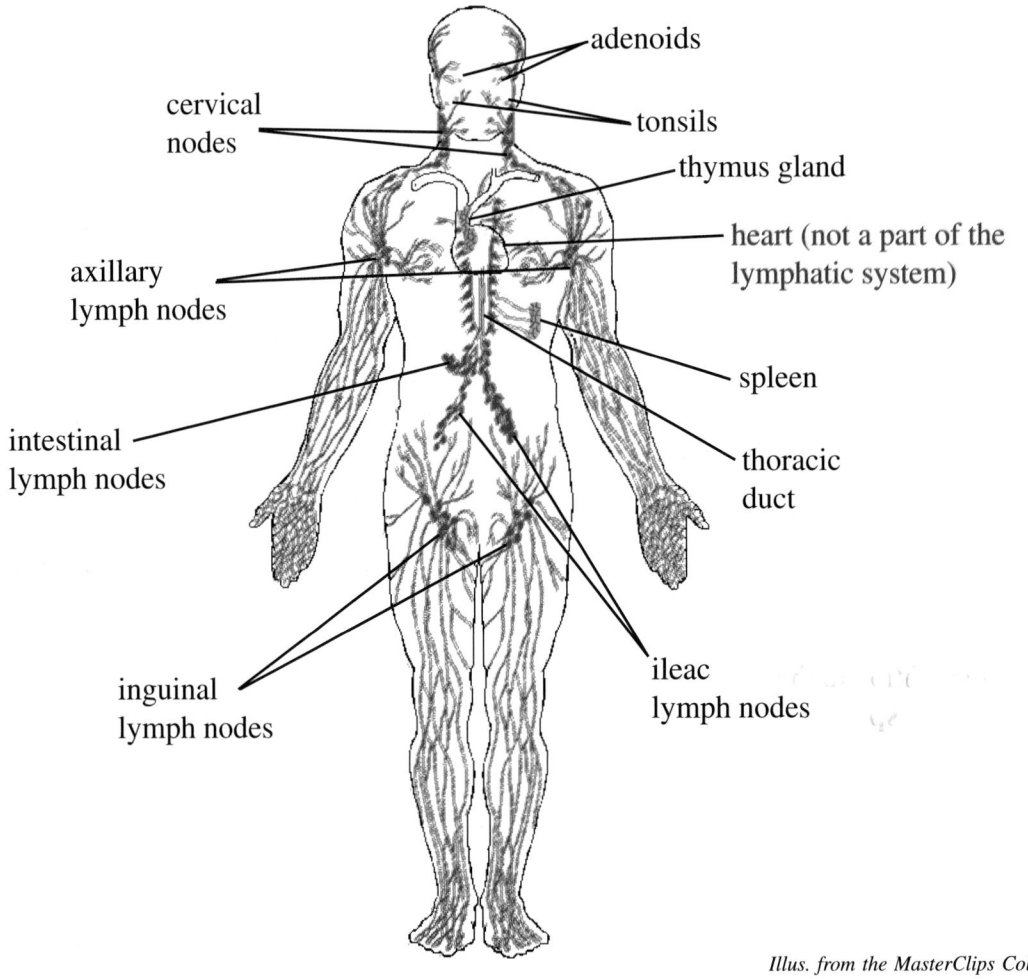

Illus. from the MasterClips Collection

The green lines in the figure represent the major lymph vessels in the body. There are many, many more lymph vessels than what are shown. These are simply the major ones. The network of lymph vessels is essentially the same size and scope as the network of arteries or veins in the body. After all, the lymph vessels must collect and clean the fluids surrounding all of the cells in the body. Thus, wherever you find capillaries, you will find lymph vessels as well. Unlike capillaries, however, lymph vessels begin as "dead-end" vessels. Remember, in capillaries the blood comes in from an artery and goes out into a vein. Thus, the capillaries provide a way in for the blood and a way out. Lymph vessels, however, are simply there to collect excess fluid. Thus, they are open-ended, like the drains of a sewer. Fluid flows into them and then makes its way back to where it is cleaned and put back into the blood supply. While in the lymphatic system, the body fluid is called **lymph**.

The green "blobs" that you see attached to the lymph vessels at different places throughout the body are called **lymph nodes**. These are the places where the lymph is cleaned before it is returned to the blood. I will discuss the lymph nodes in greater detail in the next section of this module. For right now, just be aware that they help clean the lymph that is traveling through the lymphatic system. Notice that the nodes are concentrated in certain regions. There are several nodes (the "intestinal nodes") near the small intestine, others (the "axillary nodes") near the armpits, still others (the "cervical nodes") near the neck, etc. Often when a doctor is trying to determine the nature of an illness, he or she will check these areas for swollen lymph nodes. If the doctor notices swollen nodes in those areas, it indicates that those nodes are fighting an infection.

Now you might wonder *how* the lymph travels through the lymph vessels, into the nodes, and back into the blood. Remember, blood travels through your blood vessels because your heart pumps it through. Is there a separate pump for lymph? No, there is not. Does the heart pump it, then? No, the heart pumps only blood. How, then, is lymph able to travel throughout the lymphatic system? Well, it turns out that the lymph vessels are positioned in the body so that when certain muscles contract, the lymph vessels are squeezed. This causes a gentle flow of lymph through the lymphatic system. That's pretty ingenious, isn't it? Rather than making another "heart" for the lymphatic system, God simply designed the lymph vessels to be in the right place so that muscular contractions can govern the flow of lymph. That allows the body to use the motion of muscles (which are done for some other purpose) to be used to also power the flow of lymph. What an efficient idea! Do you think some random process could come up with something so ingenious?

In addition to the lymph nodes and the lymph vessels, there are other lymph tissues to consider. The **spleen**, for example, is an organ where many white blood cells reside and reproduce. They grow and mature in the spleen and are stored up for use in fighting disease. The **tonsils** and **adenoids** work together to produce and release antibodies that attack pathogens which are eaten or inhaled. The **thymus gland** produces white blood cells and antibodies. The term "gland" is probably new to you.

Gland - A group of cells that prepare and release a chemical for use by the body

You will hear a lot more about glands when I discuss the endocrine system.

ON YOUR OWN

15.1 A chemist hands you two vials of a liquid. The chemist says that the liquids are identical in every way. However, the first vial contains lymph while the second vial does not. From where was the fluid in the first vial taken? From where was the fluid in the second vial taken?

15.2 The spleen can be removed from a sick person without killing him or her. Sometimes this is necessary. If this happens to a person, what can you predict about the person's ability to fight off disease and infection?

15.3 A person's left axillary lymph nodes are swollen. Looking at Figure 15.1, where (most likely) is the person infected?

Lymph Nodes

Scattered along the lymph vessels throughout the lymphatic system are small bean-like organs which are called lymph nodes. As I mentioned in the previous section, the lymph that travels through the lymphatic vessels gets cleaned at the lymph nodes. How does it get cleaned? Well, there is a complex "filtration" system in every lymph node. This system identifies the "bad" chemicals and organisms in the lymph and traps them, allowing the clean lymph to travel back into the bloodstream.

This filtration system is incredibly complex and well-designed. It is so complex that there is no way I can tell you the details of how it works. You must have a lot of chemistry background before you can hope to understand how the lymph nodes really work. However, I would like to point out the general features, just so you get a feeling for what's involved. To get started, then, the following figure is a simplified illustration of a lymph node.

3D Illustration by Michael Dailey

FIGURE 15.2
A Lymph Node

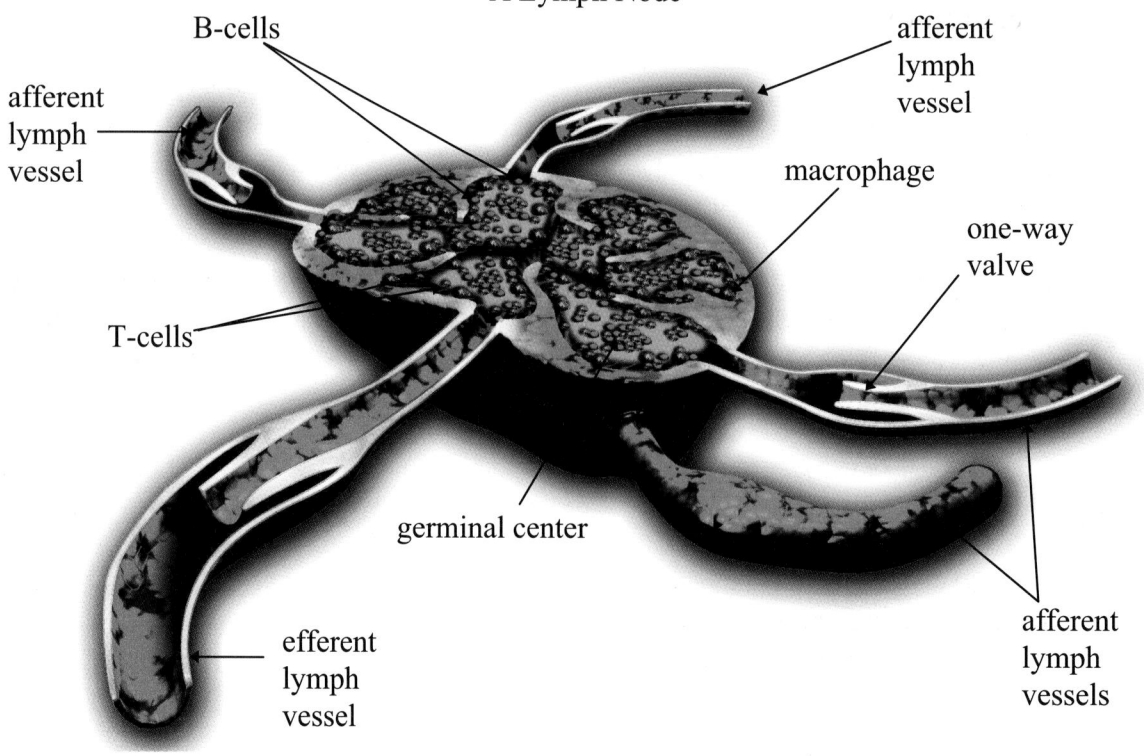

The first thing you should notice about the lymph node is that several lymph vessels (called "afferent lymph vessels") feed into it, but only one vessel (the "efferent lymph vessel") leads out. Now if you think about it, this should make sense. After all, there are many, many tiny lymph vessels that collect interstitial fluid throughout the body. Those vessels must combine together at some point into a larger vessel which will eventually dump the cleaned lymph back into the bloodstream. A lymph node, then, acts not only as a filtration system, but also a transfer station, where many vessels combine their fluid into a larger vessel. It is likely that the efferent lymph vessel leading out of one lymph node will eventually lead into another lymph node as an afferent vessel. This means that lymph usually travels through more than one lymph node (and therefore gets cleaned more than once) before getting dumped back into the bloodstream.

There is one thing that you should notice about the lymph vessels themselves. The "flaps" that are inside each lymph vessel compose a one-way valve. These valves are scattered throughout each lymph vessel, and their job is to keep the lymph moving in only one direction: back towards the heart. Because of their ingenious design, lymph can flow one way through the valve but it cannot pass back the other way. As a result, lymph travels only towards the heart, not back from where it came. Similar one-way valves can be found in veins.

The cleaning power of lymph nodes comes from the white blood cells. White blood cells found in the lymph system are called **lymphocytes** (limf' oh sites). There are many different kinds of lymphocytes, each of which performs different tasks in the lymphatic system. For example, **B-cells** produce antibodies that attack specific disease-causing microorganisms. **T-cells**, on the other hand, attack microorganisms directly. You can think about B-cells and T-cells this way: B-cells are "archers" who shoot their enemies with arrows (antibodies) from a distance, while T-cells are "swordsmen" who attack the enemy in hand-to-hand combat. Another kind of white blood cell (not technically considered a lymphocyte) is the **macrophage** (mac' roh fayj). Macrophage cells scavenge the lymph, eating bacteria and other debris.

Not only do the lymph nodes serve as transfer stations and filtering centers, they also serve as a supply station for white blood cells that can travel throughout the body. When an infection is detected by the lymph nodes, the **germinal centers** release lymphocytes. These cells mature, and some of them stay in the lymph nodes to help fight the infection. Others, however, get transferred into the bloodstream so that they can travel to the source of the infection and try to destroy it there. Once a lymphocyte leaves the blood to fight an infection in the body's tissue, it is no longer called a lymphocyte. It is called a "plasma cell." Not all lymphocytes in the blood vessels come from the lymph nodes. Others come from the spleen, the tonsils, and the thymus. Thus, the lymph nodes are just one source of white blood cells.

One of the neatest aspects of the body's lymphatic system is that it has a "memory" of the infections it has fought. Remember, one of the weapons that the lymphatic system has at its disposal is the B-cell. B-cells produce antibodies that fight specific infections. Well, when B-cells produce antibodies, they also produce **memory B-cells**. These memory cells are configured to start producing the same antibody again the moment the same infection is detected. This allows the lymphatic system to react much more quickly if the body is attacked again.

The fact that our lymph system can "remember" a previous infection is the basis of one of the greatest achievements in modern medicine: the **vaccine**.

Vaccine - A weakened or inactive version of a pathogen that stimulates the body's production of antibodies which can destroy the pathogen

When a person is infected by most pathogens, the only way to rid the person of that pathogen is for the body to make a specific antibody which will destroy it. The body can produce antibodies against many, many different pathogens. However, some pathogens are so fast-acting that the body cannot produce antibodies before it is overwhelmed. As a result, the disease kills or permanently harms the person.

There are two basic types of vaccines. The first type contains a weakened form of the pathogen itself. In this kind of vaccine, the pathogen has been weakened so that it cannot overtake your body's immune system. As a result, your lymph system recognizes it, makes the antibodies to kill it, and then makes the memory B-cells to "remember" the infection in case the organism attacks again. Since the pathogen is weakened, your body's immune system will destroy it before it can overtake your body. Thus, even though the vaccine actually contains a disease-causing pathogen, the vaccine is safe because the pathogen is so weak that your immune system will destroy it.

The other type of vaccine contains a human-made chemical that makes the body react the same as if a certain pathogen has entered the body. This type of vaccine, then, "mimics" a real pathogen, causing the lymph system to react and produce antibodies as well as memory B-cells. Regardless of the type of vaccine, the effect is the same. The vaccine causes your body to react as if it is being infected. It then forms B-cells that produce antibodies and memory B-cells that remember how to produce those antibodies. As a result, your lymph system becomes "primed" to fight off a real infection, if one should actually happen.

Think about what this means. A vaccine is *not* a cure for a disease. You can't take the vaccine *after* you have gotten sick. That's not how it works. A vaccine must be taken *before* you get sick. The vaccine then "primes" the lymph system for action in case the *real* pathogen ever infects your body. Thus, the act of giving someone a vaccine is often called **immunization**, because it makes a person immune to the disease. This name actually gives a false notion, however. There is a small percentage of people (usually less than 2%, depending on the specific vaccine) that will not respond to a vaccine. As a result, their lymphatic systems never get "primed" for an attack. As a result, if they are ever exposed to the real pathogen, they will, most likely, still get sick. A better way of thinking about it, then, is that a vaccine provides immunization for the vast majority of people, but not everyone. Many vaccines require "booster shots," to maintain immunity.

The first idea of a vaccine came from British physician Edward Jenner in 1796. There were many people in his area dying of smallpox. He noticed that cowpox, a similar sickness that struck cows, is a relatively mild disease in humans. Thus, he injected humans with cowpox and, since smallpox and cowpox are very similar, their immune systems developed antibodies that would kill both. Thus, as long as someone was injected with cowpox *before* he or she got smallpox, the person was very likely to be immune to the effects of smallpox.

The concept was improved upon significantly by the great Louis Pasteur. In 1885, he developed a vaccine against rabies. In 1954, perhaps the most widely-used vaccine was invented: the polio vaccine. Developed by the American scientist Jonas Salk, this vaccine immunized children against one of the most devastating childhood diseases. This disease, also called "infantile paralysis," affects the nerves which control muscle movement. As a result, the disease slowly takes away the patient's ability to move. Albert Sabin actually improved the vaccine later (1961). Thanks to the Sabin vaccine, polio has been nearly eliminated in most parts of the world.

There is a movement afoot these days that says vaccines are bad for you. After all, proponents say, a vaccine injects a pathogen into your body! This is just like getting infected by the pathogen. In addition, the antibodies whose production it stimulates stay in your body forever. Thus, your body "remembers" the infection, and you will always have poorer health as a result. Nothing could be farther from the truth! Since the pathogen in a vaccine is either weakened or a chemical mimic, it is not like getting infected by the real thing. Thus, the risk is minimal and the benefits are enormous. Vaccines are truly one of the most wondrous inventions that God has allowed humanity to discover!

Now if you think about this for a moment, the concept of a vaccine is, in fact, a great testament to God's power and majesty. After 3,000 years of medical science, human beings cannot fight pathogens as efficiently as God's creation (the human body) can. Thus, to protect ourselves, we simply stimulate the body to do what God designed it to do in the first place. In the case of vaccines then, human science gives the body a little push, and the body does the rest.

ON YOUR OWN

15.4 If a pathogen cannot be destroyed by antibodies, what other defenses can the lymph nodes use against it?

15.5 Which carries more lymph: an afferent lymph vessel or an efferent lymph vessel?

Tears

Before I move on to the urinary system, I want to spend a few moments talking about tears. The body produces tears in the **lacrimal** (lack' rih muhl) **gland**, and they run through tiny tubes called "tear ducts" and then flow across the eyes. Because tears contain an infection-fighting chemical for your eyes, they are related to what I was just discussing. They are not technically a part of the lymphatic system, however. They are considered to be a part of the eye.

The first thing you must realize is that your body produces tears continually, even when you do not cry. These tears run across your eyes, lubricating them and covering them with an infection-fighting chemical. After running across the eyes, they are collected in ducts that then drain into the nasal cavity. When you cry, you are producing *excess* tears, and they overflow the duct that drains them. As a result, these excess tears fall down your cheeks, and people say that you are crying.

Why do we produce excess tears and cry? Well, you can explore one reason by performing the following experiment.

EXPERIMENT 15.1

Working Your Lacrimal Glands Too Hard

BE CAREFUL...Cut the onions, not yourself!!!

Supplies:

- Three onions (any size)
- A cutting knife (In this experiment, a dull knife works better than a sharp one!)
- A freezer
- A cutting board
- A sink in which you can cut

Introduction - In this experiment, you will cut onions under three different conditions to learn why cutting onions can make you cry.

Procedure:

A. Take one onion and put it in the freezer. It needs to stay in there for at least 15 minutes.
B. If you are wearing contacts, remove them. Contacts reduce the effect of the experiment.
C. Put a second onion on the cutting board and begin cutting it into tiny pieces. Perhaps you can use them for cooking later. **BE CAREFUL!!!!!!!! KNIVES CAN BE DANGEROUS!**
D. Hold your head so that your eyes are directly over the onions.
E. Continue cutting until you start crying.
F. Get rid of the onion pieces, either by throwing them away or putting them in a container for later use in cooking.
G. Clean the cutting board.
H. Wipe away all of the tears and wait until you are no longer crying.
I. Put the cutting board in the sink and start the water running.
J. Now cut the other onion that is still out. This time, however, make sure that the onion stays under the running water while you are cutting. Cut this onion up as much as you did the first.
K. Note whether or not you cry.
L. Once again, get rid of the onion pieces and clean the cutting board.
M. When the third onion has been in the freezer for at least 15 minutes, pull it out of the freezer and begin cutting it. Put the cutting board the same place that you put it when you cut the first onion, and cut the onion up as much as you did the other two.
N. Note whether or not you cry.
O. Clean everything up.

Well, did you cry when you cut the first onion? Most likely, you did. What about when you cut the second onion? Most likely, you did not cry then. What about when you cut the third onion? People with very sensitive eyes might have cried, but most people will not have. How do we explain the results of this experiment? Well, onions have sulfur-based chemicals that are contained in tiny sacs in the onion's tissues. When you cut the first onion, those sacs "exploded," releasing the chemicals as tiny droplets in the air. When those droplets reached your eyes, a chemical reaction occurred and your eyes were irritated. This caused your lacrimal glands to produce excess tears. As a result, you cried. Your body interpreted the chemicals reaching your eyes as a possible harm to your health and, as a result, produced excess tears designed to wash the irritant out of the eyes and kill any potential invaders.

Why didn't you cry in the second part of the experiment? Well, when you cut the second onion, the sacs still "exploded," but the tiny droplets dissolved in the water coming from the faucet and thus never reached your eyes. As a result, your body had no reason to produce excess tears. Finally, you probably didn't cry in the third part of the experiment, either. When you put the onion in the freezer, one of the main chemicals that causes the chemical reaction which irritates your eyes was destroyed by the low temperature of the freezer. As a result, the chemical hit your eyes, but the chemical reaction could not occur, and your eyes were therefore not irritated.

Of course, there is another reason that we cry. Human eyes also release excess tears in response to strong emotional feelings, i.e., when we are sad, we cry. Amazingly enough, the tears that we cry when our eyes are irritated (like what happened in the first part of the experiment) are chemically quite different from the tears we cry when we are upset! Tears produced by strong emotions contain chemicals that do not appear (to any great extent) in tears produced by eye irritants. These chemicals include manganese (a chemical depressant), leucine-enkephalin (chemical which helps control pain), and the adrenocorticotrophic hormone (a chemical produced by bodies under stress). When you excrete these chemicals by crying, the net effect is to *make you feel better.* By releasing these toxins, the tears serve to chemically and physically make the crier feel less depressed!

Interestingly enough, humans are the only organisms that can cry as a result of emotion. This is, in actuality, a *real* problem for evolutionists. After all, an evolutionist is forced to assume that this property of human tears evolved in only the human race over a long time period. Think about it for a minute, though. What possible survival advantage is obtained by feeling better as a result of a good cry? The answer, of course, is none whatsoever. In fact, those who bottle up their emotions are usually more aggressive, which, according to evolutionary principles, should make them more fit to battle for survival. Thus, if anything, this particular feature of human chemistry is harmful to the species' ability to survive and would be thrown out by natural selection.

According to evolutionary theory, then, this trait should *never have evolved.* If, instead, we view the human body as a marvelously designed machine, we can assume that the tears we shed are a gift from the Designer. Since He built in us the ability for emotions, He also built in us the ability to deal with those emotions. One of those is the ability to sit down and have a good, long cry.

The Urinary System

About half of a person's weight comes from water. It is everywhere in the human body. The cells have water inside them. The interstitial fluid picked up in the lymphatic system is mostly water. Indeed, blood plasma itself is more than 90% water. In addition, we drink a lot of water. Even if you don't make a habit of drinking "plain old water," the liquids that you do drink (juice, milk, soda pop, etc.) are mostly composed of water. As you learned in Module #11, the cells in your body also *produce* water through the burning of macronutrients.

How is all of this water controlled in the body? Well, the amount of water, as well as the levels of the many substances in that water, are all controlled by the human **urinary system**.

Illus. from the MasterClips Collection

FIGURE 15.3
The Human Urinary System

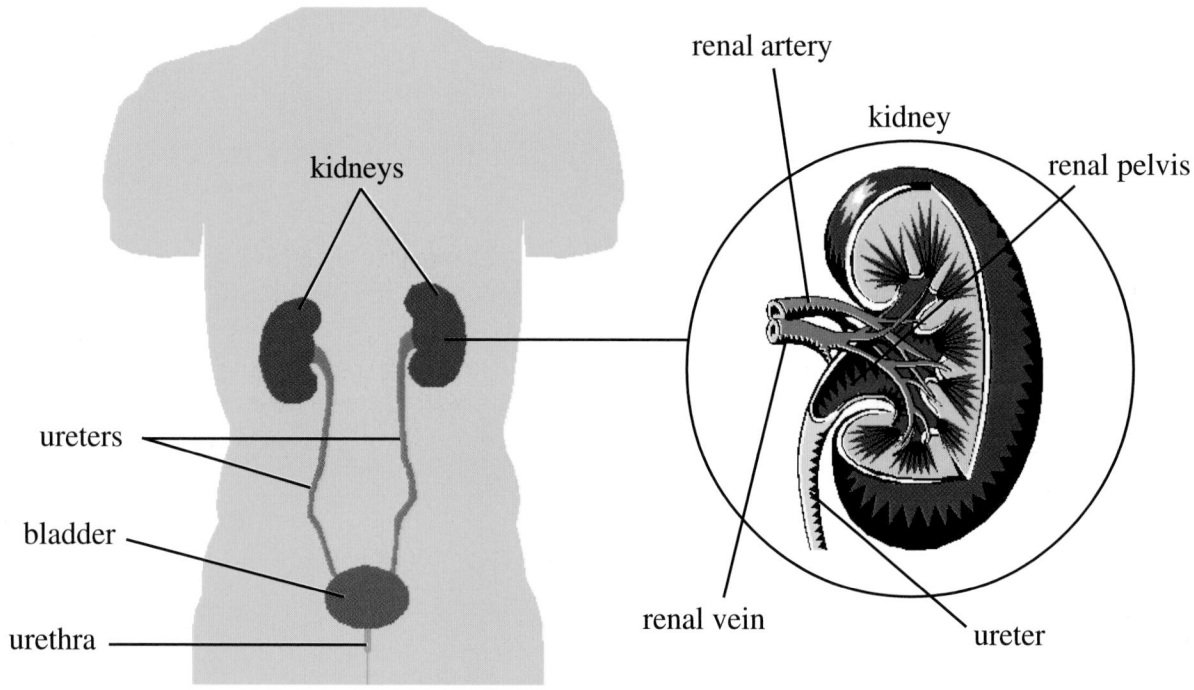

Compared to other systems you have studied so far, the urinary system might look relatively "simple." However, the task that it performs is *far* from simple!

Like the lymph nodes, the main task of the kidneys is to clean. Instead of cleaning lymph, however, the kidneys clean the blood and blood plasma. This is important because the lymph system cannot clean the way that the kidneys clean. The lymph system cleans out organisms and chemicals that it recognizes as disease-causing. The kidneys do something completely different. They clean out chemicals that are not dangerous to the body until they reach certain levels. Thus, the chemicals are not necessarily ones that cause disease. Instead, they are simply chemicals whose levels in the blood must be monitored and maintained.

How do kidneys do their job? Each kidney is actually made up of a million units called **nephrons** (nef' rons). Each nephron is a tiny filter which empties into a tiny, curving tubule. Each nephron works independently to make **urine**. Here's how it happens. The **renal artery** brings blood into the kidney. The blood supplies oxygen and nutrients to the cells of the kidneys and picks up the cells' waste products. It is important to note that the kidneys actually get much more blood than they need for their own cells. After all, they need to clean all of the blood. In fact, *every five minutes,* your kidneys end up processing all of the blood in your body!

In order to be cleaned, blood flows through a nephron where it is filtered. Nutrients as well as wastes and water are temporarily dumped into the nephron. Then, as this fluid flows through the tubule of the nephron, the cells that line the nephron *reabsorb* the proper amounts of nutrients and chemicals back into the blood. Excess chemicals are left behind in the nephron to become urine. Meanwhile, the proper amount of water is also reabsorbed from the nephron back into the blood.

The blood then leaves the kidney through the **renal vein** to travel back to the heart. Any water and chemicals that were not reabsorbed into the blood go from the nephrons into the **renal pelvis** and flow out of the kidney to the **ureter** (yur' ee ter). At this point, the mixture of water and chemicals is called urine. The urine travels through the ureter and is held in the **bladder**. Eventually, the bladder releases the urine it has stored, and the urine leaves the body through the **urethra** (yuh ree' thruh).

Now if you think about it, the job that the kidneys do is truly amazing. They filter the blood, and then they reabsorb the water and chemicals back into the blood, in just the right amounts. How in the world do they do that? Well, it's impossible for me to tell you, because first and foremost, scientists don't fully understand the process. Secondly, in order to understand it at even a basic level, you need at least a year of a solid high school chemistry course. However, I can give you an *idea* of how the kidneys work by having you perform the following experiment.

EXPERIMENT 15.2

A Model of Kidney Function

Supplies:

- A tea bag
- Three small glasses (like juice glasses)
- A paper towel
- A coffee filter
- A funnel
- Scissors
- A tea kettle or pot
- A stove
- A spoon for stirring
- A pile of 2 to 3 books (The pile needs to be at least ¾ as high as one of the glasses.)

Introduction - This experiment simulates the processes that occur in the kidney.

Procedure:

A. Start a pot or kettle of water boiling. You only need about a cup of water in the end.
B. Use the scissors to cut open the tea bag, spilling the contents into one of the two small glasses.
C. Once the water has boiled, remove it from the heat and let it cool for 1 minute. Then, **carefully** pour it into the glass that contains the contents of the tea bag. **BE CAREFUL, THE WATER IS HOT!!!!!**
D. Use the spoon to stir the hot water with the contents of the tea bag. Do this for a while, so that the water becomes a nice deep brown color. Do not try to dissolve all of the contents of the tea bag. That would be VERY hard. Just make the water brown.
E. Place a coffee filter into the funnel so that you can pour something into the filter. You may have to hold it there. Use another person's help if necessary.
F. Hold the filter/funnel combination over another one of the glasses.
G. Pick up the glass with the water/tea leaves. **BE CAREFUL - IT IS PROBABLY STILL HOT.** You can wait for it to cool off if it is too hot now.
H. Carefully pour the solution in the glass so that it fills the coffee filter. Do this slowly, so that the water filling the coffee filter never rises above either the top of the funnel or the top of the filter paper. The water will pass through the coffee filter and into the funnel. Then, it will fall down the funnel and into the glass underneath.
I. Once most of the water has drained through the filter paper and funnel, put the filter paper/funnel system aside and look at the solution in the glass that was underneath. Note its appearance.
J. Now, set that glass on the top of the pile of books.
K. Take the paper towel and fold it in half lengthwise. Fold it in half again in the same direction. Repeat that one more time. Now you should have a long, thin paper towel.
L. Take the long, thin paper towel and put one end of it into the tea in the glass so that the end touches the bottom of the glass.
M. Bend the other end of the paper towel and position the remaining empty glass so that that end of the paper towel is in that glass. DO NOT put the remaining glass on the pile of books. The glass with tea needs to be a lot higher than the remaining glass. In the end, then, you should have two glasses: one with tea in it sitting on the pile of books and one empty glass sitting on the table or counter next to the pile of books. The long, thin paper towel should have an end in both glasses, forming a "bridge" between the two.
N. Wait for an hour or so.
O. Look in the glass that was empty. Note what you see.
P. Clean everything up.

What did you see in step (I) of the experiment? If everything went well, you should have seen that after passing through the filter paper, the tea that you made was a clear brown solution with no tea leaves floating in it. Why? Well, the filter paper has tiny holes in it. The water and tea that is dissolved in the water pass through these holes. The tea leaves that were floating in the tea, however, are too big to pass through the holes. Thus, they are stopped by the filter paper. That's the first thing that the kidneys do to blood. They filter the blood, stopping any large chemicals that are floating in it.

What did you see in step (O) of the experiment? If things worked out right, you should have seen that the empty glass ended up with a little tea in it. That tea should have been a *lot* lighter than the color of the original tea. You see, the paper towel absorbed the water and tea. Because of a process a bit too difficult to explain here, the water and tea began to travel along the paper towel. The paper towel ended up holding most of the tea. Some of the water was released into the other glass, as was some of the tea. The paper towel, however, kept a larger percentage of the tea than the water. In the end, then, the tea in the second glass was weaker than the original tea. This is something like how a kidney works. The kidney is *significantly* more complicated, but the basic result is the same. The nephrons filter the water and chemicals in the water out of the blood. They then put some of the water and some of the chemicals back into the blood, holding the rest to be sent out the ureter as urine.

Now there are many differences between what your system in the experiment did and what a real kidney does. First of all, the kidneys process a *lot* more water. In the average adult, the kidneys pull about 40 gallons of water from the blood each day. They end up putting back 99% of that water (unlike the paper towel in your experiment), so that the average amount of urine an adult produces is 1 quart per day. Also, the nephrons reabsorb the chemicals from the filtered fluid in a very sophisticated way so as to separate the chemicals and decide how much goes back into the blood. This keeps the amount of water in your body very constant, as well as the levels of chemicals in that water.

Although scientists do not fully understand the kidney, medical researchers have been able to produce an artificial kidney that can work in place of a real kidney. Like all marvels of technology, the abilities of an artificial kidney pale in comparison to a *real* kidney. The artificial kidney is much less efficient and does a significantly poorer job than a real kidney. It is also *much* bigger than a real kidney. As is always the case, even the best scientists and engineers alive today cannot make anything that comes close to the efficiency, compactness, and ability of the marvelous things that God has designed in us!

When a sick person uses an artificial kidney, we say that the person is on **dialysis**. In one type of dialysis, blood is taken from the renal vein and routed into a machine that attempts to filter and clean the blood as does a real kidney. It does not do nearly as good a job, but it can be a reasonable temporary solution. Typically, people on dialysis use the artificial kidney for a set amount of time on a regular schedule. Most patients do it either while they wait for injured kidneys to heal or while they wait for a kidney transplant, in which their non-functioning kidney is replaced with a working kidney from someone else's body.

ON YOUR OWN

15.6 Suppose a person produces three quarts of urine each day. What can you conclude about the drinking habits of that person?

15.7 The bladder is not an essential part of the urinary system, but you should be glad that it is there. Why?

The Endocrine System

Have you ever heard the term **hormone** before? If you follow professional sports, you've probably heard about problems with "steroids." Well, a steroid is an example of a hormone.

Hormone - A chemical messenger released in the bloodstream that sends signals to distant cells, causing them to change their behavior in specific ways

The word "hormone" comes from the Greek word *hormao*, which means "I excite." There is a good reason for that. Hormones excite specific cells to behave in specific ways.

Hormones are released by endocrine glands which are scattered throughout the body. Trying to get a complete picture of this complicated system is extremely difficult. There are more than 200 identified hormones in the human body, and more are being discovered. They are each very specific: targeting certain types of cells in certain ways. One author has suggested that trying to understand the endocrine system in detail is comparable to memorizing all of the train, plane, and bus schedules serving New York City.

As a result, I do not want to give you a detailed view of the endocrine system. Indeed, even a rough understanding of its details requires several years of college-level chemistry. Nevertheless, I would like to discuss some of the major endocrine glands and some of what their hormones do, so that you can get a basic idea of this amazing control system in your body. The figure below illustrates the placement of some of the most important endocrine glands in the body. Please note that the arrows do not point to the glands themselves, as they are typically quite small. The arrows point only to the general locations of the glands.

FIGURE 15.4
The Locations of Some of the Important Endocrine Glands

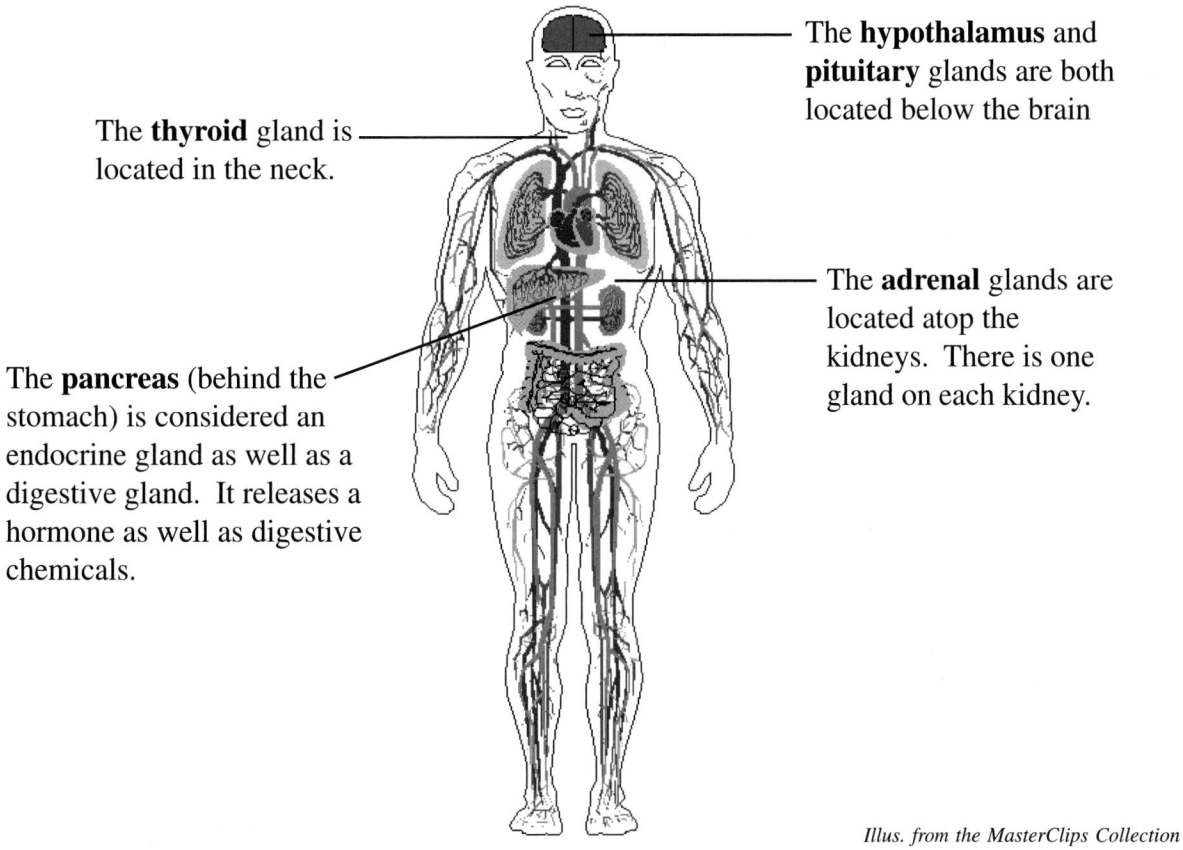

Illus. from the MasterClips Collection

The **hypothalamus** (hi poh thal' uh mus) is one of the main regulators of the endocrine system. It is part of the lower brain and makes up less than 1% of the brain's total volume. Despite the fact that it is so small, it influences a wide range of body functions. It regulates thirst, hunger, and body temperature. It also helps initiate the "fight or flight" responses such as the fast heart rate and increased blood flow which occur when we are frightened or angry. Its function in the endocrine system is to control the **pituitary** (pih two' uh teh ree) **gland**, which is often referred to as the "master endocrine gland."

The pituitary gland sits right below the hypothalamus in the brain. It, too, is very small (about the size of a pea), but its effects on the body are incredible. It is referred to as the "master endocrine gland" because the hormones that it makes and puts into the bloodstream control many other endocrine glands in the body. It produces and releases at least 10 separate hormones. I say "at least" because those are the ones that scientists have identified. There are probably more that just haven't been discovered yet. Some of these hormones specifically control other endocrine glands, while others directly affect bodily processes.

Here are a few examples of the pituitary hormones that directly affect processes in the body. The pituitary gland makes and releases human growth hormone (HGH), which is essential for the proper development of the skeleton. Another hormone made by the pituitary gland, endorphin, is a natural pain reliever. When the body is stressed, the pituitary gland releases endorphin to reduce the effects of pain. Another important hormone made and released by the pituitary gland is the antidiuretic (an tie die' uh reh' tik) hormone (ADH). This hormone controls the amount of water reabsorbed by the nephrons in the kidneys, regulating the amount of water retained in the body.

Being the "master endocrine gland," the pituitary also controls other endocrine glands. For example, the pituitary gland produces the "thyroid stimulating hormone," which is often called TSH. This hormone controls the activity of the **thyroid gland**. The main thing that the thyroid gland does is affect the basal metabolic rate. It does this by producing two hormones which speed up the rate at which cells burn macronutrients. The body is very sensitive to thyroid gland activity. If your thyroid produces too many hormones, you are said to have "hyperthyroidism." This results in a very high metabolism and high activity level. An opposite condition, "hypothyroidism," occurs when the thyroid produces too few hormones. People with this condition are lethargic, tire easily, and tend towards obesity.

I want to stop here and illustrate the complex nature of the endocrine system and why it is so difficult to learn and understand. Remember, the hypothalamus controls the pituitary gland. But the pituitary gland controls other endocrine glands. In the end, then, the endocrine system is a multi-leveled control system. Let's look at the thyroid gland as an example. The hypothalamus receives information from the brain indicating that the body is not getting enough energy. Thus, it stimulates the pituitary gland, which releases TSH. The TSH then stimulates the thyroid into producing its hormones, which results in increased metabolism! Now *that's* complicated.

The **adrenal glands** are also controlled by the pituitary gland. The "adrenocorticotropic (uh dree' no kort' uh cuh troh' pik) hormone," mercifully abbreviated as ACTH, controls the activity of the adrenal glands, which produce **cortisol** (kort' uh sol). When a person gets afraid or excited, the hypothalamus stimulates the pituitary to release ACTH. This causes the adrenal glands to produce cortisol, which causes the liver to release more glucose so that there is plenty of energy available to the body.

Although I have taught you to think of the **pancreas** as a digestive gland, it is also an endocrine gland. In addition to the digestive chemicals it produces, the pancreas makes **insulin**, a hormone that enables glucose to enter the cells so that it can be burned. The disease diabetes is a result of a pancreas that does not produce enough insulin.

ON YOUR OWN

15.8 Although most scientists refer to the pituitary gland as the "master endocrine gland," the hypothalamus could be considered the "master of the master." Why?

15.9 Suppose a person's thyroid began producing too few hormones and the person gets tired and lethargic. If a doctor determines there are no problems with the thyroid itself, what should the doctor look at next?

ANSWERS TO THE ON YOUR OWN PROBLEMS

15.1 Remember, the interstitial fluid becomes lymph only when it goes into the lymph vessels. Thus, the first vial of liquid was taken from a lymph vessel, while the second was taken from between some cells. Thus, both vials contain interstitial fluid, it's just that the first is lymph because that fluid had entered a lymph vessel.

15.2 The person will not be able to fight off disease and infection quite as well as before the spleen was removed. After all, the spleen is a part of the lymphatic system, which fights infection. Take a part of that system away, and the person's ability to fight infection decreases. Remember, however, that the lymphatic system has other means by which to protect the body. Thus, losing a spleen is far from debilitating.

15.3 Remember, the lymph nodes clean lymph that is coming into them from the lymph vessels. The figure indicates that these lymph nodes are near the arm pit, on the left side. The vessels in the diagram which feed these nodes are in the left and upper left side of the body. Thus, the infection is probably in the left arm or upper left part of the body.

15.4 Antibodies are produced by B-cells. There are also T-cells and macrophages that fight infection in different ways. The lymphatic system can use them instead.

15.5 An efferent lymph vessel carries more lymph. Remember, several afferent lymph vessels carry lymph into a lymph node and only one efferent lymph vessel carries lymph out. Thus, the efferent lymph vessels carries the lymph from several afferent lymph vessels.

15.6 Three quarts a day is more than the average amount. Since the amount of water in the body stays the same, the only way this person could produce more than the average amount of urine is by drinking more than the average amount of liquid.

15.7 The bladder holds your urine so that you release a lot of it all at once. Without the bladder, you would have a steady, slow stream of urine running out of your body. That would be bad!

15.8 The hypothalamus controls the pituitary gland.

15.9 The doctor should look at the pituitary gland. That's the gland which produces the thyroid stimulating hormone. If the thyroid is fine but producing too few hormones of its own, perhaps the problem is that it is not getting stimulated.

STUDY GUIDE FOR MODULE # 15

1. Define the following terms:

a. Gland
b. Vaccine
c. Hormone

2. Describe the main function of each of the three systems you studied in this module.

3. What two kinds of structures make up the lymphatic system? In which of these structures is the lymph actually cleaned?

4. How does lymph get pumped through the lymphatic system?

5. What gland produces tears? What two purposes do tears serve?

6. What three kinds of cells in the lymph nodes fight infection?

7. What kind of cell in the lymph nodes produces antibodies?

8. What kind of cell helps the lymphatic system "remember" an infection so that it can fight the infection better the next time?

9. Does it do any good to take a vaccine once you are sick with the disease the vaccine is supposed to fight?

10. Explain how a kidney functions. Start with the blood going into a kidney and end with it leaving the kidney.

11. What does a kidney do with any excess water or chemicals? Where do they go?

12. What is the purpose of dialysis?

Match the following glands with their function.

13. hypothalamus	a. Produces hormones that regulate the basal metabolic rate
14. thyroid	b. Produces cortisol which causes the liver to release glucose into the blood
15. pituitary	c. Produces insulin which enables glucose to enter the cells
16. adrenal	d. Controls the pituitary gland
17. pancreas	e. Produces hormones that control many of the endocrine glands

18. Which gland is often called the "master endocrine gland?"

Module #16: The Human Nervous System

Introduction

Have you ever looked inside a computer? Well, if you were to do such a thing, here is a portion of what you would see.

Photo from the MasterClips Collection

FIGURE 16.1

A Portion of a Computer's Integrated Circuit Board

This is typically referred to as a "printed circuit board." Looks pretty complicated, doesn't it? There are integrated circuit chips that do a variety of different things. Most of the actual work of the circuit board occurs in the chips. However, one chip by itself cannot accomplish a lot of useful work. Thus, there are several chips that communicate with one another. They do this by sending electronic signals through electrical pathways on the board. There are also other components like resistors and capacitors. Although the "real work" of the circuit board is done in the chips, the resistors and capacitors play a vital support role. Without them, the chips could not communicate with one another effectively.

In the end, then, a computer works because it is composed of several components that all work together to get a common job done. It is, of course, an amazingly complex process which only the best applied scientists really understand. Looking at that printed circuit board, you immediately understand that it must have been designed by someone smarter than you or me. After all, there is no way to explain the complex nature of the board nor the resulting function (a machine that can process complicated and detailed instructions) without assuming that someone thought long and hard about how to design and build it!

Well, there are a lot of similarities between your brain and that printed circuit board. Compared to your brain, of course, the printed circuit board is *incredibly* primitive and ineffective. Nevertheless, there are some striking similarities. If you were able to magnify a section of a person's brain and then get rid of certain features, you might see something like this:

FIGURE 16.2

Illus. by Megan Whitaker

A Stylized Sketch of the Layout of a Tiny Portion of the Brain

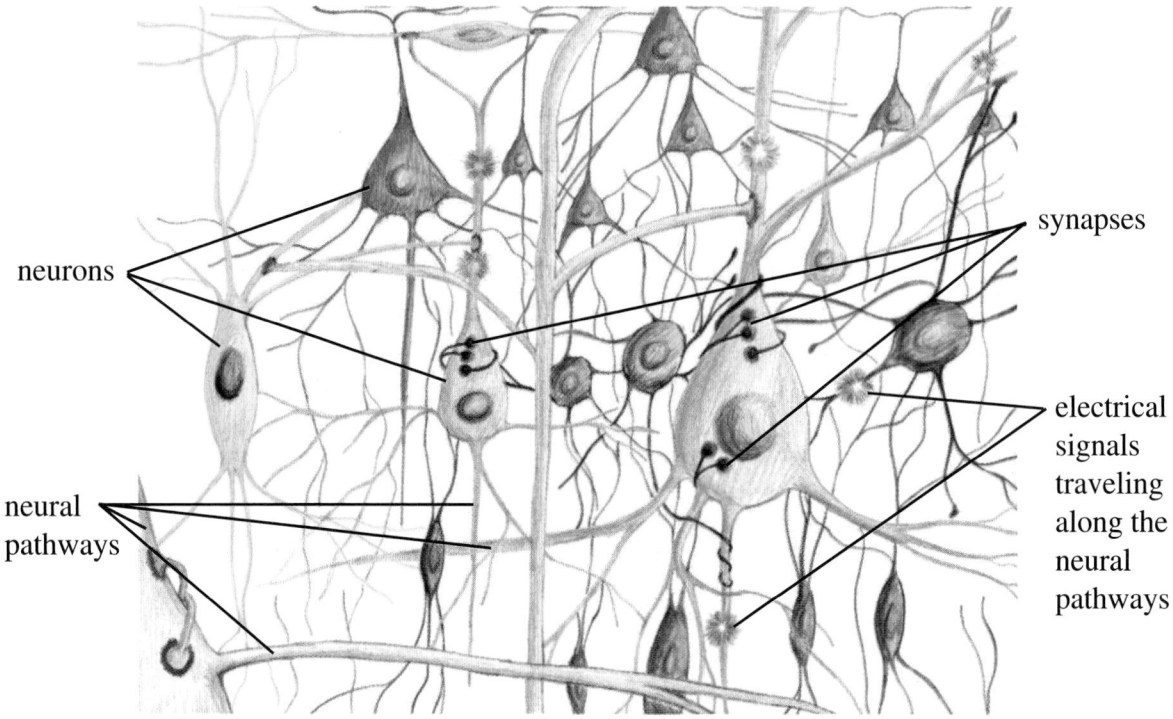

Looks pretty complicated, doesn't it? Well, like I stated a moment ago, there are really a lot of similarities between the brain and a printed circuit board. For example, the "real work" of the brain occurs in cells called **neurons**. Thus, neurons can be thought of as the "chips" of the brain. Like chips, however, neurons cannot get a lot accomplished without communicating with other neurons. Thus, there are neural pathways that connect neurons to one another. They communicate by sending electrical signals down those pathways, just like the chips on the printed circuit board communicate by sending electrical signals down electronic pathways. The point at which a neural pathway connects to another neuron is called a **synapse** (sin' aps).

What about the resistors and capacitors in a printed circuit board? Is there anything similar to them in the brain? Well, yes, there is. The neurons cannot function properly without the help of other cells called **neuroglia** (ner' oh glee' uh). Like the resistors and capacitors on a printed circuit board, these cells support the neurons and help them communicate with one another. There are actually twice as many neuroglia as neurons in the brain, and they account for nearly half of the brain's weight.

As I mentioned previously, even though there are similarities between the two, a printed circuit board is *incredibly* primitive compared to the human brain. For example, a *really complex* printed circuit board might have thirty or forty chips. Now a chip actually is composed of several thousands of working circuits, so these chips might (at most) represent as many as

100,000 to 1,000,000 individual circuits. However, the average adult brain is composed of 100 ***billion*** neurons. Now remember, these neurons must talk to one another. Most scientists who study the brain indicate that there are *trillions and trillions* of neural pathways. Indeed, there are more neural pathways in *one single human brain* than there are electronic pathways in *all of the computer systems in the world*! In addition, the brain processes information *significantly* more quickly than does a computer's printed circuit board. Scientists who study the brain, working with applied scientists who understand computers, have estimated that the brain can perform in 100 computational steps what it would take the most sophisticated computer nearly *one billion* steps to accomplish! Are you beginning to see why I say that a computer's printed circuit board is primitive compared to the brain?

Why have I spent so much time discussing the complexity of the human brain? Well, the brain runs the human **nervous system**, which essentially controls most aspects of the human body. Thus, the brain is the central focus of the human nervous system, which I want to discuss in this module. Now remember, the previous module was a little short, so this module will be a bit longer than what you are used to. As a result, you will probably spend more time on this module than you spent on most of the others.

Neurons: The Basic Unit of the Nervous System

As I mentioned in the previous section, nerve cells are called **neurons**. As you can see from Figure 16.2, neurons are very strange-looking cells. Although the shape, size, and details of neurons vary greatly throughout both the brain and the nervous system, they all have some basic characteristics in common. These are illustrated in the figure below.

Illus. from the Future Graph collection

FIGURE 16.3
A Typical Neuron

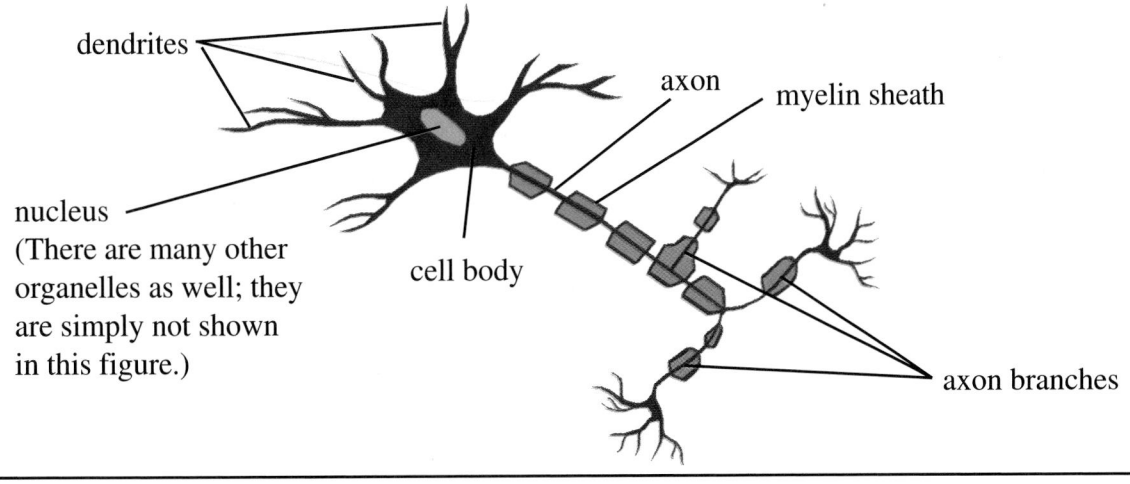

Nerve cells, like all cells in the human body, contain many organelles that perform all of the functions of life. The only organelle shown in the figure is the nucleus, but there are many others, all housed in the **cell body**. What make nerve cells look so unique are all of the fibers that shoot out of the cell body. The fibers come in two types: **dendrites** and **axons**. Both of these kinds of fibers act like electrical cords, carrying electrical signals either into or away from the cell body. In fact, that's how we distinguish between these two types of fibers. Dendrites conduct electrical signals *towards* the cell body, while axons direct signals away from the cell body.

Nerve cells have something in common with lymph nodes. Remember, several vessels carry lymph into a lymph node, but only one vessel takes the lymph away. Well, nerve cells have many, many dendrites bringing electrical signals into the cell body but only one axon sending the signal away. As shown in the figure, that axon will almost always be branched farther down the line, but at the point where it leaves the cell body, it is always one single fiber. The axon is the longest fiber of a nerve cell. Some axons span nearly 3 feet! The axon is covered by a fatty insulator called a **myelin sheath**. This sheath protects the axon and speeds up the rate at which an electrical signal can travel down it.

Okay, so that's what a neuron looks like. What, however, does a neuron do? Well, neurons have many different tasks in the body, but the majority of these tasks can be lumped into one of three groups:

1. **Neurons pass signals to other neurons.**

2. **Neurons pass signals to muscle or gland cells.**

3. **Neurons receive signals, process the information, and send out new signals to other neurons.**

The first two tasks listed are primarily performed by neurons that make up the nerves in our bodies. After all, the brain controls the actions of the body. Thus, most instructions sent to any part of the body start out in the brain. Also, the receptors in our body are constantly sending information to the brain. Our nerves pass this information along in the form of electrical signals.

The first task listed, then, is typically performed by neurons that make up the nerves in the body. They either pass information from the brain to some cell which the brain must instruct, or they send signals from a receptor to the brain. Those neurons which perform the second task listed are typically the ones at the end of a nerve. These neurons are the last in the chain of neurons which go from the brain to a cell, and they pass the signal to its final destination. Most of the neurons that perform the third task listed are a part of the brain. These neurons actually evaluate information and decide what must be done based on that information.

Think about these three tasks for a moment. Each of them requires that neurons communicate with other cells. Neurons either communicate with other neurons or with the cells that are supposed to receive signals from them. How is that accomplished? Well, the answer to that question is surprisingly complicated. You might think that an electrical signal traveling down the axon of one neuron simply gets transferred to the next neuron. Basically, you would be right. However, the process through which this happens is *incredibly* complicated.

For reasons that are too complex to explore in this course, the axons and dendrites of one neuron cannot actually touch another cell. Thus, the electrical signal cannot be transferred directly from one neuron to another, or from one neuron to a target cell. Instead, there is always a tiny gap between the end of one neuron's axon and the next cell in line. That gap is called a **synapse**. Electrical signals cannot "jump over" the synapse. Thus, something must be done to "carry" the signal across the synapse so that it can travel from the neuron which currently has the signal to the next cell in line. How is that done?

Well, an amazing thing happens when the signal reaches the end of an axon. The end of the axon is full of tiny sacs that contain chemicals which we call **neurotransmitters**. When a signal comes to the end of an axon, a neurotransmitter is released out of the sacs. The neurotransmitter then travels across the synapse, chemically interacting with the cell on the other side of the gap. The interaction between the neurotransmitter and the receiving neuron is used as a means of controlling the signal that it being passed.

How does this interaction control the signal? Well, if you think about it, your receptors are receiving an *enormous* amount of information all of the time. If all of the information from those receptors was sent to the brain, you would constantly be distracted by useless information. Things that you regularly ignore (a tight watch band, the color of the walls, etc.) would constantly distract you. Thus, based on the "importance" of the signal being processed at the synapse, the neurotransmitter might just pass the signal along, it might stop the signal altogether, or it might reduce the strength of the signal. All of this is done in a carefully controlled way so that the brain gets enough information to control the body but not too much information.

Pretty amazing, isn't it? I want to try to make it clear how complicated this is and how well our nervous system does its job. Suppose, for example, that you are running a race against several other athletes. The beginning of the race is always the same. The runners kneel at the starting line, tense up, and wait for the starter to fire his or her pistol. When the runners hear the pistol fire, they all take off as fast as they can. Especially for short races, the race is often won or lost at the start. If a runner can get off the starting line faster than his or her competitors, he or she can win the race right then and there.

Now think about this process in terms of the nervous system. The runner is tensed and poised to begin. He or she is just waiting to hear the gun. When the gun fires, the sound is converted to an electrical signal by complex processes which occur in the ear. That signal then travels along a nerve towards the brain. This is done by each neuron receiving the signal, sending it down the axon, and releasing a neurotransmitter. If the signal is strong enough (and thus too important to be ignored), the neurotransmitter then travels across the synapse to the next neuron and creates a new electrical signal in that neuron. The whole process then starts over again with the next neuron on the way to the brain.

Once the signal reaches the brain, it is then processed by several thousands of neurons. The end result is that the neurons decide whether or not this is the sound for which the runner has been waiting. The neurons in the brain then release a series of signals destined for the muscle cells in the arms, legs, and other parts of the body. These signals leave the brain and travel from neuron to neuron as described previously. However, this process is even more complicated, because the signals must be routed by the neurons to the proper muscle cells. The signals meant for the muscle cells in the arms must get to the muscle cells in the arms. Thus, the neurons not only do all of the passing that I described in the previous paragraph, but they also analyze the signals to determine their ultimate destination, and then they route the signals to the next neuron in that direction! When the signals finally reach the last neuron in the chain, they go through the final conversion from an electrical signal to neurotransmitter, and the neurotransmitter travels across the synapse to the muscle cell. The muscle cell responds to the neurotransmitter, and the race is on!

Now think about this process for a moment. Literally millions of neurons are involved in it. Neuron after neuron passes signals either from the ear to the brain or from the brain to the muscles. Each time the signal steps from one neuron to another, the signal must be converted from electrical energy to chemicals and then back to electrical energy. The neurons in the brain must process the signals they receive so that they recognize that it is the sound the runner is waiting for, and then they determine what signals to send to the muscles. The neurons involved in passing the signals from the brain to the muscles must not only pass the signals along, but send them each along the correct route until they reach their intended destination. Now think about this. *The entire process as I just described it takes about one tenth of one second!* The most powerful computer designed by humankind would be *millions* of times slower at processing the same information and sending out the same signals!

That gives you some idea of how elegantly designed the human nervous system is! However, that's not the end of the story. Remember from the introduction that the neurons represent only about one-third of the total number of cells in the brain. The other two-thirds of the cells are neuroglia. In the entire nervous system, which includes all of the nerves that run throughout the body, there are *nine times* as many neuroglia as neurons. What do these cells do? They support the neurons. What does that mean? It means they perform tasks that make it possible for the neurons to do their jobs.

Here's an example of how the neuroglia support the neurons. Have you ever noticed how a young baby's arms and legs tend to wave aimlessly and that the baby has little control over them? That's because the signals are not traveling down the baby's axons as quickly as they need to for proper control. This is due to the fact that the myelin sheath is not fully formed at birth. Remember, the myelin sheath increases the speed at which signals can travel down the axon. As the baby matures, the myelin sheath will form, and the baby will gain full control of his arms and legs. Well, guess what kinds of cells are in the myelin sheath. Neuroglia cells. In this case, then, the neuroglia help increase the speed at which a signal can travel down an axon. Of course, this is just one of the many support functions performed by the neuroglia.

ON YOUR OWN

16.1 An electrical signal is traveling towards the cell body of a neuron. Is it traveling along a dendrite or an axon?

16.2 A neuron can stay alive even if it cannot make neurotransmitters. However, it is essentially useless without them. Why?

The Basic Layout of the Human Nervous System

The neuron is the basic unit of the **nervous system**. The brain is made up of one hundred billion of them. Of course, the brain would be essentially useless without a means of getting its signals to all parts of the body. Thus, other neurons form "cords" that snake through the entire body. Those cords are called **nerves**. Nerves are bundles of neurons that carry signals to and from the brain as discussed in the previous section. Figure 16.4 gives you an idea of how all of this is arranged in the body.

FIGURE 16.4
The Human Nervous System

Illus. from the MasterClips collection

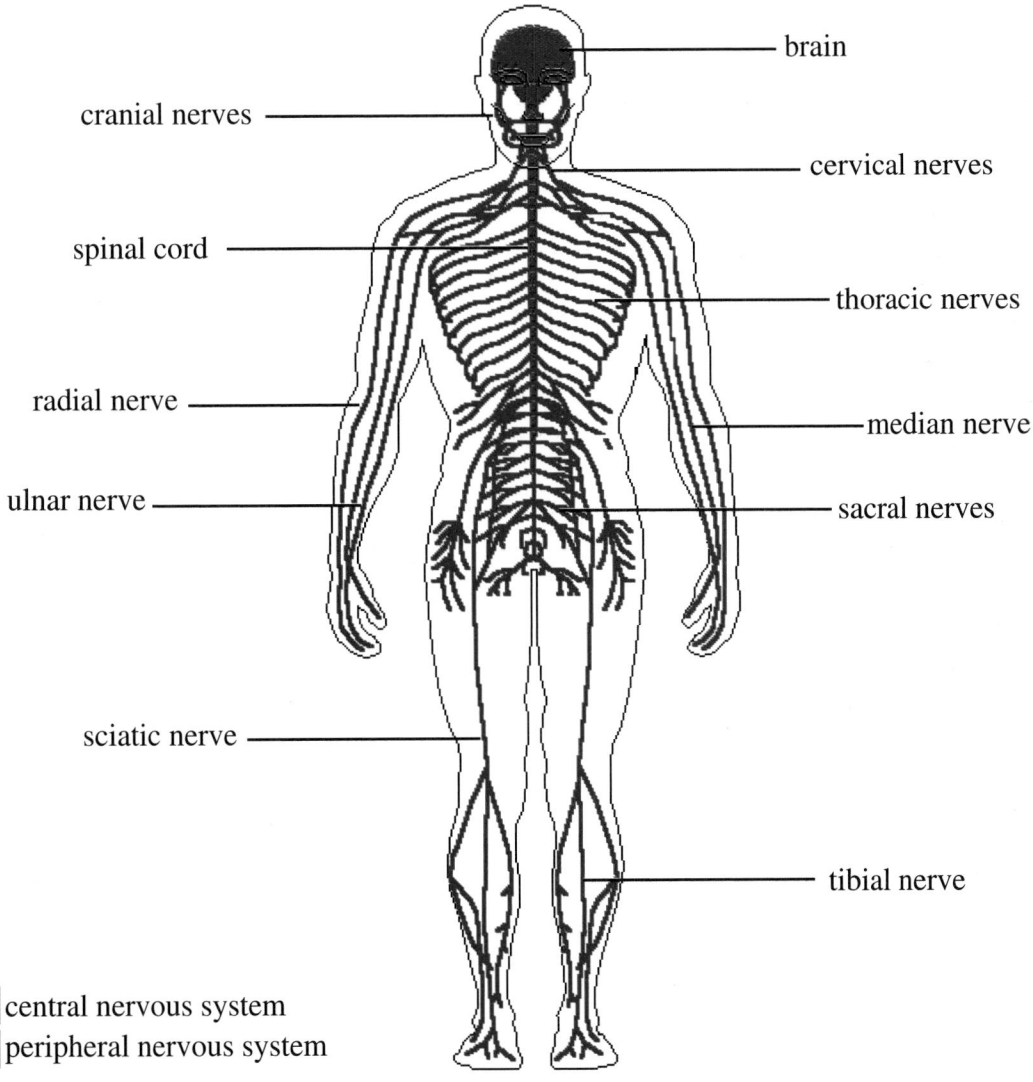

There are many more nerves in the human body than those pictured here. In fact, if you were to take every nerve in the body and lay them all end-to-end, the resulting "string" of nerves would be roughly 93,000 miles long! The nerves pictured in the figure, then, are simply the major nerves in the body. Now don't worry, I am not going to make you memorize them! I just wanted to give you an idea of the layout.

The human nervous system is split into two components: the **central nervous system** (CNS) and the **peripheral nervous system** (PNS). The CNS is composed of the brain and the spinal cord, while the PNS contains all of the other nerves of the body. The spinal cord is actually the biggest nerve in the body. It is of major importance, because signals coming from and going out to the PNS must travel through the spinal cord. If the spinal cord gets injured, then, the brain can lose control of entire sections of the body. As a result, God has protected the spinal cord by embedding it in the backbone, which is called the **vertebral** (ver' tuh bral) **column**.

The vertebral column is made up of bones called **vertebrae** (ver' tuh bruh) which are stacked on top of one another. Washer joints in between the vertebrae give the backbone flexibility. The vertebrae each have a hole in the center which lines up with the holes in the other vertebrae. These holes form a tunnel which the spinal cord passes through. Since the vertebrae are made of bone, the vertebral column forms a very safe, protected "shell" around the spinal cord. Now remember, animals with backbones are called "vertebrates." As you might imagine, then, all vertebrates have a spinal cord.

Although the spinal cord is an incredibly important part of the nervous system, the brain is an even more important part. It also has protection: the skull. The brain sits inside the skull, and the bones of the skull protect it from harm. Believe it or not, however, the skull is not the only source of protection for the brain.

The brain actually floats in the skull, which contains about half a cup of a fluid. This same fluid is found surrounding the spinal cord, so it is called **cerebrospinal** (sir ee' broh spine' uhl) **fluid**. This colorless fluid is actually produced by neuroglia in the brain and contains several chemicals. These chemicals include glucose, proteins for many different functions, and lymphocytes which guard against infection.

Although the cerebrospinal fluid provides chemicals to the brain, its main function is protection. Since the brain is floating in the fluid, the fluid serves to absorb and disperse blows that would otherwise harm the brain. Thus, the cerebrospinal fluid acts a bit like Styrofoam "peanuts" that people use in packaging materials. If you were to send a delicate vase to someone via mail, you would be careful to pack it in a thick layer of Styrofoam peanuts, knowing that the peanuts will absorb bumps and blows that would otherwise break the vase. Well, the cerebrospinal fluid does the same thing for the brain!

What does the human brain actually look like? Figure 16.5 gives you two different views of the brain.

Illus. from the MasterClips collection

FIGURE 16.5
The Human Brain

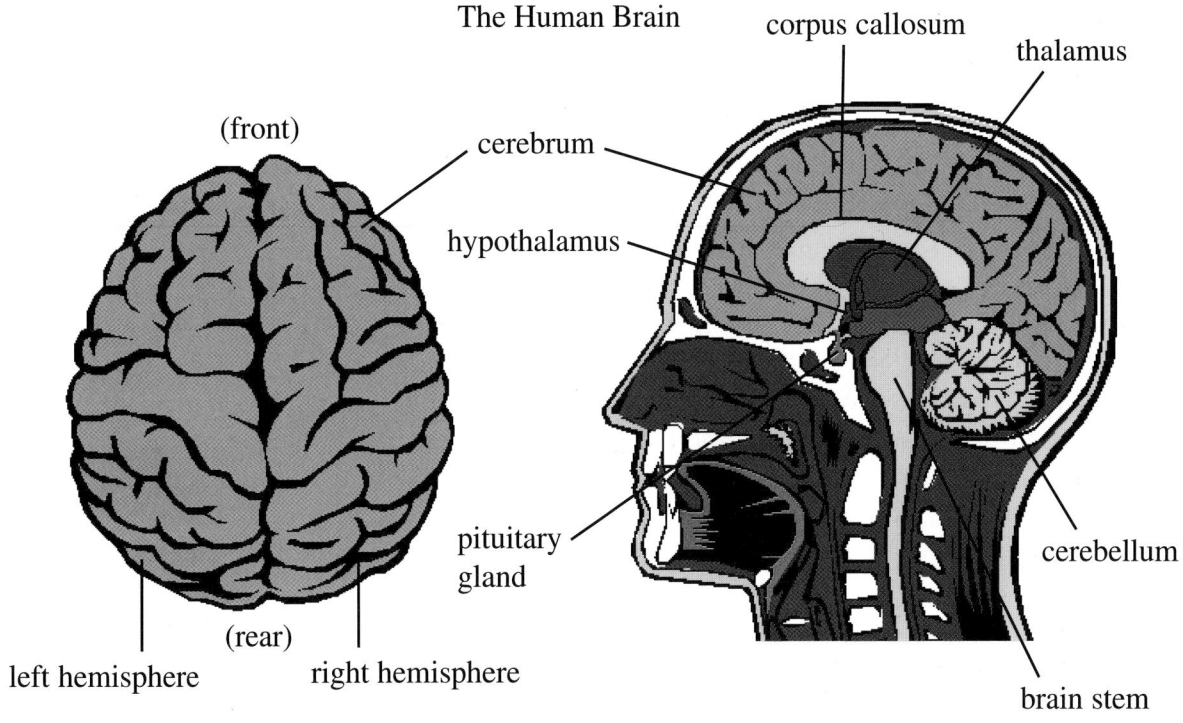

On the left-hand side of the figure, you are looking down on the brain from above. In this view, it is easy to see that the brain is divided into halves, which we call **hemispheres**. Interestingly enough, each side of the brain actually controls one side of the body. The right side of the brain controls the peripheral nervous system (PNS) on the *left* side of the body, and the left side of the brain controls the PNS on the *right* side of the body.

On the right-hand side of the figure, you are looking at a "slice" of the brain from the side. We call this a **cross-section**, and it mimics what you would see if we cut the person's brain in half right between the hemispheres and then looked at it from the side. Notice that in this view, there are some easily-identifiable structures. First of all, the gray, folded tissue that surrounds the outside of the brain is called the **cerebrum**. On the left-hand side of the figure, you only see the gray cerebrum. On the right-hand side of the figure, you can see that the cerebrum is simply the "outer layer" of the brain.

The cerebrum deals with what is often called "higher-level" brain functions. These include interpreting the signals sent from the various receptors in the body, reasoning, and memory. The tissue of the cerebrum is different depending on where you look. The outer layer of the cerebrum is covered in **gray matter**. Gray matter is composed almost exclusively of the cell bodies of neurons. Underneath the cerebrum's gray matter is **white matter**. This tissue is composed mostly of the axons of the neurons in the gray matter. The lighter color of white matter comes from the myelin which covers the axons. One of the best examples of white matter in the brain is the **corpus** (kor' pus) **callosum** (kuh la' sum), which allows the two hemispheres of the brain to exchange information.

The **cerebellum** (se ruh bel' uhm) is located in the lower portion and to the back of the brain. Its main job is to coordinate the voluntary muscles so that the body moves as instructed by the cerebrum. The finer the movement of the muscles, the more the cerebellum is involved. For example, suppose you are trying to aim a rifle at a target. The cerebellum receives signals from the cerebrum, processes those signals, and then sends detailed signals back to the muscles instructing them to move. The cerebrum receives signals from the eyes indicating how well the rifle has been aimed, and then it sends new instructions to the cerebellum. The cerebellum interprets those instructions and sends signals to the muscles to adjust so that the rifle is better aimed. This "back and forth" between the eye, cerebrum, cerebellum, and muscles continues until the cerebrum is satisfied that the rifle is aimed at the target.

The **brain stem** is right next to the cerebellum. There are actually several parts to the brain stem, but I don't want to go into that much detail. The brain stem is the general term for the area between the **thalamus** and the spinal cord. It controls the more basic functions of the human body, such as breathing, heart rate, and the pressure at which blood is pumped through the body.

The thalamus which I mentioned above acts much like a relay station in the brain. Most of the receptors in the body send their information to the thalamus, and then the thalamus relays that information to the part of the cerebrum that is designed to receive and process it. The cerebrum also sends information back to the thalamus, which the thalamus then routes to other areas of the brain or down the spinal cord for relay to the PNS.

You learned a little about the **hypothalamus** in the previous module. Mostly, however, you learned that it controls the pituitary gland. That is certainly true, but it is only one function that the hypothalamus performs. Typically, we refer to it as the "endocrine function" of the hypothalamus. The hypothalamus, however, also has non-endocrine functions. It regulates thirst, hunger, and body temperature. It also helps initiate the "fight or flight" responses such as the fast heart rate and increased blood flow which occur when we are frightened or angry.

Although I have concentrated on describing the brain and the spinal cord (which make up the CNS), please remember that the PNS is a very important part of the nervous system. After all, without the nerves which run throughout your body, the signals that are generated in the brain and passed down the spinal cord would do little good! Interestingly enough, most nerves in the PNS transmit signals both to and from the brain, while a few transmit signals only one way. For example, the facial nerve sends information from your tongue to your brain, providing you with a sense of taste. In addition, the brain sends signals to the muscles in the face along the same nerve. These signals tell the muscles how to move so that you can express yourself by "making faces." On the other hand, the olfactory nerve transmits signals only from the nose to the brain, giving you your sense of smell. No signals ever travel from the brain to the nose along the olfactory nerve.

ON YOUR OWN

16.3 An unfortunate man is in a car accident and his spinal cord is severed at the waist. Will the man be able to move his arms? What about his legs?

16.4 Although the human brain is significantly more complex than the brains of other vertebrates, the basic layout is the same. However, one part of the brain is *significantly* larger in humans than in any other vertebrates. What part of the brain would you think that is?

Our "Split" Brains

Now that you have a general idea of the basic layout of the nervous system, I want to spend a little more time on the brain itself. After all, it is the most interesting part of the entire system, so it deserves a little more attention. I want to start with the fact that the brain is composed of two hemispheres. As I mentioned in the previous section, they each control the opposite side of the PNS. Thus, the left hemisphere of the brain sends signals to and receives signals from the PNS on the right side of the body. Similarly, the right hemisphere of the brain sends signals to and receives signals from the PNS on the left side of the body.

To see one consequence of our divided brain, perform the following experiment.

EXPERIMENT 16.1
Determining a Person's Dominant Side

Supplies:

- Scissors
- A pencil
- Paper
- A ball (It needs to be small enough to be thrown with one hand, like a baseball, softball, or golf ball.)
- A coin
- Some stairs or porch steps
- A paper towel tube or rolled-up piece of thick paper
- A few people to test (8 years or older)
- A glass

Introduction - Most people have a dominant side in their PNS. For example, most people are right-handed. We would say, then, that their dominant hand is their right hand. What you may not know is that most people also have a dominant foot, eye, and ear. This experiment will help you see some trends in this area. It can be easily expanded into a science fair-type project.

Procedure:

(You will perform this procedure on as many people as you can. Try to make it at least 5 people, but the more you have, the better. DO NOT tell them what you are testing. Just ask them to do the things listed below and compile your results.)

A. Put the scissors, pencil, paper, ball, and paper towel tube on a table in front of the test subject. Ask your subject to cut a medium-sized circle out of the paper. Note which hand the subject uses to work the scissors.
B. After the subject has cut the circle out, ask him or her to write the word "hello" in the center of the circle. Note which hand the subject uses to write.
C. Ask your subject to pick up the ball and throw it to you. Note which hand the subject uses.
D. Put the ball on the ground and ask the subject to kick the ball gently. Note which leg is used.
E. Take your subject to a set of stairs or porch steps and ask him to climb the first step. Note which leg the subject lifts and sets on the step first. Have the subject do this a couple more times and note the first leg lifted each time.
F. Put the coin on the ground and ask the subject to step on it. Note which leg was used.
G. Point to an object a short distance away and ask your subject to look at the object through the paper towel tube. Note which eye the subject uses.
H. Take away the tube and have your subject point to the same object while both eyes stay open. Then ask the subject to close his or her right eye. Ask the subject whether or not his or her finger is still pointing at the object.
I. Ask the subject to open his or her right eye and close his or her left eye. Once again, ask whether or not his or her finger is still pointing at the object. In either this step or the previous step, the subject should have answered "no." Note which eye was *closed* when the subject answered "no."
J. Give the subject a glass and have him or her place it up against a wall. Then tell the subject to listen through the glass to see if he or she hears anything on the other side of the wall. Note which ear is used to press against the glass.

(This ends the tests that you do on each subject.)

K. Look at your results. Steps (A) - (C) test for which hand is dominant. Most likely, the subjects used the same hand in each step. If not, choose the hand they used in 2 of the 3 steps to determine which hand was dominant. How many of the subjects had their right hand dominant? How many had their left hand as dominant? In the overall population, roughly 90% have their right hand dominant.
L. Steps (D) - (F) test the dominance of the legs. Most people will use the same leg in each of the three tests. If not, choose the leg used in 2 of the 3 tests to determine which was dominant. How many people had their right leg dominant? How many had their left leg dominant? Roughly 85% of the population has their right leg dominant.
M. Steps (G) - (I) test which eye is dominant. Most people will have the same eye dominant in each test. If not, call this one "not determined." How many people had their right eye

dominant? How many had their left eye dominant? Roughly 70% of the population has their right eye dominant.

N. The last step determines the dominant ear. How many people had their right ear dominant? How many had their left ear dominant? Roughly 60% of the population has their right ear dominant.

O. Look at the results as a whole. Were there any subjects whose dominant side changed? For example, was there any subject whose dominant hand was their right hand but whose dominant leg was their left leg? These people are in the minority. Most people have the same side dominant for the hand, ear, leg, and eye. However, I myself am one of those exceptions. My right hand, leg, and ear are all dominant, but my left eye is dominant!

The fact that the majority of people are right-handed, right-eyed, right-legged, and right-eared is unique in Creation. All vertebrates have two hemispheres in their brains. However, people are the only vertebrates that tend to have one side (the right side) dominant over the other throughout the entire population. An individual rat, for example, might be right-eyed, but there are roughly as many right-eyed rats as left-eyed ones. Thus, the overall population has no dominant side. Humanity as a whole, however, is mostly right side dominant.

Quite frankly, scientists have no solid explanation as to why. In fact, scientists really have no idea why individuals have a dominant side at all, much less why most people tend to be right side dominant. There are many theories out there, but none of them have enough experimental evidence to back them up. In the end, then, most humans clearly have one side of the PNS dominant over the other, but we really do not know why!

There is another consequence of the fact that our brain is split into two hemispheres. Have you ever heard of a person being "right-brained" or "left-brained?" These terms have arisen as a result of experiments which show that some thinking skills are dominated by the left hemisphere of the cerebrum and some are dominated by the right hemisphere of the cerebrum. For example, the right hemisphere of the cerebrum tends to govern the ability of people to think in terms of shapes and spatial relationships. In addition, the right cerebrum tends to govern whether or not we recognize a face we have seen before. Also, musical abilities tend to come from the right side of the cerebrum. On the other hand, the left side of the cerebrum tends to dominate when it comes to thinking logically, using mathematical skills, and speaking. As a result, people who love science and math tend to be referred to as "left-brained people," while people who are talented at visualizing shapes or playing music tend to be called "right-brained people."

Despite the fact that people tend to have a dominant side to their PNS, and despite the fact that the right brain dominates in some cerebral functions while the left brain dominates in others, it is very important to remember that these two sides of the brain are in constant communication. That's the purpose of the corpus callosum that you learned about in the previous section. Thus, don't start thinking that the brain is split into two *completely separate* halves. The halves do communicate with each other; it just seems that one half tends to take more responsibility for certain functions while the other half takes responsibility for others.

ON YOUR OWN

16.5 Two accident victims are studied. The first has damage to a particular area of the right side of his brain. The second has similar damage to the same general area, but on the left side of his brain. One of the patients has had severe difficulty speaking clearly and understandably since the accident which caused the damage. The other has had no apparent speech problems after the accident. Which one (most likely) is having no speech problems?

The Brain and Blood

Although the brain makes up only 2% of an adult's weight, it uses 20% of the body's blood supply. Why? The reason is simple. It takes an enormous amount of energy to produce electrical signals, manufacture and release neurotransmitters, etc. Combine that with the fact that the brain does all of this so quickly, and you are left with an organ that requires *a lot* of energy. This means that the brain cells need a lot of oxygen and nutrients, which come from the blood supply. Thus, the brain needs a *lot* of blood.

There is, however, a "problem." The neurons of the brain are incredibly specialized cells that do their jobs very well. However, because of their unique nature, many chemicals that are necessary for other body tissues are actually toxic to the neurons of the brain. Although the brain needs lots of blood, its cells can't be exposed to many of the chemicals that are in that blood. This sounds like a real difficult problem, doesn't it? The brain needs blood, but it cannot be exposed to many of the chemicals in that blood. How would you solve such a problem?

The first thing that comes to my mind is to have a *separate* circulatory system for the brain. That way, the body can provide the brain with the blood that it needs without any of the chemicals that it can't have. Now that's a plausible solution, but there are several problems. First of all, there would have to be a separate heart, a separate area in the lungs where the brain's blood is oxygenated, and a separate kidney system to regulate the blood. Also, you would have to figure out how to get that blood to absorb nutrients from the small intestine and be cleaned and managed by the liver without mixing with the other blood supply. That's all really complicated!

Lucky for us, however, that the Designer of the human body is a *lot* smarter than you or me. God has designed an amazingly elegant solution to the problem that seems so daunting to me. He has designed the **blood-brain barrier**. To me, this is one of the most amazing aspects to the human body, yet very few people actually know about it. To best understand what the blood-brain barrier is and how elegantly it solves the problem, you need to be reminded about a few things you should have learned in Module #14.

Remember, our circulatory system is made up of veins, arteries, and capillaries. The capillaries are where blood gives up oxygen and nutrients to the cells while picking up the cells' waste products. That can happen because the walls of capillaries are only one cell thick and there are gaps in between the cells. This allows fluid to "leak" out of the capillaries and bathe the cells. The exchange of gases, nutrients, and waste products is then made possible by this fluid bathing the cells.

If this were to happen in the brain, neurons would die instantly. Thus, brain capillaries are *different* than the capillaries in the rest of the body. Their walls are still only one-cell thick, but there are no gaps in between the cells. In fact, the cells are sealed together by protein fibers. Have you ever heard the phrase, "He blew a gasket?" That actually refers to something which can happen in automobiles. Automobile engines must hold fluid inside certain chambers. These chambers are made from different metal parts which join together. Now if the makers of an engine simply put the metal pieces together and did nothing else, the fluid would leak out in between the parts where the metal pieces are joined. To prevent that, a piece of rubber called a **gasket** is placed between the pieces of metal before they are joined. The rubber seals the metal junction, and keeps the fluid from leaking out. When an automobile "blows a gasket," that rubber seal bursts, and the fluid starts leaking out. In the blood-brain barrier, proteins form gaskets in between the cells that line the capillaries, keeping the fluid in the capillaries from leaking out.

That's all well and good. It keeps the blood from exposing the brain cells to many harmful chemicals. Of course, it could also keep the blood from giving the brain cells what they need. After all, if the brain cells are separated from the blood in the capillaries, they can't get any of the things they need from the blood, can they? Yes they can! This is the real beauty of the blood-brain barrier. The cells that line these capillaries have special chemical processes which *transport* the things that the brain needs out of the blood. Each of the cells that line the capillaries, then, can be thought of as a watchdog. When a cell "sees" things that the brain needs (water, oxygen, and glucose), it transports them through the cell. Other molecules, however, are recognized as bad for the brain and they are not transported. Isn't that amazing?

Not all toxins are held back by the blood-brain barrier. For example, certain drugs can pass through the blood-brain barrier and wreak havoc on the brain cells. People who use illegal drugs looking for a "high" do not realize that they are getting around a system that God has designed to protect very sensitive brain cells. As a result, most illegal drugs that affect the brain also kill brain cells. That's one reason the term "dope" has been used to describe illegal drugs. Many of the popular illegal drugs kill brain cells, turning habitual users into dopes! Alcohol also passes through the blood-brain barrier. It passes through as easily as water, but is not good for brain tissue. Recent studies have indicated that teens who drink alcohol have trouble with memory functions and learning.

ON YOUR OWN

16.6 Would the blood-brain barrier work without the proteins in between the capillary cells? Why or why not?

The Peripheral Nervous System (PNS)

So far, I have concentrated on the brain in this module. Mostly, that's because the brain is the most important part of the nervous system. To some extent, it's also because I find the brain the most interesting part of the nervous system. However, I do want to spend the rest of this module emphasizing several parts of the PNS. In this section, I want to give you a little more general information about the PNS, and then I want to discuss specifically how the PNS works together with the brain to give us the five major senses - taste, smell, vision, touch, and hearing.

As you already know, the PNS is made up of those nerves which run off of the central nervous system (CNS). At this point, it is important to make a distinction which I have so far avoided. As I told you previously, the nerves in the PNS are made up of neurons. However, the term **nerve** has a very specific meaning to scientists. A nerve is made up of dendrites and axons, not the cell bodies of neurons. The cell bodies of neurons typically cluster together in groups. These groups are called **ganglia** (gan' glee uh). When several ganglia cluster together, it is called a **plexus**, which many people call a "nerve center." Interestingly enough, there are many animals (earthworms and shrimp, for example) that don't have real brains. Instead, they have ganglia and plexi (plural of plexus) that control their nervous systems.

The PNS is composed of three main divisions: **the autonomic** (aw toh nom' ik) **nervous system, the sensory nervous system,** and **the motor nervous system**.

Autonomic nervous system - The system of nerves which carries instructions from the CNS to the body's smooth muscles, cardiac muscle and glands

Sensory nervous system - The system of nerves which carries information from the body's receptors to the CNS

Motor nervous system - The system of nerves which carries instructions from the CNS to the skeletal muscles

I want to discuss each one of these systems briefly, just so you have some idea of what's involved with each of them.

The autonomic nervous system is by far the most fascinating component of the PNS, because it regulates the automatic processes which keep the body going. The rate and strength of the heartbeat, relaxation and contraction of smooth muscles, and the functions of many glands are all controlled by the autonomic nervous system. Information about these processes is sent to the CNS and is evaluated by the hypothalamus, brain stem, and in some cases, the spinal cord. Based on the results of the evaluation, instructions are then sent to the heart muscle, smooth muscles, and glands. This continuous monitoring, evaluation, and issuing of instructions happens throughout the body, without any conscious thought on our part!

The autonomic nervous system is composed of two parts: the **sympathetic division** and the **parasympathetic division**. These two divisions are made up of completely different nerves and ganglia and counterbalance each other in many ways. The sympathetic division increases the rate and strength of the heartbeat and raises the blood pressure. It also stimulates the liver to release more glucose in the blood, producing quick energy for the "fight or flight" response that we experience when we are frightened or angry. The parasympathetic system, on the other hand, slows the heart rate and lowers the blood pressure. In addition, it takes care of certain "housekeeping" activities such as causing the stomach to churn while it is digesting a meal. To get a quick understanding of the difference between the sympathetic and parasympathetic divisions of the autonomic nervous system, perform the following experiment.

EXPERIMENT 16.2

The Pupil of the Eye

Supplies

- A mirror
- A room with a light switch that when closed off gets *really* dark
- A candle
- Matches

Introduction - The two divisions of the nervous system tend to counterbalance one another. You will see this effect in the following experiment.

Procedure:

A. Go into a room that can be closed off and gets really dark. If you have a bathroom with a mirror which either has no window or has an easily-covered window, that is ideal.
B. Close the door but keep the light on.
C. Use the matches to light the candle. **BE CAREFUL!!! OPEN FLAMES ALWAYS HOLD AN ELEMENT OF RISK!!!**
D. Turn off the lights. The room should be completely dark except for the light from the candle.
E. Look at your face in the mirror, concentrating on just one eye.
F. Move the candle around so that you have enough light to see one eye reasonably well, but the candle is as far away as possible. **BE CAREFUL!! IF YOU HOLD THE CANDLE TOO CLOSE, YOU CAN BURN YOURSELF OR SET YOUR HAIR ON FIRE!**
G. Concentrate on the dark circle at the center of your eye. This is called your **pupil**. Notice its size. Look at it for 15 seconds or so.
H. Without changing anything else and without looking away, turn on the lights or have someone do it for you.
I. As the lights come on, watch your pupil. You should see a change.
J. If you did not see a change, try again, really concentrating on your pupil. If you have very dark eyes, you might want to watch someone else while they do the experiment, as it might be hard for you to determine where your pupil ends and the rest of the eye begins.
K. Blow out the candle and put it away.

What did you see in the experiment? You should have seen your pupil get smaller when the light was turned on. Your eye's main function is to collect light. Light enters the eye through the pupil. The larger the pupil, the more light that gets into the eye. When the surroundings are bright, the pupil needs to be small so that only a fraction of the incoming light actually gets into the eye. Otherwise, the eye would become *overloaded* with light. However, as the surroundings get darker, the eye needs to let in more light so that it can still get enough information to send to your brain. Thus, it makes the pupil bigger so that more light can come in.

When the room was dark except for the candle, there was little light striking your eyes. As a result, your autonomic nervous system caused your eye's pupil to open wide, accepting a large fraction of that light in. When you turned on the lights, suddenly a LOT more light started striking your eyes. The sensory nervous system sensed that your eye would be damaged if all of that light was allowed in for a long period of time, so the pupil closed down, and you should have seen it get smaller. You know that this was all a part of the autonomic nervous system's work, because you did not have to think about doing it. It simply happened automatically.

The reason I wanted you to do the experiment, however, was to illustrate the difference between the sympathetic and parasympathetic divisions of the autonomic nervous system. The sympathetic division of the autonomic nervous system is what caused your pupil to get large. The technical way to say it is that the sympathetic division **dilated** the pupil. When the sensory nervous system reported that too little light was getting to the eye, the sympathetic division contracted smooth muscles in the iris which then dilated the pupil. In contrast, the parasympathetic division took over when you turned the light on. When the sensory nervous system reported that too much light was getting in the eye, the parasympathetic division worked other smooth muscles in the iris, causing the pupil to constrict (get smaller).

The motor nervous system controls the voluntary muscles in the body. When you decide that it is time to turn the page in this book, for example, your brain sends signals along the motor nervous system. These signals cause the skeletal muscles in your arm and hand to contract and relax in such a way that you move your hand, grab the page, and turn it. Now, of course, while the motor nervous system is being utilized in such a way, the autonomic nervous system doesn't stop working! That's one of the amazing aspects of the human nervous system. There is no way that even the fastest computer known to man can perform as quickly as even *one part* of the human nervous system. Nevertheless, the human nervous system can handle *several parts* working simultaneously at high efficiency!

The sensory nervous system sends information to the CNS from all of the receptors scattered throughout the body. These signals are absolutely necessary for us to be able to respond to the changes that occur in our surroundings (the third criterion for life). For example, consider the act of walking outside of your home. You use your motor nervous system to contract and relax your skeletal muscles so that you can walk, open the door, and go outside. All of the while, of course, your autonomic nervous system is making your heart, blood vessels, internal organs, and glands work properly. Once you get outside, however, you may notice that it is cold. This happens because your skin's receptors send signals to the brain via the sensory nervous system indicating that the outside temperature is too low. This causes your brain to form the thought "it's cold." You can then choose to use your motor nervous system to go back inside and get a coat. Whether or not you do that, your autonomic nervous system has already kicked into action, increasing heart rate and blood pressure in an attempt to keep your insides warm. In the next few sections, I will concentrate solely on the sensory nervous system.

ON YOUR OWN

16.7 When you get cold and your autonomic nervous system increases your heart rate and blood pressure, which division (parasympathetic or sympathetic) is causing the change?

The Human Sense of Taste

When you eat food, you taste it. The foods that you like "taste good," while the foods that you don't like "taste bad." Why do we have this sense? Well, there are at least two reasons. First, God wants his people to enjoy themselves (within limits) while here on earth. Food is one source of enjoyment, so I am sure that part of the reason we have a sense of taste is simply so that we can enjoy eating. However, there is a biological reason for taste as well. When something tastes bad, we usually try to avoid eating it. Our brain has been programmed to respond to many toxic substances as "bad tasting." As a result, we avoid eating them. This helps protect us. This biological reason is especially important in animals. Animals avoid things that are bad for them based to a large extent on taste.

What gives us this sense of taste? The answer is simple. Our sense of taste comes from our tongue. If you stick your tongue out and look at it in the mirror, you will see tiny "bumps." These bumps are called **papillae** (puh pill' ee). On the sides and at the base of these papillae rest microscopic clusters of cells called **taste buds**. These cells have tiny "hairs" which are sensitive to certain chemicals. When those chemicals are detected in your saliva, the taste bud cells send signals along the sensory nerves in the tongue to your cerebrum. The brain then gives you a taste sensation, which can be either bad or good, depending on many factors.

Believe it or not, it is thought that people have only four basic senses of taste: sweet, sour, salty, and bitter. The overall taste sensation that you get when eating any food is simply the sum of these four basic tastes. It turns out that the taste buds which are most sensitive to these four tastes are located primarily in different places on the tongue. As a result, it is possible to "map" your tongue to locate the different concentrations of taste buds. Perform the following experiment to map the taste buds on your own tongue.

EXPERIMENT 16.3
Mapping Your Taste Buds

Supplies:

- Salt
- Sugar
- Water
- Lemon juice
- Onion juice (Tonic water is a substitute, but it is not as effective. To make onion juice, cut a few slices of onion and put them in a zippered plastic bag. Then strongly press a rolling pin back and forth across the bag several times. In this way, you will squeeze the juice right out of the onion! You do not need a lot of juice.)
- Several toothpicks
- 5 glasses

Introduction - This experiment will allow you to determine where the taste buds are concentrated on your tongue and to what tastes they are sensitive.

Procedure:

A. Make a strong solution of salt water in one of the three glasses. You don't need a lot.
B. Make a strong solution of sugar water in the second glass. You don't need a lot.
C. Pour some lemon juice into another glass. You don't need a lot.
D. Put onion juice in the fourth glass. You don't necessarily need to use a glass here. If you made onion juice according to the instructions above, you can just use the plastic bag.
E. Fill the fifth glass full of water.
F. Take a toothpick and dip it in the salt water. Now, stick out your tongue.
G. Touch the very tip of your tongue with the toothpick. **Touch lightly - don't hurt your tongue!** Note whether or not you taste the salty taste strongly, weakly, or not at all.
H. Dip the toothpick into the salt water again and now touch another part of your tongue - a little to the left and back a bit from the tip. Note whether or not you taste the salty taste strongly, weakly, or not at all.
I. Repeat this several times until you have tested most of the areas of your tongue. Be sure and test all of the way out to the sides of your tongue, and as far back as you can go without gagging. Also, be sure to dip the toothpick back into the solution each time before you use it to touch your tongue. As you do these tests, you should definitely notice that some parts of your tongue give you a strong salty taste, while other parts of your tongue give you little or no salty taste.
J. Draw the shape of your tongue and shade in those areas which gave you a strong salty taste.
K. Now drink the water in the fifth glass to remove any salt taste from your mouth.
L. Repeat steps (F) - (K) for the sugar water, the lemon juice, and the onion juice. For the sugar water, you are trying to taste the sweetness. The lemon juice should provide you with a sour taste for which to test, and the onion juice is a good test for sensitivity to the bitter taste.
M. Clean everything up.

What did your drawings look like in the end? Well, if you are like most people, here's what you should have seen:

FIGURE 16.6

Illus. from the MasterClips collection

The Taste Bud Concentrations in the Human Tongue

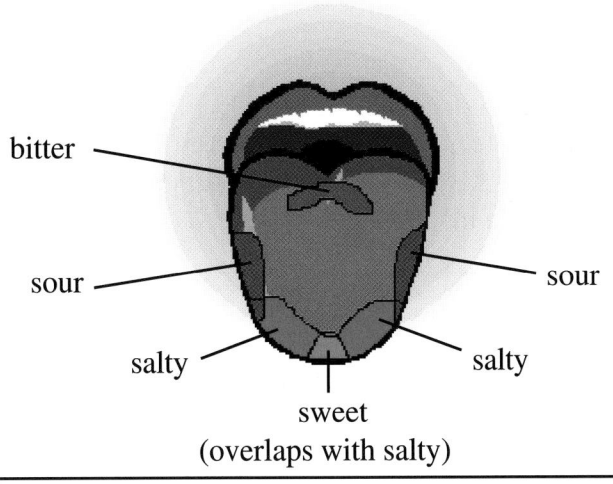

Of course, your experiment might not have produced the same "map" of taste buds, but it certainly should have given you the idea that some parts of your tongue are more sensitive to certain tastes than are others. All of this is due to the fact that your taste buds are concentrated on certain parts of your tongue, and that the different kinds of taste buds that are sensitive to different tastes tend to be clustered together. Notice in the illustration above that there is very little taste sensitivity in the center of the tongue. That's because there are few taste buds there. In the same way, the most taste sensitivity is near the front and on the sides of the tongue, because that's where the taste buds seem to be concentrated.

Interestingly enough, the pleasantness of the four basic taste sensations (sweet, sour, bitter, and salty) changes depending on the strength. In general, the sweetness taste gets more and more pleasant the stronger the sweetness is. At some point, many people will say that a taste is too sweet, but the general rule is that the more sweet the taste, the more pleasant it is. For the salty and sour tastes, however, the results are quite different. If something is lightly salted or just a bit sour, it is generally considered pleasant tasting. However, too much salt or too much sourness quickly turns unpleasant. Thus, most people only like the salty and sour tastes when they are relatively weak. The bitter taste is only considered pleasant at the weakest levels. When there is much bitterness at all, the overall effect is unpleasant to most people.

The basic reason for this once again is protection. One set of chemicals that tend to make things taste sour, for example, are called acids. Weak acids are good for us, so we consider their taste pleasant. Orange juice, for example, is considered pleasant tasting because the acid in it is a weak acid, providing a pleasant taste. Orange juice is good for you, so that works out fine. If something contains a strong acid, however, it tastes strongly sour and you will avoid it because the strong sour taste is unpleasant. This is good, because strong acids can be very dangerous if they are ingested.

ON YOUR OWN

16.8 Suppose someone ate food that was way too hot and they severely burned the middle of their tongue. The burn scars up, eliminating most of the living tissue in the center of the tongue. Would the person's sense of taste be strongly affected? Why or why not?

The Human Sense of Smell

I'm sure that at some point in your life, you have put your nose in front of a flower and inhaled the flower's scent deeply. What gives us the sense of smell which allows us to enjoy such an experience? The answer at first glance is easy: the nose. But how does the nose detect smell?

Smell begins as chemicals which are floating in the air. A flower, for example, releases chemicals into the air in order to attract insects or birds. The insects and birds will feed on the flower and, in the process, actually aid the flower in reproduction. You will learn more about that in biology class. When we inhale these chemicals, some of them will touch the roof of the nasal cavity and dissolve in the moist mucus which covers it. Millions of cells line this part of the nose, called the **olfactory** (ol fak' tor ee) **epithelium** (ep' uh theel ee uhm). Some of these cells, called **olfactory sensory cells**, have long "hairs" that stick into the mucus.

When chemicals dissolved in the mucus interact with the "hairs" of the olfactory sensory cells, they cause the cells to generate a signal which gets sent on to the brain. The brain then gives us an impression which we call "smell." The sense of smell, then, has something in common with the sense of taste. They both rely on the interaction between chemicals that make their way into the body and the hairs of certain specialized cells. The sense of smell also tends to work in tandem with the sense of taste. Perform the following experiment to see what I mean.

EXPERIMENT 16.4

The Sense of Smell and the Sense of Taste

Supplies:

- Toothpicks
- Apple
- Onion
- Blindfold
- A person to help you
- A knife
- Two paper towels

Introduction - The sense of smell affects the sense of taste. This experiment will demonstrate that fact for most people.

Procedure:

A. Make sure that your helper is not in the room when you start this experiment.
B. Cut a few bite-sized pieces from both the apple and the onion.
C. Put the pieces on a paper towel and cover them with the other paper towel.
D. Put away the rest of the apple and onion so that your helper has no idea what you have been cutting up. This is very important.
E. Blindfold your helper and have your helper pinch his or her nose to make sure he or she cannot smell.
F. Use the toothpick to spear one of the pieces and feed it to your helper. Ask him or her to identify the food by taste. Do not give him or her any hints. If he or she cannot identify the taste, don't worry about it.
G. Do this with three more pieces of food so that your helper has had two onion pieces and two apple pieces. Each time, ask the helper to identify the food by taste.
H. Now repeat steps (F) and (G), but this time allow your helper to stop pinching his or her nose. Let your helper smell the food before he or she tastes it. Once again, ask him or her to identify the food.
I. Clean everything up.

How did your helper do with the identification? Most people will not do well with their nose pinched, because the sense of smell really augments the sense of taste. Remember, we really only taste sweet, sour, bitter, and salty. Most of the rest of our impressions of the "taste" of food come from our sense of smell. Think about it. Have you ever been so sick with a cold that you can't smell anything? When that happens, most people complain that their food just doesn't taste very good. Once again, that's because taste and smell work together to give you an overall impression of food, and you usually think of it as just the food's taste. For some animals, this effect is even more pronounced. Cats, for example, get nearly all of their pleasure from the food's smell, not its taste. That's why they like strong-smelling things like tuna. To them, smell is almost everything.

There is something else in our minds which is strongly connected to our sense of smell. Have you ever noticed that smells can bring back memories? Psychology research has demonstrated that the sense of smell is the most likely sense to bring back memories. Scientists think they know why. The nerves that pass the signals from the olfactory cells to the brain are all a part of the **limbic system**, the part of the brain that deals with memories and emotions. Thus, the sense of smell is very intimately connected with our memories and emotions!

ON YOUR OWN

16.9 An air purifying system claims to clean "all of the chemicals" out of the air and leave behind a "pleasant scent" like that after a thunderstorm. What is wrong with this claim?

The Human Sense of Vision

I truly wish I could spend an entire module (perhaps more) solely on your sense of vision. Of all the wonderfully designed organs of your body, the eye is probably eclipsed only by the brain. Since the eye and the brain must work in tandem to give you your sense of vision, together they form the most remarkable system in all of Creation! To give you an idea of just how amazing this all is, consider a very simplified sketch of the human eye.

Illus. from the MasterClips collection

FIGURE 16.7
The Human Eye

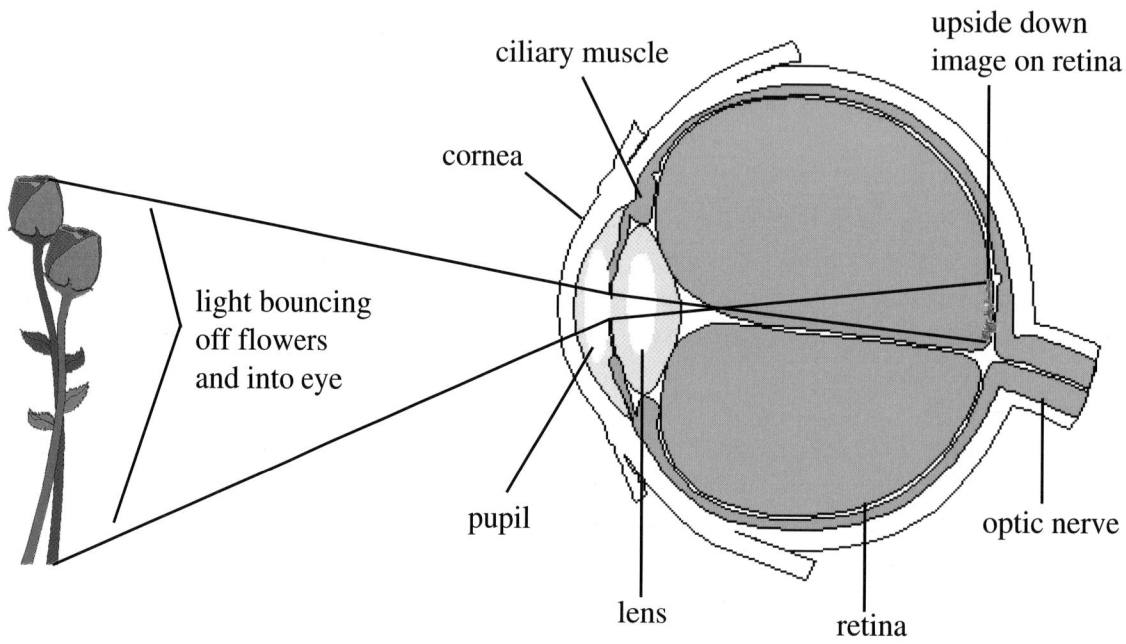

As I told you in an earlier section, the eye's function is to collect light. In order for us to see an object (like the flowers in the figure), light must bounce off the object and enter the eye. When light strikes the eye, it first passes through the transparent **cornea**. The cornea is covered with a very thin layer of clear tissue which is kept moist and clean because each blink of the eye washes it in tears produced by the lacrimal glands, which you learned about in the previous module. The light then passes through a clear liquid called the "aqueous humor" and then through the **pupil**. As you already learned, the pupil is controlled by the autonomic nervous system, automatically opening wide or closing down depending on the amount of light present. The light then passes through the **lens**, which is what the eye uses to focus the image onto the **retina**.

I want to spend at least a moment on the way that the eye focuses objects onto the retina. Have you ever watched a photographer operate a camera with a manual focus? If you have, then you have seen the photographer twisting the lens of the camera back and forth. Why does he do that? Well, in order to get a good picture, the image that he is trying to photograph must be focused precisely onto the film in the camera. When the photographer twists the lens, he is not actually twisting it. Instead, he is *moving* it back and forth. In a camera, the photographer changes the focus by moving the lens. When the lens is close to the film, it focuses objects near to the camera onto the film. When the lens is far from the film, it focuses objects far from the camera onto the film. Thus, the focus of a camera is changed by moving the position of the lens relative to the film.

That works quite well for a camera, but it would be an incredibly inefficient design for a person! Why? Well, a person needs to change the focus of his or her eye quickly. It takes time to move a lens back and forth. Also, if the lens moves, there must be room for it to move. In cameras, the lens moves back and forth within a tube that is on the front of the camera. The larger the range of focus you want, the larger the tube has to be. To give us the range that we need for focusing by that method, human eyes would have to have their lenses mounted on long tubes that would stick out of the eye. How weird would that be?

So the eye needs to focus the light from the object onto the retina, but doing so by moving the lens is simply too inefficient. How does the eye do it? It *changes the shape of the lens itself*! The lens is attached to a smooth muscle called the **ciliary** (sil' ee air ee) **muscle**. When this circular muscle is relaxed, it automatically pulls on the lens so that the lens is thin. This causes the eye to focus far away objects onto the retina. If the eye needs to focus on objects nearby, the ciliary muscle contracts, and the lens becomes fat. This mode of focusing is *significantly* more efficient than that which can be achieved by the best cameras made in the world!

Think about it. You are sitting down reading this book, focusing on the words you are reading. Suddenly, your mom calls you. You look up, and she is standing at the other end of the room. You focus on her even before you realize it! As far as you are concerned, your focus changes instantaneously. Now think about how long it would take a camera (even one with automatic focus) to do this. Suppose you are trying to take a picture of this page and then suddenly decide to surprise your mom across the room by taking a picture of her. How long would it take to get the camera to change its focus? Well, at least half a second, probably more. That is *hundreds of times slower* than the speed at which you can change the focus of your eyes!

Notice in the figure that once the image actually does get focused on the retina, it is upside down. This is a consequence of how the light travels through the lens. The reason we don't actually see things upside down is that while we are infants, we learn to link the image we see on the retina to the object in the outside world. Since we spend time as infants touching everything, we learn the correct orientation of everything, so we become accustomed to flipping the image in our mind so that we see right side up. The actual images on our retina, however, are upside down.

Okay, so now we know how an image gets focused on our retina. How does that allow us to see? Well, the retina is filled with specialized cells called **rods** and **cones**. Each of these cells has as many as 100 million molecules which are sensitive to light. The cones have molecules sensitive to three colors of light, while the rods have molecules sensitive only to light in general, not any particular color. The rods are highly sensitive to light and can react to even tiny amounts.

When there is little light, your eyes rely mostly on the rods of the retina to form images. When there is a reasonable amount of light, the cones play a more important role.

When the molecules within the rods and cones are struck by light, they set off a complex chain of chemical reactions in the cell. These chemical reactions eventually form an electrical signal, which travels down a nerve fiber and eventually into the **optic nerve**. As the signal travels towards the brain, it is partly analyzed by ganglia that exist along the way. Eventually, these "preprocessed" signals reach the cerebrum where the information is analyzed in many different parts of the brain. The brain then puts all of this information together and produces an image for you. Okay, now here's the really amazing part: all of this happens in less than *one thousandth of one second!*

Think about that for a minute. When light hits the retina of the eye, it causes millions of cells to turn on complicated chemical machinery that send signals down roughly 125 million nerves. As these 125 million signals travel down the nerves, each signal gets preprocessed by the neurons along the way. All 125 million signals get routed to the *correct* parts of the cerebrum based on the information they carry, and then the brain analyzes each signal and adds the information together to form an image in your mind. This image is sharper, clearer, and better resolved than the image produced by the best camera in the world, and all of this happens in *less than a thousandth of a second*! There is no computer today, nor any computer than any applied scientist can envision, which can process so many signals so accurately so quickly. In fact, it has been estimated that it would take a Cray supercomputer (the most powerful computer in the world) *one hundred years* of computer time to simulate what takes place *each second* in the eye and brain. How in the world can anyone believe that such a system developed by chance?

There is one more thing I want you to learn about the eye before I move on to the next section. Notice that the optic nerve enters through the back of the eye. At the point where the optic nerve enters the eye, there are no rods and cones on the retina. What is the result? Perform the following experiment to find out.

EXPERIMENT 16.5
The Human Blind Spot

Supplies:

- Two sheets of paper
- A black marker or pen

Introduction - The human eye has no rods and cones at the point where the optic nerve enters the eye. This creates a minor problem which will be demonstrated in this experiment.

Procedure:

A. On the first sheet of paper, draw a dot that is about 1/8 of an inch across and to the left of the center of the page.

B. About 4 and one-half inches to the right of the dot, draw a plus sign that is roughly the same size. In the end, what you have drawn should look like what you see below:

C. Hold the paper away from you at arm's length.
D. Close your left eye, and look at the dot, not the plus sign. Even though you are looking at the dot, you can still see the plus sign, right? That's because your eye is accepting enough light so that light bouncing off of the plus sign is still getting to your retina. Thus, you are still seeing it.
E. While constantly looking at the dot, slowly pull the paper closer and closer to your face until it essentially touches your nose. What eventually happens to the plus sign? DON'T LOOK AT IT - JUST BE AWARE OF IT.
F. If you do not see an effect the first time, try again. Keep looking at the dot, but be aware of the plus sign.
G. If you want, you can reverse the procedure for the other eye. Just close your right eye and focus on the plus sign. You should now see the same thing happen to the dot as you pull the paper closer and closer to your face.
H. On the other piece of paper, draw two solid rectangles with a space in between them. Each rectangle should be one-fourth of an inch high, and inch and one-half long, and there should be about a one-eighth inch space in between.
I. To the right of both rectangles draw a dot like the one you drew before. It should look like this:

J. Once again, hold the paper at arm's length.
K. Close your right eye.
L. Focus on the dot.
M. Pull the paper slowly towards your face. Be aware of the rectangles. What happens?

What did you see in the experiment? In the first part, you should have seen the plus sign disappear as you moved the paper towards your face. As you kept moving, it should have re-appeared. Why did that happen? Well, as you moved the paper towards your face, you eventually reached the point at which the plus sign was being focused right where the optical nerve enters your eye. At that point, there are no rods and cones, so although the image was focused there, you did not see anything, because there were no rods and cones there to detect the light! That's the blind spot in your eye. As you moved the paper even closer, the plus sign moved to another location on the retina, and you started seeing it again.

Now realize that the blind spot is not a problem under normal circumstances, because when *both* of your eyes are open, one eye will be able to see what is in the other eye's blind spot. As a result, you can see through a whole range of vision without interruption. You can confirm this yourself by repeating the experiment. When the plus sign disappears, open your other eye and see what happens. It reappears! The blind spot, then, is only a problem when one of your eyes is shut or does not work.

The second part of the experiment gives you an idea of how the brain deals with the blind spot in each eye. As you pulled the paper closer to your face, you should have seen the space in between the rectangles actually go away. At that point, the two rectangles should have appeared as one big rectangle. Why? Well, at that point, the space in between the rectangles was being focused on your blind spot. Thus, the light from it was not generating any signals. However, on both sides of the blind spot, your brain was receiving signals indicating that there were black rectangles on the paper. Thus, the brain assumed that the rectangles were actually one big rectangle and thus "filled in" what it thought "should" be in the blind spot. As a result, the two small rectangles became one larger one.

I want to give you one more fact about how your brain and your eyes work together to give you your sense of vision. Look at the figure below.

FIGURE 16.8
Circles

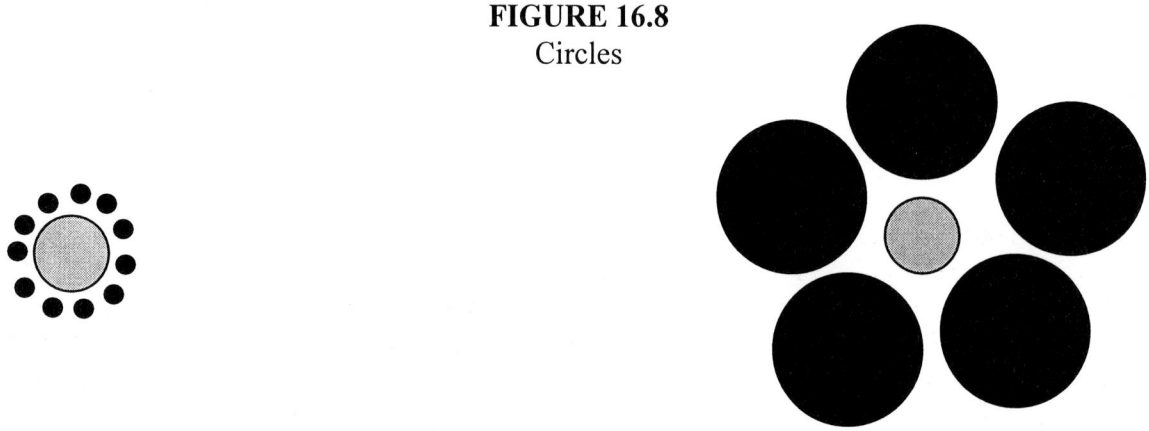

Which gray circle is bigger? Most people will say that the one on the left is. That's not true. They are both exactly the same size. Get out a ruler and see for yourself! Why do you perceive the circle on the left to be bigger? Because it is surrounded by smaller circles. The brain judges size (in part) by comparing the object in question to other objects. Since the gray circle on the left is so much larger than the black circles surrounding it, the brain judges it to be a large circle. Since the gray circle on the right is smaller than the circles surrounding it, the brain judges it to be a small circle. As a result, the brain thinks that the gray circle on the left is larger than the gray circle on the right, even though they are exactly the same size.

Have you ever seen the moon when it is low on the horizon. It looks huge compared to what it normally looks like in the sky, doesn't it? Most people think that this is because the moon is closer to the earth. That's not at all true! It is part of an eye/brain interaction, similar to the one in the figure above. When the moon is close to the horizon, the brain has plenty of things with which to compare it in terms of size. Thus, the brain gives you an accurate view of the moon's size in the sky. When the moon is high in the sky, the brain has nothing with which to compare it. Since the sky is vast and black, the brain assumes that the moon is small, and you perceive it that way. In fact, the moon's apparent size when it is near the horizon is more correct than its apparent size when it is high in the sky! Nevertheless, the *actual* size of the moon in the sky varies only a little throughout the year. When it is on the horizon, it is essentially the same size as when it is high in the sky.

Before I leave this section on the eye, you might be wondering how in the world we see all the incredible colors that we see. After all, I made the statement that your cones are sensitive to only three colors of light. How in the world do we see all of the other colors? Well, I don't want to answer that question in this course. If you take physical science next year, you will learn about it then! That should give you at least one reason to study physical science!

ON YOUR OWN

16.10 Which is more relaxing: focusing on a scene far away or focusing on a picture held in your hand? Why?

16.11 Suppose a person is born with no cone cells. Will the person be able to see? If so, what will be missing?

The Human Sense of Touch

The human sense of touch is centered on the skin. The skin if full of millions and millions of neurons which are all attached to receptors of different sorts. In order to give you all of the touch sensations that you need, the receptors on the skin are many and varied so that they respond to touch in different ways. Some respond quickly to even the slightest touch. Others are slow to respond and tend to give the nervous system information about alterations in the skin which last a much longer time. Others are quick to respond but only to very strong pressure, such as that caused by a crushing blow. As you learned in Module #11, an object doesn't even have to touch you in order for you to feel it. If something brushes up against the hairs on your skin, receptors at the base of the hair respond to the hair bending and send signals to the brain.

It is quite amazing how all of these receptors and nerves work together. I once listened to a speech given by a medical researcher who was trying to fashion a glove for people with leprosy. If you are not aware, leprosy is a disease in which the nerve endings in your skin begin to deteriorate. Thus causes you to lose your sense of touch. Although that might not sound so bad at first, think about it. Without your sense of touch, you feel no pain. Thus, if your skin gets cut, you won't even notice it. That might sound good at first, but because you do not feel the pain, you do not know you are hurt. As a result, you do not take care of the wound. People with leprosy have terrible problems with infection for that reason. Also, since a person with leprosy cannot feel pain, he or she can destroy skin without realizing it. For example, suppose you lean on a hot stove. You will immediately jerk away because you know that it is hot. A person with leprosy would not know this. Thus, he or she would continue to lean against the stove, burning his or her skin until it is completely fried. Since your skin is your first line of defense against disease, this can be a *real* problem.

The doctor, therefore, was trying to design a glove that he could put on such a person's hand. The glove would send an electrical shock to some part of the body where the nerves were not yet destroyed whenever the patient did something that would cause pain. Sounds simple enough, doesn't it? Well, the problem was that he could not adjust the sensitivity of the sensors in his glove properly. For example, if a person hit his finger with a hammer, the sensor could be set to register the blow and shock the patient. However, if the sensor was set that way, the jars from simply *using* the hammer would also cause a shock! In the end, our skin has so many different kinds of receptors that it is able to distinguish between an enormous range of touches. Such a range of sensory discrimination is simply not possible with humanity's best technology!

Although the skin is the focal point of the sense of touch, it is important to note that not all parts of the body are equally sensitive. Perform the following experiment to find out what I mean.

EXPERIMENT 16.6

The Variation in Touch Sensitivity

Supplies:

- Two well-sharpened pencils
- Some tape

Introduction - This experiment will help you learn what parts of your body are most sensitive to touch.

Procedure:

A. Tape the two pencils together, side-by-side. Make sure that the pencil points are both facing the same direction and level with one another.
B. Lightly touch the two pencil tips on your finger. Note whether you can really tell that you are being touched by two pencil points at the same time.
C. Do the same thing on the center of the palm of your hand. Once again, note whether or not you can tell that there are two pencil points touching you.
D. Do the same thing on various parts of your arm. Continue to note whether or not you can tell that there are two pencil points touching you.
E. Try other parts of your body. **BE CAREFUL ABOUT THIS. YOU CLEARLY DON'T WANT TO DO YOUR EYES OR EARS OR ANYTHING LIKE THAT. ALSO, BE GENTLE. DO NOT HURT YOURSELF BY PUSHING TOO HARD!!!** Continue to note whether or not you can tell that there are two pencil points touching you.

What did you find out? Well, most likely you were able to tell that two pencil points were touching your finger and hand, but your arm really couldn't distinguish between one pencil point and two. Why? There are many more neurons and receptors in the skin of your hand than in the skin of your arms. As a result, your arms are less sensitive to touch. This means it is harder for you to accurately sense touch on your arms. Now if you think about it, that should make sense. Your hands need to be very sensitive to touch because they handle things all of the time. Your arms are not used to give you much information from touch, so you do not need to have as many touch nerves and receptors in the skin of your arm. If you continued the experiment, you probably found that your lips, tongue, feet, and toes were the sensitive areas, while most of the rest of your body was not.

The Human Sense of Hearing

If a tree falls in the forest and no one is there to hear it, does it make a sound? Have you ever heard that question before? From a scientist's point of view, the answer is easy: YES. You see, scientists do not define sound in reference to your sense of hearing. Instead, sound is defined as a series of vibrations in the air. Indeed, that's where your hearing begins. Suppose you are listening to someone playing the violin. You hear music (hopefully good music) coming from the instrument. How is it formed?

When the violinist strokes the strings with the bow, the strings begin to vibrate back and forth. That pushes the air surrounding the violin back and forth, setting up vibrations in the air. Those vibrations then travel to you, eventually encountering your ear. That's when you start to hear it. How do vibrations in the air turn into sounds that you hear? Remember that from a scientist's viewpoint, vibrations in the air *already are* sound. However, you do not perceive them as sound until your ear goes to work.

FIGURE 16.9
The Human Ear

Illus. from the Medical Clipart Gallery

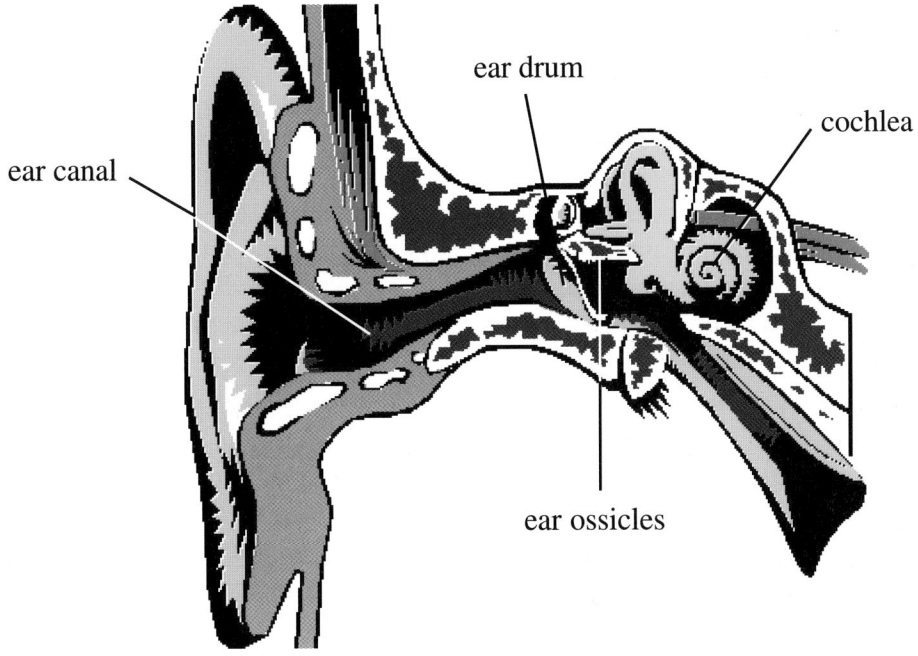

The vibrations in the air travel down the **ear canal** until they reach the **ear drum**. The ear drum is, indeed, much like a drum. It is a thin sheet of tissue stretched across the ear canal. Vibrations in the air cause the ear drum to vibrate. You will learn more about how that works when you take physical science next year. The vibrations of the ear drum cause tiny bones called **ossicles** (ah' sik uhls) to move back and forth. This movement in turn vibrates the snail-like **cochlea** (ko' klee uh), which is filled with fluid and "hair cells." These hair cells vibrate according to the pitch of the sound. When the hair cells vibrate, an electrical signal is sent via the auditory nerve to the brain, and the brain interprets the signal as sound.

If you think about it then, the ear's real job is to *transform* sound. Sound hits the ear as vibrations in the air. That's what sound really is. The ear drum transforms those vibrations in the air into vibrations in its own tissue. Those vibrations are then transformed into the rocking of the ossicles, which is then further transformed into electrical signals. The brain then takes those electrical signals and transforms them into what you call sound.

It is useful to compare the human ear to something else that transforms sound: a microphone. When you speak into a microphone, the vibrations your vocal cords set up in the air reach a thin "drum" of material. Just like the ear drum, this drum shakes in response to the air vibrations. Those shakes are then passed on to a quartz crystal. The quartz crystal has the property of producing electrical signals when it vibrates. Thus, the microphone also takes vibrations in the air and transforms them into electrical signals, somewhat like the ear.

Of course, compared to the ear, a microphone is incredibly primitive. The electrical signals produced by the hair cells within the cochlea are hundreds of times more sensitive than those produced by a quartz crystal. Thus, the depth and quality of sound you hear in your ears is significantly better than the depth and quality of sound produced by even a very sophisticated microphone!

Do We Really Use Only 10% of our Brain?

How many times have you heard the phrase, "We use less than 10% of our brain." It is a very popular saying. You hear it in advertisements, in motivational seminars, and even on the news. There is only one problem: ***it is absolutely wrong!*** There is no scientific data that lends any support to such a statement. It is simply a myth. An enormous amount of research has been done on the human brain. Doctors have found that removing even a small piece of a person's brain can have disastrous consequences. Although it is impossible for scientists to track the activity of every neuron in the brain, it is pretty apparent that all the neurons in the brain really are used. In the end, then, science tells us that we really use *all* of our brain!

How did this myth get started? No one knows for sure. In the early 1900's, a scientist named Karl Spencer Lashley performed experiments on rats where he removed large parts of their brains and demonstrated that they could still survive. This led some people to conclude that large portions of the brain go unused. Of course, the experimental data really do not justify the conclusion. After all, the rats may have survived, but Lashley didn't test to see if they could still do all of the things that they could do *before* the operation. If Lashley missed the critical parts of the brain, the rats' autonomic nervous system would have remained intact and instincts like the need to eat could have survived. However, the rats probably could not do nearly as much as before, like running mazes, learning specific behaviors, and the like.

It seems like some prominent people took those experiments and ran with them, however. American psychologist William James wrote in 1908: "We are making use of only a small part of our possible mental and physical resources". There are those that even attribute the very quote, "We only use 10% of our brain," to Albert Einstein. Regardless of its origin, this statement has been promoted by the popular media for many years. Nevertheless, as far as science can tell, it is a myth.

Summing it All Up

Well, believe it or not, you have reached the end of the course! I hope you have gotten a glimpse of why science excites me so much! Perhaps you still do not like science as much as I do. That's okay. I really hope that after taking this course, you can appreciate why some people can enjoy studying science.

I also hope you have developed a deep appreciation for all that God has given you in His Creation. From the majesty of rock formations to the intricacy of cells to the grand design of the human body, Creation screams out in testimony to its Creator. It is up to us to recognize that and give the Creator his due.

As you finish this course, I want to remind you of a quote that I gave you in the first module of the course. Robert Boyle (the founder of modern chemistry), in his last address to the Royal Society (a group of scientists in England), said the following:

"Remember to give glory to the One who authored nature."

Unfortunately, most scientists have forgotten the words of that great scientist. Do not let it happen to you!

ANSWERS TO THE ON YOUR OWN PROBLEMS

16.1. Dendrites carry signals to the neuron cell body, while axons carry signals away from the neuron cell body. Thus, the signal is traveling along a dendrite.

16.2. Without neurotransmitters, the neuron cannot communicate with other cells. All of the functions of a neuron depend on the neuron communicating with another cell.

16.3. The man will be able to move his arms but not his legs. If the spinal cord is severed at the waist, CNS signals cannot reach the PNS below the waist. Since the legs are below the waist, there will be no control over the leg muscles. However, the arms are above the waist, so the CNS can still control the PNS above the waist.

16.4. Remember, the "higher level" thinking like reasoning occurs in the cerebrum. Since humans are intellectually superior to all vertebrates, the cerebrum is significantly larger.

16.5. The first patient is having no problems speaking. The left side of the brain is primarily responsible for speech. Thus, the person with the left side of the brain damaged will be the one having trouble speaking. It was data like this that led to scientists first realizing that one hemisphere of the brain dominates the other in certain skills and functions.

16.6. The blood-brain barrier will not work without the proteins in between the cells of the capillaries. Those proteins seal the capillaries like gaskets, keeping the blood and fluid in the capillaries.

16.7. The sympathetic division of your autonomic nervous system is at work in this case. The sympathetic division increases heart rate and blood pressure.

16.8. The person's sense of taste would not be severely affected. The center of the tongue holds few taste buds, compared to other parts of the tongue.

16.9. Without chemicals in the air, there can be no scent. The air purifier marketers probably wanted to say that it cleans out all "foreign chemicals," or something like that. Note that some air purifiers do not live up to their claims and certain types can be dangerous. See http://www.epa.gov/iaq/pubs/ozonegen.html for more details.

16.10. Focusing on a scene far away will be more relaxing. When the ciliary muscle relaxes, the lens gets thinner, and that focuses on things far from the eye.

16.11. The person will be able to see, but there will be no color. There will be other problems as well, but since cones detect color, the obvious problem is that he will not see color.

STUDY GUIDE FOR MODULE #16

1. Define the following terms:

    a. Autonomic nervous system
    b. Sensory nervous system
    c. Motor nervous system

2. What are the two main types of cells in the human nervous system?

3. Identify the structures pointed out in this diagram of a neuron.

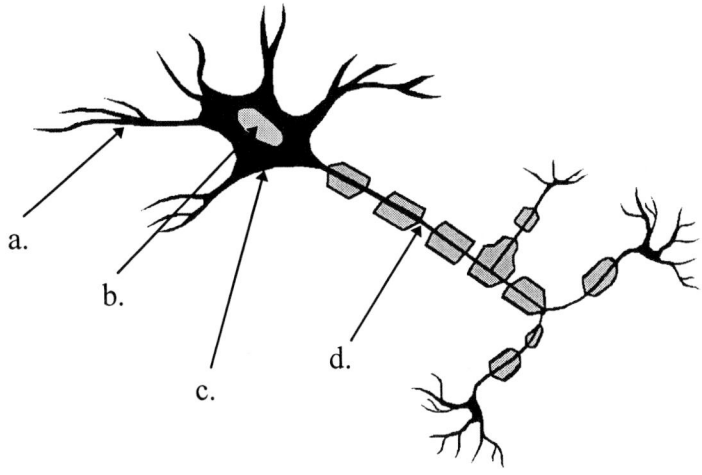

4. What do dendrites do?

5. What do axons do?

6. What is a synapse?

7. Explain how a signal crosses from the axon of a neuron to the receiving cell.

8. What is the function of neuroglia?

9. A nerve runs down the leg, carrying signals to the foot. Is it a part of the PNS or the CNS?

10. What two main structures make up the CNS?

11. What two things protect the brain?

12. What protects the spinal cord?

13. What is the brain's gray matter composed of?

14. What is the brain's white matter composed of?
15. What is the function of the corpus callosum?
16. What does the cerebellum primarily control?
17. What part of the brain deals mostly with the higher level thinking skills?
18. Do the two sides of the brain do exactly the same things?
19. What side of the PNS does the left side of the brain control?
20. What is the blood-brain barrier and why is it important?
21. What does the sympathetic division of the autonomic nervous system do?
22. What does the parasympathetic division of the autonomic nervous system do?
23. What are the four basic tastes that we can detect?
24. What portion of the tongue is least sensitive to taste? Why is it so insensitive?
25. When we smell something, what are we actually detecting?
26. What is the function of the eye's pupil?
27. What is the function of the eye's lens?
28. What is the function of the eye's ciliary muscle?
29. What cells of the retina detect light?
30. What causes an eye's blind spot?
31. Which part of the body has the most nerves related to touch: the fingers or the arm?
32. What is the function of the ear drum?
33. What is the function of the cochlea?

GLOSSARY

The numbers in parentheses refer to the page on which the definition is presented.

Absolute age – The calculated age of an artifact from a specific dating method that is used to determine when the artifact was made (128)

Appendicular skeleton – The portion of the skeleton that attaches to the axial skeleton and has the limbs attached to it (273)

Archaeology – The study of past human life as revealed by preserved relics (111)

Aristotle's dictum - The benefit of the doubt is to be given to the document itself, not assigned by the critic to himself. (114)

Arteries - Blood vessels that carry blood away from the heart (345)

Artifacts - Objects made by humans such as tools, weapons, containers, etc. (111)

Atom - The smallest stable unit of matter in Creation (218)

Autonomic nervous system - The system of nerves which carries instructions from the CNS to the body's organs (402)

Axial skeleton – The portion of the skeleton that supports and protects the head, neck, and trunk (273)

Basal metabolic rate - The minimum amount of energy required by the body every day (311)

Blind studies - Experiments in which the participants do not know whether or not they are a part of the control group (71)

Capillaries - Tiny, thin-walled blood vessels that allow the exchange of gases and nutrients between the blood and cells (345)

Carnivore - A consumer that eats only other consumers (297)

Catastrophism - The view that most of earth's geological features are the result of large-scale catastrophes such as floods, volcanic eruptions, etc. (137)

Cell - The smallest unit of life in Creation (236)

Circumference - The distance around a circle, equal to 3.1416 times the circle's diameter (103)

Consumers - Organisms that eat living producers and/or other living consumers for food (296)

Control (of an experiment) - The variable or part of the experiment to which all others can be compared (65)

Counter-example - An example that contradicts a scientific conclusion (38)

Decomposers - Organisms that break down the dead remains of other organisms (255)

Dendrochronology - The process of counting tree rings to determine the age of a tree (125)

Diameter - The length of a straight line that travels from one side of a circle to another, while passing through the center of a circle (94)

Digestion - The process by which an organism breaks down its food into small units which can be absorbed (321)

Double-blind studies - Experiments in which neither the participants nor the people analyzing the results know who is in the control group (74)

Erosion - The process by which sediments and rock fragments are carried away by wind or rain (149)

Eukaryotic cell - A cell with organelles (246)

Exoskeleton – A body covering, typically made of chitin, that provides support and protection (274)

Experimental variable - An aspect of an experiment which changes during the course of the experiment (59)

Extinct - A term applied to a species of plant or animal that was once living but now is not (172)

Force - A push or pull that changes the motion of an object (86)

Geological column - A theoretical picture in which layers of rock from around the world are meshed together into a single, unbroken record of earth's past (194)

Geology – The study of earth's history as revealed in the rocks that make up the earth (112)

Gland - A group of cells that prepare and release a chemical for use by the body (371)

Herbivore - A consumer that eats producers exclusively (297)

Hormone - A chemical released in the bloodstream that sends signals to specific cells, causing them to change their behavior in specific ways (381)

Humus - The decayed remains of once-living creatures (138)

Hypothesis - An educated guess that attempts to explain an observation or answer a question (40)

Index fossils - A fossil considered to represent a certain period in earth's past (189)

Known age - The age of an artifact as determined by a date printed on it or a reference to the artifact in a work of history (125)

Life science – A term that encompasses all scientific pursuits related to living organisms (111)

Mechanical advantage - The amount by which force or motion is magnified in a simple machine (89)

Metabolism - The process by which a living organism takes energy from its surroundings and uses it to sustain itself, develop, and grow (228)

Minerals - Inorganic crystalline substances found naturally in the earth (139)

Molecule - Two or more atoms linked together to make a substance with unique properties (218)

Motor nervous system - The system of nerves which carries instructions from the CNS to the skeletal muscles (402)

Omnivore - A consumer that eats both plants and other consumers (297)

Paleontology – The study of life's history as revealed in the preserved remains of once-living plants and animals (112)

Papyrus - A primitive form of paper, made from a long-leafed plant of the same name (2)

Pathogen - An organism that causes disease (250)

Petrifaction - The conversion of organic material into stone (164)

Photosynthesis - The process by which a plant uses the energy of sunlight and certain chemicals to produce its own food (227)

Producers - Organisms that produce their own food (295)

Prokaryotic cell - A cell that has no organelles (246)

Radiometric dating - Using a radioactive process to determine the age of an item (128)

Receptors - Special structures or chemicals that allow living organisms to sense the conditions of their surroundings (229)

Resin - A sticky, liquid substance that usually hardens when exposed to air (169)

Science - A branch of study dedicated to the accumulation and classification of observable facts in order to formulate general laws about the natural world (1)

Scientific law - A theory that has been tested by and is consistent with generations of data (40)

Sensory nervous system - The system of nerves which carries information from the body's receptors to the CNS (402)

Simple machine - A device that reduces the amount of force needed to perform a task or changes the direction of a force (86)

Spontaneous generation - The idea that living organisms can be spontaneously formed from non-living substances (9)

Symbiosis – Two or more different organisms living together so that each benefits from the other (287)

The Principle of Superposition – When artifacts are found in rock or earth that is layered, the deeper layers hold the older artifacts. (129)

The Theory of Evolution - A theory which states that all of life on this earth has a single, common ancestor that existed a long time ago (195)

Theory - An hypothesis that has been tested with a significant amount of data (40)

Unconformity - A surface of erosion that separates one layer of rock from another (155)

Uniformitarianism - The view that most of earth's geological features are the result of slow, gradual processes that have been at work for millions or even billions of years (137)

Vaccine - A weakened or inactive version of a pathogen that stimulates the body's production of antibodies which can destroy the pathogen (376)

Vegetative reproduction - The process by which the stem of a plant can form new roots and develop into a mature plant (260)

Veins - Blood vessels that carry blood back to the heart (345)

Vitamin - a chemical substance essential for the normal working of the human body (338)

Weathering - The process by which rocks are broken down by the forces of nature (146)

Index

A

absolute age, 128
acid, 286
acid, hydrochloric, 330
acid, lactic, 286
acid, stomach, 330
acids, 331
ACTH, 384
adding machine, 84
adenine, 220
adenoids, 371
ADH, 384
adrenal glands, 384
adrenocorticotrophic hormone, 377
adrenocorticotropic hormone, 384
advantage, mechanical, 89
Africa, 203
age, absolute, 128
age, known, 125
age, relative, 129
air resistance, 37
albinism, 288
Albright, William F., 121, 122
Alchemists, 12
Alchemy, 12
Alexander the Great, 8, 52
algae, 246, 252
Allegemeine Krakenhaus, 40
alveoli, 357
amber, 169
amino acids, 306
amino acids, essential, 306
amphibians, 289
Anamalia, 247
Anaximander, 4
Anaximenes, 4
angular unconformity, 155
animal cell, 237
Animalia, 245, 247, 364
antacid, 330
anthocyanin, 14
antibodies, 355
antidiuretic hormone, 384
anus, 324
aorta, 351
appendectomy, 325
appendicular skeleton, 273
appendix, 325
applied science, 83
aqueous humor, 410
archaeology, 111
Archaeopteryx, 211
Archimedes, 9
Aristotle's dictum, 118
Arizona, 255
arteries, 345
arthropod, 289
arthropods, 274, 283
articular capsule, 279
artifacts, 111
atmospheric pressure, 23
atom, 6, 218
atomic theory, 26
atoms, 4
atrium, 349
Australopithecus, 213
autonomic nervous system, 402
axial skeleton, 273
axons, 390

B

backbone, 394
backbone (of DNA), 220
Bacon, Roger, 17
bacteria, 41, 334
bacterium, 248
ball-and-socket joints, 277
basal metabolic rate, 311, 384
bases, 331
B-cells, 373
B-cells, memory, 373
beakheads, 207
Behe, Michael, 356
Bethlehem, 53
Bible, 25
biblical contradictions, 117, 118
bibliographic test, 112, 114, 123
bile, 324, 335
biology, 245
biosphere, 228
Biosphere 2, 255, 256
biotin, 339
bird, 247, 289
birds, 350
bladder, 379
blind studies, 71
block, 95
block and tackle, 98
blood, 345
blood cells, red, 354
blood cells, white, 355
blood clotting, 339
blood plasma, 354
blood platelets, 355
blood vessels, 345
blood, deoxygenated, 347
blood, oxygenated, 347
blood-brain barrier, 400
BMR, 311
Bohr Model, 30
Bohr, Niels, 30
bolus, 328
Bone Cave,Cumberland, 204
bone cells, 272
bone marrow, 267, 271, 355
bone matrix, 270
bone, compact, 271
bone, spongy, 271
botulism, 250
Boyle, Robert, 24
Bradwardine, Thomas, 18
brain hemispheres, 395
brain stem, 396
breathing, 300
bronchial tubes, 357
bronchioles, 357
bronchus, 357, 361
Bruce, F. F., 121
Burr, William Henry, 116
Burundi, 151
butter, 252
buttermilk, 252

C

calorie, 311
calorie, food, 311
Cambrian, 194
canine teeth, 327
canyons (formed quickly), 200
cap, 257
capillaries, 345
capsule, articular, 279
carbohydrates, 304
carbon dioxide, 303
carbonate residue, 166
cardiac cycle, 352
cardiac muscle, 267, 281, 349
carnivore, 297

cartilage, 278
cast, 161
cat, 247
catastrophism, 137, 197
cavern, 153
cecum, 334
cell, 236, 245
cell types, 237
cell wall, 261
cell, average size, 237
cell, eukaryotic, 246, 247
cell, prokaryotic, 246
cells, bone, 272
central nervous system, 394
central vacuole, 261
cerebellum, 396
cerebrospinal fluid, 394
cerebrum, 395
cheddar cheese, 252
cheese, 251
chemical, 217
chemical digestion, 322
chemical reaction, 14
chemical weathering, 146
Chicago Field Museum of Natural History, 211
chitin, 274
Christ, Jesus, 53, 54, 117
Christian world-view, 18, 26
chyme, 332
cilia, 283
ciliary muscle, 411
circulatory system, 345
circumference, 103
clams, 274
clams, most common fossil, 171
classification, 8, 244
classification system, 244
clay, 139
Clostridium botulinum, 250
clotting, of blood, 339
CNS, 394
coagulation, 355
cochlea, 418
codeine, 2
coelacanth, 208
collagen, 270
colon, 334
color, of skin, 287
Colorado River, 178
column, 153
column, geological, 194
combustion, 26, 298, 299, 300, 315
compact bone, 271
computer, 84, 219, 387
conditioned response, 328
cones, 411
consumer, 296
control, experimental, 65, 71
Copernican System, 19
Copernicus, Nicholas, 19
cornea, 410
corpus callosum, 395
cottage cheese, 252
cough, 328
counter-example, 38
cowpox, 374
crayfish, 274
Creation, 99, 202, 218, 231, 256, 267, 287, 295, 298, 364, 419
Creator, 27, 255, 316, 333, 334
Cretaceous, 196
criteria for life, 217
crust, of earth, 139
cry, 377
crying, 376
crystalline, 140
Cumberland Bone Cave, 204
curds, 252
Cusa, Nicholas of, 18
cutting, of a plant, 260
cytoplasm, 236, 285
cytosine, 220

D

Dalton, John, 26
Darwin, Charles, 210
Darwin, Charles R., 27
Darwin's Black Box, 356
dating, radiometric, 127
Dead Sea scrolls, 123, 124
decomposer, 296
decomposers, 255
dehydrated food, 251
delta, 152
Democritus, 4
dendrites, 390
dendrochronology, 125
density, 6
deoxygenated blood, 347
dermis, 284
descending aorta, 351
design, 287
Designer, 316, 377
Devonian, 196
dialysis, 381
diameter, 93
dictum, Aristotle's, 113
dictum, Artistotle's, 118
digestion, 321
digestion time, 324
digestion, chemical, 322
digestion, physical, 322
digestive system, human, 323
digestive tract, 335
dikes, 156
dinosaurs, 194
disaccharide, 304
disconformities, 155
dissolve, 73
DNA, 217
DNA backbone, 220
DNA, structure of, 220
dog, 27
double wedge, 101
double-blind studies, 72
drug testing experiments, 70
dust, 248, 285

E

ear, 417
ear canal, 418
ear drum, 418
earth's crust, 139
ectothermic, 310
effort, 88
Egyptian medicine (ancient), 1
Einstein, Albert, 30
electromagnetism, 29
electron microscope, 248
electron transport system, 314
elephant, 171
emotions, 377, 409
emphysema, 358
encyclopedias, 15
endocrine system, 369, 382
endorphin, 384
endoskeleton, 273
endothermic, 310, 336
energy, 217, 225, 295
ENIAC, 84
Enlightenment, 25
environmentalists, 173
epidermis, 285
epiglottis, 328, 360
eras, geological, 194
erosion, 149
eruption, 198
esophagus, 324, 326, 361
essential amino acids, 306
eukaryotic cells, 246, 252
evolution, 11, 27, 195, 210, 268, 356
exoskeleton, 274, 283
experimental variables, 59
external test, 112, 114, 119
extinct, 172
eye, 410

F

Faraday, Michael, 28
fast formation of canyons, 200
fast formation of stratified rock, 198
fat, 285
fats, 304
fats, saturated, 305
fats, unsaturated, 305
feces, 324, 334
fertilizer, 228

fingernails, 268
First Law of Thermodynamics, 29
first-class lever, 89
fish, 289, 350
fish (and oxygen), 73
five-kingdom system, 245
Fleming, Wallace, 51
flood, of Noah, 180
fluid, cerebrospinal, 394
fluid, synovial, 279
folic acid, 339
follicle, hair, 285
food calorie, 311
food poisoning, 250
fossil graveyards, 203
fossil hat, 206
fossil of a water wheel, 205
fossil pliers, 206
fossil record, 170, 211
fossilization, rapid, 206
fossils, 161
fossils, index, 189
four-chambered heart, 349
frogs, 289, 350
fructose, 304
fruit flies, 232
fulcrum, 87
Fungi, 245, 247, 255

G

Galileo Galilei, 22
gall bladder, 324, 332, 336
ganglia, 402
gasket, 401
gastric juice, 330
genealogies (of Christ), 117
general theory of relativity, 30
genetics, 28
Geocentric System, 11
geological column, 194
geology, 28, 112
germ, 41
germinal centers, 373
gills, 73, 257, 364
gland, lacrimal, 375
gland, sebaceous, 286
glucose, 226, 304
glycogen, 336
glycolysis, 314
God, 11, 15, 16, 17, 18, 20, 23, 24, 25, 26, 27, 41, 202, 218, 231, 256, 262, 267, 268, 287, 296, 364, 375, 381, 394, 400, 405, 419
goose-pimples, 285
Grand Canyon, 142
Grand Canyon, Little, 200
graphical results, 74
graphing data, 74
grass, 247
grasshopper, 247
grasshoppers, 274
gravel, 139
graveyards, of fossils, 203
gravitation, 24
gravotropism, 284
gray matter, 395
Green, William, 124
Grosseteste, Robert, 17
groundwater, 153
guanine, 220

H

hair, 268, 285
hair follicle, 285
hat as a fossil, 206
hearing, 417
heart, 349
heliocentric system, 19
hemispheres (brain), 395
hemoglobin, 354
herbivore, 297
Herodotus, 52
HGH, 383
Hiero, 10
high-temperature superconductors, 48
hinge joints, 277
hormone, 382
hormones, 369
human body, 267
human digestive system, 323
human growth hormone, 383
humus, 138
hydrochloric acid, 330
hyperthyroidism, 384
hypodermis, 285
hypothalamus, 383, 396
hypothesis, 40, 41

I

igneous rock, 139
Imhotep, 1
immunization, 374
immutability of the species, 27
impression, 166
incisor teeth, 327
inclined plane, 99
index fossils, 189
indicator, 331
Industrial Revolution, 26
infantile paralysis, 375
inferior vena cava, 351
information, 217
ingestion, 321
inorganic, 139
insects, 274
insulin, 384
intermediate link, 210, 211
internal test, 112, 116
intestinal villi, 333
intestine, large, 324, 333
intestine, small, 324, 333
intrusion, 155
invertebrate, 194
invertebrates, 274
involuntary movements, 281
involuntary muscles, 281, 308

J

jellyfish, 274
Jenner, Edward, 374
Jidejian, Nina, 53
joints, 276
joints, ball-and-socket, 277
joints, hinge, 277
joints, saddle, 278
joints, washer, 278
Josephus, Flavius, 120
Joule, James, 29
juice, gastric, 330
Jurassic, 196

K

Kant, Immanuel, 25
Karoo Beds, 203
Kepler, Johannes, 20
Kepler's Laws, 20
keratin, 285
keratinization, 268, 285
kidneys, 354
kingdoms, in classification, 245
Kitchen, K. A., 122
known age, 125
Krebs cycle, 314

L

lacrimal gland, 375
lacrimal glands, 410
lactic acid, 286
Lactobacilus, 251
laminae, 145
laminae (formed quickly), 199
lamination, 145
large intestine, 324, 333
larynx, 324, 360
Lavoisier, Antoine-Laurent, 26, 39
Law of Mass Conservation, 26
law, scientific, 40, 41
leaves, 260
lens, 410
leprosy, 415
leucine-enkephalin, 377
Leucippus, 4
lever, 87
lever, first-class, 89

lever, third class, 89
lever. second-class, 89
life science, 111
life, criteria for, 217
ligaments, 279
light bulb, 47
limbic system, 409
limitations of science, 49
Linnaeus, Carrolus, 26
Little Grand Canyon, 200
liver, 324, 335
living organism, 217
lobes (lung), 358
lobsters, 274, 350
Lowell, Percival, 45
lungs, 324, 351, 357
Lyell, Sir Charles, 28
lymph, 370
lymph nodes, 371, 372
lymph vessels, 369
lymphatic system, 369
lymphocytes, 373

M

machine, adding, 84
machine, simple, 86
macronutrients, 304, 324
macrophages, 373
maggot, 232
magma, 139
mammal, 289
mammoth, 167, 171
manganese, 377
Mari Tablets, 121
marrow, 267, 271
Mars, canals on, 45
Maryland, 204
Mass Conservation, Law of, 26
master endocrine gland, 383
master tree ring patterns, 127
Maxwell, James Clerk, 28
Mazar, Amuhai, 121
McDowell, Josh, 53, 55
McMillen, S. I., 41
mechanical advantage, 89
medicine, ancient Egyptian, 1
Mediterranean Sea, 151
medullary canal, 271
melanin, 288
membrane, 236
memories, 409
memory B-cells, 373
Mendel, Gregor, 28
messianic prophecies, 53
metabolic rate, 311
metabolic rate, basal, 311, 384
metabolism, 228
metamorphic rock, 139
metamorphosis, 232
micronutrients, 308, 324, 338
microorganism, 247
microscope, 24, 41
milk, pasteurized, 28
minerals, 139, 270, 338
missing link, 211
Mississippian, 196
mitochondrion, 314
molar teeth, 327
mold, 161
molecule, 218
Monera, 245, 246, 247, 364
monosaccharide, 304
morphine, 2
Morse Code, 221
Morse, Samuel F. B., 221
motor nervous system., 402
Mount Saint Helens, 198
mouth, 324, 326
mouth cavity, 360
movements, involuntary, 281
mucus, 360
muscle, cardiac, 281
muscles, 267
muscles, involuntary, 281, 308
muscles, skeletal, 275
muscles, smooth, 281
mushroom, 255, 257
mycelium, 256, 257
myelin sheath, 390

N

nasal cavity, 360
natural selection, 28, 377
Nebuchadnezzar, 52
nebula, 15
Neptune, 44
nerve, 402
nerve center, 402
nerves, 393
nervous system, 389
nervous system, autonomic, 402
nervous system, central, 394
nervous system, illus., 393
nervous system, motor, 402
nervous system, peripheral, 394, 395, 402
nervous system, sensory, 402
neuroglia, 388, 392
neuron, illus., 389
neurons, 388
neurotransmitters, 391
neutralization, 331
Newton, Sir Isaac, 23, 37
Nile river, 151
Noah's flood, 180
node, sinoatrial, 282
nodes, lymph, 371, 372
nonconformity, 155
nose, 408
nuclear reactor, 248
nucleotide, 220
nucleus, 237, 261
Numbers, 41

O

objective data, 72
observation, 40
Old Testament, 41
olfactory epithelium, 408
olfactory sensory cells, 408
omnivore, 297
one-way valves, 373
onion, 377
optic nerve, 412
Ordovician, 194
organelles, 236
organism, 217
organism, living, 217
organs, vestigial, 325
ossicles, 418
oxygen, 252
oxygenated blood, 347

P

pacemaker, 282
paleontology, 112
pancreas, 324, 332, 337, 384
pantothenic acid, 339
papillae, 405
papyrus, 2
paraconformities, 155
paraconformity, 208
parasympathetic division, 403
Pascal, Blaise, 23, 84
Pascal's wager, 23
past, key to present, 176
Pasteur, Louis, 28, 375
pasteurization, 28
pasteurized milk, 28
pathogen, 250
pathogenic bacteria, 250
Paul, Saint, 117
Pavlov, Ivan, 328
pectoral girdle, 273
pelvic girdle, 273
penicillin, 2
Pennsylvanian, 196
periosteum, 272
peripheral nervous system, 394, 395, 402
Permian, 196
petrifaction, 164
pharynx, 324, 326, 360
Philadelphius, Ptolemy, 51
Phlegon, 120
phloem, 365
phlogiston, 38
photosynthesis, 226, 227, 252
phototropism, 283

physical digestion, 322
physical weathering, 146
pigment, 288
pimples, goose, 285
pituitary gland, 383
placebo, 71
placoderms, 175
Planck, Max, 29
plant cell, 237
Plantae, 245, 247
plasma, blood, 354
platelets, 355
plexus, 402
pliers as a fossil, 206
Pliny the Younger, 123
PNS, 394, 402
polio, 375
polysaccharide, 304
poppy, 2
poppy seeds, 2
Precambrian, 194
premolar teeth, 327
present, as key to past, 176
primary bronchus, 357, 361
Principia, 24
Principle of Superposition, 129
printed circuit board, 387
producer, 295
prokaryotic cells, 246
proof, 37
prophecies, 55
proteins, 270, 304, 305
Protista, 245, 246, 252, 364
protozoa, 252
Psalm, 267
Pseudomonas, 248
Ptolemaic System, 11
Ptolemy, 10
pulley, 95
pulmonary artery, 351, 353
pulmonary vein, 351, 353
pulse, 352
pupil, 403, 404, 410
pyloric sphincter, 332

Q

quanta, 29
quantum mechanics, 30
Quaternary, 194

R

rabies, 375
radiometric dating, 127
rapid fossilization, 206
Raup, Dr. David, 211
receptor, 229, 241
rectum, 324, 334
Red blood cells, 354
red tide, 204
relative age, 129
relativity, special and general, 30
renal pelvis, 379
renal vein, 379
reproduction, 231
reptile, 289
resin, 169
resistance, 88
respiratory system, 345, 360
response, conditioned, 328
retina, 410
River, Colorado, 178
rock, three basic types, 139
rods, 412
root, 257
roots, 260
rust, 148

S

Sabin, ALbert, 375
saddle joints, 278
salamanders, 289
saliva, 322
Salk, Jonas, 375
Salmonella, 250
saltwater, density of, 61
sand, 139
saturated fats, 305
sauerkraut, 252
Schiaparelli, Giovanni, 45
science, 1, 83
scientia, 1
scientific law, 40, 41
scientific method, 40, 41
scientific method, failures of, 45
scorpions, 274
sebaceous gland, 286
second-class lever, 90
sedimentary rock, 139
sediments, 139
Semmelweis, Ignaz, 40, 41
sensory nervous system, 402
sheath, myelin, 390
Sickle cell anemia, 356
sills, 156
silt, 139
Silurian, 194
simple machine, 86
sinoatrial node, 282
skeletal muscles, 267, 275
skeleton, 267
skeleton, appendicular, 273
skeleton, axial, 273
skin, 229, 267, 284, 415
skin color, 287
small intestine, 324, 333
smallpox, 374
smell, 408
smooth muscles, 267, 281
snails, 274
snflowers, 284
soft palate, 328
soil, 138
Sophocles, 123
SOS, 221
sound, 417
special theory of relativity, 30
sphincter, pyloric, 332
spiders, 274
spleen, 371
sponges, 349
spongy bone, 271
spontaneous generation, 9
stalactite, 153
stalagmite, 153
stalk, 257
starch, 226, 304
stems, 260
stomach, 324, 330
stomach acid, 330
strata, 129, 143, 173
strata (formed quickly), 199
strata, fossils in, 173
stratified rock made quickly, 198
structure of DNA, 220
subjective data, 72
sucrose, 304
sugars, simple, 304
sun, 295
superconductivity, 47
superconductors, high-temperature, 48
superior vena cava, 351
supernova, 15
Superposition, Principle of, 129
superstructure, of the human body, 267
supporting documents, 116
surface tension, 69
surface tension, soap's effect on, 69
sweat, 286
symbiosis, 287, 334
sympathetic division, 403
synapse, 388, 391
synovial fluid, 279
Syria, 51
system, endocrine, 369, 382
system, lymphatic, 369
system, urinary, 369, 378

T

Tacitus, Cornelius, 120, 123
taste, 324, 405
taste buds, 405
T-cells, 373
tears, 377, 410
technology, 83, 84
teeth, 324
telescope, 22
tendon, 276

tension, surface, 69
Tertiary, 196
test, bibliographic, 112, 114, 123
test, external, 112, 114, 119
test, internal, 112, 116
thalamus, 396
Thales, 4
Thallus, 120
The Origin of Species, 27
The Pavement, 122
theory, 40, 41
Theory of Evolution, 195
Thermodynamics, First Law of, 29
third-class lever, 90
thymine, 220
thymus, 371
thyroid gland, 384
thyroid stimulating hormone, 384
toads, 289
toenails, 268
tongue, 324
tonsils, 371
topsoil, 138
touch, 415
trachea, 324, 357, 360
transistor, 84
tree, 247
tree ring patterns, 127
Triassic, 196
trilobite, 175
trilobites, 194
TSH, 384
tuatara, 207
turgor pressure, 262
Tyre, 51, 52, 53

U

unconformity, 155, 208
uniformitarianism, 137, 189, 204
uniformitarianism versus catastrophism, 206
unsaturated fats, 305
ureter, 379
urethra, 379
urinary system, 369, 378
urine, 379

V

vaccine, 374, 375
vaccines, 28
vacuole, 261
vacuum tubes, 84
valves, one-way, 373
van Leeuwenhoek, Anton, 247
van Leeuwenhoek, Antoni, 24, 41
variables, experimental, 59
vegetarian, 306
vegetative reproduction, 260
veins, 345
vena cava, inferior, 351
vena cava, superior, 351
ventricle, 349
vertebrae, 278, 394
vertebral column, 394
vertebrates, 203, 273, 394
Vesalius, Andreas, 20
vessels, lymph, 369
vestigial, 325
vestigial organs, 325
Vienna, 40
villi, 333
vinegar, 252, 299
vision, 410
vitamin A, 339
vitamin B, 339
vitamin C, 339
vitamin D, 339
vitamin E, 339
Vitamin K, 251, 334, 339
vitamins, 338
vocal chords, 362
voice box, 362
Von Freiberg, Dietrich, 17

W

washer joints, 278
Washington state, 198
water wheel fossil, 205
weathering, 146
wedge, 100
wheel and axle, 93
whey, 252
white blood cells, 355
white matter, 395
world-view, Christian, 18, 26

X

x-axis, 74
X-rays, 85
xylem, 365

Y

Yamauchi, Edwin, 121
y-axis, 74
yeast, 258